GEOGRAPHICAL ATLAS OF THE WORLD

Designed and produced by Engineering Surveys Reproduction Ltd

Cartographic Design and Production Manager
Keith Brook

Senior Cartographic Editor
Zoë Goodwin

Cartographic Editor
Lindsay Evans

Cartographers
Nicky Chapman
Mike Larby
Gill Dalton
David Handley-Clarke
Chris Major

Cartographic Consultant
Allan Marles

Cartographic Illustrator
Janos Marffy

Illustrator
Tom McArthur

The publishers wish to thank all those involved in the production of
this atlas, and in particular the photo technicians at ESR Ltd, Richard
Ross, John Gill, Michael Hodson Designs, Apollo Colour Repro Ltd,
E.S. Computing Ltd, Typogram Ltd, and Link-Line Ltd.

3155
This edition published 1997 by Colour Library Direct
©1989 CLB International, Godalming, Surrey, England
First revision 1991
Second revision 1992
Third revision 1993
Fourth revision 1995
Fifth revision 1996
Printed in Spain

ISBN 1-85833-590-6

GEOGRAPHICAL ATLAS OF THE WORLD

Foreword by WILLIAM R. MEAD

Professor Emeritus of Geography at
University College London

FOREWORD

In 1636 a bound collection of maps was published by Gerard Mercator and John Hondt with a frontispiece illustrating the titan Atlas bearing the world on his shoulders. As a result, the word 'atlas' entered the vocabulary as a synonym for a book of maps. In the seventeenth century only the very rich could afford the luxury of an atlas. Cartographic masterpieces by Dutch map engravers offered their patrons the first view of a world the horizons of which were being swiftly broadened by maritime discovery.

Today, most households can afford an atlas even if they do not own one. Certainly, the need for and the attraction of the atlas have never been greater. Never have so many people been on the move around the world. Never have so many been concerned with the impact of world events. 'Atlas-eaters', Dylan Thomas called those who were hungry for world news. The atlas, through its co-ordinates of latitude and longitude, can answer the question 'Where?'. Or, perhaps, more precisely, the index to the atlas provides the answer – hence the importance of the extended index to the Atlas of the World.

In an atlas, the science of map-making is married to the art of map presentation. Techniques of production are increasingly refined; sources of information are increasingly precise. Satellite imagery, photogrammetry and computerisation have transformed map production. Most of the Atlas of the the World consists of topographical maps, with our own respective home areas receiving generous treatment. The thematic maps of the introductory section, necessarily selective in the topics that they treat, offer perspectives on the world distribution of a number of critically important phenomena.

An atlas is no substitute for a globe. The two are complementary, for not even the larger globes can include a fraction of the information that is packed into an atlas. The task of projecting the globe onto a flat surface has taxed the ingenuity of mathematicians since the Greeks first attempted to measure the circumference of the Earth. The variety of formidably-named projections employed in the Atlas of the World illustrates the extended range of options available to present-day cartographers.

Atlases have a romantic appeal as well as a utilitarian value. The novelist Alan Sillitoe, in a memorable essay on maps, recalls the flights of fancy set in motion by his 'first cheap layer-tinted atlas'. To turn the pages of the Atlas of the World – to contemplate the controlling features of land and sea, to reflect upon the boundaries that define the outlines and shape the destinies of countries and to respond to the magic of the infinity of place-names – is to experience a stimulus to the imagination as well as to the intellect.

William R. Mead
PROFESSOR EMERITUS OF GEOGRAPHY, UNIVERSITY COLLEGE LONDON.

CONTENTS

THE WORLD IN MAPS

EUROPE

CONTINENTS AND NATIONS OF THE WORLD

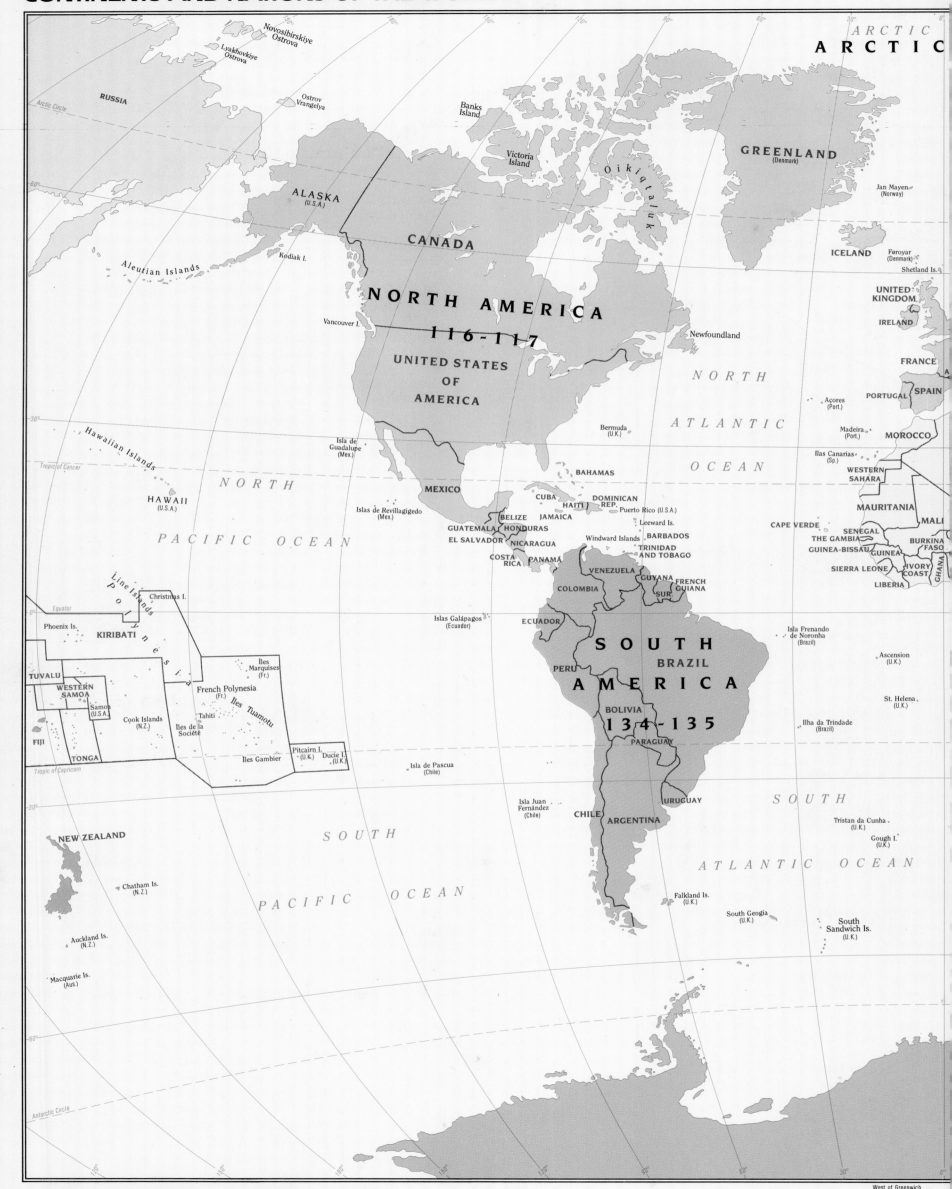

ARCTIC

ARCTIC

RUSSIA

Novosibirskiye Ostrova

Lyakhovkiye Ostrova

Arctic Circle

Ostrov Vrangelya

Banks Island

Victoria Island

Oikiqtaluk

GREENLAND (Denmark)

Jan Mayen (Norway)

ALASKA (U.S.A.)

CANADA

ICELAND

Feroyar (Denmark)

Shetland Is.

Aleutian Islands

Kodiak I.

NORTH AMERICA 116-117

Vancouver I.

UNITED STATES OF AMERICA

Newfoundland

NORTH

UNITED KINGDOM

IRELAND

FRANCE

Açores (Port.)

PORTUGAL

SPAIN

ATLANTIC

Hawaiian Islands

Tropic of Cancer

NORTH

Isla de Guadalupe (Mex.)

OCEAN

Bermuda (U.K.)

Madeira (Port.)

MOROCCO

Ilas Canarias (Sp.)

HAWAII (U.S.A.)

PACIFIC OCEAN

Islas de Revillagigedo (Mex.)

MEXICO

BAHAMAS

CUBA

HAITI

DOMINICAN REP.

JAMAICA

Puerto Rico (U.S.A.)

Leeward Is.

WESTERN SAHARA

MAURITANIA

MALI

CAPE VERDE

BELIZE

GUATEMALA HONDURAS

EL SALVADOR NICARAGUA

Windward Islands

BARBADOS

TRINIDAD AND TOBAGO

SENEGAL

THE GAMBIA

GUINEA-BISSAU GUINEA

BURKINA FASO

COSTA RICA PANAMÁ

VENEZUELA

GUYANA

FRENCH GUIANA

SIERRA LEONE

IVORY COAST

GHANA

LIBERIA

Line Islands

Christmas I.

COLOMBIA

SUR.

Equator

Phoenix Is.

Islas Galápagos (Ecuador)

ECUADOR

Isla Frenando de Noronha (Brazil)

KIRIBATI

SOUTH

Ascension (U.K.)

TUVALU

Iles Marquises (Fr.)

PERU

BRAZIL

AMERICA

St. Helena (U.K.)

WESTERN SAMOA

Samoa (U.S.A.)

French Polynesia (Fr.)

Iles Tuamotu

BOLIVIA

134-135

Ilha da Trindade (Brazil)

Cook Islands (N.Z.)

Tahiti

Iles de la Société

FIJI

TONGA

Iles Gambier

Pitcairn I. (U.K.)

Ducie I. (U.K.)

Tropic of Capricorn

PARAGUAY

Isla de Pascua (Chile)

Isla Juan Fernández (Chile)

URUGUAY

SOUTH

Tristan da Cunha (U.K.)

Gough I. (U.K.)

NEW ZEALAND

CHILE

ARGENTINA

ATLANTIC OCEAN

SOUTH

Chatham Is. (N.Z.)

PACIFIC OCEAN

Falkland Is. (U.K.)

South Georgia (U.K.)

South Sandwich Is. (U.K.)

Auckland Is. (N.Z.)

Macquarie Is. (Aus.)

Antarctic Circle

West of Greenwich

1:73,000,000 (Scale at the Equator)

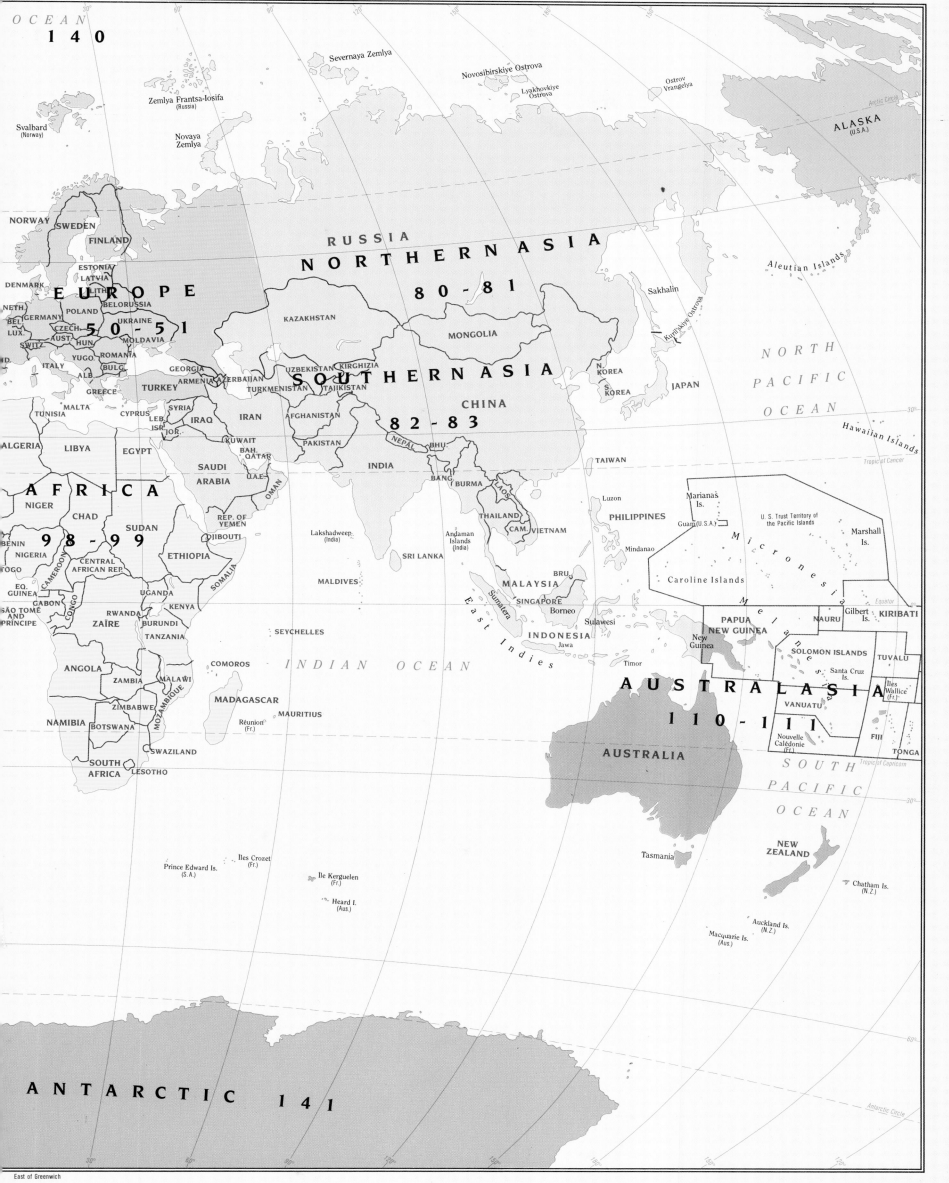

OCEAN

140

Svalbard
(Norway)

Zemlya Frantsa-Iosifa
(Russia)

Novaya
Zemlya

Severnaya Zemlya

Novosibirskiye Ostrova

Lyakhovkiye
Ostrova

Ostrov
Vrangelya

Arctic Circle

ALASKA
(U.S.A.)

NORWAY
SWEDEN
FINLAND

ESTONIA
LATVIA
DENMARK
LITH.
NETH.
BELORUSSIA
BEL.
GERMANY
POLAND
LUX.
CZECH.
UKRAINE
AUST.
SWITZ.
HUN.
MOLDAVIA
IND.
ITALY
YUGO.
ROMANIA
ALB.
BULG.
GREECE

RUSSIA

NORTHERN ASIA

80-81

KAZAKHSTAN

MONGOLIA

Sakhalin

Aleutian Islands

Kuril'skiye Ostrova

N O R T H

P A C I F I C

O C E A N

EUROPE
50-51

GEORGIA
ARMENIA
AZERBAIJAN
TURKEY
TURKMENISTAN

UZBEKISTAN
KIRGHIZIA
TAJIKISTAN

SOUTHERN ASIA

N. KOREA
S. KOREA
JAPAN

TUNISIA
MALTA
CYPRUS
SYRIA
LEB.
ISR. JOR.
IRAQ
IRAN
AFGHANISTAN

CHINA
82-83

ALGERIA
LIBYA
EGYPT
KUWAIT
BAH.
QATAR
U.A.E.
PAKISTAN

NEPAL
BHU.
TAIWAN

Tropic of Cancer

Hawaiian Islands

SAUDI
ARABIA
OMAN

INDIA
BANG.
BURMA

AFRICA

NIGER
CHAD
SUDAN
REP. OF
YEMEN
DJIBOUTI

LAOS
THAILAND
CAM.
VIETNAM

Luzon

PHILIPPINES

Marianas
Is.
Guam (U.S.A.)

U. S. Trust Territory of
the Pacific Islands

Marshall
Is.

M
i
c
r
o
n
e
s
i
a

98-99

BENIN
NIGERIA
TOGO
CENTRAL
AFRICAN REP.
CAMEROON
EQ.
GUINEA
GABON
SÃO TOMÉ
AND
PRÍNCIPE
CONGO
ZAÏRE

ETHIOPIA
SOMALIA

Lakshadweep
(India)

Andaman
Islands
(India)

SRI LANKA

Mindanao

Caroline Islands

M
e
l
a
n
e
s
i
a

MALDIVES

MALAYSIA
SINGAPORE
Borneo

Equator

RWANDA
BURUNDI
UGANDA
KENYA
TANZANIA

SEYCHELLES

East Indies

Sumatera

INDONESIA
Jawa

Sulawesi

Timor

PAPUA
NEW GUINEA
New
Guinea

NAURU

Gilbert
Is.
KIRIBATI

SOLOMON ISLANDS

BRU.

Santa Cruz
Is.

TUVALU

Iles
Wallice
(Fr.)

ANGOLA
ZAMBIA
MALAWI
COMOROS

INDIAN OCEAN

AUSTRALASIA

VANUATU

NAMIBIA
ZIMBABWE
BOTSWANA
MOZAMBIQUE
MADAGASCAR

MAURITIUS

Réunion
(Fr.)

Nouvelle
Calédonie
(Fr.)

FIJI

110-111

TONGA

SOUTH
AFRICA
SWAZILAND
LESOTHO

AUSTRALIA

S O U T H

P A C I F I C

Tropic of Capricorn

O C E A N

NEW
ZEALAND

Tasmania

Prince Edward Is.
(S.A.)

Iles Crozet
(Fr.)

Ile Kerguelen
(Fr.)

Heard I.
(Aus.)

Auckland Is.
(N.Z.)

Chatham Is.
(N.Z.)

Macquarie Is.
(Aus.)

ANTARCTIC 141

Antarctic Circle

THE SOLAR SYSTEM

Modern scientific and astronomical studies have increased our knowledge of the universe and the Earth's place within it immensely. Space exploration has solved many mysteries, but there is still much to be learnt.

The Earth is one of nine planets and numerous smaller bodies that orbit the Sun. The Sun is part of a much larger group of perhaps 100 billion stars that make up the Milky Way. This in turn is only one of the billions of galaxies in an incomprehensibly large universe.

Orbiting the Sun

Under the control of the Sun's gravitational force each planet maintains an elliptical orbit. Except for Mercury and Pluto, which are inclined 7° and 17° respectively, the orbits of the other planets lie within 3° of the plane of the Sun's equator.

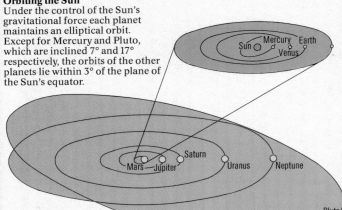

	Sun	Mercury	Venus	Earth	Mars	Jupiter	Saturn
Distance from the Sun (mean) millions of km	-	57·9	108·2	149·6	227·9	778·3	1427
Orbit (sidereal period) days	-	88	224·7	365·25	687	4332·5	10759·2
Rotation d—days hr—hours	24·6d	58·65d	243d	23·93hr	24·62hr	9·8hr	10·2hr
Orbital inclination	-	7°	3°23'	0°	1°52'	1°18'	2°29'
Equatorial diameter km	1392530	4878	12104	12756	6787	142800	120600
Mass (Earth—1)	333000	0·055	0·815	1 / 5·97x10²⁴kg	0·012	317·8	92·2
Density (water—1)	1·41	5·43	5·24	5·52	3·94	1·32	0·7
Number of satellites	-	0	0	1	2	16	17

The Sun is a huge, brilliant star at the centre of the Solar System. It is thought to be about five billion years old; halfway through its stable period of existence. The source of the Sun's immense energy is the continuous fusion of hydrogen into helium. Temperatures in the photosphere can reach 5500°C. Above the photosphere lies the chromosphere, the top layer of which contains numerous spicules that reach into the lower corona. The corona extends far beyond the Sun and produces a bright glow. Solar prominences often appear as great arches extending into the corona. The most conspicuous features on the surface of the Sun are dark blemishes called sunspots. These groups may be associated with violent solar flares.

Mercury is the smallest of the terrestrial planets and the closest to the Sun. The surface is distinctly lunar in appearance, extensively cratered, with smoother volcanic plains. Long lines of cliffs and scarps cut across the plains and craters alike. These probably resulted from crustal shortening as the planet cooled and shrank. Mercury has the greatest temperature extremes of any planet, rising to 480°C during daylight and falling to −180°C at night. This, as well as the virtual lack of atmosphere, indicates that no known form of life could survive there.

Venus is the planet most similar to Earth in both size and mass. However, it is altogether a more hostile world. A dense atmosphere (96 per cent carbon dioxide) obscures the surface under permanent cloud whilst maintaining a temperature of about 480°C. Radar mapping has revealed a landscape of highland 'continents', 'lowlands' and undulating plains. There are also shallow craters, large volcanoes and some rift valleys and trenches. Space probes have shown that the surface is strewn with smooth rocks.

Earth is the largest of the inner planets. The lower atmosphere consists mainly of nitrogen and oxygen. Ozone in the upper layers protects the Earth from the Sun's harmful radiation. The Earth is unique in having a surface largely covered with water (70 per cent), the remainder by continental land masses. Plate tectonics is the dominant process responsible for the structure of the surface, which is then subjected to erosional forces, creating a changing landscape.

Mars has a thin atmosphere which is mainly carbon dioxide (95 per cent). The mean surface temperature is about −40°C, ranging from −138°C at the winter pole to 27°C at the equator, causing strong atmospheric circulation. Dust storms can occur, enveloping the planet, and may take months to settle. Surface features include craters that are often filled with dust, lava plains and giant volcanoes such as Olympus Mons (25km high and 500km across its base), immense canyons, winding river-like valleys, the formation of which is subject to speculation, and polar ice caps which expand and contract with the seasons.

Asteroids are probably the remains of the debris from which the planets formed. They range in diameter from 1000km (the largest, Ceres), to less than 1km. The orbits of most asteroids lie between Mars and Jupiter.

Jupiter is the largest and most massive of the planets. It rotates faster than any other planet. This causes the equatorial region to bulge and the poles to flatten. The atmosphere is composed primarily of hydrogen and helium. The immense heat emanating from the planet's interior produces huge convection currents in the atmosphere. This drives strong wind systems that generate the alternate light- and dark-coloured bands of cloud that encircle the planet. A prominent feature is the Great Red Spot, which was first seen in the 17th century. It is thought to be a huge storm. Other storms have been observed, but none have survived for more than a few days. Jupiter's ring system appears to consist of particles temporarily entrapped by the planet's intense magnetic field. Its satellite system has at least 16 moons.

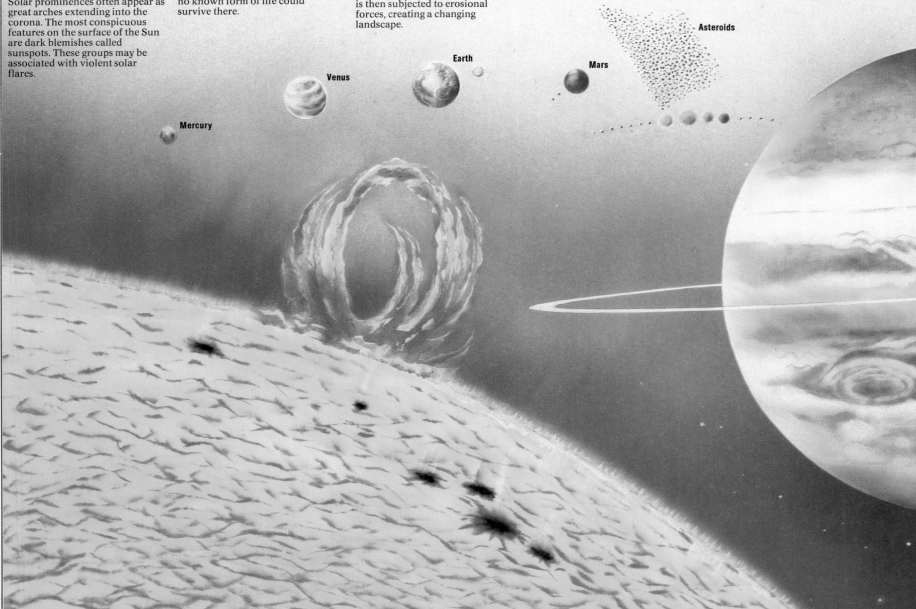

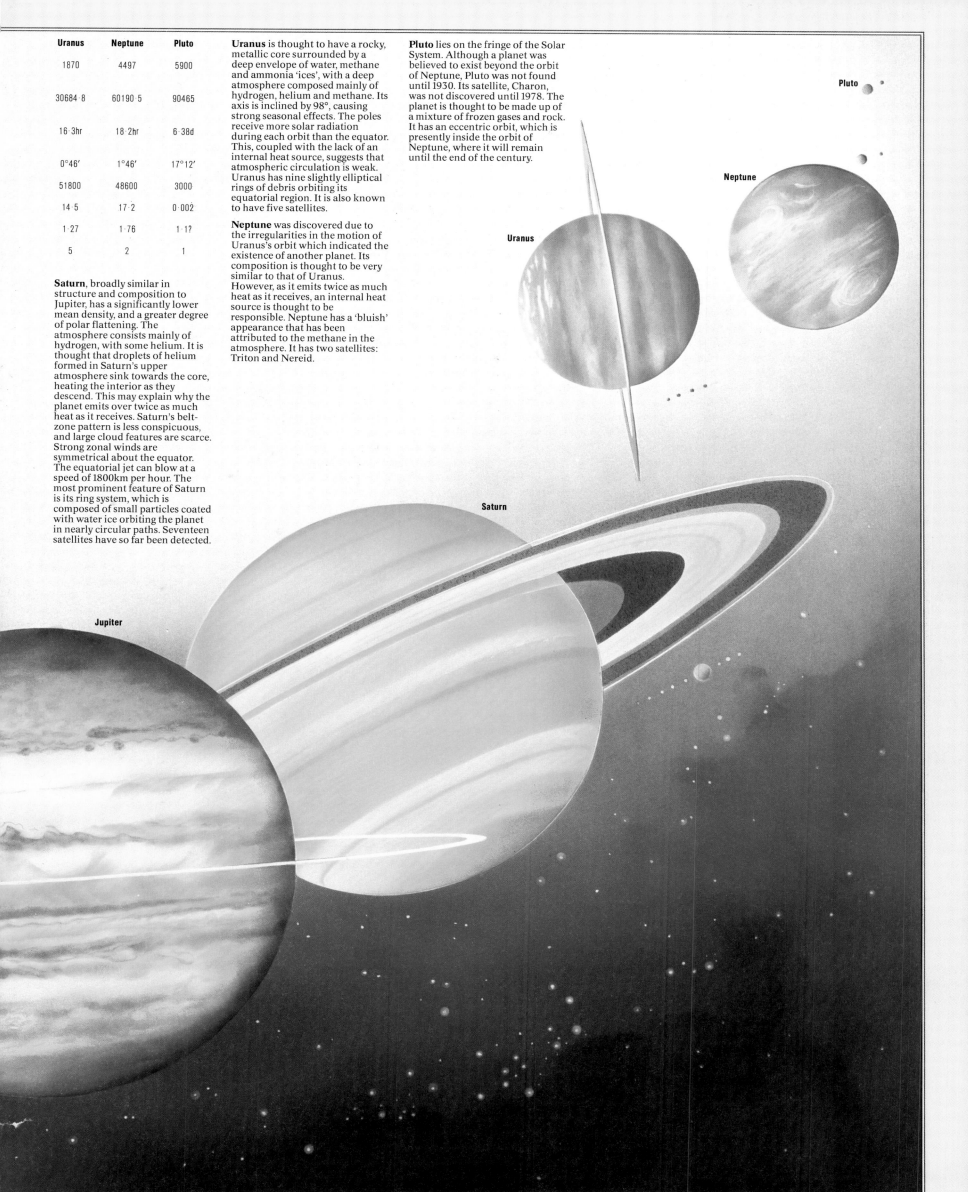

Uranus	Neptune	Pluto
1870	4497	5900
30684·8	60190·5	90465
16·3hr	18·2hr	6·38d
0°46′	1°46′	17°12′
51800	48600	3000
14·5	17·2	0·002
1·27	1·76	1·1?
5	2	1

Saturn, broadly similar in structure and composition to Jupiter, has a significantly lower mean density, and a greater degree of polar flattening. The atmosphere consists mainly of hydrogen, with some helium. It is thought that droplets of helium formed in Saturn's upper atmosphere sink towards the core, heating the interior as they descend. This may explain why the planet emits over twice as much heat as it receives. Saturn's belt-zone pattern is less conspicuous, and large cloud features are scarce. Strong zonal winds are symmetrical about the equator. The equatorial jet can blow at a speed of 1800km per hour. The most prominent feature of Saturn is its ring system, which is composed of small particles coated with water ice orbiting the planet in nearly circular paths. Seventeen satellites have so far been detected.

Uranus is thought to have a rocky, metallic core surrounded by a deep envelope of water, methane and ammonia 'ices', with a deep atmosphere composed mainly of hydrogen, helium and methane. Its axis is inclined by 98°, causing strong seasonal effects. The poles receive more solar radiation during each orbit than the equator. This, coupled with the lack of an internal heat source, suggests that atmospheric circulation is weak. Uranus has nine slightly elliptical rings of debris orbiting its equatorial region. It is also known to have five satellites.

Neptune was discovered due to the irregularities in the motion of Uranus's orbit which indicated the existence of another planet. Its composition is thought to be very similar to that of Uranus. However, as it emits twice as much heat as it receives, an internal heat source is thought to be responsible. Neptune has a 'bluish' appearance that has been attributed to the methane in the atmosphere. It has two satellites: Triton and Nereid.

Pluto lies on the fringe of the Solar System. Although a planet was believed to exist beyond the orbit of Neptune, Pluto was not found until 1930. Its satellite, Charon, was not discovered until 1978. The planet is thought to be made up of a mixture of frozen gases and rock. It has an eccentric orbit, which is presently inside the orbit of Neptune, where it will remain until the end of the century.

Pluto

Neptune

Uranus

Saturn

Jupiter

11

Designed and produced by E.S.R.

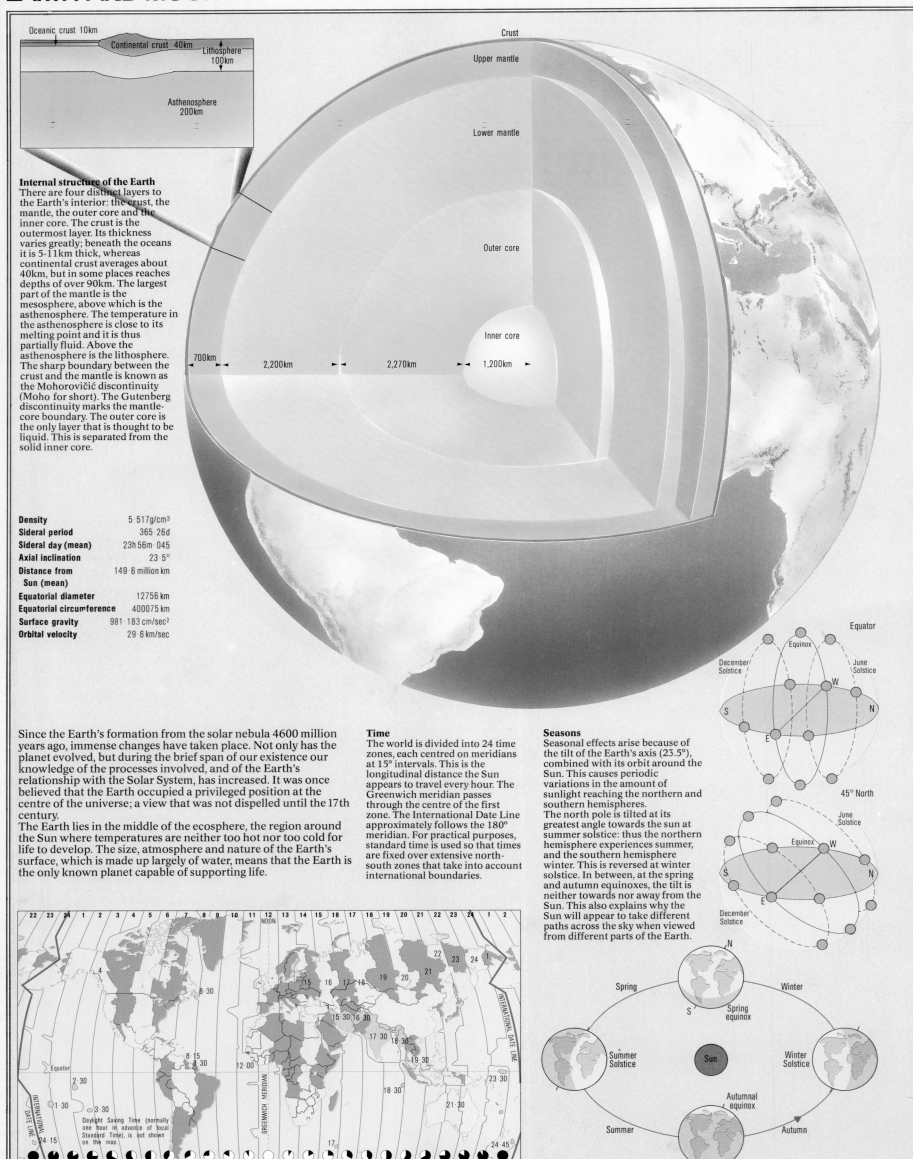

Internal structure of the Earth
There are four distinct layers to the Earth's interior: the crust, the mantle, the outer core and the inner core. The crust is the outermost layer. Its thickness varies greatly; beneath the oceans it is 5-11km thick, whereas continental crust averages about 40km, but in some places reaches depths of over 90km. The largest part of the mantle is the mesosphere, above which is the asthenosphere. The temperature in the asthenosphere is close to its melting point and it is thus partially fluid. Above the asthenosphere is the lithosphere. The sharp boundary between the crust and the mantle is known as the Mohorovičić discontinuity (Moho for short). The Gutenberg discontinuity marks the mantle-core boundary. The outer core is the only layer that is thought to be liquid. This is separated from the solid inner core.

Density	5·517g/cm³
Sideral period	365·26d
Sideral day (mean)	23h 56m 04s
Axial inclination	23·5°
Distance from Sun (mean)	149·6 million km
Equatorial diameter	12756 km
Equatorial circumference	400075 km
Surface gravity	981·183 cm/sec²
Orbital velocity	29·6 km/sec

Since the Earth's formation from the solar nebula 4600 million years ago, immense changes have taken place. Not only has the planet evolved, but during the brief span of our existence our knowledge of the processes involved, and of the Earth's relationship with the Solar System, has increased. It was once believed that the Earth occupied a privileged position at the centre of the universe; a view that was not dispelled until the 17th century.
The Earth lies in the middle of the ecosphere, the region around the Sun where temperatures are neither too hot nor too cold for life to develop. The size, atmosphere and nature of the Earth's surface, which is made up largely of water, means that the Earth is the only known planet capable of supporting life.

Time
The world is divided into 24 time zones, each centred on meridians at 15° intervals. This is the longitudinal distance the Sun appears to travel every hour. The Greenwich meridian passes through the centre of the first zone. The International Date Line approximately follows the 180° meridian. For practical purposes, standard time is used so that times are fixed over extensive north-south zones that take into account international boundaries.

Seasons
Seasonal effects arise because of the tilt of the Earth's axis (23.5°), combined with its orbit around the Sun. This causes periodic variations in the amount of sunlight reaching the northern and southern hemispheres.
The north pole is tilted at its greatest angle towards the sun at summer solstice: thus the northern hemisphere experiences summer, and the southern hemisphere winter. This is reversed at winter solstice. In between, at the spring and autumn equinoxes, the tilt is neither towards nor away from the Sun. This also explains why the Sun will appear to take different paths across the sky when viewed from different parts of the Earth.

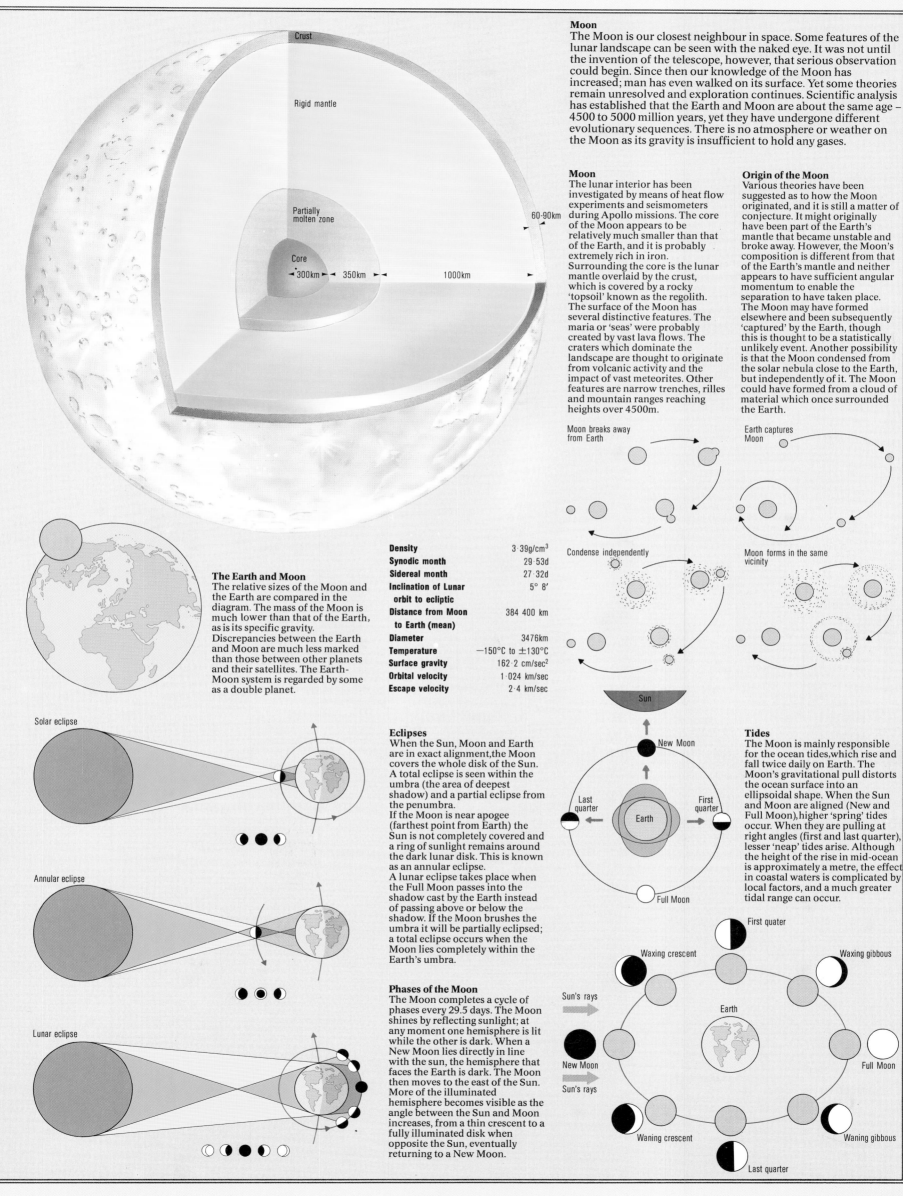

Crust

Rigid mantle

Partially molten zone

Core

◄ 300km ► ◄ 350km ► ◄ 1000km ►

60-90km

Moon
The Moon is our closest neighbour in space. Some features of the lunar landscape can be seen with the naked eye. It was not until the invention of the telescope, however, that serious observation could begin. Since then our knowledge of the Moon has increased; man has even walked on its surface. Yet some theories remain unresolved and exploration continues. Scientific analysis has established that the Earth and Moon are about the same age – 4500 to 5000 million years, yet they have undergone different evolutionary sequences. There is no atmosphere or weather on the Moon as its gravity is insufficient to hold any gases.

Moon
The lunar interior has been investigated by means of heat flow experiments and seismometers during Apollo missions. The core of the Moon appears to be relatively much smaller than that of the Earth, and it is probably extremely rich in iron. Surrounding the core is the lunar mantle overlaid by the crust, which is covered by a rocky 'topsoil' known as the regolith. The surface of the Moon has several distinctive features. The maria or 'seas' were probably created by vast lava flows. The craters which dominate the landscape are thought to originate from volcanic activity and the impact of vast meteorites. Other features are narrow trenches, rilles and mountain ranges reaching heights over 4500m.

Origin of the Moon
Various theories have been suggested as to how the Moon originated, and it is still a matter of conjecture. It might originally have been part of the Earth's mantle that became unstable and broke away. However, the Moon's composition is different from that of the Earth's mantle and neither appears to have sufficient angular momentum to enable the separation to have taken place. The Moon may have formed elsewhere and been subsequently 'captured' by the Earth, though this is thought to be a statistically unlikely event. Another possibility is that the Moon condensed from the solar nebula close to the Earth, but independently of it. The Moon could have formed from a cloud of material which once surrounded the Earth.

Moon breaks away from Earth

Earth captures Moon

Condense independently

Moon forms in the same vicinity

The Earth and Moon
The relative sizes of the Moon and the Earth are compared in the diagram. The mass of the Moon is much lower than that of the Earth, as is its specific gravity. Discrepancies between the Earth and Moon are much less marked than those between other planets and their satellites. The Earth-Moon system is regarded by some as a double planet.

Density	3·39g/cm³
Synodic month	29·53d
Sidereal month	27·32d
Inclination of Lunar orbit to ecliptic	5° 8'
Distance from Moon to Earth (mean)	384 400 km
Diameter	3476km
Temperature	−150°C to ±130°C
Surface gravity	162·2 cm/sec²
Orbital velocity	1·024 km/sec
Escape velocity	2·4 km/sec

Eclipses
When the Sun, Moon and Earth are in exact alignment, the Moon covers the whole disk of the Sun. A total eclipse is seen within the umbra (the area of deepest shadow) and a partial eclipse from the penumbra.
If the Moon is near apogee (farthest point from Earth) the Sun is not completely covered and a ring of sunlight remains around the dark lunar disk. This is known as an annular eclipse.
A lunar eclipse takes place when the Full Moon passes into the shadow cast by the Earth instead of passing above or below the shadow. If the Moon brushes the umbra it will be partially eclipsed; a total eclipse occurs when the Moon lies completely within the Earth's umbra.

Solar eclipse

Annular eclipse

Lunar eclipse

Sun

New Moon

Last quarter

First quarter

Earth

Full Moon

Tides
The Moon is mainly responsible for the ocean tides, which rise and fall twice daily on Earth. The Moon's gravitational pull distorts the ocean surface into an ellipsoidal shape. When the Sun and Moon are aligned (New and Full Moon), higher 'spring' tides occur. When they are pulling at right angles (first and last quarter), lesser 'neap' tides arise. Although the height of the rise in mid-ocean is approximately a metre, the effect in coastal waters is complicated by local factors, and a much greater tidal range can occur.

Phases of the Moon
The Moon completes a cycle of phases every 29.5 days. The Moon shines by reflecting sunlight; at any moment one hemisphere is lit while the other is dark. When a New Moon lies directly in line with the sun, the hemisphere that faces the Earth is dark. The Moon then moves to the east of the Sun. More of the illuminated hemisphere becomes visible as the angle between the Sun and Moon increases, from a thin crescent to a fully illuminated disk when opposite the Sun, eventually returning to a New Moon.

First quarter

Waxing crescent

Waxing gibbous

Sun's rays

Earth

New Moon

Full Moon

Sun's rays

Waning crescent

Waning gibbous

Last quarter

Designed and produced by E.S.R.

MOVING CONTINENTS

The Earth's development is still a matter of much conjecture and debate. Until comparatively recently the view that the structure of the Earth has remained essentially fixed throughout geological time was common. The matching of many pairs of coastlines (strictly, continental shelves) led to the first detailed geological and structural comparisons. Palaeomagnetism has probably proved to be the most influential proof of continental drift, in conjunction with palaeontology, palaeoclimatology and other geological evidence.

Plate tectonics, the field of Earth studies which encompasses the theory of continental drift, offers an explanation for many of the Earth's varied structural and geophysical phenomena. According to theory, the lithosphere consists of rigid segments called plates. These can contain both oceanic and continental crust, which 'float' across the more mobile asthenosphere. Major interactions occur along the plate margins.

Cratons over 2000 million years old
Palaeozoic rock and mobile belt
Cretaceous and Tertiary coastal basin
Mesozoic and Cenozoic mobile belt
Maximum extent of ice movement

Glossopteris
Mesosaurus

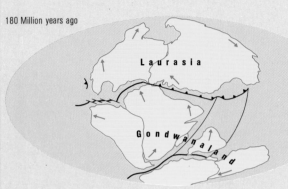

180 Million years ago

Drifting continents
180 million years ago
The fragmentation of the supercontinent Pangaea began about 200 million years ago. Two major rifts initiated the breakup. The rift zone between North America and Africa generated a northern continental group, Laurasia. The rift that separated the southern landmass of Gondwanaland sent India in a northward direction and simultaneously split South America and Africa from Australia and Antarctica.

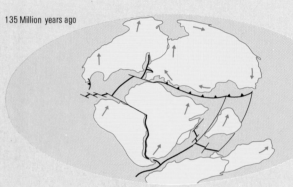

135 Million years ago

135 million years ago
Both Gondwanaland and Laurasia continued to drift northwards. Africa and South America began splitting apart to form the origins of the South Atlantic. India continued heading northwards to Asia. The southern part of the North Atlantic had widened considerably.

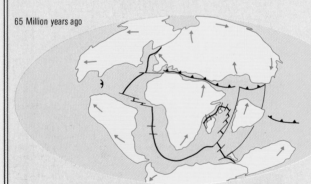

65 Million years ago

65 million years ago
South America had completely separated from Africa and the South Atlantic emerged as a full-fledged ocean. Madagascar had broken away from Africa. In the south, Australia was still connected to Antarctica.

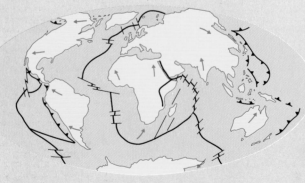

Present

Present
The northward movement of India has led to a collision with Asia, from which the Himalayas resulted. The separation of Greenland from Eurasia is also a recent event in geological time. South America has connected with North America, whilst Australia has drifted north away from Antarctica. Africa is moving away from the Arabian peninsula as the Red Sea rift widens.

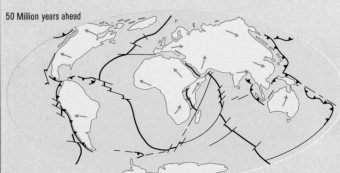

50 Million years ahead

50 million years ahead
By extrapolating plate movements into the future, important changes can be seen. A new sea emerges as East Africa parts company with the mainland. Australia and Papua New Guinea migrate north. The Baja peninsula slides past the North American plate along the San Andreas Fault. The continents will undoubtedly continue to change shape and position: exactly how must still be speculative.

Proving continental drift
Evidence to support the theory of continental drift and the idea that today's continents were once joined comes from various geological and geophysical investigations. Rocks from 'matching coastlines' such as South America and Africa, are often similar in age, type and structure. Fossil remains of the reptile *Mesosaurus* have been found on both sides of the South Atlantic. Similarly the remains of the fossil fern *Glossopteris* also indicates that the continents were once joined. Comparisons of palaeomagnetism in rocks of various ages and the Earth's changing magnetic field seems to confirm continental movement.

Plate tectonics
The mobile behaviour of the material within the asthenosphere allows the motion of lithospheric plates, which form a rigid outer shell to the Earth. Each plate moves as a distinct unit. Most earthquakes, volcanoes and mountain building occur along the plate margins.

There are three types of plate boundary: Divergent (constructive) where plates move apart and upwelling of material from the mantle creates oceanic ridges; Convergent (destructive) where plates collide, causing the lithosphere of one plate to be consumed along a subduction zone; Transform margin, along which plates slide, neither creating nor destroying the lithosphere.

Plate boundaries
Transform
Divergent (constructive)
Convergent (destructive)
Undifferentiated
Uncertain and incipient
Direction of plate movement
Volcano
Earthquake zone

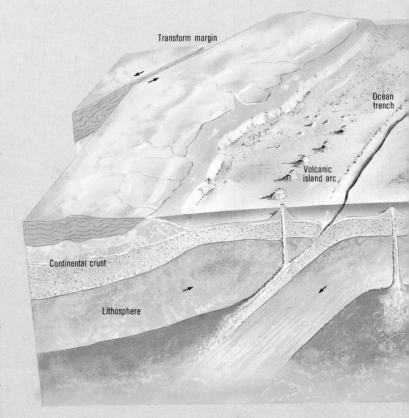

Transform margin
Ocean trench
Volcanic island arc
Continental crust
Lithosphere

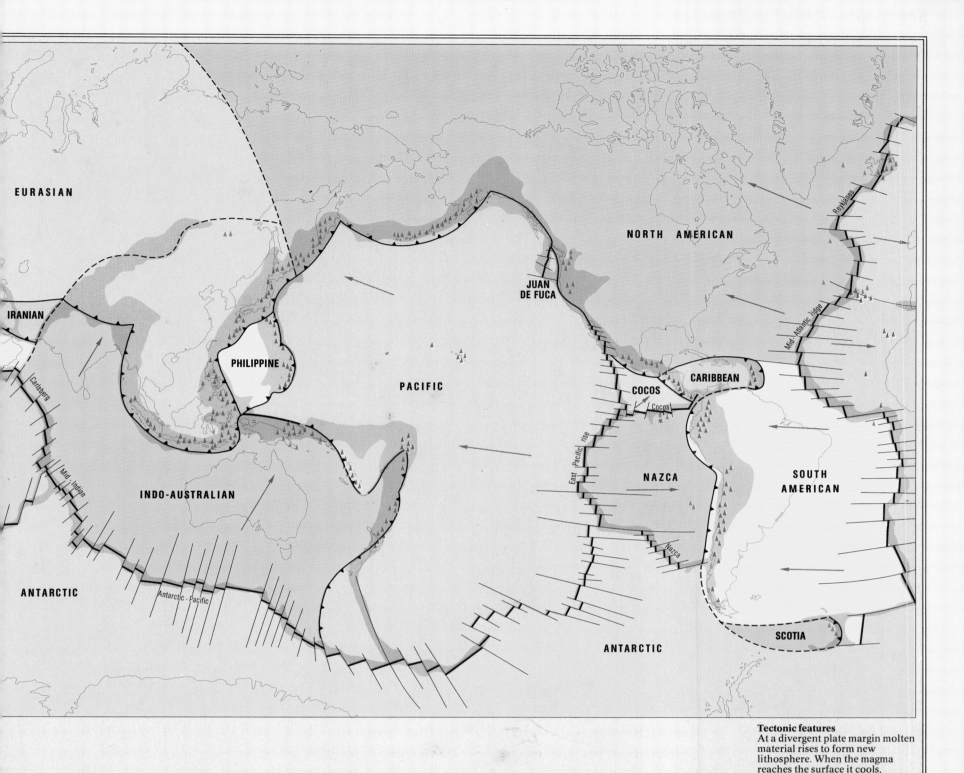

EURASIAN

IRANIAN

Carlsberg

Mid. Indian

INDO-AUSTRALIAN

ANTARCTIC

Antarctic - Pacific

PHILIPPINE

PACIFIC

NORTH   AMERICAN

JUAN
DE FUCA

Reykjanes

Mid. Atlantic Ridge

COCOS

Cocos

CARIBBEAN

East Pacific rise

NAZCA

Nazca

SOUTH
AMERICAN

ANTARCTIC

SCOTIA

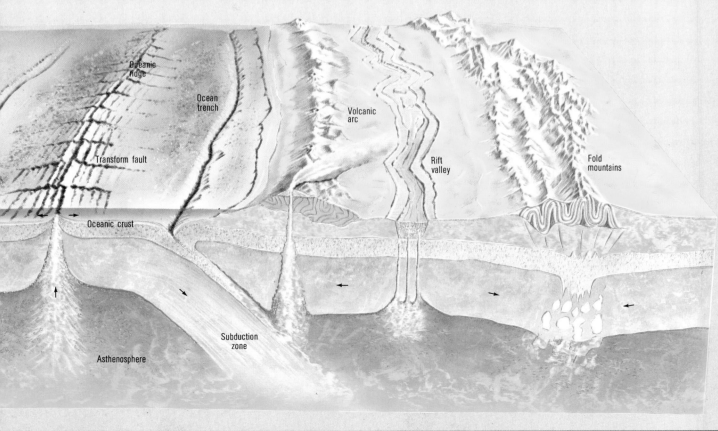

Oceanic
ridge

Ocean
trench

Transform fault

Oceanic crust

Asthenosphere

Subduction
zone

Volcanic
arc

Rift
valley

Fold
mountains

Tectonic features
At a divergent plate margin molten material rises to form new lithosphere. When the magma reaches the surface it cools, solidifies and continues to diverge. The ocean floors are thus in a state of continuous creation and spreading. The Red Sea is believed to be the site of a recently formed divergent boundary. Lateral spreading within a continent can generate large down-faulted valleys, or rifts, like the Great Rift Valley of East Africa.

Plate destruction occurs along subduction zones, often indicated by seismic activity. Continents will remain at the surface while the denser oceanic lithosphere is consumed in an ocean trench. The subducting lithosphere re-enters the Earth's interior, slowly melts and becomes reassimilated. Some magma may eventually migrate to the surface producing volcanic arcs, of which the Andes are an example. Island arcs, such as the Aleutian Islands, are often associated with descending oceanic plates.

If continental plates converge new mountain ranges will result. These are composed of deformed sedimentary rocks and fragments of volcanic arc compressed together. The most recently formed are the Himalayas, but the Alps and the Urals are also thought to have originated in this manner. At transform margins tectonic effects are less dramatic as plates slide against one another. However, as in southern California increased seismic and volcanic activity occurs.

Designed and produced by E.S.R.

THE EARTH'S LANDSCAPE

The landscape around us is the result of a complex system of natural processes. Different rocks of igneous, sedimentary or metamorphic origin comprise the underlying structure. These can be brought to the surface of the Earth by various forces. When exposed to the elements of nature they are slowly weathered, leading to the disintegration and decomposition of the rock. The debris is then carried away and deposited elsewhere. In turn this may be acted upon by other agents. The Earth's surface reflects the processes at work at any given time. Although the forces which shape the landscape appear to act very slowly, in geological terms the alterations are very swift.

The number of people inhabiting the Earth has risen exponentially, and technology has expanded in conjunction with this growth. The human impact on the landscape has thus become increasingly significant. Construction, excavation, reclamation, hydrological work and farming create the most visible features of this changing environment.

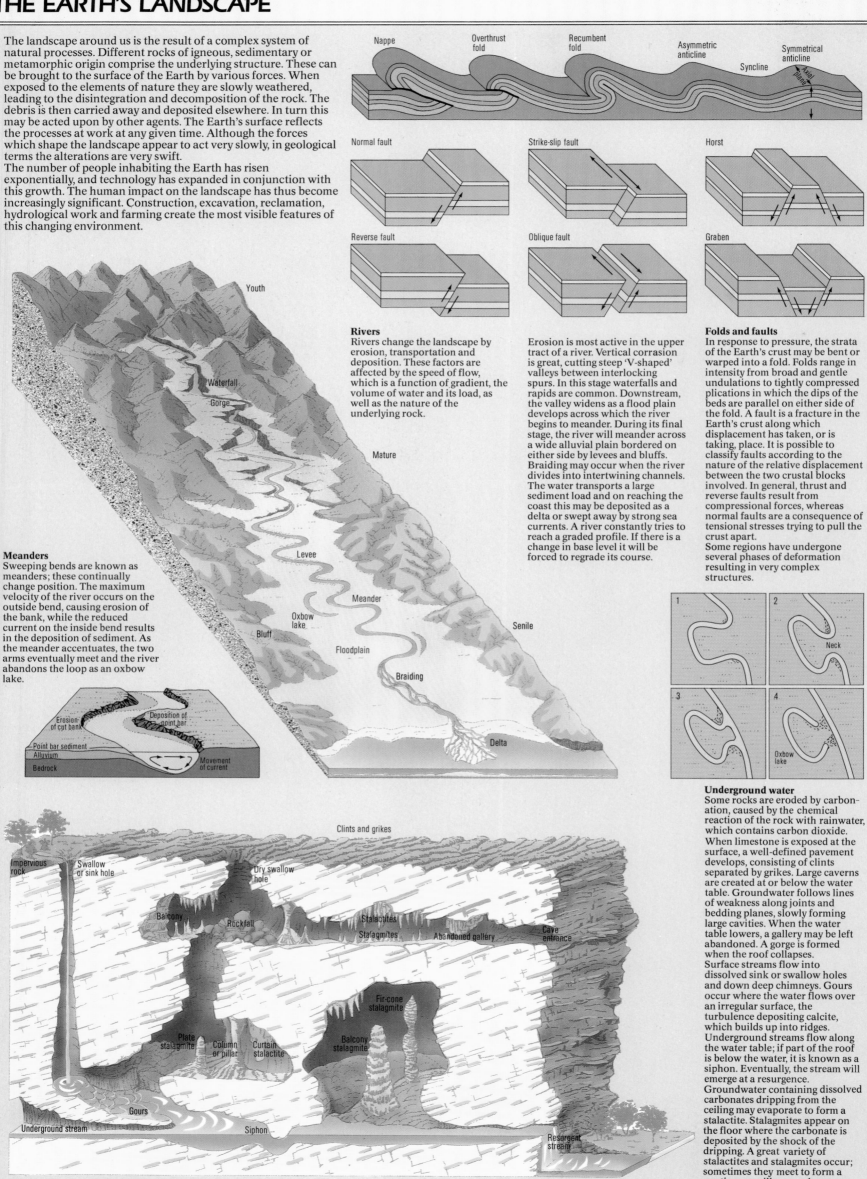

Meanders
Sweeping bends are known as meanders; these continually change position. The maximum velocity of the river occurs on the outside bend, causing erosion of the bank, while the reduced current on the inside bend results in the deposition of sediment. As the meander accentuates, the two arms eventually meet and the river abandons the loop as an oxbow lake.

Rivers
Rivers change the landscape by erosion, transportation and deposition. These factors are affected by the speed of flow, which is a function of gradient, the volume of water and its load, as well as the nature of the underlying rock.

Erosion is most active in the upper tract of a river. Vertical corrasion is great, cutting steep 'V-shaped' valleys between interlocking spurs. In this stage waterfalls and rapids are common. Downstream, the valley widens as a flood plain develops across which the river begins to meander. During its final stage, the river will meander across a wide alluvial plain bordered on either side by levees and bluffs. Braiding may occur when the river divides into intertwining channels. The water transports a large sediment load and on reaching the coast this may be deposited as a delta or swept away by strong sea currents. A river constantly tries to reach a graded profile. If there is a change in base level it will be forced to regrade its course.

Folds and faults
In response to pressure, the strata of the Earth's crust may be bent or warped into a fold. Folds range in intensity from broad and gentle undulations to tightly compressed plications in which the dips of the beds are parallel on either side of the fold. A fault is a fracture in the Earth's crust along which displacement has taken, or is taking, place. It is possible to classify faults according to the nature of the relative displacement between the two crustal blocks involved. In general, thrust and reverse faults result from compressional forces, whereas normal faults are a consequence of tensional stresses trying to pull the crust apart.

Some regions have undergone several phases of deformation resulting in very complex structures.

Underground water
Some rocks are eroded by carbonation, caused by the chemical reaction of the rock with rainwater, which contains carbon dioxide. When limestone is exposed at the surface, a well-defined pavement develops, consisting of clints separated by grikes. Large caverns are created at or below the water table. Groundwater follows lines of weakness along joints and bedding planes, slowly forming large cavities. When the water table lowers, a gallery may be left abandoned. A gorge is formed when the roof collapses.

Surface streams flow into dissolved sink or swallow holes and down deep chimneys. Gours occur where the water flows over an irregular surface, the turbulence depositing calcite, which builds up into ridges. Underground streams flow along the water table; if part of the roof is below the water, it is known as a siphon. Eventually, the stream will emerge at a resurgence. Groundwater containing dissolved carbonates dripping from the ceiling may evaporate to form a stalactite. Stalagmites appear on the floor where the carbonate is deposited by the shock of the dripping. A great variety of stalactites and stalagmites occur; sometimes they meet to form a continuous pillar or column.

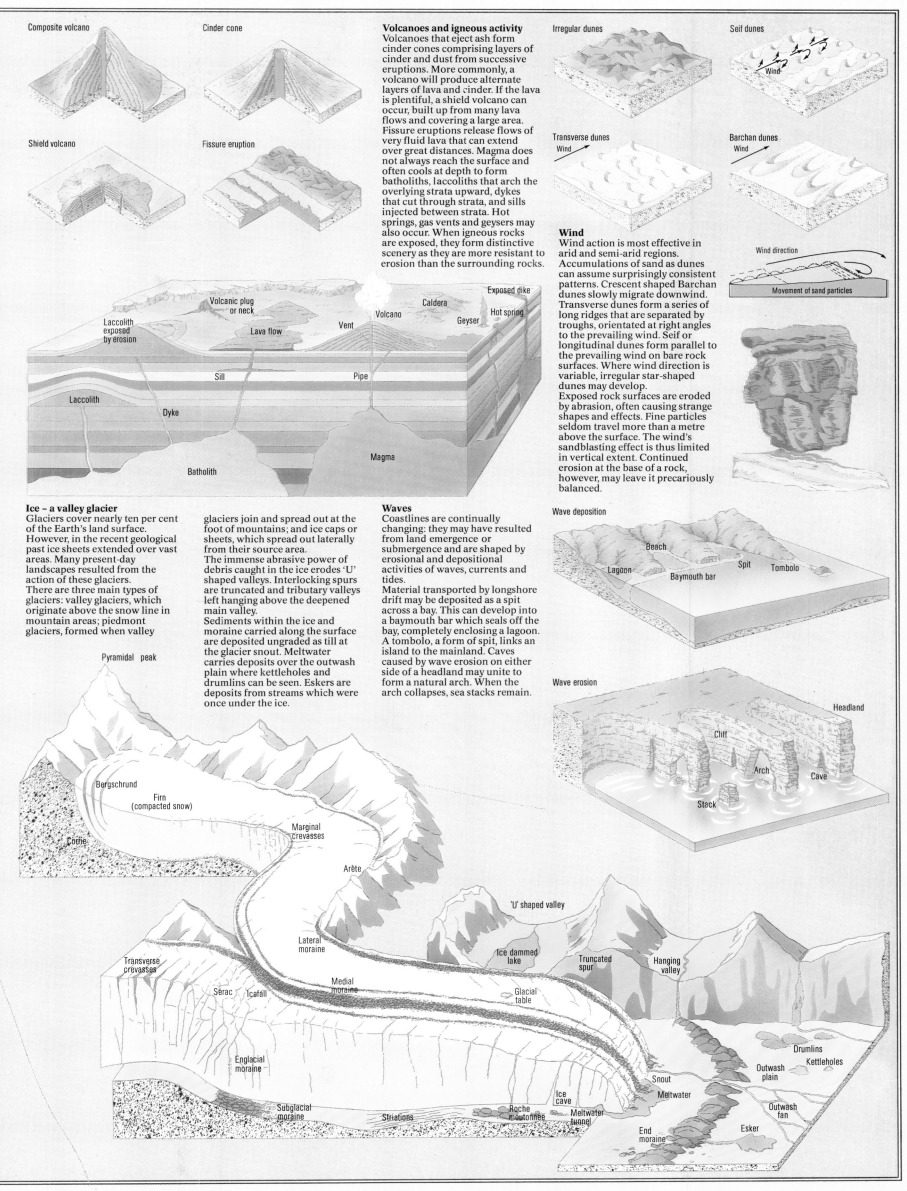

Composite volcano

Cinder cone

Shield volcano

Fissure eruption

Volcanoes and igneous activity

Volcanoes that eject ash form cinder cones comprising layers of cinder and dust from successive eruptions. More commonly, a volcano will produce alternate layers of lava and cinder. If the lava is plentiful, a shield volcano can occur, built up from many lava flows and covering a large area. Fissure eruptions release flows of very fluid lava that can extend over great distances. Magma does not always reach the surface and often cools at depth to form batholiths, laccoliths that arch the overlying strata upward, dykes that cut through strata, and sills injected between strata. Hot springs, gas vents and geysers may also occur. When igneous rocks are exposed, they form distinctive scenery as they are more resistant to erosion than the surrounding rocks.

Irregular dunes

Seif dunes — Wind

Transverse dunes — Wind

Barchan dunes — Wind

Wind

Wind action is most effective in arid and semi-arid regions. Accumulations of sand as dunes can assume surprisingly consistent patterns. Crescent shaped Barchan dunes slowly migrate downwind. Transverse dunes form a series of long ridges that are separated by troughs, orientated at right angles to the prevailing wind. Seif or longitudinal dunes form parallel to the prevailing wind on bare rock surfaces. Where wind direction is variable, irregular star-shaped dunes may develop.

Exposed rock surfaces are eroded by abrasion, often causing strange shapes and effects. Fine particles seldom travel more than a metre above the surface. The wind's sandblasting effect is thus limited in vertical extent. Continued erosion at the base of a rock, however, may leave it precariously balanced.

Wind direction

Movement of sand particles

Laccolith exposed by erosion — Volcanic plug or neck — Lava flow — Vent — Volcano — Caldera — Geyser — Hot spring — Exposed dike

Sill — Pipe

Laccolith — Dyke — Batholith — Magma

Ice – a valley glacier

Glaciers cover nearly ten per cent of the Earth's land surface. However, in the recent geological past ice sheets extended over vast areas. Many present-day landscapes resulted from the action of these glaciers.

There are three main types of glaciers: valley glaciers, which originate above the snow line in mountain areas; piedmont glaciers, formed when valley glaciers join and spread out at the foot of mountains; and ice caps or sheets, which spread out laterally from their source area.

The immense abrasive power of debris caught in the ice erodes 'U' shaped valleys. Interlocking spurs are truncated and tributary valleys left hanging above the deepened main valley.

Sediments within the ice and moraine carried along the surface are deposited ungraded as till at the glacier snout. Meltwater carries deposits over the outwash plain where kettleholes and drumlins can be seen. Eskers are deposits from streams which were once under the ice.

Waves

Coastlines are continually changing: they may have resulted from land emergence or submergence and are shaped by erosional and depositional activities of waves, currents and tides.

Material transported by longshore drift may be deposited as a spit across a bay. This can develop into a baymouth bar which seals off the bay, completely enclosing a lagoon. A tombolo, a form of spit, links an island to the mainland. Caves caused by wave erosion on either side of a headland may unite to form a natural arch. When the arch collapses, sea stacks remain.

Wave deposition

Beach — Lagoon — Spit — Tombolo — Baymouth bar

Wave erosion

Headland — Cliff — Arch — Cave — Stack

Pyramidal peak

Bergschrund — Firn (compacted snow) — Marginal crevasses — Arête — Corrie

'U' shaped valley — Ice dammed lake — Truncated spur — Hanging valley

Transverse crevasses — Sérac — Icafáll — Lateral moraine — Medial moraine — Glacial table — Englacial moraine

Subglacial moraine — Striations — Roche moutonnée — Ice cave — Meltwater tunnel — Snout — Meltwater — End moraine — Outwash plain — Drumlins — Kettleholes — Outwash fan — Esker

Designed and produced by E.S.R.

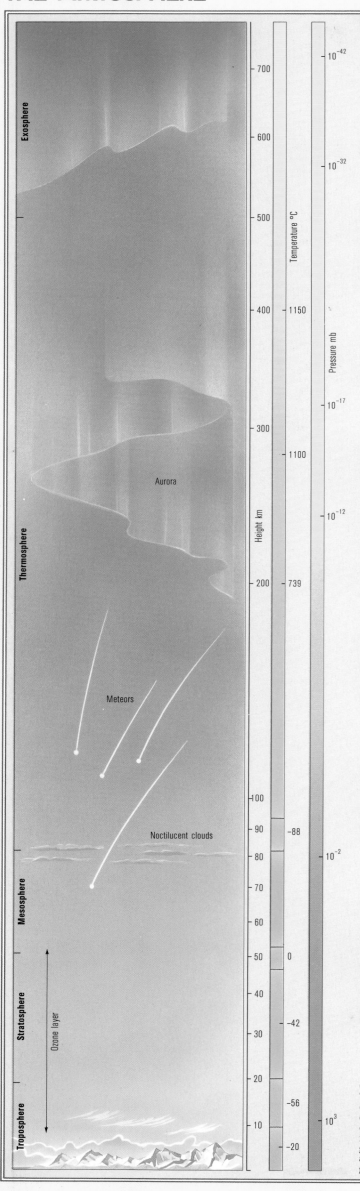

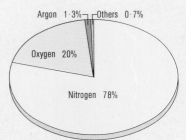

Exosphere, Thermosphere and Mesosphere
Stratosphere
Troposphere

Earth

The atmosphere, which is unlike that of any other planet, encircles and protects the Earth. Changes in the composition of the atmosphere are closely associated with the evolution of the Earth. One of the most important transitions was the increase in oxygen when photosynthetic plants evolved.

The atmosphere is a mixture of gases, the largest proportion of which is nitrogen. The most important is oxygen, without which life could not be sustained; other gases are present in quite small quantities.

Near the Earth's surface, gravitational pull increases the density of the atmosphere. We do not feel this air pressure because of the equal air pressure inside our bodies. Variation in air pressure has a major influence on weather, as does the amount of water vapour in the atmosphere. These elements are in turn affected by a number of factors such as the evaporation of water from the oceans, wind movements and the topography of the Earth.

Structure of the atmosphere
The atmosphere can be divided into various layers, depending on its physical properties. Variations in temperature and pressure result from the distribution of solar heating and help to distinguish the different zones.

Atmospheric composition
The composition of the Earth's atmosphere has changed as the planet has evolved. At present the largest proportion is formed of nitrogen followed by oxygen. Argon and carbon dioxide can also be found, as well as other inert gases such as neon and helium. The atmosphere also contains variable amounts of water vapour, up to three per cent, and small quantities of sulphur dioxide.

Argon 1·3%   Others 0·7%
Oxygen 20%
Nitrogen 78%

Exosphere merges into the vacuum of space. It is extremely rarefied and is composed mainly of hydrogen and helium.

Thermosphere absorbs ultraviolet radiation. Temperatures rise steeply with height to several thousand degrees. This region is the source of the ionosphere, disturbances in this region appear as glowing lights of varying colours – aurorae. They occur primarily over the poles because the charged particles from the Sun are channelled there by the Earth's magnetic field. Short-wave and long-wave radio transmissions are also reflected at various layers within the ionosphere.

It would appear that human activities are altering the natural atmospheric conditions of the planet. To what extent this is happening is still a matter of great debate.

The ozone (a form of oxygen), in the upper atmosphere, screens the Earth from the Sun's ultraviolet rays and is deteriorating. The use of man-made refrigerant gases such as chlorofluorocarbons (CFCs) are a contributing factor. Conversely, other pollutants, such as methane, are by a complex set of chemical reactions increasing ozone levels nearer the ground, which may be adding to the 'greenhouse effect', a phrase which has been used to describe a general warming of the atmosphere.

Since the industrial revolution, carbon dioxide levels have increased by 30 per cent. This is a direct result of burning fossil fuel and destroying vast tracts of forest. The carbon dioxide traps outgoing radiation, which leads to an increase in temperatures. It has been predicted that an average rise of 3°C is possible, and as much as 8-10°C at the poles. Sea levels would rise as a result of melting ice and thermal expansion of the oceans. Many areas of low-lying land would then be flooded and island nations swamped. Accompanying these temperature rises would be changes in rainfall patterns which could affect agricultural productivity. In general it is also thought that tropical conditions would gradually extend northwards.

Mesosphere extends to a height of about 80km and in it there is a marked fall in temperature to −120°C. Meteorites from space tend to burn out in this region as they meet increased air resistance.

Other forms of atmospheric pollution are also causing concern. Industrial emissions of sulphur oxide and nitrogen oxide dissolve in rain, which is often transported great distances before returning to Earth as sulphuric and nitric acids. Their deposition as 'acid rain' can have dire effects on ecosystems. Forests are affected, soils leached and water supplies contaminated. Exhaust-caused smogs and lead emitted from vehicles also have a detrimental effect on the atmosphere.

It is known that the atmosphere and climate of the planet have changed with time. Our knowledge, however, is far from complete in many areas. Whether changes in atmospheric conditions are natural or man-made is to some degree still a matter of speculation and controversy.

Stratosphere contains the ozone layer, which absorbs the Sun's harmful ultraviolet light. As a result, the temperature rises to about 10°C before decreasing again in the stratopause. Noctilucent clouds may form from compressed meteoric dust in this region.

Troposphere is the lowest layer of the atmosphere and contains all the climatic activities that affect us. It reaches about 8km above the poles and 15km above the equator. Pressure is at its greatest due to the weight of the layers above, and 80 per cent of the mass of the atmosphere is found here. Near ground level, visible and infrared radiation is absorbed. Temperature decreases with height until the tropopause is reached.

Greenhouse effect
The balance of the incoming and outgoing solar radiation is disturbed by the increased amount of carbon dioxide which traps infrared radiation. This causes a general warming of the atmosphere known as the greenhouse effect.

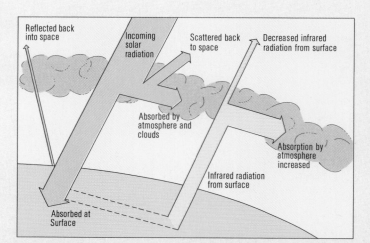

Reflected back into space
Incoming solar radiation
Scattered back to space
Decreased infrared radiation from surface
Absorbed by atmosphere and clouds
Absorption by atmosphere increased
Infrared radiation from surface
Absorbed at Surface

Clouds

Clouds can be classified on the basis of their appearance and height. The basic forms are cirrus, stratus and cumulus. Other clouds reflect one of these forms or are combinations or modifications of them.

Cirrus thin, delicate, fibrous ice-crystal clouds. Sometimes appear as hooked filaments called 'mares tails', often the first sign of an approaching depression.

Cirrocumulus thin, white ice-crystal clouds in the form of ripples, waves or globular masses all in a row. May produce a 'mackerel sky'.

Cirrostratus thin sheet of white ice-crystal clouds that may give the sky a milky look. Sometimes produce haloes around the Sun or Moon.

Altocumulus white to grey clouds often composed of separate globules. Frequently indicates unsettled weather.

Altostratus stratified veil of clouds that are generally thin and may produce very light precipitation.

Stratocumulus soft, grey clouds in globular patches or rolls. Rolls may join together to make a continuous cloud.

Stratus low uniform layer, forms dull, overcast skies. Associated with depressions, may often produce drizzle and rain.

Nimbostratus amorphous layer of dark grey clouds. One of the chief precipitation-producing clouds.

Cumulus dense, billowy clouds often characterised by flat bases. May occur as isolated clouds or closely packed.

Cumulonimbus towering cloud sometimes spreading out on top to form an 'anvil head'. Associated with heavy rainfall, thunder, lightning, hail and tornadoes.

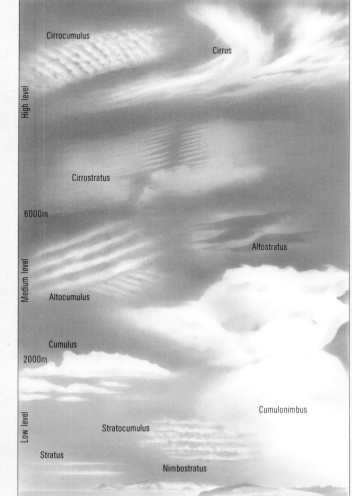

Clouds

Without clouds there would be no precipitation. Variations in the amount of precipitation from place to place as well as local differences from time to time have a significant impact not only on the nature of the physical landscape but also on people's lifestyles.

Clouds consist of microscopic drops of water or ice crystals suspended in the atmosphere. Formation occurs when air that contains water vapour becomes saturated and reaches its dew point. This is usually the result of the air rising and thus cooling. The water vapour then condenses around dust particles.

Wind

The unequal heating of the Earth by solar radiation generates pressure differences. These inequalities cause the movement of air from areas of higher pressure to areas of lower pressure. A system of general circulation is thus generated by semipermanent cells of high and low pressure over the oceans. Wind direction is then subject to deflection by the Coriolis effect, to the right in the northern hemisphere, to the left in the southern hemisphere. This is complicated by seasonal pressure changes over land, which can give rise to seasonal reversals of wind known as monsoons.

Circulation of the air
The temperature differences between the poles and the equator provide the thermal energy to drive atmospheric circulation. Warm air at the equator rises and flows towards the poles at high levels. Cold polar air moves towards the equator at low levels to replace it. Once the effect of rotation is added, the Coriolis effect, this simple convection system breaks down into smaller cells.

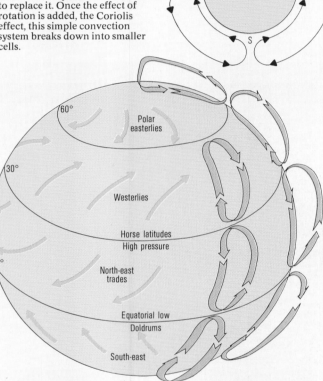

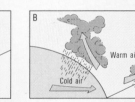

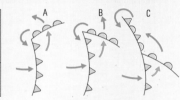

A Depression
Variable weather in the middle latitudes often results from the development of low pressure areas known as depressions, a common feature of which is the formation of warm and cold fronts. The warm, light air rises above the cool air along the warm front. Behind, the cold air forces its way under the warm air along the cold front. Gradually, the cold front catches up with the warm front and the warm air is pushed above the cold in an occlusion. In the northern hemisphere, the air circulates in an anticlockwise direction and in the southern, it circulates clockwise.

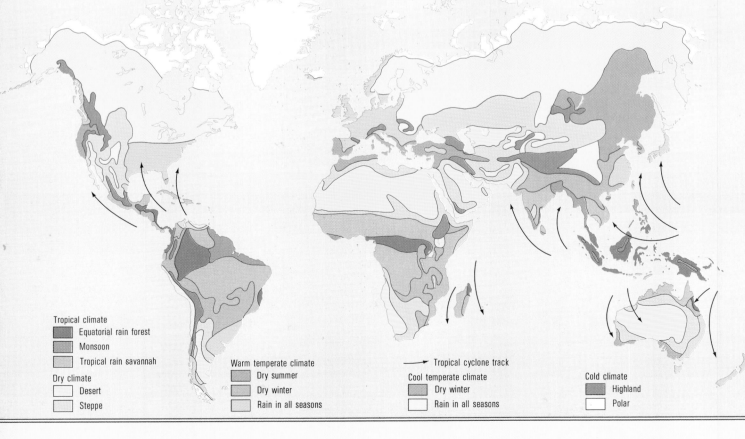

Tropical climate
- ▨ Equatorial rain forest
- ▨ Monsoon
- ▨ Tropical rain savannah

Dry climate
- ☐ Desert
- ☐ Steppe

Warm temperate climate
- ☐ Dry summer
- ☐ Dry winter
- ☐ Rain in all seasons

→ Tropical cyclone track

Cool temperate climate
- ☐ Dry winter
- ☐ Rain in all seasons

Cold climate
- ▨ Highland
- ☐ Polar

Climate
The climate of an area is its characteristic weather considered over a long period of time. Differences in latitude, prevailing air masses, either local or regional, the relative distribution of land and sea, as well as the topography, will all have an effect on the climatic conditions experienced. The most popular climatic classification is that devised by Wladimir Köppen. It is based on the seasonal variations of temperature and rainfall and their effect on vegetation growth. The range of climates can broadly be defined according to latitude. Hot, tropical climates are dominated by equatorial air masses throughout the year. Temperate climates of the mid-latitudes are very variable, subjected alternately to subpolar and subtropical air masses as well as seasonal shifts. Polar climates of high latitudes are strongly seasonal, influenced by subpolar and polar air masses. Geological evidence suggests that during other periods the planet experienced a more uniform climate. The present variable pattern may be due, in part, to the fact that the earth is still recovering from the last Ice Age, although opinion varies as to whether fluctuations in climate should be regarded as abnormal.

Designed and produced by E.S.R.

EVOLUTION OF LIFE

All living things have a common ancestry – dating as far back as the origin of life itself. It is believed that the first flickerings of life began over 3500 million years ago. Since then species have become ever more numerous and diverse, to produce the present vast array of life. Through successive geological periods the variety of life forms preserved as fossils is both astonishing and informative. It is possible to tell not only what plants and animals looked like, but also, to some extent, how they lived.

The theory of evolution helps to explain how the different kinds of flora and fauna came into existence, how they are related to each other and how they have changed. Charles Darwin was the first person to propound the theory of evolution in a scientific manner. He suggested that a process of natural selection takes place. Those plants and animals best adapted to their environment are more likely to survive and reproduce than others. As time passes an increasing proportion of individuals will have inherited the particular advantageous characteristics.

Geological time scale
Geological time is divided into named intervals. These are separated from each other by major changes in rock type, obvious breaks in succession, and abrupt changes in fossil groups.

Various dating methods place rocks and geological events in the correct chronological order. The particular fossil content in successive strata is one such method. Today, radioactive dating is the most reliable way of determining the absolute age of rocks. The basis of this involves analysis of the atomic decay of elements within the rock minerals.

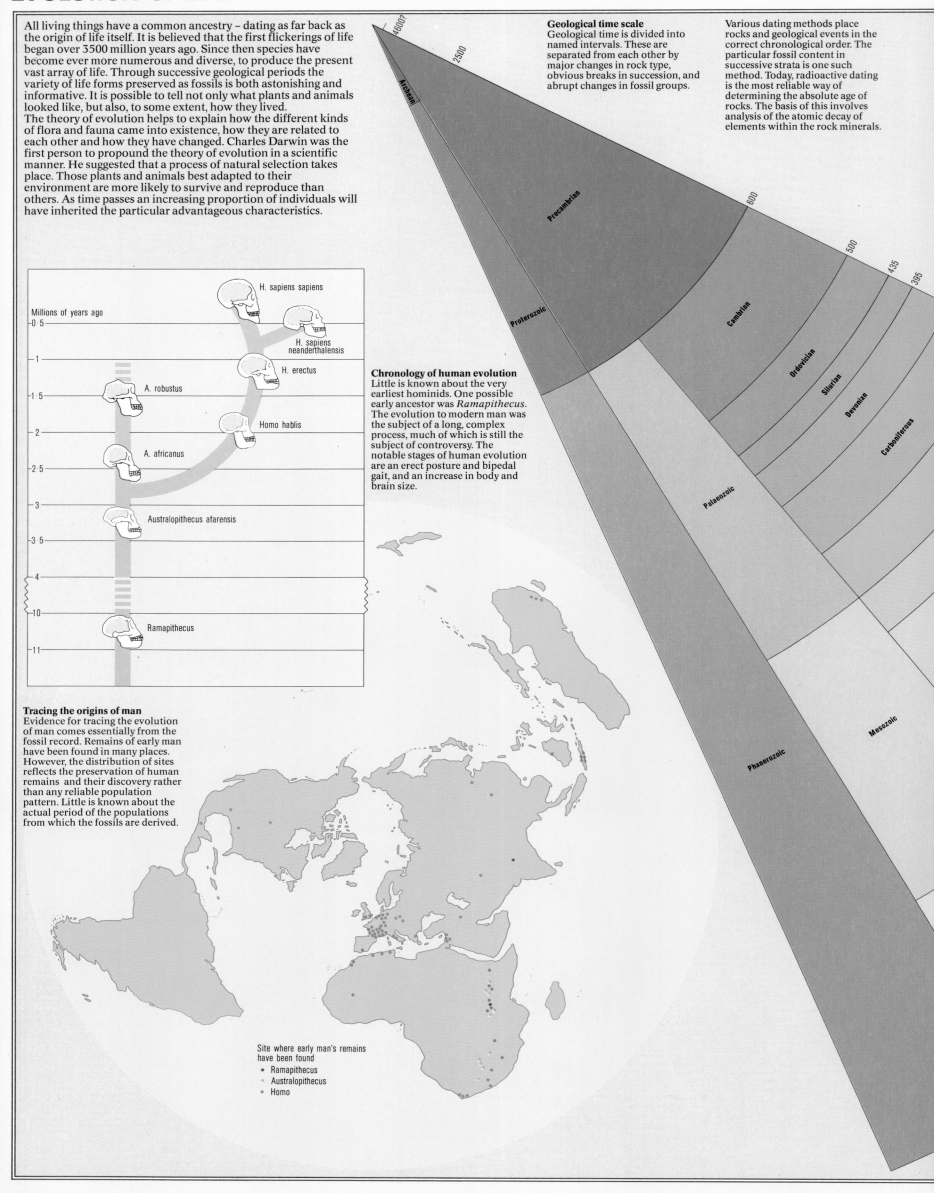

Chronology of human evolution
Little is known about the very earliest hominids. One possible early ancestor was *Ramapithecus*. The evolution to modern man was the subject of a long, complex process, much of which is still the subject of controversy. The notable stages of human evolution are an erect posture and bipedal gait, and an increase in body and brain size.

Tracing the origins of man
Evidence for tracing the evolution of man comes essentially from the fossil record. Remains of early man have been found in many places. However, the distribution of sites reflects the preservation of human remains and their discovery rather than any reliable population pattern. Little is known about the actual period of the populations from which the fossils are derived.

Site where early man's remains have been found
- Ramapithecus
- Australopithecus
- Homo

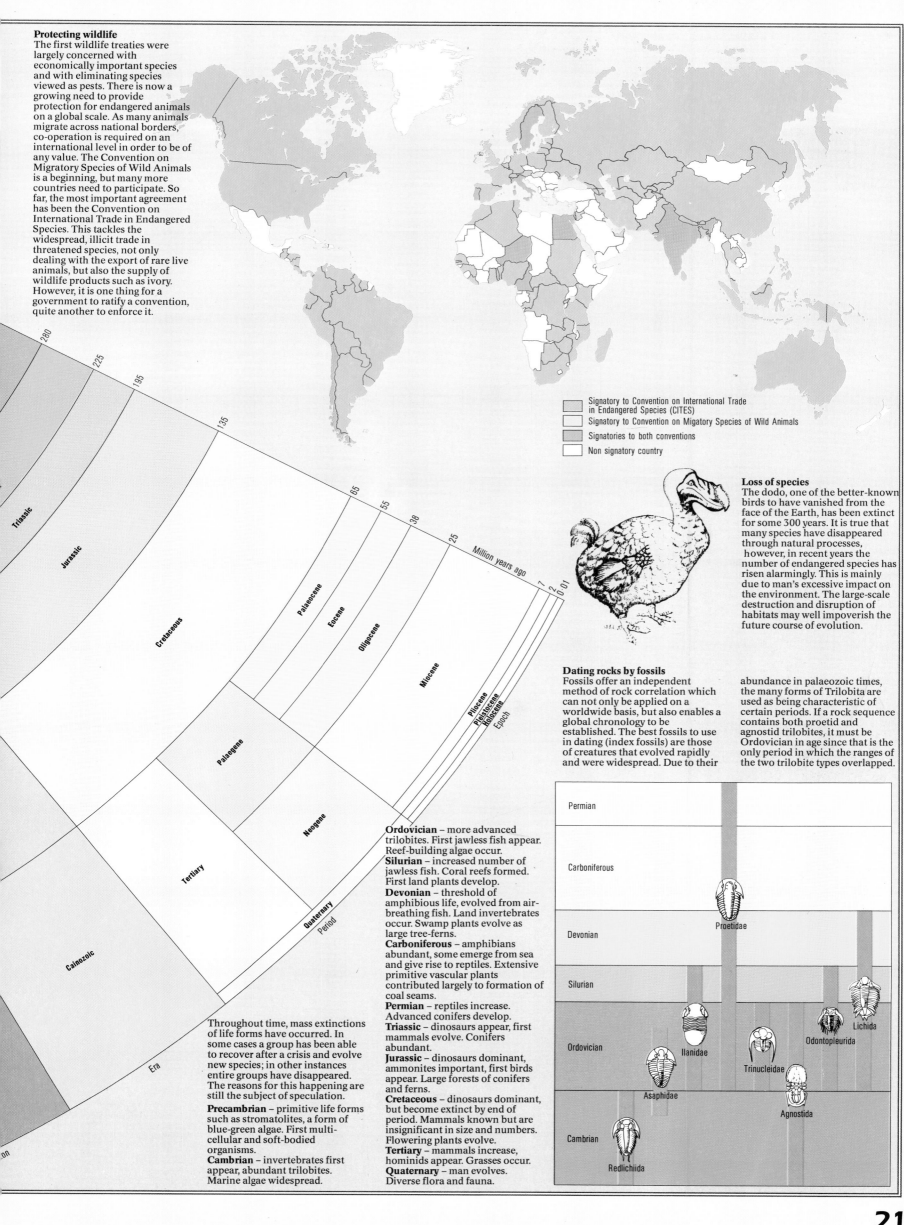

Protecting wildlife
The first wildlife treaties were largely concerned with economically important species and with eliminating species viewed as pests. There is now a growing need to provide protection for endangered animals on a global scale. As many animals migrate across national borders, co-operation is required on an international level in order to be of any value. The Convention on Migratory Species of Wild Animals is a beginning, but many more countries need to participate. So far, the most important agreement has been the Convention on International Trade in Endangered Species. This tackles the widespread, illicit trade in threatened species, not only dealing with the export of rare live animals, but also the supply of wildlife products such as ivory. However, it is one thing for a government to ratify a convention, quite another to enforce it.

Signatory to Convention on International Trade in Endangered Species (CITES)
Signatory to Convention on Migatory Species of Wild Animals
Signatories to both conventions
Non signatory country

Loss of species
The dodo, one of the better-known birds to have vanished from the face of the Earth, has been extinct for some 300 years. It is true that many species have disappeared through natural processes, however, in recent years the number of endangered species has risen alarmingly. This is mainly due to man's excessive impact on the environment. The large-scale destruction and disruption of habitats may well impoverish the future course of evolution.

Dating rocks by fossils
Fossils offer an independent method of rock correlation which can not only be applied on a worldwide basis, but also enables a global chronology to be established. The best fossils to use in dating (index fossils) are those of creatures that evolved rapidly and were widespread. Due to their abundance in palaeozoic times, the many forms of Trilobita are used as being characteristic of certain periods. If a rock sequence contains both proetid and agnostid trilobites, it must be Ordovician in age since that is the only period in which the ranges of the two trilobite types overlapped.

Throughout time, mass extinctions of life forms have occurred. In some cases a group has been able to recover after a crisis and evolve new species; in other instances entire groups have disappeared. The reasons for this happening are still the subject of speculation.

Precambrian – primitive life forms such as stromatolites, a form of blue-green algae. First multi-cellular and soft-bodied organisms.
Cambrian – invertebrates first appear, abundant trilobites. Marine algae widespread.
Ordovician – more advanced trilobites. First jawless fish appear. Reef-building algae occur.
Silurian – increased number of jawless fish. Coral reefs formed. First land plants develop.
Devonian – threshold of amphibious life, evolved from air-breathing fish. Land invertebrates occur. Swamp plants evolve as large tree-ferns.
Carboniferous – amphibians abundant, some emerge from sea and give rise to reptiles. Extensive primitive vascular plants contributed largely to formation of coal seams.
Permian – reptiles increase. Advanced conifers develop.
Triassic – dinosaurs appear, first mammals evolve. Conifers abundant.
Jurassic – dinosaurs dominant, ammonites important, first birds appear. Large forests of conifers and ferns.
Cretaceous – dinosaurs dominant, but become extinct by end of period. Mammals known but are insignificant in size and numbers. Flowering plants evolve.
Tertiary – mammals increase, hominids appear. Grasses occur.
Quaternary – man evolves. Diverse flora and fauna.

280 225 195 135 65 55 38 25 7 2 0.01

Million years ago

Triassic
Jurassic
Cretaceous
Palaeocene
Eocene
Oligocene
Miocene
Pliocene
Pleistocene
Holocene
Epoch
Palaegene
Neogene
Tertiary
Quaternary
Period
Cainozoic
Era

Permian
Carboniferous
Devonian
Silurian
Ordovician
Cambrian

Proetidae
Lichida
Odontopleurida
Ilanidae
Trinucleidae
Asaphidae
Agnostida
Redlichiida

EXPLORATION AND DISCOVERY

The early explorers who travelled beyond their own shores were
accomplished shipbuilders and seamen. The Vikings, Chinese and
Arabs were among those who first reached distant lands. Some
merchants and missionaries reached remote inland areas. Within
a relatively short space of time the great voyages of discovery had
charted the vast expanses of sea and largely determined the extent
and shape of the continental landmasses. These geographical
explorations were later expanded and consolidated by
expeditions of a more scientific nature.

Baffin Bay

Beaufort Sea

Davis Str.

Arctic Circle
Bering Str.

Hudson Str.

Bering Sea

Hudson Bay

NORTH AMERICA

NORTH ATLANTIC OCEAN

Newfoundland

Montréal

Bristol
Plymouth

NORTH PACIFIC OCEAN

Vancouver Island

Astoria (Fort George)

Missouri

Mississippi

St. Louis

San Juan

Lisboa
Huelva
Cadiz
Tanger

Tropic of Cancer

South Sandwich Is.
Hawaii

Gulf of Mexico

Bahamas

Cuba

Tombo

Vera Cruz

Tenochtitlan (Ciudad de México)

Hispaniola

Caribbean Sea

Bathurst

Panamá

Freetown

Equator

Quito

Amazon

SOUTH AMERICA

Lima
Cuzco

From England
From England

Tropic of Capricorn

Coquimbo

Buenos Aires

SOUTH ATLANTIC OCEAN

SOUTH PACIFIC OCEAN

SOUTHERN SEA
South Sandwich Is.
South Orkney Is.
South Shetland Is.
Drake Passage

Lazarev Sea

Queen Maud Land

Enderby Land

Scotia Sea

Antarctic Peninsula

WEDDELL SEA

ANTARCTICA

Bellingshausen Sea

Ronne Ice Shelf

Scott 18 1 1912
Shackleton 88°23' 1909

South Pole
Amundsen 14 12 1911

Davis Sea

Marie Byrd Land

Wilkes Land

AMUNDSEN SEA

Ross Ice Shelf

Cabo de Hornas

St. Est. de Magellanes

ROSS SEA

Dumont d'Urville Sea

INDIAN OCEAN

SOUTH PACIFIC OCEAN

Antarctic explorers
- – – – Bellingshausen 1819-21
- –·–· Weddell 1820-24
- ——— Biscoe 1831-32
- –··–·· Wilkes 1839-40
- –·–·– Ross 1840-43
- –·–·– Shackleton 1907-9
- ········ Scott 1910-12
- ——— Amundsen 1911-12
- ········ Hillary-Fuchs 1955-58

West of Greenwich

22

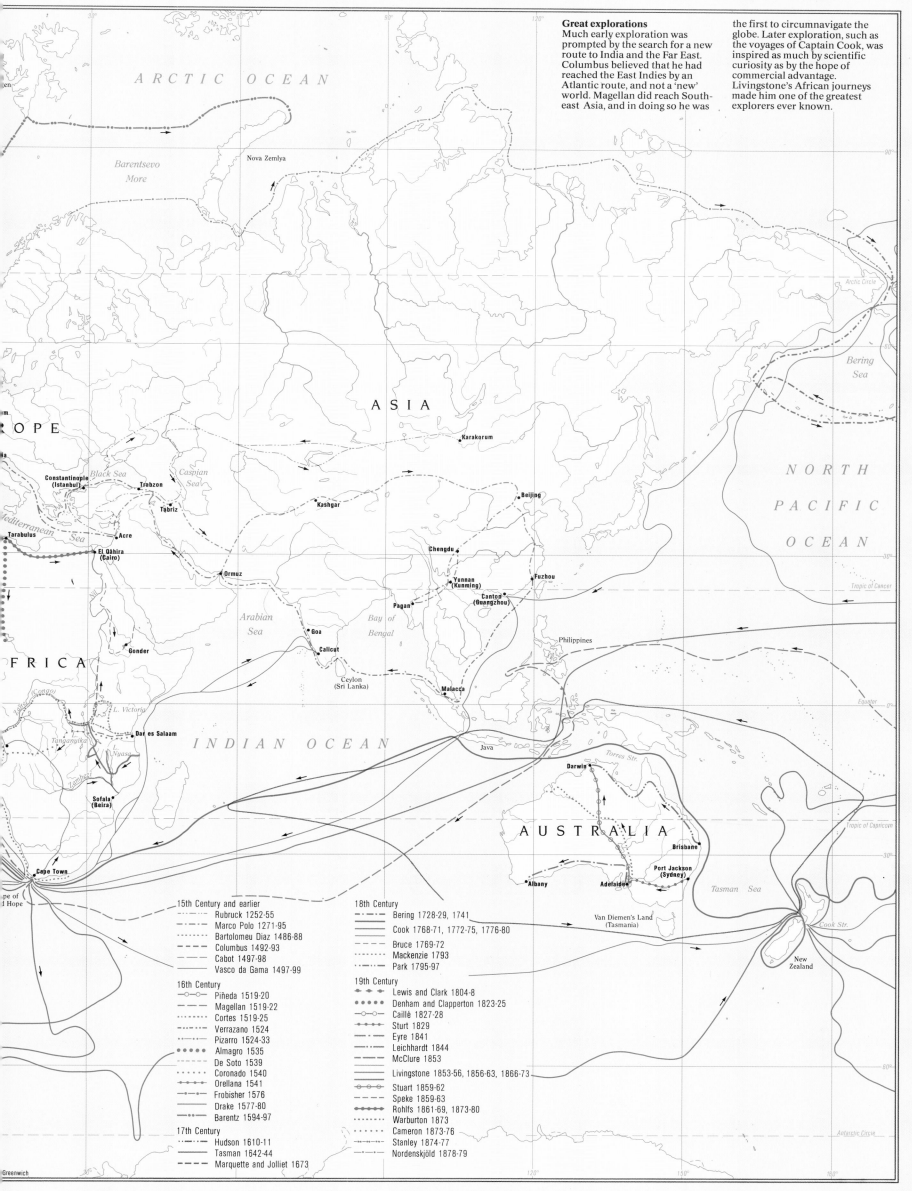

Great explorations

Much early exploration was prompted by the search for a new route to India and the Far East. Columbus believed that he had reached the East Indies by an Atlantic route, and not a 'new' world. Magellan did reach Southeast Asia, and in doing so he was the first to circumnavigate the globe. Later exploration, such as the voyages of Captain Cook, was inspired as much by scientific curiosity as by the hope of commercial advantage. Livingstone's African journeys made him one of the greatest explorers ever known.

ARCTIC OCEAN

Barentsevo More

Nova Zemlya

A S I A

Karakorum

N O R T H

Bering Sea

P A C I F I C

O C E A N

ROPE

Black Sea

Constantinople (Istanbul)

Trabzon

Caspian Sea

Tabriz

Kashgar

Beijing

Mediterranean Sea

Acre

Tarabulus

El Qâhira (Cairo)

Chengdu

Ormuz

Yunnan (Kunming)

Fuzhou

Tropic of Cancer

Pagan

Canton (Guangzhou)

Arabian Sea

Goa

Bay of Bengal

Philippines

FRICA

Calicut

Gonder

Ceylon (Sri Lanka)

Malacca

(Congo)

L. Victoria

Dar es Salaam

I N D I A N   O C E A N

Java

Equator

Tanganyika

L. Nyasa

Darwin

Torres Str.

Zambezi

Sofala (Beira)

A U S T R A L I A

Tropic of Capricorn

Brisbane

Port Jackson (Sydney)

Cape Town

Albany

Adelaide

Tasman Sea

Cook Str.

pe of d Hope

15th Century and earlier
- ‒·‒·‒ Rubruck 1252-55
- —·—·— Marco Polo 1271-95
- ············ Bartolomeu Diaz 1486-88
- ‒ ‒ ‒ Columbus 1492-93
- ——— Cabot 1497-98
- —— Vasco da Gama 1497-99

16th Century
- ‒o‒o‒ Piñeda 1519-20
- ‒ ‒ ‒ Magellan 1519-22
- ············ Cortes 1519-25
- ‒‒‒‒ Verrazano 1524
- ‒·‒·‒ Pizarro 1524-33
- ●●●●● Almagro 1535
- ‒ ‒ ‒ De Soto 1539
- ············ Coronado 1540
- ◆◆◆◆ Orellana 1541
- ‒+‒+‒ Frobisher 1576
- ‒‒‒‒ Drake 1577-80
- ——— Barentz 1594-97

17th Century
- ‒·‒·‒ Hudson 1610-11
- ——— Tasman 1642-44
- ‒ ‒ ‒ Marquette and Jolliet 1673

18th Century
- ‒·‒·‒ Bering 1728-29, 1741
- ——— Cook 1768-71, 1772-75, 1776-80
- ‒ ‒ ‒ Bruce 1769-72
- ············ Mackenzie 1793
- ·········· Park 1795-97

19th Century
- ◆◆◆◆ Lewis and Clark 1804-8
- ●●●●● Denham and Clapperton 1823-25
- ‒o‒o‒ Caillé 1827-28
- ◆◆◆◆ Sturt 1829
- ‒‒‒‒ Eyre 1841
- ‒·‒·‒ Leichhardt 1844
- ‒ ‒ ‒ McClure 1853
- ——— Livingstone 1853-56, 1856-63, 1866-73
- ‒⊙‒⊙‒ Stuart 1859-62
- ‒ ‒ ‒ Speke 1859-63
- ◆◆◆◆ Rohlfs 1861-69, 1873-80
- ············ Warburton 1873
- ·········· Cameron 1873-76
- ‒×‒×‒ Stanley 1874-77
- ‒‒‒‒ Nordenskjöld 1878-79

Van Diemen's Land (Tasmania)

New Zealand

Antarctic Circle

Greenwich

Designed and produced by E.S.R.

ORGANISATIONS AND AFFILIATIONS

Today's large number of nations is a relatively recent phenomenon. As colonialism declined, the number of independent nations grew. Some of the recently established national boundaries have created artificial divisions which often divide tribal lands and separate ethnic communities. Many newly emergent countries have been beset by instability, civil war and other turbulent events. The outcome of disputes within and between nations is now often dependent upon global opinion or intervention.

Nations are becoming more involved in each others affairs by virtue of trade, technology and aid. Also, problems such as terrorism, pollution, ecological issues and many more may be tackled more effectively through collaborative effort. An array of international and regional bodies, consultative agencies and other cohesive groupings reflect this growing interdependence of nations. There has been a rapid growth in recent years in the number of non-governmental organisations. They range from development groups like OXFAM to conservation groups such as Greenpeace and Friends of the Earth. These and other pressure groups seek to influence governments and international agencies. Some highly effective campaigns have increased world awareness of the disasters and problems faced in other parts of the globe as well as bringing to the fore many environmental issues.

League of Nations

The League of Nations was the first major organisation of the states of the world dedicated to the preservation of peace, international co-operation and improvements in human welfare. The League's lack of political success had tended to overshadow its welfare and humanitarian achievements. By January 1940 it had ceased to function effectively in political matters. In 1946 the League's assets were turned over to the United Nations.

United Nations

The United Nations formally came into existence on 24th October 1945. Of the original 51 members hardly any were African or Asian. Over 40 years later the membership has more than trebled. The UN is an association of states which have pledged themselves to maintain international peace and security, and to establish the political, economic and social conditions under which this aim can be achieved. The UN consists of the General Assembly, the Security Council, the Economic and Social Council, the Trusteeship Council, the International Court of Justice and the Secretariat. In addition, there are 18 independent specialised agencies (such as ILO, FAO, UNESCO, WHO and IMF), and some 14 major UN programmes and funds devoted to achieving economic and social progress in developing countries.

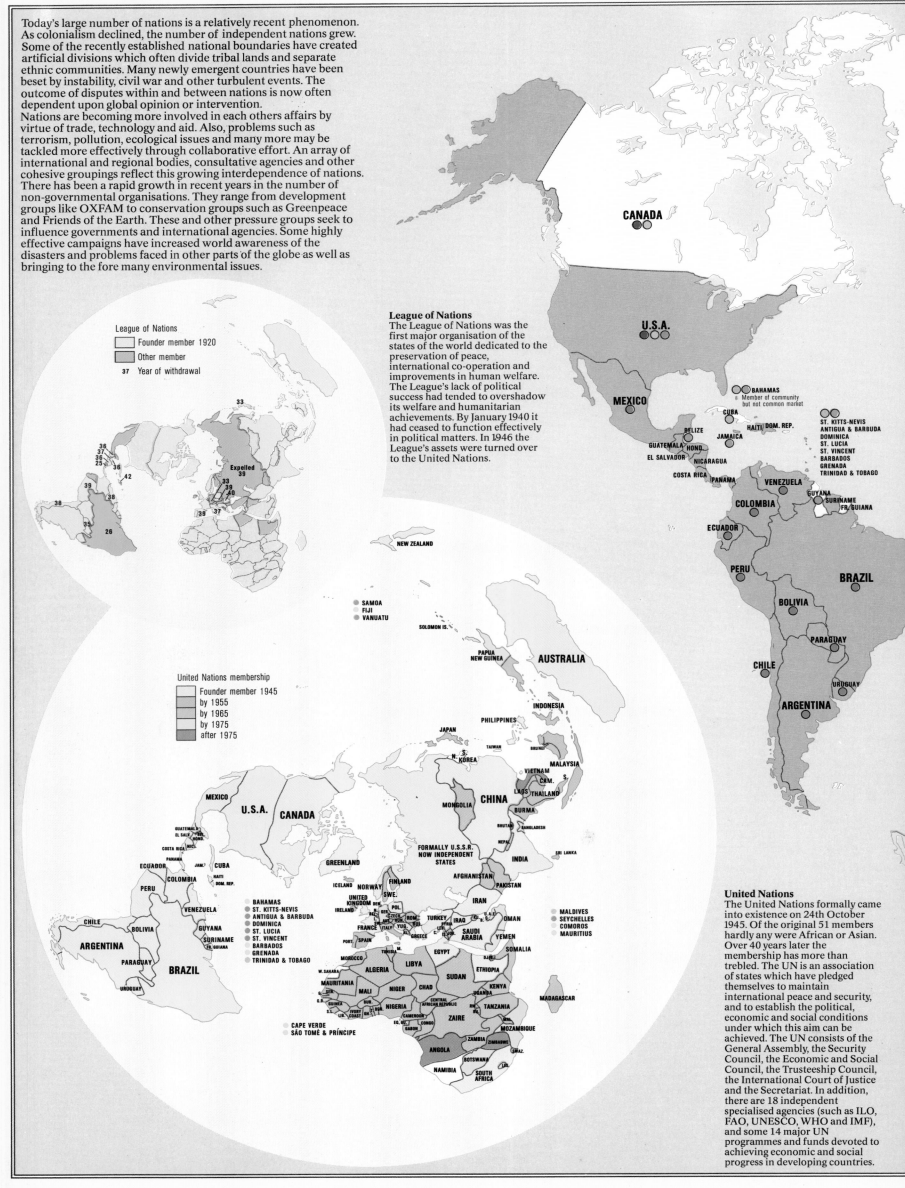

League of Nations
- Founder member 1920
- Other member
- 37 Year of withdrawal

United Nations membership
- Founder member 1945
- by 1955
- by 1965
- by 1975
- after 1975

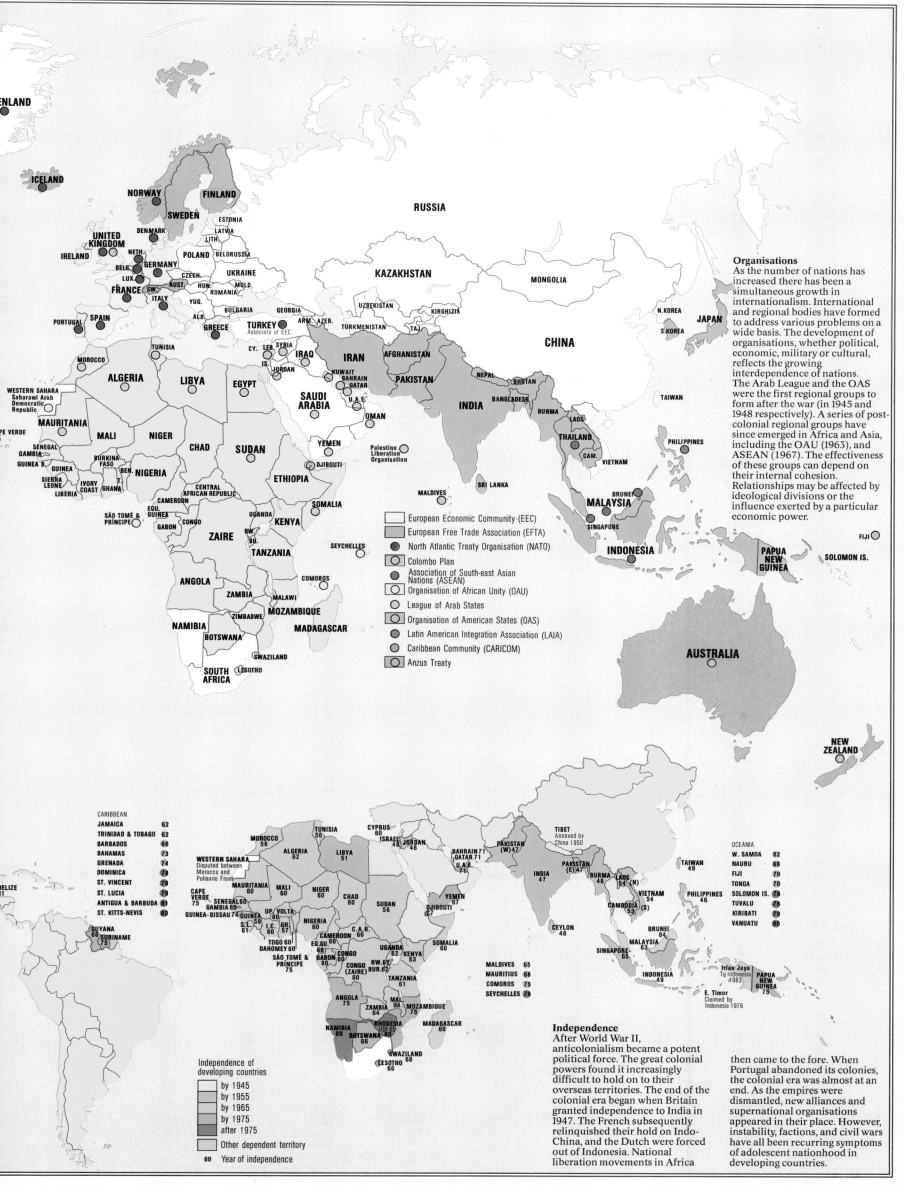

Organisations

As the number of nations has increased there has been a simultaneous growth in internationalism. International and regional bodies have formed to address various problems on a wide basis. The development of organisations, whether political, economic, military or cultural, reflects the growing interdependence of nations. The Arab League and the OAS were the first regional groups to form after the war (in 1945 and 1948 respectively). A series of post-colonial regional groups have since emerged in Africa and Asia, including the OAU (1963), and ASEAN (1967). The effectiveness of these groups can depend on their internal cohesion. Relationships may be affected by ideological divisions or the influence exerted by a particular economic power.

Legend:
- European Economic Community (EEC)
- European Free Trade Association (EFTA)
- North Atlantic Treaty Organisation (NATO)
- Colombo Plan
- Association of South-east Asian Nations (ASEAN)
- Organisation of African Unity (OAU)
- League of Arab States
- Organisation of American States (OAS)
- Latin American Integration Association (LAIA)
- Caribbean Community (CARICOM)
- Anzus Treaty

Independence

After World War II, anticolonialism became a potent political force. The great colonial powers found it increasingly difficult to hold on to their overseas territories. The end of the colonial era began when Britain granted independence to India in 1947. The French subsequently relinquished their hold on Indo-China, and the Dutch were forced out of Indonesia. National liberation movements in Africa then came to the fore. When Portugal abandoned its colonies, the colonial era was almost at an end. As the empires were dismantled, new alliances and supranational organisations appeared in their place. However, instability, factions, and civil wars have all been recurring symptoms of adolescent nationhood in developing countries.

Independence of developing countries
- by 1945
- by 1955
- by 1965
- by 1975
- after 1975
- Other dependent territory
- 60 Year of independence

CARIBBEAN
JAMAICA	62
TRINIDAD & TOBAGO	62
BARBADOS	66
BAHAMAS	73
GRENADA	74
DOMINICA	78
ST. VINCENT	79
ST. LUCIA	79
ANTIGUA & BARBUDA	81
ST. KITTS-NEVIS	83

OCEANIA
W. SAMOA	62
NAURU	68
FIJI	70
TONGA	70
SOLOMON IS.	78
TUVALU	78
KIRIBATI	79
VANUATU	80

Designed and produced by E.S.R.

Population density
Some of the most densely populated areas in the world can be found in Europe and Asia. Bangladesh has 685 people per square kilometre, whilst Australia has only two people for the same area. A low density of population can often be associated with large areas of inhospitable territory, such as Greenland.

Growth of conurbations
It has been predicted that by the year 2000 at least 50 per cent of the world's population will be urbanised. Within the last decade existing cities have been growing at an alarming rate. Some places are already merging to create vast metropolitan conurbations. By the year 2000 nearly 50 cities will have a population of five million, with at least 20 million in Mexico City. Many urban areas in the North are faced with inner city degeneration. Industry has declined and affluent people have moved out to the suburbs leaving a vacuum in the centre.
Vast shanty towns have grown up around many third world cities overwhelming the already poor services and conditions. The movement of people into cities in the hope of a 'better' life creates a further strain on the rural population whose productivity needs to increase to maintain the growing number of urban dwellers.

Population profile
The population profile shows the age group structure of a developing and a developed country. In Indonesia the broad base of the pyramid results from a high birth rate. 40 per cent of the population is under 15, with their reproductive years still to come. The economically active group for Sweden is relatively large but so is the elderly section. Combined with a low birth rate this will pose new problems for future generations.

Population potential
Many developed countries have achieved a stable population – a balanced birth rate and death rate. However high birth and death rates and a large infant mortality seems to be the norm in the third world. The high birth rate often reflects the desire for a large family due to high infant mortality, labour intensive means of subsistence, and the need for support in old age. The large increase in population threatens to outstrip economic growth. Theoretically the birth rate can be controlled. However, there are often many reasons including religious taboos, lack of effective diet, health and education which means that population growth is still a major obstacle to development. Some countries have introduced tax incentives and maternity provisions in order to try and keep families small.

Birth rate is number of births in a year per 1000 of the population.

Death rate is number of deaths in a year per 1000 of the population.

Infant mortality is annual number of deaths of children under one year per 1000 births

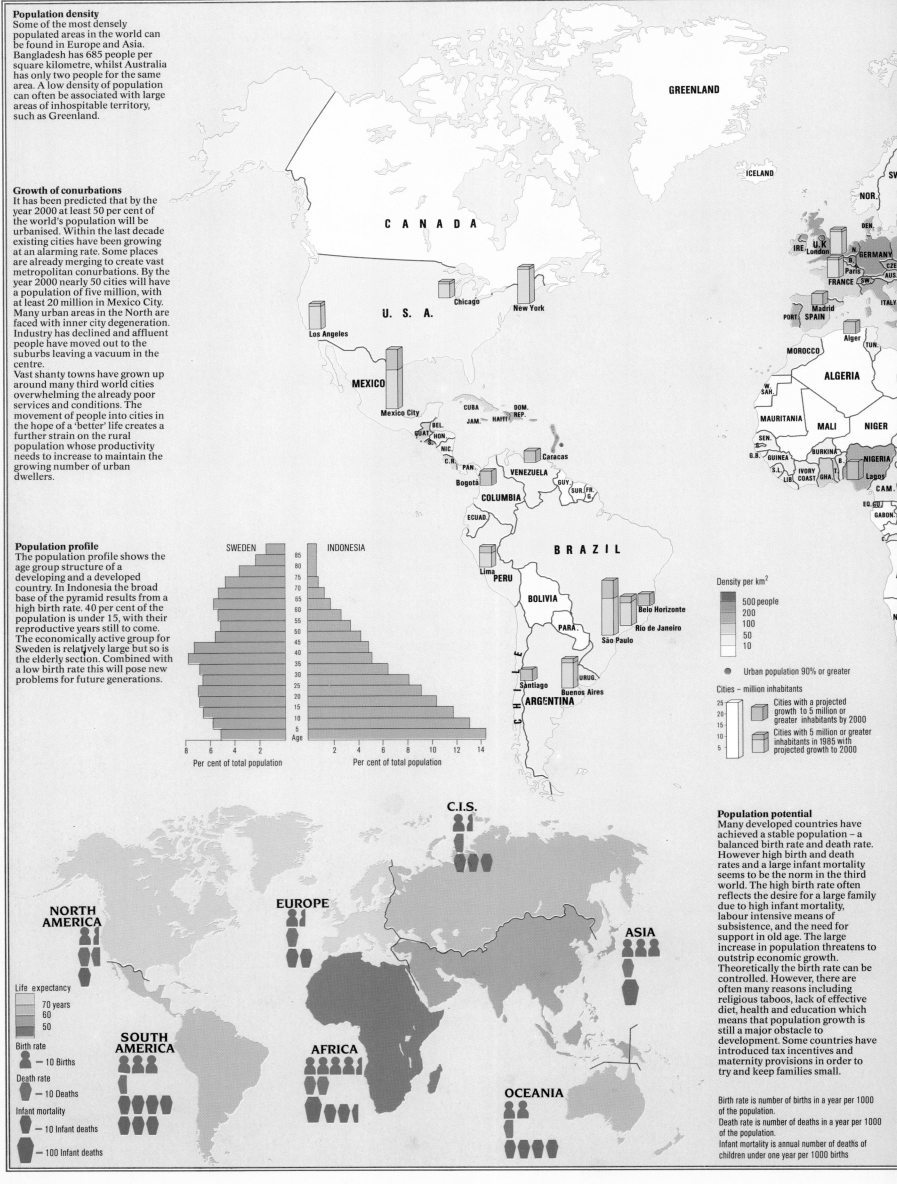

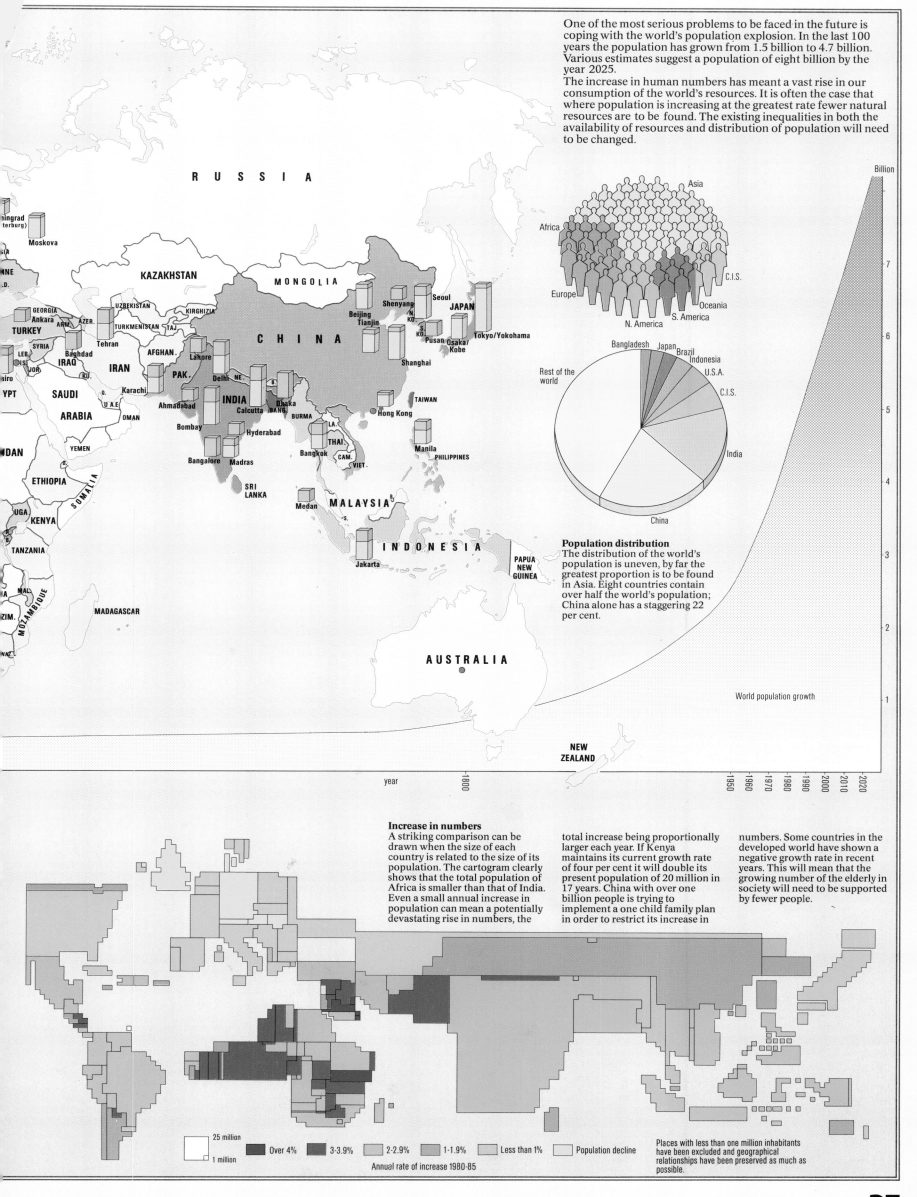

One of the most serious problems to be faced in the future is coping with the world's population explosion. In the last 100 years the population has grown from 1.5 billion to 4.7 billion. Various estimates suggest a population of eight billion by the year 2025.

The increase in human numbers has meant a vast rise in our consumption of the world's resources. It is often the case that where population is increasing at the greatest rate fewer natural resources are to be found. The existing inequalities in both the availability of resources and distribution of population will need to be changed.

Population distribution
The distribution of the world's population is uneven, by far the greatest proportion is to be found in Asia. Eight countries contain over half the world's population; China alone has a staggering 22 per cent.

World population growth

Billion

Increase in numbers
A striking comparison can be drawn when the size of each country is related to the size of its population. The cartogram clearly shows that the total population of Africa is smaller than that of India. Even a small annual increase in population can mean a potentially devastating rise in numbers, the total increase being proportionally larger each year. If Kenya maintains its current growth rate of four per cent it will double its present population of 20 million in 17 years. China with over one billion people is trying to implement a one child family plan in order to restrict its increase in numbers. Some countries in the developed world have shown a negative growth rate in recent years. This will mean that the growing number of the elderly in society will need to be supported by fewer people.

25 million
1 million

Over 4% | 3-3.9% | 2-2.9% | 1-1.9% | Less than 1% | Population decline

Annual rate of increase 1980-85

Places with less than one million inhabitants have been excluded and geographical relationships have been preserved as much as possible.

27

Designed and produced by E.S.R.

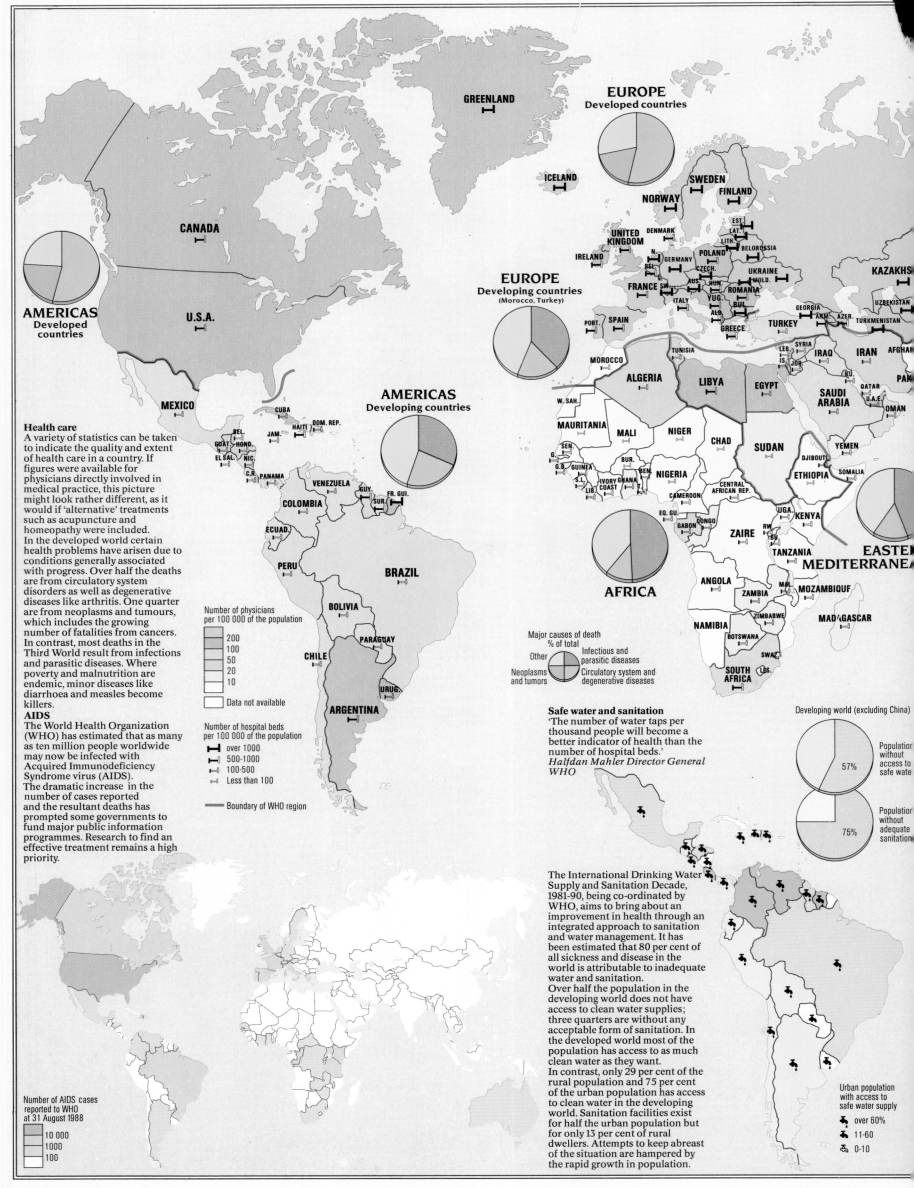

Health care
A variety of statistics can be taken to indicate the quality and extent of health care in a country. If figures were available for physicians directly involved in medical practice, this picture might look rather different, as it would if 'alternative' treatments such as acupuncture and homeopathy were included.
In the developed world certain health problems have arisen due to conditions generally associated with progress. Over half the deaths are from circulatory system disorders as well as degenerative diseases like arthritis. One quarter are from neoplasms and tumours, which includes the growing number of fatalities from cancers. In contrast, most deaths in the Third World result from infections and parasitic diseases. Where poverty and malnutrition are endemic, minor diseases like diarrhoea and measles become killers.

AIDS
The World Health Organization (WHO) has estimated that as many as ten million people worldwide may now be infected with Acquired Immunodeficiency Syndrome virus (AIDS).
The dramatic increase in the number of cases reported and the resultant deaths has prompted some governments to fund major public information programmes. Research to find an effective treatment remains a high priority.

Number of physicians per 100 000 of the population
200
100
50
20
10
Data not available

Number of hospital beds per 100 000 of the population
over 1000
500-1000
100-500
Less than 100

Boundary of WHO region

Major causes of death % of total
Other
Neoplasms and tumors
Infectious and parasitic diseases
Circulatory system and degenerative diseases

Safe water and sanitation
'The number of water taps per thousand people will become a better indicator of health than the number of hospital beds.'
Halfdan Mahler Director General WHO

Developing world (excluding China)
57%
Population without access to safe water
75%
Population without adequate sanitation

The International Drinking Water Supply and Sanitation Decade, 1981-90, being co-ordinated by WHO, aims to bring about an improvement in health through an integrated approach to sanitation and water management. It has been estimated that 80 per cent of all sickness and disease in the world is attributable to inadequate water and sanitation.
Over half the population in the developing world does not have access to clean water supplies; three quarters are without any acceptable form of sanitation. In the developed world most of the population has access to as much clean water as they want.
In contrast, only 29 per cent of the rural population and 75 per cent of the urban population has access to clean water in the developing world. Sanitation facilities exist for half the urban population but for only 13 per cent of rural dwellers. Attempts to keep abreast of the situation are hampered by the rapid growth in population.

Urban population with access to safe water supply
over 60%
11-60
0-10

Number of AIDS cases reported to WHO at 31 August 1988
10 000
1000
100

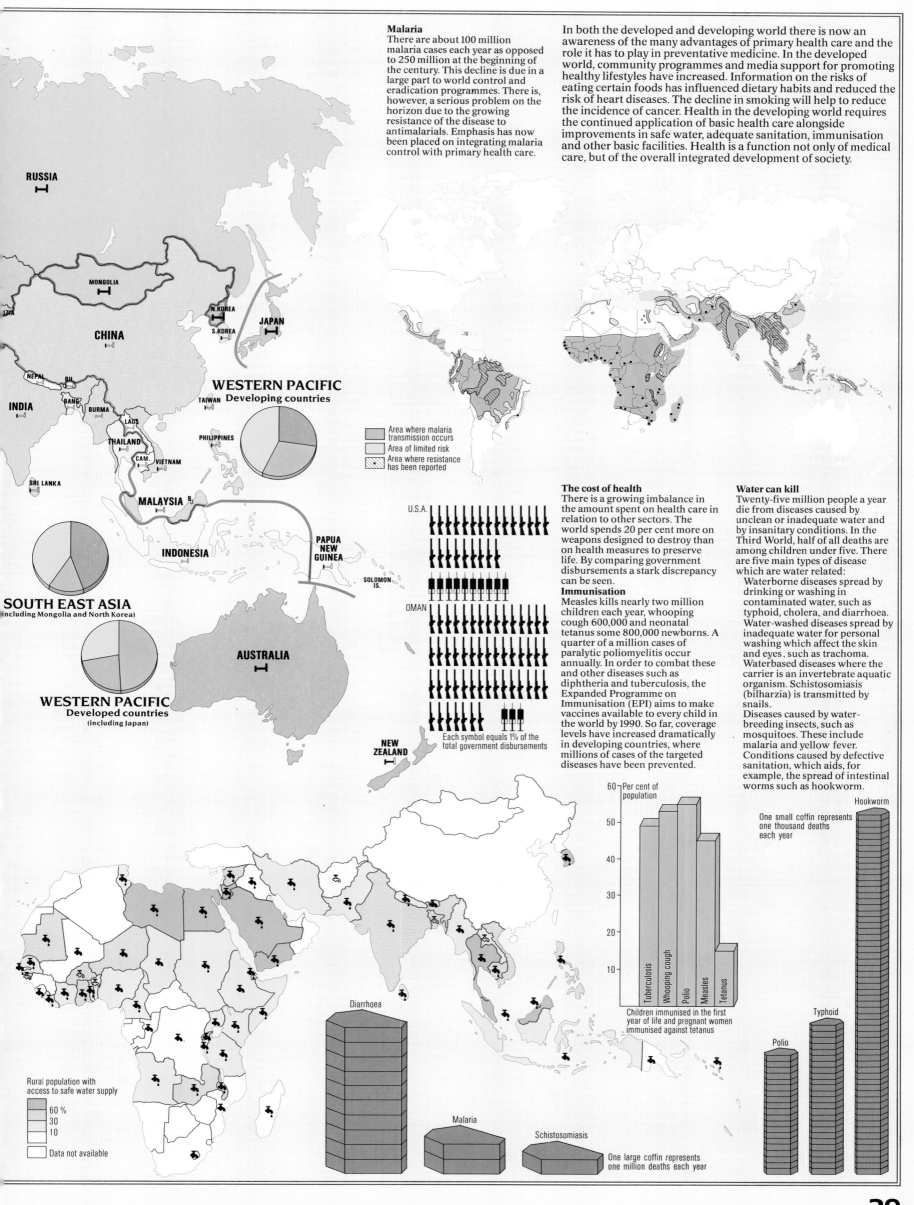

Malaria
There are about 100 million malaria cases each year as opposed to 250 million at the beginning of the century. This decline is due in a large part to world control and eradication programmes. There is, however, a serious problem on the horizon due to the growing resistance of the disease to antimalarials. Emphasis has now been placed on integrating malaria control with primary health care.

In both the developed and developing world there is now an awareness of the many advantages of primary health care and the role it has to play in preventative medicine. In the developed world, community programmes and media support for promoting healthy lifestyles have increased. Information on the risks of eating certain foods has influenced dietary habits and reduced the risk of heart diseases. The decline in smoking will help to reduce the incidence of cancer. Health in the developing world requires the continued application of basic health care alongside improvements in safe water, adequate sanitation, immunisation and other basic facilities. Health is a function not only of medical care, but of the overall integrated development of society.

RUSSIA

MONGOLIA

N. KOREA

JAPAN

S. KOREA

CHINA

TAIWAN

WESTERN PACIFIC
Developing countries

NEPAL
BH
INDIA
BANG.
BURMA
LAOS
THAILAND
CAM.
VIETNAM
SRI LANKA

PHILIPPINES

Area where malaria transmission occurs

Area of limited risk

Area where resistance has been reported

MALAYSIA

SOUTH EAST ASIA
(including Mongolia and North Korea)

INDONESIA

PAPUA NEW GUINEA

WESTERN PACIFIC
Developed countries
(including Japan)

AUSTRALIA

NEW ZEALAND

U.S.A.

OMAN

SOLOMON IS.

Each symbol equals 1% of the total government disbursements

The cost of health
There is a growing imbalance in the amount spent on health care in relation to other sectors. The world spends 20 per cent more on weapons designed to destroy than on health measures to preserve life. By comparing government disbursements a stark discrepancy can be seen.

Immunisation
Measles kills nearly two million children each year, whooping cough 600,000 and neonatal tetanus some 800,000 newborns. A quarter of a million cases of paralytic poliomyelitis occur annually. In order to combat these and other diseases such as diphtheria and tuberculosis, the Expanded Programme on Immunisation (EPI) aims to make vaccines available to every child in the world by 1990. So far, coverage levels have increased dramatically in developing countries, where millions of cases of the targeted diseases have been prevented.

Water can kill
Twenty-five million people a year die from diseases caused by unclean or inadequate water and by insanitary conditions. In the Third World, half of all deaths are among children under five. There are five main types of disease which are water related:

Waterborne diseases spread by drinking or washing in contaminated water, such as typhoid, cholera, and diarrhoea.
Water-washed diseases spread by inadequate water for personal washing which affect the skin and eyes, such as trachoma.
Waterbased diseases where the carrier is an invertebrate aquatic organism. Schistosomiasis (bilharzia) is transmitted by snails.
Diseases caused by water-breeding insects, such as mosquitoes. These include malaria and yellow fever.
Conditions caused by defective sanitation, which aids, for example, the spread of intestinal worms such as hookworm.

60 Per cent of population
50
40
30
20
10

Tuberculosis
Whooping cough
Polio
Measles
Tetanus

Children immunised in the first year of life and pregnant women immunised against tetanus

Hookworm

One small coffin represents one thousand deaths each year

Diarrhoea

Malaria

Schistosomiasis

One large coffin represents one million deaths each year

Polio

Typhoid

Rural population with access to safe water supply

60 %
30
10
Data not available

Designed and produced by E.S.R.

EDUCATION AND WORK

It has been argued that the kind of education provided by schools may be less important than 'traditional' wisdom derived from experience, especially in cultures other than those in the industrialised world. Education in the Third World has often been modelled on imported curricula which reflect the needs and conditions of a different society. Though newly independent nations introduce more suitable subjects, they may often lack the resources for relevant teaching materials.

Illiteracy
An illiterate person, one who is unable to read or write, is at a basic disadvantage in a world where literacy is an increasingly critical skill. Despite many literacy programmes, the total number of illiterates – over 800 million people, most of them in developing countries – continues to grow. These nations have only 12 per cent of the world's education budget. Most African countries spend less than ten per cent of GNP on education. There is a noticeable gap between the levels of male and female illiteracy, the latter being higher. This is often due to cultural differences and religious attitudes.

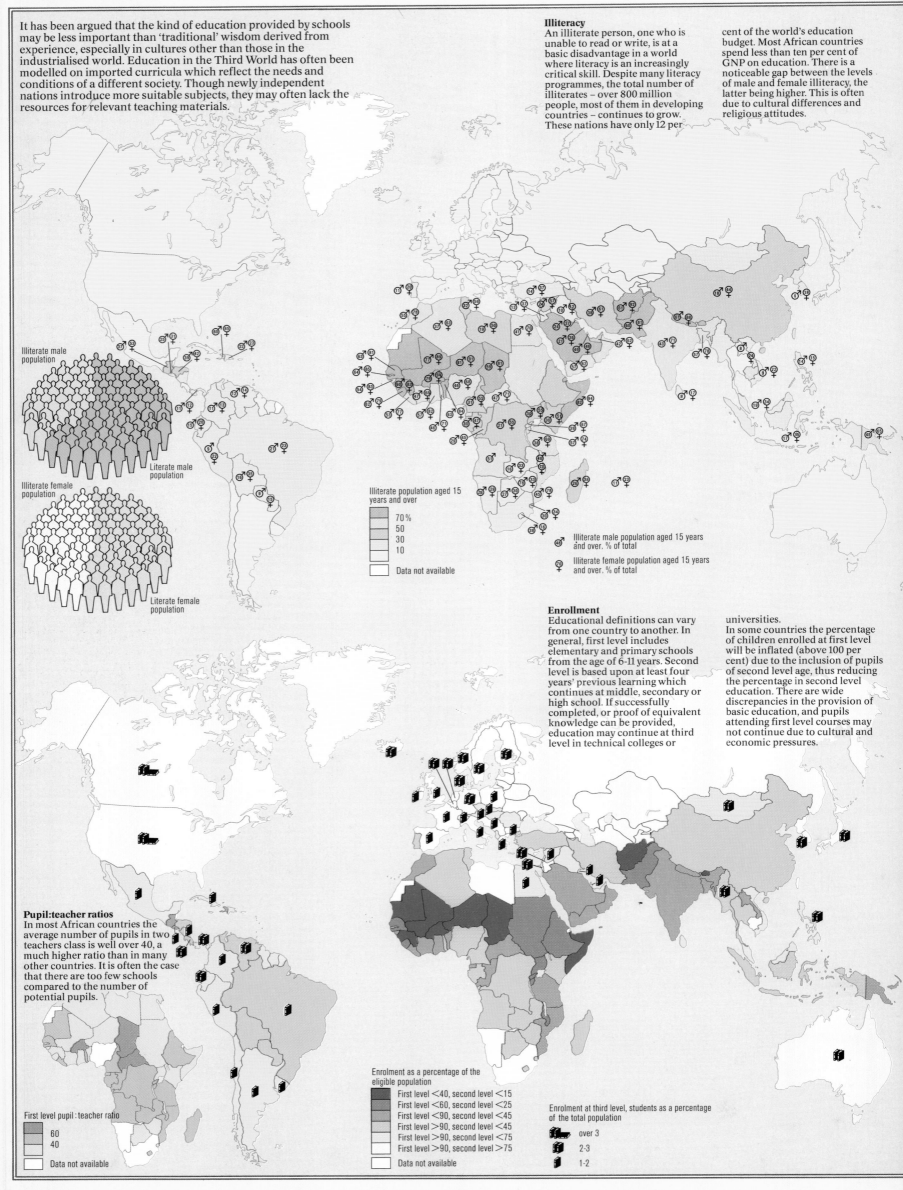

Illiterate male population

Literate male population

Illiterate female population

Literate female population

Illiterate population aged 15 years and over

70 %
50
30
10

Data not available

⚦ Illiterate male population aged 15 years and over, % of total

♀ Illiterate female population aged 15 years and over, % of total

Enrollment
Educational definitions can vary from one country to another. In general, first level includes elementary and primary schools from the age of 6-11 years. Second level is based upon at least four years' previous learning which continues at middle, secondary or high school. If successfully completed, or proof of equivalent knowledge can be provided, education may continue at third level in technical colleges or universities.
In some countries the percentage of children enrolled at first level will be inflated (above 100 per cent) due to the inclusion of pupils of second level age, thus reducing the percentage in second level education. There are wide discrepancies in the provision of basic education, and pupils attending first level courses may not continue due to cultural and economic pressures.

Pupil:teacher ratios
In most African countries the average number of pupils in two teachers class is well over 40, a much higher ratio than in many other countries. It is often the case that there are too few schools compared to the number of potential pupils.

First level pupil : teacher ratio

60
40

Data not available

Enrolment as a percentage of the eligible population

First level <40, second level <15
First level <60, second level <25
First level <90, second level <45
First level >90, second level <45
First level >90, second level <75
First level >90, second level >75

Data not available

Enrolment at third level, students as a percentage of the total population

over 3
2-3
1-2

© COLOUR LIBRARY BOOKS

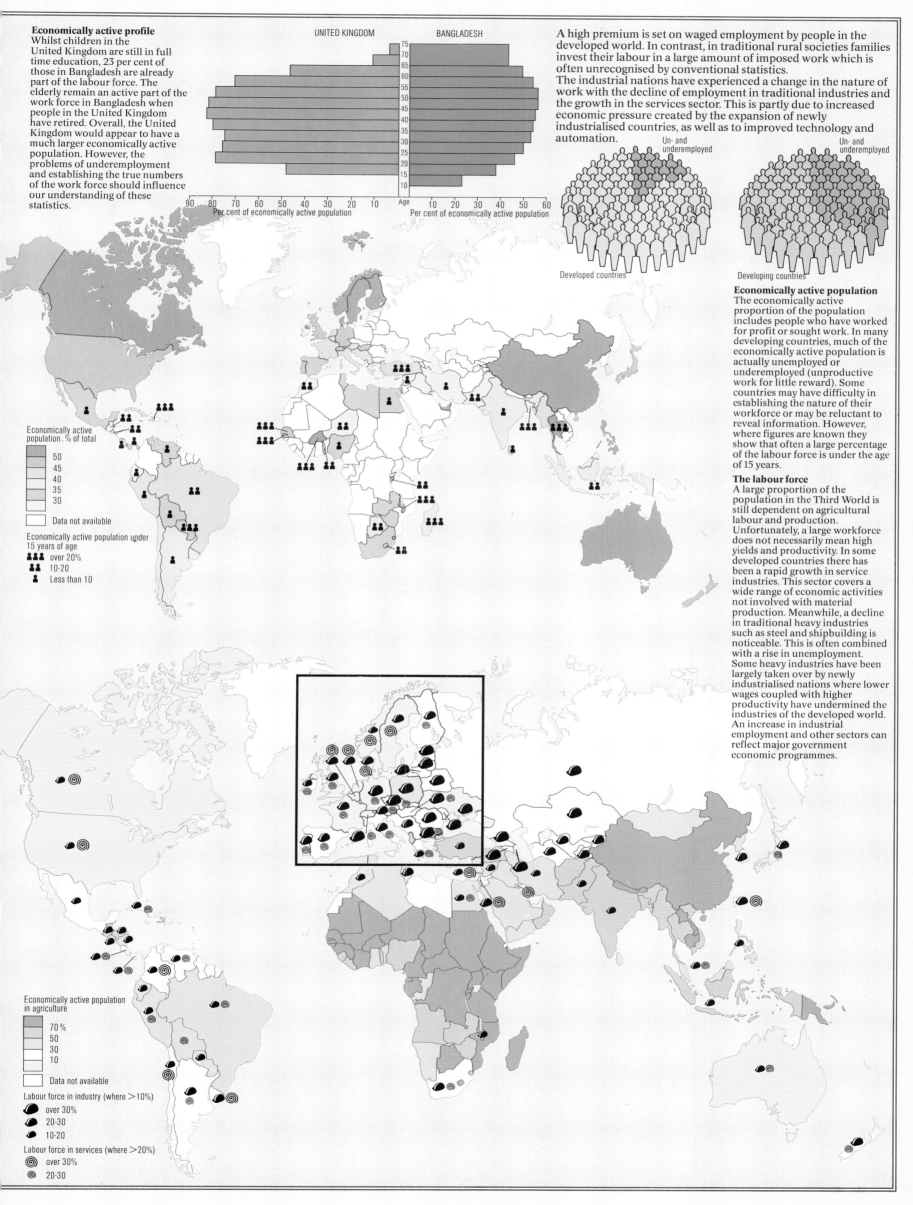

Economically active profile
Whilst children in the United Kingdom are still in full time education, 23 per cent of those in Bangladesh are already part of the labour force. The elderly remain an active part of the work force in Bangladesh when people in the United Kingdom have retired. Overall, the United Kingdom would appear to have a much larger economically active population. However, the problems of underemployment and establishing the true numbers of the work force should influence our understanding of these statistics.

UNITED KINGDOM   BANGLADESH

Age

Per cent of economically active population   Per cent of economically active population

A high premium is set on waged employment by people in the developed world. In contrast, in traditional rural societies families invest their labour in a large amount of imposed work which is often unrecognised by conventional statistics.
The industrial nations have experienced a change in the nature of work with the decline of employment in traditional industries and the growth in the services sector. This is partly due to increased economic pressure created by the expansion of newly industrialised countries, as well as to improved technology and automation.

Un- and underemployed   Un- and underemployed

Developed countries   Developing countries

Economically active population
The economically active proportion of the population includes people who have worked for profit or sought work. In many developing countries, much of the economically active population is actually unemployed or underemployed (unproductive work for little reward). Some countries may have difficulty in establishing the nature of their workforce or may be reluctant to reveal information. However, where figures are known they show that often a large percentage of the labour force is under the age of 15 years.

The labour force
A large proportion of the population in the Third World is still dependent on agricultural labour and production. Unfortunately, a large workforce does not necessarily mean high yields and productivity. In some developed countries there has been a rapid growth in service industries. This sector covers a wide range of economic activities not involved with material production. Meanwhile, a decline in traditional heavy industries such as steel and shipbuilding is noticeable. This is often combined with a rise in unemployment. Some heavy industries have been largely taken over by newly industrialised nations where lower wages coupled with higher productivity have undermined the industries of the developed world. An increase in industrial employment and other sectors can reflect major government economic programmes.

Economically active population . % of total
- 50
- 45
- 40
- 35
- 30
- Data not available

Economically active population under 15 years of age
- over 20%
- 10-20
- Less than 10

Economically active population in agriculture
- 70 %
- 50
- 30
- 10
- Data not available

Labour force in industry (where >10%)
- over 30%
- 20-30
- 10-20

Labour force in services (where >20%)
- over 30%
- 20-30

31

Designed and produced by E.S.R.

LAND USE

Over the millenia the earth's landscape has changed significantly, due in no small part to man. The population explosion has put vegetation at risk as the need for agricultural land has increased. In order to meet the demand, forests have been cleared and degraded and marginal lands exhausted. Once fertile soils are rapidly becoming mineral-stressed. The requirement for forest products has risen, leading to even greater demolition of our woodlands. Man's expansion and construction has put all land uses under pressure.

The advancing desert
Over one quarter of land is now affected by rapidly encroaching deserts. 'Desertization' refers to instances in which the process is natural. Desertification usually occurs in arid and semi-arid areas and involves additional human factors. Expanding populations move onto marginal lands, where deforestation, over-cultivation and over-grazing occur, often accompanied by drought. This reduces the productivity of the land, which quickly degrades under stress.

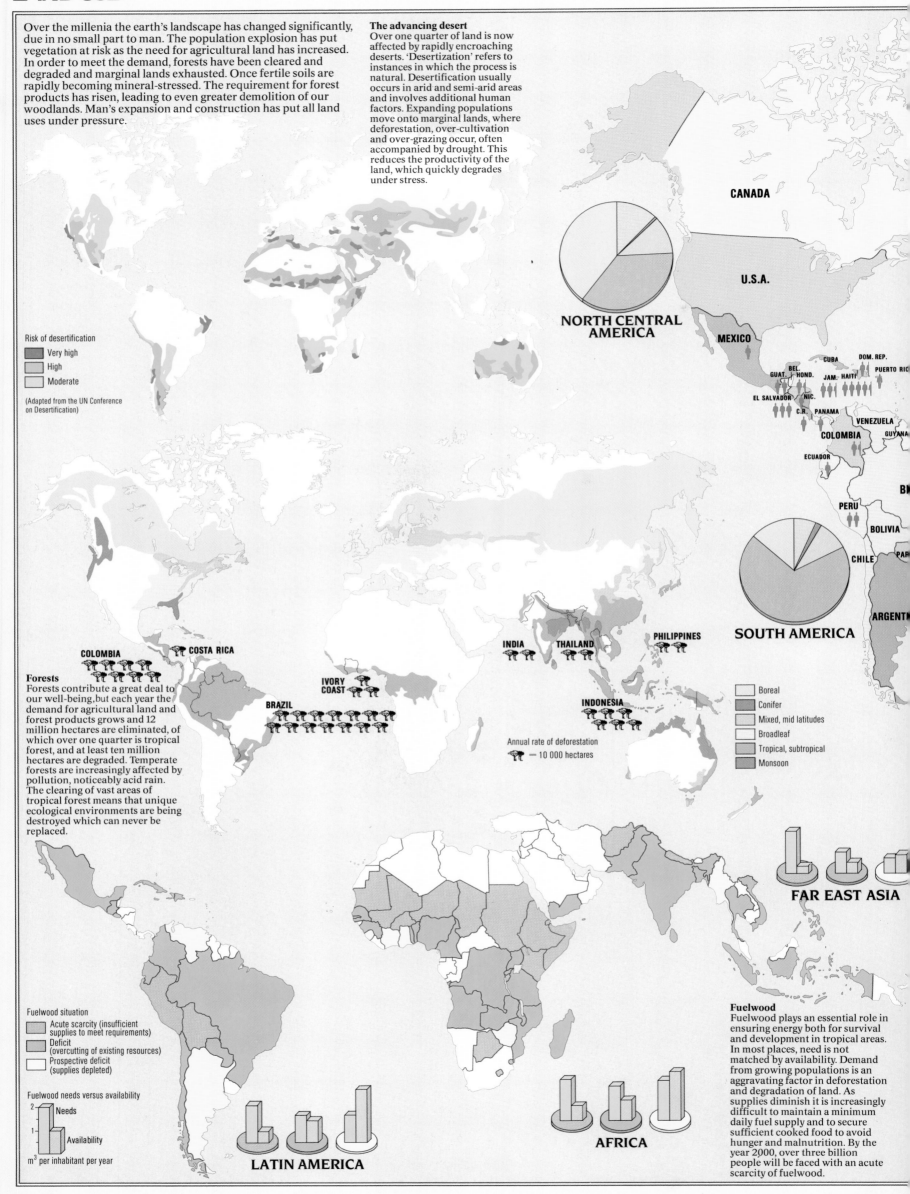

Risk of desertification
- Very high
- High
- Moderate

(Adapted from the UN Conference on Desertification)

Forests
Forests contribute a great deal to our well-being, but each year the demand for agricultural land and forest products grows and 12 million hectares are eliminated, of which over one quarter is tropical forest, and at least ten million hectares are degraded. Temperate forests are increasingly affected by pollution, noticeably acid rain. The clearing of vast areas of tropical forest means that unique ecological environments are being destroyed which can never be replaced.

Annual rate of deforestation
= 10 000 hectares

- Boreal
- Conifer
- Mixed, mid latitudes
- Broadleaf
- Tropical, subtropical
- Monsoon

NORTH CENTRAL AMERICA

SOUTH AMERICA

CANADA

U.S.A.

MEXICO

BEL. GUAT. HOND. JAM. HAITI
EL SALVADOR NIC.
C.R. PANAMA

CUBA
DOM. REP.
PUERTO RICO

VENEZUELA
GUYANA
COLOMBIA
ECUADOR

PERU
BOLIVIA
CHILE
ARGENTINA

COLOMBIA
COSTA RICA
IVORY COAST
BRAZIL

INDIA THAILAND
PHILIPPINES
INDONESIA

FAR EAST ASIA

Fuelwood
Fuelwood plays an essential role in ensuring energy both for survival and development in tropical areas. In most places, need is not matched by availability. Demand from growing populations is an aggravating factor in deforestation and degradation of land. As supplies diminish it is increasingly difficult to maintain a minimum daily fuel supply and to secure sufficient cooked food to avoid hunger and malnutrition. By the year 2000, over three billion people will be faced with an acute scarcity of fuelwood.

Fuelwood situation
- Acute scarcity (insufficient supplies to meet requirements)
- Deficit (overcutting of existing resources)
- Prospective deficit (supplies depleted)

Fuelwood needs versus availability
2 — Needs
1 — Availability
m³ per inhabitant per year

LATIN AMERICA

AFRICA

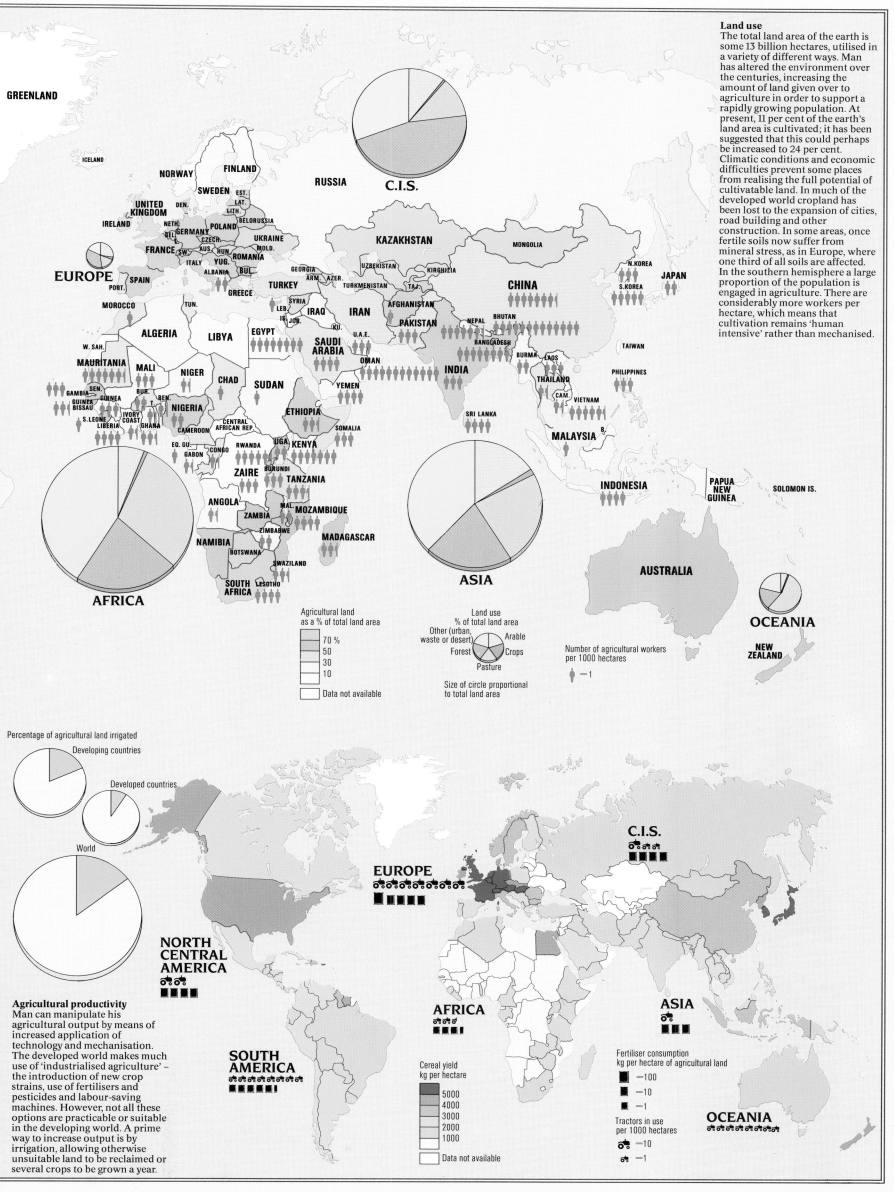

Land use

The total land area of the earth is some 13 billion hectares, utilised in a variety of different ways. Man has altered the environment over the centuries, increasing the amount of land given over to agriculture in order to support a rapidly growing population. At present, 11 per cent of the earth's land area is cultivated; it has been suggested that this could perhaps be increased to 24 per cent. Climatic conditions and economic difficulties prevent some places from realising the full potential of cultivatable land. In much of the developed world cropland has been lost to the expansion of cities, road building and other construction. In some areas, once fertile soils now suffer from mineral stress, as in Europe, where one third of all soils are affected. In the southern hemisphere a large proportion of the population is engaged in agriculture. There are considerably more workers per hectare, which means that cultivation remains 'human intensive' rather than mechanised.

Agricultural productivity

Man can manipulate his agricultural output by means of increased application of technology and mechanisation. The developed world makes much use of 'industrialised agriculture' – the introduction of new crop strains, use of fertilisers and pesticides and labour-saving machines. However, not all these options are practicable or suitable in the developing world. A prime way to increase output is by irrigation, allowing otherwise unsuitable land to be reclaimed or several crops to be grown a year.

Agricultural land
as a % of total land area

70 %
50
30
10

Data not available

Land use
% of total land area
Other (urban, waste or desert)
Forest
Pasture
Arable
Crops

Size of circle proportional to total land area

Number of agricultural workers per 1000 hectares
— 1

Percentage of agricultural land irrigated
Developing countries
Developed countries
World

Cereal yield
kg per hectare
5000
4000
3000
2000
1000

Data not available

Fertiliser consumption
kg per hectare of agricultural land
—100
—10
—1

Tractors in use
per 1000 hectares
—10
—1

Designed and produced by E.S.R.

FOOD

Enough food is produced globally to feed all of the population. Millions starve each year, millions suffer from malnutrition and are thus susceptible to disease and death. Somewhere the equation does not balance; resources are not necessarily matched to the areas of greatest demand.

Technological advances to increase output have created a new set of problems, including surpluses, mineral stressed soils, and vast erosion of topsoil. Emphasis on cash crops needs to be reversed in order for many countries to move towards self sufficiency. Combining this change with an increase in research to develop locally adapted strains and cultivation techniques relevant to local surroundings would help feed the hungry.

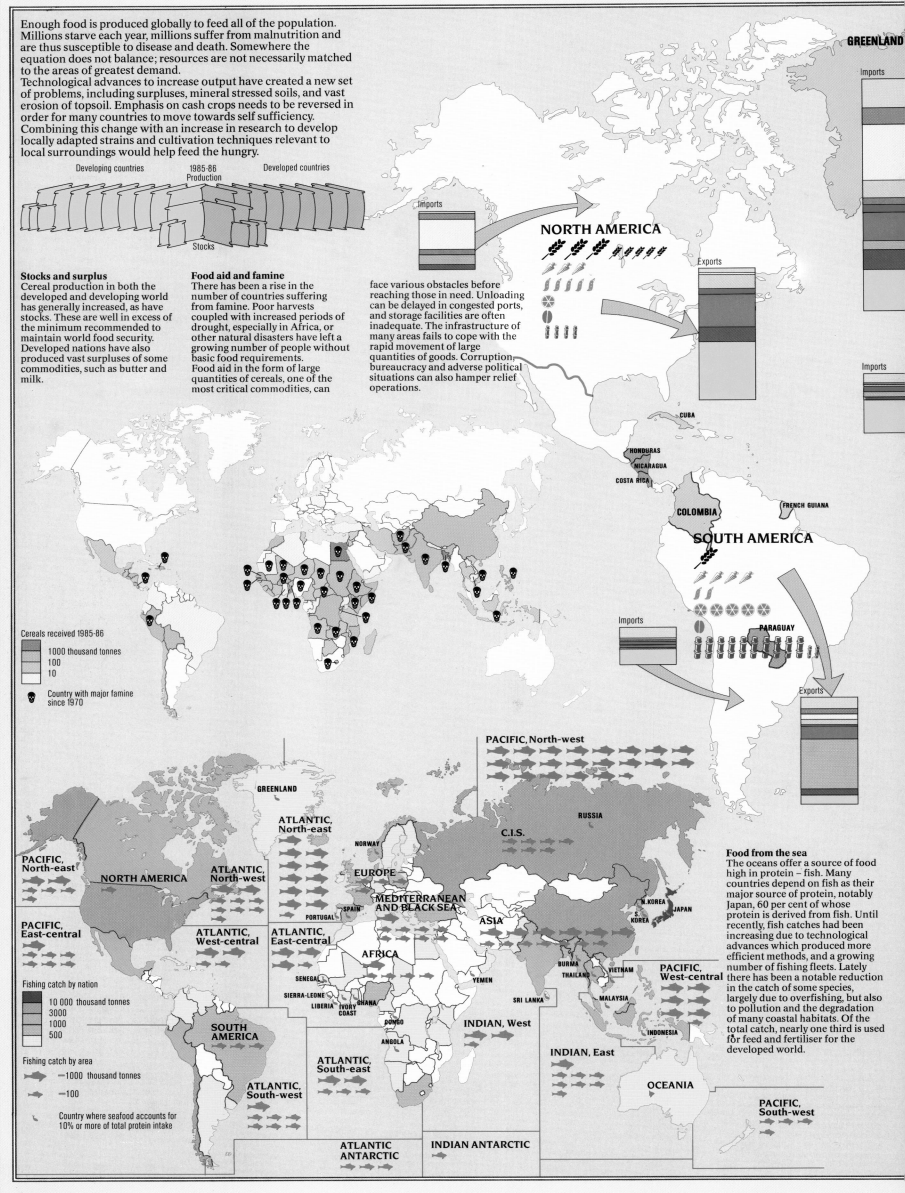

Stocks and surplus
Cereal production in both the developed and developing world has generally increased, as have stocks. These are well in excess of the minimum recommended to maintain world food security. Developed nations have also produced vast surpluses of some commodities, such as butter and milk.

Food aid and famine
There has been a rise in the number of countries suffering from famine. Poor harvests coupled with increased periods of drought, especially in Africa, or other natural disasters have left a growing number of people without basic food requirements.
Food aid in the form of large quantities of cereals, one of the most critical commodities, can face various obstacles before reaching those in need. Unloading can be delayed in congested ports, and storage facilities are often inadequate. The infrastructure of many areas fails to cope with the rapid movement of large quantities of goods. Corruption, bureaucracy and adverse political situations can also hamper relief operations.

Food from the sea
The oceans offer a source of food high in protein – fish. Many countries depend on fish as their major source of protein, notably Japan, 60 per cent of whose protein is derived from fish. Until recently, fish catches had been increasing due to technological advances which produced more efficient methods, and a growing number of fishing fleets. Lately there has been a notable reduction in the catch of some species, largely due to overfishing, but also to pollution and the degradation of many coastal habitats. Of the total catch, nearly one third is used for feed and fertiliser for the developed world.

Cereals received 1985-86
1000 thousand tonnes
100
10

Country with major famine since 1970

Fishing catch by nation
10 000 thousand tonnes
3000
1000
500

Fishing catch by area
—1000 thousand tonnes
—100
Country where seafood accounts for 10% or more of total protein intake

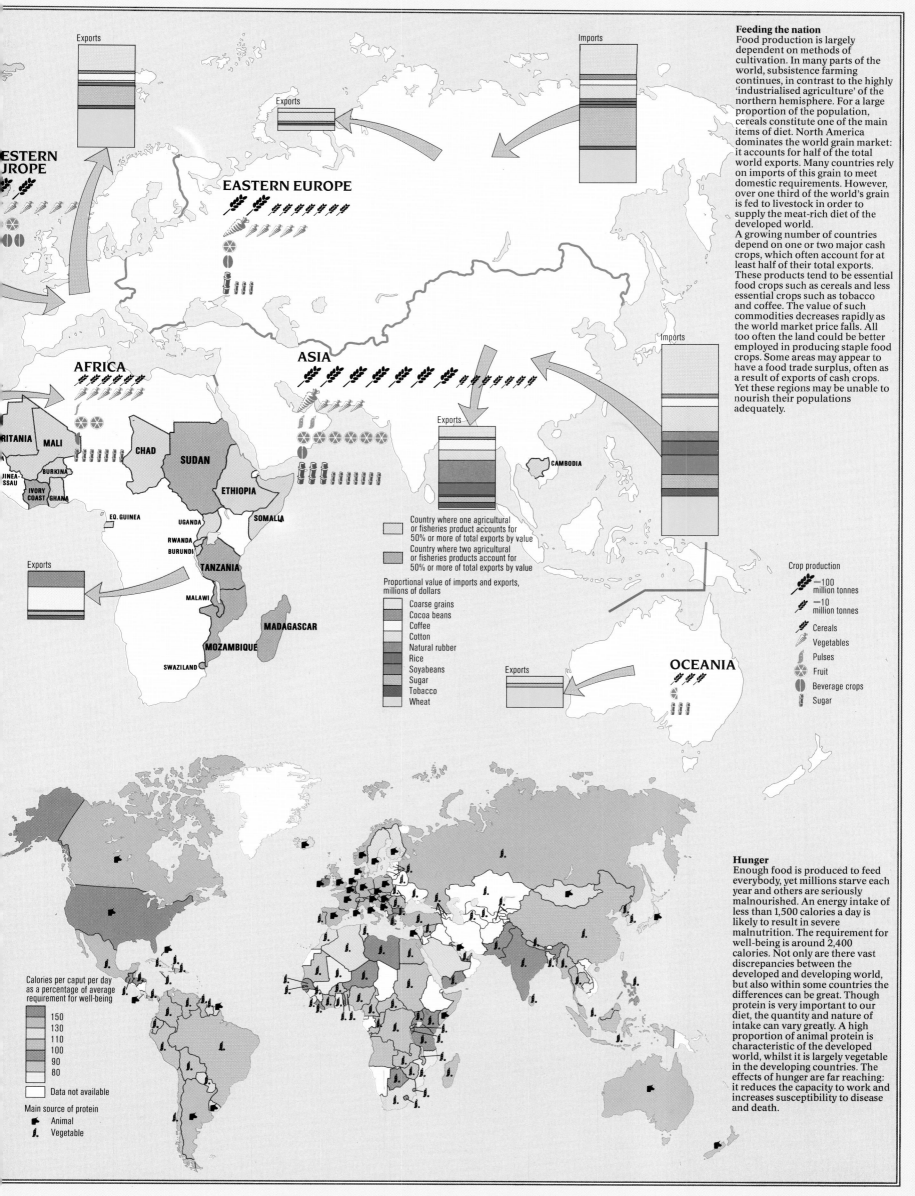

Feeding the nation

Food production is largely dependent on methods of cultivation. In many parts of the world, subsistence farming continues, in contrast to the highly 'industrialised agriculture' of the northern hemisphere. For a large proportion of the population, cereals constitute one of the main items of diet. North America dominates the world grain market: it accounts for half of the total world exports. Many countries rely on imports of this grain to meet domestic requirements. However, over one third of the world's grain is fed to livestock in order to supply the meat-rich diet of the developed world.

A growing number of countries depend on one or two major cash crops, which often account for at least half of their total exports. These products tend to be essential food crops such as cereals and less essential crops such as tobacco and coffee. The value of such commodities decreases rapidly as the world market price falls. All too often the land could be better employed in producing staple food crops. Some areas may appear to have a food trade surplus, often as a result of exports of cash crops. Yet these regions may be unable to nourish their populations adequately.

Country where one agricultural or fisheries product accounts for 50% or more of total exports by value

Country where two agricultural or fisheries products account for 50% or more of total exports by value

Proportional value of imports and exports, millions of dollars

Coarse grains
Cocoa beans
Coffee
Cotton
Natural rubber
Rice
Soyabeans
Sugar
Tobacco
Wheat

Crop production

—100 million tonnes
—10 million tonnes

Cereals
Vegetables
Pulses
Fruit
Beverage crops
Sugar

Hunger

Enough food is produced to feed everybody, yet millions starve each year and others are seriously malnourished. An energy intake of less than 1,500 calories a day is likely to result in severe malnutrition. The requirement for well-being is around 2,400 calories. Not only are there vast discrepancies between the developed and developing world, but also within some countries the differences can be great. Though protein is very important to our diet, the quantity and nature of intake can vary greatly. A high proportion of animal protein is characteristic of the developed world, whilst it is largely vegetable in the developing countries. The effects of hunger are far reaching: it reduces the capacity to work and increases susceptibility to disease and death.

Calories per caput per day as a percentage of average requirement for well-being

150
130
110
100
90
80

Data not available

Main source of protein

Animal
Vegetable

35

Designed and produced by E.S.R.

ENERGY AND MINERALS

Energy from fossil fuels is limited by geology, and supplies are being exhausted. Even if new discoveries are made and extraction is viable there is still a limit to how long these will last. There is a growing awareness of the environmental damage caused by the increased use of coal. The many problems of nuclear power have made it a high risk option, and not the energy panacea envisaged by many. As a result, interest in renewable sources of energy has grown: wind, geothermal, power from the sea, hydro and solar are all possible alternatives for the production of energy.

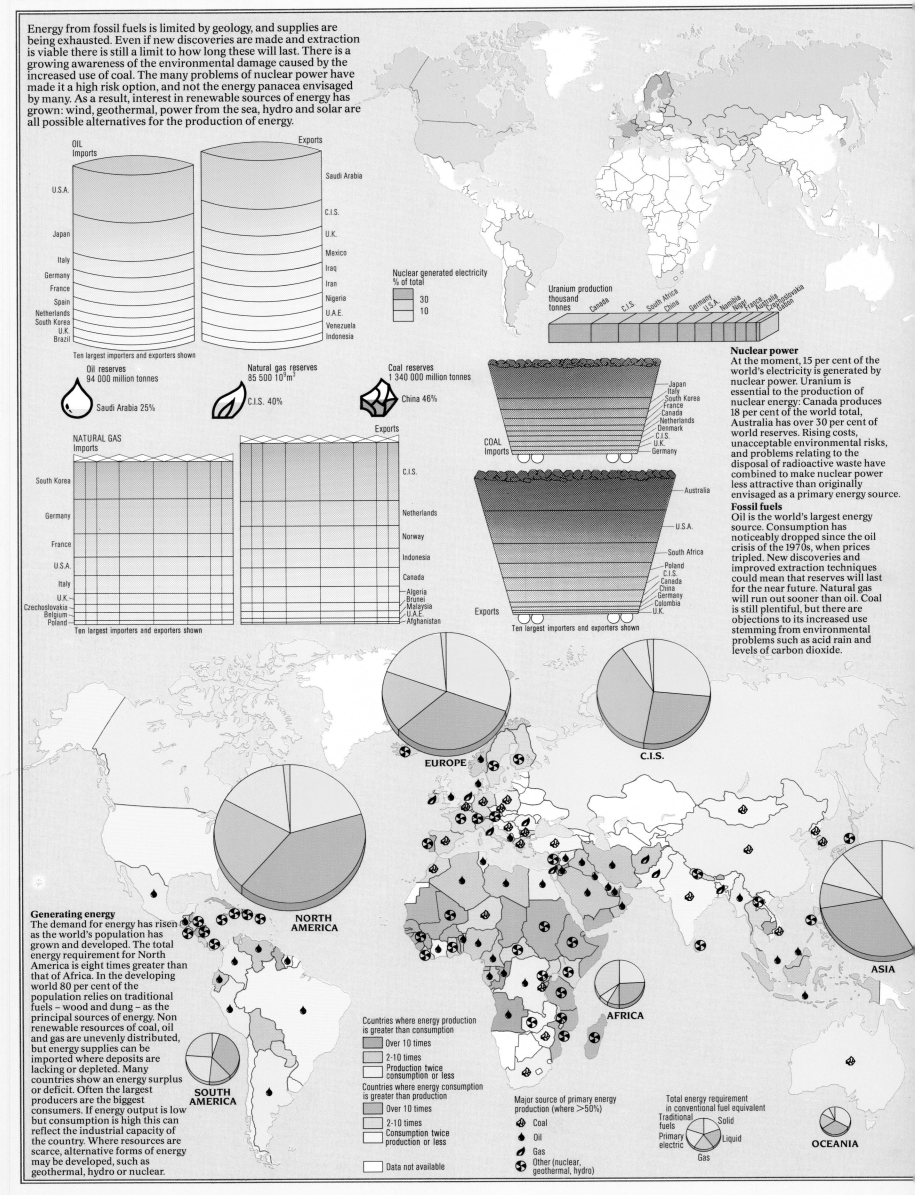

OIL
Imports
Exports

U.S.A.
Japan
Italy
Germany
France
Spain
Netherlands
South Korea
U.K.
Brazil

Saudi Arabia
C.I.S.
U.K.
Mexico
Iraq
Iran
Nigeria
U.A.E.
Venezuela
Indonesia

Ten largest importers and exporters shown

Oil reserves
94 000 million tonnes
Saudi Arabia 25%

Natural gas reserves
85 500 10⁹m³
C.I.S. 40%

Coal reserves
1 340 000 million tonnes
China 46%

Nuclear generated electricity
% of total
30
10

Uranium production
thousand
tonnes
Canada C.I.S. South Africa China Germany U.S.A. Namibia Niger France Australia Czechoslovakia Gabon

NATURAL GAS
Imports
Exports

South Korea
Germany
France
U.S.A.
Italy
U.K.
Czechoslovakia
Belgium
Poland

C.I.S.
Netherlands
Norway
Indonesia
Canada
Algeria
Brunei
Malaysia
U.A.E.
Afghanistan

Ten largest importers and exporters shown

COAL
Imports

Japan
Italy
South Korea
France
Canada
Netherlands
Denmark
C.I.S.
U.K.
Germany

Australia
U.S.A.
South Africa
Poland
C.I.S.
Canada
China
Germany
Colombia
U.K.

Exports

Ten largest importers and exporters shown

Nuclear power
At the moment, 15 per cent of the world's electricity is generated by nuclear power. Uranium is essential to the production of nuclear energy: Canada produces 18 per cent of the world total, Australia has over 30 per cent of world reserves. Rising costs, unacceptable environmental risks, and problems relating to the disposal of radioactive waste have combined to make nuclear power less attractive than originally envisaged as a primary energy source.

Fossil fuels
Oil is the world's largest energy source. Consumption has noticeably dropped since the oil crisis of the 1970s, when prices tripled. New discoveries and improved extraction techniques could mean that reserves will last for the near future. Natural gas will run out sooner than oil. Coal is still plentiful, but there are objections to its increased use stemming from environmental problems such as acid rain and levels of carbon dioxide.

EUROPE
C.I.S.
NORTH AMERICA
AFRICA
ASIA
SOUTH AMERICA
OCEANIA

Generating energy
The demand for energy has risen as the world's population has grown and developed. The total energy requirement for North America is eight times greater than that of Africa. In the developing world 80 per cent of the population relies on traditional fuels – wood and dung – as the principal sources of energy. Non renewable resources of coal, oil and gas are unevenly distributed, but energy supplies can be imported where deposits are lacking or depleted. Many countries show an energy surplus or deficit. Often the largest producers are the biggest consumers. If energy output is low but consumption is high this can reflect the industrial capacity of the country. Where resources are scarce, alternative forms of energy may be developed, such as geothermal, hydro or nuclear.

Countries where energy production is greater than consumption
Over 10 times
2-10 times
Production twice consumption or less

Countries where energy consumption is greater than production
Over 10 times
2-10 times
Consumption twice production or less

Data not available

Major source of primary energy production (where >50%)
Coal
Oil
Gas
Other (nuclear, geothermal, hydro)

Total energy requirement in conventional fuel equivalent
Traditional fuels
Primary electric
Solid
Liquid
Gas

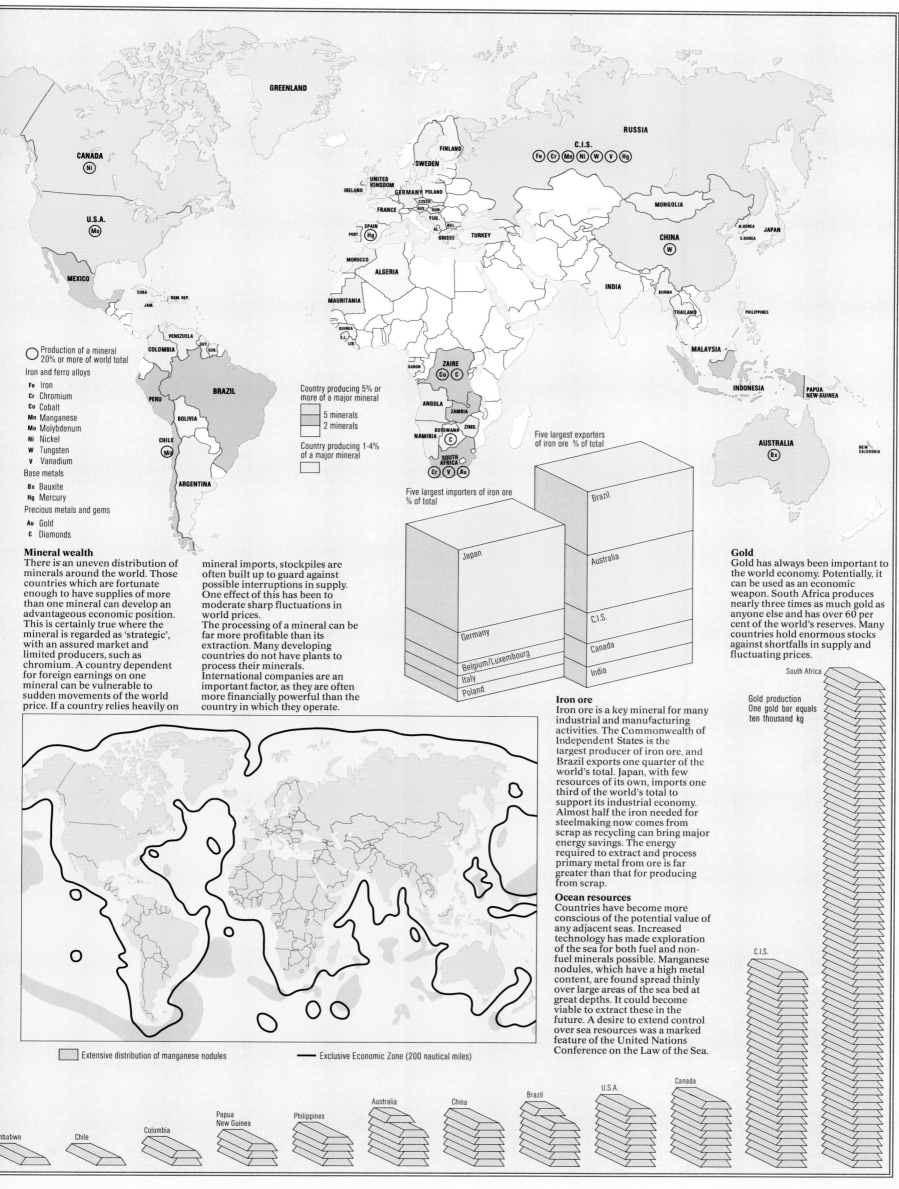

GREENLAND

CANADA (Ni)

U.S.A. (Mo)

MEXICO

CUBA
JAM.
DOM. REP.

VENEZUELA
COLOMBIA
GUY.
SUR.

PERU
BRAZIL
BOLIVIA
CHILE (Mo)
ARGENTINA

RUSSIA

FINLAND
SWEDEN

C.I.S. (Fe)(Cr)(Mn)(Ni)(W)(V)(Hg)

IRELAND
UNITED KINGDOM
GERMANY POLAND
CZECH.
FRANCE AUS. HUN.
SPAIN YUG.
PORT. (Hg) BUL.
GREECE TURKEY
AL.

MONGOLIA

N.KOREA JAPAN
S.KOREA

CHINA (W)

INDIA

MOROCCO
ALGERIA
MAURITANIA
GUINEA
S.L.
LIB.
GABON
ZAIRE (Co)(C)
ANGOLA
ZAMBIA
NAMIBIA
BOTSWANA (C)
ZIMB.
SOUTH AFRICA (Cr)(V)(Au)

BURMA
THAILAND
PHILIPPINES
MALAYSIA
INDONESIA
PAPUA NEW GUINEA

AUSTRALIA (Bx)
NEW CALEDONIA

Legend

◯ Production of a mineral 20% or more of world total

Iron and ferro alloys
Fe Iron
Cr Chromium
Co Cobalt
Mn Manganese
Mo Molybdenum
Ni Nickel
W Tungsten
V Vanadium

Base metals
Bx Bauxite
Hg Mercury

Precious metals and gems
Au Gold
C Diamonds

Country producing 5% or more of a major mineral
▨ 5 minerals
▨ 2 minerals

☐ Country producing 1-4% of a major mineral

Mineral wealth

There is an uneven distribution of minerals around the world. Those countries which are fortunate enough to have supplies of more than one mineral can develop an advantageous economic position. This is certainly true where the mineral is regarded as 'strategic', with an assured market and limited producers, such as chromium. A country dependent for foreign earnings on one mineral can be vulnerable to sudden movements of the world price. If a country relies heavily on mineral imports, stockpiles are often built up to guard against possible interruptions in supply. One effect of this has been to moderate sharp fluctuations in world prices.

The processing of a mineral can be far more profitable than its extraction. Many developing countries do not have plants to process their minerals. International companies are an important factor, as they are often more financially powerful than the country in which they operate.

Five largest importers of iron ore % of total
Japan
Germany
Belgium/Luxembourg
Italy
Poland

Five largest exporters of iron ore % of total
Brazil
Australia
C.I.S.
Canada
India

Iron ore

Iron ore is a key mineral for many industrial and manufacturing activities. The Commonwealth of Independent States is the largest producer of iron ore, and Brazil exports one quarter of the world's total. Japan, with few resources of its own, imports one third of the world's total to support its industrial economy. Almost half the iron needed for steelmaking now comes from scrap as recycling can bring major energy savings. The energy required to extract and process primary metal from ore is far greater than that for producing from scrap.

Ocean resources

Countries have become more conscious of the potential value of any adjacent seas. Increased technology has made exploration of the sea for both fuel and non-fuel minerals possible. Manganese nodules, which have a high metal content, are found spread thinly over large areas of the sea bed at great depths. It could become viable to extract these in the future. A desire to extend control over sea resources was a marked feature of the United Nations Conference on the Law of the Sea.

Gold

Gold has always been important to the world economy. Potentially, it can be used as an economic weapon. South Africa produces nearly three times as much gold as anyone else and has over 60 per cent of the world's reserves. Many countries hold enormous stocks against shortfalls in supply and fluctuating prices.

Gold production
One gold bar equals ten thousand kg

South Africa
C.I.S.
Canada
U.S.A.
Brazil
China
Australia
Philippines
Papua New Guinea
Colombia
Chile
Zimbabwe

☐ Extensive distribution of manganese nodules

—— Exclusive Economic Zone (200 nautical miles)

Designed and produced by E.S.R.

As trade has expanded, the production of goods has become increasingly specialised – components and raw materials from one country are shipped overseas for assembly or processing, then returned to their country of origin, or re-exported elsewhere. The dominance of established industrial countries is under threat from rapidly expanding industrial nations. Multinational corporations also play a large part in trade flows: they are mainly based in the developed world, which has a commanding influence on markets. Many developing countries, in order to achieve economic growth, face the dilemma between gearing production to satisfy overseas demands, while importing goods needed at home, or orientating production to domestic needs and increasing infrastructure at home. If trade is to prosper, the mutual interdependence of the developed and developing world both in demand and supply of goods needs to be recognised.

Trading partners
High productivity coupled with low wages and increased exports – over 20 per cent in the last decade – has seen South Korea emerge as one of the 'newly industrialised countries'. Textiles and clothing account for a quarter of exports; ships and electrical machinery, a third.

A declining market?
World trade on the whole is increasing. The debate as to whether this is a sustainable recovery or a temporary blip after recession continues. Industrial Europe accounts for nearly half of total world exports. In contrast, Africa's share of the market is only two per cent and real per capita income from exports seems likely to decrease. Massive growth in exports has been restricted by the growing number of trade barriers and other measures, often political, against competitors. If Third World earnings from exports are thus curtailed, spending on imports decreases, leading to increased subsidies on exported goods fuelling further protectionism from the developed world.

Balance of trade
The relationship between imports and exports is not always equal. Greater exports than imports create a trade surplus; more imports than exports means a deficit and leads to a negative balance of payments. The USA, as the world's largest consumer, has seen an increasing trade deficit, which seems likely to continue. The difference between exports and imports in the UK is also growing at an alarming rate. So far, the annual rate of deficit is worth about 3.25 per cent of national income, higher proportionally than the enormous deficit of the USA.
In contrast, Japanese economic policies stimulating high exports and low imports give rise to a large trade surplus.

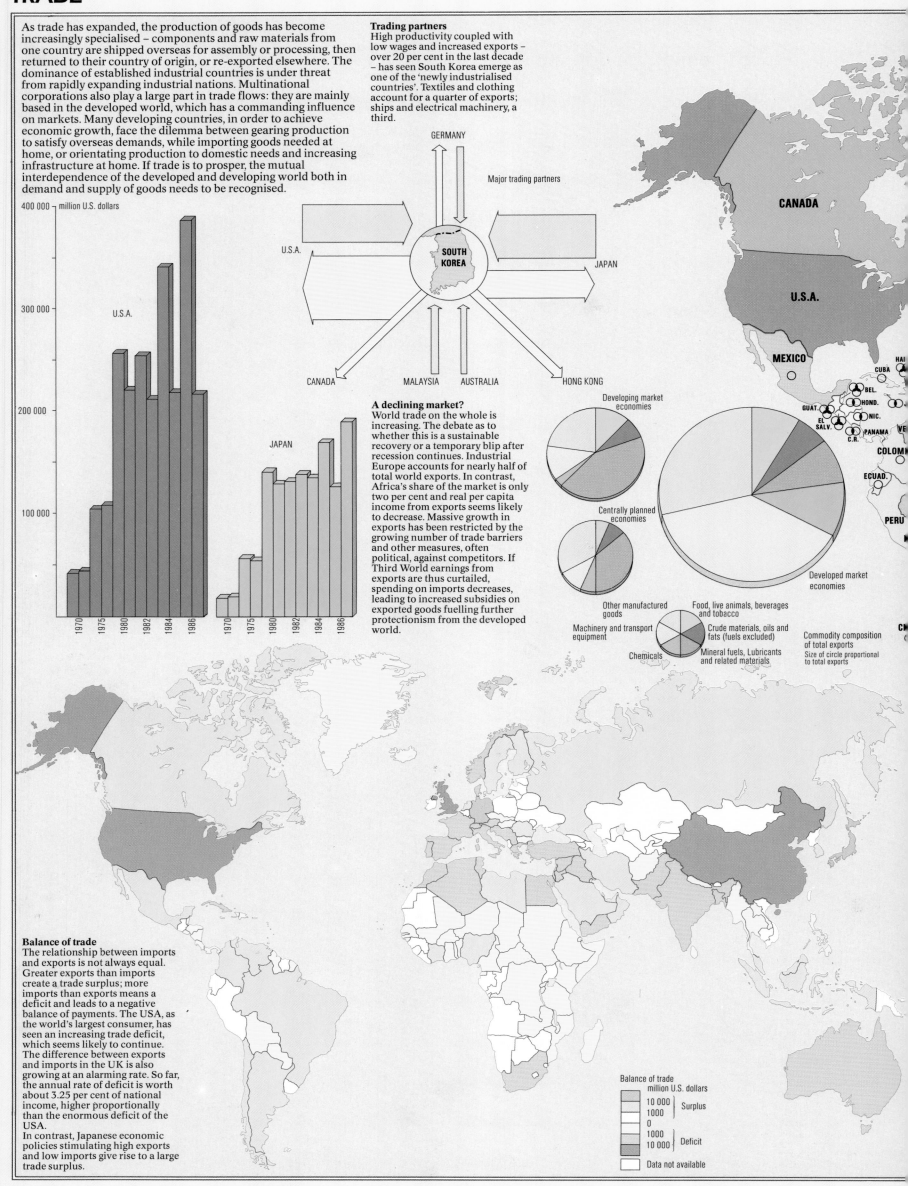

Major trading partners

GERMANY · U.S.A. · JAPAN · CANADA · MALAYSIA · AUSTRALIA · HONG KONG

SOUTH KOREA

400 000 million U.S. dollars

U.S.A.

JAPAN

1970 1975 1980 1982 1984 1986

Developing market economies

Centrally planned economies

Developed market economies

Other manufactured goods
Machinery and transport equipment
Chemicals
Food, live animals, beverages and tobacco
Crude materials, oils and fats (fuels excluded)
Mineral fuels, Lubricants and related materials

Commodity composition of total exports
Size of circle proportional to total exports

CANADA · U.S.A. · MEXICO · HAI · CUBA · BEL. · HOND. · NIC. · GUAT. · EL SALV. · PANAMA · C.R. · VE · COLOM · ECUAD. · PERU

Balance of trade
million U.S. dollars

10 000	Surplus
1000	
0	
1000	Deficit
10 000	
	Data not available

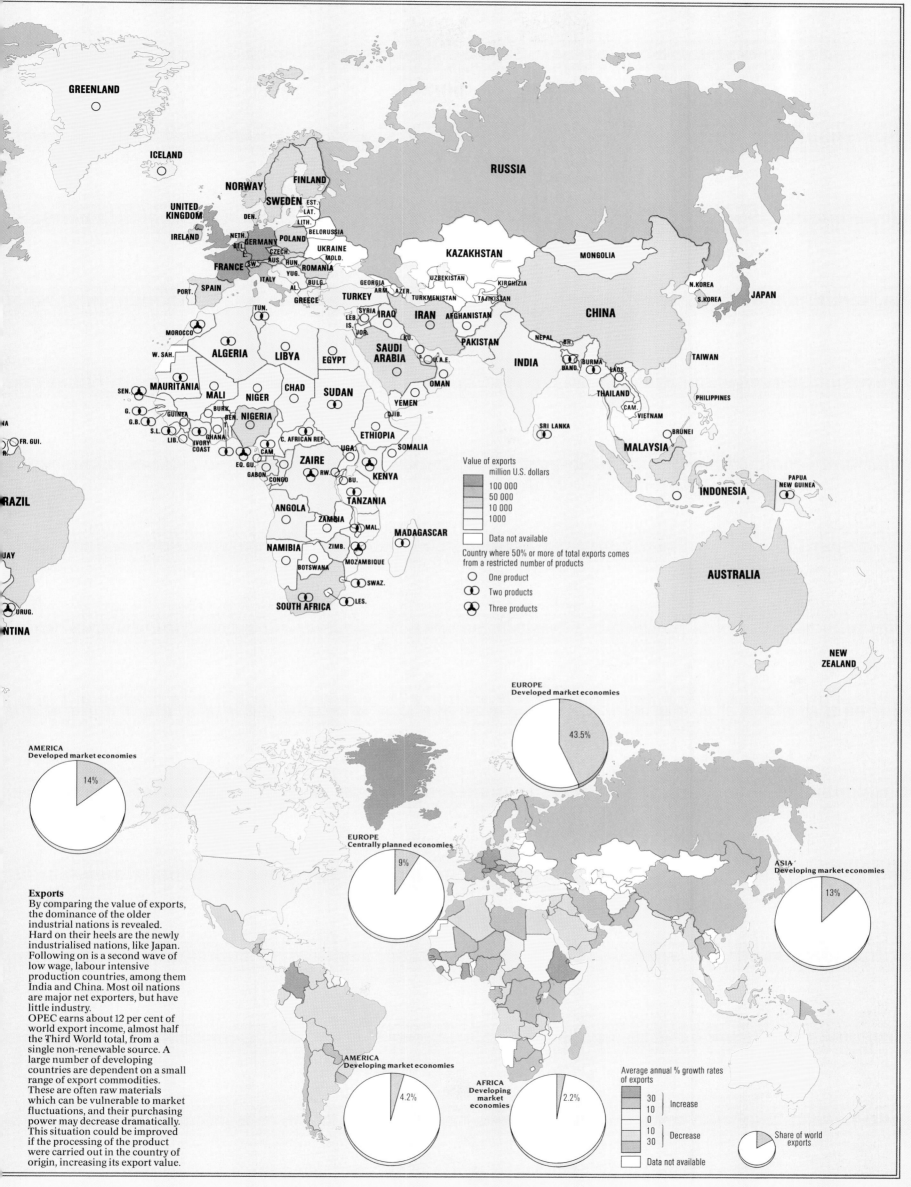

Exports

By comparing the value of exports, the dominance of the older industrial nations is revealed. Hard on their heels are the newly industrialised nations, like Japan. Following on is a second wave of low wage, labour intensive production countries, among them India and China. Most oil nations are major net exporters, but have little industry.

OPEC earns about 12 per cent of world export income, almost half the Third World total, from a single non-renewable source. A large number of developing countries are dependent on a small range of export commodities. These are often raw materials which can be vulnerable to market fluctuations, and their purchasing power may decrease dramatically. This situation could be improved if the processing of the product were carried out in the country of origin, increasing its export value.

Value of exports
million U.S. dollars
100 000
50 000
10 000
1000

Data not available

Country where 50% or more of total exports comes from a restricted number of products

One product
Two products
Three products

EUROPE
Developed market economies
43.5%

AMERICA
Developed market economies
14%

EUROPE
Centrally planned economies
9%

ASIA
Developing market economies
13%

AMERICA
Developing market economies
4.2%

AFRICA
Developing market economies
2.2%

Average annual % growth rates of exports
30
10
0
Increase
10
30
Decrease

Data not available

Share of world exports

Designed and produced by E.S.R.

WEALTH AND DEBT

The chasm between the rich and poor nations of the world is widening. Existing methods of reducing the difference involve loans and aid from governments, UN organisations and aid agencies. In the future the international economic system needs to be redesigned to finance and invest in sustainable development of national resources and programmes to combat poverty.

Aid donors
Aid has mostly been provided by the developed nations, particularly members of the Development Assistance Committee (DAC) of the Organisations of Economic Cooperation and Development (OECD). However, in recent years a growing proportion has come from the major oil producing nations. The total amount of aid donated by a country can seem enormous, but as a proportion of GNP a rather different view of the nation's generosity emerges.

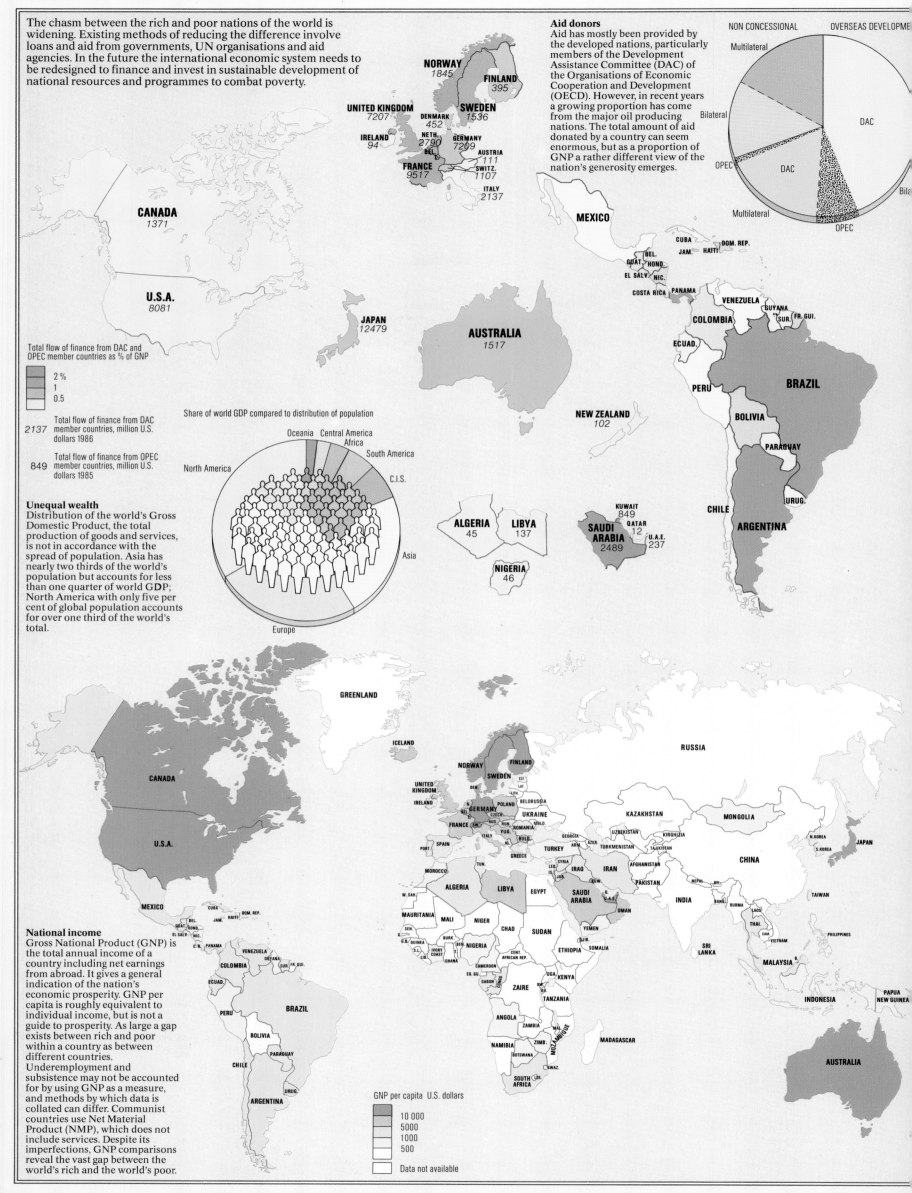

NORWAY 1845
FINLAND 395
SWEDEN 1536
UNITED KINGDOM 7207
DENMARK 452
IRELAND 94
NETH. 2790
GERMANY 7209
BEL.
FRANCE 9517
AUSTRIA 111
SWITZ. 1107
ITALY 2137

NON CONCESSIONAL   OVERSEAS DEVELOPME
Multilateral
Bilateral
DAC
OPEC
DAC
Multilateral
OPEC
Bila

CANADA 1371

U.S.A. 8081

JAPAN 12479

AUSTRALIA 1517

NEW ZEALAND 102

MEXICO
CUBA
DOM. REP.
GUAT. BEL. HOND. JAM. HAITI
EL SALV. NIC.
COSTA RICA PANAMA
VENEZUELA GUYANA
COLOMBIA SUR. FR. GUI.
ECUAD.
PERU
BRAZIL
BOLIVIA
PARAGUAY
URUG.
CHILE
ARGENTINA

ALGERIA 45   LIBYA 137
KUWAIT 849
QATAR 12
SAUDI ARABIA 2489
U.A.E. 237
NIGERIA 46

Total flow of finance from DAC and OPEC member countries as % of GNP
2 %
1
0.5

2137 Total flow of finance from DAC member countries, million U.S. dollars 1986

849 Total flow of finance from OPEC member countries, million U.S. dollars 1985

Oceania   Central America
Africa
Share of world GDP compared to distribution of population
North America
South America
C.I.S.
Asia
Europe

Unequal wealth
Distribution of the world's Gross Domestic Product, the total production of goods and services, is not in accordance with the spread of population. Asia has nearly two thirds of the world's population but accounts for less than one quarter of world GDP; North America with only five per cent of global population accounts for over one third of the world's total.

GREENLAND
ICELAND
NORWAY SWEDEN FINLAND
UNITED KINGDOM DEN.
IRELAND
CANADA
U.S.A.
MEXICO
CUBA DOM. REP.
GUAT. BEL. HOND. JAM. HAITI
EL SALV. NIC.
PANAMA
VENEZUELA GUYANA
COLOMBIA SUR. FR. GUI.
ECUAD.
PERU
BRAZIL
BOLIVIA
PARAGUAY
CHILE
URUG.
ARGENTINA

RUSSIA
POLAND BELORUSSIA
GERMANY CZECH. UKRAINE
FRANCE KAZAKHSTAN MONGOLIA
ROMANIA
YUG. BULG.
PORT. SPAIN GEORGIA UZBEKISTAN KIRGHIZIA
ITALY TURKEY ARM. AZER. TURKMENISTAN TAJIKISTAN
GREECE SYRIA IRAQ IRAN AFGHANISTAN CHINA JAPAN
MOROCCO TUN. LEB. ISR. JOR. KUW. PAKISTAN N.KOREA S.KOREA
ALGERIA LIBYA EGYPT SAUDI ARABIA NEPAL BHU. TAIWAN
W.SAH. Q. U.A.E. INDIA BURMA LAOS
MAURITANIA MALI NIGER CHAD SUDAN YEMEN OMAN BANG. THAI. VIETNAM PHILIPPINES
SEN. G.B. GUINEA BURK. CENT. AFRICAN REP. DJIB. SRI LANKA
S.L. LIB. IVORY COAST GHANA NIGERIA CAMEROON ETHIOPIA SOMALIA MALAYSIA
EQ. GU. GABON UGA. KENYA
ZAIRE
TANZANIA INDONESIA PAPUA NEW GUINEA
ANGOLA ZAMBIA MAL.
NAMIBIA ZIMB. MOZAMBIQUE MADAGASCAR
BOTSWANA
SWAZ.
SOUTH AFRICA LES.
AUSTRALIA

National income
Gross National Product (GNP) is the total annual income of a country including net earnings from abroad. It gives a general indication of the nation's economic prosperity. GNP per capita is roughly equivalent to individual income, but is not a guide to prosperity. As large a gap exists between rich and poor within a country as between different countries. Underemployment and subsistence may not be accounted for by using GNP as a measure, and methods by which data is collated can differ. Communist countries use Net Material Product (NMP), which does not include services. Despite its imperfections, GNP comparisons reveal the vast gap between the world's rich and the world's poor.

GNP per capita U.S. dollars
10 000
5000
1000
500
Data not available

40

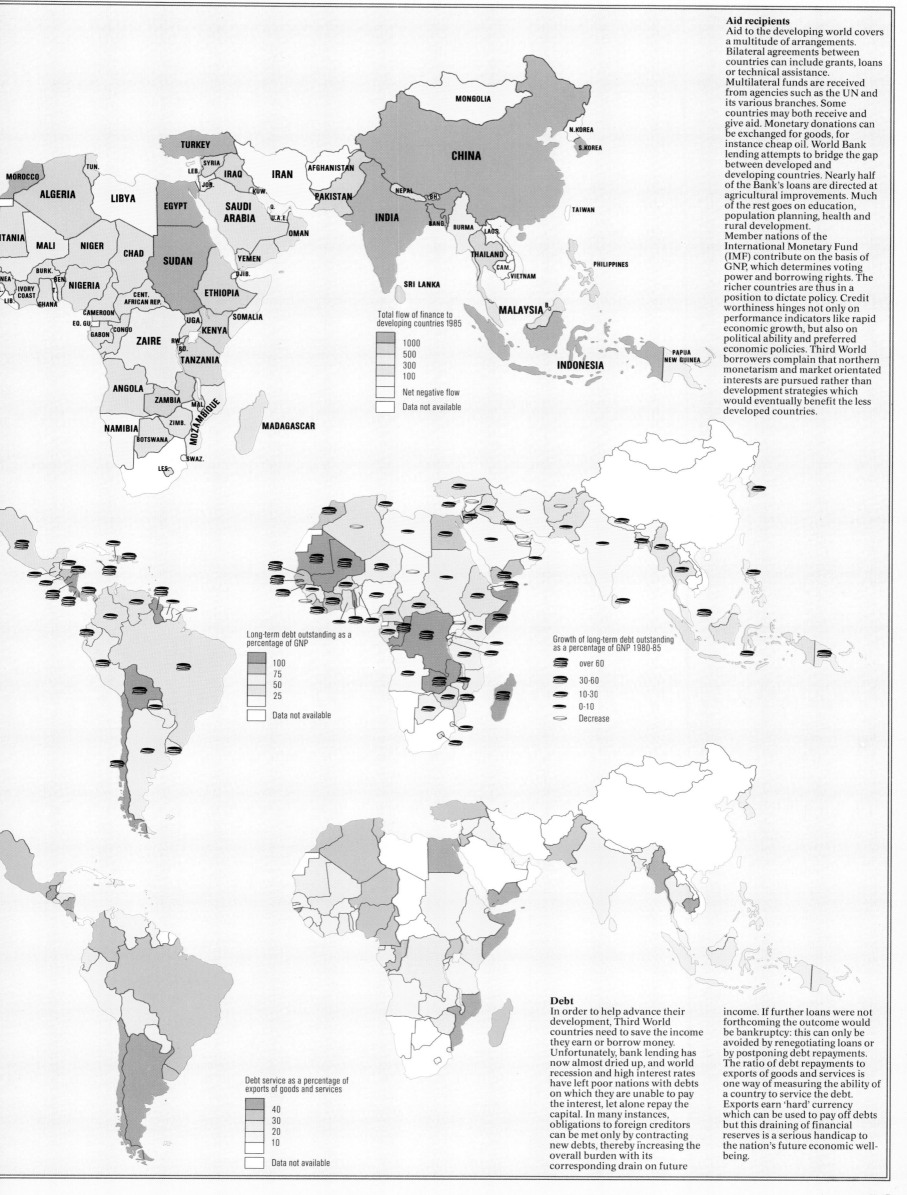

Aid recipients

Aid to the developing world covers a multitude of arrangements. Bilateral agreements between countries can include grants, loans or technical assistance. Multilateral funds are received from agencies such as the UN and its various branches. Some countries may both receive and give aid. Monetary donations can be exchanged for goods, for instance cheap oil. World Bank lending attempts to bridge the gap between developed and developing countries. Nearly half of the Bank's loans are directed at agricultural improvements. Much of the rest goes on education, population planning, health and rural development.

Member nations of the International Monetary Fund (IMF) contribute on the basis of GNP, which determines voting power and borrowing rights. The richer countries are thus in a position to dictate policy. Credit worthiness hinges not only on performance indicators like rapid economic growth, but also on political ability and preferred economic policies. Third World borrowers complain that northern monetarism and market orientated interests are pursued rather than development strategies which would eventually benefit the less developed countries.

MONGOLIA

N.KOREA

S.KOREA

CHINA

TURKEY

SYRIA

LEB.
IRAQ

IRAN

AFGHANISTAN

JOB.
KUW.

Q.
U.A.E.

TUN.

MOROCCO

ALGERIA

LIBYA

EGYPT

SAUDI
ARABIA

PAKISTAN

NEPAL

BH.

INDIA

BANG.

BURMA

LAOS

TAIWAN

OMAN

ITANIA

MALI

NIGER

CHAD

SUDAN

YEMEN

DJIB.

THAILAND

CAM.

VIETNAM

PHILIPPINES

BURK.

NEA

L

IVORY
COAST

BEN.

NIGERIA

CENT.
AFRICAN REP.

ETHIOPIA

SRI LANKA

LIB.

GHANA

CAMEROON

UGA.

SOMALIA

MALAYSIA

B.

EQ. GU.

GABON

CONGO

ZAIRE

RW.

BO.

KENYA

TANZANIA

INDONESIA

PAPUA
NEW GUINEA

ANGOLA

ZAMBIA

MAL

MOZAMBIQUE

NAMIBIA

ZIMB.

MADAGASCAR

BOTSWANA

SWAZ.

LES.

Total flow of finance to developing countries 1985

1000
500
300
100

Net negative flow

Data not available

Long-term debt outstanding as a percentage of GNP

100
75
50
25

Data not available

Growth of long-term debt outstanding as a percentage of GNP 1980-85

over 60
30-60
10-30
0-10
Decrease

Debt

In order to help advance their development, Third World countries need to save the income they earn or borrow money. Unfortunately, bank lending has now almost dried up, and world recession and high interest rates have left poor nations with debts on which they are unable to pay the interest, let alone repay the capital. In many instances, obligations to foreign creditors can be met only by contracting new debts, thereby increasing the overall burden with its corresponding drain on future income. If further loans were not forthcoming the outcome would be bankruptcy: this can only be avoided by renegotiating loans or by postponing debt repayments. The ratio of debt repayments to exports of goods and services is one way of measuring the ability of a country to service the debt. Exports earn 'hard' currency which can be used to pay off debts but this draining of financial reserves is a serious handicap to the nation's future economic well-being.

Debt service as a percentage of exports of goods and services

40
30
20
10

Data not available

Designed and produced by E.S.R.

SETTLEMENT

For scales larger than 1:2,000,000   Population

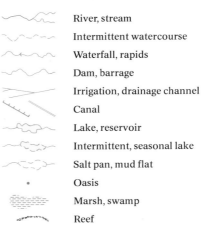 **BIRMINGHAM**	>1,000,000	
GLASGOW	500,000–1,000,000	
CARDIFF	250,000–500,000	
LIMERICK	50,000–250,000	
• **Dover**	10,000–50,000	
• Lossiemouth	5,000–10,000	
○ Church Stretton	<5,000	

CROYDON   London Borough

For scales between 1:2,000,000 and 1:12,000,000

NEW YORK	>5,000,000
RANGOON	2,500,000–5,000,000
■ **KUYBYSHEV**	1,000,000–2,500,000
• **Hyderabad**	500,000–1,000,000
• Adelaide	100,000–500,000
○ Baden-Baden	<100,000

For scales smaller than 1:12,000,000

■ **DAR ES SALAAM**	>1,000,000
• **Maracaibo**	500,000–1,000,000
• Tiranë	<500,000

Lisboa   National capital   **Winnipeg**   State, provincial capital

COMMUNICATIONS

——————	Motorway
- - - - - - -	Motorway under construction
——————	Principal road
- - - - - -	Principal road under construction
——————	Other main road
— — — —	Track, seasonal road
→┤ ├←	Road tunnel
——————	Principal railway
– – – –	Principal railway under construction
→┤ ├←	Railway tunnel
✈	International, main airport

BOUNDARIES

▬▬▬▬	International
▬ ▬▬ ▬▬	Undefined, disputed
——————	Internal, state, provincial
– – – –	Armistice, cease-fire line

The representation of a boundary in this atlas does not denote its international recognition and therefore the *defacto* situation has been depicted.

HYDROGRAPHIC FEATURES

	River, stream
	Intermittent watercourse
	Waterfall, rapids
	Dam, barrage
	Irrigation, drainage channel
	Canal
	Lake, reservoir
	Intermittent, seasonal lake
	Salt pan, mud flat
•	Oasis
	Marsh, swamp
	Reef

Depth of sea in metres

Scales larger than 1:12,000,000

0
200
3000

Scales smaller than 1:12,000,000

0
1000
5000

OTHER FEATURES

▲ 3798	Elevation above sea level (metres)
▼ -133	Depression, below sea level (metres)
≍	Pass
•—▪—•	Oil, gas pipeline with field

ENVIRONMENTAL TYPES

	Permanent ice and snow
	Mountain and moorland
	Tundra
	Coniferous forest
	Deciduous forest
	Tropical forest
	Prairie
	Temperate agriculture
	Mediterranean scrub
	Savannah
	Desert

This representation of the environment and its associated vegetation gives an overview of the landscape. It is not intended to be definitive.

CONVERSION SCALES

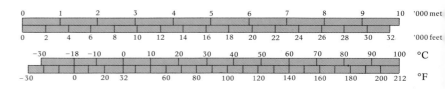

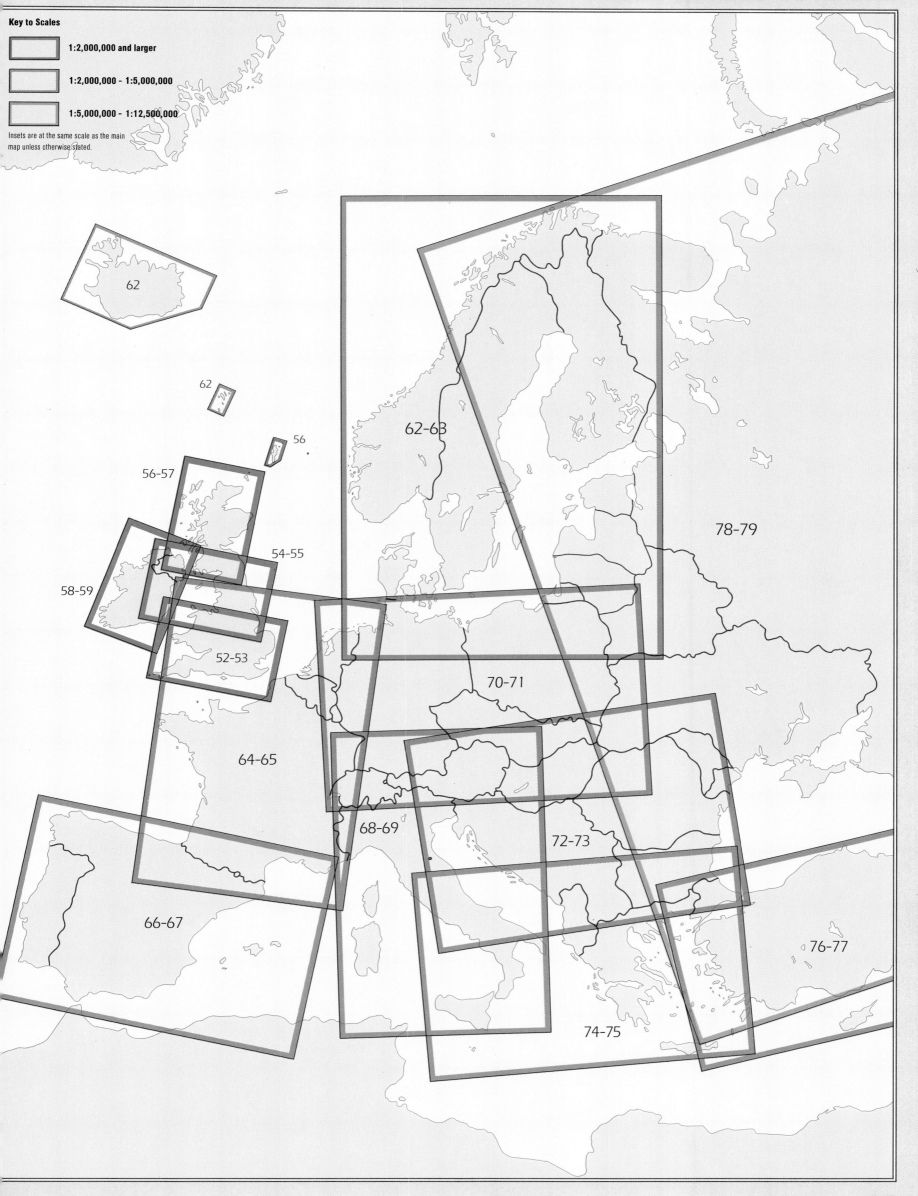

Key to Scales

1:2,000,000 and larger

1:2,000,000 – 1:5,000,000

1:5,000,000 – 1:12,500,000

Insets are at the same scale as the main
map unless otherwise stated.

62

62

62-63

78-79

56

56-57

54-55

58-59

52-53

70-71

64-65

66-67

68-69

72-73

74-75

76-77

Designed and produced by E.S.R.

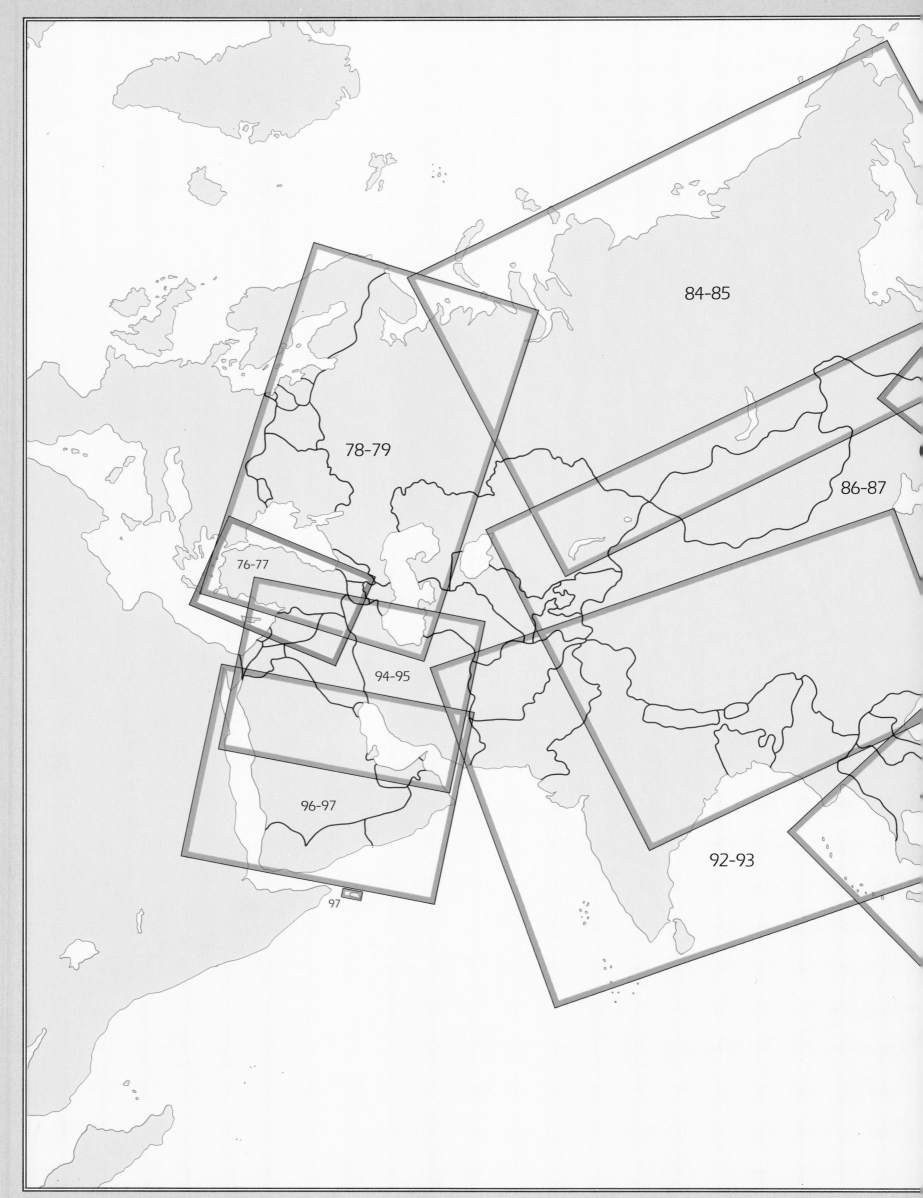

84-85

78-79

86-87

76-77

94-95

92-93

96-97

97

88-89

89

114

114

90-91

115

115

112-113

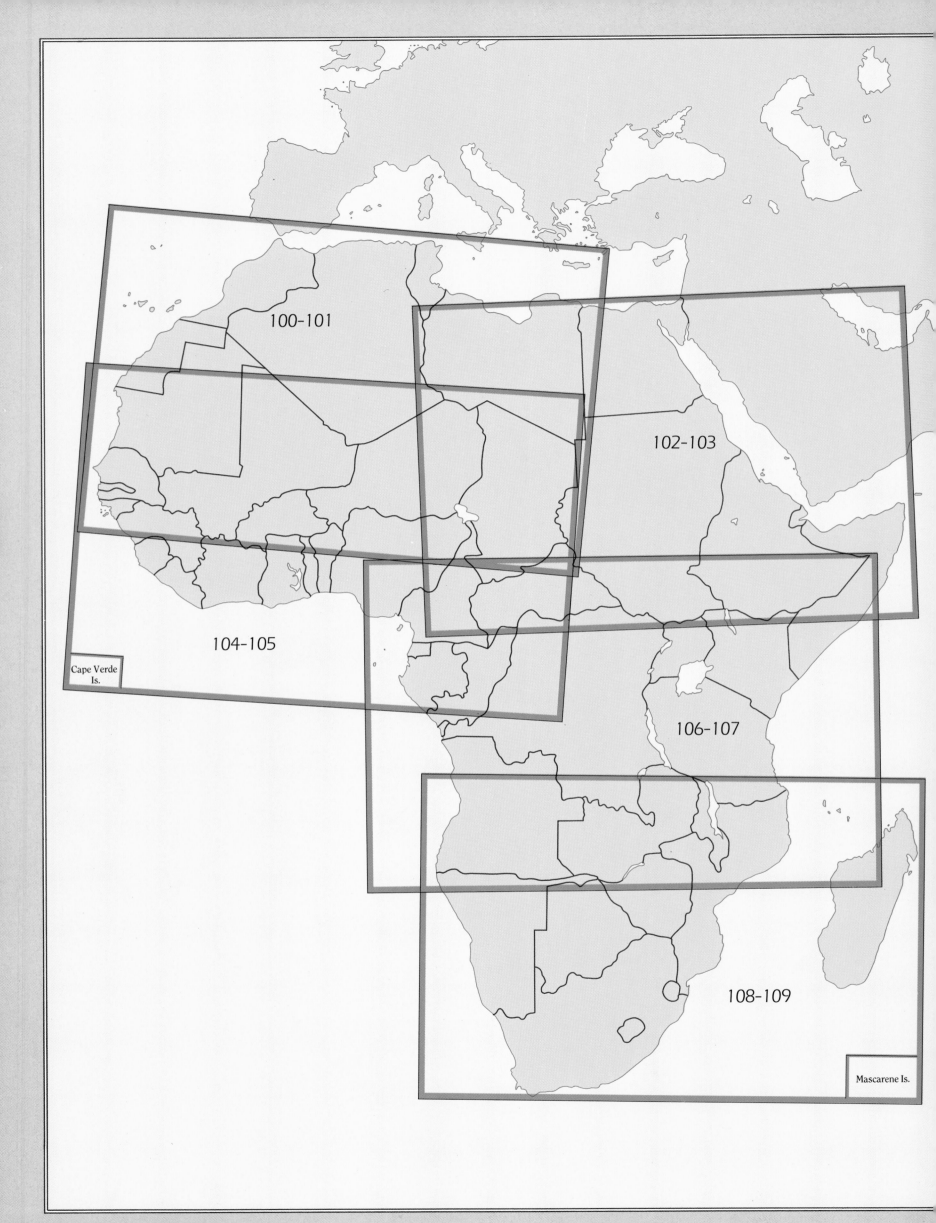

100-101

102-103

Cape Verde Is.

104-105

106-107

108-109

Mascarene Is.

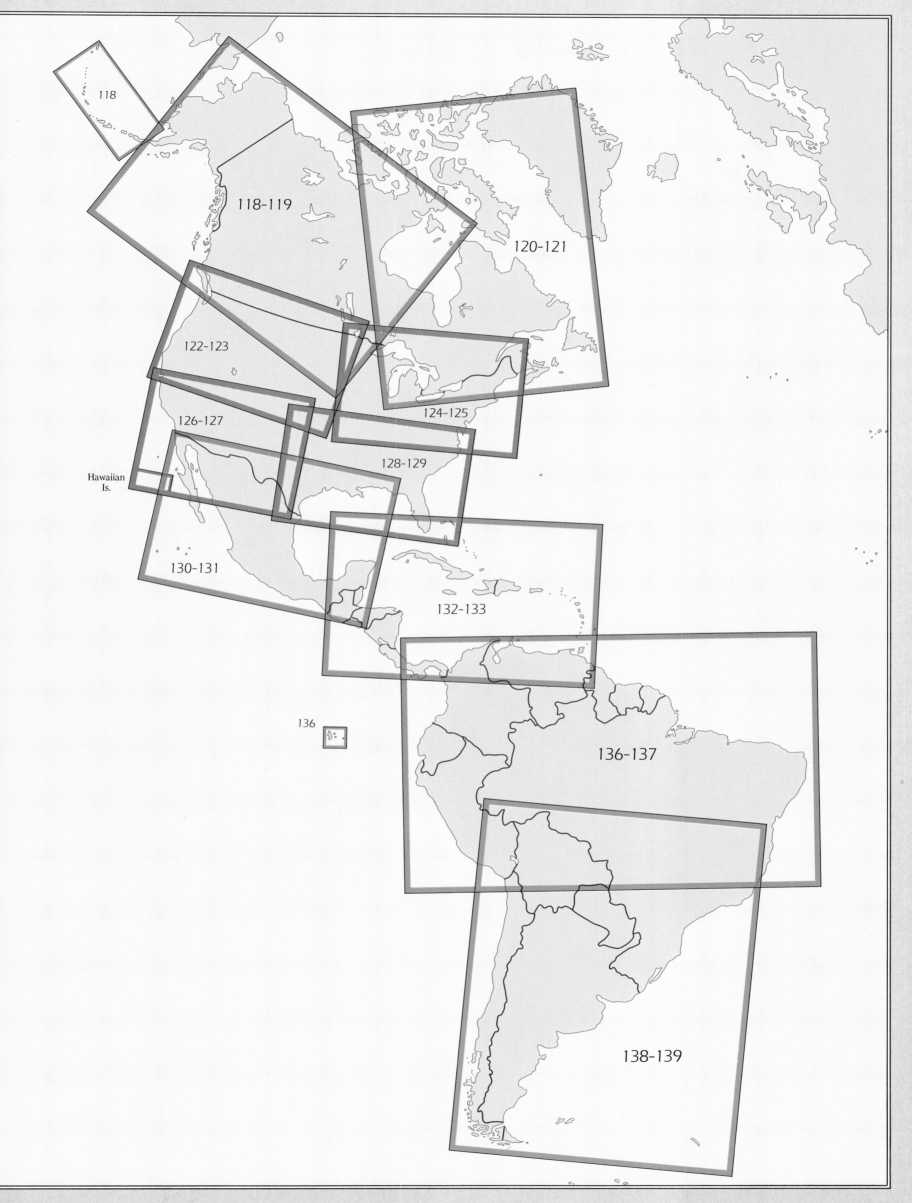

118

118-119

120-121

122-123

124-125

126-127

128-129

Hawaiian Is.

130-131

132-133

136

136-137

138-139

Designed and produced by E.S.R.

West of Greenwich

A · 150° · **B** · 120° · **C** · 90° · **D** · 60° · **E** · 30° · **F**

ARCTIC OCEAN

Ellesmere Island

Lincoln Sea

1

Queen Elizabeth Islands

Kane Basin

Baffin Bay

GREENLAND (Denmark)

Viscount Melville Sound

Banks Island

Beaufort Sea

Jan Mayen (Norway)

Ostrov Vrangelya

Pt. Barrow

Chucki Sea

Amundsen Gulf

Victoria Island

Foxe Basin

Oikiqtaluk

Davis Str.

Norweg Sea

2

Brooks Range

ALASKA (U.S.A.)

Mackenzie Mts.

Great Bear Lake

Back

ICELAND

Reykjavik

McKINLEY 6194▲

Alaska Range

Great Slave Lake

Hudson Str.

Kap Farvel

Denmark Strait

Føroyar (Denmark)

Shetland Is. (U.K.)

Bering Sea

Gulf of Alaska

Rocky Mountains

L. Athabasca

Reindeer Lake

Hudson Bay

Labrador Sea

UNITED KINGDOM

Kodiak I.

CANADA

Labrador

Dublin IRELAND

Aleutian Islands

L. Winnipeg

Great Lakes

Newfoundland

s'Gra LONDON

3

Aleutian Trench

Vancouver I.

Columbia

NORTH PACIFIC OCEAN

Great Plains

Missouri

Ottawa

Appalachian Mts.

CHICAGO

NEW YORK

PHILADELPHIA

Washington

NORTH ATLANTIC OCEAN

Açores (Port.)

PORTUGAL **SPAIN**

Madrid

Lisboa

Gt. Salt Lake

UNITED STATES OF AMERICA

SAN FRANCISCO

LOS ANGELES

Rabat

Madeira (Port.)

MOROCCO

Isla de Guadalupe (Mex.)

Rio Grande

Gulf of Mexico

Bermuda (U.K.)

Ilas Canarias (Sp.)

Al Aaiún

WESTERN SAHARA

Tropic of Cancer

Hawaiian Islands

BAHAMAS Nassau

La Habana

CUBA

West Indies

DOMINICAN REP.

Port au Prince

Puerto Rico (U.S.A.)

Leeward Is.

CAPE VERDE IS.

Praia

MAURITANIA Nouakchott

MA

Dakar

SEN

4

HAWAII (U.S.A.)

Islas de Revillagigedo (Mex.)

MEXICO CIUDAD DE MEXICO

Belmopan

BELIZE Kingston

HONDURAS Tegucigalpa

HAITI Santo Domingo

JAMAICA

Windward Is.

BARBADOS

THE GAMBIA

GUINEA BISSAU

Banjul

Bissau

Bamako

GUINEA

FA

BU

Ouagadougou

P o l y n e s i a

Line Islands

Christmas I.

GUATEMALA Guatemala

San Salvador

EL SALVADOR **NICARAGUA**

Managua

Costa Rica San José

Caribbean Sea

Caracas

TRINIDAD AND TOBAGO

VENEZUELA

Conakry

SIERRA LEONE Freetown

Yamoussoukro Lo

Monrovia

LIBERIA **IVORY COAST**

SA

Equator

Phoenix Is.

KIRIBATI

Panamá

PANAMA

Georgetown

GU SUR

Paramaribo

Cayenne

FRENCH GUIANA

Orinoco

Bogotá

COLOMBIA

Isla Fernando de Noronha (Brazil)

AND P

Islas Galápagos (Ecuador)

Quito

ECUADOR

Negro

Ascension (U.K.)

W. SOMOA

Apia

Samoa (U.S.A.)

Iles Marquises (Fr.)

French Polynesia (Fr.)

Iles Tuamotu

PERU

Cordillera

LIMA

BRAZIL

Planalto do Mato Grosso

SOUTH ATLANTIC OCEAN

St. Helena (U.K.)

5

TONGA Nuku'alofa

Cook Islands (N.Z.)

Tahiti

Iles de la Société

SOUTH PACIFIC OCEAN

La Paz

BOLIVIA

Titicaca

Brasília

Ilha da Trindade (Brazil)

Iles Gambier

Pitcairn I. (U.K.) Ducie I. (U.K.)

Salar de

PARAGUAY

Asunción

SÃO PAULO

RÍO DE JANEIRO

Tropic of Capricorn

Isla de Pascua (Easter I.) (Chile)

Pilcomayo

Chile Trench

ACONCAGUA 6960▲

Cordillera de los Andes

URUGUAY Montevideo

Tristan da Cunha (U.K.)

Gough I. (U.K.)

SOUTH ATLANTIC OCEAN

Islas Juan Fernández (Chile)

Santiago

ARGENTINA

BUENOS AIRES

Chatham Is. (N.Z.)

Patagonia

6

Falkland Is. (U.K.)

South Georgia (U.K.)

Cabo de Hornos

Scotia Sea

South Sandwich Is. (U.K.)

A · 150° · **B** · 120° · **C** · 90° · **D** · 60° · **E** · 30° · **F**

1:85,000,000 (Scale at the Equator)

ARCTIC OCEAN

1

Zemlya Frantsa-Iosifa
(Russia)

Severnaya Zemlya

Novosibirskiye Ostrova

*Karskoye
More*

*More
Laptevykh*

Novaya
Zemlya

Byrranga

Ozero Taymyr

Lyakhovkiye
Ostrova

*Vostochno
Sibirskoye
More*

*Barentsevo
More*

Nordkapp

Poluostrov
Yamal

Gydanskiy
Poluostrov

Gory

Plato
Putorana

Kolmskaya
Nizmennost

Ostrov Vrangelya

2

Lappland

SWEDEN

FINLAND

Helsingfors

Stockholm

Tallinn

ST. PETERSBURG

ESTONIA

Riga

MOSKVA

Baltic

LATVIA

LITHUANIA

Vilnius   Minsk

Berlin   BELARUS

Warszawa

POLAND

Kyiv
(Kiev)

UKRAINE

MOLDOVA

Chisinau
(Kishinev)

Budapest

Bucuresti

Beograd

Sofiya

ALBANIA

GREECE

Athinai

Valletta

MALTA

Tarabulus

Sea

LIBYA

EGYPT

Tibesti

CHAD

N'djaména

SUDAN

El Khartum

CENTRAL
AFRICAN REP

Bangui

CAMEROON

Congo
Basin

ZAIRE

Kinshasa

Luanda

ANGOLA

ZAMBIA

Lusaka

Harare

ZIMBABWE

NAMIBIA

Windhoek

BOTSWANA

Gaborone

Kalahari

Pretoria

Maputo

SOUTH
AFRICA

Maseru

LESOTHO

SWAZILAND

Mbabne

Good Hope

Orange

Ural'skiy Khrebet

*Zapadno
Sibirskaya
Ravnina*

Poluostrov
Yamal

*Sredne
Sibirskoye
Ploskogor'ye*

RUSSIA

Verkhoyanskiy Khrebet

Khrebet Cherskogo

Khrebet Kolymskiy

*Bering
Sea*

Prikaspiyskaya
Nizmennost'

Kirgiz
Step'

KAZAKHSTAN

Ozero Balkhash

Ozero Baykal

MONGOLIA

Ulaanbaatar

Gobi

Sakhalin

Sikhote Alin'

Kuril'skiye Ostrova

Aleutian   Islands

3

Black Sea

GEORGIA

T'bilisi

ARMENIA

Yerevan

AZERBAIJAN

Baku

Caspian

Aral'skoye
More

Peski
Karakumy

Kyzylkum

Tashkent

UZBEKISTAN

Bishkek

Alma-Ata

KYRGYZSTAN

Tian Shan

Tarim
Pendi

Taklimakan
Shamo

Kunlun Shan

BEIJING

TIANJIN

N. KOREA

Pyongyang

S. KOREA

Sôul

CHINA

Huang Ho

*Sea of
Japan*

JAPAN

TÔKYÔ

*NORTH
PACIFIC
OCEAN*

TURKEY

Ankara

SYRIA

Dimashq

LEB.

Bayrut

ISRAEL

IRAQ

Baghdad

JOR.

Amman

Yerushalayim

EL QÂHIRA

CYPRUS

Levkosia

TEHRAN

IRAN

Kühhä-ye Zagros

KUW.

Al Kuwayt

BAH.

Al Manamah

QAT.

Ad Dawhah

Abu Zabi

U.A.E.

SAUDI
ARABIA

Ar Riyâd

OMAN

Masqat

Red Sea

ERITREA

San'â

YEMEN

DJIB.

ETHIOPIA

Adis Abeba

SOMALIA

Muqdisho

UGANDA

Kampala

RW.

Kigali

BU.

Bujumbura

Nairobi

KENYA

Dodoma

TANZANIA

KLIMANJARO

Victoria

SEYCHELLES

TURKMENISTAN

Ashgabat

TAJIKISTAN

Dushanbe

Hindu Kush

AFGHANISTAN

Kâbul

Islamabad

PAKISTAN

Xizang
Gaoyuan

Himalaya

EVEREST

NEPAL

Kathmandu

New
Delhi

DELHI

*Thar
Desert*

KARACHI

INDIA

Deccan

BOMBAY

CALCUTTA

MADRAS

BHU.

BANG.

Dhaka

MYANMAR

Yangon

*Bay of
Bengal*

Andaman
Islands
(India)

LAOS

Viangchan

THAI-
LAND

KRUNG THEP

VIETNAM

Hanoi

HONG KONG
(U.K)

Tai-pei

TAIWAN

*Huang
Hai*

SHANGHAI

Chang Jiang

MADAGASCAR

Antananarivo

MAURITIUS

Réunion
(Fr.)

Port Louis

COMOROS

Moroni

MOZAMBIQUE CHANNEL

Lilongwe

MAL.

MOZAMBIQUE

Lakshadweep
(India)

Malé

MALDIVES

Colombo

SRI LANKA

INDIAN OCEAN

Suqutrâ
(S.Yem.)

*Arabian
Sea*

CAM.

Phnom Penh

MALAYSIA

Kuala Lumpur

SINGAPORE

Sumatera

Bandar Seri
Begawan

BRU.

Borneo

East   Indies

Java Trench

JAKARTA

Jawa

INDONESIA

Maluku

Sulawesi

PHILIPPINES

Mindanao

Luzon

MANILA

Nan Hai

Marianas
Is.

Guam (USA)

Micronesia

Caroline Islands

Marshall Is.

NAURU

Tarawa

Gilbert
Is.

Phoenix Is.

Equator

4

PAPUA
NEW
GUINEA

Port Moresby

Timor

Laut Arafura

*Laut
Timor*

SOLOMON ISLANDS

Honiara

Santa
Cruz
Is.

TUVALU

Fanafuti

Melanesia

New
Caledonia

*Coral
Sea*

Gt. Barrier Reef

VANUATU

Vila

Nouvelle
Calédonie
(Fr.)

FIJI

Suva

Iles
Wallice

W.
SAMOA

Apia

TONGA

Nuku'alofa

Tonga Trench

5

AUSTRALIA

Gt. Victoria Desert

L. Eyre

Darling

Gt. Dividing Range

C. Leeuwin

Canberra

Tropic of Capricorn

Tasman Sea

NEW ZEALAND

Wellington

Tasmania

Chatham Is.
(N.Z.)

Kermadec Trench

6

Prince Edward Is.
(S.A.)

Iles Crozet
(Fr.)

Ile Kerguelen
(Fr.)

Heard I.
(Aus.)

Auckland Is.
(N.Z.)

Macquarie Is.
(Aus.)

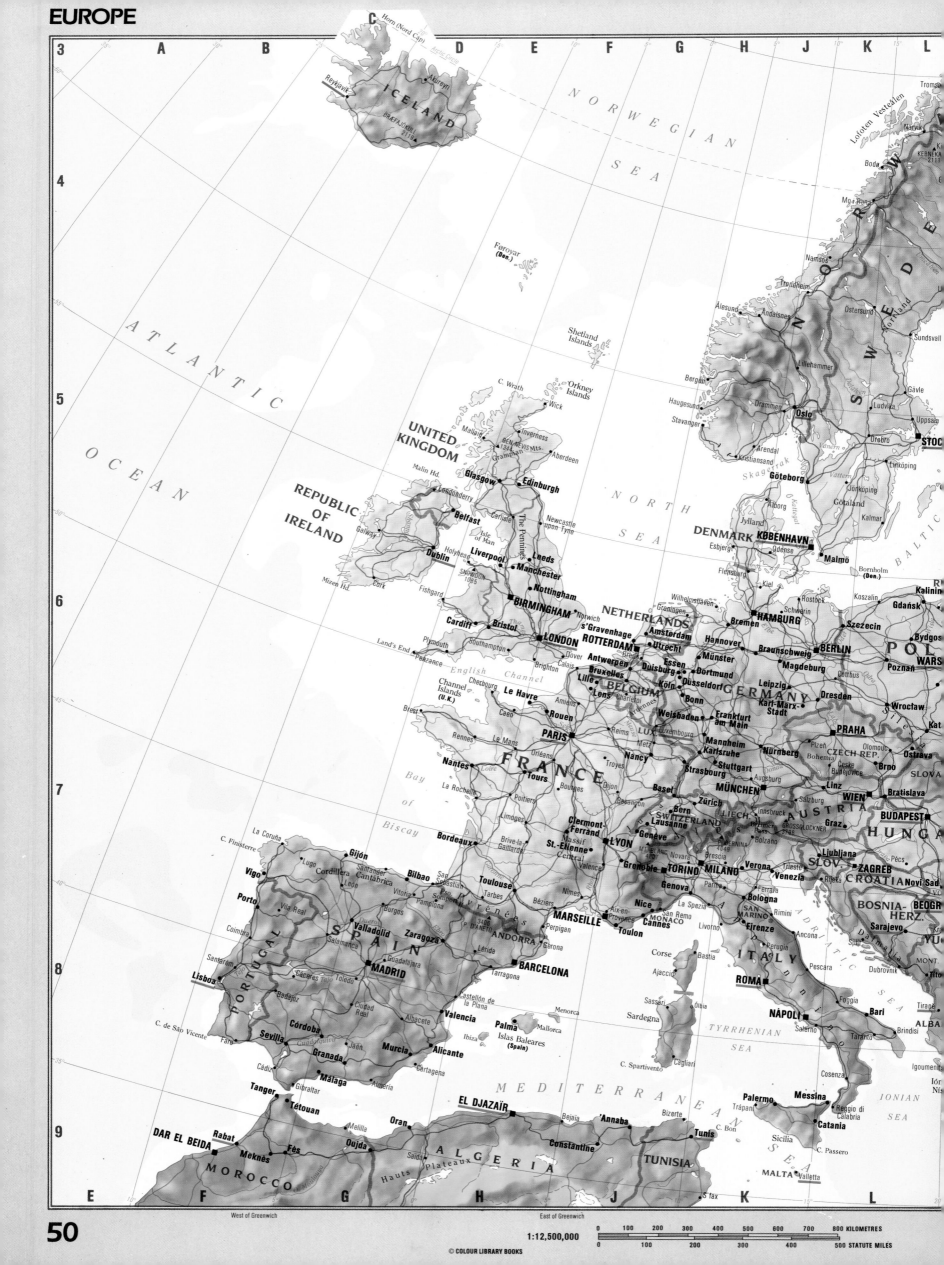

West of Greenwich   East of Greenwich

1:12,500,000

© COLOUR LIBRARY BOOKS

Designed and produced by E.S.R.

Miller Oblated Stereographic Projection

SOUTHERN ENGLAND AND WALES

Transverse Mercator Projection

1:1,175,000

© COLOUR LIBRARY BOOKS

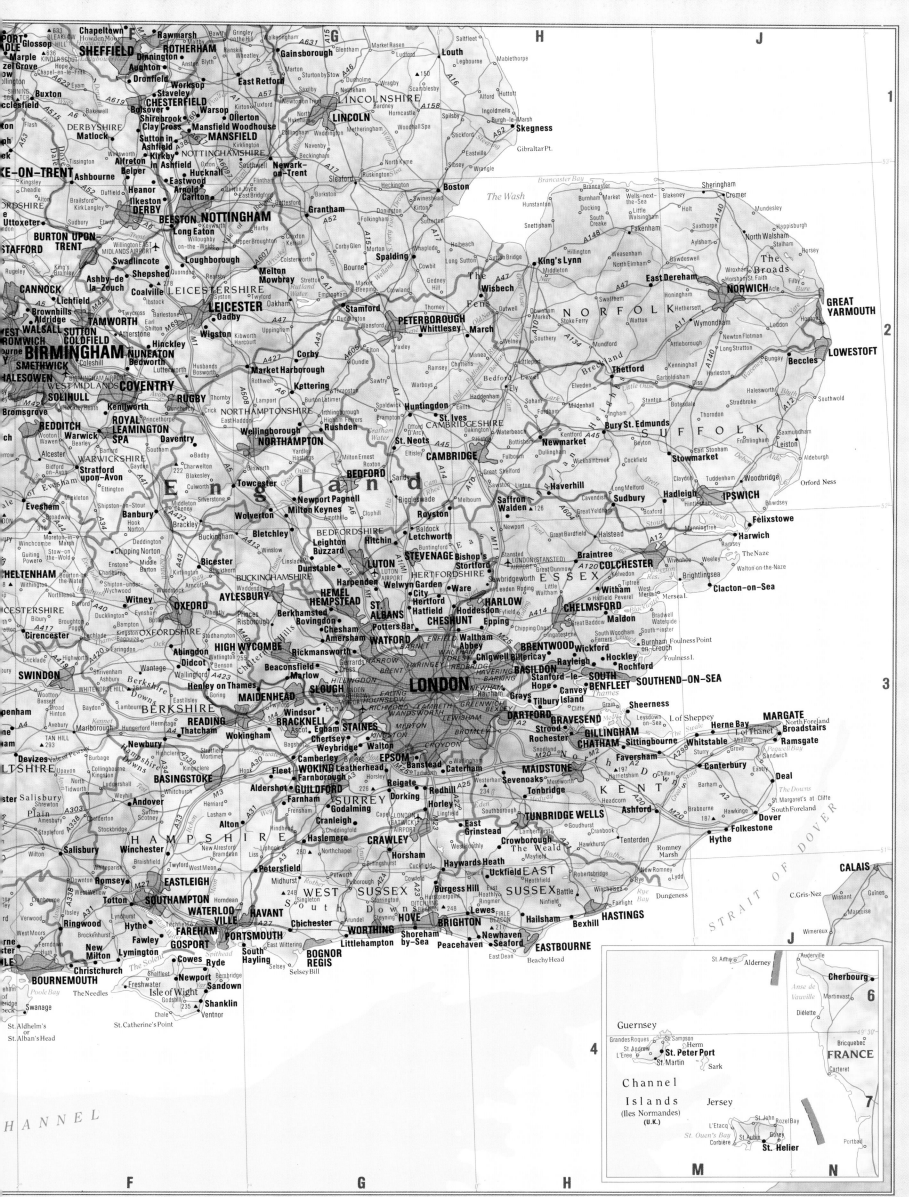

53

Transverse Mercator Projection

1:1,175,000

© COLOUR LIBRARY BOOKS

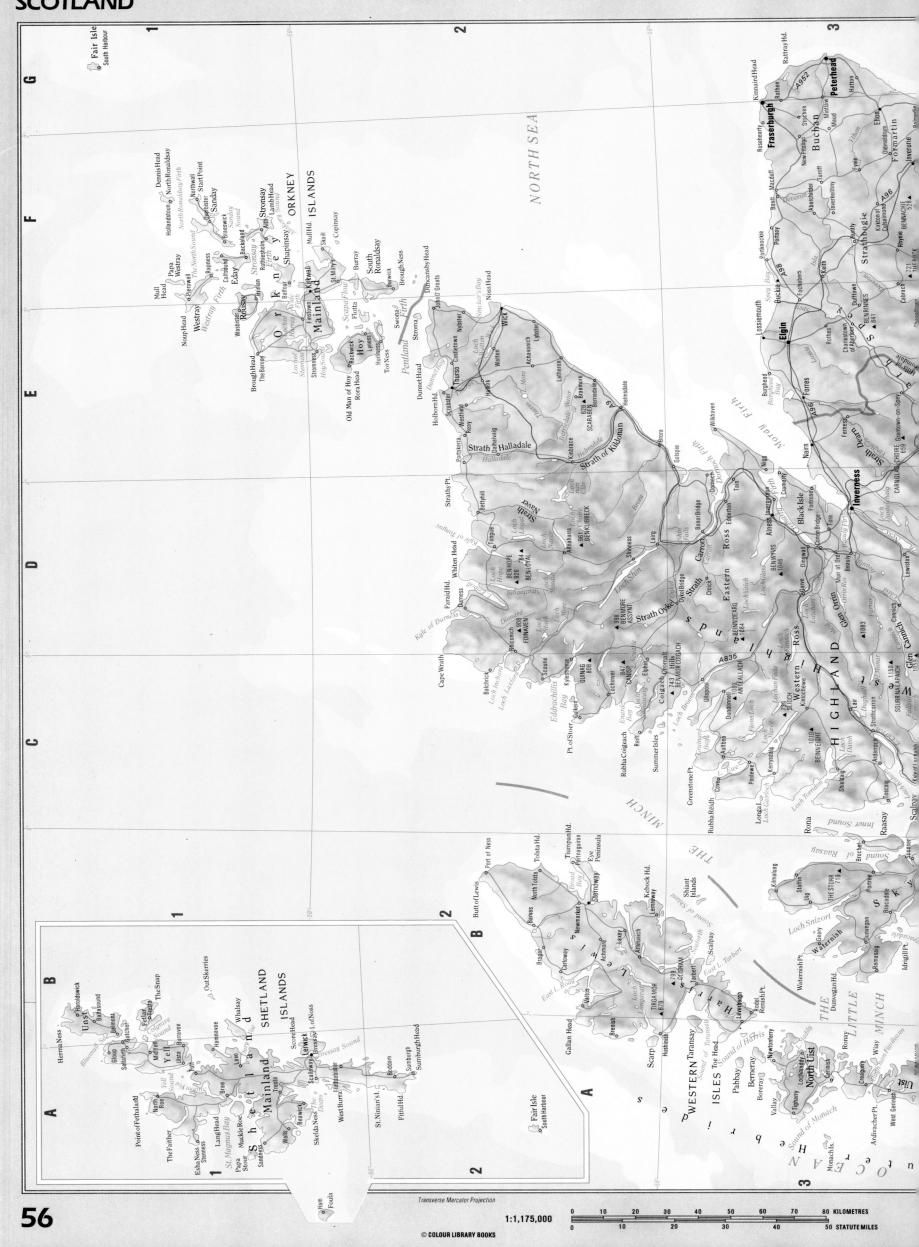

NORTH SEA

ORKNEY ISLANDS

SHETLAND ISLANDS

THE MINCH

LITTLE MINCH

WESTERN ISLES

HIGHLAND

Transverse Mercator Projection

1:1,175,000

| 0 10 20 30 40 50 60 70 80 KILOMETRES |
| 0 10 20 30 40 50 STATUTE MILES |

© COLOUR LIBRARY BOOKS

West of Greenwich

Designed and produced by E.S.R.

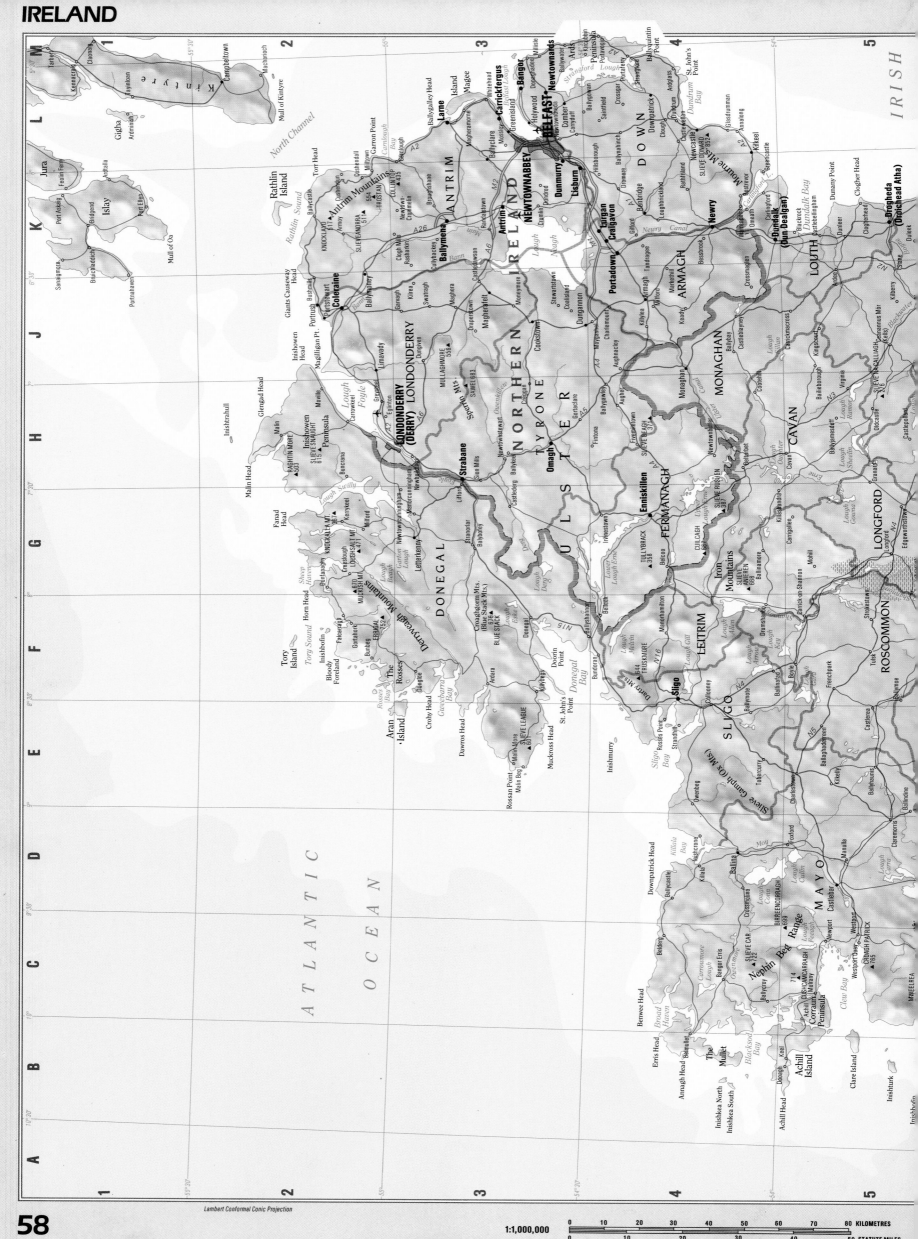

Lambert Conformal Conic Projection

© COLOUR LIBRARY BOOKS

1:1,000,000

```
0   10   20   30   40   50   60   70   80 KILOMETRES
0         10        20        30        40   50 STATUTE MILES
```

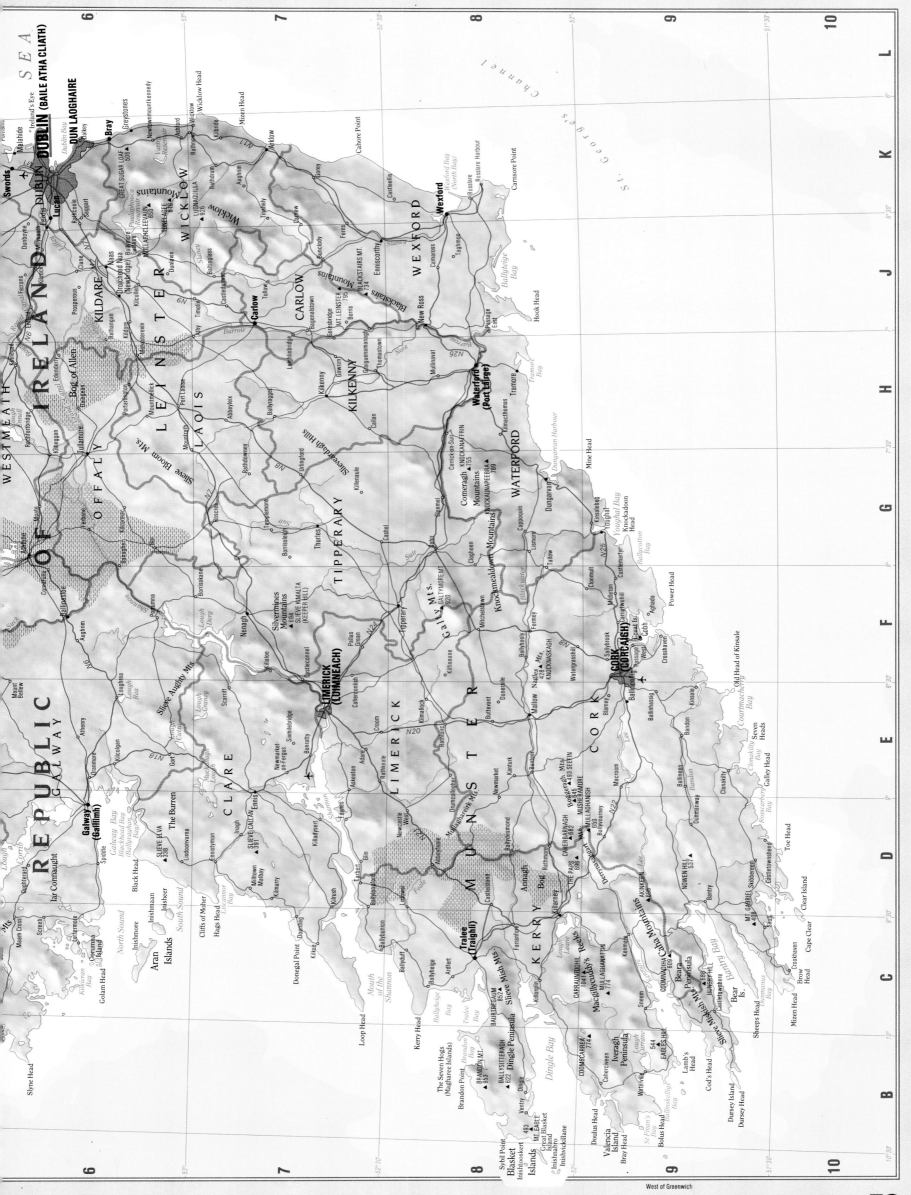

REPUBLIC OF IRELAND

I R I S H   S E A

DUBLIN (BAILE ÁTHA CLIATH)
DÚN LAOGHAIRE
Bray
Swords
Lucan
Malahide

St. George's Channel

Wexford
Rosslare Harbour

Waterford (Port Láirge)
Kilkenny
Carlow

WICKLOW
WEXFORD
CARLOW
KILKENNY
KILDARE
LAOIS
OFFALY
WESTMEATH
LEINSTER

Wicklow Mountains
LUGNAQUILLA 926
BLACKSTAIRS MT. 795
MT. LEINSTER 794

Galway (Gaillimh)
GALWAY
CLARE
Aran Islands
The Burren
Galway Bay
Cliffs of Moher

Limerick (Luimneach)
LIMERICK
TIPPERARY
Silvermines Mountains
SLIEVE KIMALTA (KEEPER HILL) 694
Galty Mts.
GALTYMORE MT. 920
Comeragh Mountains
KNOCKANAFFRIN 755
KNOCKAUNAPEEBRA 789
WATERFORD

CORK (CORCAIGH)
CORK
MUNSTER
KERRY
Tralee (Trálee)
Dingle Peninsula
BRANDON MT. 953
Macgillycuddy's Reeks
CARRAUNTOOHIL 1041
Iveragh Peninsula
Beara Peninsula
MT GABRIEL
Mizen Head
Cape Clear
Bantry Bay

West of Greenwich

Designed and produced by E.S.R.

West of Greenwich

1:5,000,000

© COLOUR LIBRARY BOOKS

0   50   100   150   200   250   300   350   400 KILOMETRES

0   50   100   150   200   250 STATUTE MILES

61

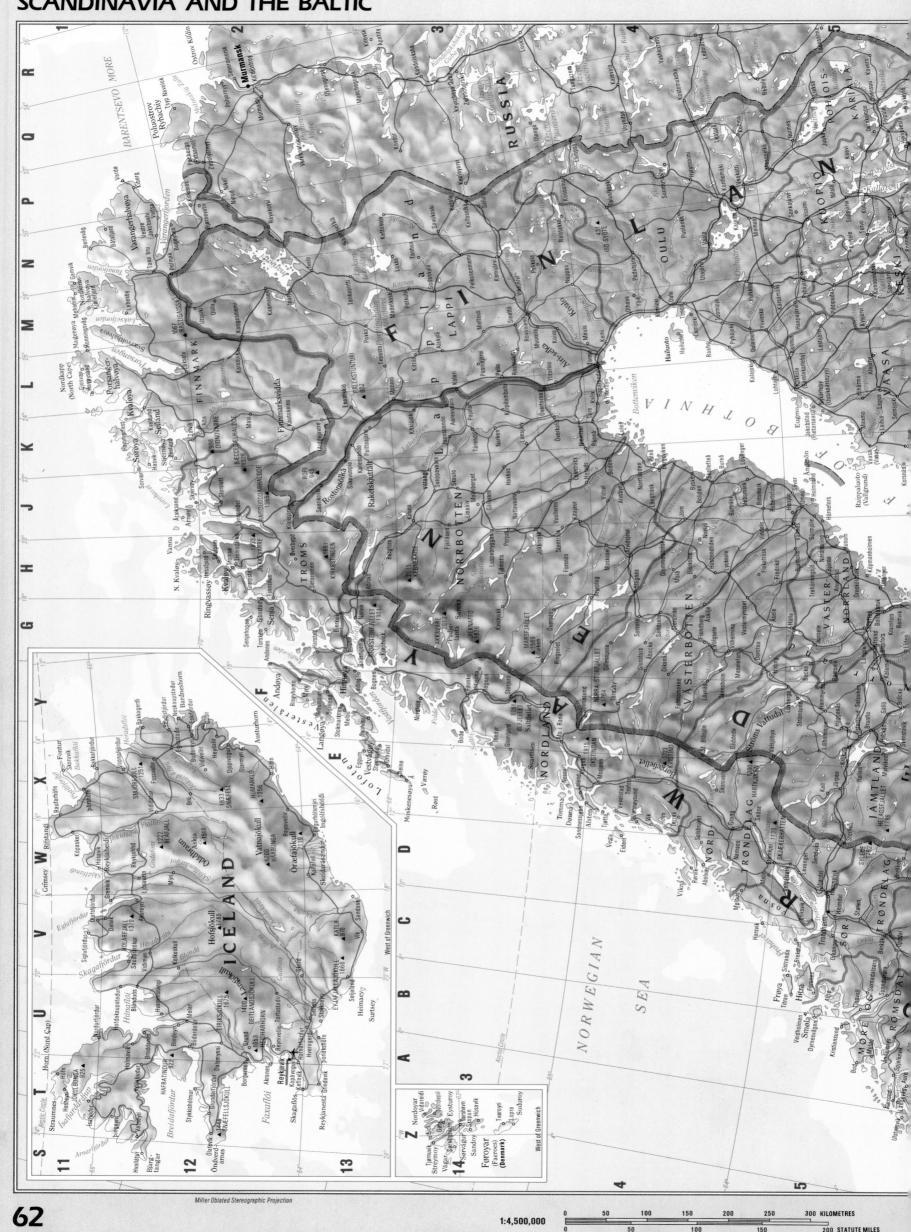

Miller Oblated Stereographic Projection

1:4,500,000

| 0 | 50 | 100 | 150 | 200 | 250 | 300 KILOMETRES |

| 0 | 50 | 100 | 150 | 200 STATUTE MILES |

© COLOUR LIBRARY BOOKS

East of Greenwich

63

BENELUX AND FRANCE

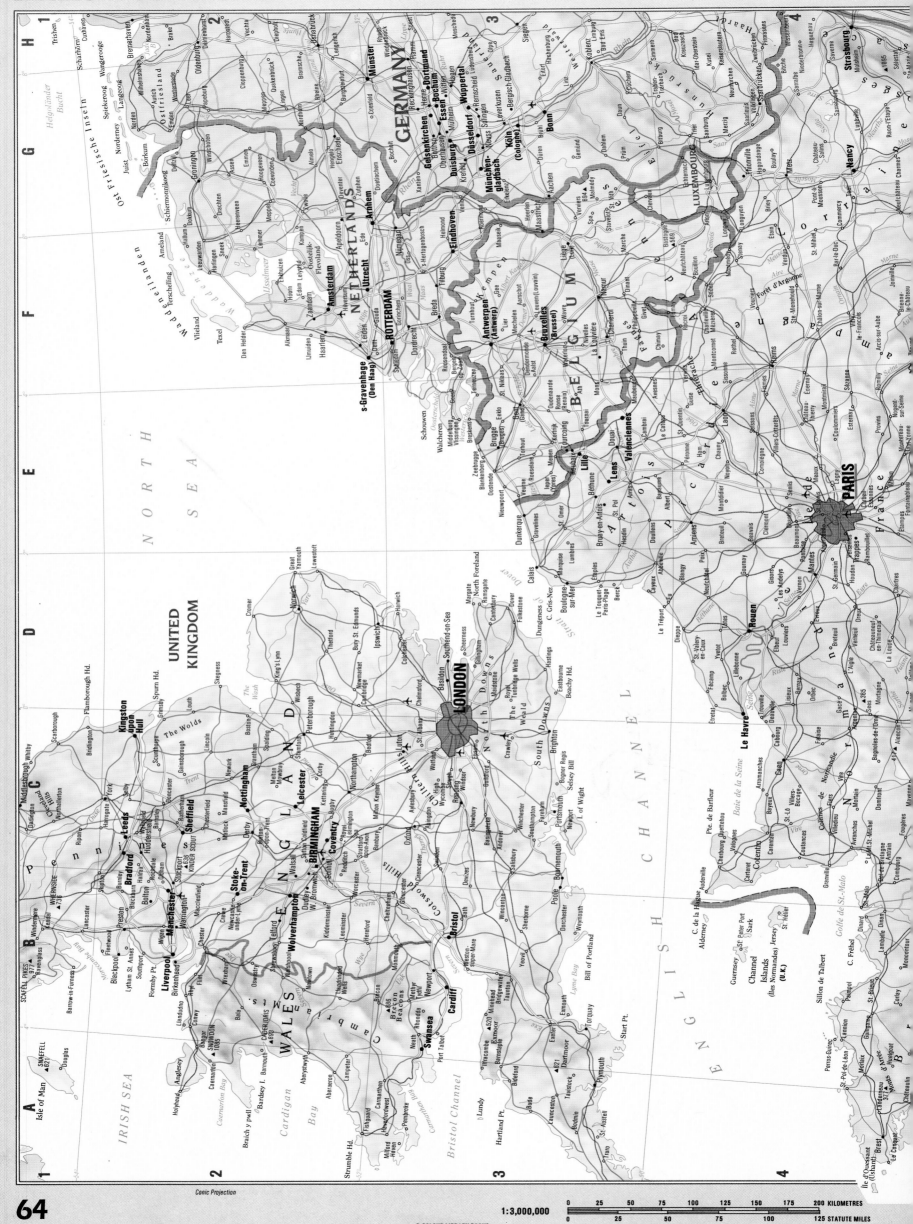

Conic Projection

1:3,000,000

© COLOUR LIBRARY BOOKS

| 0 | 25 | 50 | 75 | 100 | 125 | 150 | 175 | 200 KILOMETRES |

| 0 | 25 | 50 | 75 | 100 | 125 STATUTE MILES |

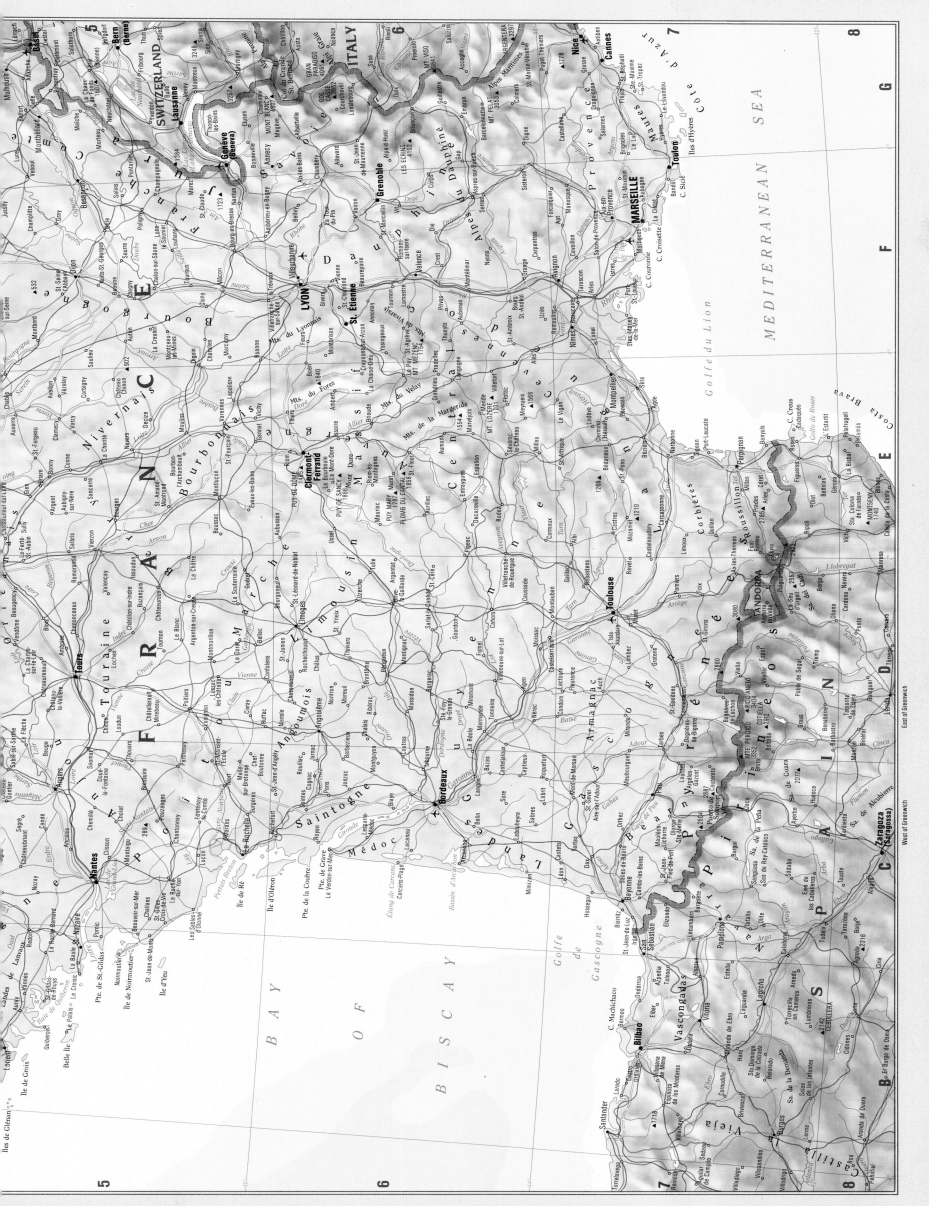

Designed and produced by E.S.R.

THE IBERIAN PENINSULA

Conic Projection

1:3,000,000

© COLOUR LIBRARY BOOKS

0 25 50 75 100 125 150 175 200 KILOMETRES
0   25   50   75   100   125 STATUTE MILES

Designed and produced by E.S.R.

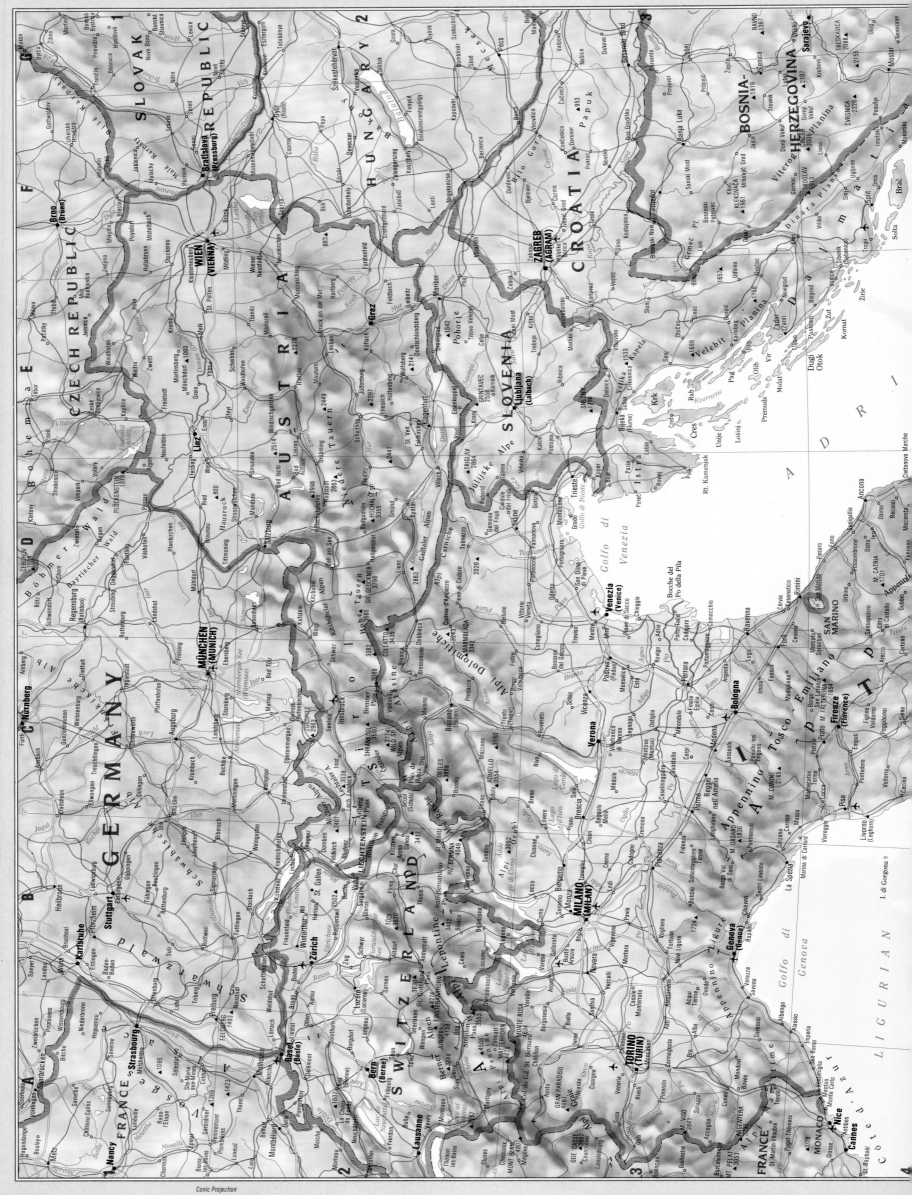

Conic Projection

1:3,000,000

0 25 50 75 100 125 150 175 200 KILOMETRES

0 25 50 75 100 125 STATUTE MILES

© COLOUR LIBRARY BOOKS

Conic Projection

1:3,000,000

© COLOUR LIBRARY BOOKS

| 0 | 25 | 50 | 75 | 100 | 125 | 150 | 175 | 200 KILOMETRES |

| 0 | 25 | 50 | 75 | 100 | 125 STATUTE MILES |

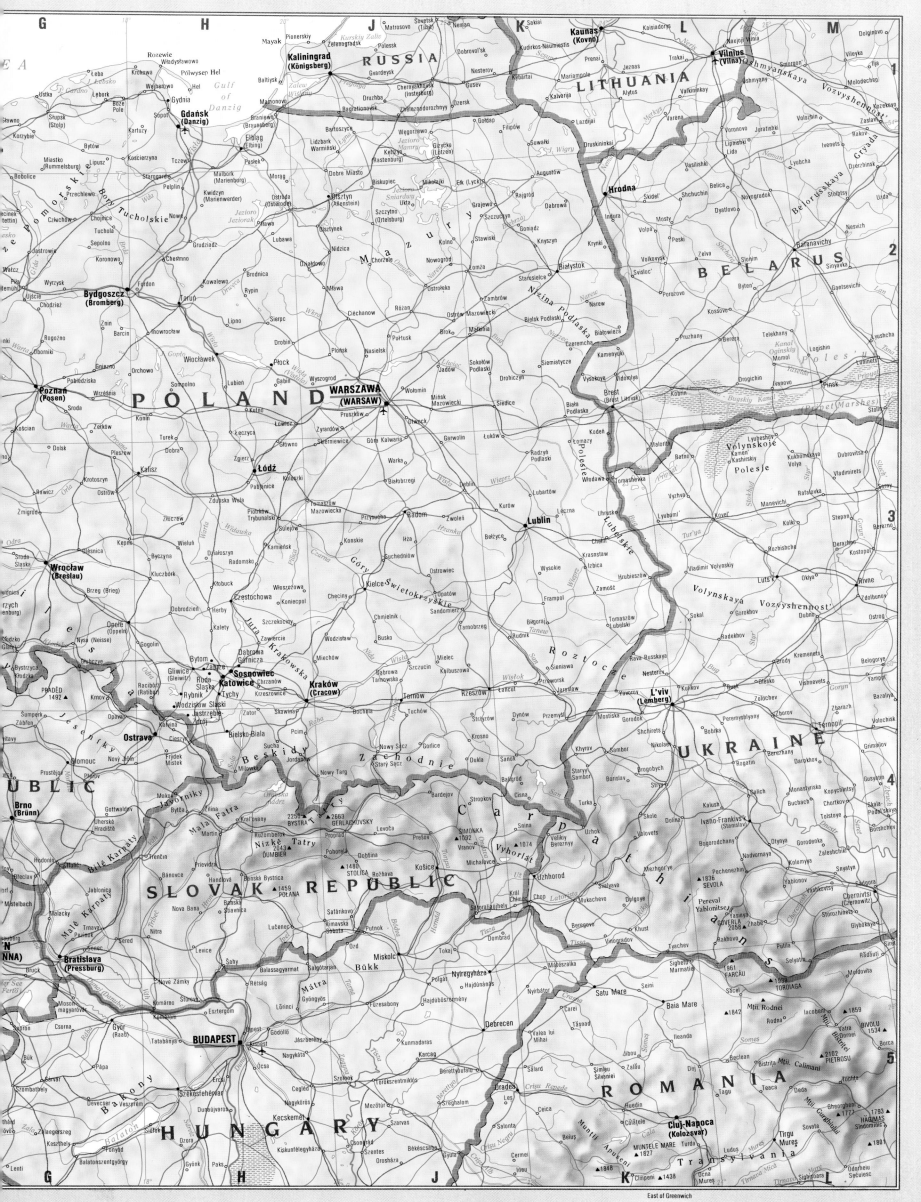

Conic Projection

1:3,000,000

0   25   50   75   100   125   150   175   200 KILOMETRES

0   25   50   75   100   125 STATUTE MILES

© COLOUR LIBRARY BOOKS

73

Conic Projection

1:3,000,000

© COLOUR LIBRARY BOOKS

SERBIA
YUGOSLAVIA
KOSOVO
MACEDONIA
Skopje

BULGARIA
SOFIYA (SOFIA)
Plovdiv

TURKEY

GREECE
Thessaloniki (Saloniki)
ATHÍNAI (ATHENS)

Peloponnisos

Pátrai (Patras)

AEGEAN SEA

Lésvos (Lesbos)
İZMİR (SMYRNA)

Thásos
Samothráki
Límnos (Lemnos)

Voríai Sporádhes (Northern Sporades)
Skópelos

Évvoia (Euboea)

Skíros

Psará
Khíos (Chios)
Sámos

Ikaría (Nikaria)

Kikládhes (Cyclades)

Ándros
Tínos
Míkonos
Síros
Páros
Náxos

Sérifos
Sífnos

Amorgós
Íos (Nios)
Astipálaia

Dhodhekánisos (Dodecanese)

Kálimnos (Calino)
Kos (Cos)

Mílos
Mílos

Thíra (Santoríni)

Sími
Tílos (Piscopi)
Khálki
Ródhos (Rhodes)

Kritikón Pélagos (Sea of Crete)

Kárpathos (Scarpanto)

Kríti (Crete)
Iráklion (Candia)
Khaniá (Canea)

Kásos

BLACK SEA
Varna
Burgas

Marmara Denizi (Sea of Marmara)
Balıkesir

East of Greenwich

75

TURKEY

Lambert Conformal Conic Projection

© COLOUR LIBRARY BOOKS

1:3,500,000

| 0 | 50 | 100 | 150 | 200 | 250 KILOMETRES |
| 0 | 25 | 50 | 75 | 100 | 125 | 150 STATUTE MILES |

East of Greenwich

Designed and produced by E.S.R.

Miller Oblated Stereographic Projection

1:8,000,000

© COLOUR LIBRARY BOOKS

East of Greenwich

Designed and produced by E.S.R.

Conic Projection

1:17,000,000

© COLOUR LIBRARY BOOKS

| 0 100 200 300 400 500 600 700 800 KILOMETRES |
| 0 100 200 300 400 500 STATUTE MILES |

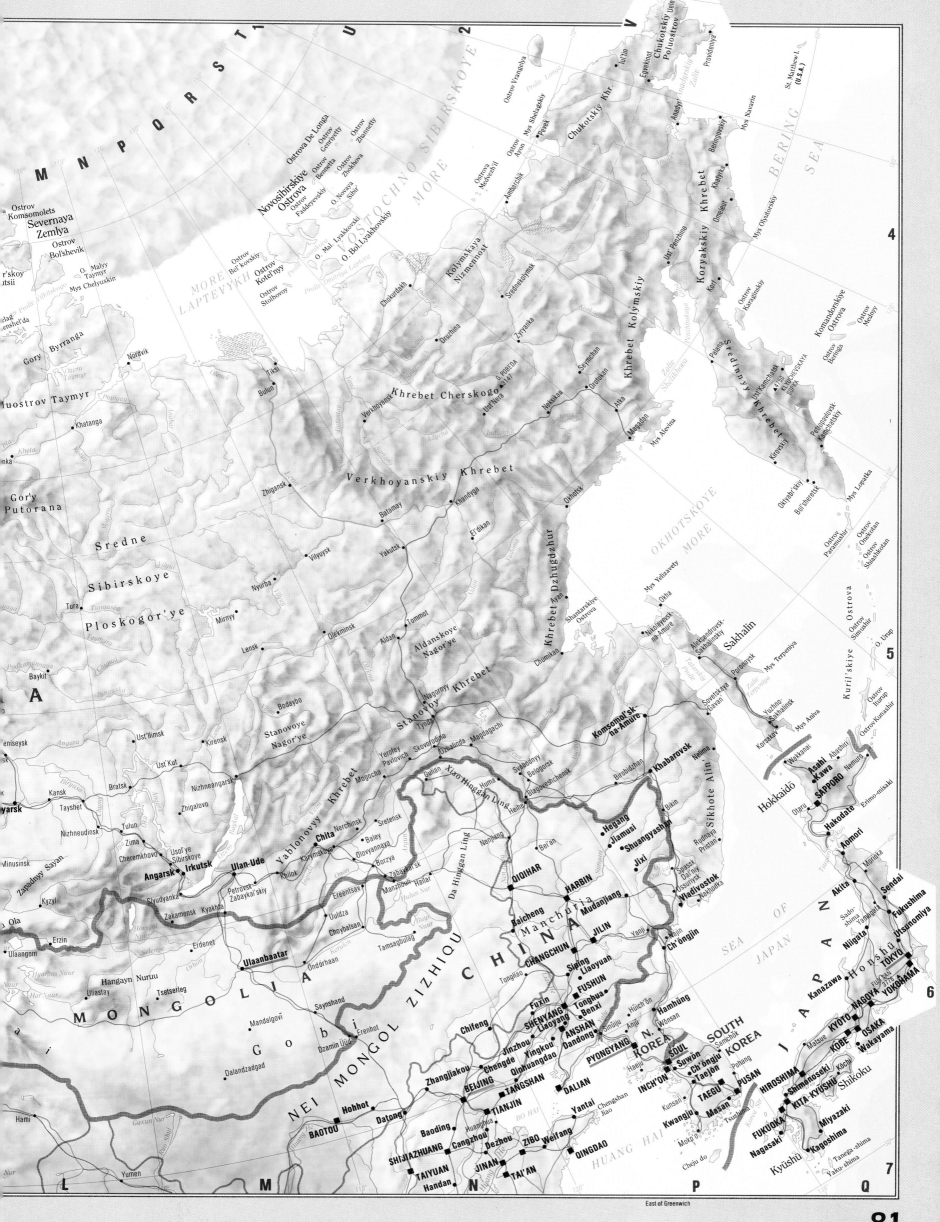

Lambert Azimuthal Equal Area Projection

1:25,000,000

© COLOUR LIBRARY BOOKS

| 200 | 400 | 600 | 800 | 1000 KILOMETRES |

| 100 | 200 | 300 | 400 | 500 | 600 STATUTE MILES |

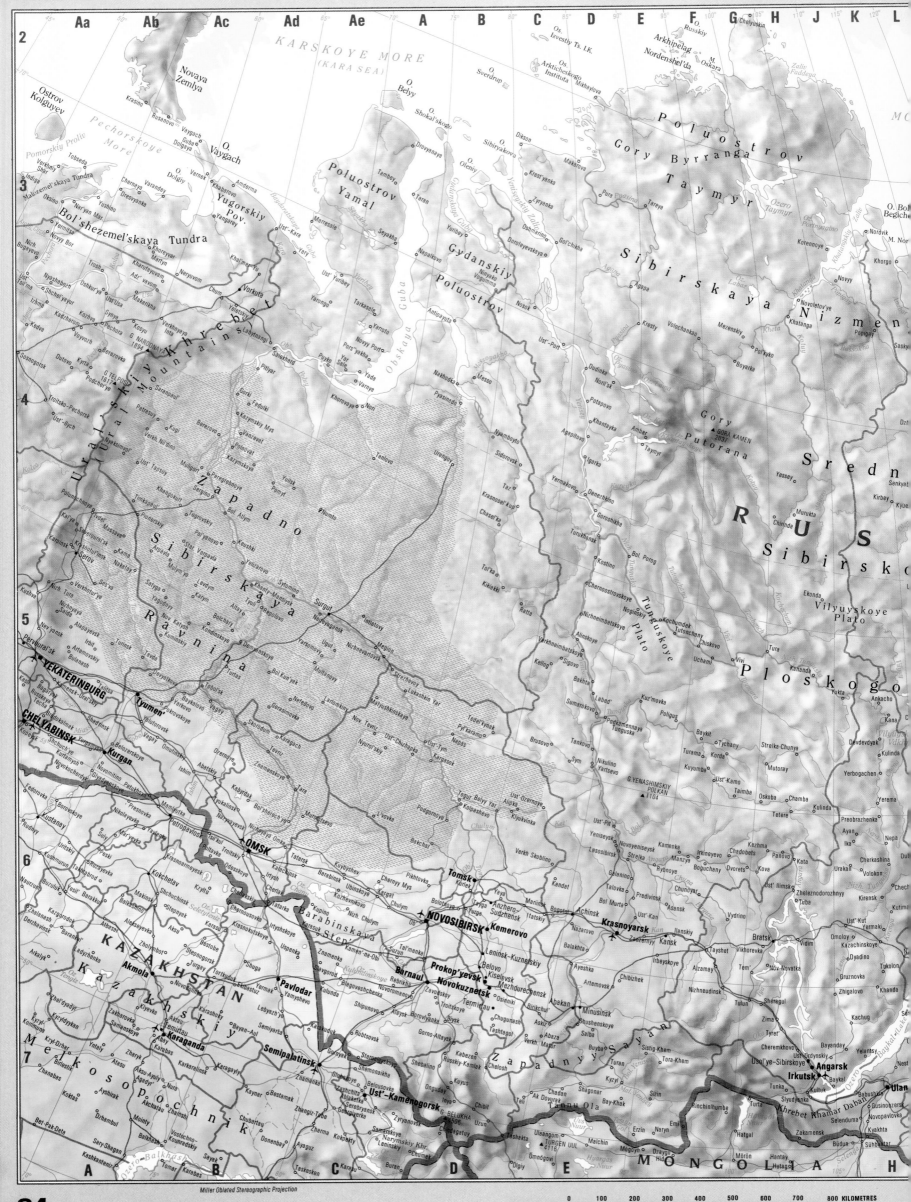

Miller Oblated Stereographic Projection

1:11,500,000

© COLOUR LIBRARY BOOKS

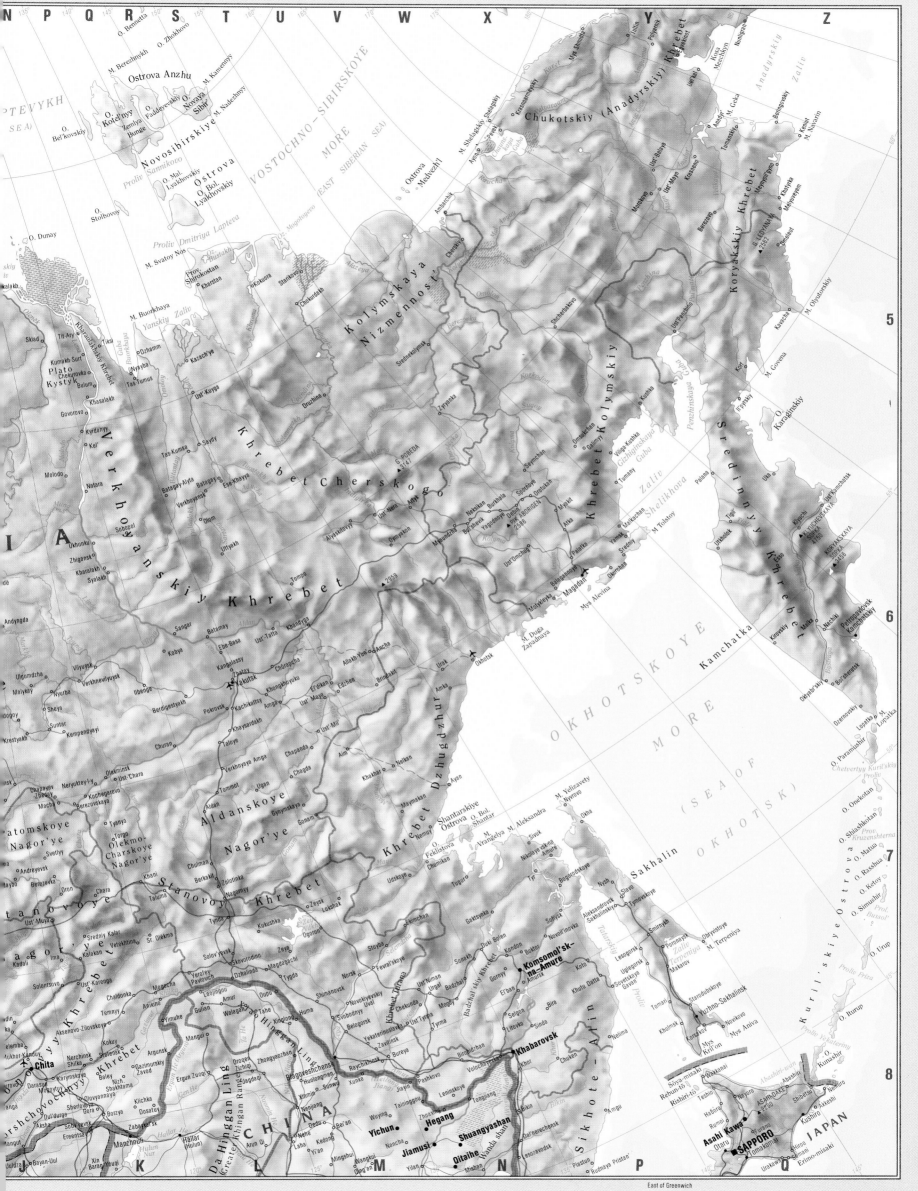

Miller Oblated Stereographic Projection

1:11,500,000

© COLOUR LIBRARY BOOKS

800 KILOMETRES

500 STATUTE MILES

East of Greenwich

Designed and produced by E.S.R.

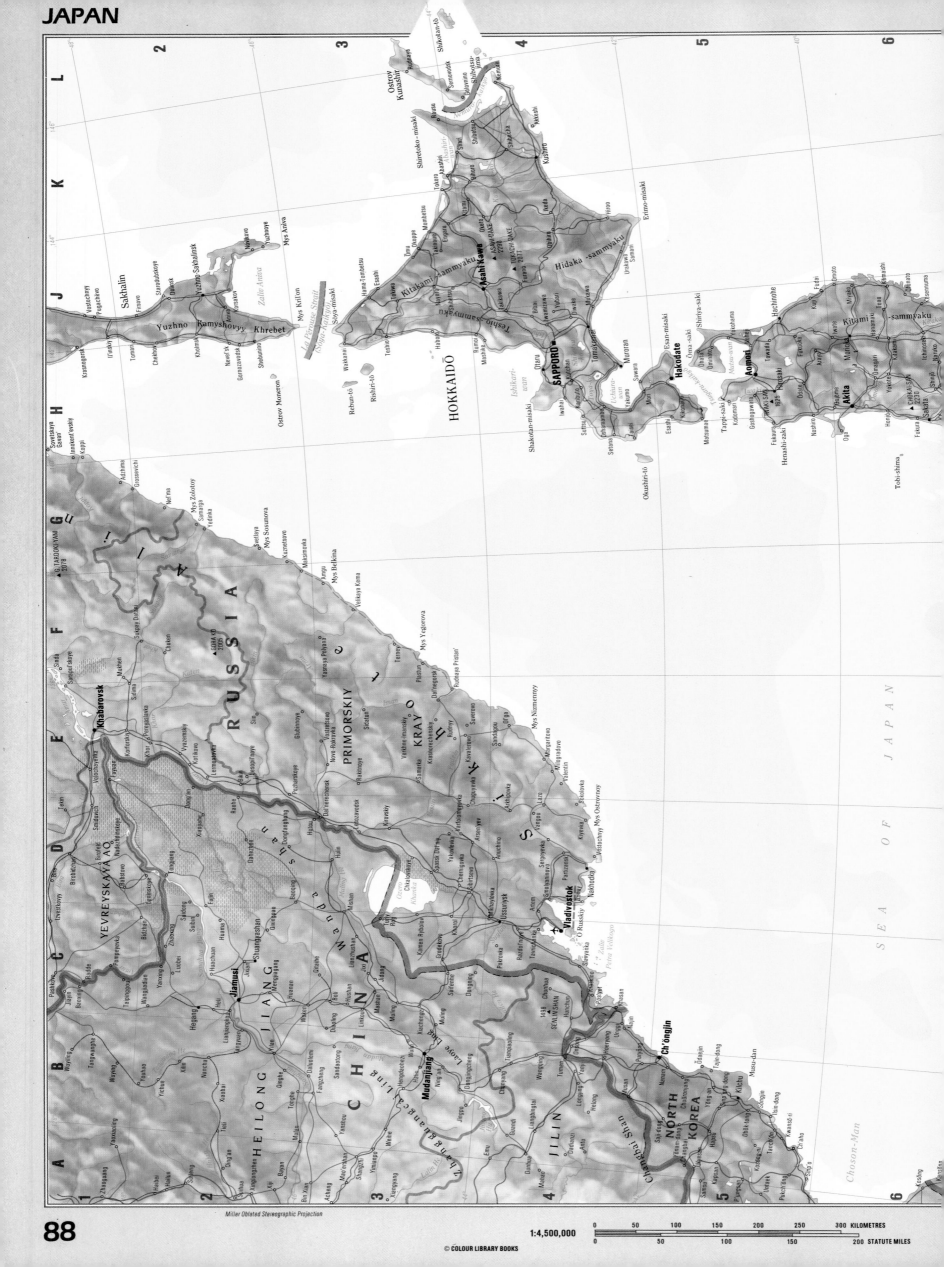

Miller Oblated Stereographic Projection

1:4,500,000

| 0 | 50 | 100 | 150 | 200 | 250 | 300 KILOMETRES |

| 0 | 50 | 100 | 150 | 200 STATUTE MILES |

© COLOUR LIBRARY BOOKS

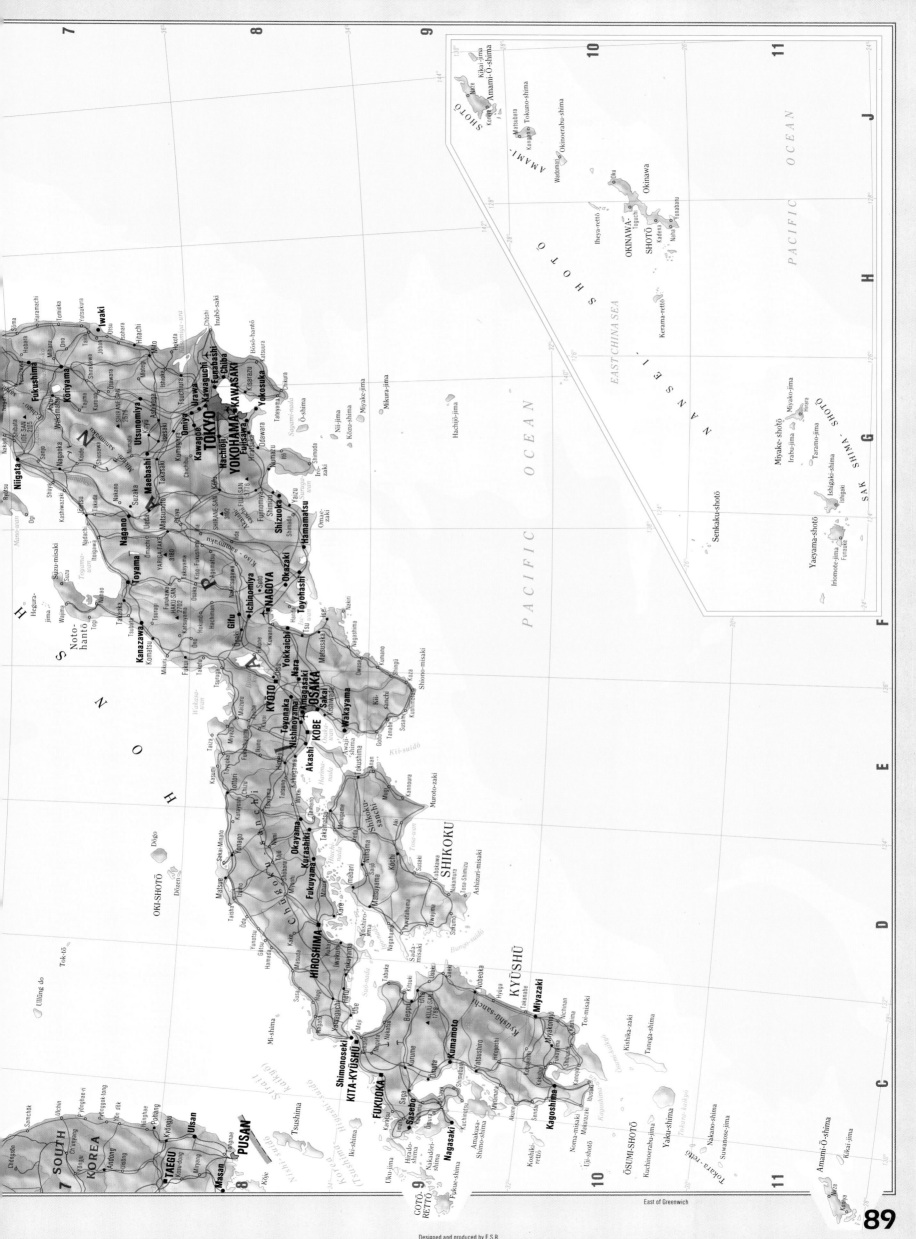

SOUTH-EAST ASIA

Mercator Projection

1:12,000,000

© COLOUR LIBRARY BOOKS

| 0 | 100 | 200 | 300 | 400 | 500 | 600 | 700 | 800 KILOMETRES |

| 0 | 100 | 200 | 300 | 400 | 500 STATUTE MILES |

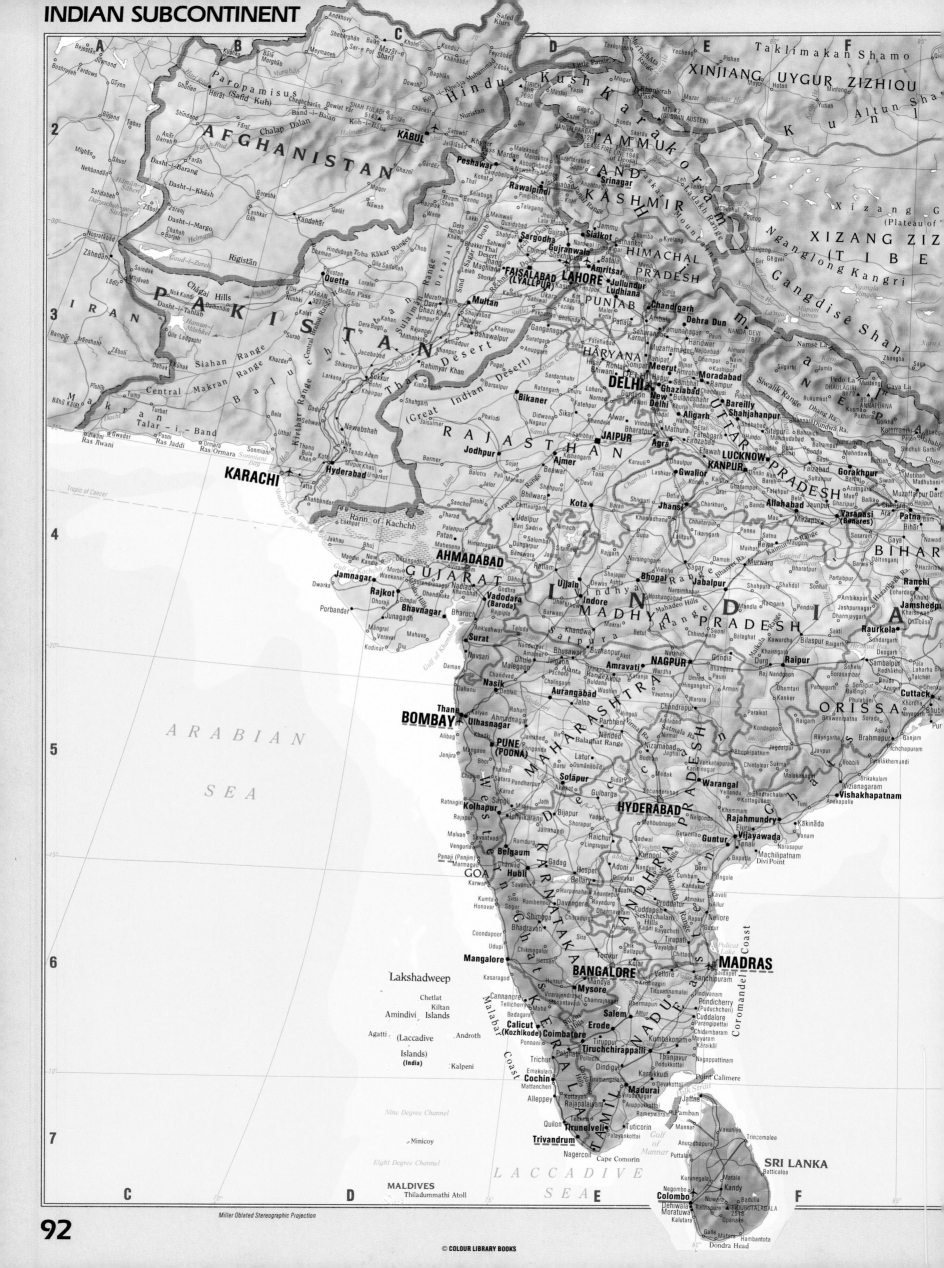

H J K L M N

Taghi Qaidam Shan Datong Shan Daban Shan Zhongwei Tongxin Yan'an Yan'an Xinxiang Heze Xuzhou
Dawusi Qaidam Pendi Delingha Tianjun Yongdeng Gaolan Huan Xian Fu Xian Linfen SHANXI Kaifeng Huaibei
QINGHAI Ulan Ula Burhan Budai Shan Golmud Xining Ledu LANZHOU Tongchuan SHAANXI Jiaozuo ZHENGZHOU HENAN ANHUE 2
Dongbolhai Shan Ngoring Hu Xiahe Tianshui Baoji Xianyang XI'AN Luoyang Pingdingshan Nanyang Zhumadian Fuyang
Tanggula Shan Tanggula Shankou Amdo Sêrtar Wudu Hanzhong SHIYAN Xiangfan Shiyan Xiangyang HUBEI WUHAN Huangshi
SICHUAN Mianyang Daba Shan Yichang Da'an Jiujiang
Lhasa Nedong Garzê CHENGDU Nanchong CHONGQING Changde CHANGSHA JIANGXI 3
Gyangzê Litang Neijiang Luzhou Zunyi HUNAN Xiangtan Zhuzhou PINGXIANG
Zigong Yibin GUIZHOU GUIYANG Shaoyang Hengyang Leiyang
ARUNACHAL PRADESH Hengduan Shan Dukou GUIYANG Guilin Shaoguan GUANGDONG
BHUTAN Thimphu ASSAM NAGALAND YUNNAN KUNMING GUANGXI Liuzhou GUANGZHOU (CANTON)
SIKKIM MEGHALAYA MANIPUR Nanning MACAO (AOMEN) (Port.)
BANGLADESH DHAKA (DACCA) MIZORAM Gejiu Maoming Zhanjiang 4
CALCUTTA CHITTAGONG MYANMAR Mandalay HANOI HAIPHONG Haikou Hainan Dao
MOUNT VICTORIA 3053 LAOS Beibu Wan (Gulf of Tongking)
Sittwe (Akyab) PHU LOI 2256 Thanh Hoa 5
YANGON (RANGOON) VIETNAM NAN HAI (SOUTH CHINA SEA) Parcel Islands Xisha Qundao (Claimed by China and Vietnam)
THAILAND Da Nang NGOC LINH 2598
Preparis North Channel KRUNG THEP (BANGKOK) CAMBODIA CHU YANG SIN 2405 6
ANDAMAN Andaman Islands (India) Phnom Penh
North Andaman Middle Andaman South Andaman Port Blair (India) HO CHI MINH (SAIGON)
Nicobar Car Nicobar Gulf of Thailand 7
Nicobar Islands (India) Little Nicobar Great Nicobar J K L
Pygmalion Pt. East of Greenwich

0 100 200 300 400 500 600 700 800 KILOMETRES
0 100 200 300 400 500 STATUTE MILES

Designed and produced by E.S.R.

93

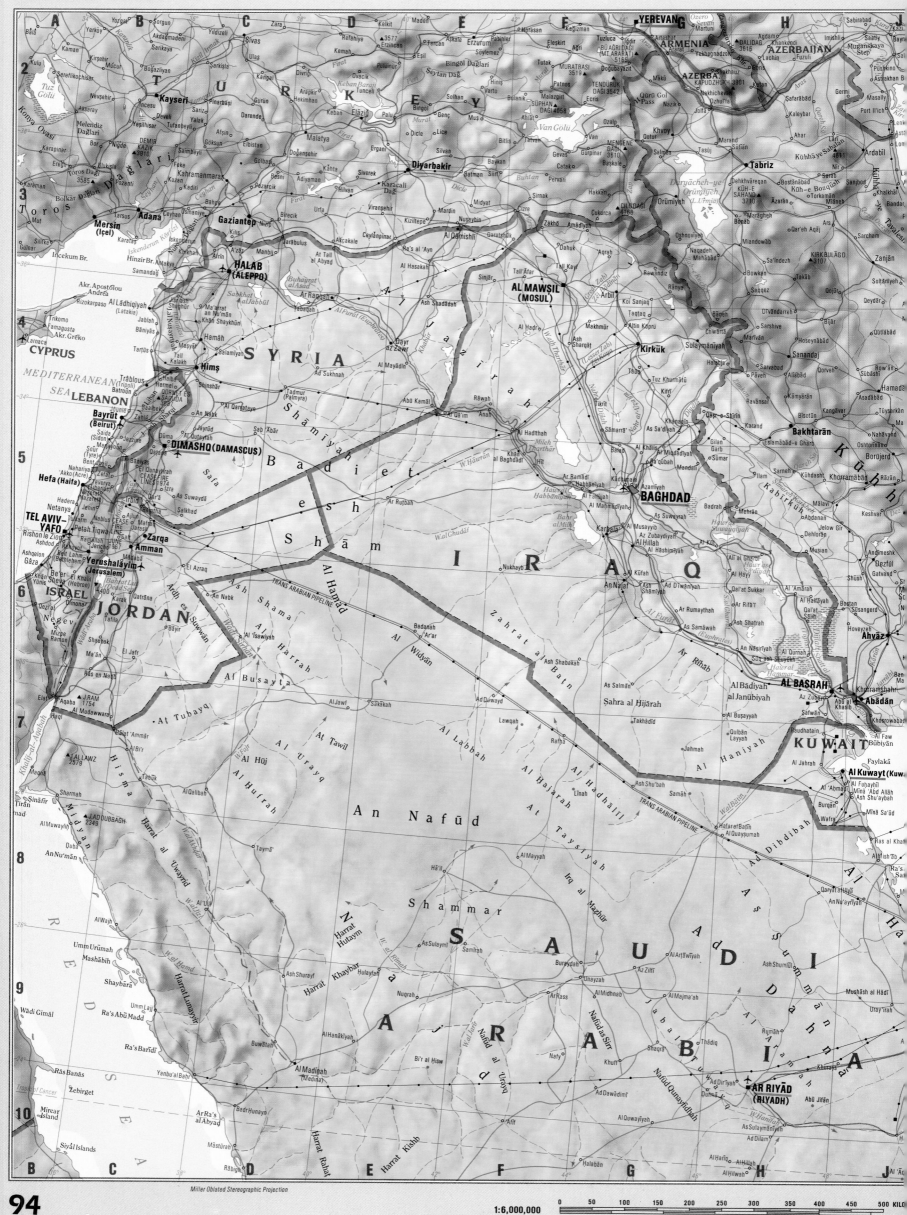

Miller Oblated Stereographic Projection

1:6,000,000

© COLOUR LIBRARY BOOKS

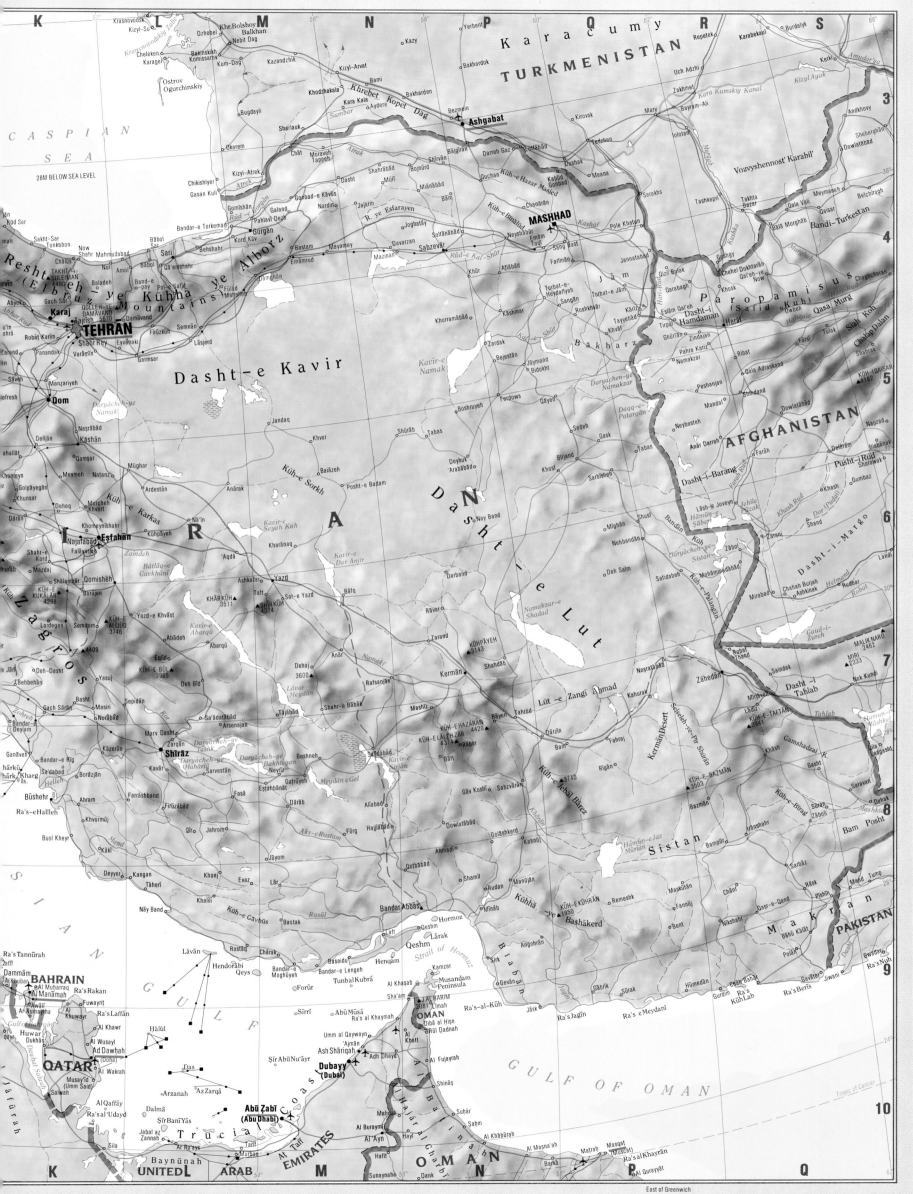

CASPIAN SEA

28M BELOW SEA LEVEL

TURKMENISTAN

Karacumy

Ashgabat

MASHHAD

AFGHANISTAN

Paropamisus (Safid Kuh)

Herat

TEHRĀN

Karaj

Elburz Mountains (Reshteh-ye Kūhhā-ye Alborz)

Dasht-e Kavir

Qom

I R A N

Dasht-e Lut

Eşfahān

Zāgros

Shīrāz

Kermān

Zāhedān

Dasht-i-Margo

PAKISTAN

Makran

Bandar Abbās

Strait of Hormuz

Qeshm

Musandam Peninsula

OMAN

GULF OF OMAN

BAHRAIN
Al Manāmah

Gulf of Bahrain

QATAR

Ad Dawḥah (Doha)

Dubayy (Dubai)

Abū Zabī (Abu Dhabi)

Trucial Coast

UNITED ARAB EMIRATES

OMAN

Tropic of Cancer

East of Greenwich

Designed and produced by E.S.R.

ARABIAN PENINSULA

Miller Oblated Stereographic Projection

AFRICA

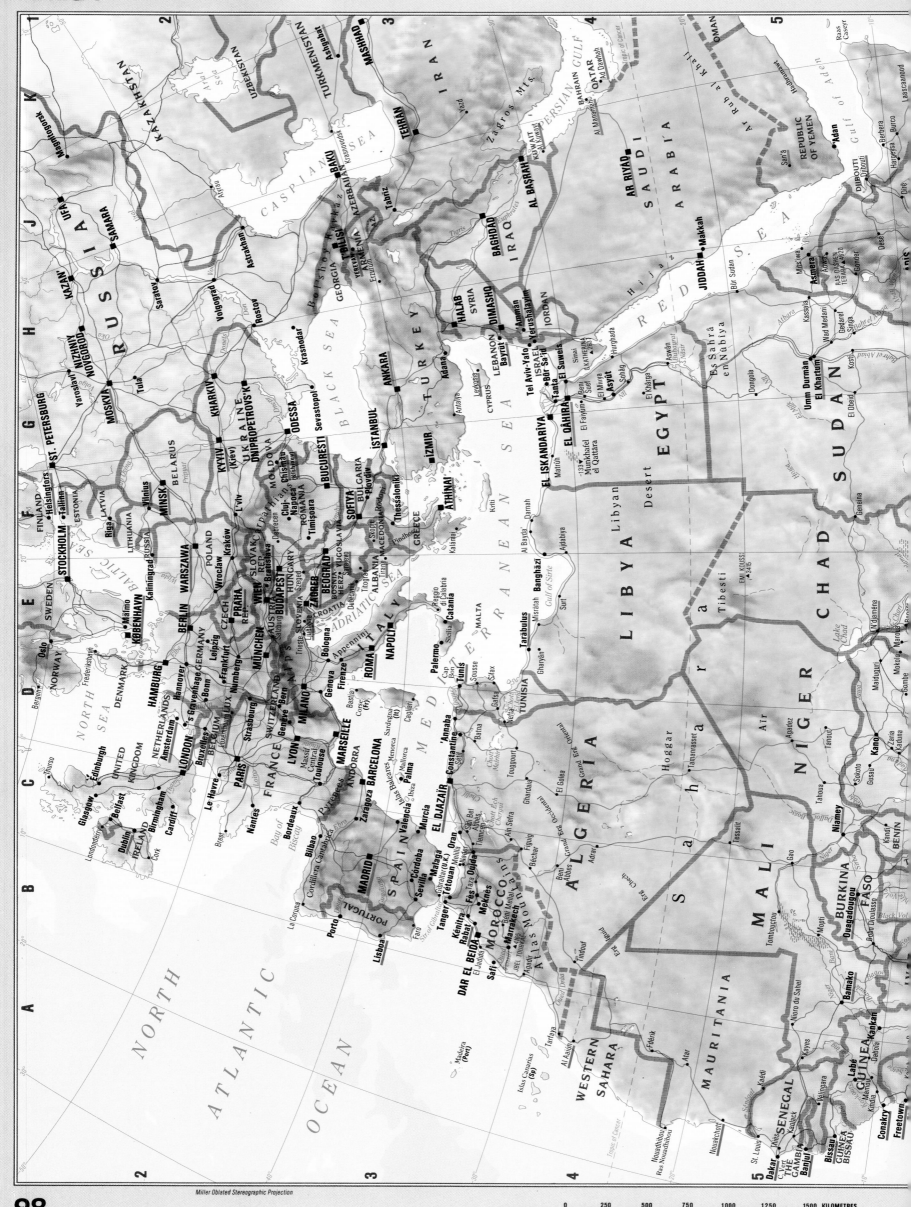

Miller Oblated Stereographic Projection

1:23,000,000

| 0 | 250 | 500 | 750 | 1000 | 1250 | 1500 KILOMETRES |

| 0 | 100 | 200 | 300 | 400 | 500 | 600 | 700 | 800 | 900 | 1000 STATUTE MILES |

© COLOUR LIBRARY BOOKS

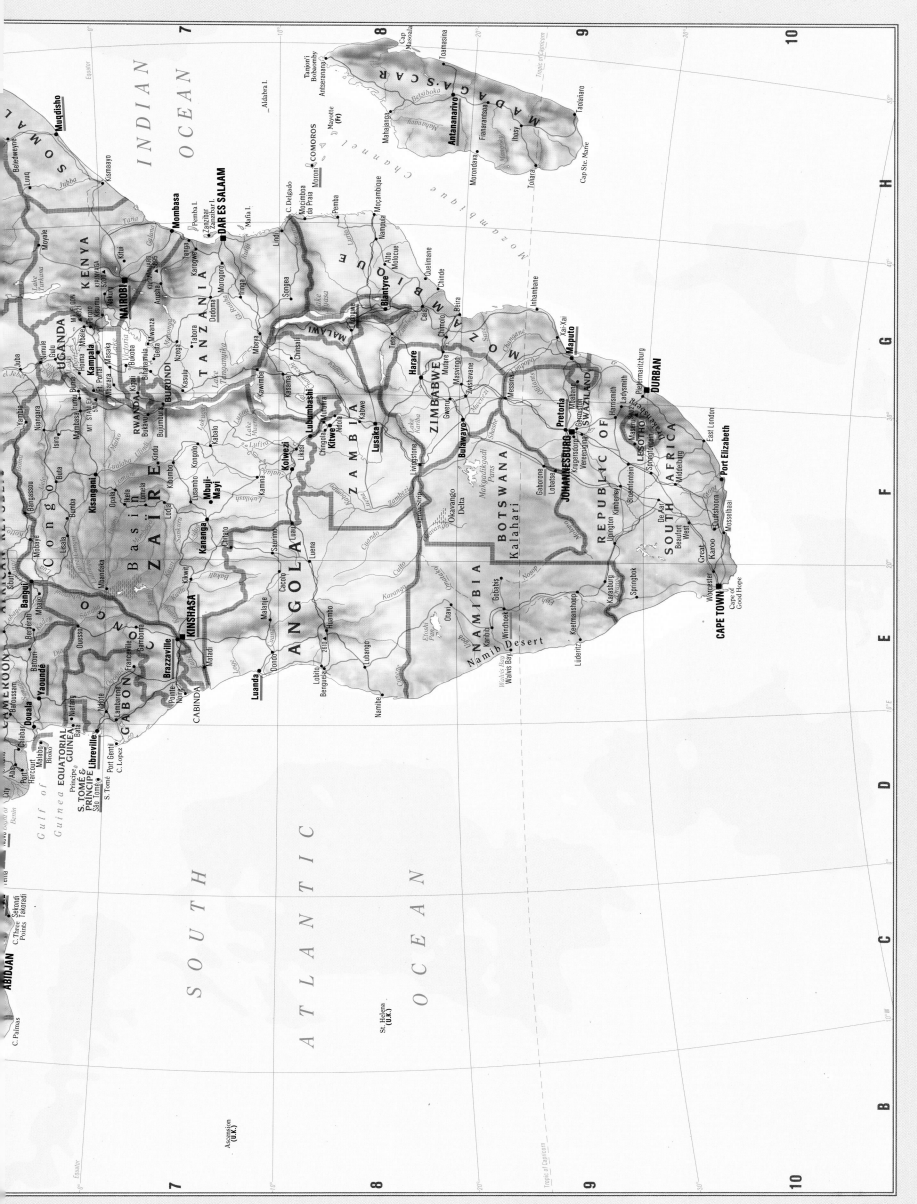

INDIAN OCEAN

SOMAL
Muqdisho
Beledweyne
Luuq

Moyale
Kismaayo

KENYA
NAIROBI
Machakos
Kitui

UGANDA
Kampala

Mombasa

DAR ES SALAAM
Zanzibar I.
Pemba I.
Mafia I.

TANZANIA
Dodoma
Tabora
Morogoro

C. Delgado
MOZAMBIQUE
Mocímboa
da Praia
Pemba

COMOROS
Moroni
Mayotte (Fr)

MADAGASCAR
Cap
Masoala
Tanjon'i
Bobaomby
Antsiranana

Antananarivo
Mahajanga
Toamasina
Fianarantsoa
Ihosy
Toliara
Taolañaro
Cap Ste. Marie
Morondava

Mozambique Channel

RWANDA
BURUNDI
Bujumbura

ZAIRE
Basin
Kisangani
Kananga
Mbuji-Mayi
Kolwezi
Lubumbashi

Congo
KINSHASA
Brazzaville
GABON
Libreville

Kitwe
Chingola
Ndola
Kabwe
ZAMBIA
Lusaka
Livingstone

MALAWI
Blantyre
Lilongwe

Harare
ZIMBABWE
Gweru
Bulawayo
Masvingo
Mutare

Maputo
SWAZILAND
Pretoria
JOHANNESBURG
Vereeniging

BOTSWANA
Gaborone
Kalahari

NAMIBIA
Namib Desert
Walvis Bay
Windhoek
Lüderitz

REPUBLIC OF
SOUTH AFRICA
Kimberley
Bloemfontein
LESOTHO
Maseru
Durban
Pietermaritzburg
East London
Port Elizabeth
CAPE TOWN
Cape of
Good Hope
Worcester
Beaufort
West
Karoo

ANGOLA
Luanda
Lobito
Benguela
Namibe

CABINDA

EQUATORIAL
GUINEA
Malabo
Bioko
S. TOMÉ &
PRÍNCIPE
São Tomé

Yaoundé
Douala

ABIDJAN

SOUTH ATLANTIC OCEAN

St. Helena (U.K.)

Ascension (U.K.)

Tropic of Capricorn

Designed and produced by E.S.R.

NORTH AFRICA

SPAIN

Faro ·
Cádiz · · Málaga · Sa. Nevada · Almería
Algeciras · Gibraltar (U.K.)
Cap Spartel · Ceuta (Sp.) · Mostaganem
Tanger · Tétouan · Melilla (Spain) · Oran · Arzew
Asilah · Cap des Trois Fourches · Beni Saf · Sidi Bel Abbès
Larache (El Araiche) · Chaouen · Ouezzane · ▲2456 · Nador · Ghazaouat · Tlemcen · Frenda
Ksar el Kebir · Sidi Kacem · Taourirt · Oujda · Jerada
Kénitra · Salé · Taza · Mecheria
DAR EL BEIDA (CASABLANCA) · **Rabat** · Sefrou · Ain Sefra
Fès · **Meknès** · Khémisset · Oulmès · Azrou · 3340 · Bouârfa
El Jadida · Settat · Khenifra · Moyen Atlas · Hauts Plat
Khouribga · Oued Zem · Figuig
Safi · Youssoufia · Kasba Tadla · **MOROCCO** · Atlas · Kénadsa · Béchar
Essaouira · Beni Mellal · Demnate · IRHIL M'GOUN · Grand Erg Occ
Oued Tensift · **Marrakech** (Marrakesh) · 4071 · Er Rachidia (Ksar es Souk) · Beni Abbès
JEBEL TOUBKAL ▲4165 · Haut · Ouarzazate ·
Cap Rhir · Anti-Atlas · Tagounite · Ksabi
Agadir · Taroudannt · Hamada du Dra · Timimoun
Tiznit · Oued Drâa
Sidi Ifni · Adrar
Tan-Tan · Oued Tigzerte · Reggane
Tarfaya (Villa Bens) · **A L G E**
Cap Juby · Tindouf
Al Aaiún (Laâyoune)
Es Semara · As Saguia al Hamra
Boujdour · Erg Iguidi
WESTERN
SAHARA · Bir Moghrein (Fort Trinquet) · Erg Chech · Tanezrouft · Posta Weygand
Tropic of Cancer
Ad Dakhla (Villa Cisneros) · Irharen
Baie de Rio de Oro
C. Barbas · Fdérik · Zouerate · Taoudenni · Tessalit
Nouadhibou (Pt. Etienne) · Aguelhok
Ras Nouadhibou (C. Blanc) · Maktéir ·
Atâr · Chinguetti · Ouarâne · El Djouf · S a h
C. Timiris · Akjoujt · **M A U R I T A N I A** · Araouane
Nouakchott · Beila · Tidjikdja · Tichitt · **M A L I**
Boutilimit · Moudjéria · Aouker · Oualata · Vallée du Tilemsi
Mederdra · Aleg · Tamchaket · L. Faguibine · Tombouctou (Timbuktu) · Bamba
Senegal · Bogué · Kiffa · Aïoun el Atrouss · Ras el Ma · Gourma-Rharous · Bourem
St. Louis · Dagana · Poder · Diorbivol · Mbout · Néma · Goundam · Gao
Louga · Kébémer · Linguère · Matam · Timbédra · Niafounké
Tivaouane · Thiès · Diourbel · Bakel · Balle · Nara · Douentza
Cape Vert · Sélibabi · Nioro du Sahel · Sokolo
Dakar · Mbour · Fatick · **S E N E G A L** · Kayes · Niono · Mopti · Bandiagara
Foundiougne · Kaolack · Kaffrine · Ségou · Djenné · Ouahigouya · Dori
Banjul (Bathurst) · Maka · Tambacounda · Bafoulabé · Kita · Bani · San · Tougan · Yako · Bani
THE GAMBIA · Brikama · Georgetown · Basse Santa Su · Kati · Déédougou · **BURKINA FASO** · Faga N'Gourma
Ziguinchor · Kolda · Vélingara · Satadougou · Kédougou · **Bamako** · Koutiala · Koudougou · **Ouagadougou**
C. Roxo · Youkounkoun · Bafing · Makana · Boromo · Tenkodogo
GUINEA · Koundara · Foula Mory · Siguiri · Sikasso · Bobo · Diébougou · Pô
BISSAU · Bafatá · Gaoual · Yambering · Bougouni · Dioulasso · Banfora · Léo · Bolgatanga
Bissau · Bolama · Boké · Telimélé · Dinguiraye · Tumu · Navrongo · Bawku
Arquipelago dos Bijagos · Pita · **Labé** · Dalaba · Dabola · Kouroussa · Gaoua · Wa · **GHANA**
Boffa · Mamou · Timbo · Faranah · Lawra · Dapaong
Cap Verga · **Kankan**
Kindia · **G U I N E A**

A · B · C · D · E

Miller Oblated Stereographic Projection · West of Greenwich

100

1:9,000,000

| 0 | 100 | 200 | 300 | 400 | 500 | 600 KILOMETRES |
| 0 | 50 | 100 | 150 | 200 | 250 | 300 | 350 | 400 STATUTE MILES |

© COLOUR LIBRARY BOOKS

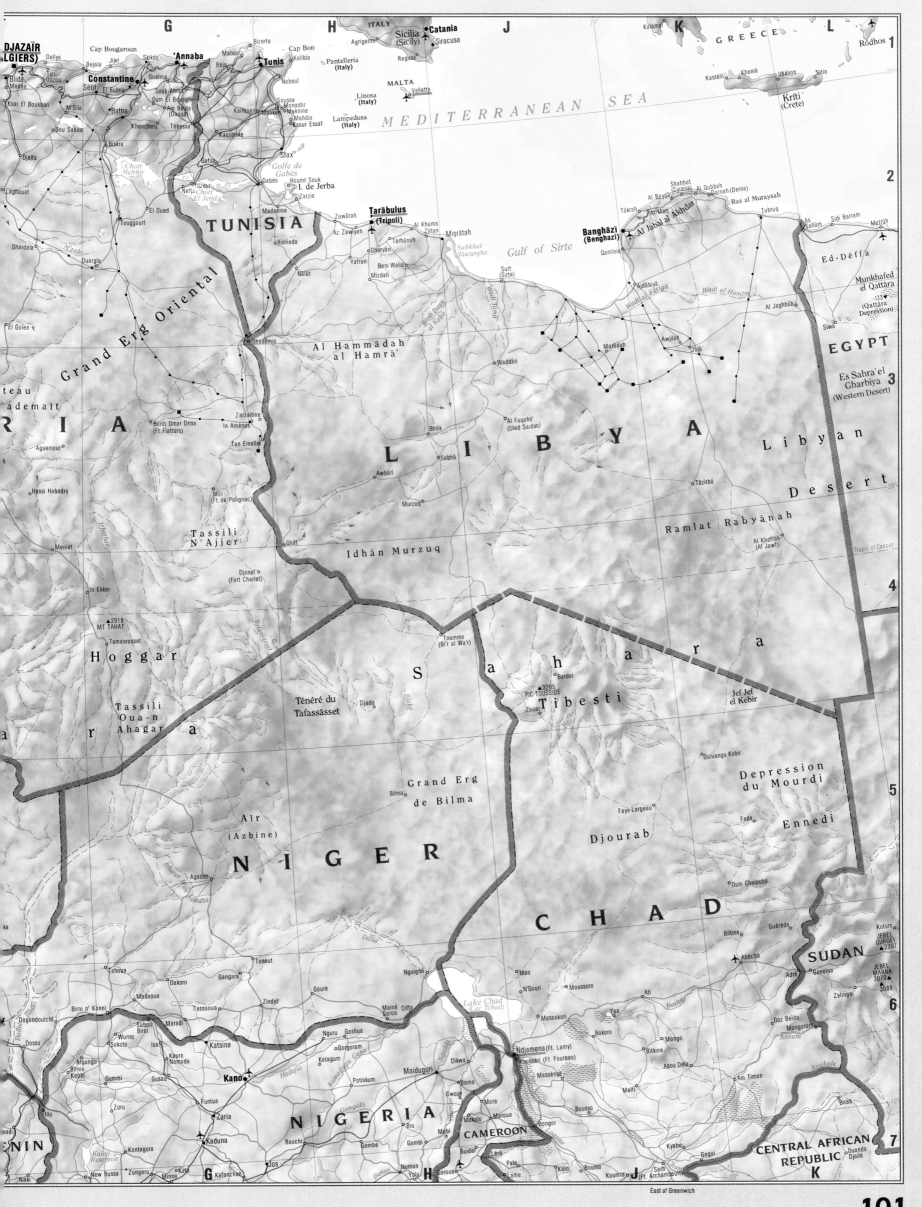

G   **H**   **J**   **K**   **L**

MEDITERRANEAN SEA

GREECE

ITALY
Sicilia (Sicily)   **Catania**
Siracusa
Agrigento   Ragusa

Pantelleria (Italy)

MALTA
Valletta

Linosa (Italy)
Lampedusa (Italy)

Kálamai
Ródhos
Kastélli   Khaniá   Iráklion   Sitía
Kríti (Crete)

DJAZAÏR (ALGIERS)
Dellys   Cap Bougaroun
Cap Djinet
Bejaia   Jijel   Skikda   **'Annaba**
Blida
Medea   Izzi Ouzou   Sétif   El Eulma   Guelma
Bizerte   Cap Bon
Mateur   Kelibia
Beja   **Tunis**
Nabeul

Constantine
Ksar El Boukhari   M'Sila   Batna   Ain Beïda (Daoud)   Souk Ahras   Tébessa
Khenchela

Bou Saâda   Biskra   Kassérine

Laghouat
Djelfa

Ghardaia
Ouargla

El Golea

Chott Melrhir
Gafsa
Nefta   Tozeur   Chott el Jerid
El Oued
Touggourt

Sousse   Monastir
Meknassy   Mahdia   Ksour Essaf
Sfax
Golfe de Gabès
Gabès   I. de Jerba
Medenine   Houmt Souk   Zarzis

TUNISIA

Remada

Zuwārah   **Tarābulus (Tripoli)**
Az Zāwiyah   Al Khums   Zlitan
Ghadāmis   Nālūt   Gharyān   Tarhūnah   Misrātah
Yafran   Bani Walid
Mizdah

Shahhat   Al Qubbah
Al Baydā' (Cyrene)   Darnah (Derna)
Tūkrah   Aj Mari   Ras al Muraysah
Banghāzī (Benghazi)   Al Jabal al Akhdar
Qamīnis
Tubruq   As Sallūm   Sidi Barrani
Matrūh

Gulf of Sirte
Surt (Sirte)
Ajdābiyā
Wadi al Farigh   Wadi al Hamīm
Sabkhat Tawurgha
Wadi Bayy al Kabīr
Al Jaghbūb

Ed-Déffa

Munkhafad el Qattāra
-133 (Qattāra Depression)
Siwa

EGYPT

Grand Erg Oriental

steau
ademaït

RIA

Aguemour
Hassi Habadra
Meniet
In Ekker

Bordj Omar Driss (Ft. Flatters)   In Amenas
Zarzaïtine
Tan Emelle
Ilizi (Ft. de Polignac)

Tassili N'Ajjer

Ghât

Djanet (Fort Charlet)

▲2918 MT TAHAT
Tamanrasset

Hoggar

Tassili Oua-n Ahagar

Waddān
Al Hammādah al Hamrā'
Birāk
Sabhā
Awbārī
Murzuq

Idhān Murzuq

Al Fuqahā' (Uled Saidan)

Tāzirbū

L   I   B   Y   A

Es Sahra'el Gharbīya (Western Desert)

Libyan

Desert

Ramlat Rabyānah

Al Khufrah (Al Jawf)

Tropic of Cancer

S   a   h   a   r   a

Toummo (Bi'r al Wa'r)

Bardai
▲3265 PIC TOUSSIDE
Zouar

Jef Jef el Kebir

Tibesti

Ténéré du Tafassásset
Djado
Bilma
Djodo
Blaka

Aïr (Azbine)

Agadez

Ounianga Kebir

Depression du Mourdi

Faya-Largeau   Fada   Ennedi

Djourab

Grand Erg de Bilma

Tahoua   Dakoro   Gangara
Tanout
Madaoua   Tessaoua   Zinder
Birni n' Konni

N   I   G   E   R

Oum Chalouba

C   H   A   D

Biltine   Guéréda
Abéché
Adré   Geneina

Mao
N'Gouri   Moussoro   Ati   Batha
Nguigmi
Maïné Soroa   Diffa   Lake Chad (Lac Tchad)
Massakori   Yao
Bokoro   Mongo
Bitkine

Kutum
JEBEL GURGEI ▲2597

SUDAN

JEBEL MARRA 3070 ▲3088
Zalingei
Goz Beïda   Mongororo

Dogondoutchi
Dosso
Kainji Reservoir
Gummi
Argungu
Birnin Kebbi
New Bussa
Kontagora
Zungeru

Illo
Sokoto
Gusau
Kaura Namoda
Isa
Wurno
Birni
Maradi
Katsina
Kano
Zaria
Funtua

Gashua   Nguru   Gorgoram
Katagum   Potiskum
Maiduguri   Dikwa   Bama
Hadejia
Kafanchan   Zaria
Kaduna   JOS
Bauchi
Gombe
Biu

N   I   G   E   R   I   A

Ndjamena (Ft. Lamy)
Kousséri (Ft. Foureau)
Massénya   Bousso
Melfi
Abou Deïa
Am Timan

Gwoza   Mora   Mokolo
Mabi   Gombi   Maroua
Yola   Bongor
Numan
Garoua
Lame
CAMEROON
Guider   Lère   Pala
Kélo   Kyabé   Sarh (Ft. Archambault)
Boumo   Koumra
Kéni
Bénoué
Mbaiki

Birao

CENTRAL AFRICAN REPUBLIC

Gagui
Ouanda Djailé

NIN

G   H   J   K

East of Greenwich

Designed and produced by E.S.R.

1   **2**   **3**   **4**   **5**   **6**   **7**

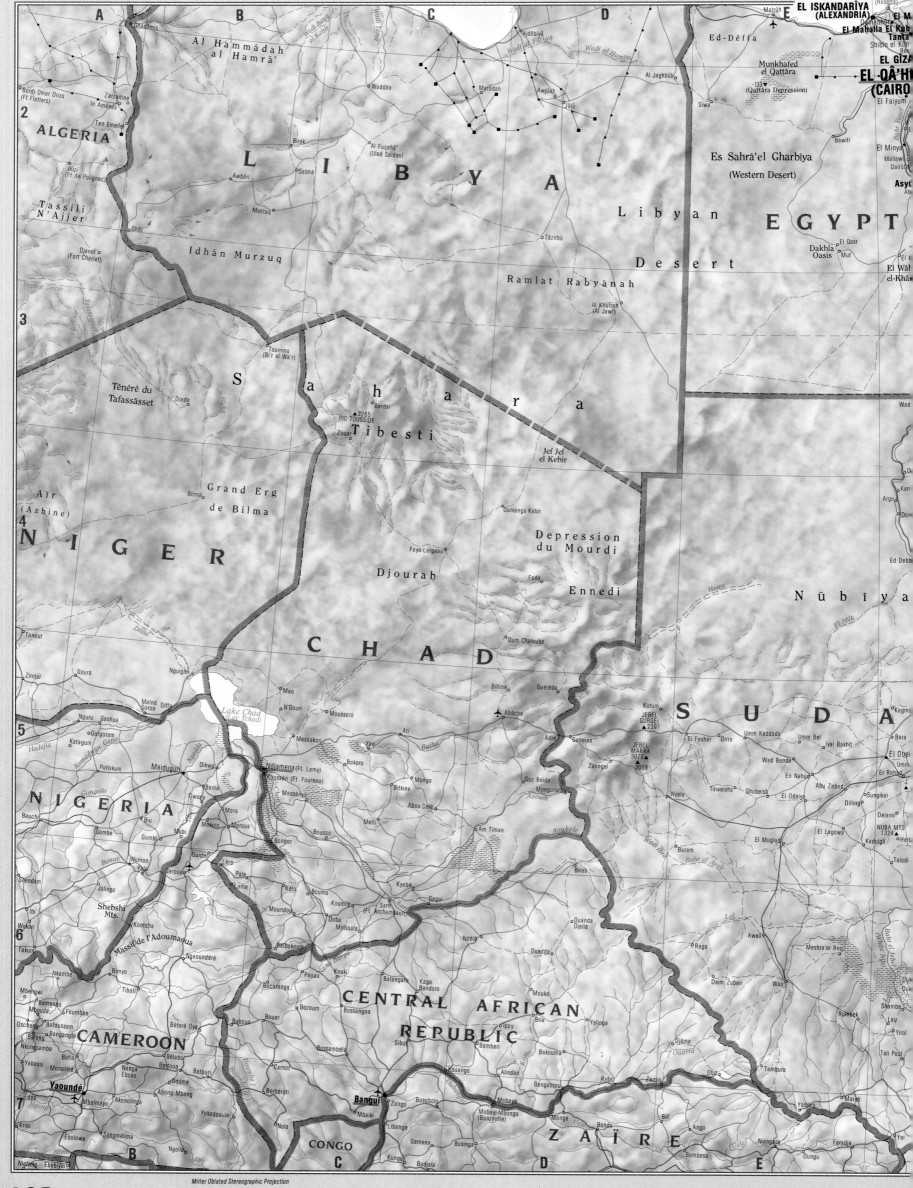

Miller Oblated Stereographic Projection

© COLOUR LIBRARY BOOKS

1:9,000,000

| 0 | 100 | 200 | 300 | 400 | 500 | 600 KILOMETRES |

| 0 | 50 | 100 | 150 | 200 | 250 | 300 | 350 | 400 STATUTE MILES |

ISRAEL **JORDAN** **IRAQ** **KUWAIT** **IRAN**

Jamietta
Sa'id
(Port Said)
ez Cazal
nà'iliya

El 'Arish
Ràs en Naqb
Ma'àn
Al Busayyah
Al Jahrah
Al Kuwayt
(Kuwait)
Mina 'Abd Allàh
Bazràjàn
Fasà
Dàràb

El Suweis
(Suez)
El Arish
Aqaba
Al Mudawwara
Ad Duwayd
Ash Shu'bah
Mina Sa'ud
Al Khafji
Farrashband
Jahrom
Fìrùzàbàd

Sinai
Peninsula
GEBEL
KATHERINA
2637
El Tor
J AL LAWZ
2579
Tabùk
Al Jawf
Sàkàkah
Ra's al Khafji
Al Batin
Khvormùj
Khonj
Làr

Ràs Muhammad
Hurghada
Magnà
Taymà
Hà'il
Al Mayyah
Al Jubayl
Busayah
Qatif
Ad Dammàm
Az Zahràn
Al Muharraq
Al Manàmah
Này Band
Bastak

Safàga
Al'Ulà
An Nafùd
Ad Dahnà
Manifah
BAHRAIN
QATAR
Ad Dawhah
(Doha)
Hàlùl
Kangan

Qena
Luxor
Mashàbih
Shaybara
Ra's Abù Madd
Al Hanàkiyah
Buraydah
Unayzah
Ar Rass
Al Hufùf
Ad Dilam
Musay'id
Ra'sal 'Udayd
Az Zarqà
Murbàn
Abù Zabì
(Abu Dhabi)

Idfu
Om Ombo
1977
GEBEL HAMATA
2260
Ra's Bàrìdì
Al Madinah
(Medina)
Yanbu'al Bahr
Badr Hunayn
AR RIYÀD
(RIYADH)
Ad Dawàdimì
Afif
Al Hariq
Harad
UNITED ARAB EMIRATES

Aswàn
Sadd al-Aswàn
(Aswan High Dam)
Lake Nasser
(Buhayrat Nàsir)
ADMIN BOUNDARY
POLITICAL BOUNDARY
Ra's Hàtibah
ArRa's al Abyad
S A U D I
Zalim
As Sùq
Al Hàniq
 Al'Ubaylah
Tropic of Cancer
Sabkhat Matti

Wàdi 'Allàqi
Abu Hamed
Halaib
JEBEL ODA
2260
JIDDAH
(JEDDA)
MAKKAH
(Mecca)
At Tà'if
A R A B I A
Turabah
As Sùu
Layla

Es Sahrâ en Nûbîya
(Nubian Desert)
Port Sudan
Suakin
Sinkat
Muhammad Qol
Al Lith
Al Qunfudhah
Qal'at Bishah
Wàdi Dawàsir
As Sulayyi
A r   R u b   a l   K h à l i
OMAN

Wàdi Amur
Berber
Atbara
Musmar
Tohamiyam
Tokar
Derudeb
Karora
Hali
Abhà
Khamis Mushayt
Najràn
W. Najràn
Sharùrah
Thamùd
Damqawt

Ed Damer
Shendi
Nak'fa
Sad'ah
Al Qatn
Tarim
Ra's Fartak

REPUBLIC
OF YEMEN
Qishn
Sayhùt

Khartoum North
El Khartum (Khartoum)
Kassala
Sebderat
Akordat
Barentu
Àsmera
Keren
Mits'iwa
Jazà'ir Farasàn
Nora
Dehalak Desert
Az Zuhrah
Amràn
3760
San'a
Harib
Bayhàn al Qàsàb
Habbàn
Al Mukallà
Ash Shihr
Riyan
Hadramawt

El Kamlin
Rufa'a
Wad Rawa
Tesenay
Àdi Ugri
Àdi K'eyah
Adigrat
Az Zaydiyah
Al Hudaydah
Bayt al Faqih
Dhamàr
Al Baydà
Ash Shaykh'Uthman
Lawdar
Ìrqah

El Mesellemiya
Wad Medani
El Managil
Aksum
3217
Adwa
Zabid
Ta'izz
Ibb
Ad Dàli'

El Hosh
Hag 'Abdulla
Gedaref
Àbiy Adi
Mek'elè
Ed
Ta'izz
At Turbah
Al Mukhà
Madinat ash Sha'b
Little Aden
Shuqrah

Sennar
Singa
4620
Dabat
Denakil
Àseb
Bab el Mandeb
Adan
(Aden)
GULF OF ADEN
Caluula
Raas Caluula
Bereeda

Kosti
Gallabat
Metema
Gonder
Sek'ot'a
Lalibela
4284
Ras el Bir
Tadjoura
Obock
1510
Qandala
Boosaaso
(Bender Qaasim)
CAL 1810
Hurdiyo
Xaafuun
Raas Xaafuun

El Jebelein
Renk
Dunkur
T'ana Hàyk'
Debre Tabor
Weldiya
DJIBOUTI
Djibouti
Saylac
Karin
Maydh
Ceerigaabo
Bandarbeyla

Ed Damazin
Guba
3533
Mot'a
Dessye
4247
Debre Birhan
Ankober
Berbera
Laas Dhuure
Qardho

Melut
Kurmuk
BIRHAN 4154
Debre Mark'os
Shiikh
Cadadley
Burco
Caynabo
Eyl

ADIS ÀBEBA
Nek'emte
3298
DENDI
A Nazrèt
Mi'eso
Dirè Dawa
Jeldèsa
Jijiga
Hargeysa
SOMALIA
Laascaanood

Nasir
Dembi Dolo
Gorè
Metu
Jima
Hosa'ina
K'ECH'A TERARA 4190
Shashemenè
E T H I O P I A
Ahmar Mountains
Hàren
Fàfàn Shèt'
Degeh Bur
K'ebri Dehar
Kaila
Raas Gabbac

Waat
Maji
3568
Bako
Gidolè
Yirga Alem
4307 BATU
Goba
Ginir
Ogadèn
Denan
K'orahè
Geladi
Jirriiban
Gaalkacyo

Pibor Post
Shewa Gimira
Negelè
Dana Wenz
Wabè Gestro Wenz
El K'oran
Hobyo
Domo

DIDINGA Hills
Nàgishot
3187
Kapoeta
Lokichokio
Lake Turkana
(Lake Rudolf)
Moysie
Dolo Odo
Luuq
Xuddur
Tayeeglow
Beledweyne
Ceelbuur
Buuloburde
Ceeldheer
KENYA
Kitgum
Kakamari

Wàbè Shabelè Wenz
Garbaharrey

East of Greenwich

Designed and produced by E.S.R.

WEST AFRICA

A | B | C | D | E

1

WESTERN SAHARA

C. Barbas

Nouadhibou (Pt. Etienne)
Ras Nouadhibou (C. Blanc)

Makteir

Ouarâne

Fdérik
Zouérate

Tropic of Cancer

Erg Chech

Tanezrouf

Taoudenni

2

C. Timiris

MAURITANIA

Atar

Chinguetti

Akjoujt

El   Djouf

Sa

Araouane

M A L I

Ag

Nouakchott
Beila

Boutilimit

Mederdra

Aleg

Moudjéria

Tidjikdja

Tichitt

A o u k e r

Tamchaket

Oualata

Araouane

Séné gal

St. Louis
Dagana
Podor
Bogué
Kaédi

Diorbivol

Matam

Kiffa

Aioun el Atrouss

Néma

Timbédra

L. Faguibine

Tombouctou
(Timbuktu)

Gourma-
Rharous

Bamba

Bourem

Niger

Louga
Kébémer
Linguère

Tivaouane

Diourbel

Sélibabi

Bakel

Kayes

Ballé

Nioro du Sahel

Nara

Ras el Ma

Goundam

Niafounké

Gao

Douentza

Cape Vert
Dakar
Thiès

Mbour
Faticko
Foundiougne
Kaolack
Katfrine

SENEGAL

Maka

Tambacounda

Bafoulabé

Satadougou

Kita

Kati

Sokolo

Niono

Ségou

Bani

San

Mopti

Bandiagara

Dori

3

THE GAMBIA
Banjul
(Bathurst)
Brikama

Georgetown
Basse Santa Su

Gambia

Bafing
Makana

Bamako

Koutiala

Sikasso

Djenné

Tougan

Ouahigouya

Yako

BURKINA FAS

Diouloulou

Kolda
Velingara

C. Roxo
Bafata
Bissau
Bolama

GUINEA BISSAU

Ziguinchor

Casamance

Youkounkoun
Koundara

Fulacunda

Arquipelago
dos Bijagos

Boké

Koula Moré

Gaoual

Yambering

Kédougou

Siguiri

Bougouni

Dédougou

Koudougou

Ouagadougou

Houndé

Diébougou

Lep

Pô

Tenkodogo

Telimélé

Labé
Pita
Dalaba

Dinguiraye

GUINEA

Timbo
Dabola

Kouroussa

Massigui

Bobo
Dioulasso

Banfora

Gaoua

Lawra

Tumu

Navrongo

Bolgatanga

Bawku

Cap Verga

Boffa

Mamou

Kindia

Faranah

Kankan

Wa

Bole

Damongo

White Volta

Tamale

Yendi

Conakry

Dubréka
Forécariah

Kanbia
Port Loko

**SIERRA
LEONE**

Makeni
Magburaka

Koba

Rokel

Kabala

Kissidougou

Odienné

Boundiali

Korhogo

Kong

Bouna

Daboya

Kintampo

Kete

Salaga

Freetown

Moyamba
Shenge
Sherbro

Lunsar

Sefadu
Pendembu
Segbwema

Guékedou

Macenta

Beyla

1236▲

Touba

Ségueéla

Mankono

Katiola

Dabakala

Bondoukou

IVORY COAST

GHANA

Sunyani

Mampong

Yawri Bay

Bo
Pujehun

Kenema

Wologisi
Mts.

Nzérékoré

Lola
Biankouma

Man

Zuénoula

Bouaké

Kumasi

Mataeso

Ahosombo
Dam

4

Sherbro Island

Bonthe

Gbarnga

MTS. NIMBA
±152

Daloa
Bouaflé

Duékoué

Yamoussoukro

Sinfra

Abengourou

Dimbokro

Aya-Yehino

Bekwai

Awaso

Obuasi
Koforidua

Oda

Akuse

Tototá
Robertsport

LIBERIA

Saint Paul

Guiglo

Gagnoa

Agboville

Anyama
Bingerville

Enchi

Dunkwa

Asamankese

Winneba

Tema

Monrovia

Buchanan

Zwedru

Soubré

ABIDJAN

Abboisso

Nsuta

Tarkwa

Salpond

Accra

Timbo

Greenville
(Sinoe)

Sasstown

Harper
C. Palmas

Grand
Lahou

Sassandra

San Pédro

Tabou

Axim

Sekondi Takoradi

Dixcove

Cape Three Points

Cape Coast

5

A T L A N T I C

O C E A N

104

Miller Oblated Stereographic Projection

West of Greenwich

1:9,000,000

| 0 | 100 | 200 | 300 | 400 | 500 | 600 | KILOMETRES |

| 0 | 50 | 100 | 150 | 200 | 250 | 300 | 350 | 400 | STATUTE MILES |

Inset: CAPE VERDE

B | L | C

7

Santo Antão
Porto Novo
Mindelo
São Vicente

São Nicolau

Sal

**CAPE
VERDE**

Boa Vista

Fogo
Brava

São Tiago

Maio

Praia

6

Equator

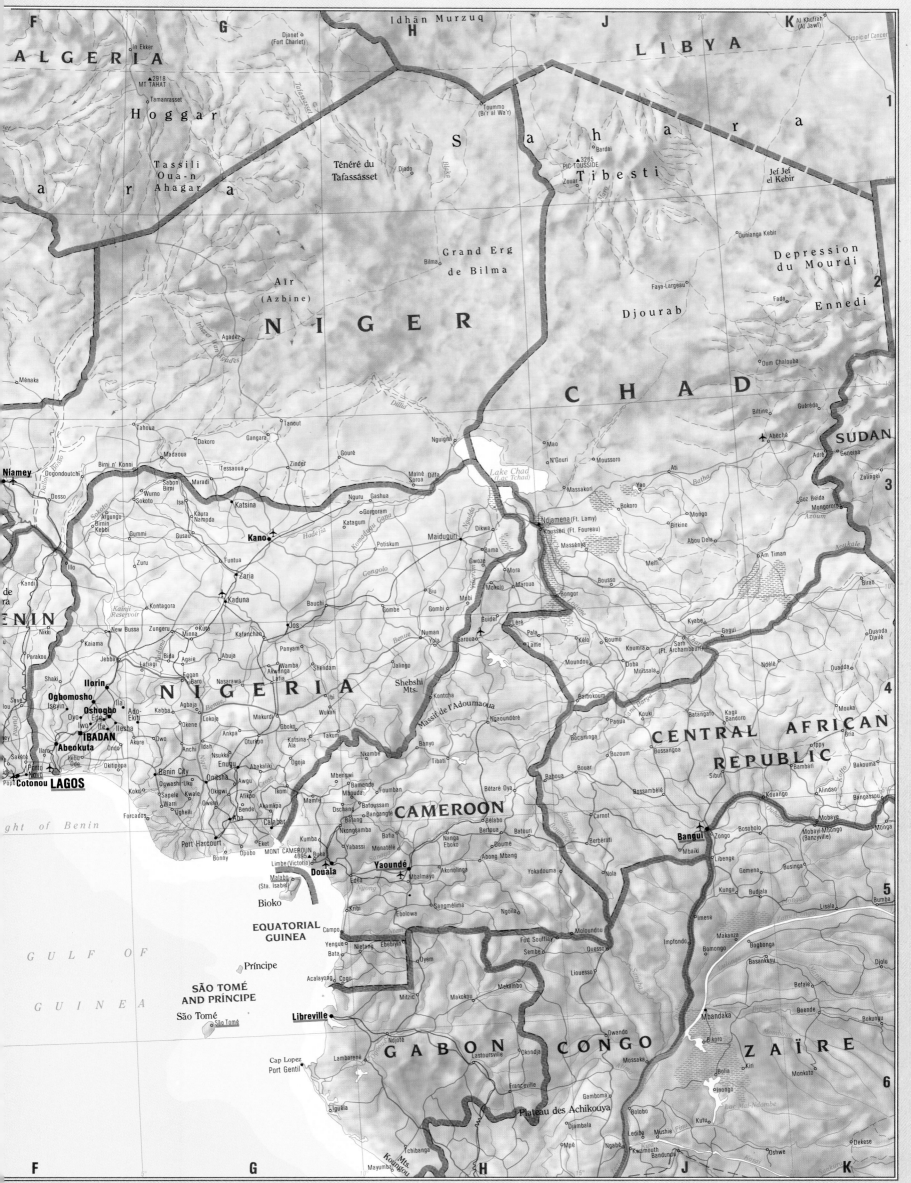

ALGERIA

F   G   H   J   K

LIBYA

In Ekker
Djanet
(Fort Charlet)
Toummo
(Bi'r al Wa'r)
Al Khufrah
(Al Jawf)
Tropic of Cancer

1

▲2918
MT TAHAT
Tamanrasset

Hoggar

Idhān Murzuq

S   a   h   a   r   a

Bardai
PIC TOUSSIDE ▲3265
Zouar

Tibesti
Jef Jef
el Kebir

Tassili
Oua-n
Ahagar

Ténéré du
Tafassâsset

Djado

Bilma

Grand Erg
de Bilma

Ounianga Kebir

Depression
du Mourdi

2

Aïr
(Azbine)

Faya-Largeau

Fada   Ennedi

Ménaka

N   I   G   E   R

C   H   A   D

Oum Chalouba

Tahoua
Dakoro
Gangara   Tanout

Nguigmi

Mao

Guéréda

Biltine

Abéché   SUDAN

Adré   Geneina

3

Niamey

Birni n' Konni
Dogondoutchi
Dosso

Madaoua
Tessaoua
Zinder

Gouré

Maïné
Soroa   Diffa

Lake Chad
(Lac Tchad)

N'Gouri

Moussoro

Massakori

Bokoro

Yao   Ati

Batha

Mongo

Goz Beida

Mongororo
Azoum

Zalingei

Sabon
Birni
Wurno
Sokoto   Isa

Maradi
Katsina

Nguru   Gashua

Gorgoram

Katagum

Maiduguri

Ndjamena (Ft. Lamy)
Kousséri (Ft. Foureau)

Massènya

Bitkine   Abou Deïa

Melfi   Am Timan

Birao

Argungu
Birnin
Kebbi
Gummi   Kaura
Namoda

Kano

Hadejia

Komadugu Gana

Dikwa
Bama

Massakori

Bongor

Kano

Zuru
Gusau

Funtua

Potiskum

Gwoza

Mokolo
Mora
Maroua

Mondou

Sarh
(Ft. Archambault)

Ndélé

Ouanda
Djalé

Ouadda

4

Zaria

Zungeru
Kaduna

Bauchi

Jos   Gombe
Gombi

Mubi

Guider   Lére
Pala
Lame

Kélo
Boumo
Koumra   Doba
Moissala

Gagui   Ouanda

Kaga
Bandoro   Mouka

Ippy   Bria

Kainji
Reservoir

New Bussa   Kontagora

Minna   Kafanchan

Panyam   Biu

Numan   Yola

Kontcha

Massif de l'Adoumaoua

Batangafo

Bossangoa

Bambari

BENIN

Nikki

Kaiama

Jebba   Agaie
Bida

Lafiagi   Abuja

Nasarawa
Lafia

Wamba
Akwanga

Shendam   Ibi   Wukari

Shebshi
Mts.   Jalingo

Takum

Ngaoundéré

Banyo   Tibati

Bocaranga

Bozoum   Bouar

Bouca   Sibut

CENTRAL AFRICAN

Bakouma

Perakou

Shaki   Ilorin

Oghomosho   Iseyin
Ogbomosho   Oyo   Ila
Oshogbo   Ife
Iwo   Ilesha
Ado-
Ekiti

IBADAN   Ondo

Abeokuta

Okitipupa

N   I   G   E   R   I   A

Kabba
Agbaja

Okene
Lokoja
Anchi   Idah

Makurdi
Oturkpo

Nkambe

Mbengwi

Foumban

Nanga
Eboko

Bétaré Oya

Babua

Baboua
Bouar

Carnot

Bossèmbélé

REPUBLIC   Bambari

Bangassou

Ilaro
Ijebu
Ode

Saketé
Porto
Novo

Popo   Cotonou   LAGOS

ght of Benin

Bight of Benin

Benin City

Sapele   Kwale
Warri
Ughelli

Forcados

Ogwashi-Uku

Onitsha

Koko

Enugu
Awgu
Okigwi
Owerri

Aba

Abakaliki

Afikpo
Ikom

CAMEROON

Bamende
Mbouda
Dschang
Batang
Bangangte

Bafoussam

Bafia

Yaoundé

Bertoua   Batouri

Berbérati

Nola

Gamboula

Mobaye

Bangui   Zongo
Mbaiki

Bosobolo

Libenge

Mobayi-Mbongo
(Banzyville)

Monga

Aliindao

Kouango

Gemena
Businga

Port Harcourt

Opobo
Bonny

Calabar
Eket

Kumba
Buea

Akamkpa

Mamfe

MONT CAMEROUN
4095 ▲

Limbe (Victoria)

Douala

Malabo
(Sta. Isabel)

Bioko

Nkongsamba
Yabassi
Monatélé

Edéa

Kribi

Mbalmayo

Sangmélima

Ngoila

Abong Mbang

Akonolinga

Yokadouma

Moloundou

Nola

Quesso

Sembé

Liouesso

Impfondo

Ngabé

Makanza

Bomongo

Bogbonga

Basankusu

Lisala   Bumba

5

EQUATORIAL
GUINEA

Campo

Yengue
Bata

Acalayong

Nietang
Ebebiyin

Oyem

Mitzic

Cogo

GULF OF

Príncipe

SÃO TOMÉ
AND PRÍNCIPE

São Tomé
São Tomé

Makokou

Mekambo

Fort Souflay

Bikoro

Djolu

Befale

Boende

GUINEA

Libreville

Kango   Booué

Lastoursville

Okondja

Owando

Mossaka   Mbandaka

Bolia   Kiri

Inongo

Monkoto

ZAÏRE

6

Cap Lopez
Port Gentil

Lambaréné

GABON   CONGO

Francaville   Gamboma

Bolobo

Mushie

Kutu

Oshwe

Dekese

Iguéla

Ndjolé

Mayumba
Mts.
Koumou

Tchibanga

Plateau des Achikouya

Mpé

Ngabé

Djambala

Pwamouth

Lediba

Bandundu

East of Greenwich

Designed and produced by E.S.R.

105

F   G   H   J   K

EQUATORIAL AFRICA

Miller Oblated Stereographic Projection

1:9,000,000

0   100   200   300   400   500   600 KILOMETRES
0   50   100   150   200   250   300   350   400 STATUTE MILES

© COLOUR LIBRARY BOOKS

107

SOUTHERN AFRICA

Miller Oblated Stereographic Projection

1:9,000,000

© COLOUR LIBRARY BOOKS

| 0 | 100 | 200 | 300 | 400 | 500 | 600 KILOMETRES |

| 0 | 50 | 100 | 150 | 200 | 250 | 300 | 350 | 400 STATUTE MILES |

F   **G**   **H**   **J**   **K**

TANZANIA

Lindi
Mikindani
Mtwara
Makondi
945
Kitangari
Plateau
Masasi
C. Delgado
Palma
Songea
Tunduru
Mocimboa da Praia
Mueda

Chilumba
Mzuzu
Songea
Mecula
Mueda

Grande
Comore
COMOROS
Moroni
Moheli
Anjouan
Dzaoudzi
Mayotte
(France)

Tanjon'i Bobaomby
Antseranana
(Diego-Suárez)
Nosy
Mitsio
Nosy Bé
Hell-Ville
Ambilobe
Vohimarina
(Vohémar)

MALAWI
Livingstone Mts
Lake Nyasa (Lake Malawi)
Chilumba
Mzuzu
Nkhotakota
Dowa
Salima
Lichinga
Matgoca
Mecula
Marrupa
Montepuez
Balama
Pemba
Mecufi

Lundazi
Kasungu
Chipata (Ft. Manning)
Lilongwe
Zomba
Limbe
Blantyre
Namuli
2419
Gurué
Alta Molócue
Lugela
Gilé
Namapa
Maúa
Lalaua
Nampula
Nametil
Namaponda
Mogincual
Moma
Angoche

Massif du
Tsaratanana
▲2876
Analalava
Antsohihy
Befandriana
Maroantsetra
Sambava
Andapa
Antalaha
C. Masoala
Mananara

Mahajanga
Port-Bergé
Marovoay
Amboro-Boeny
Miarinarivo
Tsaratanana
Nosy Boraha
(Sainte-Marie)
Ambodifototra
Fenoarivo Atsinanana

C. St. André
Toraka Vestale
Besalampy
Mahabe
Maevatanana
Stampiky

Juan de Nova
(France)

Morafenobe
Maintirano
A'tomainty
Ankazobe
Tsiroanomandidy
Miarinarivo
Antsalova
Bekopaka
Soavinandriana
Arivonimamo
Antananarivo
(Tananarive)
Toamasina
(Tamatave)
Vavatenina
A'tondrazaka
Anjozorobe
Moramanga
Andevoranto
Vatomandry
Anosibe
an'Ala
Belo-Tsiribihina
Ambatolampy
Antsirabe
Betafo

Mahabo
Morondava
Miandrivazo
A'tofinandrahana
Ambositra
Fandriana
Marolambo
Nosy-Varika

Manja
Béroroha
Tsitondroina
A'himahasoa
Fianarantsoa
Vohilava
Mananjary

Morombe
Ankiliabo
Ambalavao
Ikongo
Manakara
Ambalavao
Ikongo
Vohipeno
Ankazoabo
Ihosy
Farafangana

Fitsitika
Toliara
(Tuléar)
Soalara
Betioky
Bekily
Mi. de l'Ivakoany
1956
Vangaindrano

Itampolo
Ampanihy
Midongy
Atsimo
Ambovombe
Taolañaro
(Fort Dauphin)
C. Sainte Marie
Faux Cap

MOZAMBIQUE
Mutoko
Macosse
Caia
Mopeia Velha
Quelimane
Chinde

Cabora
Bassa Dam
Tete
Moatize
Chiromo
2054▲
CHIPERONE
Nsanje (Port Herald)
Chemba
Mutarara
Namacurra
Pebane

Nova
Vanduzi
Inchope
Gorongoza
Muanza

Mutare
(Umtali)
Chimoio
Dombe
Buzi
Beira
Nova Sofala

Chimanimani
Espungabera
Algueirão

Machanga
Nova Mambone
Inhassôro
I. do Bazaruto
I. Benguérua
Vilanculos
P. S. Sebastião

Massangena
Madade
Maxela
Massinga

Chigubo
Mabalane
Homoine
Inhambane

Massangir
Panda
Inharrime

Chókwè
Chibuto
Xai-Xai
Magude
Manhiça

Maputo
Baía de Maputo
C. de Santa Maria
Bela Vista

Makatini
Flats
Ubombo
Lake
St. Lucia
Cape Saint Lucia

MADAGASCAR
Plateau du Bemaraha
Manambolo
Massif du Makay
Mangoky
Onilahy
Andringitra
Beampingaratra

Bassas
da India
(France)

I. de l'Europa
(France)

Tropic of Capricorn

I N D I A N

O C E A N

J   **K**

MAURITIUS
Port Louis
Beau Bassin
Curepipe
Mahébourg

Réunion
(France)
St. Denis
St. Benoit
St. Pierre

*Mascarene
Islands*

6   **7**

L

F   **G**   **H**

Bonne Projection

1:19,000,000

© COLOUR LIBRARY BOOKS

East of Greenwich

| 0 | 200 | 400 | 600 | 800 KILOMETRES |
| 0 | 100 | 200 | 300 | 400 | 500 STATUTE MILES |

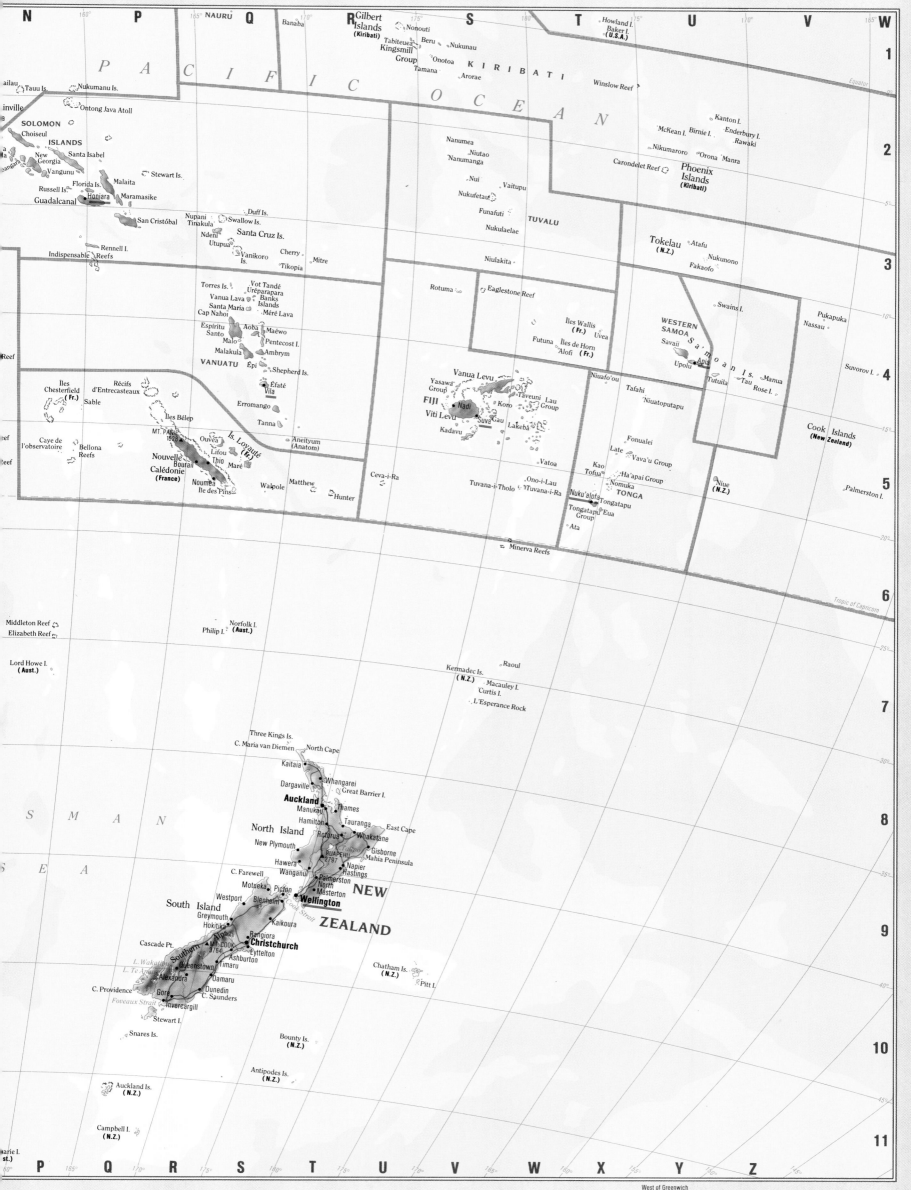

N P Q R S T U V W

NAURU
Banaba

Gilbert
Islands
(Kiribati)

Nonouti
Beru Nukunau

Howland I.
Baker I.
(U.S.A.)

1

P A C I F I C

Tabiteuea
Onotoa
Tamana
Arorae

KIRIBATI

Winslow Reef

Equator

ailau
Tauu Is.
Nukumanu Is.
inville

Ontong Java Atoll

O C E A N

Kanton I.
McKean I. Birnie I. Enderbury I.
Nikumaroro Orona Rawaki

2

SOLOMON
Choiseul
ISLANDS
New
Georgia
Vangunu
Russell Is.
Florida Is.
Honiara
Guadalcanal

Santa Isabel

Stewart Is.

Malaita
Maramasike

San Cristóbal

Nupani
Tinakula
Ndeni
Utupua

Duff Is.
Swallow Is.
Santa Cruz Is.
Vanikoro
Is.

Cherry
Tikopia

Mitre

Nanumea
Niutao
Nanumanga

Nui Vaitupu

Nukufetau

Funafuti TUVALU

Nukulaelae

Niulakita

Carondelet Reef

Phoenix
Islands
(Kiribati)

Tokelau
(N.Z.)

Atafu

Nukunono

Fakaofo

3

Indispensable Reefs
Rennell I.

Reef

Torres Is.
Vot Tandé
Uréparapara
Vanua Lava
Banks
Santa Maria Islands
Cap Nahoi
Méré Lava
Espíritu Aoba
Santo Maéwo
Malo Pentecost I.
Malakula Ambrym
VANUATU Épi
Shepherd Is.
Êfaté
Vila

Rotuma
Eaglestone Reef

Îles Wallis
Uvea
Futuna Îles de Horn
Alofi (Fr.)

WESTERN
SAMOA
Savaii
Upolu Apia

Swains I.

Samoan Is.
Manua
Tutuila Tau Rose I.

Pukapuka
Nassau

Suvorov I.

4

Îles
Chesterfield
(Fr.)
Récifs
d'Entrecasteaux
Sable

Îles Bélep

Erromango

Tanna

Vanua Levu
Yasawa
Group Taveuni
Koro Lau
FIJI Group
Viti Levu Ovalau
Suva Lakeba
Kadavu

Niuafo'ou
Tafahi
Niuatoputapu

Fonualei
Late Vava'u Group
Kao Vava'u Group
Tofua
Nomuka Ha'apai Group
Nuku'alofa TONGA

Cook Islands
(New Zealand)

5

Caye de
l'observatoire
Bellona
Reef

MT. PANIÉ
1628
Nouvelle
Calédonie
(France)
Nouméa
Île des Pins

Ouvéa Is. Loyauté
Lifou (Fr.)
Thio Maré
Bouraíl
Walpole Matthew
Hunter

Ceva-i-Ra

Tuvana-i-Tholo
Vatoa
Ono-i-Lau
Tuvana-i-Ra

Ata

Tongatapu
Tongatapu 'Eua
Group

Niue
(N.Z.)

Palmerston I.

6

Minerva Reefs

Tropic of Capricorn

Middleton Reef
Elizabeth Reef

Lord Howe I.
(Aust.)

Philip I.
Norfolk I.
(Aust.)

Raoul
Kermadec Is.
(N.Z.)
Macauley I.
Curtis I.
L'Esperance Rock

7

T A S M A N

Three Kings Is.
C. Maria van Diemen
North Cape
Kaitaia
Whangarei
Dargaville Great Barrier I.
Auckland
Manukau Thames
Hamilton Tauranga
North Island Rotorua East Cape
New Plymouth Whakatane
RUAPEHU Gisborne
Hawera 2797 Mahia Peninsula
Wanganui Napier
C. Farewell Palmerston Hastings
Motueka North
Picton Masterton NEW
Westport Blenheim Wellington
South Greymouth Kaikoura
Island Hokitika ZEALAND
Cascade Pt. MT. COOK
3764 Rangiora
Southern Christchurch
L. Wakatipu Alps Lyttelton
L. Te Anau Queenstown Ashburton
Alexandra Timaru
C. Providence Gore Oamaru
Foveaux Strait Invercargill Dunedin
C. Saunders
Stewart I.

Chatham Is.
(N.Z.)
Pitt I.

8

S E A

9

10

Snares Is.
Bounty Is.
(N.Z.)

Antipodes Is.
(N.Z.)

Auckland Is.
(N.Z.)

Campbell I.
(N.Z.)

arie I.
st.)

P Q R S T U V W X Y Z

West of Greenwich

Designed and produced by E.S.R.

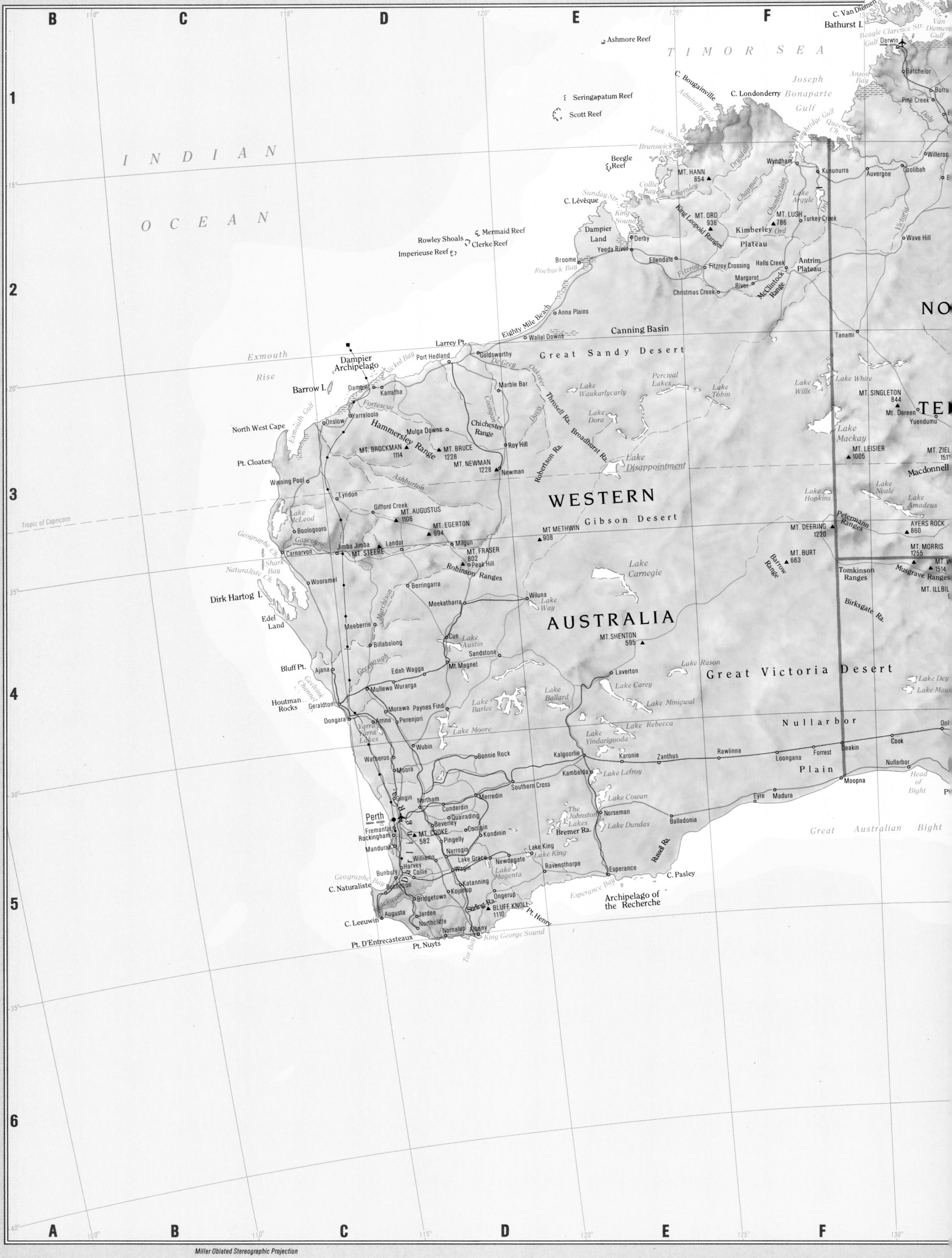

B
C
D
E
F
1
2
3
4
5
6
A
B
C
D
E
F
INDIAN OCEAN
TIMOR SEA
Tropic of Capricorn
Ashmore Reef
Seringapatum Reef
Scott Reef
Beegle Reef
Rowley Shoals
Mermaid Reef
Clerke Reef
Imperieuse Reef
Melville I.
C. Van Diemen
Bathurst I.
Beagle Gulf
Clarence Str.
Van Diemen Gulf
Dundas Str.
Darwin
Batchelor
Anson Bay
Joseph Bonaparte Gulf
C. Bougainville
Admiralty Gulf
C. Londonderry
Cambridge Gulf
Queens Ch.
Pine Creek
Daly
York Sound
Brunswick Bay
Drysdale
Wyndham
Kununurra
Auvergne
Coolibah
Willeroo
MT. HANN 854
Collier Bay
Charnley
Chapman
Chamberlain
Lake Argyle
Ord
Victoria
C. Lévêque
Sunday Str.
King Sound
King Leopold Ranges
MT. ORD 936
MT. LUSH 786
Turkey Creek
Kimberley Plateau
Wave Hill
Dampier Land
Derby
Yeeda River
Broome
Roebuck Bay
Ellendale
Fitzroy
Fitzroy Crossing
Halls Creek
Antrim Plateau
Margaret River
McClintock Range
Christmas Creek
Anna Plains
Eighty Mile Beach
Wallal Downs
Canning Basin
Tanami
NO
Larrey Pt.
Port Hedland
Goldsworthy
De Grey
Oakover
Great Sandy Desert
Exmouth Rise
Dampier Archipelago
Nickol Bay
Barrow I.
Dampier
Karratha
Marble Bar
Lake Waukarlycarly
Percival Lakes
Lake Tobin
Lake Wills
Lake White
MT. SINGLETON 844
Mt. Doreen
Yuendumu
TE
Fortescue
Onslow
Yarraloola
Exmouth Gulf
North West Cape
Coongan
Chichester Range
Throssel Ra.
Davis
Lake Dora
Lake Mackay
Hammersley Range
Mulga Downs
MT. BROCKMAN 1114
MT. BRUCE 1228
MT. NEWMAN 1228
Roy Hill
Newman
Broadhurst Ra.
Lake Disappointment
MT. LEISIER 1005
MT. ZIEL 1511
Macdonnell
Pt. Cloates
Robertson Ra.
Winning Pool
Ashburton
Lyndon
WESTERN
Lake Hopkins
Lake Neale
Lake Amadeus
Lake McLeod
Boologooro
Gifford Creek
MT. AUGUSTUS 1106
MT. EGERTON 994
Gibson Desert
MT METHWIN 908
MT. DEERING 1220
Petermann Ranges
AYERS ROCK 860
Geographe Ch.
Gascoyne
Carnarvon
Jimba Jimba
MT. STEERE
Landor
Milgun
MT. FRASER 802
Peak Hill
Robinson Ranges
MT. MORRIS 1255
MT. BURT 663
Barrow Range
Shark Bay
Naturaliste Ch.
Wooramel
Berringarra
Lake Carnegie
Tomkinson Ranges
Musgrave Ranges
MT. ILLBIL
Dirk Hartog I.
Murchison
Meekatharra
Wiluna
Lake Way
Birksgate Ra.
Edel Land
AUSTRALIA
Meeberrie
Billabalong
Cue
Lake Austin
MT. SHENTON 595
Sandstone
Bluff Pt.
Ajana
Greenough
Edah Wagga
Mt. Magnet
Lake Rason
Laverton
Great Victoria Desert
Lake Dey
Lake Maurice
Geelvink Channel
Houtman Rocks
Geraldton
Mullewa Wurarga
Lake Ballard
Lake Carey
Lake Minigwal
Morawa
Paynes Find
Lake Barlee
Dongara
Arrino
Perenjori
Yarra Yarra Lakes
Lake Moore
Lake Rebecca
Lake Yindarlgooda
Nullarbor
Ool
Wubin
Watheroo
Bonnie Rock
Kalgoorlie
Karonie
Zanthus
Rawlinna
Loongana
Forrest
Deakin
Cook
Nullarbor
Moora
Kambalda
Lake Lefroy
Plain
Moopna
Head of Bight
Southern Cross
Gingin
Northam
Merredin
Cunderdin
Lake Cowan
Eyre
Madura
Perth
Fremantle
Rockingham
Quairading
Beverley
Corrigin
MT. COOKE 582
Kondinin
Pingelly
The Johnston Lakes
Norseman
Lake Dundas
Bremer Ra.
Balladonia
Mandurah
Narrogin
Williams
Lake Grace
Newdegate
Lake King
Ravensthorpe
Russell Ra.
Great Australian Bight
Harvey
Bunbury
Collie
Wagin
Lake Magenta
Esperance
C. Pasley
Geographe Bay
C. Naturaliste
Busselton
Katanning
Kojonup
Ongerup
Esperance Bay
Archipelago of the Recherche
Bridgetown
Stirling Ra.
BLUFF KNOLL 1110
Pt. Henry
Augusta
Jardee
Northcliffe
C. Leeuwin
Nornalup
Albany
King George Sound
Tor Bay
Pt. D'Entrecasteaux
Pt. Nuyts
Darling
110°
115°
120°
125°
130°
15°
20°
25°
30°
35°
40°

Miller Oblated Stereographic Projection

1:10,500,000

0 100 200 300 400 500 600 700 800 KILOMETRES

0 100 200 300 400 500 STATUTE MILES

NEW GUINEA AND PACIFIC ISLES

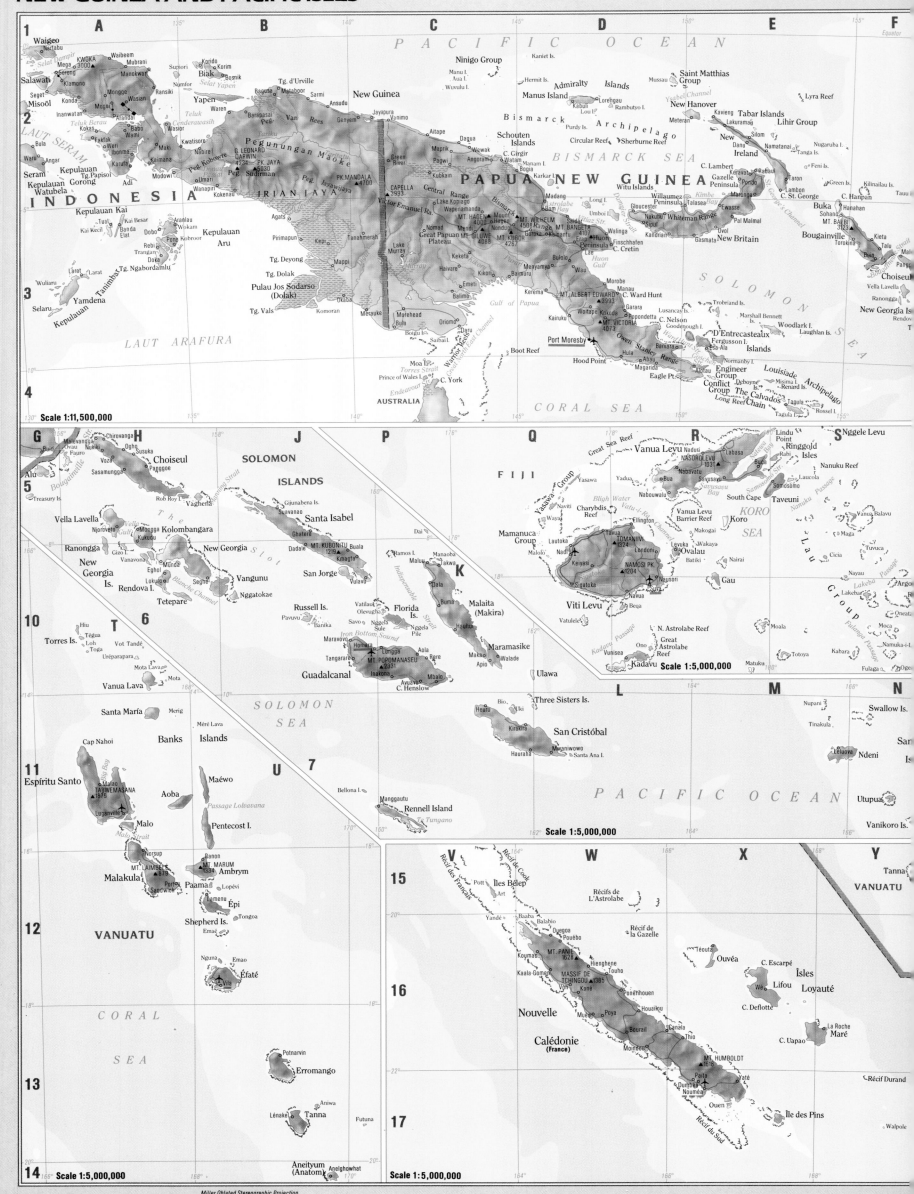

Scale 1:11,500,000

Miller Oblated Stereographic Projection

North Island

NEW
ZEALAND

South Island

TASMAN SEA

PACIFIC OCEAN

Auckland
Wellington
Christchurch
Dunedin

Stewart Island

Chatham I.
Chatham
Islands
Pitt I.

East of Greenwich

1:4,500,000

| 0 | 50 | 100 | 150 | 200 | 250 | 300 KILOMETRES |
| 0 | 50 | 100 | 150 | 200 STATUTE MILES |

Designed and produced by E.S.R.

NORTH AMERICA

Lambert Azimuthal Equal Area Projection

1:20,000,000

| 0 | 100 | 200 | 300 | 400 | 500 | 600 | 700 | 800 | 900 | 1000 KILOMETRES |

| 0 | 100 | 200 | 300 | 400 | 500 | 600 STATUTE MILES |

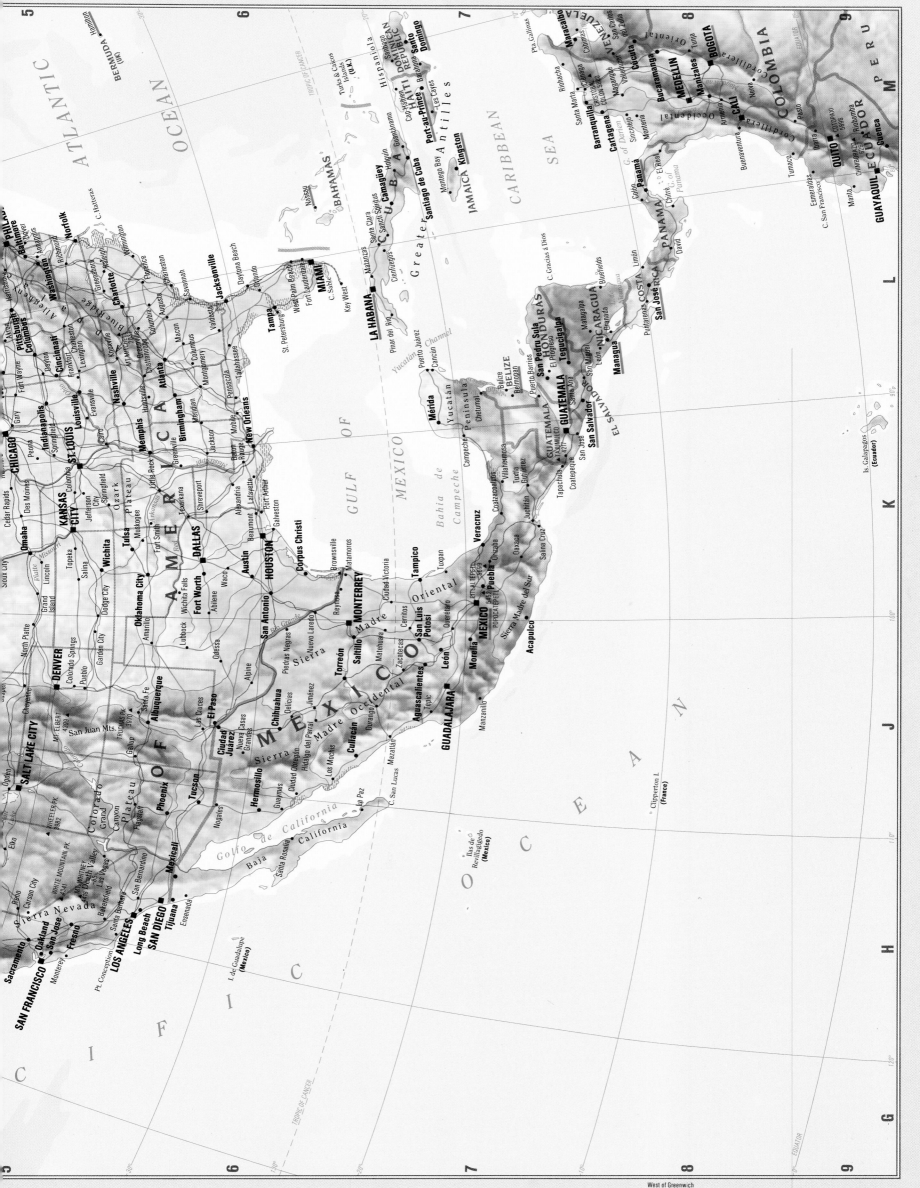

ATLANTIC OCEAN

BERMUDA (UK)
Hamilton

BAHAMAS
Nassau

Turks & Caicos Islands (U.K.)

Hispaniola
HAITI
DOMINICAN REPUBLIC
Santo Domingo
Port-au-Prince
Cap-Haïtien
Les Cayes

Greater Antilles

CUBA
La Habana
Santa Clara
Cienfuegos
Sancti Spíritus
Camagüey
Holguín
Santiago de Cuba
Guantánamo

JAMAICA
Kingston
Montego Bay

CARIBBEAN SEA

VENEZUELA
Maracaibo
Cabimas
Barquisimeto
Valencia
Maracay
CARACAS
San Carlos
San Cristóbal
Cumaná
Pta. Gallinas
Riohacha

COLOMBIA
Cordillera Oriental
Cúcuta
Bucaramanga
BOGOTÁ
MEDELLÍN
Manizales
Tunja
Barranquilla
Cartagena
Santa Marta
Sincelejo
Montería
CALI
Armenia
Ibagué
Neiva
Pasto
Buenaventura

PANAMA
Panamá
Colón
G. of Darien
G. of Panama
David
Chitré

COSTA RICA
San José
Puntarenas
Limón
C. Gracias á Dios

ECUADOR (Ecuador)
QUITO
Esmeraldas
Ibarra
Manta
GUAYAQUIL
Riobamba
Cuenca
C. San Francisco
Tumaco

PERU

EQUATOR
Is. Galápagos (Ecuador)

UNITED STATES OF AMERICA

PHILA.
Baltimore
Washington
Norfolk
Richmond
Dover
Annapolis
C. Hatteras
Wilmington
Raleigh
Greensboro
Charlotte
Blue Ridge
Florence
Columbia
Charleston
Savannah
Augusta
Macon
Columbus
Montgomery
Tallahassee
Jacksonville
Daytona Beach
Orlando
Valdosta
Pensacola
Mobile
Meridian
Jackson

Appalachians
Pittsburgh
Columbus
Cincinnati
Dayton
Frankfort
Lexington
Louisville
Evansville
Nashville
Knoxville
Chattanooga
Huntsville
Birmingham
Atlanta

CHICAGO
Gary
Fort Wayne
Indianapolis
Springfield
Peoria
ST. LOUIS
Cairo
Memphis
Little Rock
Ozark Plateau
Fort Smith
Muskogee
Tulsa
Wichita

KANSAS CITY
Topeka
Jefferson City
Columbia
Springfield
Des Moines
Cedar Rapids
Omaha
Lincoln
Sioux City

Grand Island
North Platte

Colorado Springs
Pueblo
DENVER
Cheyenne

SALT LAKE CITY
Ogden
Provo

Grand Canyon
Flagstaff
Phoenix
Tucson
Nogales
Mexicali
Tijuana
Ensenada

San Diego
Long Beach
LOS ANGELES
San Bernardino
Santa Barbara
Bakersfield
Fresno
San Jose
Oakland
SAN FRANCISCO
Sacramento
Monterey
Carson City
Reno
Elko

Sierra Nevada
Mt. Whitney 4418
Death Valley
Las Vegas
White Mountain Pk. 4341

Colorado Plateau
Wheeler Pk.

San Juan Mts.
Mt. Elbert 4399
Santa Fe
Albuquerque
Gallup
Las Cruces
El Paso
Ciudad Juárez
Nuevo Casas Grandes

Tucumcari 3971
Amarillo
Garden City
Dodge City
Lubbock
Wichita Falls
Abilene
Odessa
Alpine

Oklahoma City
DALLAS
Fort Worth
Waco
Austin
San Antonio
HOUSTON
Corpus Christi
Brownsville
Matamoros
Laredo
Nuevo Laredo
Piedras Negras

Fort Worth
Texarkana
Shreveport
Alexandria
Baton Rouge
Lafayette
Port Arthur
Beaumont
Galveston
New Orleans

MEXICO

Chihuahua
Delicias
Hidalgo del Parral
Jiménez
Torreón
Saltillo
MONTERREY
Reynosa
Ciudad Victoria

Sierra Madre Oriental
Sierra Madre Occidental

Hermosillo
Guaymas
Ciudad Obregón
Los Mochis
Culiacán
Durango
Mazatlán
Tepic
Zacatecas
Aguascalientes
San Luis Potosí
GUADALAJARA
León
Querétaro
Cerritos
Matehuala

MEXICO
Morelia
POPOCATÉPETL 5452
Puebla
Orizaba 5610
CITLALTÉPETL 5699
Acapulco
Sierra Madre del Sur
Oaxaca
Veracruz
Tampico
Tuxpan
Coatzacoalcos
Villahermosa
Tuxtla Gutiérrez
Salina Cruz
Juchitán

Gulf of California
Golfo de California
La Paz
Santa Rosalía
C. San Lucas

Baja California

GULF OF MEXICO
Bahía de Campeche
Yucatán Peninsula
Mérida
Campeche
Chetumal
Cancún
Puerto Juárez

TROPIC OF CANCER

MIAMI
Tampa
St. Petersburg
West Palm Beach
Fort Lauderdale
Key West
C. Sable

GUATEMALA
GUATEMALA
TAJUMULCO 4220
Santa Ana
San José
Coatepeque
Tapachula
Quetzaltenango

BELIZE
BELIZE
Belmopan

HONDURAS
San Pedro Sula
El Progreso
Puerto Barrios
Puerto Cortés

NICARAGUA
Managua
León
Matagalpa
Bluefields
Granada

EL SALVADOR
SAN SALVADOR
San Miguel

Tegucigalpa

PACIFIC OCEAN

Ilas de Revillagigedo (Mexico)

Clipperton I. (France)

West of Greenwich

Designed and produced by E.S.R.

ALASKA

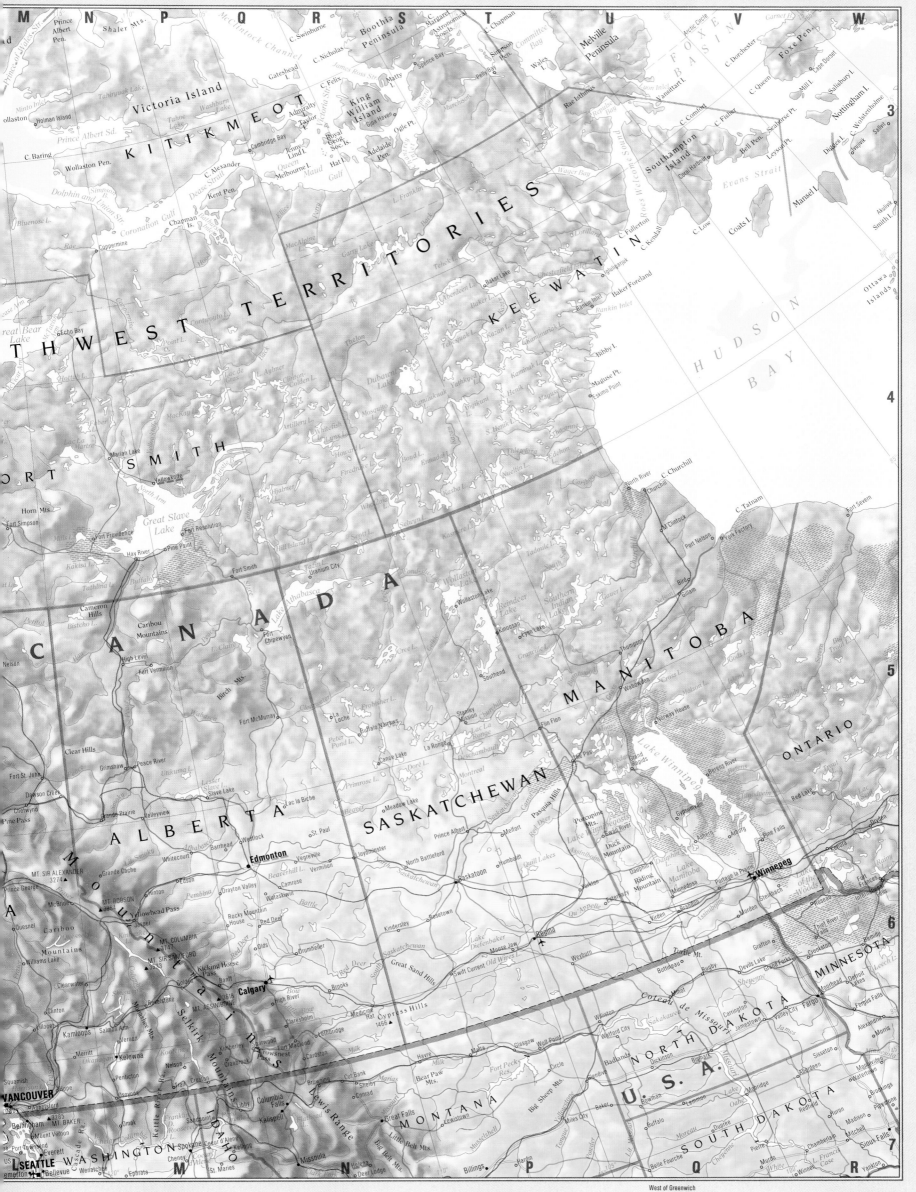

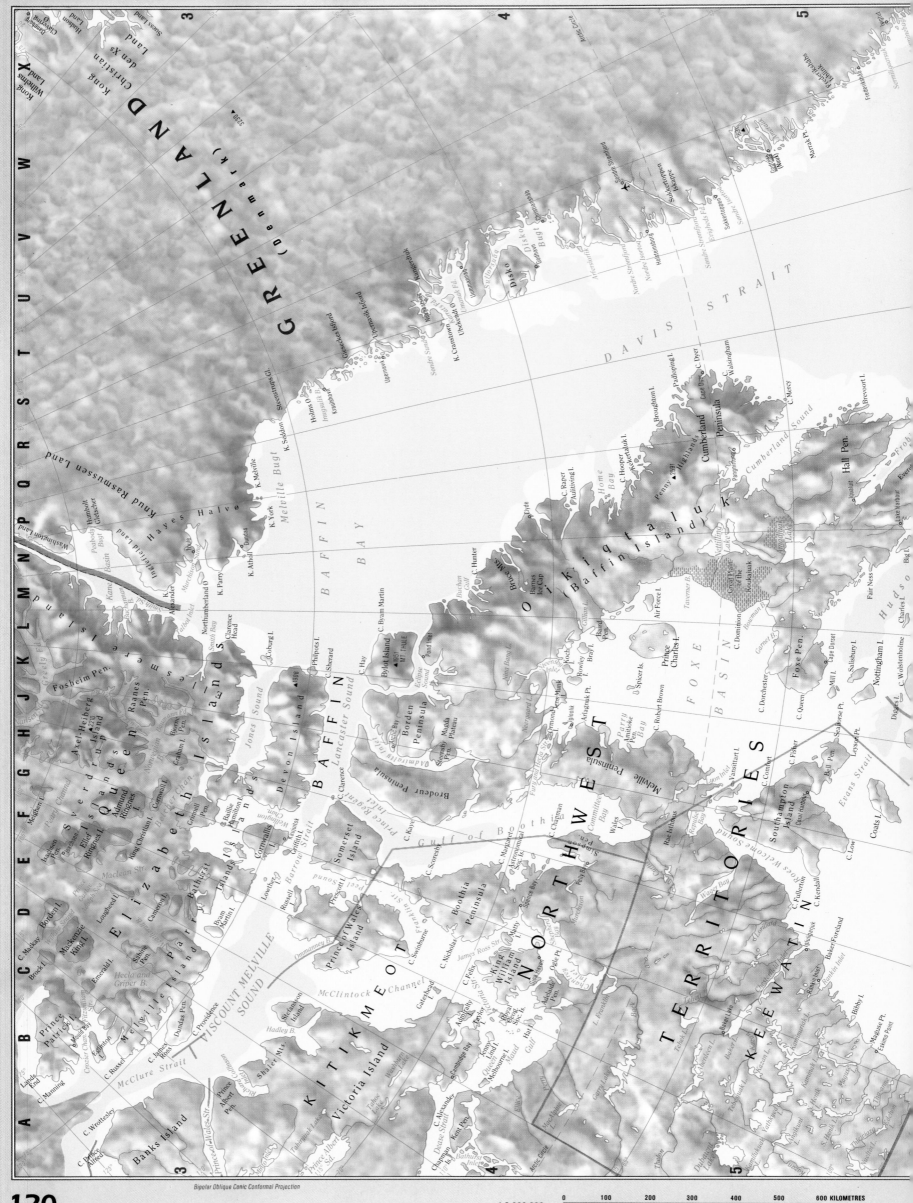

EASTERN CANADA

GREENLAND (Denmark)

Kong Wilhelms Land

Kong Christian den Xs Land

Knud Rasmussen Land

Hayes Halvø

Washington Land
Inglefield Land
Humboldt Gletscher
Peabody Bugt

Melville Bugt

BAFFIN BAY

DAVIS STRAIT

Disko Bugt

Disko

Arctic Circle

Godthåb (Nuuk)

Marrak Pt.

Cumberland Peninsula

Cumberland Sound

Hall Pen.

C. Mercy

Qikiqtaluk

Baffin Island

Foxe Basin

Foxe Peninsula

HUDSON

Ellesmere Island

Queen Elizabeth Islands

Devon Island

Lancaster Sound

Jones Sound

BAFFIN

Borden Peninsula

Brodeur Peninsula

Prince Regent Inlet

Melville Peninsula

Southampton Island

Roes Welcome Sound

Melville Island

Banks Island

Victoria Island

Prince Patrick I.

Mackenzie King I.

KITIKMEOT

VISCOUNT MELVILLE SOUND

McClintock Channel

Somerset Island

Prince of Wales Island

Boothia Peninsula

King William Island

Gulf of Boothia

NORTHWEST TERRITORIES

KEEWATIN

Bipolar Oblique Conic Conformal Projection

1:9,000,000

0 100 200 300 400 500 600 KILOMETRES

0 50 100 150 200 250 300 350 400 STATUTE MILES

© COLOUR LIBRARY BOOKS

Designed and produced by E.S.R.

Bipolar Oblique Conic Conformal Projection

1:5,000,000

| 0 | 50 | 100 | 150 | 200 | 250 | 300 | 350 | 400 KILOMETRES |

| 0 | 50 | 100 | 150 | 200 | 250 STATUTE M|

Designed and produced by E.S.R.

West of Greenwich

Bipolar Oblique Conic Conformal Projection

1:5,000,000

© COLOUR LIBRARY BOOKS

| 0 | 50 | 100 | 150 | 200 | 250 | 300 | 350 | 400 KILOMETRE |

| 0 | 50 | 100 | 150 | 200 | 250 STATUTE M |

125

SOUTHWEST UNITED STATES

© COLOUR LIBRARY BOOKS

1:5,000,000

| 0 | 50 | 100 | 150 | 200 | 250 | 300 | 350 | 400 KILOMETRES |
| 0 | | 50 | 100 | 150 | 200 | | 250 STATUTE MI |

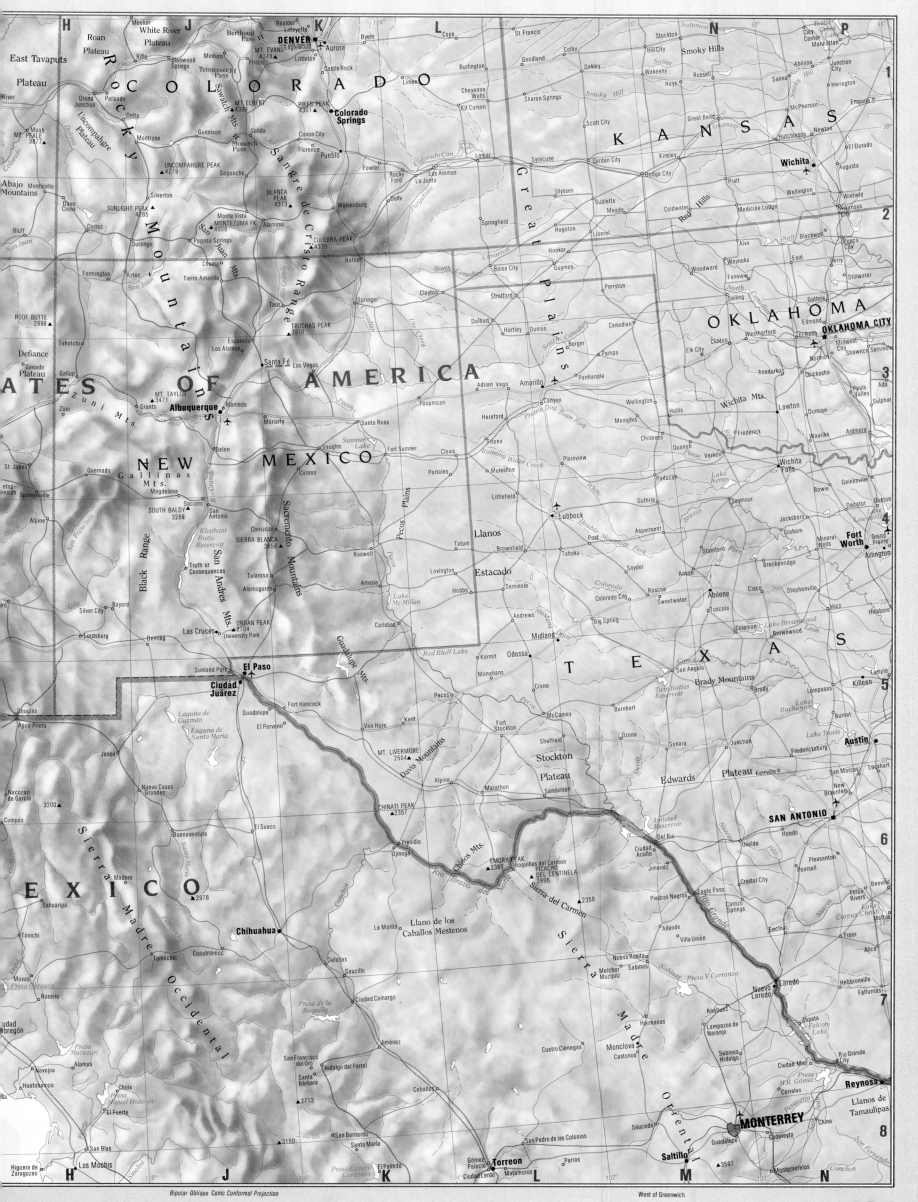

Bipolar Oblique Conic Conformal Projection

West of Greenwich

Designed and produced by E.S.R.

SOUTHEAST UNITED STATES

Bipolar Oblique Conic Conformal Projection

1:5,000,000

© COLOUR LIBRARY BOOKS

MEXICO

Tijuana
Mexicali
El Centro
National City
Pta. la Banda
Ensenada
Santo Tomas
C. Colonet
Sa. San Pedro Martir
CERRO DE LA ENCANTADA 3088
Pta. Estrella
San Felipe
El Rosario
Pta. Baja
Ba. de San Quentin
I. Cedros
Punta Prieta
Rosario
Guerrero Negro
I. Angel de la Guarda
I. Tiburón
I. San Lorenzo
Pta. San Gabriel
Ba. Sebastián Vizcaíno
Pta. Eugenia
Pta. San Pablo
Sierra Vizcaíno
Desierto de Vizcaíno
San Ignacio
Sta. Rosalia
VOLCAN LAS TRES VIRGENES 1996
I. San Marcos
Magdalena
Pta. Concepción
Ba. de Ballenas
San José de Gracia
Pta. San Juanico
Loreto
Ligui
I. Carmen
I. Sta. Catalína
I. Sta. Cruz
I. San José
Ejido Insurgentes
Llano de la Magdalena
Sierra de la Giganta
I. Magdalena
C. San Lázaro
PICO CÚPULA 1524
I. Espíritu Santo
I. Sta. Margarita
Ba. de la Paz
La Paz
San Pedro
Pta. Arena de las Ventas
I. Cerralvo
Todos Santos
Sa. de S. Lazaro 2046
Pta. Arena
San José del Cabo
San Lucas
Cabo San Lucas

PACIFIC OCEAN

Islas Revillagigedo (Mex.)
I. Clarión
I. Roca Partida
I. San Benedicto
I. Socorro

Tropic of Cancer

GOLFO DE CALIFORNIA

Sonoran Desert
Gran Desierto
Yuma
San Luis Rio Colorado
El Golfo de Santa Clara
Desemboque
San Felipe
Pto. Peñasco
Ba. de San Jorge
El Sahuaro
Puerto Libertad
Bahia Kino
Hermosillo
Guaymas
Cabo Haro
Empalme
Ciudad Obregón
Navojoa
Huatabampo
Los Mochis
Guasave
Isla de Altamura
Navolato
Culiacán
La Cruz
Mazatlán
Rosario
Acaponeta
Santiago Ixcuintla
Islas Marías
I. María Madre
I. María Magdalena
Tuxpan
Tepic
Compostela
Sayulita
Puerto Vallarta
Ba. de Banderas
Cabo Corrientes
Chamela
Pta. Farallón
Autlán
NEVADO DE COLIMA 4339
Manzanillo
Tecomán

ARIZONA
Gila Bend
Casa Grande
Globe
San Carlos L.
Safford
Eloy
Green Valley
Tuscon
Benson
Nogales
Nogales
Douglas
Agua Prieta
Sonoita
Imuris
Santa Ana
Cananea
Caborca
Cumpás
Nacozari de García
Aconchi
Ures
Sahuaripa
Tónichi
Movas
Rosarito
Onavas
La Cienaguita
Presa Obregón
Alamos
Chiox
El Fuerte
San Blas
Higuera de Zaragoza
Guamúchil
Venustiano Carranza
CERRO HUEHUENTO 3150
Durango
El Salto
Mezquital

Elephant Butte Res.
Truth or Consequences
Carrizozo
Roswell
Pecos
Lubbock
Tatum
Tularosa
Artesia
Lovington
Seminole
San Andres Mts.
ORGAN PK. 2704
NEW MEXICO
Deming
Las Cruces
Bayard
Lordsburg
L. McMillan
Hobbs
Big Spring
Carlsbad
El Paso
Ciudad Juárez
Red Bluff L.
Odessa
Midland
Fort Hancock
El Porvenir
Van Horn
Kent
McCamey
Pecos
Crane
Janos
La. de Sta. María
Laguna de Guzmán
MT. LIVERMORE 2554
Sheffield
Fort Stockton
Stockton Plateau
Nuevo Casas Grandes
Buenaventura
El Sueco
Alpine
Marathon
Sanderson
CHINATI PK. 2357
Madera
3200
2978
Cuauhtémoc
Chihuahua
Ojinaga
Presidio
Rio Bravo del Norte
EMORY PK. 2389
PICACHO DEL CENTINELA 2696
Boquillas del Carmen
Conchos
La Morita
Llano de los Caballos Mesteños
Sierra del Carmen
2358
Ciudad Camargo
Presa de la Boquilla
Jiménez
Melchor Muzquiz
San Francisco del Oro
Hidalgo del Parral
Cuatro Ciénegas
Castano
Ceballos
3150
San Bernardo
San Pedros de las Colonias
Gómez Palacio
Ciudad Lerdo
Torreón
Matamoros
El Palmito
Santiago Papasquiaro
Cuencamé
Guadalupe Victoria
Juan Aldama
San Tib
Vicente Guerrero
Río Grande
Sombrerete
MEX
Fresnillo
Valparaiso
Zacatecas
Jerez
Villanueva
Pabellón Arteaga
Aguascalientes
Tlaltenango
Jalpa
Sierra de los Huicholes
Jalostotitlán
Magdalena
Ixtlán
Tepatitlán
Atotonilco
GUADALAJARA
Ameca
Cocula
Zacoalco
Ocotlán
La Barca
Sehuayo
Zapotlanejo
Hidal
CERRO DES MORONADE 2740
Zacoalco
Laguna de Chapala
Zamo
Jiquilpan
Puréperi
Sayula
Ciudad Guzmán
Colima
VOLCAN EL PARICUTIN 2774
Apatzingán
Chihuatlán
Tuxpan
2764
Arteaga
Playa Azul

Tropic of Cancer

Bipolar Oblique Conic Conformal Projection

130

1:6,500,000

| 0 | 50 | 100 | 150 | 200 | 250 | 300 | 350 | 400 KILOMETRES |

| 0 | 50 | 100 | 150 | 200 | 250 STATUTE MILES |

© COLOUR LIBRARY BOOKS

GULF OF MEXICO

BAHÍA DE CAMPECHE

Yucatán

BELIZE

GUATEMALA

HONDURAS

DALLAS
Fort Worth
Irving
Garland
Greenville
Arlington
HOUSTON
Pasadena
SAN ANTONIO
Austin
Corpus Christi
McAllen
Reynosa
MONTERREY
Matamoros
Llanos de Tamaulipas
Tampico
Ciudad Madero
Querétaro
Puebla
Veracruz
CIUDAD DE MÉXICO
Toluca
Cuernavaca
Acapulco
Oaxaca
Villahermosa
Mérida
Campeche
GUATEMALA
San Pedro Sula

MISSISSIPPI
ALABAMA
GEORGIA
FLORIDA
LOUISIANA
Shreveport
Jackson
Mobile
Pensacola
Baton Rouge
NEW ORLEANS
Beaumont

131

CENTRAL AMERICA AND THE CARIBBEAN

Bipolar Oblique Conic Conformal Projection

© COLOUR LIBRARY BOOKS

1:7,000,000

0 50 100 150 200 250 300 350 400 KILOMETRES

0 50 100 150 200 250 STATUTE MILES

NORTH ATLANTIC OCEAN

CARIBBEAN SEA

Venezuela Basin

Lesser Antilles

Cayman Trench

JAMAICA
Kingston
Montego Bay

Cap-Haïtien
HAITI
Port-au-Prince
Les Cayes

DOMINICAN REPUBLIC
Santo Domingo
Santiago
Barahona

Puerto Rico (U.S.A.)
San Juan
Ponce

Virgin Is. (U.K.-U.S.A.)
St. Croix (U.S.A.)
ST. KITTS-NEVIS
ANTIGUA & BARBUDA
Montserrat (U.K.)
Guadeloupe (Fr.)
DOMINICA
Roseau
Martinique (Fr.)
Fort-de-France
ST. LUCIA
Castries
BARBADOS
Bridgetown
ST. VINCENT
Kingstown
GRENADA
St. George's
Windward Islands

Leeward Islands

Aruba (Neth.)
Curaçao (Neth.)

TRINIDAD & TOBAGO
Port of Spain

I. de Margarita (Ven.)

PANAMÁ
Panamá
Colón
Golfo de Panamá

Isla Malpelo (Col.)

ECUADOR
QUITO
COTOPAXI 5896
V. CHIMBORAZO
Cuenca
GUAYAQUIL
Golfo de Guayaquil
Manta
Esmeraldas
Equator

COLOMBIA
BOGOTÁ
MEDELLÍN
CALI
Manizales
Pereira
Ibagué
Armenia
Neiva
Pasto
Buenaventura
Cúcuta
Bucaramanga
Cordillera Occidental
Cordillera Central
Cordillera Oriental
Sincelejo
Montería
Golfo del Darién

VENEZUELA
CARACAS
Valencia
Maracaibo
Barquisimeto
Maracay
Los Teques
Guarenas
Cabimas
San Cristóbal
Mérida
Cord. de Mérida
Golfo de Venezuela
Punta Gallinas
Santa Marta
Barranquilla
Cartagena
Valledupar
Puerto Carreño
Barcelona
Cumaná
Maturín
Ciudad Bolívar
Ciudad Guayana
MT. RORAIMA 2810
Serra Pacaraima
Orinoco
Llanos

GUYANA
Georgetown

SURINAME
Paramaribo

FRENCH GUIANA (France)
Cayenne
Serra de Tumucumaque
Cabo Orange

PERÚ
LIMA
Callao
Trujillo
Chiclayo
Chimbote
Piura
Punta Aguja
Cuzco
Juliaca
Arequipa
Ica
NEVADO DE HUASCARÁN 6768
NEVADO DE AMPATO 6310
Huancayo
Pucallpa
Iquitos
Leticia
Cordillera de los Andes

BOLIVIA
La Paz
NEVADO DE ILLAMPÚ 6485
Trinidad
Riberalta
Cobija

BRAZIL
BRASÍLIA
BELÉM
FORTALEZA
RECIFE
SALVADOR
Manaus
São Luís
Teresina
Natal
C. de São Roque
João Pessoa
Olinda
Campina Grande
Maceió
Aracaju
Feira de Santana
Valença
Ilhéus
Vitória da Conquista
Propriá
Cadaxá
Mossoró
Itapipoca
Sobral
Juazeiro do Norte
Iguatú
Parnaíba
Floriano
Carolina
Barreiras
Barra
Ibotirama
Goiás
Goiânia
Anápolis
Rondonópolis
Cuiabá
Cachimbo
Vilhena
Pôrto Velho
Rio Branco
Cruzeiro do Sul
Tefé
Santarém
Macapá
Ilha de Marajó
Selvas
Planalto de Mato Grosso
Serra dos Parecis
Serra do Roncador
Campos
Montes Claros
Barragem de Sobradinho
São Francisco
Tocantins
Xingu
Tapajós
Teles Pires
Roosevelt
Madeira
Purús
Juruá
Negro
Amazonas

Equator

134

Bipolar Oblique Conic Conformal Projection

1:16,000,000

| 0 | 100 | 200 | 300 | 400 | 500 | 600 | 700 | 800 KILOMETRES |

| 0 | 100 | 200 | 300 | 400 | 500 STATUTE MILES |

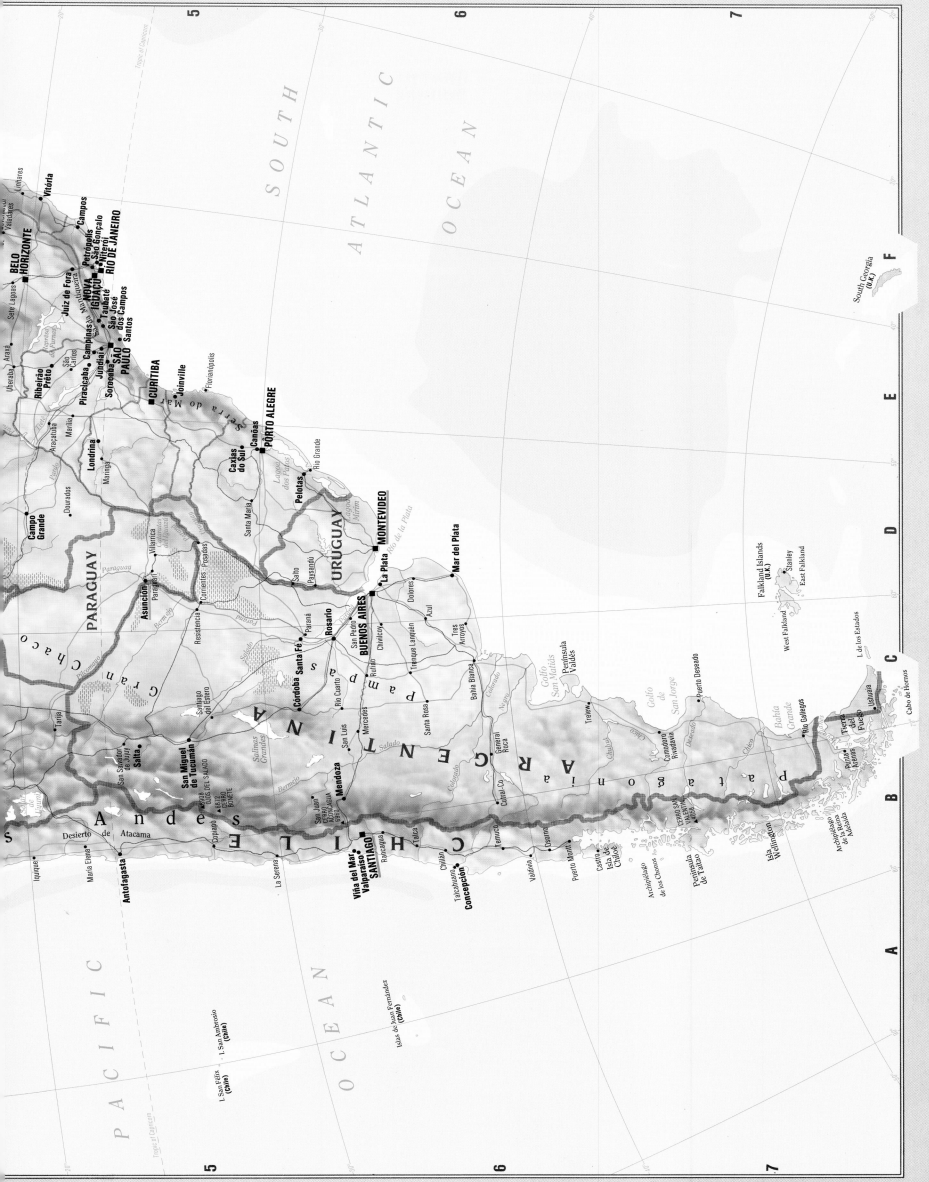

West of Greenwich

Designed and produced by E.S.R.

Bipolar Oblique Conic Conformal Projection

© COLOUR LIBRARY BOOKS

1:11,000,000

0   100   200   300   400   500   600   700   800 KILOMETRES
0   100   200   300   400   500 STATUTE MILES

NORTH ATLANTIC OCEAN

Paramaribo Nieuw Amsterdam
Totness Groningen Moengo Albina
                    Saint Iracoubo Sinnamary
Affobakka   Laurent Roura Cayenne
URINAME   FRENCH   Kaw Guisanbourg
        GUIANA Inini Cabo Orange
Pontoetoe   (France) Oiapoque Cabo Caciporé
Oranje Malavate Bienvenu Punta Grande
Gebergte Serra Lombarda Regina Ilha de Maracá
Kapiting Tumucumaque Serra Amapá
Serra   AMAPÁ
Merirumã Serra do Navio Ponta Grossa
Azuari   Pôrto Grande Mouths of
                            the Amazon
        Ilha Grande Macapá
Oriximiná do Gurupá Chaves
Óbidos Almeirim Soure Salinópolis
Juruti Monte Gurupá Ponta de Pedras Viana Capanema Curuça Tijoca
Alegre Curuá Melgaço Igarapé-Miri Ilha de Marajó BELÉM Viseu Ilhas de São João
Santarém Cametá Moju São José do Gurupi
Belterra Pombal Baião Abaetetuba Mocajuba Turiaçu Marassumé
Tauari Altamira Tucurui Cajapió Alcântara Tutóia Camocim Acaraú
PARÁ Areão Jacundá São Luís Rosário Araioses Paranaíba Itapipoca
Nova Carajari Marabá São João Viana Itapecuru Mirim FORTALEZA
Maranhão Sobrado do Araguaia Imperatriz Pimentel Chapadinha Piracuruca Tianguá Sobral Maranguape Cascavel
Tucuparé Carajás Cachoeira Guaribas Serra dos Carajás Bacabal Coroatá Miguel Alves Piripiri Jpu Baturité Punta da Maceió
São Félix Serra do Gurupi Codó Peritoró Pedreiras Campo Maior Crateús Russas Areia Branca
BRAZIL Serra das Graduais MARANHÃO Teresina Senador Pompeu Quixadá Limoeiro Mossoró Macau Touros
Serra Conceição do Araguaia São João Presidente Dutra RIO GRANDE Açu Pta. do Calcanhar
do Cachimbo do Araguaia Barra do Valença Picos CEARÁ DO NORTE Cabo de São Roque
Cachimbo Araguacema Corda Colinas PIAUÍ Pau dos Ferros Natal
Pau d' Arco Paranaidji Serra das Carolina Araras Floriano Varzea Grande Arneiroz Campos Sales Patu Currais Novos Canguaretama
Couto Magalhães Pastos Bons Oeiras Crato Juàzeiro Cajazeiras Patos Sta. Luzia Nova Cruz
Planalto do Loreto Flores do Norte Jaicós Chapada do Araripe PARAÍBA João Pessoa
Cachoeira Araguaina Uruçuí Eliseu Martins Simplicio Mendes Monteiro Campina Cabo Branco
Von Martius Pedro Afonso Paulistana São João do Piauí Oricuri Grande Goiana
Apiacás Miracema do Norte Bom Jesus São Raimundo Nonato Parnamirim Parnamirim Olinda
dos Gaúchos Lizardo Serra do Piauí Rajada Cabrobó Caruaru RECIFE
Campo de Diauarum Gilbues Redenção Nova Remanso Petrolina PERNAMBUCO Vitória de Jaboatão
Mato Grosso Cristalândia Barra Juàzeiro Nova Sento Sé Uauá Canudos Sta. Antão Palmares
GROSSO Pôrto Nacional Formosa do Rio Prêto Xique-Xique Pão de Açucar ALAGOAS União dos Palmares
Campo de Diauarum Natividade Serra da Piranhas Propriá Maceió
Serra do Roncador Peixe Tabatinga Irecê Senhor do Bonfim Euclides da Cunha Japaratuba São Miguel dos Campos
Mato Grosso Alvorada Barreiras Capixaba Jacobina Queimadas SERGIPE Pontal do Manguinha
Nobres Taguatinga Angical Morpara Morro do Chapéu Tucano Ribeira do Pombal Aracaju
Pedra San Miguel Arraias Santana BAHIA Ipupiara Mundo Novo Serrinha Estância
do Araguaia Alto Araguaia São Domingos Ibotirama Andaraí Itaberaba Riachão do Jacuípe Inhambupe
Cuiabá Ceres Riacho de Santana Bom Jesus da Lapa Palmeiras Ipirá Alagoinhas
Poconé GOIÁS Cavalcante Macaúbas Nazaré Castro Feira de Santana
Guiratinga Iporá Goiás Uruaçu Carinhanha Manga Novo Acre Alves Santo Amaro
Rondonópolis DISTRITO Niquelândia Cocos Caetité Jequié Cachoeira SALVADOR
Anhumas Caiapônia Paraúna FEDERAL Sítio da Abadia Brumado Valença I. de Tinharé
Alto Araguaia Itaberaí BRASÍLIA Urandi Condeúba Ubaitaba I. Boipeba
Alto Coité Inhumas 1678 Formosa Januária Monte Azul Vitória da Ponta do Mutá
MATO GROSSO Leopoldo Bulhões Conquista Cabo Tromba Grande
Alto Sucuriú GOIÂNIA Brasília Barrocão Una Itabuna
DO SUL Hidrolândia Cristalina Bocaiúva Pedra Azul Itapetinga Ilhéus
Rio Verde Paracatu Piraporu Rio Pardo de Minas Salto da Divisa
Morrinhos Pirapora Montes Claros Araçuaí Itambé Ponta Santo Antônio
Itumbiara Canoeiros MINAS Capelinha Jequitinhonha Pôrto Seguro
Araguari Coromandel Corinto Diamantina Seiro Chagas Caravelas Ponta da Baleia
Uberlândia Patos de Minas GERAIS PICO DE ITAMBÉ Teófilo Otôni Helvécia
Patrocinio Abaeté 2040 Guanhães Governador
Três Marias Curvelo ESPÍRITO SANTO
Ituiutaba Prata Valadares Serra dos Aimorés São Mateus

Equator

West of Greenwich

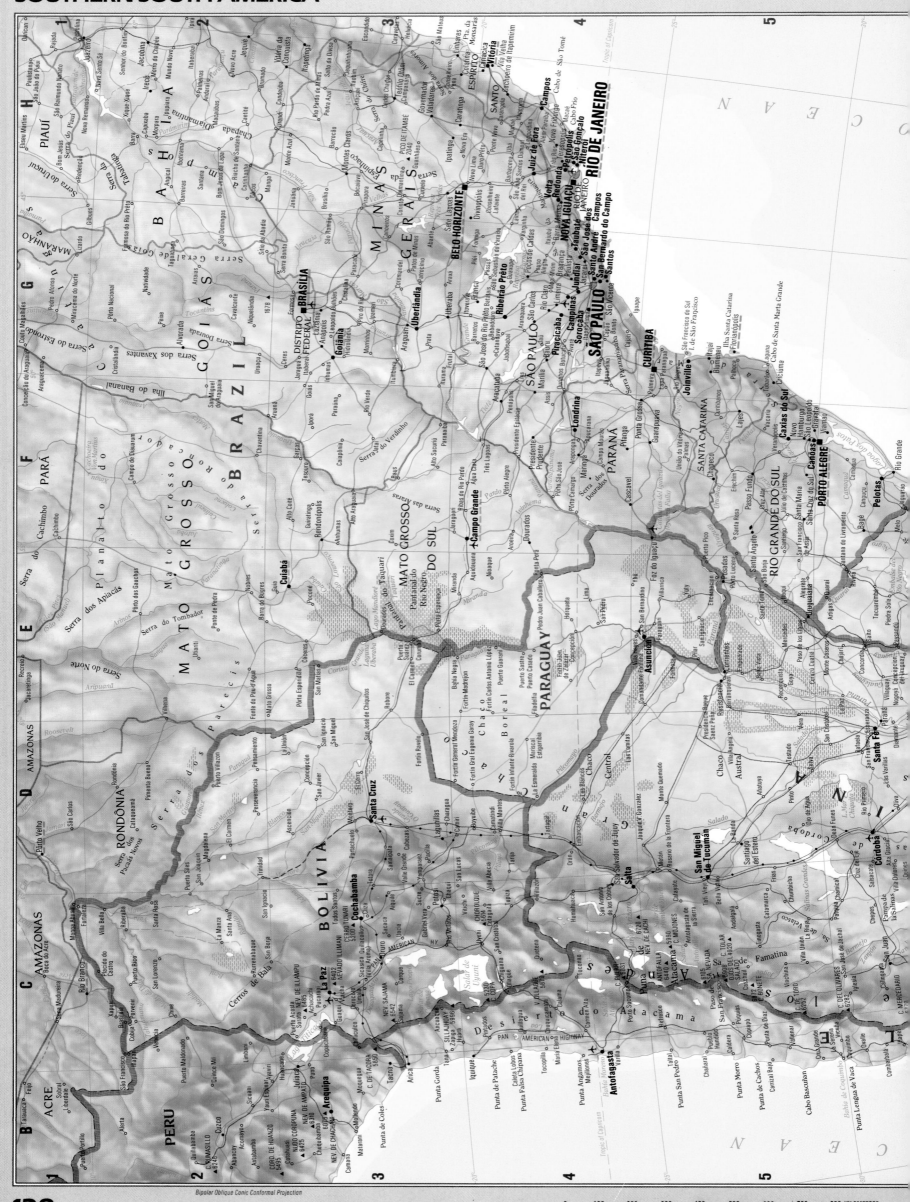

Bipolar Oblique Conic Conformal Projection

1:11,000,000

| 0 | 100 | 200 | 300 | 400 | 500 | 600 | 700 | 800 KILOMETRES |

| 0 | 100 | 200 | 300 | 400 | 500 STATUTE MILES |

© COLOUR LIBRARY BOOKS

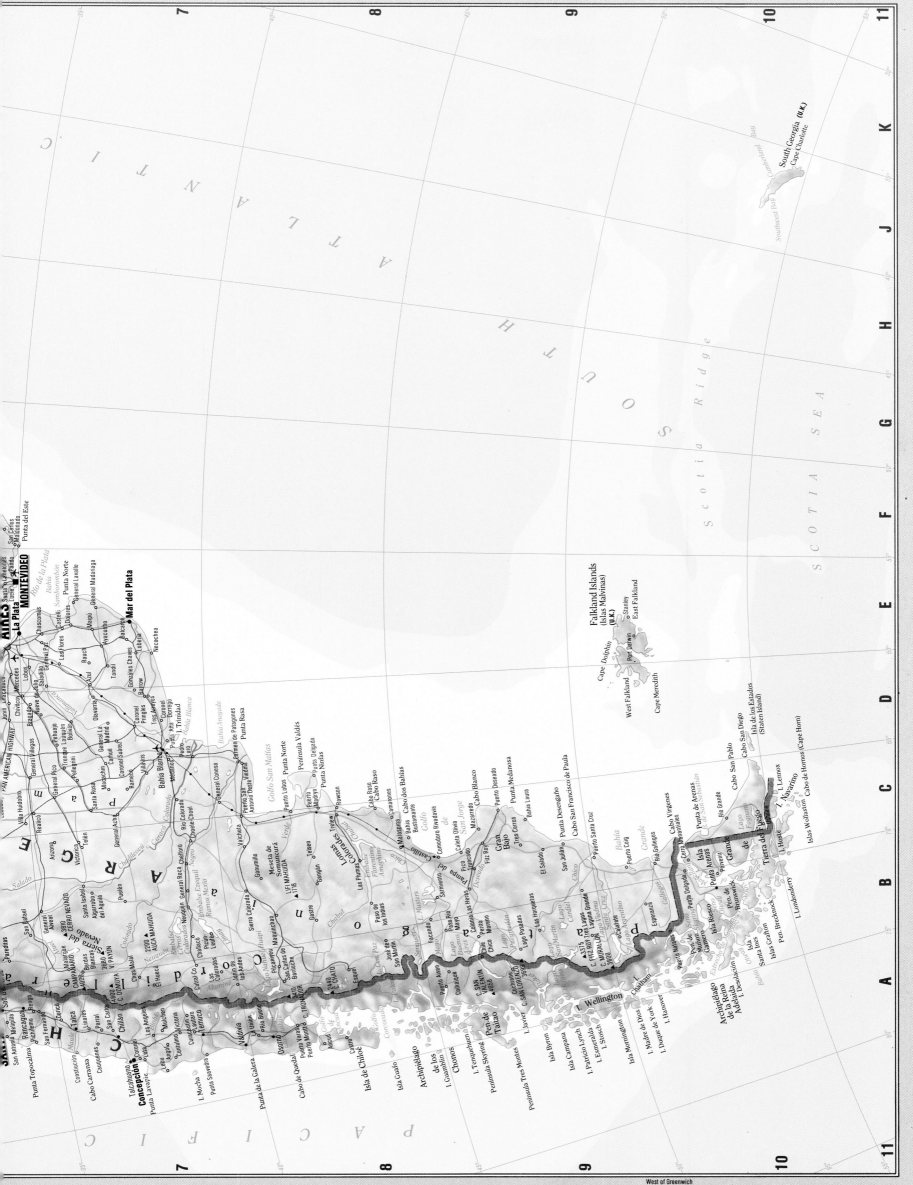

South Georgia (U.K.)
Cape Charlotte
Cumberland Bay
Southwest Bay

ATLANTIC
SOUTH
OCEAN

SCOTIA SEA
Scotia Ridge

Falkland Islands
(Islas Malvinas)
(U.K.)

Cape Dolphin
Stanley
East Falkland
West Falkland
Port Darwin
Cape Meredith

MONTEVIDEO
La Plata
Mar del Plata

San Carlos
Maldonado
Punta del Este
Sauce
Rocha
Lazcano
Bahía
Samborombón
Punta Norte
Río de la Plata
General Lavalle
Dolores
Castelli
Chascomús
General Madariaga
Maipú
Saladillo
General Belgrano
Las Flores
Ayacucho
Rauch
Azul
Tandil
Balcarce
Cobijar
Gonzáles Chaves
Barrow
Necochea
Tres Arroyos
Coronel
Pringles
Coronel
Dorrego
I. Trinidad
Punta Alta
Bahía Blanca
Coronel Suárez
Bahía Anegada
Carmen de Patagones
Punta Rasa
Viedma
Bahía Blanca
San Antonio Oeste
Península Valdés
Golfo San Matías
Punta Norte
Puerto Lobos
Punta Delgada
Puerto Madryn
Punta Ninfas
Rawson
Trelew
Golfo Nuevo

Cabo Raso
Cabo dos Bahías
Camarones
Bahía
Bustamante
Comodoro Rivadavia
Caleta Olivia
Golfo
San Jorge
Cabo Blanco
Puerto Deseado
Punta Medanosa
Bahía Laura
Puerto Santa Cruz
Bahía
Grande
Punta San Francisco de Paula
Río Gallegos
Cabo Vírgenes
Punta de Arenas
B. de San Sebastián
Isla
Grande
de
Tierra del Fuego
Cabo San Pablo
Cabo San Diego
Isla de los Estados
(Staten Island)
I. Lennox
I. Navarino
I. Hoste
Islas Wollaston
Cabo de Hornos (Cape Horn)

Concepción
Talcahuano
Chillán
San Antonio
Punta Topocalma
Constitución
Cabo Carranza
Punta Lavapié
I. Mocha
Punta de la Galera
Valdivia
Puerto Montt
Puerto Varas
Ancud
Castro
Isla de Chiloé
Cabo de Quedal
Isla Guafo
Archipiélago
de los
Chonos
I. Guamblín
Pen. de
Taitao
I. Tenquehuén
Península Tres Montes
Isla Byron
I. Patricio Lynch
I. Campana
I. Esmeralda
I. Stosch
I. Madre de Dios
I. Duque de York
I. Hanover
Wellington
I. Chatham
Archipiélago
de la Reina
Adelaida
I. Javier
Pen. de
Brunswick
Isla
Riesco
Punta Arenas
Estrecho de Magallanes
Pen. de
Muñoz
Gamero
Isla Santa Inés
Islas Clarence
Isla
Desolación
Pen. Brecknock
I. Londonderry

PAN AMERICAN HIGHWAY

West of Greenwich

139

Polar Stereographic Projection

Scale 1:30,000,000 (Approx.)

© COLOUR LIBRARY BOOKS

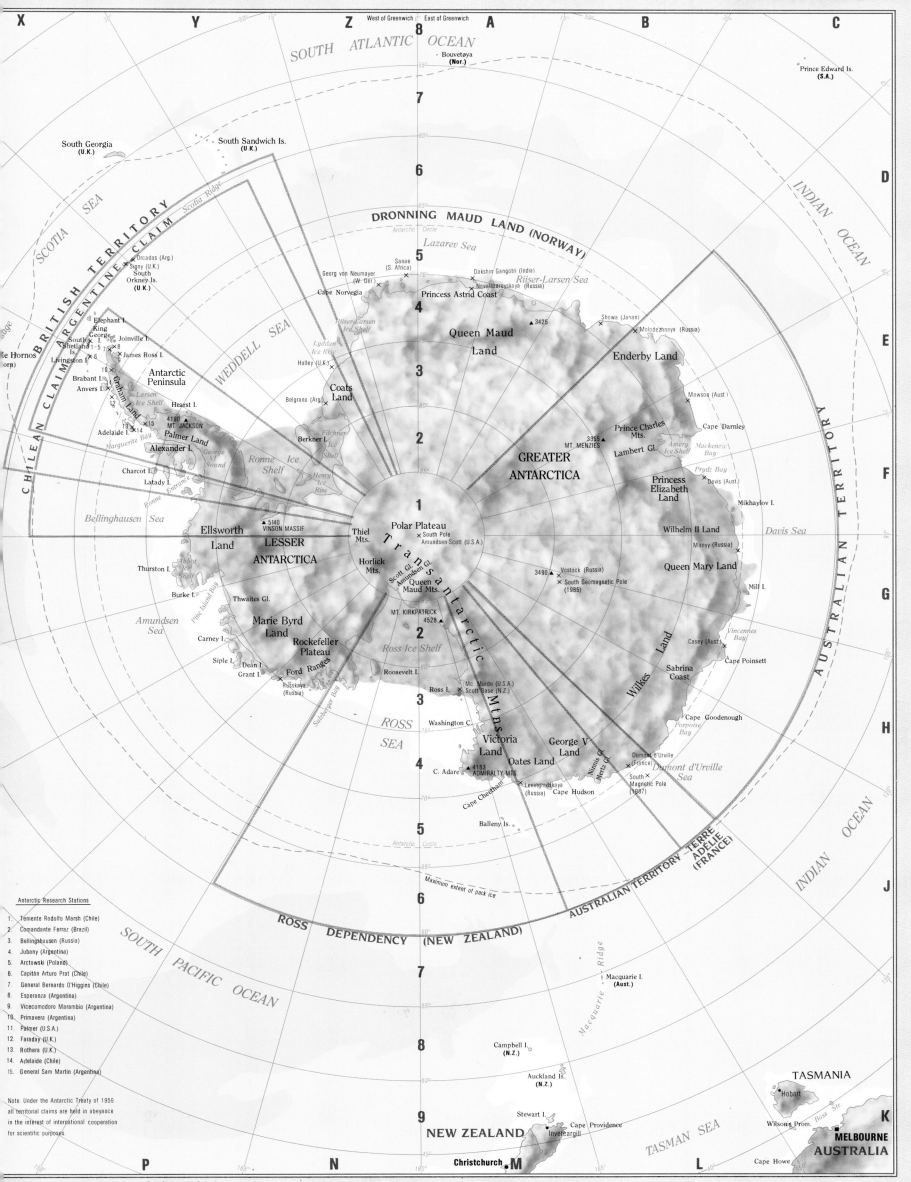

THE WORLD

A B C D E F

1

GREENLAND
(Denmark)

Svalbard
(Norway)

Zemlya Frantsa-Iosifa
(U.S.S.R.)

Severnaya Zemlya

Novosibirskiye O

More
Laptevykh

Lyakhovskiye
Ostrova

Ko

2

Jan Mayen
(Norway)

Nordkapp

Barentsevo
More

Karskoye
More

Novaya
Zemlya

Poluostrov
Yamal

Gydanskiy
Poluostrov

Plato
Putorana

Gory

Byrranga

Sredne

Verkhoyanskiy

Khrebet Cherskogo

Denmark Strait

Norwegian
Sea

Arctic Circle

ICELAND

Reykjavík

Føroyar
(Denmark)

Shetland Is.
(U.K.)

Lappland

SWEDEN

NORWAY

FINLAND

Helsingfors

Oslo   Stockholm

Tallinn

ST. PETERSBURG

København

ESTONIA

LATVIA

LITH.

Rīga

Vilnius

MOSKVA

Ozero
Ladozhskoye

Beloye
More

Pechora

Ural'skiy Khrebet

Sukhona

Zapadno

Sibirskaya

Ravnina

RUSSIA

Sibirskoye

Ploskogor'ye

Vilyuy

Khrebet

Okhotsk
More

Sakhalin

Kolyma

Yenisey

Sikhote Alin'

Kuril'skiy

3

NORTH

ATLANTIC

OCEAN

UNITED
KINGDOM

Dublin

IRELAND

LONDON

NETH.
Amsterdam

's Gravenhage

BEL.
Bruxelles

GERMANY

Berlin

POLAND

Warszawa

CZECH
REP.

Praha

SLOVAK
REP.

Bratislava

AUST.

Wien

HUNG.

Budapest

Kyyiv
(Kiev)

BELARUS

Minsk

UKRAINE

Dnjepr

MOLDOVA

Chisinau
(Kishinev)

Prikaspiyskaya
Nizmennost'

Kirgiz
Step'

Aral'skoye

KAZAKHSTAN

Ozero Balkhash

Irtysh

Ozero Baykal

Altai

MONGOLIA

Ulaanbaatar

Gobi

BEIJING

TIANJIN

N. KOREA

Pyŏngyang

S. KOREA

SŎUL

Sea of
Japan

JAPAN

TŌKYŌ

LUX.

FRANCE

PARIS

Bern

SWITZ.

AND.

CROAT.

SLOV.

Beograd

BOS.-
HERZ.

YUGO.

ROM.

Bucuresti

BULG.

Sofiya

MACE.

ALB.

Tirane

Roma

Madrid

SPAIN

PORTUGAL

Lisboa

Açores
(Port.)

Madeira
(Port.)

Ilas Canarias
(Sp.)

GREECE

Athínai

Ankara

TURKEY

GEORGIA

T'bilisi

ARMENIA

Yerevan

EL'BRUS
▲5642

Black Sea

Caspian
Sea

AZER.

Baku

TURKMENISTAN

Ashgabat

Tashkent

UZBEKISTAN

Kyzylkum

Bishkek

Alma-Ata

KYRGYZSTAN

Dushanbe

TAJIK.

Tyan Shan

Karakumy

Tarim
Pendi

▲154

Kunlun Shan

Taklimakan
Shamo

Xizang
Gaoyuan

CHINA

SHANGHAI

Huang
Hai

Chang Jiang

Huang He

Tai-pei

TAIWAN

HONG KONG
(U.K.)

4

Mediterranean

Rabat

MOROCCO

El Djazair

Tunis

TUNISIA

Valletta

MALTA

Tarābulus

Sea

CYPRUS

Levkosia

SYRIA

LEB.

Bayrūt

Dimashq

IRAQ

Baghdad

Amman

JOR.

El Qâhira

ISRAEL

Yerushalayim

▼-133

TEHRĀN

ye Zagros

Kūhhā

IRAN

AFGHANISTAN

Kābul

Hindu Kush

Islamabad

PAKISTAN

New
Delhi

DELHI

Thar
Desert

NEPAL

Kathmandu

EVEREST

Himalaya

BHU.

Thimpu

8848▲

BANG.

Dhaka

MYANMAR

Hanoi

LAOS

Viangchan

THAI-
LAND

KRUNG THEP

CAM.

Phnom Penh

VIETNAM

Nan Hai

MANILA

Luzon

PHILIPPINES

Mindanao

Marianas
Is.

Guam (U.S.A.)

Caroline Islands

M

WESTERN
SAHARA

Al Aaiun

ALGERIA

Atlas Mountains

Tropic of Cancer

LIBYA

Hoggar

Sahara

Tibesti

EGYPT

Nil

SAUDI
ARABIA

Ar Riyâd

Al Kuwayt

KUW.

Al Manamah

BAH.

QAT.

Ad Dawhah

Abu Zabi

U.A.E.

Masqat

OMAN

Red Sea

Arabian
Sea

KARACHI

BOMBAY

Deccan

INDIA

CALCUTTA

MADRAS

Bay of
Bengal

Lakshadweep
(India)

Andaman
Islands
(India)

Colombo

SRI LANKA

MALAYSIA

Kuala Lumpur

SINGAPORE

Sumatera

BRU.

Bandar Seri
Begawan

Borneo

Sulawesi

Maluku

5

CAPE
VERDE

Praia

Dakar

THE
GAMBIA

Banjul

GUINEA-
BISSAU

Bissau

SEN.

MALI

Nouakchott

MAURITANIA

Bamako

BUR.
FASO

Ouagadougou

Niamey

NIGER

CHAD

N'djaména

L. Chad

NIGERIA

El Khartum

SUDAN

ERITREA

Asmera

San'a

YEMEN

Suqutrā
(S. Yem.)

DJIB.

Adis Abeba

ETHIOPIA

SOMALIA

Muqdisho

Malé

MALDIVES

Laut
Timor

Timor

Java Trench

JAKARTA

Jawa

East Indies

INDONESIA

Laut Arafura

PAPUA
NEW
GUINEA

New
Guinea

Gt.

GUINEA

Conakry

SIERRA LEONE

Freetown

Monrovia

LIBERIA

IVORY
COAST

Yamoussoukro

GH.

Accra

Lomé

Porto Novo

Lagos

Libreville

GABON

EQ. GUINEA

Malabo

Yaoundé

CAMEROON

SÃO TOMÉ
AND PRÍNCIPE

Bangui

CENTRAL
AFRICAN REP.

Brazzaville

Kinshasa

Congo
Basin

ZAIRE

UGANDA

Kampala

RW.

Kigali

Bujumbura

BU.

5895▲

Nairobi

KENYA

Dodoma

TANZANIA

KILIMANJARO

Victoria

Victoria

SEYCHELLES

COMOROS

Moroni

Ascension
(U.K.)

Luanda

Equator

ANGOLA

ZAMBIA

Lusaka

Lilongwe

MAL.

Harare

ZIMBABWE

MOZAMBIQUE

Mozambique Channel

MADAGASCAR

Antananarivo

Réunion
(Fr.)

Port Louis

MAURITIUS

INDIAN OCEAN

AUSTRALIA

L. Eyre

Gt. Victoria Desert

C. Leeuwin

St. Helena
(U.K.)

Ilha da Trindade
(Brazil)

SOUTH

ATLANTIC

OCEAN

Tropic of Capricorn

NAMIBIA

Windhoek

BOTSWANA

Gaborone

Kalahari

Orange

Pretoria

Mbabne

Maputo

SWAZILAND

SOUTH
AFRICA

Maseru

LESOTHO

Cape of Good Hope

Tristan da Cunha
(U.K.)

Gough I.
(U.K.)

6

Canberra

Tasmania

Iles Crozet
(Fr.)

Prince Edward Is.
(S.A.)

Ile Kerguelen
(Fr.)

Heard I.
(Aus.)

South
Sandwich Is.
(U.K.)

A B C D E F

Mercator Projection

1:85,000,000 (Scale at the Equator)

© COLOUR LIBRARY BOOKS

G　East of Greenwich　West of Greenwich　H　J　K　L　M

ARCTIC OCEAN

Lincoln Sea

Queen
Elizabeth
Islands

Ellesmere
Island

Kane
Basin

1

tochno
irskoye
tore

Banks
Island

Viscount Melville
Sound

Baffin Bay

GREENLAND
(Denmark)

Ostrov Vrangelya

Chucki
Sea

Pt. Barrow

Beaufort Sea

Amundsen
Gulf

Victoria Island

Oikiqtaluk

Denmark Strait

2

rebet Kolymskiy

Brooks Range

ALASKA
(U.S.A)
Yukon

Mackenzie Mts.

Great Bear Lake

Foxe
Basin

Arctic Circle

McKINLEY
6194 ▲
Alaska Range

Rock

Great Slave Lake

Hudson Str.

Reykjavik
ICELAND

Bering
Sea

Gulf of Alaska

Kodiak I.

L. Athabasca

Reindeer Lake

Hudson Bay

Labrador Sea

Kap Farvel

60°

3

Aleutian　Islands

Aleutian Trench

Vancouver I.

CANADA

L. Winnipeg

*Great
Lakes*

Labrador

Newfoundland

NORTH
PACIFIC
OCEAN

NORTH
ATLANTIC
OCEAN

Açores
(Port.)

Columbia

Great
Plains

Missouri

Ottawa
St. Lawrence

**UNITED STATES
OF
AMERICA**

Gt. Salt Lake

SAN FRANCISCO

CHICAGO
Appalachian Mts.
NEW YORK
PHILADELPHIA
Washington

30°

LOS ANGELES

Mississippi

Bermuda
(U.K.)

Hawaiian

Isla de
Guadalupe
(Mex.)

Rio Grande

Gulf of Mexico

BAHAMAS
Nassau

Tropic of Cancer

4

Islands

HAWAII
(U.S.A.)

Islas de Revillagigedo
(Mex.)

MEXICO
**CIUDAD DE
MÉXICO**

La Habana
CUBA

West Indies

DOMINICAN REP.

**CAPE
VERDE**

Belmopan
BELIZE
HONDURAS
GUATEMALA
Guatemala
San Salvador
EL SALVADOR
Managua
San José
COSTA RICA

Port au Prince
HAITI
Kingston
JAMAICA
Tegucigalpa
NICARAGUA
Panamá
PANAMA

Puerto Rico(U.S.A)
Santo Domingo

Leeward Is.

BARBADOS
Windward Is.
**TRINIDAD
AND TOBAGO**

Praia

Caribbean Sea

Caracas
VENEZUELA
Bogotá
COLOMBIA
Orinoco

Georgetown
GUY-
Paramaribo
SUR
Cayenne
FRENCH GUIANA

Marshall Is.

P
o
l
y
n

Line
Islands

Christmas I.

Quito
EQUADOR

Equator
0°

5

NAURU
Tarawa
Gilbert
Is.

Phoenix Is.

KIRIBATI

Islas Galápagos
(Ecuador)

Negro

Amazon

Isla Fernando
de Noronha
(Brazil)

e
s
i
a

Iles Marquises
(Fr.)

PERU

BRAZIL
Planalto do
Mato Grosso

ON ISLANDS
ara
Santa
Cruz
Is.
TUVALU
Fanafuti

SAMOA
W.
Apia
SAMOA
(U.S.A.)
Iles Wallice
(Fr.)

French Polynesia
(Fr.)

SOUTH
PACIFIC
OCEAN

LIMA

Cordillera

Brasília

Ilha da Trindade
(Brazil)

UATU
Vila
FIJI
Suva

TONGA
Nuku'alofa
Tonga
Trench

Tahiti
Iles
Société

Iles Tuamotu

Iles de la

Iles Gambier

Pitcairn I.
(U.K.) Ducie I.
(U.K.)

Isla de Pascua
(Easter I.)
(Chile)

La Paz
BOLIVIA
Salar de
Uyuni

PARAGUAY
Asunción

SÃO PAULO
RÍO DE JANEIRO

Tropic of Capricorn

de

los

Paraná

Normanke Trench

Islas Juan
Fernández
(Chile)

ACONCAGUA
6960
Santiago

ARGENTINA
Buenos Aires

URUGUAY
Montevideo

30°

6

an Sea
W ZEALAND
Wellington

Chatham Is.
(N.Z.)

Andes

Patagonia

Chile Trench

SOUTH
ATLANTIC
OCEAN

Auckland Is.
(N.Z.)

arie Is.
us.)

Falkland Is.
(U.K.)

South Georgia
(U.K.)

South
Sandwich
Is. (U.K.)

Cabo de Hornos

Scotia Sea

G　H　180°　J　150°　K　120°　L　90°　M　60°　30°

GLOSSARY AND ABBREVIATIONS

Language abbreviations in glossary

Afr	Afrikaans	*Dut*	Dutch	*I-C*	Indo-Chinese	*Mal*	Malay	*S-C*	Serbo-Croat
Alb	Albanian	*Fin*	Finnish	*Ice*	Icelandic	*Mlg*	Malagasy	*Som*	Somali
Ar	Arabic	*Fr*	French	*Ind*	Indonesian	*Mon*	Mongolian	*Sp*	Spanish
Ber	Berber	*Gae*	Gaelic	*It*	Italian	*Nor*	Norwegian	*Swe*	Swedish
Bul	Bulgarian	*Ger*	German	*Jap*	Japanese	*Per*	Persian	*Th*	Thai
Bur	Burmese	*Gr*	Greek	*Khm*	Khmer	*Pol*	Polish	*Tib*	Tibetan
Ch	Chinese	*Heb*	Hebrew	*Kor*	Korean	*Por*	Portuguese	*Tu*	Turkish
Cz	Czech	*Hin*	Hindi	*Lao*	Laotian	*Rom*	Romanian	*Vt*	Vietnamese
Dan	Danish	*Hun*	Hungarian	*Lat*	Latvian	*Rus*	Russian	*Wel*	Welsh

Glossary

A

Abar (*Ar*) – wells
Abyar (*Ar*) – wells
Adasi (*Tu*) – island
Adrar (*Ber*) – mountains
Ain (*Ar*) – spring, well
Akra (*Gr*) – cape, point
Alb (*Ger*) – mountains
Alpen (*Ger*) – mountains
Alpes (*Fr*) – mountains
Alpi (*It*) – mountains
Alto (*Por*) – high
-alv (*Swe*) – river
-alven (*Swe*) – river
Appenino (*It*) – mountain range
Aqabat (*Ar*) – pass
Archipielago (*Sp*) – archipelago
Arquipielago (*Por*) – archipelago
Arrecife (*Sp*) – reef
Ayia (*Gr*) – saint
Ayios (*Gr*) – saint
Ayn (*Ar*) – spring, well

B

Bab (*Ar*) – strait
Bad (*Ger*) – spa
Badiyah (*Ar*) – desert
Bælt (*Dan*) – strait
Baharu (*Mal*) – new
Bahia (*Sp*) – bay
Bahr (*Ar*) – bay, canal, lake, stream
Bahrat (*Ar*) – lake
Baia (*Por*) – bay
Baie (*Fr*) – bay
Baja (*Sp*) – lower
Ban (*Khm, Lao, Th*) – village
-bana (*Jap*) – cape, point
Banco (*Sp*) – bank
-bandao (*Ch*) – peninsula
Bandar (*Per*) – bay
Baraji (*Tu*) – reservoir
Barqa (*Ar*) – hill
Barragem (*Por*) – reservoir
Bassin (*Fr*) – basin, bay
Batin (*Ar*) – depression
Beinn (*Gae*) – mountain
Beloyy (*Rus*) – white
Ben (*Gae*) – mountain
Bereg (*Rus*) – bank, shore
Berg (*Ger*) – mountain
Berge (*Afr*) – mountains
Bheinn (*Gae*) – mountain
Biar (*Ar*) – wells
Bir (*Ar*) – well
Bi'r (*Ar*) – well
Birkat (*Ar*) – well
Birket (*Ar*) – well
Boca (*Sp*) – river mouth
Bocche (*It*) – mouths, estuary
Bodden (*Ger*) – bay
Bogazi (*Tu*) – strait
Boka (*S-C*) – gulf, inlet
Bol'shoy (*Rus*) – big
Bol'shoye (*Rus*) – big
Bory (*Pol*) – forest
Bratul (*Rom*) – river channel
Bucht (*Ger*) – bay
Bugt (*Dan*) – bay
Buhayrat (*Ar*) – lagoon, lake
Bukit (*Mal*) – hill, mountain
Bukt (*Nor*) – bay
Bulak (*Rus*) – spring
Burnu (*Tu*) – cape, point
Burun (*Tu*) – cape, point
Busen (*Ger*) – bay
Buyuk (*Tu*) – big

C

Cabo (*Por, Sp*) – cape, point
Cachoeira (*Sp*) – waterfall
Cap (*Fr*) – cape, point
Campos (*Sp*) – upland
Cao Nguyen (*Th*) – plateau, tableland
Cataratas (*Sp*) – waterfall
Cayi (*Tu*) – stream
Cayo (*Sp*) – islet, rock
Cerro (*Sp*) – hill
Chaco (*Sp*) – jungle
Chaine (*Fr*) – mountain chain
Chapada (*Por*) – hills
Ch'eng (*Ch*) – town
Chiang (*Ch*) – river
Chiang (*Th*) – town
Chott (*Ar*) – marsh, salt lake
Chute (*Fr*) – waterfall
Cienaga (*Sp*) – marshy lake
Ciudad (*Sp*) – city, town
Co (*Tib*) – lake
Col (*Fr*) – pass
Colinas (*Sp*) – hills
Cordillera (*Sp*) – mountain range
Costa (*Sp*) – coast, shore
Cote (*Fr*) – coast, slope
Coteau (*Fr*) – hill, slope
Coxilha (*Por*) – mountain pasture
Cuchillas (*Sp*) – hills

D

Dag (*Tu*) – mountain
Dagi (*Tu*) – mountain
Daglari (*Tu*) – mountains
-dake (*Jap*) – peak
-dal (*Nor*) – valley
Dao (*Ch*) – island
Darreh (*Per*) – valley
Daryacheh (*Per*) – lake
Dasht (*Per*) – desert
Denizi (*Tu*) – sea
Desierto (*Sp*) – desert
Djebel (*Ar*) – mountain
-djik (*Dut*) – dyke
Do (*Kor, Jap, Vt*) – island
Dolina (*Rus*) – valley
Dolok (*Ind*) – mountain
Dolna (*Bul*) – lower
Dolni (*Cz*) – lower
-dong (*Kor*) – village
-dorp (*Afr*) – village
Dur (*Ar*) – mountains

E

Eiland (*Dut*) – island
Eilanden (*Dut*) – islands
-elva (*Nor*) – river
Embalse (*Sp*) – reservoir
Erg (*Ar*) – sandy desert
Estero (*Sp*) – bay, estuary, inlet
Estrecho (*Sp*) – strait
Etang (*Fr*) – lagoon, pond
Ezers (*Lat*) – lake

F

Feng (*Ch*) – mountain, peak
Fels (*Ger*) – rock
Firth (*Gae*) – estuary
-fjall (*Swe*) – mountains
Fjeld (*Dan*) – mountain
-fjell (*Nor*) – mountain
-floi (*Ice*) – bay
-fjoraur (*Ice*) – fjord
Forde (*Ger*) – inlet
Foret (*Fr*) – forest
-foss (*Ice*) – waterfall

G

-gan (*Jap*) – rock
Gang (*Ch*) – harbour
Ganga (*Hin*) – river
Gata (*Jap*) – inlet, lagoon
Gave (*Fr*) – torrent
Gebel (*Ar*) – mountain
Gebirge (*Ger*) – mountains
Ghat (*Hin*) – range of hills
Ghubbat (*Ar*) – bay
Glen (*Gae*) – valley
Gletscher (*Ger*) – glacier
Gobi (*Mon*) – desert
Golfe (*Fr*) – bay, gulf
Golfo (*It, Sp*) – bay, gulf
Golu (*Tu*) – lake
Gora (*Bul*) – forest
Gora (*Pol, Rus*) – mountain
-gorod (*Rus*) – small town
Gory (*Pol, Rus*) – mountains
Grada (*Rus*) – mountain range
Grad (*Bul, Rus, S-C*) – city, town
Gross (*Ger*) – big
Gryada (*Rus*) – ridge
Guba (*Rus*) – bay
-gunto (*Jap*) – island group
Gunung (*Ind, Mal*) – mountain

H

Hadh (*Ar*) – sand dunes
Hafen (*Ger*) – harbour, port
Haff (*Ger*) – bay, lagoon
Hai (*Ch*) – sea
Haixia (*Ch*) – strait
-holm (*Dan*) – island
Halvo (*Dan*) – peninsula
-hama (*Jap*) – beach
-hamar (*Ice*) – mountain
Hamada (*Ar*) – plateau
Hammadah (*Ar*) – plain, stony desert
Hamun (*Per*) – marsh
-hanto (*Jap*) – peninsula
Harrat (*Ar*) – lava field
Hav (*Swe*) – gulf
Havet (*Nor*) – sea
-havn (*Dan, Nor*) – harbour
Hawr (*Ar*) – lake
He (*Ch*) – river
Heide (*Ger*) – heath, moor
-hisar (*Tu*) – castle
Ho (*Ch*) – river
Hohe (*Ger*) – hills
Horn (*Ger*) – peak, summit
Hu (*Ch*) – lake
-huk (*Swe*) – cape, point

I

Idd (*Ar*) – well
Idhan (*Ar*) – sand dunes
Ile (*Fr*) – island
Iles (*Fr*) – islands
Ilha (*Por*) – island
Ilhas (*Por*) – islands
Insel (*Ger*) – island
Inseln (*Ger*) – islands
Irq (*Ar*) – sand dunes
Irmak (*Tu*) – large river
Isfjord (*Dan*) – glacier
Iskappe (*Dan*) – icecap
Isla (*Sp*) – island
Islas (*Sp*) – islands
Isola (*It*) – island
Isole (*It*) – islands
Istmo (*Sp*) – isthmus

J

Jabal (*Ar*) – mountain
-jarvi (*Fin*) – lake
Jaza 'ir (*Ar*) – islands
Jazirat (*Ar*) – island
Jazovir (*Bul*) – reservoir
Jbel (*Ar*) – mountain
Jebel (*Ar*) – mountain
Jezero (*Alb, S-C*) – lake
Jezioro (*Pol*) – lagoon, lake
Jezirat (*Ar*) – island
-jiang (*Ch*) – river
Jibal (*Ar*) – mountain
Jiddat (*Ar*) – gravel plain
-jima (*Jap*) – island
-joki (*Fin*) – river
-jokull (*Ice*) – glacier

K

Kaap (*Afr*) – cape, point
-kai (*Jap*) – bay, sea
-kaikyo (*Jap*) – strait
Kanaal (*Dut*) – canal
Kap (*Ger*) – cape, point
-kapp (*Nor*) – cape, point
Kas (*Khm*) – island
Kavir (*Per*) – desert
-kawa (*Jap*) – river
Kenet (*Alb*) – inlet
Kep (*Alb*) – cape, point
Kepulauan (*Ind*) – archipelago, islands
Kereb (*Ar*) – hill, ridge
Khalij (*Ar*) – bay, gulf
Khawr (*Ar*) – wadi
Khrebet (*Ru*) – mountain range
Kiang (*Ch*) – river
Klein (*Afr, Ger*) – small
Ko (*Th*) – island
-ko (*Jap*) – inlet, lake
Koh (*Khm*) – island
Kolpos (*Gr*) – gulf
Kolymskoye (*Rus*) – mountain range
Korfezi (*Tu*) – bay, gulf
Kosa (*Rus*) – spit
Kotlina (*Cz, Pol*) – basin, depression
Kraj (*Cz, Pol, S-C*) – region
Krasnyy (*Rus*) – red
Kray (*Rus*) – region
Kreis (*Ger*) – district
Kryazh (*Rus*) – mountains
Kucuk (*Tu*) – small
Kuh (*Per*) – mountain
Kuhha (*Per*) – mountains
Kum (*Rus*) – sandy desert
Kyst (*Dan*) – coast
Kyun (*Bur*) – island
Kyunzu (*Bur*) – islands

L

La (*Tib*) – pass
Lac (*Fr*) – lake
Lacul (*Rom*) – lake
Laem (*Th*) – point
Lago (*It, Por, Sp*) – lake
Lagoa (*Por*) – lagoon
Laguna (*Sp*) – lagoon, lake
Lam (*Th*) – stream
Lande (*Fr*) – heath, sandy moor
Laut (*Ind*) – sea
Ling (*Ch*) – mountain range
Liman (*Rus*) – bay, gulf
Limni (*Gr*) – lagoon, lake
Llano (*Sp*) – plain, prairie
Llanos (*Sp*) – plains, prairies

J

Llyn (*Wel*) – lake
Loch (*Gae*) – lake
Lough (*Gae*) – lake

M

Mae Nam (*Th*) – river
Mala (*S-C*) – small
Malaya (*Rus*) – small
Male (*Cz*) – small
Maloye (*Rus*) – small
Malyy (*Rus*) – small
Mar (*Por, Sp*) – sea
Mare (*It*) – sea
Masirah (*Ar*) – channel
Massif (*Fr*) – mountains
Mato (*Por*) – forest
Meer (*Afr, Dut, Ger*) – lake, sea
Menor (*Por, Sp*) – lesser, smaller
Mer (*Fr*) – sea
Mesa (*Sp*) – tableland
Minami (*Jap*) – south
-misaki (*Jap*) – cape, point
Mont (*Fr*) – mountain
Montagna (*It*) – mountain
Montagne (*Fr*) – mountain
Montagnes (*Fr*) – mountains
Montana (*Sp*) – mountain
Montanas (*Sp*) – mountains
Monte (*It, Por, Sp*) – mountain
Monti (*It*) – mountains
More (*Rus*) – sea
Mull (*Gae*) – cape, point, promontory
Munkhafad (*Ar*) – depression
Muntii (*Rom*) – mountains
Mynydd (*Wel*) – mountain
Mys (*Rus*) – cape, point

N

-nada (*Jap*) – gulf, sea
Nadrz (*Cz*) – reservoir
Nafud (*Ar*) – desert, dune
Nagor'ye (*Rus*) – highland, uplands
Nagy- (*Hun*) – great
Nahr (*Ar*) – river
Namakzar (*Per*) – desert, salt flat
Nei (*Ch*) – inner
Ness (*Gae*) – cape, promontory
Neu (*Ger*) – new
Nevada (*Sp*) – snow capped mountains
Nevado (*Sp*) – mountain
Ngoc (*Vt*) – mountain peak
-nisi (*Gr*) – island
Nisoi (*Gr*) – islands
Nisos (*Gr*) – island
Nizhnyaya (*Rus*) – lower
Nizina (*Pol*) – depression, lowland
Nizmennost' (*Rus*) – lowland
Noord (*Dut*) – north
Nord (*Dan, Fr, Ger*) – north
Norte (*Por, Sp*) – north
Nos (*Bul, Rus*) – point, spit
Nosy (*Mlg*) – island
Nova (*Bul*) – new
Nova (*Cz*) – new
Novaya (*Rus*) – new
Nove (*Cz*) – new
Novi (*Bul*) – new
Nudo (*Sp*) – mountain
Nuruu (*Mon*) – mountain range
Nuur (*Mon*) – lake

O

Ø (*Dan*) – island
Oblast' (*Rus*) – province

144

Occidental (*Fr, Rom, Sp*) – western
Oki (*Jap*) – bay
-oog (*Ger*) – island
Ojo (*Sp*) – spring
Orasul (*Rom*) – city
Ori (*Gr*) – mountains
Oriental (*Fr, Rom, Sp*) – eastern
Ormos (*Gr*) – bay
Oros (*Gr*) – island
Ort (*Ger*) – cape, point
Ostrov (*Rus*) – island
Ostrova (*Rus*) – islands
Otok (*S-C*) – island
Otoki (*S-C*) – islands
Ouadi (*Ar*) – wadi, dry watercourse
Oued (*Ar*) – dry river bed, wadi
Ovasi (*Tu*) – plain
Ozero (*Rus*) – lake

P

Pampa (*Sp*) – plain
Paniai (*Ind*) – lake
Paso (*Sp*) – pass
Passage (*Fr*) – pass
Passo (*It*) – pass
Pasul (*Rom*) – pass
Pelagos (*Gr*) – sea
Pendi (*Ch*) – basin
Pengunungnan (*Ind*) – mountain range
Peninsola (*It*) – peninsula
Peninsule (*Fr*) – peninsula
Pereval (*Rus*) – pass
Peski (*Rus*) – desert, sands
Phnom (*Khm*) – hill, mountain
Phu (*Vt*) – mountain
Pic (*Fr*) – peak
Picacho (*Sp*) – peak
Pico (*Sp*) – peak
Pik (*Rus*) – peak
Pingyuan (*Ch*) – plain
Pizzo (*It*) – peak
Planalto (*Por*) – plateau
Plana (*S-C, Sp*) – plain
Planina (*Bul, S-C*) – mountains
Plato (*Afr, Bul, Rus*) – plateau
Ploskogor'ye (*Rus*) – plateau
Ploskogorje (*Rus*) – plateau
Poco (*Ind*) – peak

Pohorie (*Cz*) – mountain range
Pointe (*Fr*) – cape, point
Pojezierze (*Pol*) – plateau
Poluostrov (*Rus*) – peninsula
Polwysep (*Pol*) – peninsula
Ponta (*Por*) – cape, point
Presa (*Sp*) – reservoir
Proliv (*Sp*) – strait
Pueblo (*Sp*) – village
Puerto (*Sp*) – harbour, pass
Pulau (*Ind, Mal*) – island
Puna (*Sp*) – desert plateau
Puncak (*Ind*) – peak
Punta (*It, Sp*) – cape, point
Puy (*Fr*) – peak

Q

Qalamat (*Ar*) – well
Qalib (*Ar*) – well
Qararat (*Ar*) – depression
Qolleh (*Per*) – mountain
Qornet (*Ar*) – peak
Qundao (*Ch*) – archipelago

R

Ramlat (*Ar*) – dunes
Ra's (*Ar, Per*) – cape, point
Ras (*Ar*) – cape, point
Rass (*Som*) – cape, point
Ravnina (*Rus*) – plain
Recife (*Por*) – reef
Represa (*Por*) – dam
Reshteh (*Per*) – mountain range
-retto (*Jap*) – island chain
Rijeka (*S-C*) – river
Rio (*Por, Sp*) – river
Riviere (*Fr*) – river
Rt (*S-C*) – cape, point
Rubha (*Gae*) – cape, point
Ruck (*Ger*) – mountain
Rucken (*Ger*) – ridge
Rud (*Per*) – river
Rudohorie (*Cz*) – mountains
Rzeka (*Pol*) – river

S

Sabkhat (*Ar*) – salt flat
Sagar (*Hin*) – lake
Sahara (*Ar*) – desert

Sahl (*Ar*) – plain
Sahra (*Ar*) – desert
Sa'id (*Ar*) – highland
-saki (*Jap*) – cape, point
Salar (*Sp*) – salt pan
Salina (*Sp*) – salt pan
San (*Sp*) – saint
-san (*Jap*) – mountain
-sanchi (*Jap*) – mountainous area
Sankt (*Ger, Swe*) – saint
-sanmyaku (*Jap*) – mountain range
Santa (*Por*) – saint
Sao (*Por*) – saint
Sar (*Kur*) – mountain
Satu (*Rom*) – village
Sawqirah (*Ar*) – bay
Se (*I-C*) – river
See (*Ger*) – lake
-sehir (*Tu*) – town
Selat (*Ind*) – channel, strait
-selka (*Fin*) – bay
Selva (*Sp*) – forest
Serra (*Por*) – mountain range
Serrania (*Sp*) – mountains
-seto (*Jap*) – channel, strait
Severnaya (*Rus*) – southern
Sfintu (*Rom*) – saint
Shamo (*Ch*) – desert
Shan (*Ch*) – mountains
Shandi (*Ch*) – mountainous area
Shatt (*Ar*) – river mouth, river
-shima (*Jap*) – islands
Shiqqat (*Ar*) – interdune trough
-shoto (*Jap*) – group of islands
Sierra (*Sp*) – mountain range
Sint (*Afr, Dut*) – saint
Slieve (*Gae*) – range of hills
So (*Dan, Nor*) – lake
Soder- (*Swe*) – southern
Sondre (*Dan, Nor*) – southern
Song (*Vt*) – river
Spitze (*Ger*) – peak
Sredne (*Rus*) – middle
Stadt (*Ger*) – town
Stara (*Cz*) – old
Staraya (*Rus*) – old
Stenon (*Gr*) – strait, pass
Step' (*Rus*) – plain, steppe
Strelka (*Rus*) – spit
Stretto (*It*) – strait

-suido (*Jap*) – channel, strait
Sund (*Swe*) – sound, strait
Szent- (*Hun*) – saint

T

-take (*Jap*) – peak
Tall (*Ar*) – hill
Tallat (*Ar*) – hills
Tanggula (*Tib*) – pass
Tanjong (*Ind, Mal*) – cape, point
Tanjon'i (*Mlg*) – cape, point
Tanjung (*Ind, Mal*) – cape, point
Tao (*Ch*) – island
Taraq (*Ar*) – hills
Tassili (*Ber*) – rocky plateau
Tau (*Rus*) – mountains
Taung (*Bur*) – mountain, south
Tekojarvi (*Fin*) – reservoir
Tell (*Ar*) – hill
Teluk (*Ind*) – bay
Tenere (*Fr*) – desert
Terre (*Fr*) – land
Thale (*Th*) – lake
Thamad (*Ar*) – well
Tirat (*Ar*) – canal
Tjarn (*Swe*) – lake
Tso (*Tib*) – lake
Tonle (*Khm*) – lake
Tutul (*Ar*) – hills

U

Ujung (*Ind*) – cape, point
-ura (*Jap*) – inlet
Urayq (*Ar*) – sand ridge
Uruq (*Ar*) – dunes
Ust (*Rus*) – river mouth
Uul (*Mon*) – mountain

V

Valea (*Rom*) – valley
-varos (*Hun*) – town
-varre (*Nor*) – mountain
-vatten (*Swe*) – lake
Vaux (*Fr*) – valleys
Velika (*S-C*) – big
Velikaya (*Rus*) – big
Verkhne (*Rus*) – upper
-vesi (*Fin*) – lake, water
Ville (*Fr*) – town
Vinh (*Vt*) – bay

Virful (*Rom*) – peak
Vodokhranilishche (*Rus*) – reservoir
Volcan (*Sp*) – volcano
Vorota (*Rus*) – strait
Vostochnyy (*Rus*) – eastern
Vozvyshennost' (*Rus*) hills, upland
Vpadina (*Rus*) – depression

W

Wadi (*Ar*) – river, stream
Wahat (*Ar*) – oasis
Wai (*Ch*) – outer
Wald (*Ger*) – forest
Wan (*Ch*) – bay
Wasser (*Ger*) – lake, water
Wenz (*Ar*) – river
Wielka (*Pol*) – big

X

Xan (*Ch*) – strait
Xi (*Ch*) – stream, west
Xia (*Ch*) – gorge, lower
Xian (*Ch*) – county
Xiao (*Ch*) – small
Xu (*Ch*) – island

Y

Yam (*Heb*) – lake
-yama (*Jap*) – mountain
Yarimadasi (*Tu*) – peninsula
Yazovir (*Bul*) – reservoir
Ye (*Bur*) – island
Yoma (*Bur*) – mountain range
Yugo- (*Rus*) – southern
Yuzhnyy (*Rus*) – southern

Z

Zaki (*Jap*) – cape, point
Zalew (*Pol*) – bay, inlet
Zaliv (*Rus*) – bay
-zan (*Jap*) – mountain
Zapadno (*Rus*) – western
Zatoka (*Pol*) – bay
Zee (*Dut*) – sea
Zemiya (*Rus*) – island, land
-zhen (*Ch*) – town

Abbreviations

A

A. – Alp, Alpen, Alpi
Akr. – Akra
And. – Andorra
Arch. – Archipelago
Arr. – Arrecife
Aust. – Australia
Ay. – Ayios

B

B. – Bahia, Baia, Baie, Bay, Bucht, Bukt
Ba. – Bahia
Bang. – Bangladesh
Bah. – Bahrain
Bel. – Belgium
Ben. – Benin
Bg. – Berg
Bhu. – Bhutan
Bk. – Bukit
Bol. – Bol'shoy, Bol'shoye
Bos. – Bosnia-Herzegovina
Br. – Burnu, Burun
Bru. – Brunei
Bt. – Bukit
Bu. – Burundi
Bü. – Büyük
Bulg. – Bulgaria
Bur. Faso – Burkina Faso

C

C. – Cabo, Cap, Cape, Cerro
Cam. – Cambodia
Can. – Canal, Canale
Cga. – Cienaga
Chan. – Channel
Co. – Cerro
Col. – Columbia
Cord. – Cordillera
Cr. – Creek
Czech. – Czech Rep.

D

D. – Dag, Dagi, Daglari, Daryacheh
D.C. – District of Columbia
Den. – Denmark
Djib. – Djibouti

E

E. – East
Eq. – Equatorial
Est. – Estrecho

F

Fd. – Fjord
Fk. – Fork
Fr. – France
Ft. – Fort

G

G. – Golfe, Golfo, Guba, Gulf, Gora, Gunung
Gd. – Grand
Gde – Grande
Geb. – Gebirge
Gen. – General
Geog. – Geographical
Ger. – Germany
Gh. – Ghana
Gl. – Glacier
Gr. – Grande, Gross
Gt. – Great
Guy. – Guyana

H

Har. – Harbor
Hd. – Head
Hung. – Hungary

I

I. – Ile, Ilha, Insel, Isla, Island, Isle, Isola, Isole

Is. – Ilhas, Iles, Islands, Islas, Isles
Isth. – Isthmus

J

J. – Jabal, Jbel, Jebel, Jezioro, Jezero, Jazair
Jor. – Jordan

K

K. – Kap, Kuh, Kuhha, Koh, Kolpos
Kan. – Kanal, Kanaal
Kep. – Kepulauan
Khr. – Khrebet
Kör. – Körfezi
Kuw. – Kuwait

L

L. – Lac, Lacul, Lago, Lake, Limni, Llyn, Loch, Lough
Lag. – Lagoon, Laguna
Leb. – Lebanon
Liech. – Liechtenstein
Lit. – Little
Lux. – Luxembourg

M

M. – Mys
Mal. – Malawi
Mex. – Mexico
Mgne. – Montagne
Mt. – Mont, Mount, Mountain
Mti. – Monti
Mtii. – Muntii
Mts. – Monts, Mounts, Mountains

N

N. – Nord, North, Nos
Neb.– Nebraska
Neth. – Netherlands

Nev. – Nevado
N.H. – New Hampshire
Nizh. – Nizhnyaya
Nizm. – Nizmennost
Nor. – Norway
N.Z. – New Zealand

O

O. – Ost, Ostrov
Os. – Ostova
Oz. – Ozero

P

P. – Point
Pass. – Passage
Penn. – Pennsylvania
Peg. – Peganungan
Pen. – Peninsola, Peninsula, Peninsule
Pk. – Peak, Puncak
Pl. – Planina
Pol. – Poluostrov
Port. – Portugal
Prom. – Promontory
Pt. – Point
Pta. – Ponta, Punta
Pte. – Pointe
Pto. – Puerto, Punto

Q

Qat. – Qatar

R

R. – Reshteh
Ra. – Range
Rep. – Republic
Res. – Reservoir
Rés. – Réservoir
Rom. – Romania
Rw. – Rwanda

S

S. – Shatt, South
Sa. – Serra, Sierra
S.A. – South Africa
Sd. – Sound, Sund
Sp. – Spain
Sprs. – Springs
St. – Saint, Sint
Sta. – Santa
Ste. – Sainte
Str. – Strait
Sur. – Suriname
Switz. – Switzerland

T

Tg. – Tanjong, Tanjung
Tk. – Teluk

U

U.A.E. – United Arab Emirates
U.K. – United Kingdom
U.S.A. – United States of America

V

V. – Volcano
Vdkhr. – Vodokhranilishche
Ven. – Venezuela
Verkh. – Verkhne
Vn. – Volcan
Vol. – Volcan, Volcano

W

W. – Wadi, Wald, West

Y

Y. – Yarimadasi

Z

Zal. – Zaliv

INDEX

The index includes an alphabetical list of all names appearing in the map section of the atlas. Names on the maps and in the index are generally in the local language. For names in languages not written in the Roman alphabet, the officially accepted transliteration system has been used.

Most features are indexed to the largest scale map on which they appear. Extensive features are usually indexed to maps that show the features completely or show them in their relationship to surrounding areas. For extensive regional features, locations are given for the approximate center of the feature, those for linear features are given at the position of the name.

Each entry in the index is located by a page number and an alphanumeric grid reference on that particular page. The grid is defined by letters, positioned at the top and at the bottom of the map spread, and numbers, shown at the sides of the spread. For example, Bandung in Indonesia has the reference 90 D7. It can thus be found on page 90 in the grid square D7.

Where two identical names are referenced to the same page and grid square, it should be noted that they relate to different adjacent features. For example, the name Avon appears twice in the index and in both cases it is referenced to 52 E3. These two entries locate firstly the county of Avon and secondly the River Avon.

Name	Page	Grid
Adda	68	B2
Adda	68	B3
Ad Dakhla	100	B4
Ad Dali	96	G10
Ad Dammam	97	K3
Ad Darb	96	F8
Ad Dawadimi	96	G4
Ad Dawhah	97	K4
Ad Dila	97	K7
Ad Dilam	96	H5
Ad Diriyah	96	H4
Ad Duwaniyah	94	G6
Ad Duwayd	96	F1
Adel	124	C6
Adelaide *Antarctic*	141	V5
Adelaide *Australia*	113	H5
Adelaide *Bahamas*	129	P8
Adelaide Island	141	V5
Adelaide Peninsula	120	G4
Aden	96	G10
Aden, Gulf of	103	J5
Adh Dhayd	97	M4
Adi	114	A2
Adi Ark'ay	96	C10
Adi Dairo	96	D9
Adige	68	C3
Adigrat	96	D9
Adiguzel Baraji	76	C3
Adi Keyah	96	D9
Adilabad	92	E5
Adilcevaz	77	K3
Adin	122	D7
Adirondack Mountains	125	N4
Adis Abeba	103	G6
Adi Ugri	96	D9
Adiyaman	77	H4
Adjud	73	J2
Adjuntas, Presa de las	131	K6
Adka	118	Ac9
Adlington	55	G3
Admello	68	C2
Admiralty Gulf	112	F1
Admiralty Inlet	120	J3
Admiralty Island *Canada*	119	Q2
Admiralty Island *U.S.A.*	118	J4
Admiralty Islands	114	D2
Admund Ringnes Island	120	G2
Ado-Ekiti	105	G4
Adonara	91	G7
Adoni	92	E5
Adorf	70	E3
Adoumaoua, Massif de l'	105	H4
Adour	65	C7
Adra	66	E4
Adrano	69	E7
Adrar	100	E3
Adre	102	D5
Adria	68	D3
Adrian *Michigan*	124	J6
Adrian *Texas*	127	L3
Adriatic Sea	68	E4
Adwa	96	D9
Adwick le Street	55	H3
Adycha	85	P3
Adzhima	88	G1
Adzvavom	78	K2
Aegean Sea	75	H3
Afafura, Laut	91	K7
Afanasevo	78	J4
Affobakka	137	F3
Affric	56	C3
Afghanistan	92	B2
Afgooye	107	J2
Afif	96	F5
Afikpo	105	G4
Afmadow	107	H2
Afognak Island	118	E4
Afon Efyrnwy	52	D2
Afrin	77	G4
Afsin	77	G3
Afyon	76	D3
Agadez	101	G5
Agadir	100	D2
Agadyr	86	C2
Agaie	105	G4
Agalta, Sierra de	132	E7
Agano	89	G7
Agapa *Russia*	84	D2
Agapa *Russia*	84	D2
Agapitovo	84	D3
Agartala	93	H4
Agaruut	87	K3
Agats	114	B3
Agatti	92	D6
Agattu Island	118	Aa9
Agbaja	105	G4
Agboville	104	E4
Agdam	94	H2
Agde	65	E7
Agematsu	89	F8
Agen	65	D6
Aghada	59	F9
Agha Jari	95	J6
Agiabampo, Estero de	130	E4
Agin	77	H3
Agira	69	E7
Aglasun	76	D4
Agnanda	75	F4
Agno	68	C3
Agnone	69	E5
Agout	65	D7
Agra	92	E3
Agram	72	C3
Agreda	67	F2
Agri	69	F5
Agri	77	K3
Agrigento	69	D7
Agrinion	75	F3
Agropoli	69	E5
Agua Clara	138	F4
Aguadas	136	B2
Aguadilla	133	P5
Aguanaval	130	H5
Agua Prieta	127	H5
Aguascalientes	130	H7
Agua, Volcan de	132	B7
Aguelhok	100	F5
Aguemour	101	F3
Aguilar de Campoo	66	D1
Aguilas	67	F4
Aguja, Cabo de la	133	K9
Aguja, Punta	136	A5
Agulhas, Kaap	108	D6
Agusan	91	H4
Ahar	94	H2
Aheim	62	A5
Ahimahasoa	109	J4
Ahipara Bay	115	D1
Ahititi	115	E3
Ahlat	77	K3
Ahmadabad	92	D4
Ahmadi	95	N8
Ahmadnagar	92	D5
Ahmadpur	92	D3
Ahmar Mountains	103	H6
Ahoskie	129	P2
Ahram	95	K7
Ahtari	62	L5
Ahtarinjarvi	62	L5
Ahuachapan	132	C8
Ahvaz	94	J6
Ahvenanmaa	63	H6
Ahwar	96	H10
Aiddejavrre	62	K2
Aidhipsos	75	G3
Aigen	68	D1
Aigues	65	F6
Aiken	129	M4
Ailao Shan	93	K4
Ailsa Craig	57	C5
Aim	85	N5
Aimores, Serra dos	138	H3
Ain	65	F5
Ain Beida	101	G1
Ain Bessem	67	H4
Ain Defla	67	G4
Ain El Hadjel	67	H5
Ain Oulmene	67	J5
Ain Sefra	100	E2
Ainsworth	123	Q6
Aioun el Atrouss	100	D5
Aiquile	138	C3
Air	101	G5
Airbangis	90	B5
Airdrie	57	E5
Aire *France*	64	F4
Aire *U.K.*	55	J3
Airedale	55	H3
Aire-sur-l'Adour	65	C7
Air Force Island	120	M4
Airgin Sum	87	L3
Airi-selka	62	L3
Aisne	64	E4
Aitape	114	C2
Aith	56	F1
Aix-en-Provence	65	F7
Aix-les-Bains	65	F6
Aiyina	75	G4
Aiyinion	75	G2
Aiyion	75	G3
Aizawl	93	H4
Aizpute	63	J8
Aizu-Wakamatsu	89	G7
Ajaccio	69	B5
Ajana	112	C4
Ajanta Range	92	E4
Ajdabiya	101	K2
Ajlun	94	B5
Ajman	97	M4
Ajmer	92	D3
Akaishi-sanchi	89	G8
Akalkot	92	E5
Akamkpa	105	G4
Akaroa Head	115	D5
Akbou	67	J4
Akbulak	79	K5
Akcaabat	77	H2
Akcaakale	77	H4
Akcadag	77	G3
Akcakoca	76	D2
Akcaova	76	C4
Akcay	76	C4
Akchatau	86	C2
Ak Daglari	76	C4
Akdagmadeni	77	F3
Ak Dovurak	84	E6
Akershus	63	D6
Akeshir Golu	76	D3
Aketi	106	D2
Akgevir	77	J4
Akhalkalaki	77	K2
Akhaltsikhe	77	K2
Akhdar, Al Jabal al	101	K2
Akhdar, Jabal	97	N5
Akhdar, Wadi	96	C3
Akheloos	75	F3
Akhiok	118	E4
Akhisar	76	B3
Akhmim	103	F2
Akhtubinsk	79	H6
Akhtyrka	79	E5
Aki	89	D9
Akimiski Island	121	K7
Akincilar	77	H2
Akinkeen	59	D9
Akinli	77	J4
Akita	88	H6
Akjoujt	100	C5
Akkavare	62	J3
Akkeshi	88	K4
Akko	94	B5
Akkoy	76	B4
Akkus	77	G2
Aklavik	118	H2
Akmola	84	A6
Akniste	63	L8
Akola	92	E4
Akonolinga	105	H5
Akordat	96	C9
Akoren	76	E4
Akot	92	E4
Akpatok Island	121	N5
Akpinar	76	E3
Akqi	86	D3
Akranes	62	T12
Akron	125	K6
Aksar	77	K2
Aksaray	76	E3
Aksay *China*	86	G4
Aksay *Kazakhstan*	79	J5
Aksehir	76	D3
Akseki	76	D4
Aksenovo-Zilovskoye	85	K6
Aks-e Rostam	95	M7
Aksha	85	J6
Akshimrau	79	J7
Aksu *China*	86	E3
Aksu *Turkey*	76	D4
Aksu *Kazakhstan*	79	J5
Aksu-Ayuly	86	C2
Aksu Cayi	76	D4
Aksum	96	D9
Aksumbe	86	B3
Aktau *Kazakhstan*	84	A6
Aktau *Kazakhstan*	79	J7
Akti	75	H2
Aktogay	86	D2
Akulivik	120	L5
Akun Island	118	Ae9
Akune	89	C9
Akure	105	G4
Akureyri	62	V12
Akuse	104	F4
Akutan Island	118	Ae9
Akwanga	105	G4
Akyab	93	H4
Akyatan Golu	76	F4
Akyazi	76	D2
Akyurt	76	E2
Akzhar	86	C3
Al Aaiun	100	C3
Alabama *U.S.A.*	129	J4
Alabama *U.S.A.*	129	J4
Alaca	76	F2
Alacahan	77	G3
Alacam	77	F2
Alacam Daglari	76	C3
Alacran, Arrecife	131	Q6
Alagoas	137	K5
Alagoinhas	137	K6
Alagon *Spain*	66	C2
Alagon *Spain*	67	F2
Al Ahmadi	97	J2
Al Ajaiz	97	N7
Alajarvi	62	K5
Alajuela	132	E9
Alakanuk	118	C3
Alakol, Ozero	86	E2
Alakyla	62	L3
Al Amarah	94	H6
Alameda *California*	126	A2
Alameda *New Mexico*	127	J3
Alamicamba	132	E8
Alamo	126	E2
Alamogordo	127	K4
Ala, Monti di	69	B5
Alamos	127	H7
Alamosa	127	K2
Aland	63	H6
Alands hav	63	M6
Alanya	76	E4
Alaotra, Lake	109	J3
Alapayevsk	84	Ad5
Al Aqulah	97	J5
Alarcon, Embalse de	66	E3
Al Artawiyah	96	G3
Alasehir	76	C3
Al Ashkhirah	97	P6
Alaska	118	E3
Alaska, Gulf of	118	F4
Alaska Peninsula	118	Af8
Alaska Range	118	E3
Alassio	68	B4
Alatna	118	E2
Alatyr	78	H5
Alausi	136	B4
Alaverdi	77	L2
Alavus	62	K5
Al Ayn	97	M4
Alayor	67	J3
Alayskiy Khrebet	86	C4
Al Azamiyah	77	L6
Alazeya	85	S2
Alba	68	B3
Al Bab	77	G4
Albacete	67	F3
Alba de Tormes	66	D2
Al Badi	96	H5
Al Badi	77	J5
Alba Iulia	73	G2
Albak	63	D8
Alba, Mount	115	B6
Albanel, Lake	121	M7
Albania	74	E2
Albano	137	F4
Albany *Australia*	112	D5
Albany *Canada*	121	K7
Albany *Georgia*	129	K5
Albany *Kentucky*	124	H8
Albany *New York*	125	P5
Albany *Oregon*	122	C5
Albarracin	67	F2
Al Basrah	94	H6
Albatross Bay	113	J1
Albatross Point	115	E3
Al Bayda	96	G10
Albayrak	77	L3
Albemarle	129	M3
Albemarle Island	136	A7
Albemarle Sound	129	P2
Albenga	68	B3
Albentosa	67	F2
Alberche	66	D2
Alberga	113	G4
Albergaria-a-Velha	66	B2
Alberique	67	F3
Albert	64	E3
Alberta	119	M5
Albert Edward, Mount	114	D3
Albert Kanaal	64	F3
Albert, Lake	107	F2
Albert Lea	124	D5
Albert Nile	107	F2
Albertville *France*	65	G6
Albertville *Zaire*	107	E4
Albi	65	E7
Albina	137	G2
Al Bir	96	C2
Al Birk	96	E7
Albocacer	67	G2
Albo, Monti	69	B5
Alboran, Isla de	66	E5
Alborg	63	D8
Alborg Bugt	63	D8
Alborz, Reshteh-ye Kuhta ye	95	K3
Albro	113	K3
Albufeira	66	B4
Albu Gharz, Sabkhat	77	J5
Albuquerque	127	J3
Al Buraymi	97	M4
Albury	113	K6
Al Busayyah	94	H6
Al Buzun	97	K9
Alcacer do Sal	66	B3
Alcala de Henares	66	E2
Alcamo	69	D7
Alcanices	66	C2
Alcaniz	67	F2
Alcantara	66	C3
Alcantara	137	J4
Alcantara, Embalse de	66	C3
Alcaraz	66	E3
Alcaraz, Sierra de	66	E3
Alcaudete	66	D4
Alcazar de San Juan	66	E3
Alcester	53	F2
Alchevsk	79	F6
Alcolea del Pinar	66	E2
Alcoutim	66	C4
Alcoy	67	F3
Alcubierre, Sierra de	67	F2
Alcublas	67	F3
Alcudia	67	H3
Aldabra Islands	82	C7
Aldama	131	K6
Aldan *Russia*	85	M5
Aldan *Russia*	85	N4
Aldanskoye Nagorye	85	M5
Alde	53	J2
Aldeburgh	53	J2
Aldeia Nova	66	C4
Alderley Edge	55	G3
Alderney	53	M6
Aldershot	53	G3
Aldridge	53	F2
Aleg	100	C5
Alegrete	138	E5
Aleksandra, Mys	85	P6
Aleksandriya	79	E6
Aleksandrov	78	F4
Aleksandrovac	73	F4
Aleksandrov Gay	79	H5
Aleksandrovsk	78	K4
Aleksandrovskoye	79	G7
Aleksandrovsk-Sakhalinskiy	85	Q6
Aleksandry, Ostrov	80	F1
Alekseyevka *Kazakhstan*	84	A6
Alekseyevka *Russia*	79	F5
Aleksin	78	F5
Alem Paraiba	138	H4
Alencon	64	D4
Alenquer	137	G4
Alentejo	66	C3
Alenuihaha Channel	126	S10
Aleppo	77	G4

Name	Page	Grid
Aleria	69	B4
Alerta	136	C6
Ales	65	F6
Aleshki	78	H2
Alessandria	68	B3
Alessio	74	E2
Alesund	62	B5
Aleutian Islands	118	Ab9
Aleutian Range	118	D4
Aleutian Trench	143	H3
Alevina, Mys	85	S5
Alexander Archipelago	118	J4
Alexander Bay	108	C5
Alexander, Cape	119	P2
Alexander City	129	K4
Alexander Island	141	V4
Alexander, Kap	120	M2
Alexandra *Australia*	113	K6
Alexandra *New Zealand*	115	B6
Alexandretta	77	G4
Alexandria *Egypt*	102	E1
Alexandria *Romania*	73	H4
Alexandria *South Africa*	108	E6
Alexandria *U.K.*	57	D5
Alexandria *Louisiana*	128	F5
Alexandria *Minnesota*	124	C4
Alexandria *Virginia*	125	M7
Alexandroupolis	75	H2
Aleysk	84	C6
Al Fallujah	77	K6
Alfambra *Spain*	67	F2
Alfambra *Spain*	67	F2
Alfaro	136	B4
Alfatar	73	J4
Al Faw	94	J7
Alfeld	70	C3
Alfios	75	F4
Alford *Grampian, U.K.*	56	F3
Alford *Lincolnshire, U.K.*	55	K3
Alfreton	55	H3
Al Fuhayhil	97	J2
Al Fujayrah	97	N4
Al Fuqaha	101	J3
Al Furat	77	J5
Algard	63	A7
Algarrobo del Aguila	139	C7
Algarve	66	B4
Algatart	86	C3
Algeciras	66	D4
Algena	96	D8
Alger, Baie d	67	H4
Algeria	101	F3
Al Ghaydah	97	L8
Alghero	69	B5
Algiers	101	F1
Algoa Bay	108	E6
Algodoes	137	K5
Algodonales	66	D4
Algona	124	C5
Algonquin Park	125	L4
Algueirao	109	F4
Al Hadd	97	P5
Al Hadithah	94	F4
Al Hadr	77	K5
Al Halfayah	94	H6
Al Hallaniyah	97	N8
Al Hamar	96	H5
Alhambra	66	E4
Al Hanakiyah	96	E4
Al Hariq	96	H5
Al Hasa	97	J3
Al Hasakah	77	J4
Al Hashimiyah	94	G5
Al Hawtah	96	H9
Al Hayy	94	H5
Al Hillah *Iraq*	94	G5
Al Hillah *Saudi Arabia*	96	H5
Al Hilwah	96	H5
Al Hudaydah	96	F9
Al Hufuf	96	J4
Al Huraydah	97	J9
Aliabad	94	H4
Aliabad	95	M7
Aliaga	76	B3
Aliaga	67	F2
Aliakmon	75	G2
Ali al Gharbi	94	H5
Alibag	92	D5
Alibey, Ozero	73	L3
Alibunar	73	F3
Alicante	67	F3
Alice	128	C7
Alice, Punta	69	F6
Alice Springs	113	G3
Aligarh	92	E3
Aligudarz	95	J5
Alijuq, Kuh-e	95	K6
Al Ikhwan	97	N10
Alima	106	C3
Alindao	102	D6
Alingsas	63	E8
Alinskoye	84	D4
Alipka	84	D5
Al Isawiyah	94	C6
Alisos	126	G5
Alistati	75	G2
Aliwal North	108	E5
Al Jaghbub	101	K2
Al Jahrah	97	H2
Al Jawarah	97	N7
Al Jawf *Libya*	101	K4
Al Jawf *Saudi Arabia*	96	D2
Al Jazirah	77	J4
Al Jubayl	97	J3
Aljustrel	66	B4
Al Kalban	97	P6
Al Kamil	97	P5
Al Khaburah	97	N5
Al Khalis	94	G5
Al Khaluf	97	P6
Al Khasab	97	N3
Al Khatt	97	N4
Al Khawr	97	K4
Al Khubar	97	K3
Al Khufrah	101	K4
Al Khums	101	H2
Al Khuraybah	97	J9
Al Khuwayr	97	K3
Alkmaar	64	F2
Al Kufah	94	G5
Al Kut	94	G5
Al Kuwayt	97	H2
Allada	105	F4
Al Ladhiqiyah	77	F5
Allahabad	92	F3
Allahuekber Daglari	77	K2
Allakh-Yun	85	P4
Allanmyo	93	J5
Allanridge	108	E5
Allaqi, Wadi	103	F3
Allariz	66	C1
Alldays	108	E4
Allegheny	125	L6
Allegheny Mountains	124	J8
Allegheny Plateau	125	K7
Allen *Philippines*	91	G3
Allen *U.K.*	52	C4
Allen, Bog of	59	H6
Allendale	129	M4
Allende	127	M6
Allen, Lough	58	F4
Allenstein	71	J2
Allentown	125	N6
Alleppey	92	E7
Aller	70	D2
Allerston	55	J2
Allevard	65	G6
Allgauer Alpen	68	C2
Alliance *Nebraska*	123	N6
Alliance *Ohio*	125	K6
Allier	65	E5
Allik	121	Q6
Al Lith	96	E6
Alloa	57	E4
Al Luhayyah	96	F9
Allur	92	F6
Alma *Canada*	125	Q2
Alma *Michigan*	124	H5
Alma *Nebraska*	123	Q7
Alma-Ata	86	D3
Almaciles	66	E4
Almada	66	B3
Al Maddah	96	F7
Almaden	66	D3
Al Madinah	96	D4
Almagro	66	E3
Al Mahmudiyah	94	G5
Al Majmaah	96	G4
Almalyk	86	B3
Al Manamah	97	K3
Almanor, Lake	122	D7
Almansa	67	F3
Al Mansuriyah	96	F9
Almanzor, Pic de	66	D2
Al Mariyah	97	L5
Al Marj	101	K2
Al Masnaah	97	N5
Al Mawsil	77	K4
Al Mayadin	77	J5
Al Mayyah	96	F3
Almazan	66	E2
Almeirim	137	G4
Almelo	64	G2
Almendra, Embalse de	66	C2
Almeria	66	E4
Almeria, Golfo de	66	E4
Almetyevsk	78	J5
Almhult	63	F8
Al Midhnab	96	G4
Almina, Punta	66	D5
Al Miqdadiyah	94	G5
Almiropotamos	75	H3
Almiros	75	G3
Almirou, Kolpos	75	H5
Al Mishab	96	J3
Almodovar	66	B4
Almond	57	E4
Almonte	66	D3
Almora	92	E3
Al Mubarraz	97	J4
Al Mudawwara	94	B7
Al Mudaybi	97	P5
Al Mudayrib	97	P5
Al Muharraq	97	K3
Al Mukalla	97	J9
Al Mukha	96	F10
Almuradiel	66	E3
Al Musaymir	96	G10
Al Musayyib	94	G5
Almus Baraji	77	G2
Al Muwayh	96	E5
Al Muwaylih	96	B3
Aln	57	G5
Alness	56	D3
Alnwick	55	H1
Alofi	111	T4
Alor	91	G7
Alora	66	D4
Alor, Kepulauan	91	G7
Alotau	114	E4
Alpe-d'Huez	65	G6
Alpena	124	J4
Alpercatas, Serra das	137	J5
Alpine *Arizona*	127	H4
Alpine *Texas*	127	L5
Alps	50	J6
Alpu	76	D3
Al Qaffay	97	K4
Al Qaim	77	J5
Al Qalibah	96	C2
Al Qamishli	94	E3
Al Qaryatayn	77	G5
Al Qatif	97	J3
Al Qatn	97	J9
Al Qaysumah	96	H2
Al Qubbah	101	K2
Alqueva, Barragem de	66	C3
Alquippa	125	K6
Al Qunfudhah	96	E7
Al Qurayni	97	L6
Al Qurayyat	97	P5
Al Qurnah	94	H6
Al Qutayfah	94	C5
Al Quwayiyah	96	G4
Al Quzah	97	J9
Al Ramadi	77	K6
Als	70	C1
Alsace	64	G4
Alsask	123	K2
Alsasua	67	E1
Alsek	118	H4
Alsfeld	70	C3
Alsh, Loch	56	C3
Alsten	62	E4
Alstermo	63	F8
Alston	55	G2
Alta	62	P2
Altaelv	62	K2
Altafjord	62	K1
Alta Gracia	138	D6
Altagracia	133	M9
Altai	86	G2
Altamaha	129	M5
Altamira	137	G4
Altamura	69	F5
Altamura, Isla de	130	E5
Alta, Sierra	67	C2
Altay *Russia*	84	Ae4
Altay *China*	86	F2
Altay *Mongolia*	86	H2
Altdorf	68	B2
Altenburg	70	E3
Altinekin	76	E3
Altinhisar	76	F3
Altinkaya	76	D4
Altin Kopru	77	L5
Altinova	76	B3
Altinozu	77	G4
Altintas	76	D3
Altkirche	65	G5
Altmark	70	D2
Altmuhl	70	D4
Altnaharra	56	D2
Alto Araguaia	138	F3
Alto Coite	138	F3
Alto Molocue	109	G3
Alton *Hampshire, U.K.*	53	G3
Alton *Staffordshire, U.K.*	53	F2
Altoona	125	L6
Alto Sucuriu	138	F3
Altrincham	55	G3
Altun Shan	92	F1
Alturas	122	D7
Al Ubaylah	97	K6
Alucra	77	H2
Aluksne	63	M8
Al Ula	96	C3
Alumine	139	B7
Al Uqayr	97	K4
Alur Setar	90	C4
Al Uwayja	96	G5
Alva	128	C2
Alvarado	131	M8
Alvaro Obregon	131	N8
Alvdal	63	H5
Alvdalen	63	F6
Alvito	66	C3
Alvorada	137	H6
Alvsborg	63	E8
Alvsbyn	62	J4
Al Wajh	96	C3
Al Wakrah	97	K4
Alwar	92	E3
Alwen Reservoir	55	F3
Alwinton	57	F5
Al Wusayl	97	K4
Alyaskitovyy	85	Q4
Alyat	94	J2
Alyth, Forest of	57	E4
Alytus	71	L1
Alzamay	84	F5
Amadeus, Lake	112	G3
Amadiyah	77	K4
Amadjuak Lake	120	M5
Amagasaki	89	E8
Amager	63	E9
Amahai	91	H6
Amakusa-Shimo-shima	89	C9
Amal	63	E7
Amalfi	69	E5
Amalias	75	F4
Amalner	92	E4
Amami-O-shima	89	B11
Amami-shoto	89	J10
Amandola	69	D4
Amantea	69	F6
Amanzimtoti	108	F6
Amapa	137	G3
Amapa	137	G3
Amarante	66	B2
Amarapura	93	J4
Amargosa	126	D3
Amarillo	127	M3
Amaro	69	E4
Amasiya	77	K2
Amasra	76	E2
Amasya	77	F2
Amatignak Island	118	Ac9
Amatrice	69	D4
Amazon	137	G4
Amazonas	137	G4
Amazon, Mouths of the	137	G4
Ambala	92	E2
Ambalavao	109	J4
Ambanja	109	J2
Ambar	84	E3
Ambarchik	85	U3
Ambarnyy	78	E2
Ambato	136	B4
Ambato-Boeny	109	J3
Ambatolampy	109	J3
Amberg	70	D4
Ambergris Cay	132	D5
Amberieu-en-Bugey	65	F6
Ambert	65	E6
Ambikapur	92	F4
Ambilobe	109	J2
Amble-by-the-Sea	55	H1
Ambleside	55	G2
Ambodifototra	109	J3
Amboise	65	D5
Ambon *Indonesia*	91	H6
Ambon *Indonesia*	91	H6
Ambositra	109	J4
Ambovombe	109	J5
Ambriz	106	B4
Ambrym	114	U12
Amchitka Island	118	Ab9
Amchitka Pass	118	Ab9
Amdassa	91	J7
Amderma	84	Ad3
Amdo	93	H2
Ameca	130	G7
Amecameca	131	K8
Amendolara	69	F6
Ameralik	120	R5
American	122	D8
American Falls Reservoir	122	H6
American Samoa	111	U5
Americus	129	K4
Amersham	53	G3
Amery Ice Shelf	141	E5
Ames	124	D5
Amesbury	53	F3
Amfiklia	75	G3
Amfilokhia	75	F3
Amfipolis	75	G2
Amfissa	75	G3
Amga *Russia*	85	N4
Amga *Russia*	85	N4
Amgu	88	F3
Amguema	85	Y3
Amgun	85	P6
Amherst *Canada*	121	P8
Amherst *Virginia*	125	L8
Amiata, Monte	69	C4
Amiens	64	E4
Amikino	85	L6
Amilhayt, Wadi al	97	L7
Amindivi Islands	92	D6
Amirante Islands	82	D7
Amistad Reservoir	127	M6
Amitioke Peninsula	120	K4
Amka	85	Q5
Amland	64	F2
Amlia Island	118	Ad9
Amlwch	55	E3
Amman	94	B6
Ammanford	52	C3
Ammer	70	D4
Ammersee	70	D5
Amol	95	L3
Amorgos *Greece*	75	H4
Amorgos *Greece*	75	J4
Amos	125	L2
Amot *Buskerud, Norway*	63	C7
Amot *Telemark, Norway*	63	C7
Amotfors	63	E7
Ampana	91	G6
Ampanihy	109	H4
Ampato, Nevado de	138	B3
Amposta	67	G2
Ampthill	53	G2
Amqui	125	S2
Amran	96	F9
Amravati	92	E4
Amritsar	92	D2
Amroha	92	E3
Amrum	70	C1
Amsterdam *Netherlands*	64	F2
Amsterdam *U.S.A.*	125	N5
Am Timan	102	D3
Amuay	133	M9
Amundsen Glacier	141	P1
Amundsen-Scott	141	A1
Amundsen Sea	141	S5

Name	Page	Grid
Amuntai	90	F6
Amur *China*	87	N1
Amur *Russia*	85	Q6
Amursk	85	P6
Amurskaya Oblast	85	M6
Amur, Wadi	103	F4
Amvrakikos Kolpos	75	F3
Amvrosiyevka	79	F6
Anabar	84	J2
Anaco	133	Q10
Anaconda	122	H4
Anadarko	128	C3
Anadyr *Russia*	85	W4
Anadyr *Russia*	85	X4
Anadyrskiy Khrebet	85	W3
Anafi *Greece*	75	H4
Anafi *Greece*	75	H4
Anafjallet	62	E5
Anah	77	J5
Anaheim	126	D4
Anahuac	128	B7
Anakapalle	92	F5
Anaktuvuk	118	E2
Analalava	109	J2
Anambas, Kepulauan	90	D5
Anamur	76	E4
Anamur Burun	76	E4
Anan	89	E9
Ananes	75	H4
Anantapur	92	E6
Anantnag	92	E2
Ananyev	73	K2
Ananyevo	86	D3
Anapolis	138	J3
Anapu	137	G4
Anar	95	M6
Anarak	95	L5
Anar Darreh	95	Q5
Anatuya	138	D5
Anaua	136	E3
Anavilhanas, Arquipielago das	136	E4
A Nazret	103	G6
Anbei	86	H3
Ancenis	65	C5
Ancha	85	P4
Anchi	105	G4
Anchorage	118	F3
Anchor Island	115	A6
Ancohuma, Nevado	138	C3
Ancona	68	D4
Ancrum	57	F4
Ancuabe	109	G2
Ancuaque	138	C3
Ancud	139	B8
Ancud, Golfo de	139	B8
Anda	87	P2
Andalgala	138	C5
Andalsnes	62	B5
Andalucia	66	D4
Andalusia	129	J5
Andaman Islands	93	H6
Andaman Sea	93	J6
Andamarca	136	C6
Andam, Wadi	97	P6
Andanga	78	H4
Andapa	109	J2
Andarai	137	J6
Andeba Ye Midir Zerf Chaf	96	E9
Andeg	78	J2
Andenes	62	G2
Andermatt	68	B2
Anderson *Canada*	118	K2
Anderson *Indiana*	124	H6
Anderson *Missouri*	124	C8
Anderson *S. Carolina*	129	L3
Anderson Bay	113	K7
Andes	136	B2
Andevoranto	109	J3
Andfjorden	62	G2
Andhra Pradesh	92	E5
Andikithira	75	G5
Andimeshk	94	J5
Andimilos	75	H4
Andiparos	75	H4
Andipaxoi	75	F3
Andirin	77	G4
Andizhan	86	C3
Andkhovy	95	S3
Andoas	136	B4
Andong	89	B7
Andongwei	87	M4
Andorra	66	G1
Andorra la Vella	67	G1
Andover	53	F3
Andoya	62	F2
Andraitx	67	H3
Andrascoggin	125	Q4
Andravidha	75	F4
Andreafsky	118	C3
Andreanof Islands	118	Ac9
Andrews	127	L4
Andreyevka	79	J5
Andreyevo Ivanovka	73	L2
Andreyevsk	85	J5
Andria	69	F5
Andrijevica	72	E4
Andringitra	109	J4
Andros	132	H2
Andros *Greece*	75	H4
Andros *Greece*	75	H4
Androth	92	D6
Andujar	66	D3
Andulo	106	C5
Andyngda	85	K3
Anegada	133	Q5
Anegada, Bahia	139	D8
Aneho	105	F4
Aneityum	114	U13
Anelghowhat	114	U14
Aneto, Pic D'	67	G1
Angamos, Punta	138	B4
Angar	114	A2
Angara	84	E5
Angara Basin	140	A1
Angarsk	84	G6
Ange	62	F5
Angel de la Guarda, Isla	126	F6
Angeles	91	G2
Angel Falls	136	E2
Angelholm	63	E8
Angelino	128	E5
Angellala	113	K4
Angermanalven	62	G5
Angermunde	70	F2
Angers	65	C5
Angeson	62	J5
Angical	138	J6
Angicos	137	K5
Angikuni Lake	119	R3
Anglesey	54	E4
Ango	106	E2
Angoche	109	G3
Angohran	95	N8
Angol	139	B7
Angola	106	C5
Angola *Indiana*	124	H6
Angoram	114	C2
Angostura, Presa de la	131	N9
Angouleme	65	D6
Angoumois	65	D6
Angren	86	B3
Anguila Islands	132	H3
Anguilla	133	R5
Angus, Braes of	57	E4
Anholt	63	D8
Anhua	93	M3
Anhui	93	N2
Anhumas	138	F3
Aniak	118	D3
Anidhros	75	H4
Animas, Punta de las	126	F6
Anina	73	F3
Aniva	88	J2
Aniva, Mys	88	J2
Aniva, Zaliv	88	J2
Aniwa	114	U13
Anjalankoski	63	M6
Anjou	65	C5
Anjouan	109	H2
Anjozorobe	109	J3
Anju	87	P4
Ankacho	84	H4
Ankang	93	L2
Ankara	76	E3
Ankazoabo	109	H4
Ankazobe	109	J3
Ankiliabo	109	H4
Anklam	70	E2
Ankleshwar	92	D4
Ankober	103	G6
Ankpa	105	G4
Anlong	93	L3
Anlu	93	M2
Anna	79	G5
Annaba	101	G1
Annaberg-Buchholz	70	E3
An Nabk *Saudi Arabia*	94	C6
An Nabk *Syria*	94	C4
Anna Creek	113	H4
Annagh Bog	59	D8
Annagh Head	58	B4
Annagh Island	59	C5
An Najaf	94	G6
Annalong	58	L4
Annan *U.K.*	57	E5
Annan *U.K.*	55	F2
Annandale	57	E5
Anna Plains	112	E2
Annapolis	125	M7
Annapurna	92	F3
Ann Arbor	124	J5
An Nasiriyah	94	H6
Ann, Cape	125	Q5
Annecy	65	G6
Annenskiy-Most	78	F3
Annfield Plain	55	H2
An Nhon	93	L6
Anniston	129	K4
Annonay	65	F6
An Nuayriyah	97	J3
An Numan	96	B3
Ano Arkhanai	75	H5
Anosibe an Ala	109	J3
Ano Viannos	75	H5
Anoyia	75	H5
Anqing	87	M5
Ansbach	70	D4
Anse de Vauville	53	N6
Anserma	136	B2
Anshan	87	N3
Anshun	93	L3
Ansley	123	Q7
Anson	127	N4
Anson Bay	112	G1
Ansongo	100	F5
Anston	55	H3
Anstruther	57	F4
Ansudu	114	B2
Antabamba	136	C6
Antakya	77	G4
Antalaha	109	K2
Antalya	76	D4
Antalya Korfezi	76	D4
Antananarivo	109	J3
Antarctic Peninsula	141	W5
An Teallach	56	C3
Antequera	66	D4
Anti-Atlas	100	D3
Antibes	65	G7
Anticosti Island	121	P8
Antigo	124	F4
Antigua	133	S6
Antigua and Barbuda	133	S6
Antigua Guatemala	132	B7
Antioch	126	B2
Antipayuta	84	B3
Antipodes Islands	111	S11
Antlers	128	E3
Antofagasta	138	B4
Antofagasta de la Sierra	138	C5
Antofalla, Salar de	138	C5
Antofalla, Volcan	138	C5
Antonio, Ponta Santo	137	K7
Antonovo	73	J4
Antrain	64	C4
Antrim *U.K.*	58	K3
Antrim *U.K.*	58	K3
Antrim Mountains	58	K2
Antrim Plateau	112	F2
Antsalova	109	H3
Antseranana	109	J2
Antsirabe	109	J3
Antsohihy	109	J2
Antu	88	B4
Antufush	96	F9
An-tung	87	N7
Antwerp	64	F3
Antwerpen	64	F3
Anuchino	88	D4
Anugul	92	F4
Anundsjo	62	H5
Anupgarh	92	D3
Anuradhapura	92	F7
Anvers Island	141	V6
Anxi	86	H3
Anxious Bay	113	G5
Anyama	104	E4
Anyang	87	L4
Anyemaqen Shan	93	J2
Anyudin	78	K3
Anzhero-Sudzhensk	84	D5
Anzhu, Ostrova	85	Q1
Anzio	69	D5
Aoba	114	T11
Aola	114	K6
Aomori	88	H5
Aosta	68	A3
Aoukale	102	D5
Aouker	100	D5
Apalachee Bay	129	K6
Apalachicola	129	K6
Apaporis	136	D4
Aparri	91	G2
Apatity	62	Q3
Apatzingan	130	H8
Apeldoorn	64	F2
Apia	111	U4
Apiacas, Serra dos	137	F5
Apin-Apin	90	F4
Apio	114	K6
Apizaco	131	K8
Apolda	70	D3
Apollonia	75	H4
Apopka, Lake	129	M6
Apostle Islands	124	E3
Apostolou Andrea, Akra	76	F5
Apostolovo	79	E6
Appennino	68	C4
Appleby-in-Westmorland	55	G2
Appleton	124	F4
Apsheronsk	79	F7
Apt	65	F7
Apucarana	138	F4
Apure	136	D2
Apurimac	136	C6
Apuseni, Muntii	73	G2
Aq	77	L3
Aqaba	94	B7
Aqaba, Gulf of	103	F2
Aqabah, Khalij-al-	96	B2
Aqal	86	D3
Aqda	95	L5
Aqiq	96	D7
Aqrah	77	K4
Aqueda	66	C2
Aquidauana	138	E4
Ara	92	F3
Arababad	95	N5
Araban	77	G4
Arabatskaya Strelkha, Kosa	79	F6
Araba, Wadi	94	B6
Arab, Bahr el	102	E5
Arabelo	136	E3
Arabian Desert	103	F2
Arabian Sea	97	N8
Arab, Shatt al	94	H6
Arac	76	E2
Aracaju	137	K6
Aracati	137	K4
Aracatuba	138	F4
Aracena	66	C4
Aracena, Sierra de	66	C4
Araçuai *Brazil*	138	H3
Araçuai *Brazil*	137	H3
Arad	73	F2
Aradah	97	L5
Arafuli	96	D9
Aragats	77	L2
Aragon	67	F1
Araguacema	137	H5
Aragua de Barcelona	136	E2
Araguaia	137	H5
Araguaine	137	H5
Araguari	137	G3
Araioses	137	J4
Arak	95	J4
Arakamchechen, Ostrov	118	A3
Arakan Yoma	93	H5
Arakhthos	75	F3
Arakli	77	J2
Araks	77	K2
Aral	86	E3
Aralik	77	L3
Aralqi	86	F4
Aral Sea	98	J2
Aralsk	86	A2
Aralskoye More	80	G5
Aramah, Al	96	H4
Aranda de Duero	66	E2
Arandai	114	A2
Aran Island	58	E3
Aran Islands	59	C6
Aranjuez	66	E2
Aranlau	114	A3
Araouane	100	E5
Arapahoe	123	Q7
Arapawa Island	115	E4
Arapiraca	137	K5
Arapkir	77	H3
Arapongas	138	F4
Ar'ar	94	E6
Araracuara	136	C4
Araraquara	138	G4
Araras, Serra das *Maranhao, Brazil*	137	H5
Araras, Serra das *Mato Grosso do Sul, Brazil*	138	F3
Ararat	77	L3
Araripe, Chapada do	137	K5
Arar, Wadi	94	E6
Aras	77	K2
Arato	89	H6
Arauca *Colombia*	136	C2
Arauca *Venezuela*	136	D2
Aravalli Range	92	D3
Araxa	138	G3
Araya	88	H5
Araya, Peninsula de	136	E1
Arba	67	F1
Arbatax	69	B6
Arbil	77	L4
Arboga	63	F7
Arboleda, Punta	127	H7
Arborg	119	R5
Arbra	63	G6
Arbroath	57	F4
Arbus	69	B6
Arcachon	65	C6
Arcachon, Bassin d	65	C6
Arcadia	129	M7
Arcata	122	B7
Arc Dome	122	F8
Archidona	66	D4
Arcis-sur-Aube	64	F4
Arco	122	H6
Arcos de la Frontera	66	D4
Arctic Bay	120	J3
Arctic Ocean	140	A1
Arctic Red	118	J2
Arctic Red River	118	J2
Arctowski	141	W6
Arda	73	H5
Ardabil	94	J2
Ardahan	77	K2
Ardalstangen	63	B6
Ardanuc	77	K2
Ardara	58	F3
Ardarroch	56	C3
Ardee	58	J5
Ardennes	64	F3
Ardentinny	57	D4
Ardesen	77	J2
Ardestan	95	L5
Ardfert	59	C8
Ardglass	58	L4
Ardgour	57	C4
Ardh es Suwwan	94	C6
Ardila	66	C3
Ardino	73	H5
Ardivachar Point	56	A3
Ardlussa	57	C5
Ardminish	57	C5
Ardmore	128	D3
Ardnacross Bay	57	C5
Ardnamurchan	57	B4
Ardnamurchan Point	57	B4
Ardnave Point	57	B5
Ardrossan	57	D5
Ards Peninsula	58	L3
Ardtalla	57	B5
Ardvasar	57	C3
Ardvule, Rubha	56	A3
Areao	137	H4
Arecibo	133	P5

Name	Page	Grid
Aube	64	F4
Aubenas	65	F6
Aubigny-sur-Nere	65	E5
Aubry Lake	118	K2
Auburn *Australia*	113	L4
Auburn *Alabama*	129	K4
Auburn *California*	126	B1
Auburn *Indiana*	124	H6
Auburn *Maine*	125	Q4
Auburn *Nebraska*	124	C6
Auburn *New York*	125	M5
Aubusson	65	E6
Auca Mahuida	139	C7
Auce	63	K8
Auch	65	D7
Auchavan	57	E4
Auchengray	57	E5
Auchterarder	57	E4
Auckland	115	E2
Auckland Islands	141	M8
Aude	65	E7
Auderville	64	C4
Audierne, Baie 'd	65	A5
Aue	70	E3
Augher	58	H4
Aughnacloy	58	J4
Aughrim *Galway, Ireland*	59	F6
Aughrim *Wicklow, Ireland*	59	K7
Aughton	55	H3
Augsburg	70	D4
Augusta *Australia*	112	D5
Augusta *Georgia*	129	M4
Augusta *Italy*	69	E7
Augusta *Kansas*	128	D2
Augusta *Maine*	125	R4
Augusta *Montana*	122	H4
Augustine Island	118	E4
Augustow	71	K2
Augustus, Mount	112	D3
Auletta	69	E5
Aulia	103	F4
Aulitiving Island	120	N4
Aulne	64	B4
Aultbea	56	C3
Aumont	65	E6
Aupalak	121	N6
Aurangabad	92	E5
Auray	65	B5
Aurdal	63	C6
Aure *Norway*	62	B5
Aure *Norway*	62	C5
Aurich	70	B2
Aurillac	65	E6
Aurkuning	90	E6
Aurora *Colorado*	123	M8
Aurora *Illinois*	124	F6
Aurora *Missouri*	124	D8
Aurora *Nebraska*	123	R7
Au Sable	124	J4
Auskerry Sound	56	F1
Aust-Agder	63	D7
Austin *Minnesota*	124	D5
Austin *Nevada*	126	D1
Austin *Texas*	128	D5
Austin, Lake	112	D4
Australia	110	F6
Australian Capital Territory	113	K6
Austria	68	D2
Austurhorn	62	X12
Autazes	136	F4
Authie	64	D3
Autlan	130	G8
Autun	65	F5
Auvergne *Australia*	112	G2
Auvergne *France*	65	E6
Auxerre	65	E5
Avallon	65	E5
Avanos	76	F3
Avare	138	G4
Avas	75	H2
Avcilar	76	C2
Avebury	53	F3
Aveiro *Portugal*	66	B2
Aveiro *Portugal*	66	B2
Avellino	69	E5
Avelon Peninsula	121	R8
Aversa	69	E5
Aves, Isla de	133	R7
Avesnes	64	E3
Avesta	63	G6
Aveyron	65	E6
Avezzano	69	D4
Avgo	75	H5
Aviemore	57	E3
Aviemore, Lake	115	C6
Avigliano	69	E5
Avignon	65	F7
Avila	66	D2
Avila, Sierra de	66	D2
Aviles	66	D1
Avisio	68	C2
Aviz	66	C3
Avlum	63	C8
Avoca *Australia*	113	J6
Avoca *Iowa*	124	C6
Avola	69	E7
Avon *Devon, U.K.*	52	D4
Avon *Hampshire, U.K.*	53	F4
Avon *U.K.*	52	E3
Avon *U.K.*	52	E3
Avonmouth	52	E3
Avon Park	129	M7
Avon Water	57	D5
Avranches	64	C4
Avrig	73	H3
Avuvavu	114	K6
Awaji-shima	89	E8
Awali	97	K3
Awanui	115	D1
Awarik, Uruq al	96	H7
Awarua Point	115	A6
Awa-shima	89	G6
Awash Wenz	103	H5
Awaso	104	E4
Awatere	115	D4
Awbari	101	H3
Aweil	102	E6
Awe, Loch	57	C4
Awful, Mount	115	B6
Awgu	105	G4
Awjilah	101	K2
Axbridge	52	E3
Axe *Dorset, U.K.*	52	E4
Axe *Somerset, U.K.*	52	E3
Axel-Heiberg Island	120	H2
Axim	104	E5
Axios	75	G2
Ax-les-Thermes	65	D7
Axminster	52	D4
Ayabe	89	E8
Ayacucho *Argentina*	139	E7
Ayacucho *Peru*	136	C6
Ayaguz	86	F2
Ayamonte	66	C4
Ayan *Russia*	84	H5
Ayan *Russia*	85	P5
Ayancik	76	F2
Ayas	76	E3
Ayaviri	136	C6
Ayayei	96	C10
Aya-Yenahin	104	E4
Aybasti	77	G2
Aydarkul, Ozero	86	B3
Aydere	95	N2
Aydin	76	B4
Aydinca	77	G2
Aydincik	76	E4
Aydin Daglari	76	C3
Ayerbe	67	F1
Ayeshka	84	E6
Ayia Anna	75	G3
Ayia Marina	75	J5
Ayios	75	G4
Ayios Andreas	75	G4
Ayios Evstratios	75	H3
Ayios Kirikos	75	J4
Ayios Nikolaos *Greece*	75	F3
Ayios Nikolaos *Greece*	75	H5
Ayios Petros	75	F3
Aykathonisi	75	J4
Aykhal	84	J3
Aylesbury	53	G3
Ayllon	66	E2
Aylmer, Lake	119	P3
Aylsham	53	J2
Ayn al Bayda	77	G5
Ayni	86	B4
Ayn Tarfawi	77	K5
Ayn, Wadi al	97	M5
Ayod	102	F6
Ayon	85	V3
Ayon, Ostrov	85	V3
Ayora	67	F3
Ayr *U.K.*	57	D5
Ayr *U.K.*	57	D5
Ayranci	76	E4
Ayre, Point of	54	E2
Aysgarth	55	H2
Ayshirak	86	C2
Aytos	73	J4
Ayun	97	L8
Ayutthaya	93	K6
Ayvacik	76	B3
Ayvali	76	D4
Azambuja	66	B3
Azamgarh	92	F3
Azaran	94	H3
Azaz	77	G4
Azazga	67	J4
Azbine	101	G5
Azerbaijan	79	H7
Azezo	96	C10
Azogues	136	B4
Azoum	102	D5
Azov, Sea of	79	F6
Azovskoye More	79	F6
Azpeitia	66	E1
Azraq, Bahr el	103	F5
Azrou	100	D2
Aztec	127	H2
Azuaga	66	D3
Azuari	137	G3
Azuero, Peninsula de	132	G11
Azul *Argentina*	139	E7
Azul *Mexico*	131	Q9
Azul, Cordillera	136	B5
Azur, Cote d'	65	G7
Azvaday	76	E2
Az Zabadani	77	G6
Az Zafir	96	E7
Az Zahran	97	K3
Az Zarqa	97	L4
Az Zawiyah	101	H2
Az Zaydiyah	96	F9
Az Zilfi	96	G3
Az Zubaydiyah	94	G5
Az Zubayr	94	H6
Az Zuhrah	96	F9
Az Zuqur	96	F9

B

Name	Page	Grid
Baaba	114	W16
Baalbek	77	G5
Baamonde	66	C1
Baardheere	107	H2
Babadag	73	K3
Babaeski	76	B2
Babahoyo	136	B4
Babai Gaxun	87	J3
Baba, Koh-i-	92	C2
Babar	91	H7
Babar, Kepulauan	91	H7
Babayevo	78	F4
Babbacombe Bay	52	D4
Babelthuap	91	J4
Babine Lake	118	K5
Babo	114	A2
Babol	95	L3
Babol Sar	95	L3
Baboua	102	B6
Babruysk	79	D5
Babstovo	88	D1
Babushkin	84	H6
Babuyan *Philippines*	91	F4
Babuyan *Philippines*	91	G2
Babuyan Channel	91	G2
Babuyan Islands	91	G2
Bacabal	137	J4
Bacan	91	H6
Bacau	73	J2
Baccegalhaldde	62	J2
Back	119	R2
Backa	63	E6
Backaland	56	F1
Backa Topola	72	E3
Backe	62	G5
Bac Ninh	93	L4
Bacolod	91	G3
Bacup	55	G3
Badagara	92	E6
Badajoz	66	C3
Badalona	67	H2
Badanah	94	E6
Bad Aussee	68	D2
Badby	53	F2
Bad Doberan	70	D1
Bad Ems	70	B3
Baden	68	B2
Baden-Baden	70	C4
Badenoch	57	D4
Badgastein	68	D2
Bad Homburg	70	C3
Badiet esh Sham	94	D5
Bad Ischl	68	D2
Bad Kissingen	70	D3
Bad Kreuznach	70	B4
Bad Lands	123	N4
Bad Mergentheim	70	C4
Badminton	52	E3
Bad Neustadt	70	D3
Bad Oldesloe	70	D2
Ba Don	93	L5
Badong	93	M2
Badrah	94	G5
Badr Hunayn	96	D5
Bad Segeberg	70	D2
Bad Tolz	70	D5
Badulla	92	F7
Bad Wildungen	70	C3
Badzhal	85	N6
Badzhalskiy Khrebet	85	N6
Bae Can	93	L4
Baena	66	D4
Baeza	136	B4
Bafa Golu	76	B4
Bafang	105	H4
Bafata	104	C3
Baffin Bay *Canada*	120	H3
Baffin Bay *U.S.A.*	128	D7
Baffin Island	120	L3
Bafia	105	H5
Bafing Makana	100	C6
Bafoulabe	100	C6
Bafoussam	105	H4
Bafq	95	M6
Bafra	77	F2
Bafra Burun	77	F2
Baft	95	N7
Bafwasende	106	E2
Bagamoya	107	G4
Bagan Datuk	90	C5
Bagansiapiapi	90	C5
Baganyuvam	78	K2
Bagaryak	84	Ad5
Bagdad	126	F3
Bagdere	77	J3
Bage	138	F6
Bagenalstown	59	J7
Baggs	123	L7
Baghdad	77	L6
Bagherhat	93	G4
Bagheria	69	D6
Baghlan	92	C1
Bagh nam Faoilean	56	A3
Bagisli	77	L4
Bagneres-de-Bigorre	65	D7
Bagneres-de-Luchon	65	D7
Bagnoles-de-l'Orne	64	C4
Bagnolo Mella	68	C3
Bagoe	104	D3
Bagrationovsk	71	J1
Bagshot	53	G3
Baguio	91	G2
Bagusa	114	B2
Bahamas	132	J2
Baharampur	93	G4
Bahau	90	C5
Bahaur	90	E6
Bahawalpur	92	D3
Bahce	77	G4
Bahia	137	J6
Bahia Blanca	139	D7
Bahia Bustamante	139	C9
Bahia, Islas de la	132	D6
Bahia Kino	126	G6
Bahia Laura	139	C9
Bahia Negra	138	E4
Bahias, Cabo dos	139	C8
Bahr	96	E7
Bahr, Abu	97	J6
Bahraich	92	F3
Bahrain	97	K3
Bahrain, Gulf of	97	K4
Bahr Sayqal	77	G6
Bahu Kalat	95	Q9
Baia de Maputo	109	F5
Baia Mare	73	G2
Baian, Band-i-	92	C2
Baiao	137	H4
Baiazeh	95	M5
Baibokoum	102	C6
Baicheng *Jilin, China*	87	N2
Baicheng *Xinjiang Uygur Zizhiqu, China*	86	E3
Baie Comeau	125	R2
Baie-du-Poste	121	M7
Baiji	77	K5
Baiju	87	N5
Baikal, Lake	84	H6
Baile Atha Cliath	59	K6
Baile Herculane	73	G3
Bailieborough	58	J5
Baillie Hamilton Island	120	H2
Baillie Island	118	K1
Bailundo	106	C5
Baimuru	114	C3
Bainbridge	129	K5
Bain-de-Bretagne	65	C5
Baing	91	G8
Bains-les-Bains	65	G4
Baird Inlet	118	C3
Baird Mountains	118	C2
Baird Peninsula	120	L4
Bairin Youqi	87	M3
Bairin Zuoqi	87	M3
Bairnsdale	113	K6
Baise	65	D7
Baixingt	87	N3
Baiyanghe	86	F3
Baja	72	E2
Baja, Punta	126	E6
Bajgiran	95	P3
Bajil	96	F9
Bajmok	72	E3
Bakchar	84	C5
Bakel	104	C3
Baker *Chile*	139	B9
Baker *California*	126	E3
Baker *Montana*	123	M4
Baker *Oregon*	122	F5
Baker Foreland	119	S3
Baker Island	111	T1
Baker Lake	119	R3
Baker, Mount	122	D3
Bakersfield	126	C3
Bakewell	55	H3
Bakharden	95	N2
Bakhardok	95	P2
Bakharz	95	P4
Bakhchisaray	79	E7
Bakhmach	79	E5
Bakhta	84	D4
Bakhtaran	94	H4
Bakhtegan, Daryacheh-ye	95	L7
Bakhty	86	F2
Bakinskikh Komissarov	95	M2
Bakir	76	B3
Bakkafjordur	62	X11
Bakkafloi	62	X11
Bakkagerdi	62	Y12
Baklan	76	C4
Bako	103	G6
Bakongan	90	B5
Bakony	72	D2
Bakouma	102	D6
Baku	79	H7
Bakwanga	106	D4
Bala	52	D2
Bala	76	E3
Balabac	91	F4
Balabac Strait	90	F4
Balabio	114	W16
Bala, Cerros de	136	D6
Balacita	73	G3
Balad	77	L6
Baladch	95	K3
Balagannoye	85	R5
Balaghat	92	F4
Balaghat Range	92	E5
Balaguer	67	G2
Balaikarangan	90	E5
Balaka	107	F5

Name	Page	Ref
Balakhta	84	E5
Balakleya	79	F6
Balakovo	79	H5
Bala Lake	52	D2
Balama	109	G2
Balambangan	91	F4
Bala Morghab	95	R4
Balangir	92	F4
Balashov	79	G5
Balassagyarmat	72	E1
Balaton	72	D2
Balatonszentgyorgy	72	D2
Balazote	66	E3
Balbi, Mount	114	E3
Balboa	132	H10
Balbriggan	58	K5
Balcarce	139	E7
Balchik	73	K4
Balchrick	56	C2
Balclutha	115	B7
Bald Knob	128	G3
Baldock	53	G3
Baleares, Islas	67	H3
Balearic Islands	67	H3
Baleia, Ponta da	137	K7
Baleine, Grande Riviere de la	121	L6
Baleine, Riviere a la	121	N6
Baler	91	G2
Balerno	57	E5
Balestrand	63	B6
Baley	85	K6
Balfes Creek	113	K3
Balfour	56	F1
Balguntay	86	F3
Balhaf	97	J10
Bali	90	F7
Baligrod	71	K4
Balikesir	76	B3
Balik Golu	77	K3
Balikpapan	90	F6
Bali, Laut	90	F7
Balimbing	91	F4
Balimo	114	C3
Balinqiao	87	M3
Balintang Channel	91	G2
Balkashino	84	Ae6
Balkh	92	C1
Balkhash	86	C2
Balkhash, Ozero	86	C2
Balladonia	112	E5
Ballaghaderreen	58	E5
Ballandean	113	L4
Ballangen	62	G2
Ballantrae	57	C5
Ballao	69	B6
Ballarat	113	J6
Ballard, Lake	112	E4
Ballasalla	54	E2
Ballash	92	F4
Ballater	57	E3
Balle	100	D5
Ballenas, Bahia de	126	F7
Ballenas, Canal de las	126	F6
Balleny Islands	141	L5
Ballia	92	F3
Ballina	58	D4
Ballinafad	58	F4
Ballinamore	58	G4
Ballinasloe	59	F6
Ballincollig	59	E9
Ballindine	58	E5
Ballineen	59	E9
Ballinhassig	59	E9
Ballinluig	57	E4
Ballinskelligs Bay	59	B9
Ball Peninsula	120	K5
Ballsh	74	E2
Ballybay	58	J4
Ballybofey	58	G3
Ballybunion	59	C7
Ballycastle Ireland	58	D4
Ballycastle U.K.	58	K2
Ballyclare	58	L3
Ballycotton Bay	59	G9
Ballycroy	58	C4
Ballydesmond	59	D8
Ballyduff	59	C8
Ballygalley Head	58	L3
Ballygawley	58	H4
Ballygowan	58	L4
Ballyhaunis	58	E5
Ballyheige	59	C8
Ballyheige Bay	59	C8
Ballyhooly	59	F8
Ballyjamesduff	58	H5
Ballykeel	58	H3
Ballylongford	59	D7
Ballymahon	59	G5
Ballymena	58	K3
Ballymoe	58	F5
Ballymoney	58	J2
Ballymore Eustace	59	J6
Ballymote	58	E4
Ballynahinch	58	L4
Ballyquintin Point	58	M4
Ballyragget	59	H7
Ballyshannon	58	F3
Ballysitteragh	59	B8
Ballyteige Bay	59	J8
Ballyvaghan Bay	59	D6
Ballyvourney	59	D9
Ballywater	58	M3
Balmedie	56	F3
Balonne	113	K4
Balotra	92	D3
Balrampur	92	F3
Balranald	113	J5
Bals	73	H3
Balsas Brazil	137	H5
Balsas Mexico	131	J8
Balsas Peru	136	B5
Balsta	63	G7
Balta	79	D6
Baltanas	66	D2
Baltasound	56	A1
Balti	73	J2
Baltic Sea	63	G9
Baltim	102	F1
Baltimore	125	M7
Baltinglass	59	J7
Baluchistan	92	C3
Balurghat	93	G3
Balvicar	57	C4
Balya	76	B3
Balykshi	79	J6
Bam	95	N3
Bam	95	P7
Bama	105	H3
Bamako	100	D6
Bamba	100	E5
Bambari	102	D6
Bamberg Germany	70	D4
Bamberg U.S.A.	129	M4
Bambesa	106	E2
Bamenda	105	H4
Bami	95	N2
Bamian	92	C2
Bam Posht	95	R8
Bampton	53	F3
Bampur	95	Q8
Banaba	111	Q2
Banadia	133	M11
Banagher	59	G6
Banalia	106	E2
Banam	93	L6
Bananal, Ilha do	137	G6
Ban Aranyaprathet	93	K6
Banas	92	E3
Banas, Ras	96	C5
Bana, Wadi	96	G10
Banaz	76	C3
Banbridge	58	K4
Banbury	53	F2
Banchory	57	F3
Bancroft	125	M4
Banda	92	F3
Banda Aceh	90	B4
Banda Elat	91	J7
Banda, Kepulauan	91	H6
Banda, Laut	91	H7
Bandama Blanc	104	D4
Bandan Kuh	95	Q6
Banda, Punta la	126	D5
Bandar Abbas	95	N8
Bandarbeyla	103	K6
Bandar-e Anzali	94	J3
Bandar-e Deylam	95	K6
Bandar-e Lengeh	95	M8
Bandar e Mashur	94	J6
Bandar-e Moghuyeh	95	M8
Bandar-e Rig	95	K7
Bandar-e Torkeman	95	M3
Bandar Khomeyni	94	J6
Bandar Seri Begawan	90	E5
Bande	66	C1
Band-e-pay	95	L3
Bandiagara	100	E6
Bandirma	76	B2
Bandol	65	F7
Bandon Ireland	59	E9
Bandon Ireland	59	E9
Bandundu	106	C3
Bandung	90	D7
Baneh	94	G4
Banes	133	K4
Banff Canada	122	G2
Banff U.K.	56	F3
Banfora	104	E3
Bangalore	92	E6
Bangangte	105	H4
Bangassou	102	D7
Bangeta, Mount	114	D3
Banggai	91	G6
Banggai, Kepulauan	91	G6
Banggi	91	F4
Banghazi	101	K2
Bangka	90	D6
Bangkalan	90	E7
Bangkaru	90	B5
Bangka, Selat	90	D6
Bangko	90	D6
Bangkok	93	K6
Bangkok, Bight of	93	K6
Bangladesh	93	G4
Bangor Down, U.K.	58	L3
Bangor Gwynedd, U.K.	54	E3
Bangor U.S.A.	125	R4
Bangor Erris	58	C4
Bang Saphan Yai	93	J6
Bangui Central African Rep.	102	C7
Bangui Philippines	91	G2
Bangweulu, Lake	107	E5
Bangweulu Swamps	107	E5
Ban Hat Yai	93	K7
Ban Houei Sai	93	K4
Bani	100	D6
Baniara	114	D3
Banika	114	J6
Bani Khatmah	96	G7
Bani Maarid	96	H7
Bani Walid	101	H2
Baniyas	94	B5
Baniyas	94	B4
Bani Zaynan, Hadh	97	J6
Banja Luka	72	D3
Banjarmasin	90	E6
Banjul	104	B3
Banka Banka	113	G2
Ban Kantang	93	J7
Ban Keng Phao	93	L6
Bankfoot	57	E4
Ban Khemmarat	93	L5
Ban Khok Kloi	93	J7
Banks Island Australia	114	C4
Banks Island British Columbia, Canada	118	J5
Banks Island NW.Territories, Canada	119	L1
Banks Islands	111	Q4
Banks Peninsula	115	D5
Banks, Point	118	E4
Banks Strait	113	K7
Ban Kui Nua	93	J6
Bankura	93	G4
Bankya	73	G4
Ban Mae Sariang	93	J5
Banmauk	93	J4
Ban Me Thuot	93	L6
Bann	58	K3
Ban Nabo	93	L5
Ban Na San	93	J7
Bannockburn	108	E4
Bannu	92	D2
Banolas	67	H1
Banovce	71	H4
Ban Pak Chan	93	J6
Ban Sao	93	K5
Banska Bystrica	71	H4
Banska Stiavnica	71	H4
Bansko	73	G5
Banstead	53	G3
Banswara	92	D4
Bantaeng	91	F7
Ban Takua Pa	93	J7
Ban Tan	93	K6
Banteer	59	E8
Ban Tha Sala	93	J7
Bantry	59	D9
Bantry Bay	59	C9
Banya	73	H4
Banyak, Kepulauan	90	B5
Banyo	105	H4
Banyuls	65	E7
Banyuwangi	90	E7
Banzyville	106	D2
Baoding	87	M4
Baofeng	93	M2
Baoji	93	L2
Baoqing	88	D2
Baoshan	93	J4
Baoting	93	L5
Baotou	87	L3
Baoxing	88	C1
Bapatla	92	F5
Bapaume	64	E3
Baqubah	77	L6
Bar Ukraine	73	J1
Bar Yugoslavia	77	E1
Bara	102	F5
Baraawe	107	H2
Barabai	90	F6
Bara Banki	92	F3
Barabinsk	84	B5
Barabinskaya Step	84	B6
Baracoa	133	K4
Baraganul	73	J3
Barahona	133	M5
Barail Range	93	H3
Baraka	96	C8
Barakkul	84	Ae6
Baram	90	E5
Baran	92	E3
Baranavichy	71	L2
Barang, Dasht-i-	95	Q5
Barankul	84	Ae6
Baranof Island	118	H4
Baraoltului, Muntii	73	H2
Barapasai	114	B2
Barat Daya, Kepulauan	91	H7
Barbacena	138	H4
Barbados	133	T6
Barbas, Cap	100	B4
Barbastro	67	G1
Barberton South Africa	108	F5
Barberton U.S.A.	125	K6
Barbezieux	65	C6
Barbuda	133	S6
Barcaldine	113	K3
Barcelona Spain	67	H2
Barcelona Venezuela	136	E2
Barcelonnette	65	G6
Barcelos Brazil	136	E4
Barcelos Portugal	66	B2
Barcin	71	G2
Barcoo	113	J3
Barcs	72	D3
Barda	79	H7
Bardai	102	C3
Bardas Blancas	139	C7
Barddhaman	93	G4
Bardejov	71	J4
Bardneshorn	62	Y12
Bardney	55	J3
Bardsey Island	52	C2
Bareilly	92	E3
Barentsevo More	78	F2
Barentsoya	80	D2
Barents Sea	78	F2
Barentu	103	G4
Bareo	90	F5
Barfleur, Point de	64	C4
Barford	53	F2
Bargrennan	57	D5
Barguzinskiy Khrebet	84	H6
Barh	92	G3
Barhaj	92	F3
Barham	53	J3
Bar Harbor	125	R4
Bari	69	F5
Baridi, Ra's	96	C4
Barika	67	J5
Barinas	136	C2
Baring, Cape	119	M1
Baripada	92	G4
Bari Sadri	92	D4
Barisal	93	H4
Barisan, Pegunungan	90	C6
Barito	90	E6
Barka	97	N5
Barkan, Ra's-e	95	J7
Barking	53	H3
Barkley Sound	122	B3
Barkly East	108	E6
Barkly Tableland	113	H2
Barkol	86	F3
Barkston	53	G2
Barle	52	D3
Bar-le-Duc	64	F4
Barlee, Lake	112	D4
Barlestone	53	F2
Barletta	69	F5
Barmby Moor	55	J3
Barmer	92	D3
Barmouth	52	D2
Barnard Castle	55	H2
Barnaul	84	C6
Barnes Ice Cap	120	M3
Barnet	53	G3
Barnhart	127	M5
Barnoldswick	55	G3
Barnsley	55	H3
Barnstaple	52	C3
Barnstaple Bay	52	C3
Baro	105	G4
Baroda	92	D4
Barony, The	56	E1
Barquilla	66	D3
Barquinha	66	B3
Barquisimeto	136	D1
Barra Brazil	137	J6
Barra U.K.	57	A4
Barra do Bugres	138	E3
Barra do Corda	137	H5
Barra Head	57	A4
Barra Mansa	138	H4
Barranca Peru	136	B4
Barranca Venezuela	133	L10
Barrancabermeja	136	C2
Barrancas	133	R10
Barrancos	66	C3
Barranqueras	138	E5
Barranquilla	136	C1
Barra, Sound of	57	A3
Barre	125	P4
Barreiras	137	H6
Barreiro	66	B3
Barren Island, Cape	110	L10
Barren Islands	118	E4
Barren River Lake	124	H8
Barretos	138	G4
Barrhead Canada	119	N5
Barrhead U.K.	57	F4
Barrhill	57	D5
Barrie	125	L4
Barrier, Cape	115	E2
Barriere	122	D2
Barrington Tops	113	L5
Barrocao	138	H3
Barrow Argentina	139	D7
Barrow Ireland	59	H8
Barrow U.S.A.	118	D1
Barrowford	55	G3
Barrow-in-Furness	55	F2
Barrow Islands	112	D3
Barrow, Point	118	D1
Barrow Range	112	F4
Barrow Strait	120	G3
Barry	52	D3
Barry's Bay	125	M4
Barsalpur	92	D3
Barsi	92	E5
Barstow	126	D3
Bar-sur-Aube	64	F4
Bar-sur-Seine	64	F4
Barth	70	E1
Bartica	136	F2
Bartin	76	E2
Bartle Frere, Mount	113	K2
Bartlesville	128	D2
Barton Philippines	91	F3
Barton U.S.A.	125	P4
Barton-upon-Humber	55	J3
Bartoszyce	71	J1
Barumun	90	C5
Barus	90	B5

Name	Page	Ref
Baruun Urt	87	L2
Barvas	56	B2
Barwani	92	D4
Barwon	113	K4
Barysaw	63	Q9
Barysh	79	H5
Basaidu	95	M8
Basankusu	106	C2
Basco	91	G1
Bascunan, Cabo	138	B5
Basel	68	A2
Basento	69	F5
Bashakerd, Kuhha-ye	95	P8
Bashi Haixia	87	N7
Basht	95	K6
Basilan *Philippines*	91	G4
Basilan *Philippines*	91	G4
Basildon	53	H3
Basingstoke	53	F3
Baskale	77	L3
Baskatong, Reservoir	125	N3
Baskil	77	H3
Baskoy	77	K2
Basle	68	A2
Basoko	106	D2
Bassano del Grappa	68	C3
Bassar	104	F4
Bassas da India	109	G4
Bassein	93	H5
Bassenthwaite	55	F2
Bassenthwaite Lake	55	F2
Basse Santa Su	104	C3
Basseterre	133	R6
Basse Terre	133	S6
Bassett	123	Q6
Bassila	105	F4
Bass Strait	113	K6
Bastad	63	E8
Bastak	95	M8
Bastam	95	M3
Basti	92	F3
Bastia	69	B4
Bastogne	64	F4
Bastrop *Louisiana*	128	G4
Bastrop *Texas*	128	D5
Basyurt	77	J3
Bata	105	G5
Batabano, Golfo de	132	F3
Batagay	85	N3
Batagay-Alyta	85	N3
Batakan	90	E6
Bataklik Golu	76	E4
Batala	92	E2
Batalha	66	B3
Batamay	85	M4
Batan	91	G1
Batang	93	J2
Batangafo	102	C6
Batangas	91	G3
Batanghari	90	C6
Batan Islands	91	G1
Batatais	138	G4
Batavia	125	L5
Bataysk	79	F6
Batchelor	112	G1
Batesville	128	G3
Bath *U.K.*	52	E3
Bath *U.S.A.*	125	M5
Batha	102	C5
Bathgate	57	E5
Bathurst *Australia*	113	K5
Bathurst *Canada*	125	T3
Bathurst *Gambia*	104	B3
Bathurst Inlet	119	P2
Bathurst Island	112	G1
Bathurst Islands	120	F2
Batie	104	E4
Batiki	114	R8
Batinah, Al	97	N4
Batin, Wadi al	96	H2
Batiscan	125	P3
Batitoroslar	76	D4
Batlaq-e Gavkhuni	95	L5
Batley	55	H3
Batman *Turkey*	77	J4
Batman *Turkey*	77	J4
Batna	101	G1
Baton Rouge	128	G5
Batouri	105	H5
Batroun	77	F5
Batsfjord	62	N1
Battambang	93	K6
Batticaloa	92	F7
Battle *Canada*	119	N5
Battle *U.K.*	53	H4
Battle Creek	124	H5
Battle Harbour	121	Q7
Battle Mountain	122	F7
Batu	103	G6
Batubetumbang	90	D6
Batum	77	J2
Batumi	77	J2
Batu Pahat	90	C5
Batuputih	91	F5
Baturaja	90	D6
Baturite	137	K4
Baubau	91	G7
Bauchi	105	G3
Bauda	92	H4
Baudette	124	C2
Baudo	136	B2
Baudouinville	107	E4
Bauge	65	C5
Bauhinia Downs	113	K3
Baukau	91	H7
Bauld, Cape	121	Q7
Baumann Fjord	120	J2
Baunie	113	L4
Baurtregaum	59	C8
Bauru	138	G4
Baus	138	F3
Bautzen	70	F3
Bawdeswell	53	J2
Bawdsey	53	J2
Bawean	90	E7
Bawku	104	E3
Bawiti	102	E2
Bawtry	55	H3
Baxley	129	L5
Bayamo	132	J4
Bayamon	133	P5
Bayan	88	A2
Bayan-Aul	84	B6
Bayandalay	87	J3
Bayanday	84	H6
Bayan Harshan	93	J2
Bayanhongor	86	J2
Bayan Mod	87	J3
Bayan Obo	87	K3
Bayano, Laguna	132	H10
Bayan-Ondor	86	H3
Bayantsagaan	86	H3
Bayantsogt	87	K2
Bayan-Uul	87	L2
Bayard *Nebraska*	123	N7
Bayard *New Mexico*	127	H4
Bayat *Turkey*	76	D3
Bayat *Turkey*	76	F2
Bayburt	77	J2
Bayfield	124	E3
Bayhan al Qasab	96	G9
Bayindir	76	B3
Bayir	94	C6
Baykadam	86	B3
Baykal	84	G6
Baykalovo	84	Ae5
Baykal, Ozero	84	H6
Baykan	77	J3
Bay-Khak	84	E6
Baykit	84	F4
Baynunah	97	L5
Bayombong	91	G2
Bayona	66	B1
Bayonne	65	C7
Bayo Point	91	G3
Bayram-Ali	95	R3
Bayramic	76	B3
Bayramiy	94	J2
Bayramtepe	76	C2
Bayreuth	70	D4
Bayrut	76	F6
Bay Saint Louis	128	H5
Bayt al Faqih	96	F9
Baytown	128	E6
Bayy al Kabir, Wadi	101	H2
Baza	66	E4
Bazaliya	71	M4
Bazar-Dyuzi	79	H7
Bazaruto, Ilha do	109	G4
Bazas	65	C6
Bazman	95	Q8
Bazman, Kuh-e-	95	Q7
Bcharre	77	F5
Beach	123	N4
Beachy Head	53	H4
Beaconsfield	53	G3
Beadnell Bay	55	H1
Beagh, Lough	58	G2
Beagle Gulf	112	G1
Beagle Reef	112	E2
Beal	57	G5
Bealanana	109	J2
Beaminster	52	E4
Beampingaratra	109	J4
Bear	122	J6
Beara Peninsula	59	C9
Beardmore	124	G2
Beardstown	124	E6
Bear Island *Canada*	121	K7
Bear Island *Ireland*	59	C9
Bear Lake	122	J7
Bearley	53	F2
Bearn	65	C7
Bear Paw Mount	122	K3
Bearsden	57	D5
Beartooth Range	123	K5
Beata, Cabo	133	M6
Beata, Isla	133	M6
Beatrice	123	R7
Beatty	126	D2
Beattyville	125	M2
Beau Basin	109	L7
Beaucaire	65	F7
Beaufort *Malaysia*	90	F4
Beaufort *U.S.A.*	129	M4
Beaufort Sea	118	H1
Beaufort West	108	D6
Beaugency	65	D5
Beauly *U.K.*	56	D3
Beauly *U.K.*	56	D3
Beauly Firth	56	D3
Beaumaris	54	E3
Beaumont *France*	64	E4
Beaumont *California*	126	D4
Beaumont *Texas*	128	E5
Beaune	65	F5
Beaurepaire	65	F6
Beauvais	64	E4
Beauvoir-sur-Mer	65	B5
Beaver *Saskatchewan, Canada*	119	P5
Beaver *Yukon, Canada*	118	K3
Beaver Dam *Kentucky*	124	G8
Beaver Dam *Wisconsin*	124	F5
Beaverhill Lake	119	N5
Beawar	92	D3
Beazley	139	C6
Bebedouro	138	G4
Bebington	55	F3
Beccles	53	J2
Becej	72	F3
Becerrea	66	C1
Bechar	100	E2
Becharof Lake	118	D4
Bechet	73	G4
Beckingham	55	J3
Beckley	125	K8
Beclean	73	H2
Bedale	55	H2
Bedarieux	65	E7
Bede, Point	118	E4
Bedford *U.K.*	53	G2
Bedford *U.S.A.*	124	G7
Bedford Level	53	H2
Bedfordshire	53	G2
Bedlington	55	H1
Bedwas	52	D3
Bedworth	53	F2
Beer Sheva	94	B6
Beeston	53	F2
Beeswing	57	E5
Beeville	128	D6
Befale	106	D2
Befandriana	109	J3
Begejska Kanal	72	F3
Begoml	63	N10
Behbehan	95	K6
Behraamkale	76	B3
Behshahr	95	L3
Beian	87	P2
Beibu Wan	93	L4
Beihai	93	L4
Beijing	87	M4
Beila	100	B5
Beinn a' Ghlo	57	E4
Beinn Bheigier	57	B5
Beinn Dearg *Highland, U.K.*	56	D3
Beinn Dearg *Tayside, U.K.*	57	E4
Beinn Dorain	57	D4
Beinn Eighe	56	C3
Beinn Fhada	56	C3
Beinn Ime	57	D4
Beinn Mhor	56	A3
Beinn na Caillich	57	C3
Beinn Resipol	57	C4
Beinn Sgritheall	57	C3
Beipiao	87	N3
Beira	109	F3
Beirut	76	F6
Bei Shan	86	H3
Beit Lahm	94	B6
Beius	73	G2
Beja	66	C3
Beja	101	G1
Bejaia	101	G1
Bejaia, Golfe de	67	J4
Bejar	66	D2
Bejestan	95	P4
Beji	92	C3
Bekdast	79	J7
Bekescsaba	73	F2
Bekily	109	J4
Bekopaka	109	H3
Bekwai	104	E4
Bela *India*	92	F3
Bela *Pakistan*	92	C3
Belabo	105	H5
Belaga	90	E5
Belang	91	G5
Bela Palanka	73	G4
Belarus	71	L2
Bela Vista	109	F5
Belawan	90	B5
Belaya *Russia*	78	K4
Belaya *Russia*	85	W3
Belaya-Kalitva	79	G6
Belaya Kholunitsa	78	J4
Belayan	90	F5
Belcher Channel	120	G2
Belcher Islands	121	L6
Belchiragh	94	S4
Belchite	67	F2
Belcoo	58	G4
Belderg	58	C4
Belebey	78	J5
Beledweyne	103	J7
Belem	137	H4
Belen *Turkey*	76	E4
Belen *U.S.A.*	127	J3
Belep, Iles	114	V15
Belesar, Embalse de	66	C1
Belev	79	F5
Belfast *New Zealand*	115	D5
Belfast *U.K.*	58	L3
Belfast Lough	58	L3
Belfield	123	N4
Belford	57	G5
Belfort	65	G5
Belgaum	92	D5
Belgium	64	E3
Belgorod	79	F5
Belgorod-Dnestrovskiy	79	E6
Belgrade	72	F3
Belgrano	141	X3
Belica	71	L2
Beli Lom	73	J4
Beli Manastir	72	E3
Belimbing	90	C7
Belin	65	C6
Belinskiy	79	G5
Belinyu	90	D6
Belitsa	73	G5
Belitung	90	D6
Belize	132	C6
Belkina, Mys	88	F3
Belknap, Mount	122	H8
Belkovskiy, Ostrov	85	P1
Bella Bella	118	K5
Bellac	65	D5
Bella Coola	118	K5
Bellaire	128	E6
Bellary	92	E5
Bella Vista *Argentina*	138	C5
Bella Vista *Argentina*	138	E5
Belleek	58	F4
Bellefontaine	124	J6
Belle Fourche *South Dakota*	123	N5
Belle Fourche *Wyoming*	123	M5
Belle Glade	129	M7
Belle Ile	65	B5
Belle Isle	121	Q7
Belleme	64	D4
Belleville *Canada*	125	M4
Belleville *Illinois*	124	F7
Belleville *Kansas*	123	R8
Bellevue *Idaho*	122	G6
Bellevue *Washington*	122	C4
Belley	65	F6
Bellingham *U.K.*	57	F5
Bellingham *U.S.A.*	122	C3
Bellinghaussen Sea	141	U5
Bellingshausen	141	W6
Bellinzona	68	B2
Bello	136	B2
Bellona Island	114	J7
Bellona Reefs	111	N6
Bellpuig	67	G2
Bellshill	57	D5
Belluno	68	D2
Bell Ville	138	D6
Belly	122	H3
Belmont	56	A1
Belmonte *Portugal*	66	C2
Belmonte *Spain*	66	E3
Belmopan	132	C6
Belmullet	58	B4
Belogorsk	79	E6
Belogorye	71	M4
Belogradchik	73	G4
Belo Horizonte	138	K4
Beloit	124	F5
Belokorovichi	79	D5
Belomorsk	78	E3
Belorado	66	E1
Belorechensk	79	F7
Beloren	76	E4
Belorusskaya Gryada	71	L2
Belot, Lac	118	K2
Belo-Tsiribihina	109	H3
Belousovka	84	C6
Belovo	84	D6
Beloye More	78	F2
Beloye Ozero	78	F3
Belozersk	78	F4
Belozerskoye	84	Ae5
Belper	55	H3
Belsay	57	G5
Belterra	137	F4
Belton	55	J3
Belturbet	58	H4
Belukha, Gora	86	F2
Belvedere Marittimo	69	E6
Belvidere	124	F5
Belvoir, Vale of	53	G2
Belyando, River	113	K3
Belyayevka	73	L2
Belyy, Ostrov	85	A2
Belyy Yar	84	D5
Belzyce	71	K3
Bemaraha, Plateau du	109	J3
Bembridge	53	F4
Bemidji	124	C3
Benabarre	67	G1
Ben Alder	57	D4
Benalla	113	K6
Benares	92	F3
Benavente	66	D2
Ben Avon	57	E3
Benbaun	59	C5
Ben Chonzie	57	E4
Bencorr	59	C5
Ben Cruachan	57	C4
Bend	122	D5
Bende	105	G4
Bender Qaasim	103	J5
Bendigo	113	J6
Benesov	70	F4
Benevento	69	E5
Bengbu	87	M5
Benghazi	101	K2

Name	Page	Grid
Bengkalis	90	C5
Bengkulu	90	C6
Bengo, Baia do	106	B4
Bengoi	91	J6
Bengtsfors	63	E7
Benguela	106	B5
Benguerua, Ilha	109	G4
Benha	102	F1
Ben Hope	56	D2
Beni *Bolivia*	136	D6
Beni *Zaire*	107	E2
Beni Abbes	100	E2
Benicarlo	67	G2
Benidorm	67	F3
Beni Mazar	102	F2
Beni Mellal	100	D2
Benin	105	F4
Benin, Bight of	105	F4
Benin City	105	G4
Beni Saf	100	E1
Beni Suef	102	F2
Ben Klibreck	56	D2
Ben Lawers	57	D4
Ben Ledi	57	D4
Ben Lomond	57	D4
Ben Loyal	56	D2
Ben Lui	57	D4
Ben Macdui	57	E3
Ben MorCoigach	56	C3
Ben More *Central, U.K.*	57	D4
Ben More *Strathclyde, U.K.*	56	B4
Ben More Assynt	56	D2
Benmore, Lake	115	C6
Bennachie	56	F3
Benn Cleuch	57	E4
Bennetta, Ostrov	85	R1
Ben Nevis	57	C4
Bennington	125	P5
Benoni	108	E5
Be, Nosy	109	J2
Ben Rinnes	56	E3
Bensheim	70	C4
Benson *U.K.*	53	F3
Benson *U.K.*	126	G5
Ben Starav	57	C4
Bent	95	P8
Bentinck Island	93	J6
Bent Jbail	94	B5
Bentley	55	H3
Benton	128	F3
Benton Harbor	124	G5
Bentung	90	C5
Benue	105	G4
Ben Venue	57	D4
Ben Vorlich	57	D4
Benwee	58	C5
Benwee Head	58	C4
Ben Wyvis	56	D3
Benxi	87	N3
Beo	91	H5
Beograd	72	F3
Beppu	89	C9
Beqa	114	R9
Berat	74	E2
Berau, Teluk	114	A2
Berber	103	F4
Berbera	103	J5
Berberati	102	C7
Berck	64	D3
Berdichev	79	D6
Berdigestyakh	85	M4
Berdyansk	79	F6
Berea	124	H8
Bereeda	103	K5
Beregovo	79	C6
Berens	119	R5
Berens River	119	R5
Bere Regis	52	E4
Berettyo	73	F2
Berettyoujfalu	73	F2
Bereza	71	L2
Berezhany	71	L4
Berezhnykh, Mys	85	Q1
Berezina	78	D5
Berezino	78	D5
Berezna	79	E5
Berezniki	78	K4
Berezno	71	M3
Berezovka *Russia*	78	K3
Berezovka *Russia*	85	K5
Berezovka *Russia*	85	T3
Berezovka *Ukraine*	79	E6
Berezovo *Russia*	84	Ae4
Berezovo *Russia*	85	W4
Berezovskaya	85	K5
Berg	108	C6
Berga	67	G1
Bergama	76	B3
Bergamo	68	B3
Bergeforsen	62	G5
Bergen *Germany*	70	E1
Bergen *Norway*	63	J6
Bergen op Zoom	64	F3
Bergerac	65	D6
Bergfors	62	H2
Bergisch-Gladbach	70	B3
Bergsviken	62	J4
Berhala, Selat	90	C6
Beringa, Ostrov	81	T4
Bering Glacier	118	G3
Beringovskiy	85	X4
Bering Sea	143	H3
Bering Strait	118	B2
Berislav	79	E6
Beris, Ra's	95	Q9
Berja	66	E4
Berkak	62	C5
Berkakit	85	L5
Berkeley *U.K.*	52	E3
Berkeley *U.S.A.*	126	A2
Berkhamsted	53	G3
Berkner Island	141	W3
Berkovitsa	73	G4
Berkshire	53	F3
Berkshire Downs	53	F3
Berkshire Mountains	125	P5
Berlevag	62	N2
Berlin *Germany*	70	E2
Berlin *U.S.A.*	125	Q4
Bermeja, Sierra	66	D4
Bermejo *Argentina*	138	C6
Bermejo *Argentina*	138	D4
Bermeo	66	E1
Bermillo de Sayago	66	C2
Bermuda	117	N5
Bern	68	A2
Bernau	70	E2
Bernay	64	D4
Bernburg	70	D3
Berne	68	A2
Berner Alpen	68	A2
Berneray *U.K.*	57	A4
Berneray *U.K.*	56	A3
Bernina, Piz	68	B2
Beroroha	109	J4
Berounka	70	E4
Berre, Etang de	65	F7
Berriedale	56	E2
Berriedale Water	56	E2
Berrigan	113	K6
Berringarra	112	D4
Berrouaghia	67	H4
Berry *Australia*	113	L5
Berry *France*	65	E5
Berryessa, Lake	122	C8
Berry Head	52	D4
Berry Islands	132	J1
Bershad	73	K1
Berthoud Pass	123	L8
Bertoua	105	H5
Beru	111	S2
Beruri	136	E4
Berwick	125	M6
Berwick-upon-Tweed	57	F5
Berwyn Mountains	52	D2
Berzence	72	D2
Besalampy	109	H3
Besancon	65	G5
Besar, Kai	91	J7
Besbre	65	E5
Beshneh	95	M7
Besiri	77	J4
Beskidy Zachodnie	71	H4
Beslan	79	G7
Besni	77	G4
Bessarabia	73	K2
Bessarabka	73	K2
Bessbrook	58	K4
Bessemer *Alabama*	129	J4
Bessemer *Winconsin*	124	F3
Bestamak *Kazakhstan*	86	D2
Bestamak *Kazakhstan*	79	K6
Bestobe	84	A6
Bestuzhevo	78	G3
Betafo	109	J3
Betanzos	66	B1
Betare Oya	105	H4
Bethal	108	E5
Bethanie	108	C5
Bethany	124	C6
Bethel	118	C3
Bethel Park	125	L6
Bethesda *U.K.*	54	E3
Bethesda *U.S.A.*	125	M7
Bethlehem *Israel*	94	B6
Bethlehem *South Africa*	108	E5
Bethulie	108	E6
Bethune *France*	64	D4
Bethune *France*	64	E3
Betioky	109	H4
Betpak-Dala	86	B2
Bet-Pak-Data	86	B2
Betroka	109	J4
Betsiamites	125	R2
Betsiboka	109	J3
Bettiah	92	F3
Bettyhill	56	D2
Betul	92	E4
Betwa	92	E4
Betws-y-coed	54	F3
Beuvron	65	D5
Beverley *Australia*	112	D5
Beverley *U.K.*	55	J3
Beverly Hills	126	C3
Bexhill	53	H4
Beykoz	76	C2
Beyla	104	D4
Beylul	96	F10
Beyneu	79	K6
Beypazari	76	D2
Beypinar	77	G3
Beysehir	76	D4
Beysehir Golu	76	D4
Beyton	53	H2
Beytussebap	77	K4
Bezhetsk	78	F4
Beziers	65	E7
Bezmein	95	P2
Bhadgaon	92	G3
Bhadrachalam	92	F5
Bhadrakh	92	G4
Bhadravati	92	E6
Bhagalpur	92	G3
Bhakkar	92	D2
Bhamo	93	J4
Bhandara	92	E4
Bhanrer Range	92	F4
Bharatpur *Pradesh, India*	92	F4
Bharatpur *Rajasthan, India*	92	E3
Bharuch	92	D4
Bhatinda	92	D2
Bhatpara	93	G4
Bhavnagar	92	D4
Bhawanipatna	92	F5
Bhilwara	92	D3
Bhima	92	E5
Bhiwani	92	E3
Bhopal	92	E4
Bhopalpatnam	92	F5
Bhor	92	D5
Bhubaneshwar	92	G4
Bhuj	92	C4
Bhumiphol Dam	93	J5
Bhusawal	92	E4
Bhutan	93	G3
Bia	136	D4
Biaban	95	N8
Biabanak	95	S5
Biak	114	B2
Biala Podlaska	71	K2
Bialobrzegi	71	J3
Bialowieza	71	K2
Bialystok	71	K2
Bianco	69	F6
Biankouma	104	D4
Biaro	91	H5
Biarritz	65	C7
Biasca	68	B2
Biba	102	F2
Bibai	88	H4
Bibala	106	B5
Bibby Island	119	S3
Biberach	70	C4
Bibury	53	F3
Bicester	53	F3
Bicheno	113	K7
Bickle Knob	125	L7
Bida	105	G4
Bidar	92	E5
Biddeford	125	Q5
Biddulph	55	G3
Bidean Nam Bian	57	C4
Bideford	52	C3
Bideford Bay	52	C3
Bidford-on-Avon	53	F2
Bidokht	95	P4
Bidzhan *Russia*	88	C1
Bidzhan *Russia*	88	C2
Biebrza	71	K2
Biel	68	A2
Bielefeld	70	C2
Biella	68	B3
Bielsko-Biala	71	H4
Bielsk Podlaski	71	K2
Bien Hoa	93	L6
Bienne	68	A2
Bienveneu	137	G3
Bienville, Lac	121	M6
Biferno	69	E5
Biga	76	B2
Bigadic	76	C3
Big Bay	114	T11
Big Belt Mountains	122	J4
Big Blue	123	R7
Bigbury Bay	52	D4
Biggar *Canada*	123	K1
Biggar *U.K.*	57	E5
Biggleswade	53	G2
Big Horn	123	K5
Big Horn Mountains	123	L5
Big Island	120	M5
Big Pine	126	C2
Big Piney	123	J6
Big Sheep Mountains	123	L4
Big Sioux	123	R5
Big Snowy Mount	122	K4
Big Spring	127	M4
Big Stone Gap	124	J8
Big Timber	123	J5
Big Trout Lake	119	T4
Bihac	72	C3
Bihar	92	G4
Bihar	92	G3
Biharamulo	107	F3
Bihoro	88	K4
Bihu	87	M6
Bijagos, Arquipelago dos	104	B3
Bijapur	92	E5
Bijar	94	H4
Bijeljina	72	E3
Bijelo Polje	72	E4
Bijie	93	L3
Bijnor	92	E3
Bikaner	92	D3
Bikin *Russia*	88	E2
Bikin *Russia*	88	F2
Bikoro	106	C3
Bilad Bani Bu Ali	97	P5
Bilad Ghamid	96	E6
Bilad Zahran	96	E6
Bilaspur	92	F4
Bila Tserkva	79	E6
Bilauktaung Range	93	J6
Bilbao	66	E1
Bilchir	85	J6
Bilecik	76	C2
Biled	73	F3
Bile Karpaty	71	G4
Bilesha Plain	107	H2
Bilgoraj	71	K3
Bili	106	E2
Bilin	93	J5
Billabalong	112	D4
Billericay	53	H3
Billingham	55	H2
Billings	123	K5
Billingshurst	53	G3
Bilma	101	H5
Bilma, Grand Erg de	101	H5
Biloela	113	L3
Bilo Gora	72	D3
Biloxi	128	H5
Biltine	102	D5
Bilugyun	93	J5
Binalud, Kuh-e	95	P3
Binatang	90	E5
Binder	87	L2
Bindloe Island	136	A7
Bindura	108	F3
Binefar	67	G2
Binga	108	E3
Bingara	113	L4
Bingerville	104	E4
Bingham	125	R4
Binghamton	125	N5
Bingley	55	H3
Bingol	77	J3
Bingol Daglari	77	J3
Binjai *Indonesia*	90	B5
Binjai *Indonesia*	90	D5
Binongko	91	G7
Bintan	90	C5
Bintuhan	90	C6
Bintulu	90	E5
Bin Xian *Heilongjiang, China*	88	A3
Bin Xian *Shaanxi, China*	93	L2
Binyang	93	L4
Bio	114	K7
Biobio	139	B7
Biograd	72	C4
Bioko	105	G5
Bir	92	E5
Bira *Russia*	88	D1
Bira *Russia*	88	D1
Bira *Russia*	85	P7
Birag, Kuh-e	95	Q8
Birak	101	H3
Bir al Hisw	96	E4
Bir al War	101	H4
Birao	102	D5
Biratnagar	93	G3
Bir Butayman	77	H4
Birca	73	G4
Birch Island	122	D2
Birch Mountains	119	N4
Bird	119	S4
Bird Island	133	R7
Birdlip	53	E3
Birdum	113	G2
Birecik	77	G4
Bireun	90	B4
Bir Fardan	97	J5
Bir Ghabalou	67	H4
Bir Hadi	97	K7
Birhan	103	G5
Birikchul	84	D6
Birjand	95	P5
Birkenhead *New Zealand*	115	E2
Birkenhead *U.K.*	55	F3
Birksgate Range	112	F4
Birlad *Romania*	73	J2
Birlad *Romania*	73	J2
Birlestik	86	B2
Birmingham *U.K.*	53	F2
Birmingham *U.S.A.*	129	J4
Bir Moghrein	100	C3
Birnie Island	111	U2
Birnin Kebbi	105	F3
Birni nKonni	101	G6
Birobidzhan	88	D1
Birofeld	88	D1
Birr	59	G6
Bir, Ras el	103	H5
Birreencorragh	58	C5
Birrimbah	112	G2
Birsk	78	K4
Birtle	123	P2
Birtley	55	H2
Biryusa	84	F5
Birzai	63	L8
Biscay, Bay of	65	B6
Bischofshofen	68	D2
Biscotasi Lake	124	J3
Bisert	78	K4
Bisevo	72	D4
Bisha	96	C9
Bishah, Wadi	96	F6
Bishkek	86	C3
Bishnupur	93	G4
Bishop	126	C2
Bishop Auckland	55	H2
Bishop Burton	55	J3
Bishop's Castle	52	D2
Bishops Falls	121	Q8
Bishop's Stortford	53	H3
Bishri, Jbel	77	H5

Name	Page	Grid	Name	Page	Grid	Name	Page	Grid	Name	Page	Grid
Biskra	101	G2	Blanc, Cap	69	B7	Bogazkaya	77	F2	Bolvadin	76	D3
Biskupiec	71	J2	Blanche Channel	114	H6	Bogazkopru	76	F3	Bolyarovo	73	J4
Bislig	91	H4	Blanche, Lake	113	H4	Bogazliyan	76	F3	Bolzano	68	C2
Bismarck Archipelago	114	D2	Blanchland	55	G2	Bogbonga	106	C2	Bom	114	D3
Bismarck Range	114	D3	Blanc, Mont	65	G6	Bogen	62	L2	Boma	106	B4
Bismark	123	P4	Blanco	136	E7	Boggeragh Mountains	59	E8	Bombala	113	K6
Bismil	77	J4	Blanco, Cabo	139	C9	Boghar	67	H5	Bombay	92	D5
Bismo	63	C6	Blanco, Cape	122	B6	Bogia	114	D2	Bomili	106	E2
Bisotun	94	H4	Blanda	62	V12	Bognes	62	G2	Bom Jesus	137	J5
Bispfors	62	G5	Blandford Forum	53	E4	Bognor Regis	53	G4	Bom Jesus da Lapa	137	J6
Bissau	104	B3	Blanes	67	H2	Bogo	91	G3	Bomlafjord	63	A7
Bissett	123	S2	Blangy	64	D4	Bogodukhov	79	F5	Bomlo	63	A7
Bistcho Lake	119	M4	Blankenberge	64	E3	Bogong, Mount	113	K6	Bomongo	106	C2
Bistretu	73	G4	Blanquilla, Isla	136	E1	Bogor	90	D7	Bonab	94	H3
Bistrita *Romania*	73	H2	Blantyre	107	G6	Bogorodchany	71	L4	Bonaire	133	N8
Bistrita *Romania*	73	J2	Blarney	59	E9	Bogorodskoye *Russia*	78	J4	Bonaire Trench	133	N9
Bistritei, Muntii	73	H2	Blasket Islands	59	A8	Bogorodskoye *Russia*	85	Q6	Bona, Mount	118	G3
Bitburg	70	B3	Blavet	65	B5	Bogota	136	C3	Bonar Bridge	56	D3
Bitche	64	G4	Blaydon	55	H2	Bogotol	84	D5	Bonavista	121	R8
Bitik	79	J5	Blaye	65	C6	Bogra	93	G4	Bonavista Bay	121	R8
Bitkine	102	C5	Bleadon	52	E3	Boguchany	84	F5	Bon, Cap	101	H1
Bitlis	77	K3	Bleaklow Hill	55	H3	Boguchar	79	G6	Bondo	106	D2
Bitola	73	F5	Bled	72	C2	Bogue	100	C5	Bondokodi	91	F7
Bitonto	69	F5	Blekinge	63	F8	Bogue Chitto	128	G5	Bondoukou	104	E4
Bitterfontein	108	C6	Bletchley	53	G3	Boguslav	79	E6	Bone	69	A7
Bitterroot	122	G4	Bleus, Monts	107	F2	Bo Hai	87	K4	Bo'ness	57	E4
Bitterroot Range	122	G4	Blida	101	F1	Bohemia	70	E4	Bonete, Cerro	138	C5
Bitti	69	B5	Bligh Water	114	R8	Bohmer Wald	70	E4	Bone, Teluk	91	G6
Biu	105	H3	Blind River	124	J3	Bohol	91	G4	Bongabong	91	G3
Bivolu	73	H2	Blisworth	53	G2	Bohol Sea	91	G4	Bongor	102	C5
Biwa-ko	89	E8	Block Island	125	Q6	Boiano	69	E5	Bonham	128	D4
Biyad, Al	96	H5	Bloemfontein	108	E5	Boigul	114	C3	Bonifacio	69	B5
Biyagundi	96	C9	Blois	65	D5	Boipeba, Ilha	137	K6	Bonifacio, Strait of	69	B5
Biysk	84	D6	Blonduos	62	U12	Bois Blanc Island	124	H4	Bonn	70	B3
Bizerta	69	B7	Bloodvein	123	R2	Boisdale, Loch	57	A3	Bonners Ferry	122	F3
Bizerte	101	G1	Bloody Foreland	58	F2	Boise *U.S.A.*	122	F6	Bonnetable	64	D4
Bjargtangar	62	S12	Bloomfield	124	D6	Boise *U.S.A.*	122	F6	Bonneval	64	D4
Bjelovar	72	D3	Bloomington *Illinois*	124	F6	Boise City	127	L2	Bonneville	65	G5
Bjerkvik	62	L2	Bloomington *Indiana*	124	G7	Bois, Lac des	118	K2	Bonneville Salt Flats	122	H7
Bjorklinge	63	G6	Bloomington *Minnesota*	124	D4	Boissevain	123	P3	Bonnie Rock	112	D5
Bjorksele	62	H4	Bloomsbury	113	K3	Boizenburg	70	D2	Bonny *France*	65	E5
Bjorna	62	H5	Blouberg	108	E4	Bojana	74	E2	Bonny *Nigeria*	105	G5
Bjorneborg *Finland*	63	J6	Blubberhouses	55	H3	Bojnurd	95	N3	Bonnyrigg	57	E4
Bjorneborg *Sweden*	63	F7	Bludenz	68	B2	Boka	73	F3	Bono	69	B5
Bjornevatn	62	N2	Bluefield	125	K8	Boka Kotorska	72	E4	Bonobono	91	F4
Bjornoya	80	C2	Bluefields	132	F9	Boke	104	C3	Bonorva	69	B5
Bjurholm	62	H5	Blue Mountain Lake	125	N5	Bokhara	113	K4	Bonthe	104	C4
Bjursas	63	F6	Blue Mountain Peak	132	J5	Boknafjord	63	A7	Bontoc	91	G2
Bla Bheinn	56	B3	Blue Mountains	122	E5	Bokol	107	G2	Booligal	113	J5
Black *Alaska*	118	G2	Bluemull Sound	56	A1	Bokoro	102	C5	Boologooro	112	C3
Black *Arizona*	127	H4	Bluenose Lake	119	M2	Boksitogorsk	78	E4	Boone *Iowa*	124	D5
Black *Arkansas*	128	G3	Blue Ridge	129	K3	Boktor	85	P6	Boone *N. Carolina*	129	M2
Black *New York*	125	N5	Blue Ridge Mountains	129	L3	Bokungu	106	D3	Booneville *Mississippi*	128	H3
Blackadder Water	57	F5	Blue Stack	58	F3	Bolama	104	B3	Booneville *New York*	125	N5
Blackall	113	K3	Blue Stack Mountains	58	F3	Bolanos	130	H7	Booroorban	113	J5
Black Bay	124	F2	Bluff *New Zealand*	115	B7	Bolan Pass	92	C3	Boosaaso	103	J5
Black Belt	129	J4	Bluff *U.S.A.*	127	H2	Bolbec	64	D4	Boothia, Gulf of	120	J4
Blackburn	55	G3	Bluff Knoll	112	D5	Bolchary	84	Ae5	Boothia Peninsula	120	H3
Black Canyon City	126	F3	Bluff Point	112	C4	Bole	104	E4	Bootle	55	F3
Blackdown Hills	52	D4	Bluff, Punta	126	F6	Boleslawiec	70	F3	Boot Reefs	114	C3
Blackfoot	122	H6	Blumenau	138	G5	Bolgatanga	104	E3	Bopeechee	113	H4
Blackford	57	E4	Blunt	123	Q5	Bolgrad	79	D6	Boquilla, Presa de la	127	K7
Black Head	59	D6	Blyth *Northumberland, U.K.*	55	H1	Boli	88	C3	Boquillas del Carmen	127	L6
Blackhead Bay	59	D6	Blyth *Nottinghamshire, U.K.*	55	H3	Bolia	106	C3	Bor *Sudan*	102	F6
Blackhill	55	H3	Blyth *Suffolk, U.K.*	53	J2	Boliden	62	J4	Bor *Turkey*	76	F4
Black Hills	123	N5	Blythe	126	E4	Bolinao	91	F2	Bor *Yugoslavia*	73	G3
Black Isle	56	D3	Blythe Bridge	53	E2	Bol Irgiz	79	H5	Boraha, Nosy	109	J3
Black Mesa	126	G2	Blytheville	128	H3	Bolivar	139	D7	Borah Peak	122	H5
Blackmill	52	D3	Bo	104	C4	Bolivar *Missouri*	124	D8	Boras	63	E8
Black Mountain	52	D3	Boac	91	G3	Bolivar *Tennessee*	128	H3	Borasambar	92	F4
Black Mountains	52	D3	Boa Fe	136	C5	Bolivar, Cerro	133	R11	Borazjan	95	K7
Blackpool	55	F3	Boa Vista *Cape Verde*	104	L7	Bolivar, Pico	133	M10	Borba	136	F4
Black Range	127	J4	Boa Vista *Amazonas, Brazil*	136	D4	Bolivia	138	C3	Borborema, Planalto da	137	K5
Black River Falls	124	E4	Boa Vista *Roraima, Brazil*	136	E3	Boljevac	73	F4	Borca	73	H2
Blackrock	58	K5	Bobai	93	M4	Bolkhov	79	F5	Borcka	77	J2
Black Rock Desert	122	E7	Bobaomby, Tanjoni	109	J2	Bollington	55	G3	Bordeaux	65	C6
Black Sea	51	P7	Bobbili	92	F5	Bollnas	63	G6	Borden Island	120	D2
Blacksod Bay	58	B4	Bobbio	68	B3	Bollon	113	K4	Borden Peninsula	120	K3
Blackstairs Mount	59	J7	Bobo Dioulasso	104	E3	Bollstabruk	62	G5	Borders	57	F5
Blackstairs Mountains	59	J7	Bobolice	71	G2	Bolmen	63	E8	Bordertown	113	J6
Blackthorn	53	F3	Bobr	70	F3	Bolobo	106	C3	Bordeyri	62	U12
Black Volta	104	E4	Bobrinents	79	E6	Bologna	68	C3	Bordj-Bou-Arreridj	67	J4
Black Water	57	E4	Bobrka	71	L4	Bologoye	78	E4	Bordj Bounaama	67	G5
Blackwater *Australia*	113	K3	Bobrov	79	G5	Bolotnoye	84	C5	Bordj Omar Driss	101	G3
Blackwater *Meath, Ireland*	58	J5	Bobures	133	M10	Boloven, Cao Nguyen	93	L5	Borensberg	63	F7
Blackwater *Waterford, Ireland*	59	F8	Boca del Pao	136	E2	Bolsena, Lago di	69	C4	Boreray	56	A3
Blackwater *Essex, U.K.*	53	H3	Boca do Acre	136	D5	Bolsherechye	84	A5	Borga	63	L6
Blackwater *Hampshire, U.K.*	53	G3	Boca Grande	136	E2	Bolsheretsk	85	T6	Borgarnes	62	U12
Blackwaterfoot	57	C5	Bocaiuva	138	H3	Bolshevik	85	R4	Borgefjellet	62	E4
Blackwater Lake	119	L3	Boca Mavaca	136	D3	Bolshevik, Ostrov	81	M2	Borger	127	M3
Blackwater Reservoir *Highland, U.K.*	57	D4	Bocaranga	102	C6	Bolshezemelskaya Tundra	78	K2	Borgholm	63	G8
Blackwater Reservoir *Tayside, U.K.*	57	E4	Boca Raton	129	M7	Bolshoy Anyuy	85	U3	Borgo San Lorenzo	68	C4
Blackwell	128	D2	Bochnia	71	J4	Bolshoy Atlym	84	Ae4	Borgosesia	68	B3
Blackwood	112	D5	Bocholt	70	B3	Bolshoy Balkhan, Khrebet	95	M2	Borgo Val di Taro	68	B3
Blaenavon	52	D3	Bochum	70	B3	Bolshoy Begichev, Ostrov	84	J2	Borgo Valsugana	68	C2
Blafjall	62	W12	Bodalla	113	L6	Bolshoy Chernigovka	79	J5	Borislav	71	K4
Blagodarnyy	79	G6	Boddam	56	A2	Bolshoy Kavkaz	77	L1	Borisoglebsk	79	G5
Blagoevgrad	73	G4	Boden	62	J4	Bolshoy Kunyak	84	A5	Borispol	79	E5
Blagoveshchensk *Russia*	78	K4	Bodensee	70	C5	Bolshoy Lyakhovskiy, Ostrov	85	Q2	Borja	67	F2
Blagoveshchensk *Russia*	85	M6	Bodhan	92	E5	Bolshoy Murta	84	E5	Borkovskaya	78	H2
Blagoyevo	78	H3	Bodmin	52	C4	Bolshoy Pit	84	E5	Borkum	70	B2
Blair Atholl	57	E4	Bodmin Moor	52	C4	Bolshoy Porog	84	E3	Borlange	63	F6
Blairgowrie	57	E4	Bodo	62	F3	Bolshoy Shantar, Ostrov	85	P5	Borlu	76	C3
Blaka	101	H4	Bodrum	76	B4	Bolshoy Usa	78	K4	Bormida	68	B3
Blakely	129	K5	Bodva	71	J4	Bolshoy Yenisey	84	E6	Bormio	68	C2
Blakeney	53	J2	Bodza, Pasul	73	J3	Bolshoy Yugan	84	A5	Borneo	90	E5
Blakesley	53	F2	Boen	65	F6	Bolsover	55	H3	Bornholm	70	F1
Blanca, Bahia	139	D7	Boende	106	D3	Boltana	67	G1	Bornholmsgatset	63	F9
Blanca, Costa	67	F3	Boffa	104	C3	Bolt Head	52	D4	Bornova	76	B3
Blanca Peak	127	K2	Bogalusa	128	H5	Bolton *Greater Manchester, U.K.*	55	G3	Borohoro Shan	86	E3
Blanca, Punta	126	E6	Bogan	113	K5	Bolton *Northumberland, U.K.*	57	G5	Boroko	91	G5
Blanca, Sierra	127	K4	Bogaz	76	E2	Bolu	76	D2	Boromo	104	E3
			Bogazkale	76	F2	Bolucan	77	G3	Boronga Islands	93	H5
						Bolus Head	59	B9	Borongan	91	H3

Feature	Pg	Ref
Chapeltown *S. Yorkshire, U.K.*	55	H3
Chapleau	124	J3
Chaplygin	79	F5
Chapman	112	F2
Chapman, Cape	120	J4
Chapman Islands	119	P2
Chaqui	138	C3
Chara *Russia*	85	K5
Chara *Russia*	85	K5
Charagua	138	D3
Charak	95	M8
Charambira, Punta	136	B3
Charcot Island	141	U5
Chard	52	E4
Chardzhev	80	H6
Charente	65	C6
Chari	102	C5
Charikar	92	C1
Chariton *U.S.A.*	124	D6
Chariton *U.S.A.*	124	D6
Charkhari	92	E3
Charlemount	58	J4
Charleroi	64	F3
Charlesbourg	125	Q3
Charles, Cape	125	N8
Charles City	124	D5
Charles Island *Canada*	120	M5
Charles Island *Ecuador*	136	A7
Charleston *Illinois*	124	F7
Charleston *Missouri*	124	F8
Charleston *S. Carolina*	129	N4
Charleston *W. Virginia*	125	K7
Charlestown	58	E5
Charlestown of Aberlour	56	E3
Charleville	113	K4
Charleville-Mezieres	64	F4
Charlotte	129	M3
Charlotte Amalie	133	Q5
Charlotte, Cape	139	J10
Charlotte Harbour	129	L7
Charlottesville	125	L7
Charlottetown	121	P8
Charlton	113	J6
Charlton Island	121	L7
Charmes	64	G4
Charnley	112	F2
Charolles	65	F5
Charters Towers	113	K3
Chartres	64	D4
Charwelton	53	F2
Charybdis Reef	114	Q8
Charyn	86	D3
Chascomus	139	E7
Chaselka	84	C3
Chaslands Mistake	115	B7
Chasong	87	P3
Chasovo	78	J3
Chasseeneuil	65	D6
Chat	95	M3
Chateaubriant	65	C5
Chateau Chinon	65	E5
Chateaudun	65	D4
Chateau-Gontier	65	C5
Chateau-la-Valliere	65	D5
Chateaulin	64	A4
Chateauneuf-en-Thimerais	64	D4
Chateauneuf-sur-Loire	65	E5
Chateaurenault	65	D5
Chateauroux	65	D5
Chateau-Salins	64	G4
Chateau-Thierry	64	E4
Chatellerault	65	D5
Chatham *New Brunswick, Canada*	125	T3
Chatham *Ontario, Canada*	124	J5
Chatham *U.K.*	53	H3
Chatham, Isla	139	B10
Chatham Island *Ecuador*	136	A7
Chatham Island *New Zealand*	115	F7
Chatham Islands	115	G7
Chatillon	68	A3
Chatillon-sur-Indre	65	D5
Chatillon-sur-Seine	65	F5
Chato, Cerro	139	B8
Chattahoochee	129	K5
Chattanooga	129	K3
Chatteris	53	H2
Chatyrtash	86	D3
Chaudiere	125	Q3
Chaumont	64	F4
Chaunskaya Guba	85	V3
Chauny	64	E4
Chautauqua Lake	125	L5
Chavantina	138	G6
Chaves *Brazil*	137	H4
Chaves *Portugal*	66	C2
Chaviva	136	C3
Chay Khanah	77	L5
Chaykovskiy	78	J4
Chazhegovo	78	J3
Cheadle	55	G3
Cheb	70	E3
Cheboksary	78	H4
Cheboygan	124	H4
Chechen , Ostrov	79	H7
Chech, Erg	100	D3
Chechuysk	84	H5
Checiny	71	J3
Chedabucto Bay	121	P8
Cheddar	52	E3
Cheduba	93	H5
Cheetham, Cape	141	L4
Chef-Boutonne	65	C5
Chehalis	122	C4
Chehel Dokhtaran	95	R4
Cheju	87	P5
Cheju do	87	P5
Chekhov	88	H2
Chekunda	85	N6
Chekuyevo	78	F3
Chelan	122	D4
Chelan, Lake	122	D3
Chela, Serra da	106	B6
Cheleken	95	L2
Chelforo	139	C7
Cheliff, Oued	100	F1
Chelkar	51	U6
Chelm	71	K3
Chelmsford	53	H3
Chelmuzhi	78	F3
Chelosh	84	D6
Cheltenham	53	E3
Chelva	67	F3
Chelyabinsk	84	Ad5
Chelyuskin	84	G1
Chelyuskin, Mys	81	M2
Chemba	109	F3
Chemille	65	C5
Chemnitz	70	E3
Chenab	92	D2
Cheney	122	F4
Chengde	87	M3
Chengdu	93	K2
Chenghai	87	M7
Chengjiang	93	K4
Chengshan Jiao	87	N4
Chenonceaux	65	D5
Chen Xian	93	M3
Chepen	136	B5
Chepes	139	C6
Chepstow	52	E3
Chequamegon Bay	124	E3
Cher	65	E5
Cherangany Hills	107	G2
Cheraw	129	N3
Cherbourg	64	C4
Cherchell	101	F1
Cherdyn	78	K3
Cheremkhovo	84	C6
Cheremosh	71	L4
Cherepovets	78	F4
Cherevkovo	78	H3
Cherkashina	84	H5
Cherkasy	79	E6
Cherkessk	79	G7
Cherlak	84	A6
Cherlakskiy	84	A6
Cherlmno	71	H2
Chermoz	78	K4
Chernaya *Russia*	78	K2
Chernaya *Russia*	78	K2
Cherni	73	G4
Chernigovka *Russia*	88	D3
Chernigovka *Ukraine*	79	F6
Chernihiv	79	E5
Chernikovsk	78	K5
Cherni Lom	73	J4
Chernivtsi	73	H1
Chernobyl	79	E5
Chernoostrovskoye	84	D4
Chernousovka	84	A6
Chernushka	78	K4
Chernutyevo	78	H3
Chernyakhovsk	71	J1
Chernyshevskiy	85	J4
Chernyye Zemli	79	H6
Chernyy Mys	84	C5
Chernyy Otrog	79	K5
Cherokee	124	C5
Cherokee Sound	129	P7
Cherry	111	Q4
Cherskiy	85	U3
Cherskogo, Khrebet	85	Q3
Chertkovo	79	G6
Chertsey *New Zealand*	115	C5
Chertsey *U.K.*	53	G3
Chervonograd	79	C5
Chervonoznamenka	73	L2
Cherwell	53	F3
Chesapeake	125	M8
Chesapeake Bay	125	M8
Chesham	53	G3
Cheshire	55	G3
Cheshkaya Guba	78	H2
Cheshunt	53	G3
Chesil Beach	52	E4
Chester *U.K.*	55	G3
Chester *Illinois*	124	F8
Chester *Montana*	122	J3
Chester *S. Carolina*	129	M3
Chesterfield	55	H3
Chesterfield, Iles	113	M2
Chesterfield Inlet	119	S3
Chester-le-Street	55	H2
Chesters	57	F5
Chesterton Range	113	K4
Chesuncook Lake	125	R3
Chetlat	92	D6
Chetumal	131	Q8
Chetvertyy Kurilskiy Proliv	85	S7
Chetwynd	119	L4
Cheviot Hills	57	F5
Cheviot, The	57	F5
Chew	52	E3
Chew Valley Lake	52	E3
Cheyenne *S. Dakota*	123	P5
Cheyenne *Wyoming*	123	M7
Cheyenne Wells	127	L1
Chhapra	92	F3
Chhatarpur	92	E4
Chhindwara	92	E4
Chia-i	87	N7
Chiange	106	B6
Chiani	69	D4
Chiari	68	B3
Chiatura	77	K1
Chiautla	131	K8
Chiavari	68	B3
Chiavenna	68	B2
Chiba	89	H8
Chibia	106	B6
Chibit	84	D6
Chibizhek	84	E6
Chibougamau	125	N2
Chibougamau Lake	125	N2
Chibuto	109	F4
Chicago	124	G6
Chicama	136	B5
Chicapa	106	D4
Chichagof Island	118	H4
Chichester	53	G4
Chichester Range	112	D3
Chichibu	89	G8
Chichigalpa	132	D8
Chickasha	128	D3
Chicko	119	L5
Chiclayo	136	B5
Chico *Argentina*	139	C10
Chico *Argentina*	139	C8
Chico *U.S.A.*	122	D8
Chicoutimi	125	Q2
Chicualacuala	109	F4
Chidambaram	92	E6
Chiddingfold	53	G3
Chidley, Cape	121	P5
Chiefland	129	L6
Chiemsee	70	E5
Chieng-Mai	93	J5
Chienti	68	D4
Chieti	69	E4
Chifeng	87	M3
Chifre, Serra do	138	H3
Chiguana	138	C4
Chigubo	109	F4
Chigwell	53	H3
Chihli, Gulf of	87	K4
Chihuahua	127	J6
Chihuatlan	130	G8
Chiili	86	B3
Chijinpu	86	H3
Chik Ballapur	92	E6
Chikishlyer	95	L3
Chikmagalur	92	E6
Chikura	89	G8
Chi, Lam	93	K5
Chilamate	132	E8
Chilapa	131	K9
Chilas	92	D1
Chilca	136	B6
Chilca, Punta	136	B6
Childers	113	L4
Childress	127	M3
Chile	139	B7
Chile Chico	139	B9
Chilete	136	B5
Chilham	53	H3
Chilia, Bratul	73	K3
Chilik *Kazakhstan*	86	D3
Chilik *Kazakhstan*	79	J5
Chililabombwe	107	E5
Chillagoe	113	J2
Chillan	139	B7
Chillicothe *Missouri*	124	D7
Chillicothe *Ohio*	124	J7
Chilliculco	138	C3
Chiloe, Isla de	139	B8
Chilpancingo	131	K9
Chiltern Hills	53	G3
Chilumba	107	F5
Chi-lung	87	N6
Chilwa, Lake	107	G6
Chimanimani	109	F3
Chimay	64	F3
Chimborazo, Volcan	136	B4
Chimbote	136	B5
Chimishliya	73	K2
Chimkent	86	B3
Chimoio	109	F3
China	128	C8
Chinandega	132	D8
Chinati Peak	127	K6
Chinchilla	113	L4
Chinchilla de Monte Aragon	67	F3
Chinchon	66	E2
Chinchorro, Banco	131	R8
Chindagatuy	86	F2
Chinde	109	G3
Chindwin	93	H4
Chingola	107	E5
Chinguetti	100	C4
Chin Hills	93	H4
Chiniot	92	D2
Chinju	87	P4
Chinon	65	D5
Chinsali	107	F5
Chintalnar	92	F5
Chioggia	68	D3
Chios	75	H3
Chipata	107	F5
Chiperone	109	G3
Chipinge	109	F4
Chiplun	92	D5
Chipoka	107	F5
Chi Pou	93	L6
Chippenham	53	E3
Chippewa	124	E4
Chippewa Falls	124	E4
Chipping	55	G3
Chipping Norton	53	F3
Chipping Ongar	53	H3
Chipping Sodbury	52	E3
Chiputneticook Lakes	125	S4
Chiquinquira	136	C2
Chirchik	86	B3
Chiredzi	109	F4
Chirikof Island	118	D4
Chirimba	84	E5
Chirinda	84	G3
Chirique, Golfo de	132	F11
Chirk	52	D2
Chiromo	107	G6
Chirovanga	114	H5
Chirpan	73	H4
Chirripo	132	F10
Chishmy	78	K5
Chisinau	79	D6
Chisinau	73	K2
Chiskovo	84	F4
Chisone	68	A3
Chisos Mountains	127	L6
Chistopol	78	J4
Chita	85	J6
Chitato	106	D4
Chitembo	106	C5
Chitina	118	G3
Chitinskaya Oblast	85	K6
Chitradurga	92	E6
Chitral	92	D1
Chittagong	93	H4
Chittaurgarh	92	D4
Chittoor	92	E6
Chitungwiza	108	F3
Chiume	106	D6
Chiusi	69	C4
Chiva	67	F3
Chivasso	68	A3
Chivato, Punta	126	G7
Chive	136	D6
Chivhu	108	F3
Chivilcoy	139	D6
Chizha	78	G2
Chizha Vtoraya	79	H5
Chizu	89	E8
Chkalovskoye	88	D3
Chmielnik	71	J3
Choctawhatchee	129	K5
Chodziez	71	G2
Choele-Choel	139	C7
Choire, Loch	56	D2
Choiseul	114	H5
Choix	127	H7
Chojnice	71	G2
Chokai-san	88	H6
Chokurdakh	85	R2
Chokwe	109	F4
Cholderton	53	F3
Cholet	65	C5
Chollerton	57	F5
Choluteca	132	D8
Choma	106	E6
Chomutov	70	E3
Chona	84	H4
Chon Buri	93	K6
Chongan	87	M6
Chongjin	88	B5
Chongju	87	P4
Chongli	87	M3
Chongming Dao	87	M5
Chongqing	93	L3
Chongren	87	M6
Chongson	89	B7
Chongyang	93	M3
Chonos, Archipielago de los	139	B8
Chon Thanh	93	L6
Chop	79	C6
Chorley	55	G3
Chorolque	138	C4
Chortkov	79	D6
Chorzele	71	J2
Chos-Malal	139	B7
Choson-Man	87	P4
Choszczno	70	F2
Chota	136	B5
Choteau	122	H4
Choybalsan	87	L2
Christchurch *New Zealand*	115	D5
Christchurch *U.K.*	53	F4
Christiansfeld	63	C9
Christianshab	120	R4
Christie Bay	119	N3
Christmas Creek	112	F2
Christmas Island *Australia*	83	J8
Christmas Island *Kiribati*	143	H4
Chrzanow	71	H3
Chu	86	C3
Chubartau	86	D2
Chubut	139	C8
Chudleigh	52	D4
Chudovo	78	E4
Chudskoye Ozero	63	M7
Chugach Mountains	118	G3
Chugoku-sanchi	89	D8

Combourg	**64**	C4
Comeragh Mountains	**59**	G8
Comfort, Cape	**120**	K4
Comilla	**93**	H4
Comitan	**131**	N9
Committee Bay	**120**	J4
Como	**68**	B3
Comodoro Rivadavia	**139**	C9
Como, Lago di	**68**	B3
Comorin, Cape	**92**	E7
Comoros	**109**	H2
Compiegne	**64**	E4
Comporta	**66**	B3
Compostela	**130**	G7
Conakry	**104**	C4
Conara Junction	**113**	K7
Concarneau	**65**	B5
Conceicao do Araguaia	**137**	H5
Concepcion *Bolivia*	**138**	D3
Concepcion *Chile*	**138**	B7
Concepcion *Panama*	**132**	F10
Concepcion *Paraguay*	**138**	E4
Concepcion del Oro	**130**	J5
Concepcion del Uruguay	**138**	E6
Concepcion, Punta	**126**	G7
Conception Bay	**121**	R8
Conception Island	**133**	K3
Conception, Point	**126**	B3
Concho	**127**	M5
Conchos *Mexico*	**128**	C8
Conchos *Mexico*	**127**	K6
Concord *California*	**126**	A2
Concord *N. Carolina*	**129**	M3
Concord *New Hampshire*	**125**	Q5
Concordia *Argentina*	**138**	E6
Concordia *U.S.A.*	**123**	R8
Condamine	**113**	L4
Condeuba	**138**	J6
Condolobin	**113**	K5
Condom	**65**	D7
Conecuh	**129**	J5
Conegliano	**68**	D3
Conflict Group	**114**	E4
Confolens	**65**	D5
Congjiang	**93**	L3
Congleton	**55**	G3
Congo	**106**	B3
Congo	**106**	D2
Congo Basin	**99**	E6
Conisbrough	**55**	H3
Coniston	**55**	F2
Coniston Water	**54**	E2
Connah's Quay	**55**	F3
Connaught	**58**	D5
Conneaut	**125**	K6
Connecticut *U.S.A.*	**125**	P6
Connecticut *U.S.A.*	**125**	P6
Connellsville	**125**	L6
Conn, Lough	**58**	D4
Connors Range	**113**	K3
Conon	**56**	D3
Conon Bridge	**56**	D3
Conrad	**122**	J3
Conselheiro Lafaiete	**138**	H4
Conselheiro Pena	**138**	H3
Consett	**55**	H2
Con Son	**93**	L7
Constance, Lake	**70**	C5
Constancia dos Baetas	**136**	E5
Constanta	**73**	K3
Constantina	**66**	D4
Constantine	**101**	G1
Constantine Bay	**52**	B4
Constantine, Cape	**118**	D4
Constantinople	**76**	C2
Constitucion	**139**	B7
Contamana	**136**	C5
Contas	**137**	J6
Contratacion	**136**	C2
Contrexeville	**64**	F4
Contulmo	**139**	B7
Contwoyto Lake	**119**	N2
Conway *Arkansas*	**128**	F3
Conway *New Hampshire*	**125**	Q5
Conway *S. Carolina*	**129**	N4
Conway Bay	**54**	F3
Conwy	**54**	F3
Coober Pedy	**113**	G4
Cook	**112**	G5
Cook, Cape	**122**	A2
Cookeville	**129**	K2
Cook Inlet	**118**	E3
Cook Islands	**143**	H5
Cook, Mount	**115**	C5
Cook, Recif de	**114**	W15
Cookstown	**58**	J3
Cook Strait	**115**	E4
Cooktown	**113**	K2
Coolibah	**112**	G2
Coolidge	**126**	G4
Cooma	**113**	K6
Coomnadiha	**59**	C9
Coomscarrea	**59**	B9
Coonamble	**113**	K5
Coondapoor	**92**	D6
Coongan	**112**	D3
Coopers Creek	**113**	H4
Cooroy	**113**	L4
Coosa	**129**	J4
Coos Bay *U.S.A.*	**122**	B6
Coos Bay *U.S.A.*	**122**	B6
Cootamundra	**113**	K5
Cootehill	**58**	H4
Copacabana	**138**	C3
Copa, Cerro	**138**	C4
Cope	**123**	N8
Copenhagen	**63**	E9
Copiapo	**138**	B5
Copinsay	**56**	F2
Copkoy	**76**	B2
Copper	**118**	G3
Copper Center	**118**	F3
Coppermine *Canada*	**119**	M2
Coppermine *Canada*	**119**	N2
Copper Mount	**122**	F2
Copplestone	**52**	D4
Copsa Mica	**73**	H2
Coquet	**57**	G5
Coquimbo	**138**	B5
Coquimbo, Bahia de	**138**	B5
Corabia	**73**	H4
Coracora	**136**	C7
Coral Harbour	**120**	K5
Coral Sea Plateau	**113**	K2
Corantijn	**136**	F3
Corbeil-Essonnes	**64**	E4
Corbiere	**53**	M7
Corbieres	**65**	E7
Corbigny	**65**	E5
Corbin	**124**	H8
Corbones	**66**	D4
Corbridge	**55**	G2
Corby	**53**	G2
Corby Glen	**53**	G2
Corcaigh	**59**	E9
Corcovado, Golfo	**139**	B8
Corcubion	**66**	B1
Cordele	**129**	L5
Cordoba	**131**	L8
Cordoba *Argentina*	**138**	D6
Cordoba *Spain*	**66**	D4
Cordoba, Sierras de	**138**	D6
Cordova	**136**	B6
Cordova	**118**	F3
Corfe	**52**	D4
Corfu *Greece*	**74**	E3
Corfu *Greece*	**74**	E3
Coria	**66**	C2
Corigliano Calabro	**69**	F6
Corinda	**113**	H2
Corinth *Greece*	**75**	G4
Corinth *U.S.A.*	**128**	H3
Corinth, Gulf of	**75**	G3
Corinto *Brazil*	**138**	H3
Corinto *Nicaragua*	**132**	D8
Corixa Grande	**138**	E3
Cork *Ireland*	**59**	E9
Cork *Ireland*	**59**	E9
Corlay	**64**	B4
Corleone	**69**	D7
Corlu	**76**	B2
Cornafulla	**59**	F6
Corner Brook	**121**	Q8
Cornhill-on-Tweed	**57**	F4
Corning	**125**	M5
Corn Islands	**132**	F8
Cornudilla	**66**	E1
Cornwall *U.K.*	**52**	C4
Cornwall *Canada*	**125**	N4
Cornwallis Island	**120**	H2
Cornwall Island	**120**	H2
Coro	**136**	D1
Coroata	**137**	J4
Corocoro	**138**	C3
Coromandel *Brazil*	**138**	G3
Coromandel *New Zealand*	**115**	E2
Coromandel Coast	**92**	F6
Coromandel Peninsula	**115**	E2
Corona	**127**	K3
Coronado, Bahia de	**132**	E10
Coronation Gulf	**119**	N2
Coronel	**139**	B7
Coronel Dorrego	**139**	D7
Coronel Pringles	**139**	D7
Coronel Suarez	**139**	D7
Corovode	**75**	F2
Corps	**65**	F6
Corpus Christi	**128**	D7
Corpus Christi Bay	**128**	D7
Corpus Christi, Lake	**128**	D6
Corque	**138**	C3
Corran	**57**	C4
Corraun Peninsula	**58**	C5
Corrib, Lough	**59**	D6
Corrientes *Argentina*	**138**	E5
Corrientes *Peru*	**136**	B4
Corrientes, Cabo *Colombia*	**136**	B2
Corrientes, Cabo *Cuba*	**132**	E4
Corrientes, Cabo *Mexico*	**130**	G7
Corrigan	**128**	E5
Corrigin	**112**	D5
Corry	**125**	L6
Corryvreckan, Gulf of	**57**	C4
Corse	**69**	B4
Corse, Cap	**68**	B4
Corsewall Point	**57**	C5
Corsica	**69**	B4
Corsicana	**128**	D4
Corte	**69**	B4
Cortegana	**66**	C4
Cortez	**127**	H2
Cortina d'Ampezzo	**68**	D2
Cortland	**125**	M5
Cortona	**68**	C4
Corubal	**104**	C3
Coruche	**66**	B3
Coruh	**77**	J2
Corum	**76**	F2
Corumba	**138**	E3
Corumba	**138**	G3
Corunna	**66**	B1
Corvallis	**122**	C5
Corve	**52**	E2
Corwen	**52**	D2
Cos	**75**	J4
Cosamaloapan	**131**	M8
Cosamozza	**69**	B4
Cosenza	**69**	F6
Cosiguina, Volcan	**132**	D8
Cosmoledo Islands	**82**	C7
Cosne	**65**	E5
Costa, Cordillera de la	**133**	N9
Costa Rica	**132**	E9
Costesti	**73**	H3
Cotabato	**91**	G4
Cotacachi	**136**	B3
Cotagaita	**138**	C4
Cotahuasi	**138**	B3
Cotentin	**64**	C4
Cotiella	**67**	G1
Cotonou	**105**	F4
Cotopaxi	**136**	B4
Cottage Grove	**122**	C6
Cottbus	**70**	F3
Cottingham	**55**	J3
Cottonwood	**126**	F3
Coubre, Pointe de la	**65**	C6
Coulommiers	**64**	E4
Coulonge	**125**	M3
Council Bluffs	**124**	C6
Coupar Angus	**57**	E4
Courantyne	**136**	F3
Courchevel	**65**	G6
Couronne, Cap	**65**	F7
Courtenay	**122**	B3
Courtmacsherry Bay	**59**	E9
Coutances	**64**	C4
Couto Magalhaes	**137**	H5
Coutras	**65**	C6
Cove	**56**	C3
Coventry	**53**	F2
Covilha	**66**	C2
Covington *Kentucky*	**124**	H7
Covington *Virginia*	**125**	L8
Cowall	**57**	C4
Cowan, Lake	**112**	E5
Cowbit	**53**	G2
Cowbridge	**52**	D3
Cowdenbeath	**57**	E4
Cowes	**53**	F4
Cowfold	**53**	G4
Cowlitz	**122**	C4
Cowra	**113**	K5
Coxim	**138**	F3
Coxs Bazar	**93**	H4
Coxwold	**55**	H2
Cozumel	**131**	R7
Cozumel, Isla de	**131**	R7
Cracow	**71**	H3
Cradock	**108**	E6
Craig	**123**	L7
Craigavon	**58**	K4
Craignure	**57**	C4
Crail	**57**	F4
Crailsheim	**70**	D4
Craiova	**73**	G3
Cramlington	**55**	H1
Cranborne	**53**	F4
Cranbrook	**122**	G3
Crane	**127**	L5
Cranleigh	**53**	G3
Cranstown, Kap	**120**	Q3
Craponne-sur-Arzon	**65**	E6
Crasna *Romania*	**73**	G2
Crasna *Romania*	**73**	J2
Crater Lake	**122**	C6
Crateus	**137**	J5
Crati	**69**	F6
Crato	**137**	K5
Cravo Norte	**136**	C2
Crawford	**123**	N6
Crawford Point	**91**	F3
Crawfordville	**129**	K5
Crawley	**53**	G3
Crazy Mountains	**123**	J4
Creach Bheinn	**57**	C4
Creag Meagaidh	**57**	D3
Creagorry	**56**	A3
Crediton	**52**	D4
Cree *Canada*	**119**	P4
Cree *U.K.*	**57**	D5
Cree Lake	**119**	P4
Creeslough	**58**	G2
Creetown	**54**	E2
Creggan	**58**	H3
Creggs	**58**	F5
Crema	**68**	B3
Cremona	**68**	B3
Crepaja	**72**	F3
Creran, Loch	**57**	C4
Cres *Croatia*	**72**	C3
Cres *Croatia*	**72**	C3
Crescent	**122**	D6
Crescent City	**122**	B7
Crest	**65**	F6
Creston	**124**	C6
Crestview	**129**	J5
Crete	**75**	H5
Cretin, Cape	**114**	D3
Creus, Cap	**67**	H1
Creuse	**65**	D5
Crevillente	**67**	F3
Crewe	**55**	G3
Crewkerne	**52**	E4
Crianlarich	**57**	D4
Criccieth	**52**	C2
Criciuma	**138**	G5
Crick	**53**	F2
Crickhowell	**52**	D3
Cricklade	**53**	F3
Crieff	**57**	E4
Criffel	**55**	F2
Crikvenica	**72**	C3
Crimea	**79**	E6
Cristalandia	**137**	H6
Cristalina	**138**	G3
Cristobal Colon, Pico	**136**	C1
Crisu Alb	**73**	F2
Crisu Negru	**73**	F2
Crisu Repede	**73**	G2
Crna Reka	**73**	F5
Crni Drim	**72**	F5
Croaghgorm Mountains	**58**	F3
Croagh Patrick	**58**	C5
Croatia	**72**	C3
Crocketford	**57**	E5
Crockett	**128**	E5
Croggan	**57**	C4
Crohy Head	**58**	F3
Croick	**56**	D3
Croisette, Cap	**65**	F7
Croke, Mount	**112**	D5
Croker Island	**112**	G1
Cromalt Hills	**56**	C2
Cromar	**57**	F3
Cromarty	**56**	D3
Cromarty Firth	**56**	D3
Cromdale, Hills of	**56**	E3
Cromer	**53**	J2
Cromwell	**115**	B6
Crook	**55**	H2
Crooked *Canada*	**122**	D5
Crooked *U.S.A.*	**119**	L4
Crooked Island	**133**	K3
Crooked Island Passage	**133**	K3
Crookham	**57**	F4
Crookhaven	**59**	C10
Crookston	**124**	B3
Croom	**59**	E7
Crosby *Isle of Man, U.K.*	**54**	E2
Crosby *Merseyside, U.K.*	**55**	F3
Crosby *U.S.A.*	**124**	D3
Cross	**105**	G4
Crossett	**128**	G4
Cross Fell	**55**	G2
Crossgar	**58**	L4
Cross Hands	**52**	C3
Crosshaven	**59**	F9
Cross Lake	**119**	R5
Crossmaglen	**58**	J4
Crossmolina	**58**	D4
Cross Sound	**118**	H4
Crossville	**129**	K3
Crotone	**69**	F6
Crouch	**53**	H3
Crowborough	**53**	H3
Crowle	**55**	J3
Crowley's Ridge	**128**	G3
Crowsnest Pass	**119**	N6
Croxton Kerrial	**53**	G2
Croydon *Australia*	**113**	J2
Croydon *U.K.*	**53**	G2
Crozet, Iles	**142**	C6
Crozier Channel	**120**	C2
Cruces, Punta	**136**	B2
Crudgington	**52**	E2
Crumlin	**58**	K3
Cruz Alta	**138**	F5
Cruz, Cabo	**132**	J5
Cruz del Eje	**138**	C6
Cruzeiro do Sul	**136**	C5
Cruz Grande *Chile*	**138**	B5
Cruz Grande *Mexico*	**131**	K9
Crymych	**52**	C3
Crystal City	**127**	N6
Crystal Falls	**124**	F3
Csongrad	**72**	F2
Csorna	**72**	D2
Cuamba	**109**	G2
Cuando	**106**	D6
Cuangar	**106**	C6
Cuango	**106**	C4
Cuanza	**106**	C4
Cuatro Cienegas	**127**	L7
Cuauhtemoc	**127**	J6
Cuautla	**131**	K8
Cuba	**132**	G4
Cubango	**106**	C6
Cubara	**133**	L11
Cubuk	**76**	E2
Cuchi	**106**	C5
Cuchilla Grande	**138**	E6
Cuchivero	**136**	D2
Cuchumatanes, Alto	**132**	B7
Cuckfield	**53**	G3
Cucuta	**136**	C2
Cuddalore	**92**	E6
Cuddapah	**92**	E6
Cudgwa	**113**	K6
Cue	**112**	D4
Cuellar	**66**	D2
Cuenca	**136**	B4
Cuencame	**130**	H5
Cuenca, Serrania de	**66**	E2
Cuernavaca	**131**	K8
Cuero	**128**	D6

Name	Page	Grid
Deception	108	D4
Deception	120	M5
Dechang	93	K3
Decize	65	E5
Decorah	124	E5
Deda	73	H2
Deddington	53	F3
Dedeagach	75	H2
Dedegol Daglari	76	D4
Dedekoy	76	E2
Dedougou	104	E3
Dedu	87	P2
Dee *Cheshire, U.K.*	55	G3
Dee *Dumfries and Galloway, U.K.*	54	F2
Dee *Grampian, U.K.*	57	F3
Dee, Linn of	57	E4
Deep River	125	M3
Deeps, The	56	A2
Deering, Mount	112	F4
Deer Lake	121	Q8
Deer Lodge	122	H4
Defiance	124	H6
Defiance Plateau	127	H3
Deflotte, Cape	114	X16
De Funiak Springs	129	J5
Degeberga	63	F9
Degeh Bur	103	H6
Degelis	125	R3
Degerhamn	63	G8
Deggendorf	70	E4
De Grey	112	E3
Dehaj	95	M6
Dehak	95	R8
Dehalak Deset	103	H4
Deh Bid	95	L6
Deh-Dasht	95	K6
Deheq	95	K5
Dehiwala	92	E7
Dehkhvareqan	94	G3
Dehloran	94	H5
Dehra Dun	92	E2
Deh Salm	95	P6
Dehui	87	P3
Deim Zubeir	102	E6
Dej	73	G2
De Kalb *Illinois*	124	F6
De Kalb *Texas*	128	E4
Dekemhare	96	D9
Dekese	106	D3
Delami	102	F5
Delano	126	C3
Delaram	95	R5
Delaware *Ohio*	124	J6
Delaware *Pennsylvania*	125	N6
Delaware *U.S.A.*	125	N7
Delaware Bay	125	N7
Delcevo	73	G5
Delemont	68	A2
Delft	64	F2
Delfzijl	64	G2
Delgada, Punta	131	L8
Delgado, Cabo	109	H2
Delgerhaan	87	J2
Delgo	102	F3
Delhi *India*	92	E3
Delhi *India*	92	E3
Delhi *Colorado*	127	L2
Delhi *New York*	125	N5
Delice *Turkey*	76	E3
Delice *Turkey*	76	F2
Delicias	127	K6
Delijan	95	K4
Delingha	93	J1
Delitzsch	70	E3
Delle	65	G5
Dellys	101	F1
Delmenhorst	70	C2
Delnice	72	C3
De Long Mountains	118	C2
Deloraine	113	K7
Delray Beach	129	M7
Del Rio	127	M6
Delsbo	63	G6
Delta *Colorado*	127	H1
Delta *Utah*	126	F1
Delta Junction	118	F3
Delvin	58	H5
Dema	78	J5
Demanda, Sierra de la	66	E1
Demba	106	D4
Dembi Dolo	103	F6
Demer	64	F3
Demerara	136	F2
Deming	127	J4
Demini	136	E3
Demirci	76	C3
Demir Kazik	76	F4
Demirkoy	76	B2
Demmin	70	E2
Demnate	100	D2
Demopolis	129	J4
Dempo, Gunung	90	C6
Demyanskoye	84	Ae5
Denakil	103	H5
Denan	103	H6
Denau	86	B4
Denbigh	55	F3
Denbigh, Cape	118	C3
Denby Dale	55	H3
Dendang	90	D6
Dendermonde	64	F3
Dendi	103	G6
Denezhkino	84	D3
Dengkou	87	K3
Dengqen	93	J2
Den Haag	64	F2
Den Helder	64	F2
Denia	67	G3
Deniliquin	113	K6
Denio	122	E7
Denison *Iowa*	124	C6
Denison *Texas*	128	D4
Denison, Mount	118	E4
Denizli	76	C4
Denmark	63	B9
Denmark Strait	116	S2
Dennis Head	56	F1
Denny	57	E4
Denpasar	90	F7
Densongi	91	G6
Denta	73	F3
Denton	128	D4
D'Entrecasteaux Islands	114	E3
D'Entrecasteaux, Point	112	D5
Denver	123	M8
Deogarh	92	F4
Deoghar	92	G4
Deolali	92	D5
Deosai, Plains of	92	E2
Dep	85	M6
Deqen	93	J3
Deqing	93	M4
De Queen	128	E3
Dera Bugti	92	C3
Dera Ghazikhan	92	D2
Dera Ismail Khan	92	D2
Derajat	92	D2
Derazhno	71	M3
Derazhnya	73	J1
Derbent	79	H7
Derby *Australia*	112	E2
Derby *U.K.*	53	F2
Derbyshire	55	H3
Derekoy	76	B2
Dereli	77	H2
Derg	58	G3
Dergachi	79	F5
Derg, Lough *Donegal, Ireland*	58	G3
Derg, Lough *Tipperary, Ireland*	59	F7
De Ridder	128	F5
Derik	77	J4
Derinkuyu	76	F3
Derna	101	K2
Derong	93	J3
Derravaragh, Lough	58	H5
Derry	58	H2
Derrynasaggart Mountains	59	D9
Derryveagh Mountains	58	F2
Derudeb	103	G4
Derveni	75	G3
Derventa	72	D3
Derwent *Australia*	113	K7
Derwent *Derbyshire, U.K.*	55	H3
Derwent *N. Yorkshire, U.K.*	55	J2
Derwent Reservoir	55	H2
Derwent Water	54	E2
Derzhavinsk	84	Ae6
Desaguadero *Argentina*	138	C6
Desaguadero *Bolivia*	138	C3
Descanso	126	D4
Deschambault Lake	119	Q5
Deschutes	122	D5
Dese	103	G5
Deseado	139	C9
Desemboque	126	F5
Desengano, Punta	139	C9
Desert Center	126	E4
Desert Peak	122	H7
Des Moines *U.S.A.*	124	D6
Des Moines *U.S.A.*	124	D6
Desna	79	E5
Desolacion, Isla	139	B10
Des Plaines	124	G5
Dessau	70	E3
Destna	71	G3
Dete	108	E3
Detmold	70	C3
Detour, Point	124	G4
Detroit	124	J5
Detroit Lakes	124	C3
Deutschlandsberg	68	E2
Deva	73	G3
Devakottai	92	E7
Devdevdyak	84	H4
Devecikonagi	76	C3
Devecser	72	D2
Devegedcidi Baraji	77	H3
Develi	76	F3
Deventer	64	G2
Deveron	56	F3
Devils	127	M5
Devil's Bridge	52	D2
Devils Lake	123	Q3
Devils Paw	118	J4
Devils Tower	123	M5
Devin	73	H5
Devizes	53	F3
Devli	92	E3
Devnya	73	J4
Devoll	75	F2
Devon	52	D4
Devon Island	120	J2
Devonport	115	E2
Devrek	76	D2
Devrekani	76	E2
Devrez	76	E2
Devyatkova	84	Ae5
Dewangiri	93	H3
Dewas	92	E4
De Witt	128	G3
Dewsbury	55	H3
Dey-Dey, Lake	112	G4
Deyhuk	95	N5
Deylaman	95	J3
Deyong, Tanjung	114	B3
Deyyer	95	K8
Dez	94	J5
Dezful	94	J5
Dezhneva, Mys	118	B2
Dezhou	87	M4
Dhaka	93	G4
Dhamar	96	G9
Dhampur	92	E3
Dhamtari	92	F4
Dhanbad	92	G4
Dhandhuka	92	D4
Dhang Range	92	F3
Dhankuta	93	G3
Dhar	92	E4
Dharmapuri	92	E6
Dharmavaram	92	E6
Dharmjaygarh	92	F4
Dharwad	92	D5
Dhaulagiri	92	F3
Dhaulpur	92	E3
Dhenkanal	92	G4
Dhenousa	75	H4
Dhermatas, Akra	75	G3
Dhermi	74	E2
Dheskati	75	F3
Dhespotiko	75	H4
Dhialvos Zakinthou	75	F4
Dhidhimotikhon	75	J2
Dhikti Ori	75	H5
Dhirfis	75	G3
Dhodhekanisos	75	J4
Dhomokos	75	G3
Dhoraji	92	D4
Dhoxaton	75	H2
Dhrangadhra	92	D4
Dhrepanon, Akra	75	G3
Dhuburi	93	G3
Dhule	92	D4
Dia	75	H5
Diamante	138	D6
Diamantina *Australia*	113	H4
Diamantina *Brazil*	138	H3
Diamantina, Chapada	137	J6
Diamond Lake Junction	122	D6
Diaoling	88	B3
Diavata	75	G2
Diba al Hisn	97	N4
Dibaya	106	D4
Dibdibah, Ad	96	H2
Dibrugarh	93	H3
Dickinson	123	N4
Dickson	129	J2
Dicle	77	J4
Didcot	53	F3
Didinga Hills	103	F7
Didnovarre	62	K1
Didwana	92	D3
Die	65	F6
Diebougou	104	E3
Diefenbaker, Lake	123	L2
Diego-Suarez	109	J2
Dielette	53	N6
Dien Bien Phu	93	K4
Diepholz	70	C2
Dieppe	64	D4
Dietfurt	70	D4
Diffa	101	H6
Digby	121	N9
Digges Island	120	L5
Digne	65	G6
Digoin	65	F5
Digor	77	K2
Digul	114	C3
Diinsoor	107	H2
Dijlah, Nahr	77	K5
Dijon	65	F5
Dikakah, Ad	97	K7
Dikanas	62	G4
Dikbiyik	77	G2
Dikili	76	B3
Dikson	84	C2
Dikwa	105	H3
Dili	91	H7
Di Linh	93	L6
Dilizhan	77	L2
Dillia	101	H5
Dilling	102	E5
Dillingen	70	D4
Dillingham	118	D4
Dillon	122	H5
Dilolo	106	D5
Dimapur	93	H3
Dimashq	77	G6
Dimbelenge	106	D4
Dimbokro	104	E4
Dimbo vita	73	H3
Dimitrovgrad *Bulgaria*	73	H4
Dimitrovgrad *Russia*	78	H5
Dimona	94	B6
Dimovo	73	G4
Dinagat	91	H3
Dinajpur	93	G3
Dinan	64	B4
Dinanagar	92	E2
Dinant	64	F3
Dinar	76	D3
Dinara Planina	72	D3
Dinard	64	B4
Dinas Head	52	C2
Dinbych	55	F3
Dinbych-y-pysgod	52	C3
Dinder	96	B10
Dindigul	92	E6
Dinek	76	E4
Dinggye	93	G3
Dingle	59	B8
Dingle Bay	59	B8
Dingle Peninsula	59	B8
Dinguiraye	104	C3
Dingwall	56	D3
Dingxi	93	K1
Dingxin	86	H3
Dingxing	87	M4
Dinh Lap	93	L4
Dinnington	55	H3
Dinosaur	123	K7
Dionard	56	D2
Diorbivol	104	C2
Diouloulou	104	B3
Diourbel	104	B3
Dipolog	91	G4
Dir	92	D1
Direction, Cape	113	J1
Dire Dawa	103	H6
Direkli	77	G3
Dirk Hartogs Island	112	C4
Dirra	102	E5
Dirranbandi	113	K4
Disappointment, Cape	122	B4
Disappointment, Lake	112	E3
Discovery Bay	113	J6
Dishna *Egypt*	103	F2
Dishna *U.S.A.*	118	D3
Disko	120	R4
Disko Bay	120	R4
Disna *Belarus*	63	M9
Disna *Belarus*	63	N9
Dispur	93	H3
Diss	53	J2
Dissen	96	E8
Distrito Federal	138	G3
Ditchling Beacon	53	G4
Ditinn	104	C3
Dittaino	69	E7
Ditton Priors	52	E2
Diu	92	D4
Divandarreh	94	H4
Divinopolis	138	G4
Divi Point	92	F5
Divisor, Serra do	136	C5
Divnoye	79	G6
Divrigi	77	H3
Dixcove	104	E4
Dixon Entrance	118	J5
Diyadin	77	K3
Diyala	94	G4
Diyarbakir	77	J4
Diza	77	L3
Dja	105	H5
Djado	101	H4
Djambala	106	B3
Djanet	101	G4
Djelfa	101	F2
Djema	102	E6
Djenne	100	E6
Djibouti	103	H5
Djibouti	103	H5
Djolu	106	D2
Djougou	105	F4
Djourab	102	C4
Djupivogur	62	X12
Djurdjura	67	J2
Djursland	63	D8
Dmitriya Lapteva, Proliv	85	Q2
Dmitrov	78	F4
Dnepr	79	E6
Dneprovskaya Nizmennost	79	D5
Dneprovsko-Bugskiy Kanal	71	L2
Dnestr	73	K2
Dnestrovskiy Liman	73	L2
Dniprodzerzhynsk	79	E6
Dnipropetrovsk	79	F6
Dno	78	E4
Doaktown	125	T3
Doba	102	C6
Dobbiaco	68	D2
Dobeln	70	E3
Dobiegniew	70	F2
Dobo	114	A3
Doboj	72	E3
Dobra	71	H3
Dobre Miasto	71	J2
Dobric	73	J4
Dobrodzien	71	H3
Dobrogea	73	K3
Dobrovolsk	71	K1
Dobrush	79	E5
Dobryanka	78	K4
Dobsina	71	J4
Dobson	115	C5
Dochart	57	D4
Docking	53	H2
Dodecanese	75	J4
Dodge City	127	M2
Dodman Point	52	C4
Dodoma	107	G4
Doetinchem	64	G3
Dofa	91	H6
Dogai Coring	93	G2
Doganbey	76	D4

Doganhisar	76	D3
Dogankent	76	F4
Dogansehir	77	G3
Doganyol	77	H3
Doganyurt	76	E2
Dog Creek	122	C2
Dogen Co	93	H2
Dog Lake	124	F2
Dogo	89	D7
Dogondoutchi	101	F6
Dogubeyazit	77	L3
Dogukardeniz Daglari	77	J2
Doha	97	K4
Doi Luang	93	K5
Dojran	73	G5
Dojransko Jezero	73	G5
Doka *Indonesia*	114	A3
Doka *Sudan*	96	B10
Dokkum	64	G2
Dokshitsy	63	M9
Dokurcun	76	D2
Dolak	114	B3
Dolak, Tanjung	91	K7
Dolanog	52	D2
Dolbeau	125	P2
Dol-de-Bretagne	64	C4
Dole	65	F5
Dolgellau	52	D2
Dolginovo	71	M1
Dolgiy, Ostrov	84	Ac3
Dolgoye	71	K4
Dolina	79	C6
Dolinsk	88	J2
Dolinskaya	79	E6
Dollar	57	E4
Dollar Law	57	E5
Dolni Kralovice	70	F4
Dolok, Tanjung	114	A3
Dolomitche, Alpi	68	C2
Dolo Odo	103	H7
Dolores *Argentina*	139	E7
Dolores *Uruguay*	139	E6
Dolores *U.S.A.*	122	K8
Dolphin and Union Strait	119	N1
Dolphin, Cape	139	E10
Dolsk	71	G3
Domanic	76	C3
Dombas	63	C5
Dombe	109	F3
Dombe Grande	106	B5
Dombovar	72	E2
Dombrad	73	F1
Dome, Puy de	65	E6
Domett	115	D5
Domfront	64	C4
Dominica	133	S7
Dominical	132	F10
Dominican Republic	133	M5
Dominion, Cape	120	M4
Domo	103	J6
Domodossola	68	B2
Domuya, Cerro	139	B7
Don *Grampian, U.K.*	56	F3
Don *S. Yorkshire, U.K.*	55	H3
Don *Russia*	79	G6
Donaghadee	58	L3
Donaldsville	128	G5
Donau	68	E1
Donauworth	70	D4
Don Benito	66	D3
Doncaster	55	H3
Dondo	106	B4
Dondra Head	92	F7
Donegal *Ireland*	58	F3
Donegal *Ireland*	58	G3
Donegal Bay	58	F3
Donegal Point	59	C7
Donenbay	86	D2
Doneraile	59	E8
Donetsk	79	F6
Dongan *Heilongjiang, China*	88	E2
Dongan *Hunan, China*	93	M3
Dongara	112	C4
Dongbolhai Shan	93	G2
Dongchuan	93	K3
Dongfang	93	L5
Dongfanghong	88	D2
Donggala	91	F6
Dong Hoi	93	L5
Dongjingcheng	88	B3
Dongliu	87	M5
Dongluk	86	F4
Dongning	88	C3
Dongola	102	F4
Dongping	87	M4
Dongshan	87	N5
Dongsheng	87	K4
Dongtai	87	N5
Donguena	106	B6
Dong Ujimqin Qi	87	M2
Dongxi Lian Dao	87	M5
Donington	53	G2
Doniphan	124	E8
Donji Vakuf	72	D3
Donna	62	E3
Donner Pass	122	D8
Donnington	52	E2
Dooagh	58	B5
Doon	57	D5
Doonbeg	59	C7
Doonerak, Mount	118	E2
Doon, Loch	57	D5
Doorin Point	58	F3
Dor	95	R6
Dorada, Costa	67	G2
Dora, Lake	112	E3
Dora Riparia	68	A3
Dorbiljin	86	E2
Dorchester	52	E4
Dorchester, Cape	120	L4
Dordogne	65	C6
Dordrecht	64	F3
Dore	65	E6
Dore Lake	119	P5
Dore, Mont	65	E6
Dorgali	69	B5
Dori	104	E3
Dorking	53	G3
Dormo, Ras	96	F10
Dornbirn	68	B2
Dornie	56	C3
Dornoch	56	D3
Dornoch Firth	56	D3
Dorofeyevskaya	84	C2
Dorohoi	73	J2
Dorotea	62	G4
Dorovitsa	78	H4
Dorset	52	E4
Dortdivan	76	E2
Dortmund	70	B3
Dortyol	77	G4
Doruokha	84	J2
Dorutay	77	L3
Dosatuy	85	K7
Dosso	101	F6
Dossor	79	J6
Dothan	129	K5
Douai	64	E3
Douala	105	G5
Douarnenez	64	A4
Double Mountain Fork	127	M4
Doubs	65	F5
Doubtful Sound	115	A6
Doubtless Bay	115	D1
Doue-la-Fontaine	65	C5
Douentza	100	E5
Douglas *South Africa*	108	D5
Douglas *Isle of Man, U.K.*	54	D2
Douglas *Strathclyde, U.K.*	57	E5
Douglas *Arizona*	127	H5
Douglas *Georgia*	129	L5
Douglas *Wyoming*	123	M6
Doullens	64	E3
Doulus Head	59	B9
Doume	105	H5
Doune	57	D4
Dourada, Serra	137	H6
Dourados *Brazil*	138	E3
Dourados *Brazil*	138	F4
Dourados, Serra dos	138	F4
Douro	66	B2
Dove	55	H3
Dove Dale	55	H3
Dover *U.K.*	53	J3
Dover *Delaware*	125	N7
Dover *New Hampshire*	125	Q5
Dover *Ohio*	125	K6
Dover-Foxcroft	125	R4
Dover, Strait of	53	J4
Dovrefjell	62	C5
Dowa	107	F5
Dowlatabad *Afghanistan*	95	R5
Dowlatabad *Afghanistan*	95	S3
Dowlatabad *Iran*	95	N7
Dowlat Yar	92	C2
Down	58	L4
Downham Market	53	H2
Downpatrick	58	L4
Downpatrick Head	58	D4
Downs, The	53	J3
Downton	53	F4
Dow Rud	94	J5
Dowshi	92	C1
Dozen	89	D7
Draa, Oued	100	D3
Drac	65	F6
Dracevo	73	F5
Drachten	64	G2
Dragalina	73	J3
Dragasani	73	H3
Dragoman	73	G4
Dragonera, Isla	67	H3
Dragon's Mouth	133	S9
Dragsfjard	63	K6
Draguignan	65	G7
Dra, Hamada du	100	D3
Drake	123	P4
Drakensberg	108	E6
Drake Passage	141	V7
Drama	75	H2
Drammen	63	H7
Drangedal	63	C7
Draperstown	58	J3
Dras	92	E2
Drau	68	E2
Drava	72	E3
Dravograd	72	C2
Drawa	70	F2
Drawsko, Jezioro	71	G2
Drayton Valley	119	N5
Dren	73	G4
Drenewydd	52	D2
Dresden	70	E3
Dresvyanka	78	K2
Dreux	64	D4
Drin	75	F2
Drina	72	E3
Drin i zi	74	E1
Drobak	63	H7
Drobin	71	H2
Drogheda	58	K5
Drogichin	71	L2
Drogobych	79	C6
Drohiczyn	71	K2
Droichead Atha	58	K5
Droichead Nua	59	J6
Droitwich	53	E2
Drokiya	73	J1
Drome	65	F6
Dromedary, Cape	113	L6
Dromore	58	K4
Dronfield	55	H3
Dronne	65	D6
Dronning Maud Land	141	Z5
Dropt	65	D6
Drovyanaya	84	A2
Drumcollogher	59	E8
Drumheller	122	H2
Drummond	122	H4
Drummond Islands	124	J3
Drummond Range	113	K3
Drummondville	125	P4
Drumochter, Pass of	57	D4
Drumshanbo	58	F4
Druridge Bay	55	H1
Druskininkai	71	K1
Druzhba *Kazakhstan*	86	E2
Druzhba *Russia*	71	J1
Druzhina	85	R3
Drvar	72	D3
Drweca	71	H2
Dry	112	G2
Dry Bay *Canada*	121	N6
Dry Bay *U.S.A.*	118	H4
Dryden	124	D2
Drysdale, River	112	F2
Dschang	105	H4
Duab	94	J4
Dualo	91	G6
Duarte, Pico	133	M5
Duba	96	B3
Dubai	97	M4
Dubawnt Lake	119	Q3
Dubayy	97	M4
Dubbagh, Jambal Ad	96	B3
Dubbo	113	K5
Dubenskiy	79	K5
Dublin *Ireland*	59	K6
Dublin *Ireland*	59	K6
Dublin *U.S.A.*	129	L4
Dublin Bay	59	K6
Dubna	78	F4
Dubno	79	D5
Du Bois	125	L6
Dubois *Idaho*	122	H5
Dubois *Wyoming*	123	K6
Dubossary	79	D6
Dubreka	104	C4
Dubrovitsa	71	M3
Dubrovka *Russia*	79	E5
Dubrovka *Russia*	79	G6
Dubrovnik	72	E4
Dubrovskoye	84	J5
Dubuque	124	E5
Duchang	87	M6
Duchesne *U.S.A.*	123	J7
Duchesne *U.S.A.*	123	J7
Duchess	113	H3
Ducie Island	143	J5
Duck	129	J3
Ducklington	53	F3
Duck Mountain	119	Q5
Duddington	53	G2
Dudinka	84	D3
Dudley	53	E2
Duenas	66	D2
Duero	66	D2
Duffield	53	F2
Duff Islands	114	N6
Dufftown	56	E3
Dufton	55	G2
Dugi Otok	72	C3
Duisburg	70	B3
Dukambiya	96	C9
Dukat	73	G4
Duk Fadiat	102	F6
Duk Faiwil	102	F6
Dukhan	97	K4
Duki Bolen	85	P6
Dukla	71	J4
Dukou	93	K3
Dulan	93	J1
Duldurga	85	J6
Duleek	58	K5
Dulga-Kyuyel	84	J4
Dulgalakh	85	N3
Dullingham	53	H2
Dull Lake	118	C3
Dulnain	56	E3
Dulovo	73	J4
Duluth	124	D3
Duma	77	G6
Dumaguete	91	G4
Dumai	90	C5
Dumaran	91	F3
Dumas *Arkansas*	128	G4
Dumas *Texas*	127	M3
Dumbarton	57	D5
Dumbea	114	X17
Dumbier	71	H4
Dumfries	55	F1
Dumfries and Galloway	57	E5
Dumitresti	73	J3
Dumka	93	G4
Dumlu	77	J2
Dumlupinar	76	C3
Dumoine	125	M3
Dumont d'Urville	141	K5
Dumont d'Urville Sea	141	J6
Dumyat	103	F1
Duna	72	E2
Dunaj	71	H5
Dunajec	71	J3
Dunany Point	58	K5
Dunarea	73	J3
Dunaujvaros	72	E2
Dunav	73	H4
Dunay *Moldova*	73	K3
Dunay *Russia*	88	D4
Dunayevtsy	73	J1
Dunay, Ostrov	85	L2
Dunbar *Australia*	113	J2
Dunbar *U.K.*	57	F4
Dunblane	57	E4
Dunboyne	59	K6
Duncan *Canada*	122	C3
Duncan *U.S.A.*	128	D3
Duncan Passage	93	H6
Duncansby Head	56	E2
Dunchurch	53	F2
Dundaga	63	K8
Dundalk *Ireland*	58	K4
Dundalk *U.S.A.*	125	M7
Dundalk Bay	58	K5
Dundas	120	M2
Dundas, Lake	112	E5
Dundas Peninsula	120	D3
Dundas Strait	112	G1
Dun Dealgan	58	K4
Dundee *South Africa*	108	F5
Dundee *U.K.*	57	F4
Dundonald	57	D5
Dundonnell	56	C3
Dundrennan	54	F2
Dundrod	58	K3
Dundrum	58	L4
Dundrum Bay	58	L4
Dundwa Range	92	F3
Dunecht	57	F3
Dunedin *New Zealand*	115	C6
Dunedin *U.S.A.*	129	L6
Dunfanaghy	58	G2
Dunfermline	57	E4
Dungannon	58	J3
Dungarpur	92	D4
Dungarvan	59	G8
Dungarvan Harbour	59	G8
Dungeness	53	H4
Dungiven	58	J3
Dungloe	58	F3
Dungu	107	E2
Dungun	90	C5
Dunholme	55	J3
Dunhua	88	B4
Dunhuang	86	F3
Dunkeld	113	J6
Dunkerque	64	E3
Dunkirk	125	L5
Dunkur	103	G5
Dunkwa	104	E4
Dun Laoghaire	59	K6
Dunlavin	59	J6
Dunleer	58	K5
Dunmanus Bay	59	C9
Dunmanway	59	D9
Dunmore Town	132	J2
Dunmurry	58	K3
Dunnet Bay	56	E2
Dunnet Head	56	E2
Dunoon	57	D5
Dunragit	54	E2
Duns	57	F4
Dunseith	123	P3
Dunsford	52	D4
Dunstable	53	G3
Dunstan Mountains	115	B6
Dunster	52	D3
Duntelchaig, Loch	56	D3
Duntroon	115	C6
Dunvegan	56	B3
Dunvegan Head	56	B3
Dupang Ling	93	M3
Dupree	123	P5
Duque de York, Isla	139	A10
Du Quoin	124	F7
Duragan	76	F2
Durance	65	F7
Durand, Recif	114	Y17
Durango *Mexico*	130	G5
Durango *U.S.A.*	127	J2
Durankulak	73	K4
Durant	128	D3
Durazno	138	E6
Durazzo	74	E2
Durban	108	F6
Durcal	66	E4
Durdevac	72	D2
Durelj	87	J4
Duren	70	B3
Durg	92	F4
Durgapur *Bangladesh*	93	H3
Durgapur *India*	93	G4
Durham *U.K.*	55	H2

Name	Page	Ref
El Sahuaro	126	F5
El Salado	139	C9
El Salto	130	G6
El Salvador	132	C8
El Sam'an de Apure	133	N11
El Sauzal	126	D5
Elsham	55	J3
El Socorro	126	F5
Elster	70	E3
Elsterwerda	70	E3
El Sueco	127	J6
El Suweis	103	F2
El Tambo	136	B4
Eltham	115	E3
El Thamad	96	B2
El Tigre	133	Q10
El Tih	96	A2
Eltisley	53	G2
El Tocuyo	133	N10
Elton *U.K.*	53	G2
Elton *Russia*	79	H6
El Tule	131	L9
El Tur	96	A2
Eluru	92	F5
Elvanfoot	57	E5
Elvas	66	C3
Elveden	53	H2
Elverum	63	D6
El Viejo	133	L11
El Vigia	136	C2
Elwy	55	F3
Ely *Cambridgeshire, U.K.*	53	H2
Ely *Mid Glamorgan, U.K.*	52	D3
Ely *Minnesota*	124	E3
Ely *Nevada*	126	E1
Elze	70	C2
Ema	63	M7
Emae	114	U12
Emamrud	95	M3
Emam Taqi	95	P4
Eman	63	G8
Emao	114	U12
Emba	79	K6
Embarcacion	138	D4
Embleton	55	H1
Embona	75	J4
Embrun	65	G6
Embu	107	G3
Emden	70	B2
Emerald	113	K3
Emerald Island	120	D2
Emerson	123	R3
Emet	76	C3
Emeti	114	C3
Emi	84	F6
Emigrant Pass	122	F7
Emin	86	E2
Emine, Nos	73	J4
Emirdag	76	D3
Emir Dagi	76	D3
Emita	113	K7
Emmaboda	63	F8
Emmaste	63	K7
Emmen	64	G2
Emory Peak	127	L6
Empalme	126	G7
Empangeni	109	F5
Empedrado	138	E5
Empingham	53	G2
Empoli	68	C4
Emporia *Kansas*	128	D1
Emporia *Virginia*	125	M8
Ems	70	B2
Emu	88	B4
Enard Bay	56	C2
Encantada, Cerro Del La	126	E5
Encarnacion	138	E5
Enchi	104	E4
Encinal	128	C6
Encontrados	136	C2
Encounter Bay	113	H6
Endau	90	C5
Ende	91	G7
Endeavour Strait	113	J1
Enderbury Island	111	U2
Enderby Land	141	D5
Endicott Mountains	118	C2
Ene	136	C6
Enez	76	B2
Enfield *Ireland*	59	J6
Enfield *U.K.*	53	G3
Engano, Cabo	133	N5
Engano, Cape	91	G2
Engaru	88	J3
Engels	79	H5
Enggano	90	C7
Engger Us	87	J3
Engineer Group	114	E4
Englehart	125	L3
Englewood	123	M8
English Channel	50	G5
Enguera	67	F3
Enguera, Sierra de	67	F3
Enid	128	D2
Enkhuizen	64	F2
Enkoping	63	G7
Enna	69	E7
Ennadai Lake	119	Q3
En Nahud	102	E5
Ennedi	102	D4
Ennell, Lough	59	H6
Ennerdale Water	55	F2
Enning	123	N5
Ennis *Ireland*	59	E7
Ennis *U.S.A.*	128	D4
Enniscorthy	59	J7
Enniskillen	58	G4
Ennistymon	59	D7
Enns	68	E1
Enonkoski	62	N5
Enontekio	62	K2
Enrekang	91	N5
Enschede	64	G2
Ensenada	126	D5
Enshi	93	L2
Enstone	53	F3
Entebbe	107	F2
Enterprise	129	K5
Entinas, Punta de las	66	E4
Entraygues	65	E6
Entrecasteaux, Recifs d'	111	N5
Enugu	105	G4
Enurmino	70	C4
Enz	70	C4
Eo	66	C1
Eolie	69	E6
Epano Fellos	75	H4
Epanomi	75	G2
Epernay	64	E4
Ephrata	122	E4
Epi	114	U12
Epinal	64	G4
Epping	53	H3
Eppynt, Mynydd	52	D2
Epsi	77	J4
Epsom	53	G3
Eqlid	95	L6
Equatorial Guinea	105	G5
Equeipa	136	E2
Erap	114	D3
Erbaa	77	G2
Erba, Jebel	96	C6
Ercek	77	K3
Ercis	77	K3
Ercsi	72	E2
Erdek	76	B2
Erdemli	76	F4
Erdenet	87	J2
Erdre	65	C5
Erechim	138	F5
Ereenstav	87	M2
Eregli *Turkey*	76	D2
Eregli *Turkey*	76	F4
Erek Dagi	77	K3
Erenhot	87	L3
Erentepe	77	K3
Eresma	66	D2
Eressos	75	H3
Erfelek	76	F2
Erfurt	70	D3
Ergani	77	H3
Ergene	76	B2
Ergli	63	L8
Ergun He	85	K6
Ergun Zuoqi	87	N1
Eriboll, Loch	56	D2
Ericht, Loch	57	D4
Ericiyas Dagi	76	F3
Erie	125	K5
Erie, Lake	125	K5
Erikousa	74	E3
Erimanthos	75	F4
Erimo-misaki	88	J5
Eriskay	57	A3
Erkelenz	70	B3
Erkilet	76	F3
Erkowit	96	C7
Erlandson Lake	121	N6
Erlangen	70	D4
Erldunda	113	G4
Erme	52	D4
Ermelo	108	F5
Ermenak	76	E4
Ernakulam	92	E7
Erne	58	H5
Erne, Lower Lough	58	G4
Erne, Upper Lough	58	G4
Erode	92	E6
Eromanga	113	J4
Er Rachidia	100	E2
Er Rahad	102	F5
Errego	109	G3
Errigal	58	F2
Erris Head	58	B4
Errochty, Loch	57	D4
Errogie	56	D3
Erromango	114	U13
Erseke	75	F2
Erskine	124	C3
Ertai	86	G2
Eruh	77	K4
Erwigol	86	F3
Eryuan	93	J3
Erzen	74	E2
Erzgebirge	70	E3
Erzin	84	F6
Erzincan	77	H3
Erzurum	77	J3
Esa-Ala	114	E3
Esan-misaki	88	H5
Esashi *Japan*	88	H5
Esashi *Japan*	88	J3
Esbjerg	63	C9
Esbo	63	N6
Escalona	66	D2
Escambia	129	J5
Escanaba	124	G4
Escarpe, Cape	114	X16
Escocesa, Bahia de	133	N5
Escondido *Brazil*	138	J3
Escondido *U.S.A.*	126	D4
Escrick	55	H3
Escuintla	132	B7
Ese-Khayya	85	N3
Esemer	77	K3
Esen	76	C4
Esendere	77	L4
Esfahan	95	K5
Esfarayen, Reshteh ye	95	N3
Eshan	93	K4
Esha Ness	56	A1
Esh Sheikh, Jbel	77	G6
Esino	68	D4
Esk	57	E5
Eskdale	57	E5
Eske, Lough	58	F3
Eskifjordur	62	Y12
Eskilstuna	63	G7
Eskimalatya	77	H3
Eskimo Lakes	118	J2
Eskimo Point	119	S3
Eskipazar	76	E2
Eskishir	76	D3
Esla	66	D1
Eslamabad-e Gharb	94	H4
Eslam Qaleh	95	Q4
Esme	76	C3
Esmeralda, Isla	139	A9
Esmeraldas	136	B3
Espalion	65	E6
Espanola *Canada*	125	K3
Espanola *U.S.A.*	127	J3
Espanola, Isla	136	A7
Espenberg, Cape	118	C2
Esperance	112	E5
Esperance Bay	112	E5
Esperanza *Antarctic*	141	W6
Esperanza *Argentina*	139	B10
Esperanza *Argentina*	138	D6
Espiel	66	D3
Espinhaco, Serra da	138	H3
Espinho	66	B2
Espinosa de los Monteros	66	E1
Espirito Santo	138	H3
Espiritu Santo	114	T11
Espiritu Santo, Cape	91	H3
Espiritu Santo, Isla	130	D5
Espiye	77	H2
Espoo	63	N6
Esposende	66	B2
Espot	67	G1
Espungabera	109	F4
Esquel	139	B8
Es Sahra en Nubiya	96	B6
Essaouira	100	D2
Es Semara	100	C3
Essen	70	B3
Essex	53	H3
Essex, Punta	136	A7
Esslingen	70	C4
Esso	85	T5
Estacado, Llanos	127	L4
Estados, Isla de los	139	D10
Estahbanat	95	M7
Estancia	138	K6
Estcourt	108	E5
Este	68	C3
Esteli	132	D8
Estella	67	E1
Estepona	66	D4
Este, Punta del	139	F6
Esterhazy	123	N2
Esternay	64	E4
Estes Park	123	M7
Estevan	123	N3
Estherville	124	C5
Eston	55	H2
Estonia	63	L7
Estrela, Sierra da	66	C2
Estrella, Punta	126	E5
Estremadura	66	B3
Estremoz	66	C3
Estrondo, Serra do	137	H5
Esztergom	72	E2
Etah	92	E3
Etain	64	F4
Etampes	64	E4
Etaples	64	D3
Etawah	92	E3
Ethiopia	103	G6
Etive, Loch	57	C4
Etna, Monte	69	E7
Eton	53	G3
Etosha Pan	108	C3
Etretat	64	D4
Ettington	53	F2
Ettlingen	70	C4
Ettrick	57	E5
Ettrick Forest	57	E5
Etwall	53	F2
Eu	64	D3
Eua	111	U6
Euboea	75	H3
Euclid	125	K6
Euclides da Cunha	137	K6
Eufaula	129	K5
Eufaula Lake	128	E3
Eugene	122	C5
Eugenia, Punta	126	E7
Eunice	128	F5
Euphrates	94	G6
Eupora	128	H4
Eure	64	D4
Eureka *California*	122	B7
Eureka *Montana*	122	G3
Eureka *Nevada*	126	D1
Eureka Sound	120	J2
Europa, Ile de l	109	H4
Europa, Picos de	66	D1
Europa Point	66	D4
Eutaw	129	J4
Evans, Lake	121	L7
Evans, Mount	123	M8
Evans Strait	120	K5
Evanston *Illinois*	124	G5
Evanston *Wyoming*	122	J7
Evansville	124	G7
Evaux-les-Bains	65	E5
Evaz	95	L8
Evenlode	53	F3
Everard, Cape	113	K6
Everard, Lake	113	G5
Everest, Mount	92	G3
Everett	122	C4
Everett Mountains	120	N5
Everglades, The	129	M7
Evesham	53	F2
Evesham, Vale of	53	F2
Evigheds Fjord	120	R4
Evisa	69	B4
Evje	63	B7
Evora	66	C3
Evreux	64	D4
Evropos	75	G2
Evros	75	J2
Evrotas	75	G4
Evvoia	75	H3
Evvoikos Kolpos	75	G3
Ewasse	114	E3
Ewe, Loch	56	C3
Ewes	57	E5
Exbourne	52	D4
Exe	52	D4
Exeter	52	D4
Exford	52	D3
Exmoor	52	D3
Exmouth	52	D4
Exmouth Gulf	112	C3
Exo Hora	75	F4
Expedition Range	113	K3
Exploits	121	Q8
Exton	52	D3
Extremadura	66	C3
Exuma Sound	132	J2
Eyakit-Terde	85	J3
Eyam	55	H3
Eyasi, Lake	107	F3
Eyemouth	57	F4
Eye Peninsula	56	B2
Eyjafjallajokull	62	U13
Eyjafjordur	62	V11
Eyl	103	J6
Eynesil	77	H2
Eynsham	53	F3
Eyre	112	F5
Eyre Creek	113	H4
Eyre Mountains	115	B6
Eyre North, Lake	113	H4
Eyre Peninsula	113	H5
Eyre South, Lake	113	H4
Eysturoy	62	Z14
Eyvanaki	95	L4
Ezequil Ramos Mexia, Embalse	139	C7
Ezine	76	B3

F

Name	Page	Ref
Faber Lake	119	M3
Faborg	63	D9
Fabriano	68	D4
Facatativa	136	C3
Facundo	139	C9
Fada	102	D4
Fada NGourma	104	F3
Faddeya, Zaliv	84	H2
Faddeyevskiy, Ostrov	85	Q1
Faenza	68	C3
Faeros	62	Z14
Fafen Shet	103	H6
Fagaras	73	H3
Fagersta	63	F6
Faget	73	G3
Fagnano, Lago	139	C10
Fagnes	64	F3
Faguibine, Lac	100	E5
Fagurholsmyri	62	W13
Fahraj	95	P7
Fairbanks	118	F3
Fairborn	124	J7
Fairfield	126	A1
Fair Isle	56	A2
Fairlie	115	C6
Fairlight *Australia*	113	J2
Fairlight *U.K.*	53	H4
Fairmont *Minnesota*	124	C5
Fairmont *W. Virginia*	125	K7
Fair Ness	120	M5
Fairview	128	C2
Fairweather, Mount	118	H4
Faisalabad	92	D2
Faith	123	N5
Faither, The	56	A1
Faizabad	92	F3
Fajr, Wadi	96	D2

Name	Page	Ref
Fakaofo	111	U3
Fakenham	53	H2
Fakfak	91	J6
Fakse Bugt	63	E9
Faku	87	N3
Fal	52	C4
Falaise	64	C4
Falam	93	H4
Falavarjan	95	K5
Falcarragh	58	F2
Falcone, Capo del	69	B5
Falcon Lake	128	C7
Falfurrias	128	C7
Falkenberg	63	E8
Falkenburg	70	E3
Falkensee	70	E2
Falkirk	57	E4
Falkland	57	E4
Falkland Islands	139	E10
Falkonera	75	G4
Falkoping	63	E7
Fall Line Hills	129	J4
Fallon	126	C1
Fall River	125	Q6
Fall River Pass	123	M7
Falls City	124	C6
Falmouth	52	B4
Falmouth Bay	52	B4
Falsa Chipana, Punta	139	B4
False Bay	108	C6
False Pass	118	Af9
False Pera Head	113	J1
Falset	67	G2
Falster	63	E9
Falsterbo	63	E9
Falterona, Monte	68	C4
Falticeni	73	J2
Falun	63	F6
Famatina, Sierra de	138	C5
Fanad Head	58	G2
Fandriana	109	J4
Fangak	102	F6
Fangcheng	93	M2
Fangdou Shan	93	L2
Fangshan	87	M4
Fang Xian	93	M2
Fangzheng	88	B3
Fannich, Loch	56	D3
Fannuj	95	P8
Fano	63	C9
Fano	68	D4
Fanquier	122	E3
Fan Si Pan	93	K4
Faraday	141	V5
Faraday, Cape	120	L2
Faradje	107	E2
Farafangana	109	J4
Farah	95	R5
Farah Rud	95	R5
Faraid Head	56	D2
Farallon, Punta	130	G8
Faranah	104	C3
Farasan, Jazair	96	E8
Farcau	71	L5
Fareham	53	F4
Farewell, Cape	115	D4
Farewell Spit	115	D4
Far Falls	123	T2
Fargo	123	R4
Faridpur	93	G4
Farigh, Wadi al	101	K2
Farila	63	F6
Fariman	95	P4
Faringdon	53	F3
Farjestad	63	G8
Farmington Maine	125	Q4
Farmington Missouri	124	E8
Farmington New Mexico	127	H2
Farnborough	53	G3
Farnham	53	G3
Farnworth	55	G3
Faro	63	H8
Faro Brazil	137	F4
Faro Portugal	66	C4
Farosund	63	H8
Farquhar Islands	82	D8
Farrai	75	F3
Farranfore	59	C8
Farrar	56	D3
Farrashband	95	L7
Farsala	75	G3
Farsi	95	R5
Farsund	63	B7
Fartak, Ra's	97	L9
Farvel, Kap	116	Q3
Fasa	95	L7
Fasad	97	L7
Fasano	69	F5
Faske Bugt	70	E1
Fastov	79	D5
Fatehabad	92	E3
Fatehgarh	92	E3
Fatehpur Rajasthan, India	92	D3
Fatehpur Uttar Pradesh, India	92	F3
Fatezh	79	F5
Fatick	104	B3
Fatima	66	B3
Fatmomakke	62	F4
Fatsa	77	G2
Fatuna	111	T4
Faurei	73	J3
Fauro Vaghena	114	H5
Fausing	63	D8
Fauske	62	F3
Faux Cap	109	J5
Faversham	53	H3
Fawley	53	F4
Fawr, Fforest	52	D3
Faxafloi	62	T12
Faxalven	62	G5
Faya-Largeau	102	C4
Fayetteville Arkansas	128	E2
Fayetteville N. Carolina	129	N3
Fayetteville Tennessee	129	J3
Faylaka	97	J2
Fazilka	92	D2
Fderik	100	C4
Feale	59	D8
Fear, Cape	129	P4
Feather	122	D8
Featherston	115	E4
Fecamp	64	D4
Fedorovka	84	Ad6
Fedulki	84	Ae4
Feeagh, Lough	58	C5
Fegu	87	L4
Fehmarn	70	D1
Fehmer Boelt	70	D1
Feijo	136	C5
Feilding	115	E4
Feira de Santana	137	K6
Feistritz	68	E2
Fei Xian	87	M4
Feke	77	F4
Feklistova, Ostrov	85	P5
Felahiye	77	F3
Felanitx	67	H3
Feldbach	68	E2
Feldberg	68	A2
Feldkirch	68	B2
Feldkirchen	68	E2
Felipe Carillo Puerto	131	Q8
Felix, Cape	120	G4
Felixstowe	53	J3
Felling	55	H2
Feltre	68	C2
Femer Balt	63	D9
Femund	63	D5
Fener Burun	77	H2
Fengcheng	87	M6
Fengdu	93	L3
Fenggang	93	L3
Fengjie	93	L2
Fengning	87	M3
Fengshan	93	L4
Fengtai	93	N2
Fengxian	93	N3
Fengzhen	87	L3
Fen He	87	L4
Feni Island	114	E2
Fenoarivo Atsinanana	109	J3
Fens, The	53	H2
Fenxi	87	L4
Fenyang	87	L4
Fenyi	93	M3
Feodosiya	79	F6
Feolin Ferry	57	B5
Ferbane	59	G6
Ferdows	95	P4
Fergana	86	B3
Fergus Falls	124	B3
Fergusson Island	114	E3
Ferkessedougou	104	D4
Fermanagh	58	G4
Fermo	68	D4
Fermoy	59	F8
Fernandina Beach	129	M5
Fernandina, Isla	136	A7
Fernando de Noronha, Isla	48	E5
Ferness	56	E3
Fernie	122	G3
Ferns	59	K7
Ferrai	75	J2
Ferrans	59	J6
Ferrara	68	C3
Ferrat, Cap	67	F5
Ferreira do Alentejo	66	B3
Ferrenafe	136	B5
Ferriday	128	G5
Ferrol, Peninsula de	136	B5
Ferto	68	F2
Fes	100	D2
Fessenden	123	Q4
Fetesti	73	J3
Fethaland, Point of	56	A1
Fethiye	76	C4
Fethiye Korfezi	76	C4
Fetisovo	79	J7
Fetlar	56	B1
Fetsund	63	D7
Fetzara El Hadjar	69	A7
Feurs	65	F6
Fevralskoye	85	N6
Feyzabad	92	D1
Ffestiniog	52	D2
Fianarantsoa	109	J4
Fiandberg	62	G4
Fichtel-gebirge	70	D3
Ficksburg	108	E5
Fidenza	68	C3
Fier	74	E2
Fife Ness	57	F4
Figeac	65	E6
Figline Valdarno	68	C4
Figueira da Foz	66	B2
Figueira de Castelo Rodrigo	66	C2
Figueres	67	H1
Figuig	100	E2
Figuiro dos Vinhos	66	B3
Fiji	114	Q8
Filadelfia	138	D4
Filby	53	J2
Filchner Ice Shelf	141	X3
Filey	55	J2
Filey Bay	55	J2
Filiasi	73	G3
Filiatra	75	F4
Filipow	71	K1
Filipstad	63	F7
Fillmore California	126	C3
Fillmore Utah	126	F1
Fimi	106	C3
Finale Emilia	68	C3
Final, Punta	126	E6
Findhorn	56	E3
Findik	77	G3
Findikli	77	J2
Findikpinari	76	F4
Findlay	124	J6
Fingoe	109	F3
Finike	76	D4
Finisterre, Cabo	66	B1
Finke Australia	113	G4
Finke Australia	113	H4
Finland	63	L6
Finland, Gulf of	63	L7
Finnmark	62	L1
Finnmarksvidda	62	K2
Finnsnes	62	M2
Finschhafen	114	D3
Finsteraarhorn	68	B2
Finstown	56	E1
Fintona	58	H4
Fionn Loch	56	C3
Fionnphort	57	B4
Firat	77	H3
Firedrake Lake	119	Q3
Firenze	68	C4
Firle Beacon	53	H4
Firozabad	92	E3
Firozpur	92	D2
Firsovo	88	J2
Firuzabad	95	L7
Firuzkuh	95	L4
Fish	108	C4
Fisher, Cape	120	K5
Fishguard	52	C3
Fitchburg	125	Q5
Fitful Head	56	A2
Fitsitika	109	H4
Fitzgerald	129	L5
Fitz Roy	139	C9
Fitzroy	112	F2
Fitz Roy, Cerro	139	B9
Fitzroy Crossing	112	F2
Fitzwilliam Strait	120	C2
Fiuggi	69	D5
Fiume	72	C3
Fiumicino	69	D5
Fivemiletown	58	H4
Fizi	107	E3
Fjallasen	62	J3
Fladdabister	56	A2
Flagstaff	126	G3
Flakatrask	62	H4
Flamborough	55	J2
Flamborough Head	55	J2
Flaming	70	E3
Flaming Gorge Reservoir	123	K7
Flamingo	129	M8
Flash	55	H3
Flasjon	62	F4
Flathead	122	G3
Flathead Lake	122	G4
Flathead Range	122	G3
Flattery, Cape	122	B3
Fleet	53	G3
Fleetwood	55	F3
Flekkefjord	63	B7
Flen	63	G7
Flensburg	70	C1
Flers	64	C4
Flesberg	63	C7
Fleurance	65	D7
Flims	68	B2
Flinders Island	113	K6
Flinders Reefs	113	K2
Flin Flon	119	Q5
Flint U.K.	55	F3
Flint Georgia	129	K5
Flint Michigan	124	J5
Flintham	53	G2
Flisa	63	E6
Flix	67	G2
Fliyos	76	E2
Floka	75	F4
Florac	65	E6
Florence Italy	68	C4
Florence Alabama	129	J3
Florence Arizona	126	G4
Florence Colorado	127	K1
Florence Oregon	122	B6
Florence S. Carolina	129	N3
Florencia	136	B3
Florentino Ameghino, Embalse	139	C8
Flores Brazil	137	J5
Flores Guatemala	132	C6
Flores Indonesia	91	G7
Floreshty	79	D6
Flores, Laut	91	F7
Floresta	137	K5
Floriano	137	J5
Florianopolis	138	G5
Florida Uruguay	139	E6
Florida U.S.A.	129	L6
Florida Islands	114	K6
Florida Keys	129	M8
Florida, Straits of	129	N8
Floridia	69	E7
Florina	75	F2
Floro	63	A6
Flotta	56	E2
Flumen	67	F2
Fly	114	C3
Foca	76	B3
Foca	72	E4
Fochabers	56	E3
Focsani	73	J3
Foggia	69	E5
Fogi	91	H6
Fogo	104	L7
Fogo Island	121	R8
Fohr	70	C1
Foinaven	56	D2
Foix	65	D7
Folda	62	F3
Folegandros	75	H4
Foligno	69	D4
Folkestone	53	J3
Folkingham	53	G2
Folkston	129	L5
Follonica	69	C4
Foltesti	73	K3
Fond-du-Lac Canada	119	Q4
Fond du Lac U.S.A.	124	F5
Fonni	69	B5
Fonsagrada	66	C1
Fonseca, Golfo de	132	D8
Fontainebleau	64	E4
Fonte Boa	136	D4
Fonte do Pau-d'Agua	136	F6
Fontenay-le-Comte	65	C5
Font-Romeu	65	E7
Fontur	62	X11
Fonualei	111	U5
Fonyod	72	D2
Foraker, Mount	118	E3
Forbes	113	K5
Forcados	105	G4
Forcalquier	65	F7
Forde	63	A6
Fordham	53	H2
Fordon	71	H2
Ford Ranges	141	Q3
Fordyce	128	F4
Forecariah	104	C4
Foreland Point	52	D3
Forel, Mount	116	R2
Forest Canada	124	K5
Forest U.S.A.	128	H4
Forestier Peninsula	113	K7
Forest Park	129	K4
Forestville	125	R2
Forez, Monts du	65	E6
Forfar	57	F4
Forgandenny	57	E4
Fork	123	K5
Forks	122	B4
Forli	68	D3
Formartin	56	F3
Formby	55	F3
Formby Point	55	F3
Formentera	67	G3
Formentor, Cabo de	67	H3
Formia	69	D5
Formiga	138	G4
Formosa	87	N7
Formosa Argentina	138	E5
Formosa Brazil	138	G3
Formosa do Rio Preto	137	H6
Foroyar	62	Z14
Forres	56	E3
Forrest	112	F5
Forrest City	128	G3
Forsayth	113	J2
Forsnas	62	H3
Forsnes	62	C5
Forssa	63	K6
Forsyth Missouri	124	D8
Forsyth Montana	123	L4
Fort Albany	121	K7
Fortaleza Bolivia	136	D5
Fortaleza Brazil	137	K4
Fort Archambault	102	C6
Fort Beaufort	108	E6
Fort Benton	123	J4
Fort Bragg	122	C8
Fort Charlet	101	G4
Fort Chipewyan	119	N4
Fort Collins	123	M7
Fort Coulonge	125	M4
Fort-Dauphin	109	J5
Fort-de-France	133	S7
Fort de Polignac	101	G3
Fort Dodge	124	C5
Fortescue	112	D3
Fort Flatters	101	G3
Fort Foureau	105	J3
Fort Frances	124	D2
Fort Franklin	118	L2
Fort Good Hope	118	K2
Forth	57	D4
Fort Hall	107	G3
Fort Hancock	127	K5

Forth, Firth of 57 F4
Fortin Carlos Antonio Lopez 138 E4
Fortin General Mendoza 138 D4
Fortin Gral Eugenio Garay 138 D4
Fortin Infante Rivarola 138 D4
Fortin Juan de Zalazar 138 E4
Fortin Madrejon 138 E4
Fortin Ravelo 138 D3
Fort Jameson 107 F3
Fort Kent 125 R3
Fort Lamy 102 C5
Fort Lauderdale 129 M7
Fort Liard 118 L3
Fort Macleod 122 H3
Fort McMurray 119 N4
Fort McPherson 118 J2
Fort Madison 124 E6
Fort Manning 107 F5
Fort Morgan 123 N7
Fort Myers 129 M7
Fort Nelson 119 L4
Fort Norman 118 K3
Fortore 69 E5
Fort Payne 129 K3
Fort Peck 123 L3
Fort Peck Dam 123 L4
Fort Peck Reservoir 123 L4
Fort Pierce 129 M7
Fort Portal 107 F2
Fort Providence 119 M3
Fort Qu'Appelle 123 N2
Fort Randall 118 Af8
Fort Resolution 119 N3
Fortrose 56 D3
Fort Rosebery 107 E5
Fort Saint James 118 L5
Fort Saint John 119 L4
Fort Scott 124 C8
Fort Severn 120 J6
Fort Shevchenko 79 J7
Fort Simpson 119 L3
Fort Smith *Canada* 119 N3
Fort Smith *U.S.A.* 128 E4
Fort Soufflay 106 B2
Fort Stockton 127 L5
Fort Sumner 127 K3
Fort Trinquet 100 D1
Fortuna 122 B7
Fortune Bay 121 Q8
Fort Valley 129 L4
Fort Vermilion 119 M4
Fort Victoria 108 F4
Fort Walton Beach 129 J5
Fort Wayne 124 H6
Fort William 57 C4
Fort Worth 128 D4
Fort Yukon 118 F2
Forur 95 M8
Foshan 93 M4
Fosheim Peninsula 120 K2
Fosna 62 D5
Fossombrone 68 D4
Fossvellir 62 X12
Foster 113 K6
Fougeres 64 C4
Foula 56 A2
Foula Morie 104 C3
Foulden 57 F4
Foulness Island 53 H3
Foulness Point 53 H3
Foulwind, Cape 115 C4
Foumban 105 H4
Foundiougne 104 B3
Fountainhall 57 F5
Four Mountains, Islands of the 118 Ad9
Fournoi 75 J4
Foveaux Strait 115 B7
Fowey *U.K.* 52 C4
Fowey *U.K.* 52 C4
Fowler 127 K1
Fowler, Point 112 G5
Fowlers Bay 112 G5
Fowman 94 J3
Fox *Canada* 118 K4
Fox *U.S.A.* 124 F6
Foxe Basin 120 L4
Foxe Peninsula 120 L5
Foxford 58 D5
Fox Islands 118 Ae9
Foxton 115 E4
Foyers, Falls of 56 D3
Foyle 58 H3
Foyle, Lough 58 H2
Foynes 59 D7
Foz do Iguacu 138 F5
Fraga 67 G2
Framington 125 Q5
Framlingham 53 J2
Frampol 71 K3
Franca 138 G4
Francais, Recif des 114 V15
France 65 C5
France, Ile de 64 E4
Frances *Australia* 113 J6
Frances *Canada* 118 K3
Franceville 106 B3
Franche Comte 65 G5
Francis Case, Lake 123 Q6
Francisco Escarcega 131 P8
Francistown 108 E4
Francois Lake 118 K5
Frangista 75 F3
Frankfort *Indiana* 124 G6

Frankfort *Kentucky* 124 H7
Frankfurt 70 F2
Frankfurt am Main 70 C3
Frankischer Alb 70 D4
Franklin *Indiana* 124 H7
Franklin *Louisiana* 128 G6
Franklin *N. Carolina* 129 L3
Franklin *Pennsylvania* 125 L6
Franklin *Tennessee* 129 J3
Franklin Bay 118 K2
Franklin D Roosevelt Lake 122 E3
Franklin, Lake 119 R2
Franklin Mountains 118 K3
Franklin, Point 118 D1
Franklin Strait 120 G3
Frank's Peak 123 K6
Fransta 62 G5
Frantsa-Iosifa, Zemlya 80 G2
Frascati 69 D5
Fraserburg 108 D6
Fraserburgh 56 F3
Fraserdale 125 K2
Fraser Island 113 L4
Fraser, Mount 112 D4
Frasertown 115 F3
Frauenfeld 68 B2
Fray Bentos 138 E6
Frazer 122 D2
Freckleton 55 G3
Fredericia 63 C9
Frederick *Maryland* 125 M7
Frederick *Oklahoma* 128 C3
Frederick Reef 110 M6
Fredericksburg 125 M7
Frederick Sound 118 J4
Fredericktown 124 E8
Fredericton 125 S4
Frederikshab 120 S5
Frederikshabs Isblink 120 S5
Frederikshavn 63 D8
Frederiksted 133 Q6
Fredonia 125 L5
Fredrika 62 M4
Fredrikshamn 63 M6
Fredrikstad 63 D7
Freeling, Mount 113 G3
Freeport *Illinois* 124 F5
Freeport *Texas* 128 E6
Freeport City 132 H1
Freer 128 C7
Freetown 104 C4
Fregenal de la Sierra 66 C3
Frehel, Cap 64 B4
Freiberg 70 E3
Freiburg 70 B4
Freising 70 D4
Freistadt 68 E1
Frejus 65 G7
Fremantle 112 D5
Fremont *California* 126 A2
Fremont *Nebraska* 123 R7
Fremont *Utah* 122 J8
French 125 K1
French Broad 129 L2
French Guiana 136 G3
Frenchman 123 L3
Frenchpark 58 F5
French Polynesia 143 J5
Frenda 100 F1
Frensham 53 G3
Fresco 137 G5
Freshfield, Mount 122 F2
Freshwater 53 F4
Fresnillo 130 H6
Fresno 126 C2
Freu, Cabo del 67 H3
Frias 138 C5
Fribourg 68 A2
Fridaythorpe 55 J2
Friedrichshafen 70 C5
Friesach 68 E2
Frio 127 N6
Frio, Cabo 138 H4
Friona 127 L3
Frisco 123 L8
Friza, Proliv 85 R7
Frobisher Bay 120 N5
Frobisher Lake 119 P4
Frodsham 55 G3
Frohavet 62 C5
Frolovo 79 G6
Frome *Dorset, U.K.* 52 E4
Frome *Somerset, U.K.* 52 E3
Frome, Lake 113 H5
Fronteira 66 C3
Frontera 131 N8
Front Royal 125 L7
Frosinone 69 D5
Froya 62 C5
Frutal 138 G3
Frydek Mistek 71 H4
Fteri 75 F3
Fuan 87 M6
Fudai 88 H5
Fuding 87 N6
Fudzin 88 E3
Fuengirola 66 D4
Fuente el Fresno 66 E3
Fuente Obejuna 66 D3
Fuentesauco 66 D2
Fuentes de Onoro 66 C2
Fuerte 127 H7
Fuerteventura 100 C3
Fufeng 93 L2

Fuga 91 G2
Fuhai 86 F2
Fujian 87 M6
Fu Jiang 93 L2
Fujin 88 D2
Fujinomiya 89 G8
Fuji-san 89 G8
Fujisawa 89 G8
Fukang 86 F3
Fukaura 88 G5
Fukuchiyama 89 E8
Fukue-shima 89 B9
Fukui 89 F7
Fukuoka *Japan* 89 C9
Fukuoka *Japan* 88 H5
Fukura 88 G6
Fukushima 89 H7
Fukuyama *Japan* 89 C10
Fukuyama *Japan* 89 D8
Fulacunda 104 B3
Fulad Mahalleh 95 L3
Fulaga 114 S9
Fulanga Passage 114 S9
Fulda *Germany* 70 C3
Fulda *Germany* 70 C3
Fullerton 126 D4
Fullerton, Cape 119 T3
Fulufjallet 63 E6
Fulwood 55 G3
Fumas, de Represa 138 G4
Fumay 64 F4
Fumel 65 D6
Funabashi 89 H8
Funadalen 62 E5
Funafuti 111 S3
Funauke 89 F11
Funchal 100 B2
Fundao 66 C2
Fundy, Bay of 121 N8
Funing *Jiangsu, China* 87 M5
Funing *Yunnan, China* 93 L4
Funtua 105 G3
Fuqing 87 M6
Furancungo 109 F2
Furano 88 J4
Furg 95 M7
Furmanov 78 G4
Furmanovka 86 C3
Furmanovo 79 H6
Furneaux Group 113 K7
Furstenfeld 68 E2
Furstenwalde 70 F2
Furth 70 D4
Furukawa *Japan* 89 F7
Furukawa *Japan* 88 H6
Fury and Hecla Strait 120 K4
Fushun 87 N3
Fusui 93 L4
Futuna 114 U13
Fuwayrit 97 K3
Fu Xian 93 L1
Fuxin 87 N3
Fuyang 93 N2
Fuyu 87 N2
Fuyuan 86 F2
Fuyun 86 F2
Fuzesabony 72 F2
Fuzhou *Fujian, China* 87 M6
Fuzhou *Jiangxi, China* 87 M6
Fuzhoucheng 87 N4
Fuzuli 94 H2
Fyfield 53 H3
Fyn 63 D9
Fyne, Loch 57 C4
Fyresdal 63 C7
Fyvie 56 F3

G

Gaalkacyo 103 J6
Gabas 65 C7
Gabbac, Raas 103 K6
Gabela 106 B5
Gabes 101 H2
Gabes, Golfe de 101 H2
Gabgaba, Wadi 103 F3
Gabin 71 H2
Gabon 106 B3
Gaborone 108 E4
Gabriel, Mount 59 C9
Gabriel Vera 138 C3
Gabrik 95 P9
Gabrovo 73 H4
Gace 64 D4
Gach Sar 95 K3
Gach Saran 95 K6
Gacko 72 E4
Gadag 92 E5
Gaddede 62 F4
Gador, Sierra de 66 E4
Gadsden 129 K3
Gadwal 92 E5
Gadyach 79 E5
Gaesti 73 H3
Gaeta 69 D5
Gaeta, Golfo di 69 D5
Gafsa 101 G2
Gagarin 78 E4
Gagnoa 104 D4
Gagnon 121 N7
Gagra 79 G7
Gagui 102 C6

Gaibanda 93 G3
Gaidhouronisi 75 H5
Gailey 53 E2
Gaillac 65 D7
Gaillimh 59 D6
Gailtaler Alpen 68 D2
Gainesville *Florida* 129 L6
Gainesville *Georgia* 129 L3
Gainesville *Texas* 128 D4
Gainford 55 H2
Gainsborough 55 J3
Gairdner, Lake 113 H5
Gairloch, Loch 56 C3
Gai Xian 87 N3
Gaktsynka 85 P6
Galana 107 G3
Galand 95 M3
Galanino 84 E5
Galapagos, Islas 136 A7
Galashiels 57 F5
Galati 73 K3
Galatz 73 K3
Galax 125 K8
Galela 91 H5
Galena *Alaska* 118 D3
Galena *Illinois* 124 E5
Galena *Kansas* 124 C8
Galeota Point 136 E1
Galera, Punta de la 139 B7
Galesburg 124 E6
Galeton 125 M6
Galgate 55 G3
Galich *Russia* 78 G4
Galich *Ukraine* 71 L4
Galicia 66 C1
Galilee, Lake 113 K3
Galimyy 85 T4
Gallabat 103 G5
Gallan Head 56 A2
Gallarate 68 B3
Gallatin 129 J2
Galle 92 F7
Gallegos 139 B10
Galley Head 59 E9
Gallinas Mountains 127 J3
Gallinas, Punta 136 C1
Gallipoli *Italy* 69 F5
Gallipoli *Turkey* 76 B2
Gallivare 62 J3
Gallo 67 F2
Gallo 62 F5
Gallo, Capo 69 D6
Galloway 54 E2
Galloway, Mull of 54 E2
Gallup 127 H3
Galmisdale 57 B4
Galtymore Mount 59 F8
Galty Mountains 58 F8
Galveston 128 E6
Galveston Bay 128 E6
Galveston Island 128 E6
Galway *Ireland* 59 D6
Galway *Ireland* 59 E6
Galway Bay 59 D6
Gambell 118 A3
Gambia, The 104 B3
Gambier, Iles 143 J5
Gamboma 106 C3
Gamkunoro, Gunung 91 H5
Gamlakarleby 62 K5
Gamleby 63 G3
Gamshadzai Kuh 95 Q7
Gamvik 62 N1
Ganado 127 H3
Gananoque 125 M4
Ganaveh 95 K7
Gand 64 E3
Gandadiwata, Bukit 91 F6
Gandajika 106 D4
Gandak 92 F3
Gander 121 R8
Gander Lake 121 R8
Gandesa 67 G2
Gandhi Sagar 92 E4
Gandia 67 F3
Ganga 93 G3
Ganga, Mouths of the 93 G4
Gangan 139 C8
Ganganagar 92 D3
Gangara 101 G6
Gangdise Shan 92 F2
Ganges 93 G4
Gangew Taungdan 93 J4
Gangtok 93 G3
Gangu 93 L2
Ganjam 92 G5
Gan Jiang 87 M6
Gannat 65 E5
Gannett Peak 123 K6
Gansu 93 K2
Gantheaume, Cape 113 H6
Gantsevichi 71 M2
Ganyushkino 79 H6
Ganzhou 87 L6
Gao 100 E5
Gaoan 93 N3
Gaohe 93 M4
Gaolan 93 K1
Gaoqing 87 M4
Gaoua 104 E3
Gaoual 104 C3
Gaoyou Hu 87 M5
Gap 65 G6
Gar 92 E2

Gobabis **108** C4
Gobi **87** K3
Gobo **89** E9
Gochas **108** C4
Godafoss **62** W12
Godalming **53** G3
Godavari **92** F5
Godbout **125** S2
Goderich **125** K5
Godhavn **120** R4
Godhra **92** D4
Godollo **72** E2
Gods **119** S4
Godshill **53** F4
Gods Lake **119** S5
Godthab **120** R5
Godwin Austen **92** E1
Goeland, Lac au **121** L8
Goes **64** E3
Gogama **125** K3
Goginan **52** D2
Gogland, Ostrov **63** M6
Gogolin **71** H3
Goiana **137** L5
Goiania **138** G3
Goias *Brazil* **138** F3
Goias *Brazil* **137** H6
Gojome **88** H6
Gokceada **76** A2
Gokcekaya Baraji **76** D2
Gokdere **77** G2
Gokirmak **76** F2
Gokova Korfezi **76** B4
Goksu *Turkey* **76** E4
Goksu *Turkey* **77** F4
Goksun **77** G3
Goktas **77** J2
Goktepe **76** E4
Gol **63** C6
Golaghat **93** H3
Golam Head **59** C6
Golashkerd **95** N8
Golbasi *Turkey* **76** E3
Golbasi *Turkey* **77** G4
Golcar **55** H3
Golchikha **84** C2
Golconda **122** F7
Golcuk **76** C2
Golcuk Daglari **76** B3
Goldap **71** K1
Gold Coast **113** L4
Golden **122** F2
Golden Bay **115** D4
Goldendale **122** D5
Golden Hinde **122** B3
Goldsboro **129** P3
Goldsworthy **112** D3
Gole **77** K2
Golebert **77** K2
Goleniow **70** F2
Golfito **132** F10
Golfo Aranci **69** B5
Golgeli Daglari **76** C4
Golhisar **76** C4
Golija Planina **72** F4
Golkoy **77** G2
Golmarmara **76** B3
Golmud **93** H1
Golo **69** B4
Golova **76** D4
Golovanevsk **73** L1
Golovnino **88** K4
Golpayegan **95** K5
Golpazari **76** D2
Goma **107** E3
Gombe **105** H3
Gombi **105** H3
Gomera **100** B3
Gomez Palacio **127** L8
Gomishan **95** M3
Gonaives **133** L5
Gonam *Russia* **85** M5
Gonam *Russia* **85** N5
Gonave, Golfe de la **133** L5
Gonave, Ile de la **133** L5
Gonbad-e Kavus **95** M3
Gonda **92** F3
Gondal **92** D4
Gonder **103** G5
Gondia **92** F4
Gonen *Turkey* **76** B2
Gonen *Turkey* **76** B3
Gongbogyamda **93** H3
Gongolo **105** H3
Gongpoquan **86** H3
Goniadz **71** K2
Gonumillo **139** C8
Gonzales *California* **126** B2
Gonzales *Texas* **128** D6
Gonzales Chaves **139** D7
Goob Weyn **107** H3
Goodenough, Cape **141** J5
Goodenough Island **114** E3
Good Hope, Cape of **108** C6
Gooding **122** G6
Goodland **123** P8
Goole **55** J3
Goolgowi **113** K5
Goomen **113** L4
Goondiwindi **113** L4
Goose Bay **121** P7
Goose Creek **129** M4
Goose Lake **122** D7
Goplo, Jezioro **71** H2
Goppingen **70** C4
Gora Kalwaria **71** J3
Gorakhpur **92** F3
Gorazde **72** E4
Gorda, Punta **138** B3
Gordes **76** C3
Gordonsville **125** L7
Gore **115** B7
Gore **103** G6
Gorele **77** H2
Goresbridge **59** J7
Gorey *Ireland* **59** K7
Gorey *U.K.* **53** M7
Gorgan **95** M3
Gorgan, Rud-e **95** M3
Gorgona, Isola di **68** B4
Gorgoram **105** H3
Gori **77** L1
Gorice **75** F2
Gorinchem **64** F3
Goris **94** H2
Gorizia **68** D3
Gorka **78** H3
Gorkha **92** F3
Gorki *Belarus* **78** E5
Gorki *Russia* **84** Ae3
Gorki *Russia* **78** H4
Gorkovskoye Vodokhranilishche **78** G4
Gorlev **63** D9
Gorlice **71** J4
Gorlitz **70** F3
Gornji Milanovac **72** F3
Gornji Vakuf **72** D4
Gorno-Altaysk **84** D6
Gornozavodsk **88** H2
Gornyak **84** C6
Gornyy *Russia* **79** H5
Gornyy *Russia* **85** P6
Gorodenka **73** H1
Gorodets **78** G4
Gorodok **71** K4
Gorodovikovsk **79** G6
Goroka **114** D3
Gorokhov **71** L3
Gorong, Kepulauan **91** J6
Gorongoza **109** F3
Gorontalo **91** G5
Goroshikha **84** D3
Gorran Haven **52** C4
Gorseinon **52** C3
Gort **59** E6
Gortaclare **58** H3
Gortahork **58** F2
Gorumna Island **59** C6
Goryn **79** D5
Gorzow Wielkopolski **70** F2
Goschen Strait **114** E4
Gosforth **55** H1
Goshogawara **88** H5
Gospic **72** C3
Gosport **53** F4
Gostivar **73** F5
Gota **62** Z14
Gota Kanal **63** G7
Gotaland **63** E8
Goteborg **63** H8
Goteborg Och Bohus **63** D7
Gotene **63** E7
Gotha **70** D3
Gothenburg **63** D8
Gotland **63** H8
Goto-retto **89** B9
Gotse Delchev **73** G5
Gotska Sandon **63** H7
Gotsu **89** D8
Gottingen **70** C3
Gottwaldov **71** G4
Gouda **64** F2
Goudhurst **53** H3
Gough Island **48** F6
Gouin, Reservoir **125** N2
Goulais **124** J3
Goulburn **113** K5
Goulburn Islands **113** G1
Goundam **100** E5
Gourdon **65** D6
Goure **101** H6
Gourma-Rharous **100** E5
Gournay **64** D4
Gourock **57** D5
Govena, Mys **85** V5
Goverla **71** L4
Governador Valadares **138** H3
Governor's Harbour **132** J2
Govind Pant Sagar **92** F4
Govorovo **85** M2
Gowanbridge **115** D4
Gowanda **125** L5
Gower **52** C3
Gowna, Lough **58** G5
Goya **138** E5
Goynucek **77** F2
Goynuk *Turkey* **76** D2
Goynuk *Turkey* **77** J3
Goz Beida **102** D5
Gozne **76** F4
Gozo **74** C4
Goz Regeb **96** B8
Graaff Reinet **108** D6
Gracac **72** C3
Gradaus, Serra dos **137** G5
Grado *Italy* **68** D3
Grado *Spain* **66** C1
Gradoli **69** C4
Gradsko **73** F5
Grafham Water **53** G2
Grafton *Australia* **113** L4
Grafton *N. Dakota* **123** R3
Grafton *W. Virginia* **125** K7
Grafton, Islas **139** B10
Graham **128** C4
Graham Island *British Columbia, Canada* **118** J5
Graham Island *NW. Territories, Canada* **120** H2
Graham Land **141** V5
Grahamstown **108** E6
Graie, Alpi **68** A3
Graiguenamanagh **59** J7
Grain **53** H3
Grajau **137** H4
Grajewo **71** K2
Grampian **56** E3
Grampian Mountains **57** D4
Grampound **52** C4
Gramsh **75** F2
Gran **137** F3
Granada *Nicaragua* **132** E9
Granada *Spain* **66** E4
Granard **58** H5
Gran Bajo **139** C9
Granby *Canada* **125** P4
Granby *U.S.A.* **123** L7
Gran Canaria **100** B3
Gran Chaco **138** D4
Grand *Canada* **125** K5
Grand *Michigan* **124** H5
Grand *Missouri* **124** C6
Grand *S. Dakota* **123** P5
Grand Bahama **132** H1
Grand Bois, Coteau de **124** C3
Grand Canal *China* **87** M5
Grand Canal *Ireland* **59** H6
Grand Canyon *U.S.A.* **126** F2
Grand Canyon *U.S.A.* **126** F2
Grand Cayman **132** G5
Grand Coulee **122** E4
Grand Coulee Dam **122** E4
Grande *Brazil* **138** G4
Grande *Mexico* **131** L9
Grande *Nicaragua* **132** E8
Grande, Bahia **139** C10
Grande Cache **119** M5
Grande, Cienaga **133** K10
Grande Comore **109** H2
Grande Miquelon **121** Q8
Grande O'Guapay **138** D3
Grande Prairie **119** M4
Grande, Punta **137** G3
Grande, Rio **127** M6
Grande Ronde **122** F5
Gran Desierto **126** E5
Grandes Rocques **53** M7
Grand Falls *New Brunswick, Canada* **125** S3
Grand Falls *Newfoundland, Canada* **121** Q8
Grand Forks **123** R4
Grand Island **123** Q7
Grand Isle **128** H6
Grand Junction **127** H1
Grand Lahou **104** E4
Grand Lake *New Brunswick, Canada* **128** G6
Grand Lake *Newfoundland, Canada* **121** Q8
Grand Lake *U.S.A.* **125** S3
Grand Lake O' the Cherokees **128** E2
Grand-Lieu, Lac de **65** C5
Grand Manan Island **125** S4
Grand Marais *Michigan* **124** H3
Grand Marais *Minnesota* **124** E3
Grand-Mere **125** P3
Grandola **66** B3
Grand Popo **105** F4
Grand Prairie **128** D4
Grand Rapids *Canada* **119** R5
Grand Rapids *Michigan* **124** H5
Grand Rapids *Minnesota* **124** D3
Grandrieu **65** E6
Grand Saint Bernard, Col du **68** A3
Grand Santi **137** G3
Graney, Lough **59** E7
Grangemouth **57** E4
Grange-over-Sands **55** G2
Grangesberg **63** F6
Grangeville **122** F5
Granite Peak **123** K5
Granitola, Capo **69** D7
Granna **63** F7
Granollers **67** H2
Gran Pajonal **136** C6
Gran Paradiso **68** A3
Grantham **53** G2
Grant Island **141** R4
Grant, Mount **122** E8
Grantown-on-Spey **56** E3
Grants **127** J3
Grantshouse **57** F4
Grants Pass **122** C6
Granville **64** C4
Granville Lake **119** Q4
Grasby **55** J3
Gras, Lac de **119** N3
Grasmere **55** F2
Graso **63** H6
Grasse **65** G7
Grassrange **123** K4
Grass Valley **122** D8
Grassy **113** J7
Grassy Knob **125** K7
Gratens **65** D7
Graus **67** G1
Gravatai **138** F5
Gravdal **62** E2
Gravelines **64** E3
Grave, Pointe de **65** C6
Gravesend **53** H3
Gravois, Pointe-a- **133** L5
Gray **65** F5
Grayling **124** H4
Grays **53** H3
Grays Harbor **122** B4
Graz **68** E2
Great Abaco **132** J1
Great Artesian Basin **113** J4
Great Astrolabe Reef **114** R9
Great Australian Bight **112** F5
Great Ayton **55** H2
Great Baddow **53** H3
Great Bahama Bank **132** H2
Great Bardfield **53** H3
Great Barrier Island **115** E2
Great Barrier Reef **113** K2
Great Basin **122** F7
Great Bear Lake **119** L2
Great Bend **127** N1
Great Blasket Island **59** A8
Great Budworth **55** G3
Great Cumbrae **57** D5
Great Dividing Range **113** K3
Great Driffield **55** J2
Great Dunmow **53** H3
Greater Antarctica **141** D2
Greater Antilles **132** G4
Greater Khingan Range **87** N2
Greater London **53** G3
Greater Manchester **55** G3
Great Exuma Island **132** K3
Great Falls **122** J4
Great Fish **108** E6
Great Gable **55** F2
Great Guana Cay **132** J2
Great Harwood **55** G3
Great Inagua **133** L4
Great Indian Desert **92** D3
Great Island **59** F9
Great Karas Berg **108** C5
Great Karoo **108** D6
Great Lakes **143** L3
Great Longton **55** H2
Great Malvern **52** E2
Great Mercury Island **115** E2
Great Nicobar **93** H7
Great North East Channel **114** C3
Great Ormes Head **54** F3
Great Ouse **53** H2
Great Papuan Plateau **114** C3
Great Plains **123** J2
Great Ruaha **107** G4
Great Sacandaga Lake **125** N5
Great Salt Lake **122** H7
Great Salt Lake Desert **122** H7
Great Sand Hills **123** K2
Great Sandy Desert **112** E3
Great Sankey **55** G3
Great Sea Reef **114** R8
Great Sitkin Island **118** Ac9
Great Slave Lake **119** N2
Great Smeaton **55** H2
Great Stour **53** J3
Great Sugar Loaf **59** K6
Great Torrington **52** C4
Great Victoria Desert **112** F4
Great Wall of China, The **87** L4
Great Whernside **55** H2
Great Witley **52** E2
Great Yarmouth **53** J2
Great Yeldham **53** H2
Great Zab **94** F3
Gredos, Sierra de **66** D2
Greece **75** F3
Greeley **123** M7
Greely Fjord **120** K1
Green *Kentucky* **124** G8
Green *Wyoming* **123** J6
Green Bay *U.S.A.* **124** G4
Green Bay *U.S.A.* **124** G4
Green Bell, Ostrov **80** H1
Greenbrier **125** K8
Greencastle **58** K4
Greeneville **129** L2
Greenfield **125** P5
Green Hammerton **55** H2
Greenhead **55** G2
Green Island **115** C6
Greenisland **58** L3
Green Islands **114** E2
Greenland **116** Q1
Greenlaw **57** F4
Greenlough **112** D4
Greenlowther **57** D5
Green Mountains **125** P5
Greenock **57** D5
Green River *Papua New Guinea* **114** C2
Green River *Utah* **127** G1
Green River *Wyoming* **123** K7
Greensboro **129** N2
Greensburg **125** L6
Greenstone Point **56** C3
Green Valley **126** G5

Name	Page	Grid
Halab	94	C3
Halaban	96	G5
Halabja	94	G4
Halaib	103	G3
Halat Ammar	96	C2
Halaveden	63	F7
Halawa *Hawaii*	126	S10
Halawa *Hawaii*	126	T10
Halba	77	G5
Halberstadt	70	D3
Halcon, Mount	91	G3
Halden	63	D7
Haldensleben	70	D2
Halesowen	53	E2
Halesworth	53	J2
Halfeti	77	G4
Halfin, Wadi	97	N6
Halfmoon Bay	115	B7
Halfway	119	L4
Hali	96	E7
Haliburton Highlands	125	L4
Halifax *Canada*	121	P9
Halifax *U.K.*	55	H3
Halifax Bay	113	K2
Halikarnassos	76	B4
Halileh, Ra's-e	95	K7
Halin	88	B3
Halisah	77	G4
Halitpasa	76	B3
Halkapinar	76	F4
Halkett, Cape	118	E1
Halla	62	G5
Halladale	56	E2
Hallanca	136	B5
Halland	63	E8
Hallandsas	63	E8
Halle	70	C3
Hallefors	63	F7
Hallen	62	F5
Halley	141	Y3
Hallingdal	63	C6
Hallingskarvet	63	B6
Hall Peninsula	120	N5
Halls Creek	112	F2
Hallstavik	63	H6
Hallum	64	F2
Halmahera	91	H5
Halmahera, Laut	91	H6
Halmstad	63	E8
Hals	63	D8
Halsinge-skogen	63	F6
Halsingland	63	G6
Halstead	53	H3
Halton Lea Gate	55	G2
Halul	97	L4
Ham *France*	64	E4
Ham *U.K.*	56	A2
Hamada	89	D8
Hamad, Al	94	D6
Hamadan	94	J4
Hamah	94	C4
Hamam	77	G4
Hamamatsu	89	F8
Hamar	63	D6
Hamata, Gebel	96	B4
Hama-Tombetsu	88	J3
Hambantota	92	F7
Hambleton	55	G3
Hamburg *U.S.A.*	124	C6
Hamburg *Germany*	70	D2
Hamdaman, Dasht-i	95	Q4
Hamd, Wadi al	96	C4
Hame	63	L6
Hameln	70	C2
Hamhung	87	P4
Hami	86	F3
Hamilton	113	H3
Hamilton *Bermuda*	117	N5
Hamilton *Canada*	125	L5
Hamilton *New Zealand*	115	E2
Hamilton *U.K.*	57	D5
Hamilton *Alabama*	129	J3
Hamilton *Montana*	122	G4
Hamilton *Ohio*	124	H7
Hamilton Inlet	121	Q7
Hamim, Wadi al	101	K2
Hamina	63	M6
Hamitabat	76	D4
Hamm	70	B2
Hammar, Hawr al	94	H6
Hammarstrand	62	G5
Hammeenlinna	63	L6
Hammerdal	62	F5
Hammerfest	62	K1
Hammersley Range	112	D3
Hammond *Indiana*	124	G6
Hammond *Louisiana*	128	G5
Hammond *Montana*	123	M5
Hamnavoe	56	A1
Hampden	115	C6
Hampshire	53	F3
Hampshire Downs	53	F3
Hampton *Arkansas*	128	F4
Hampton *S. Carolina*	129	M4
Hampton *Virginia*	125	M8
Hamra , Al Hammadah al	101	H3
Hamrange	63	G6
Hamrin, Jebel	77	L5
Hamun-i Mashkel	92	B3
Hamur	77	K3
Hanahan	114	E3
Hanak	77	K2
Hanalei	126	R9
Hanamaki	88	H6
Hancheng	93	M1
Hancock	125	L7
Handa	89	F8
Handan	87	L4
Handeni	107	G4
Handlova	71	H4
Hanford	126	C2
Hangang	87	P4
Hangayn Nuruu	86	H2
Hanggin Houqi	87	K3
Hanggin Qi	87	K4
Hango	63	K7
Hangzhou	87	N5
Hangzhou Wan	87	N5
Hanhongor	87	J3
Hani	77	J3
Hanifah, Wadi	96	H4
Hanish al Kabir	96	F10
Haniyah, Al	94	H7
Han Jiang	87	M7
Hanko	63	K7
Hanksville	126	G1
Hanna	122	H2
Hannah Bay	121	L7
Hannibal	124	E7
Hann, Mount	112	F2
Hannover	70	C2
Hano-bukten	63	F9
Hanoi	93	L4
Hanover *Canada*	125	K4
Hanover *South Africa*	108	D6
Hanover *U.S.A.*	125	P5
Hanover, Isla	139	B10
Hanpan, Cape	114	E2
Han Pijesak	72	E3
Han Shui	93	M2
Hanson Bay	115	F6
Hanstholm	63	C8
Hantay	86	J2
Hanyuan	93	K3
Hanzhong	93	L2
Haparanda	62	L4
Happisburgh	53	J2
Hapsu	88	B5
Hapur	92	E3
Haql	96	B2
Hara	87	K2
Harad *Saudi Arabia*	97	J4
Harad *Yemen*	96	F8
Harads	62	J3
Haramachi	89	H7
Harare	108	F3
Harasis, Jiddat al	97	N7
Harbin	87	P2
Harbiye	77	G4
Harbour Breton	121	Q8
Harby	53	G2
Hardangerfjord	63	B6
Hardanger-Jokulen	63	B6
Hardangervidda	63	B6
Hardin	123	L5
Hardoi	92	F3
Hardy	128	G2
Hare Bay	121	Q7
Harer	103	H6
Harewood	55	H3
Hargeysa	103	H6
Hargigo	96	D9
Har Hu	93	J1
Harib	96	G9
Haridwar	92	E3
Harihari	115	C5
Harima-nada	89	E8
Harim, Jambal Al	97	N4
Hari-Rud	95	S4
Harjedalen	62	E5
Harlan	124	C6
Harlem	123	K3
Harleston	53	J2
Harlingen	64	F2
Harlow	53	H3
Harlowton	123	K4
Harmancik	76	C3
Harmil	96	E8
Harney Basin	122	D6
Harney Lake	122	E6
Harnosand	62	G5
Haro	66	E1
Haro, Cabo	126	G7
Haroldswick	56	A1
Harpanahalli	92	E6
Harpenden	53	G3
Harper	104	D5
Harper Passage	115	C5
Harpstedt	70	C2
Harrah, Ad	94	D6
Harran	77	H4
Harray, Loch of	56	E1
Harricanaw	125	M2
Harrietsham	53	H3
Harrington	55	F2
Harris	56	B3
Harrisburg *Illinois*	124	F8
Harrisburg *Pennsylvania*	125	M6
Harrismith	108	E5
Harrison	128	F2
Harrison Bay	118	E1
Harrisonburg	125	L7
Harrison, Cape	121	Q7
Harrison Lake	122	D3
Harrisonville	124	C7
Harris Ridge	140	A1
Harris, Sound of	56	A3
Harrogate	55	H3
Harrow	53	G3
Harsit	77	H2
Harstad	62	G2
Harsvik	62	D4
Hart	118	H2
Hartbees	108	D5
Hartberg	68	E2
Harteigen	63	B6
Hartford	125	P6
Harthill	57	E5
Hartkjolen	62	E4
Hartland	52	C4
Hartland Point	52	C3
Hartlepool	55	H2
Hartley	127	L3
Hartola	63	M6
Hartsville	129	M3
Hartwell Reservoir	129	L3
Hartz	108	E5
Harut	97	L8
Harvey *Australia*	112	D5
Harvey *U.S.A.*	124	G6
Harwich	53	J3
Haryana	92	E3
Harz	70	D3
Hasan Dagi	76	F3
Hashish, Ghubbat	97	P6
Haskoy	77	K2
Haslemere	53	G3
Haslingden	55	G3
Hassa	77	G4
Hassan	92	E6
Hassankeyf	77	J4
Hassela	63	L5
Hassi Habadra	101	F3
Hassleholm	63	E8
Hastings *Australia*	113	K7
Hastings *New Zealand*	115	F3
Hastings *U.K.*	53	H4
Hastings *Michigan*	124	H5
Hastings *Nebraska*	123	Q7
Hastveda	63	E8
Hasvik	62	K1
Haswell	55	H2
Hatanbulag	87	K3
Hatchie	128	H3
Hatfield *Hertfordshire, U.K.*	53	G3
Hatfield *S. Yorkshire, U.K.*	55	H3
Hatfield Peverel	53	H3
Hatgal	86	J1
Hathras	92	E3
Hatibah, Ra's	96	D6
Ha Tien	93	K6
Ha Tinh	93	L5
Hatip	76	E4
Hat Island	120	G4
Hato	136	A2
Hatohudo	91	H7
Hatskiy	84	D5
Hatteras, Cape	129	Q3
Hattiesburg	128	H5
Hatton	56	G3
Hattras Passage	93	J6
Hatunsaray	76	E4
Hatuoto	91	H6
Haugesund	63	A7
Haughton	53	E2
Hauhui	114	K6
Haukivesi	62	N5
Haukivuori	63	M5
Hauraha	114	K7
Hauraki Gulf	115	E2
Haut Atlas	100	D2
Hauts Plateaux	100	E2
Havana	124	E6
Havant	53	F4
Havasu	126	F3
Havasu, Lake	126	E3
Havel	70	E2
Havelock North	115	F3
Haverfordwest	52	C2
Haverhill *U.K.*	53	H2
Haverhill *U.S.A.*	125	Q5
Havoysund	62	L1
Havran	76	B3
Havre	123	K3
Havre-Saint-Pierre	121	P7
Havsa	76	B2
Havza	77	F2
Hawaii *U.S.A.*	126	R10
Hawaii *U.S.A.*	126	T11
Hawaya, Al	97	J6
Hawea, Lake	115	B6
Hawera	115	E3
Hawes	55	G2
Haweswater Reservoir	55	G2
Hawick	57	F5
Hawke	121	Q7
Hawke Bay	115	F3
Hawke, Cape	113	L5
Hawkesbury	125	N4
Hawkhurst	53	H3
Hawkinge	53	J3
Hawknest Point	133	K2
Hawnby	55	H2
Hawng Luk	93	J4
Hawra	97	J9
Hawran, Wadi	94	E5
Hawsker	55	J2
Hawthorne	126	C1
Haxby	55	H2
Hay *New South Wales, Australia*	113	J5
Hay *Northern Territory, Australia*	113	H3
Hay *Canada*	119	M3
Hayden	123	L7
Hayes	119	R4
Hayes Halvo	120	N2
Hayes, Mount	118	F3
Hayjan	96	G8
Hayl	97	N4
Hayl, Wadi al	77	H5
Haymana	76	E3
Hayrabolu	76	B2
Hay River	119	M3
Hays	96	F10
Hays	123	Q8
Haywards Heath	53	G4
Hazaran, Kuh-e	95	N7
Hazard	124	J8
Hazar Golu	77	H3
Hazaribag	92	G4
Hazaribagh Range	92	F4
Hazar Masjed, Kuh-e	95	P3
Hazel Grove	55	G3
Hazelton *Canada*	118	K4
Hazelton *U.S.A.*	125	N6
Hazen Bay	118	B3
Hazlehurst	128	G5
Hazro	77	J3
Headcorn	53	H3
Head of Bight	112	G5
Healdsburg	126	A1
Healesville	113	K6
Heanor	55	H3
Heard Islands	142	D6
Hearst	124	J2
Hearst Island	141	V5
Heart	123	P4
Heathfield	53	H4
Heathrow	53	G3
Hebbronville	128	C7
Hebden Bridge	55	G3
Hebei	87	M4
Hebel	113	K4
Heber City	122	J7
Hebi	87	L4
Hebrides, Sea of the	57	A4
Hebron *Canada*	121	P6
Hebron *Israel*	94	B6
Hebron *N. Dakota*	123	N4
Hebron *Nebraska*	123	R7
Hecate Strait	118	J5
Hechi	93	L4
Hechuan	93	L2
Heckington	53	G2
Hecla and Griper Bay	120	D2
Hector, Mount	115	E4
Hede	62	E5
Hedland, Port	112	D3
Hedmark	63	D6
Heerenveen	64	F2
Heerlen	64	F3
Hefa	94	B5
Hefei	87	M5
Hefeng	93	M3
Hegang	87	Q2
Hegura-jima	89	F7
Heiban	102	F5
Heide	70	C1
Heidelberg	70	C4
Heidharhorn	62	U12
Heighington	55	H2
Heilbron	108	E5
Heilbronn	70	C4
Heiligenhafen	70	D1
Heiligenstadt	70	D3
Heilong Jiang *China*	88	B2
Heilongjiang *China*	88	D1
Heimaey	62	U13
Heimdal	62	D5
Heinavesi	62	N5
Heinola	63	M6
Heinze Islands	93	J6
Hejing	86	F3
Hekimhan	77	G3
Hel	71	H1
Helagsfjallet	62	E5
Helena *Arkansas*	128	G3
Helena *Montana*	122	J4
Helen Island	91	J5
Helensburgh	57	D4
Helensville	115	E2
Helgoland	70	B1
Helgolander Bucht	70	B1
Heli	88	C2
Heligenblut	68	D2
Helleh	95	K7
Hellin	67	F3
Hell's Mouth	52	C2
Hell-Ville	109	J2
Helmand	95	R6
Helmond	64	F3
Helmsdale *U.K.*	56	E2
Helmsdale *U.K.*	56	E2
Helong	88	B4
Hel, Polwysep	71	H1
Helsingborg	63	E8
Helsingfors	63	L6
Helsingor	63	E8
Helsinki	63	K6
Helston	52	B4
Helvecia	137	K7
Helvellyn	55	F2
Hemel Hempstead	53	G3
Hempstead	128	D5
Hemsworth	55	H3

Name	Page	Ref
Henan	93	M2
Henares	66	E2
Henashi-zaki	88	G5
Henbury	113	G3
Hendek	76	D2
Henderson *Kentucky*	124	G8
Henderson *N. Carolina*	129	N2
Henderson *Nevada*	126	E3
Henderson *Texas*	128	E4
Hendersonville	129	L3
Hendorabi	95	L8
Hendota	124	F6
Hendrik Verwoerd Dam	108	E6
Hengdaohezi	88	B3
Hengduan Shan	93	J3
Hengelo	64	G2
Hengshan *Hunan, China*	93	M3
Hengshan *Shanxi, China*	87	K4
Hengshui	87	M4
Heng Xian	93	L4
Hengyang	93	M3
Henley-on-Thames	53	G3
Hennebont	65	B5
Henqam	95	M8
Henrietta Maria, Cape	121	K6
Henryetta	128	E3
Henry Ice Rise	141	W2
Henry Mountains	126	G1
Henry Point	112	D5
Henslow, Cape	114	K6
Hentiyn Nuruu	87	K2
Henty	113	K6
Henzada	93	J5
Heppner	122	E5
Hepu	93	L4
Hequ	87	L4
Heradsfloi	62	X12
Herat	95	R4
Herault	65	E7
Herbertville	115	F4
Herby	71	H3
Heredia	132	E9
Hereford *U.K.*	52	E2
Hereford *U.S.A.*	127	L3
Hereford and Worcester	52	E2
Hereke	76	C2
Heretaniwha Point	115	B5
Herford	70	C2
Herington	123	R8
Herisau	68	B2
Herlen Gol	87	L2
Herm	53	M7
Hermanas	127	M7
Herma Ness	56	B1
Hermanus	108	C6
Hermel	94	C4
Hermiston	122	E5
Hermitage	53	F3
Hermitage Bay	121	Q8
Hermit Islands	114	D2
Hermon, Mount	77	G6
Hermosillo	126	G6
Hernad	73	F1
Herne	70	B3
Herne Bay	53	J3
Herning	63	C8
Herrera del Duque	66	D3
Herriard	53	F3
Herrick	113	K7
Herroro, Punta	131	R8
Hersbruck	70	D4
Herschel Island	118	H2
Hertford	53	G3
Hertfordshire	53	G3
Hervey Bay	113	L3
Herzberg	70	D3
Hesdin	64	E3
Hessfjord	62	M2
Hesteyri	63	T11
Hestra	63	E8
Heswall	55	F3
Hethersett	53	J2
Hetton-le-Hole	55	H2
Heuru	114	K7
Heversham	55	G2
Hexham	55	G2
He Xian *Anhui, China*	87	M5
He Xian *Guangxi, China*	93	M4
Heydalir	62	X12
Heysham	55	G2
Heyuan	87	L7
Heywood	55	G3
Heze	93	N1
Hialeah	129	M8
Hibak, Al	97	L6
Hibaldstow	55	J3
Hibbing	124	D3
Hibernia Reef	110	F4
Hickory	129	M3
Hicks Cays	132	C6
Hico	128	C4
Hidaka-sammyaku	88	J4
Hidalgo del Parral	127	K7
Hiddensee	70	E1
Hidrolandia	138	G3
Hieflau	68	E2
Hienghene	114	W16
Hierro	100	B3
Higashi-suido	89	B8
Higham Ferrers	53	G2
Highampton	52	C4
Highbury	113	J2
Highclere	53	F3
High Force	55	G2
High Hesket	55	G2
Highland	56	C3
Highland Park	124	G5
High Level	119	M4
High Point	129	N3
High River	122	H2
High Street	55	G2
High Wycombe	53	G3
Higuera de Zaragozao	127	H8
Higuey	133	N5
Hiiumaa	63	K7
Hijar	67	F2
Hijaz	96	E6
Hikman, Barr al	97	P6
Hikone	89	F8
Hikurangi	115	E1
Hildesheim	70	C2
Hill City	123	Q8
Hillingdon	53	G3
Hillington	53	H2
Hill Island Lake	119	N3
Hillsboro *N. Dakota*	123	R4
Hillsboro *Ohio*	124	J7
Hillsboro *Texas*	128	D5
Hillsborough	58	K4
Hilo	126	T11
Hilpsford Point	55	F2
Hilton Head Island	129	M4
Hilvan	77	H4
Hilversum	64	F2
Hima	96	G7
Himachal Pradesh	92	E2
Himalaya	92	E3
Himare	74	E2
Himatnagar	92	D4
Himeji	89	E8
Himmerland	63	C8
Himmetdede	76	F3
Hims	94	C4
Hinche	133	L5
Hinchinbrook Island	118	F3
Hinckley	53	F2
Hinderwell	55	J2
Hindhead	53	G3
Hindley	55	G3
Hindmarsh, Lake	113	J6
Hindon	53	E3
Hindubagh	92	C2
Hindu Kush	92	D1
Hindupur	92	E6
Hinganghat	92	E4
Hingoli	92	E5
Hinis	77	J3
Hinnoya	62	F2
Hinojosa del Duque	66	D3
Hintlesham	53	J2
Hinton	119	M5
Hinzir Burun	77	F4
Hirado-shima	89	B9
Hirakud Reservoir	92	F4
Hirara	89	G11
Hiratsuka	89	G8
Hiroshima	89	D8
Hirfanli Baraji	76	E3
Hirlau	73	J2
Hiroo	88	J4
Hirosaki	88	H5
Hiroshima	89	D8
Hirschberg	70	F3
Hirsova	73	J3
Hirtshals	63	C8
Hirwaun	52	D3
Hisar	92	E3
Hisma	96	C2
Hissjon	62	J5
Hit	94	F5
Hitachi	89	H7
Hitchin	53	G3
Hitoyoshi	89	C9
Hitra	62	C5
Hiu	114	T10
Hiuchi-nada	89	D8
Hiz	53	G2
Hizan	77	K3
Hjalmaren	63	G7
Hjalmer Lake	119	P3
Hjelmeland	63	B7
Hjorring	63	C8
Ho	104	F4
Hoa Binh	93	L4
Hobara	89	H7
Hobart	113	K7
Hobbs	127	L4
Hoboksar	86	F2
Hobro	63	C8
Hobyo	103	J6
Hocalar	76	C3
Hochalm Spitze	68	D2
Ho Chi Minh	93	L6
Hochstadt	70	D4
Hockley	53	H3
Hockley Heath	53	F2
Hodal	92	E3
Hodder	55	G3
Hoddesdon	53	G3
Hodge Beck	55	H2
Hodmezovasarhely	72	F2
Hodna, Monts du	67	J5
Hodnet	52	E2
Hodonin	71	G4
Hoea	126	T10
Hoeryong	88	B4
Hof	70	D3
Hofdakaupstadur	62	U12
Hofmeyr	108	E6
Hofn *Iceland*	62	T11
Hofn *Iceland*	62	X12
Hofors	63	G6
Hofsjokull	62	V12
Hofu	89	C8
Hoganas	63	E8
Hoggar	101	G4
Hogsby	63	G8
Hogsty Reef	133	L4
Hohe Rhon	70	C3
Hohe Tauern	68	D2
Hohhot	87	L3
Hoh Xil Shan	92	G1
Hoi An	93	L5
Hoima	107	F2
Hokensas	63	F7
Hokianga Harbour	115	D1
Hokitika	115	C5
Hokkaido	88	H3
Hokksund	63	C7
Hokota	89	H7
Hokou	93	K4
Hokuno	89	F8
Holarfjall	62	V12
Holbeach	53	H2
Holborn Head	56	E2
Holbrook	127	G3
Holdenville	128	D3
Holderness	55	J3
Holdrege	123	Q7
Holguin	132	J4
Holic	71	G4
Holitna	118	D3
Holjes	63	E6
Hollabrunn	68	F1
Holland	124	G5
Hollandstoun	56	F1
Hollis	128	C3
Hollywood	129	M7
Holm	62	E4
Holman Island	119	M1
Holmavik	62	U12
Holme-on-Spalding-Moor	55	J3
Holmes Chapel	55	G3
Holmes Reef	113	K2
Holmfirth	55	H3
Holms O	120	Q3
Holmsund	62	J5
Holoin Gun	86	J3
Holstebro	63	C8
Holsteinsborg	120	R4
Holsworthy	52	C4
Holt	53	J2
Holton *Canada*	121	Q7
Holton *U.S.A.*	124	C7
Holy Cross	118	D3
Holyhead	54	E3
Holyhead Bay	55	E3
Holy Island *Gwynedd, U.K.*	54	E3
Holy Island *Northumberland, U.K.*	55	H1
Holy Island *Strathclyde, U.K.*	57	C5
Holyoke *Colorado*	123	N7
Holyoke *Massachusetts*	125	P5
Holywell	55	F3
Holywood *Dumfries and Galloway, U.K.*	57	E5
Holywood *Down, U.K.*	58	L3
Homalin	93	H4
Hombre Muerto, Salar de	138	C5
Home Bay	120	N4
Home Hill	113	K2
Home Point	115	E1
Homer	128	F4
Homer Tunnel	115	A6
Hommelvik	62	D5
Hommersak	63	D6
Homoine	109	G4
Homs	77	G5
Homyel	79	E5
Honavar	92	D6
Honaz Dagi	76	C4
Hon Chong	93	K6
Hondo *Mexico*	131	Q8
Hondo *U.S.A.*	128	C6
Honduras	132	C7
Honduras, Golfo de	132	C6
Honefoss	63	D6
Honesdale	125	N6
Honey Lake	122	D7
Hong Kong	87	L7
Hongliuyuan	86	H3
Hongo	86	G2
Hongor *Mongolia*	87	L2
Hongor *Mongolia*	87	L2
Hongshui He	93	L4
Hong, Song	93	K4
Hongsong	87	P4
Honguedo Strait	121	P8
Hongxing Sichang	86	F3
Hongze	87	M5
Hongze Hu	87	M5
Honiara	114	J6
Honingham	53	J2
Honiton	52	D4
Honjo	88	G6
Hon Khoai	93	K7
Honningsvag	62	L1
Honohina	126	T11
Honokaa	126	T10
Honolulu	126	S10
Honshu	89	E7
Hood	119	N2
Hood Canal	122	C4
Hood Island	136	A7
Hood, Mount	122	D5
Hood Point	114	D4
Hood River	122	D5
Hoogeveen	64	G2
Hooghly	93	G4
Hook	53	G3
Hooker	127	M2
Hook Head	59	J8
Hook Norton	53	F3
Hooper, Cape	120	N4
Hoor	63	E9
Hoorn	64	F2
Hoover Dam	126	E2
Hopa	77	J2
Hope *Canada*	122	D3
Hope *U.K.*	55	H3
Hope *U.S.A.*	128	F4
Hopedale	121	P6
Hopelchen	131	Q8
Hope, Loch	56	D2
Hopen	80	D2
Hope Pass	115	C5
Hope, Point	118	B2
Hopes Advance, Cape	121	N5
Hopetown	108	D5
Hopewell	125	M8
Hopkins Lake	112	F3
Hopkinsville	124	G8
Hoquiam	122	C4
Horasan	77	K2
Horby	63	E9
Hordaland	63	B6
Horezu	73	G3
Horley	53	G3
Horlick Mountains	141	R1
Horlivka	79	F6
Hormoz	95	N8
Hormuz, Strait of	97	N3
Horn *Austria*	68	E1
Horn *Iceland*	62	T11
Hornavan	62	G3
Horn, Cape	139	C10
Horncastle	55	J3
Horndal	63	G6
Horndean	53	F4
Hornefors	62	H5
Hornepayne	124	H2
Horn Head	58	G2
Horn, Iles de	111	T4
Horningsham	52	E3
Horn Mountains	119	L3
Hornos, Cabo de	139	C11
Hornsea	55	J3
Horovice	70	E4
Horqin Youyi Qianqi	87	N2
Horqin Zuoyi Houqi	87	N3
Horqueta	138	E4
Horsehoe Bend	122	F6
Horsens	63	C9
Horsey	53	J2
Horsforth	55	H3
Horsham *Australia*	113	J6
Horsham *U.K.*	53	G3
Horsham Saint Faith	53	J2
Horsley	53	G3
Horsovsky Tyn	70	E4
Horten	63	D7
Horton	118	L2
Horwich	55	G3
Hosaina	103	G6
Hosap	77	K3
Hose Mountains	90	E5
Hoseynabad	94	H4
Hoshangabad	92	E4
Hoshiarpur	92	E2
Hospet	92	E5
Hospitalet	67	H2
Hossegor	65	C7
Hoste, Isla	139	C11
Hotamis	76	E4
Hotan	92	F1
Hotazel	108	D5
Hoti	91	J6
Hoting	62	G4
Hot Springs *Arkansas*	128	F3
Hot Springs *S. Dakota*	123	N6
Hottah Lake	119	M2
Hotte, Massif de la	133	K5
Houailou	114	W16
Houdan	64	D4
Houghton	124	F3
Houghton-le-Spring	55	H2
Houlton	125	S3
Houma *China*	93	M1
Houma *U.S.A.*	128	G6
Houmt Souk	101	H2
Hounde	104	E3
Hounslow	53	G3
Houston *Mississippi*	128	H4
Houston *Texas*	128	E6
Houtman Rocks	112	C4
Hova	63	F7
Hovd	86	G2
Hovd Gol	86	G2
Hove	53	G4
Hoveyzeh	94	J6
Hovingham	55	J2
Hovlya	79	G6
Hovsgol	87	K3
Hovsgol Nuur	86	J1
Howa	102	E4
Howakil	96	E9
Howard City	124	H5

Name	Page	Grid
Kariba, Lake	108	E3
Karibib	108	C4
Kariboto	88	H4
Karigasniemi	62	L2
Karikari, Cape	115	D1
Karima	103	F4
Karimata, Kepulauan	90	D6
Karimata, Selat	90	D6
Karimganj	93	H4
Karimnagar	92	E5
Karimunjawa, Kepulauan	90	E7
Karin	103	J5
Karistos	75	H3
Kariz	95	Q4
Karkaralinsk	86	D2
Karkaralong, Kepulauan	91	H5
Karkar Island	114	D2
Karkas, Kuh-e	95	L5
Karkkila	63	L6
Karlino	70	F1
Karliova	77	J3
Karl-Marx-Stadt	70	E3
Karlobag	72	C3
Karlovac	72	C3
Karlovo	73	H4
Karlovy Vary	70	E3
Karlsborg	63	F7
Karlskoga	63	F7
Karlskrona	63	F8
Karlsruhe	70	C4
Karlstad *Sweden*	63	E7
Karlstad *U.S.A.*	124	B2
Karlstadt	70	C4
Karmanovka	79	J6
Karmoy	63	A7
Karnafuli Reservoir	93	H4
Karnal	92	E3
Karnali	92	F3
Karnataka	92	E6
Karnobat	73	J4
Karonie	112	E5
Karora	103	G4
Karossa, Tanjung	91	F7
Karousadhes	74	E3
Karoy	86	D2
Karpathos *Greece*	75	J5
Karpathos *Greece*	75	J5
Karpathos Straits	75	J5
Karpathou, Stenon	75	J5
Karpenision	75	F3
Karpinsk	84	Ad5
Karpogory	78	G3
Karratha	112	D3
Karrats Fjord	120	R3
Karree Berge	108	D6
Kars *Turkey*	77	K2
Kars *Turkey*	77	K2
Karsakpay	86	B2
Karsamaki	62	L5
Karsanti	76	F4
Karshi *Kazakhstan*	79	J7
Karshi *Uzbekistan*	80	H6
Karsiyaka	76	B3
Karskoye More	84	A2
Karsun	78	H5
Kartal	76	C2
Kartayel	78	J3
Kartuni	133	T11
Kartuzy	71	H1
Karufa	91	J6
Karun	94	J6
Karvina	71	H4
Karwar	92	D6
Karym	84	Ae4
Karymskoye	85	J6
Kas	76	C4
Kasai	106	C3
Kasaji	106	D5
Kasama	107	F5
Kasane	108	E3
Kasanga	107	F4
Kasangulu	106	C3
Kasaragod	92	D6
Kasar, Ras	96	D7
Kasba Lake	119	Q3
Kasba Tadla	100	D2
Kasempa	106	E5
Kasese	107	F2
Kashaf	95	Q3
Kashan	95	K5
Kashary	79	G6
Kashgar	86	D4
Kashi	86	D4
Kashima	89	C9
Kashin	78	F4
Kashipur	92	E3
Kashira	78	F5
Kashiwazaki	89	G7
Kashkanteniz	86	C2
Kashkarantsy	78	F2
Kashmar	95	P4
Kasimov	78	G5
Kasin	92	D2
Kasiruta	91	H6
Kaskinen	62	J5
Kasko	62	J5
Kas Kong	93	K6
Kasli	84	Ad5
Kasmere Lake	119	Q4
Kasongo	106	E3
Kasongo-Lunda	106	C4
Kasos	75	J5
Kasos, Stenon	75	J5
Kaspiyskiy	79	H6
Kassala	103	G4
Kassandra	75	G2
Kassel	70	C3
Kasserine	101	G1
Kastamonu	76	E2
Kastaneai	75	J2
Kastelli	75	G5
Kastellorizon	76	C4
Kastoria	75	F2
Kastorias, Limni	75	F2
Kastornoye	79	F5
Kastron	75	H3
Kasulu	107	F3
Kasumi	89	E8
Kasumiga-ura	89	H7
Kasungu	107	F5
Kata	84	G5
Kataba	106	E6
Katagum	105	H3
Katahdin, Mount	125	R4
Katako Kombe	106	D3
Katanning	112	D5
Katastari	75	F4
Katav Ivanovsk	78	K5
Katchall	93	H7
Katen	88	F2
Katerini	75	G2
Katha	93	J4
Katherina, Gebel	103	F2
Katherine	112	G1
Kathmandu	92	G3
Kati	100	D6
Katihar	93	G3
Katikati	115	E2
Katiola	104	D4
Katla	62	V13
Katlabukh, Ozero	73	K3
Katmai Volcano	118	E4
Kato Nevrokopion	75	G2
Katoomba	113	L5
Kato Stavros	75	G2
Katowice	71	H3
Katrineholm	63	G7
Katrine, Loch	57	D4
Katsina	105	G3
Katsina Ala	105	G4
Katsuura	89	H8
Katsuyama	89	F7
Kattavia	75	J5
Kattegat	63	D8
Kauai	126	R9
Kauai Channel	126	R10
Kauhajoki	62	K5
Kauiki Head	126	S10
Kaujuitok	120	H3
Kaulakahi Channel	126	Q9
Kaunakakai	126	S10
Kaunas	71	K1
Kaura Namoda	105	G3
Kaushany	73	K2
Kautokeino	62	K2
Kavacha	85	V4
Kavaje	74	E2
Kavak	77	G2
Kavaklidere	76	C4
Kavalerovo	88	E3
Kavali	92	E6
Kavalla	75	H2
Kavar	95	L7
Kavarna	73	K4
Kavgamis	77	H4
Kavieng	114	E2
Kavir, Dasht-e	95	M4
Kavir-e Namak	95	N4
Kavungo	106	D5
Kavusshap Daglari	77	K3
Kaw	137	G3
Kawagoe	89	G8
Kawaguchi	89	G8
Kawaihae	126	T10
Kawakawa	115	E1
Kawambwa	107	E4
Kawardha	92	F4
Kawasaki	89	G8
Kawerau	115	F3
Kawhia	115	E3
Kawhia Harbour	115	E3
Kawimbe	107	F4
Kawkareik	93	J5
Kawthaung	93	J7
Kayak Island	118	G4
Kayan	91	F5
Kaydak, Sor	79	J7
Kaye, Cape	120	H3
Kayenta	127	G2
Kayes	100	C6
Kaymaz	76	D3
Kaynar	86	D2
Kaynarca	76	D2
Kayseri	76	F3
Kayuagung	90	C6
Kazachinskoye	84	H5
Kazachye	85	P2
Kazakh	77	L2
Kazakhskiy Melkosopochnik	86	C2
Kazakhskiy Zaliv	79	J2
Kazakhstan	79	J6
Kazan	78	H4
Kazan *Turkey*	76	E2
Kazan	119	R3
Kazan Lake	119	R3
Kazanluk	73	H4
Kazan-retto	83	N4
Kazatin	79	D6
Kazbek	77	L1
Kazerun	95	K7
Kazgorodok	84	Ae6
Kazhim	78	J3
Kazi Magomed	94	J1
Kazim Karabekir	76	E4
Kaztalovka	79	H6
Kazumba	106	D4
Kazy	95	N2
Kazym	84	Ae4
Kazymskaya	84	Ae4
Kazymskiy Mys	84	Ae4
Kea *Greece*	75	H4
Kea *Greece*	75	H4
Keady	58	J4
Keal, Loch na	57	B4
Kearny	126	G4
Keaukaha	126	T11
Keban	77	H3
Keban Baraji	77	H3
Kebemer	104	B2
Kebezen	84	D6
Kebnekaise	62	H3
Kebock Head	56	B2
Kebri Dehar	103	H6
Kech a Terara	103	G6
Kechika	118	K4
Keciborlu	76	D4
Kecskemet	72	E2
Kedainiai	63	K9
Kedgwick	125	S3
Kediri	90	E7
Kedong	87	P2
Kedougou	104	C3
Kedva	78	J3
Keel	58	B5
Keelby	55	J3
Keele	118	K3
Keele Peak	118	J3
Keeler	126	D2
Keene	125	P5
Keeper Hill	59	F7
Keetmanshoop	108	C5
Keewatin *N.W. Territories, Canada*	119	R3
Keewatin *Ontario, Canada*	124	C2
Kefallinia	75	F3
Kefamenanu	91	G7
Kefken	76	D2
Keflavik	62	T12
Keglo Bay	121	N6
Kegulta	79	G6
Kehsi Mansam	93	J4
Keighley	55	H3
Keitele *Kaskisuomi, Finland*	62	L5
Keitele *Kuopio, Finland*	62	M5
Keith	56	F3
Keith Arm	119	L2
Keiyasi	114	Q8
Kekertaluk Island	120	N4
Keketa	114	C3
Kel	85	M3
Kelang	90	C5
Keld	55	G2
Keles	76	C3
Kelibia	101	H1
Kelkit *Turkey*	77	G2
Kelkit *Turkey*	77	H2
Keller Lake	119	L3
Kellett, Cape	118	K1
Kellog	84	D4
Kellogg	122	F4
Kelloselka	62	N3
Kells	58	J5
Kelme	63	K9
Kelmentsy	73	J1
Kelo	102	C6
Kelolokan	91	F5
Kelowna	122	E3
Kelsey Bay	122	B2
Kelso *New Zealand*	115	B6
Kelso *U.K.*	57	F5
Keluang	90	C5
Kelvedon	53	H3
Kem	78	E3
Kemah	77	H3
Kemaliye	77	H3
Kemalpasa	77	J2
Kemalpasar	76	B3
Kemano	118	K5
Kemerovo	84	D5
Kemi	62	L4
Kemijarvi *Finland*	62	L3
Kemijarvi *Finland*	62	M3
Kemijoki	62	L3
Kemmerer	123	J7
Kempen	64	F3
Kempendyayi	85	K4
Kemp, Lake	127	N4
Kemps Bay	132	H2
Kempsey	113	L5
Kempten	70	D5
Kempt, Lac	125	N3
Kempton	113	K7
Ken	92	F3
Kenadsa	100	E2
Kenai	118	E3
Kenai Mountains	118	E4
Kenai Peninsula	118	F3
Kendal	55	G2
Kendall, Cape	120	J5
Kendari	91	G6
Kendawangan	90	E6
Kendraparha	92	G4
Kendyrliki	86	F2
Kenema	104	C4
Kenete Karavastas	74	E2
Kenge	106	C3
Kengtung	93	J4
Kenhardt	108	D5
Kenilworth	53	F2
Kenitra	100	D2
Keniut	85	X4
Kenli	87	M4
Kenmare *Ireland*	59	C9
Kenmare *Ireland*	59	C9
Kenmore	57	D4
Kennacraig	57	C5
Kennebec	125	R4
Kenner	128	G5
Kennet	53	F3
Kennewick	122	E4
Kenninghall	53	J2
Kenn Reef	113	M3
Kenogami	121	K7
Keno Hill	118	H3
Kenora	124	C2
Kenosha	124	G5
Kent *U.K.*	53	H3
Kent *U.S.A.*	127	K5
Kentau	86	B3
Kentford	53	H2
Kentmere	55	G2
Kent Peninsula	119	P2
Kentucky *U.S.A.*	124	G8
Kentucky *U.S.A.*	124	H8
Kentucky Lake	124	F8
Kentwood	128	G5
Kenya	107	G2
Keokea	126	S10
Keokuk	124	E6
Keos	75	H4
Kepi	91	K7
Kepno	71	G3
Keppel Bay	113	L3
Kepsut	76	C3
Kerala	92	E6
Kerama-retto	89	H10
Keravat	114	E2
Kerch	79	F6
Kerchenskiy Proliv	79	F6
Kerema	114	D3
Keremeos	122	E3
Keren	103	G4
Kerguelen, Ile	142	D6
Keri	75	F4
Kericho	107	G3
Kerinci, Gunung	90	C6
Keriya He	92	F1
Kerki	95	S3
Kerkinitis, Limni	75	G2
Kerkira *Greece*	74	E3
Kerkira *Greece*	74	E3
Kerma	102	F4
Kermadec Islands	111	T8
Kermadec Trench	143	H6
Kerman	95	N6
Kerman Desert	95	P7
Kermen	73	J4
Kermit	127	L5
Kern	126	C2
Keros	78	J3
Kerpineny	73	K2
Kerrera	57	C4
Kerrville	127	N5
Kerry	59	C8
Kerry Head	59	C8
Kerrykeel	58	G2
Keruh	90	C4
Kerulen	87	L2
Kesalahti	63	N6
Kesan	76	B2
Kesap	77	H2
Kesennuma	88	H6
Keshvar	94	J5
Keskin	76	E3
Keski-Suomi	62	K5
Keskozero	78	E3
Keswick	55	F2
Keszthely	72	D2
Ket	84	D5
Keta	104	F4
Keta, Ozero	84	E3
Ketapang	90	D6
Ketchikan	118	J4
Kete	104	E4
Ketmen, Khrebet	86	E3
Ketoy, Ostrov	85	S7
Ketrzyn	71	J1
Kettering	53	G2
Kettle Ness	55	J2
Kettle River Range	122	E3
Kettlewell	55	G2
Kettusoja	62	N3
Keurus-selka	63	L5
Keushki	84	Ae4
Kew	133	M4
Kewanee	124	F6
Keweenaw	124	G3
Keweenaw Bay	124	G3
Keweenaw Point	124	G3
Keyano	121	M7
Keyaygyr	86	D3

Name	Page	Grid
Kirsanov	79	G5
Kirsehir	76	F3
Kirtgecit	77	K3
Kirthar Range	92	C3
Kirtlington	53	F3
Kirton	55	J3
Kiruna	62	J3
Kiryu	89	G7
Kisa	63	F8
Kisamou, Kolpos	75	G5
Kisangani	106	E2
Kisar	91	H7
Kisarazu	89	G8
Kiselevsk	84	D6
Kishanganj	93	G3
Kishangarh	92	D3
Kishb, Harrat	96	E5
Kishika-zaki	89	C10
Kishiwada	89	E8
Kishorganj	93	H4
Kishorn, Loch	56	C3
Kisii	107	F3
Kiska Island	118	Ab9
Kiskunfelegyhaza	72	E2
Kiskunhalas	72	E2
Kislovodsk	79	G7
Kismaayo	107	H3
Kiso-Fukushima	89	F8
Kiso-sammyaku	89	F8
Kispest	72	E2
Kissidougou	104	C4
Kissimmee	129	M7
Kisumu	107	F3
Kita	100	D6
Kitajaur	62	J3
Kitakami *Japan*	88	H6
Kitakami *Japan*	88	H6
Kitakami-sanmyaku	88	J3
Kita-kyushu	89	C9
Kitale	107	G2
Kitami	88	J4
Kitami-sammyaku	88	H6
Kitangari	107	G5
Kitay, Ozero	73	K3
Kit Carson	127	L1
Kitchener	125	K5
Kitee	62	P5
Kitgum	107	F2
Kithira *Greece*	75	G4
Kithira *Greece*	75	G4
Kithnos *Greece*	75	H4
Kithnos *Greece*	75	H4
Kitikmeot	119	N1
Kitimat	118	K5
Kitinen	62	M3
Kitkiojoki	62	K3
Kitsuki	89	C9
Kittanning	125	L6
Kittila	62	L3
Kitui	107	G3
Kitunda	107	F4
Kitwe	107	E5
Kitzbuhel	68	D2
Kitzbuheler Alpen	68	D2
Kitzingen	70	D4
Kivalo	62	L3
Kivijarvi	62	L5
Kivu, Lake	107	E3
Kiyevka	88	D4
Kiyevskoye Vodokhranilishche	79	E5
Kiyikoy	76	C2
Kizel	78	K4
Kizema	78	H3
Kizilagac	77	J3
Kizilcaboluk	76	C4
Kizilcadag	76	C4
Kizilhisar	76	C4
Kizilirmak	76	E2
Kizil Irmak	77	F2
Kizilkaya	76	D4
Kiziloren	76	E4
Kiziltepe	77	J4
Kizlyar	79	H7
Kizyl-Arvat	95	N2
Kizyl-Atrek	95	M3
Kizyl Ayak	95	S3
Kizyl-Su	95	L2
Kjollefjord	62	M1
Kjopsvick	62	L2
Kladanj	72	E3
Kladno	70	F3
Kladovo	73	G3
Klagenfurt	68	E2
Klaipeda	63	L9
Klamath *U.S.A.*	122	B7
Klamath *U.S.A.*	122	C7
Klamath Falls	122	D6
Klamath Mountains	122	C6
Klamono	91	J6
Klaralven	63	J6
Klatovy	70	E4
Klekovaca	72	D3
Klenak	72	E3
Klerksdorp	108	E5
Klichka	85	K7
Klimovichi	79	E5
Klin	78	F4
Klinovec	70	E3
Klintsovka	79	H5
Klintsy	79	E5
Klisura	73	H4
Kljuc	72	D3
Klobuck	71	H3
Klodzka *Poland*	71	G3
Klodzko *Poland*	71	G3
Klos	75	F2
Klosterneuberg	68	F1
Klosters	68	B2
Klrovskiy	79	H6
Kluane	118	H3
Kluane Lake	118	H3
Kluczbork	71	H3
Klyevka	84	A6
Klyuchevskaya Sopka	85	U5
Klyuchi	85	U5
Klyukvinka	84	D5
Kmagta	114	J6
Kmanjab	108	B3
K2, Mount	92	E1
Knapdale	57	C5
Knaresborough	55	H2
Knife	123	N4
Knight Island	118	F3
Knighton	52	D2
Knin	72	D3
Knjazevac	73	G4
Knockadoon Head	59	G9
Knockalla Mount	58	G2
Knockanaffrin	59	G8
Knockaunapeebra	59	G8
Knocklayd	58	K2
Knockmealdown Mountains	59	G8
Knocknaskagh	59	F8
Knottingley	55	H3
Knox, Cape	118	J5
Knoxville *Iowa*	124	D6
Knoxville *Tennessee*	129	L3
Knoydart	57	C3
Knud Rasmussen Land	120	P2
Knutholstind	63	C6
Knutsford	55	G3
Knyazhaya Guba	62	Q3
Knyazhevo	78	G4
Knysna	108	D6
Knyszyn	71	K2
Koba	90	D6
Kobarid	72	B2
Kobayashi	89	C10
Kobberminebugt	120	R5
Kobelyaki	79	E6
Kobenhavn	63	E9
Koblenz	70	B3
Kobowre, Pegunungan	91	K6
Kobrin	71	L2
Kobroor	91	J7
Kobuk	118	D2
Kobuleti	77	J2
Kobya	85	M4
Koca *Turkey*	76	B3
Koca *Turkey*	76	C3
Koca *Turkey*	76	E2
Kocapinar	77	K3
Kocarli	76	B4
Koceljevo	72	E3
Koch Bihar	93	G3
Kochechum	84	G3
Kochegarovo	85	K5
Kocher	70	C4
Kochi	89	D9
Koch Island	120	L4
Kochkorka	86	D3
Koch Peak	122	J5
Kochumdek	84	E4
Koden	71	K3
Kodiak	118	E4
Kodiak Island	118	E4
Kodima	78	G3
Kodinar	92	D4
Kodok	103	F6
Kodomari	88	H5
Kodyma	73	L2
Kofcaz	76	B2
Koffiefontein	108	D5
Koflach	68	E2
Koforidua	104	E4
Kofu	89	G8
Koge	63	E9
Kogilnik	73	K2
Ko, Gora	88	F2
Kohat	92	D2
Kohima	93	H3
Koh-i Qaisar	95	S5
Kohtla-Jarve	63	M7
Koide	89	G7
Koi Sanjaq	94	G3
Koitere	62	P5
Koivu	62	L3
Koje	89	B8
Kojonup	112	D5
Kokand	86	B3
Kokas	91	J6
Kokchetav	84	Ae6
Kokemaenjoki	63	K6
Kokenau	91	K6
Kokkola	62	K5
Koko	105	G4
Kokoda	114	D3
Kokomo	124	G6
Kokpekty	86	E2
Koksoak	121	N6
Kokstad	108	E6
Koktas	86	C2
Kokubu	89	C10
Kokuora	85	R2
Kokura	89	C9
Kokuy	85	K6
Kok-Yangak	86	C3
Kola	62	Q2
Kolaka	91	G6
Kolar	92	E6
Kolari	62	K3
Kolarovgrad	73	J4
Kolasin	72	E4
Kolay	77	F2
Kolberg	70	F1
Kolbuszowa	71	J3
Kolchugino	78	F4
Kolda	104	C3
Kolding	63	C9
Kole	106	D3
Kolguyev, Ostrov	78	H2
Kolhapur	92	D5
Kolin	70	F3
Kolki	71	L3
Kolkuskull	62	V12
Kollabudur	62	T12
Koln	70	B3
Kolno	71	J2
Koloa	126	R10
Kolobrzeg	70	F1
Kologriv	78	G4
Kolombangara	114	H5
Kolomna	78	F4
Kolono	91	G6
Koloubara	72	F3
Kolozsvar	73	G2
Kolpashevo	84	C5
Kolpino	78	E4
Kolskiy Poluostrov	78	F2
Koltubanovskiy	79	J5
Kolva *Russia*	78	K3
Kolva *Russia*	78	K2
Kolwezi	106	E5
Kolyma	85	U3
Kolymskaya Nizmennost	85	T3
Kolymskiy, Khrebet	85	T4
Komadugu Gana	105	H3
Komandorskiye Ostrova	81	T4
Komarno	71	H5
Komarom	72	E2
Komatsu	89	F7
Komering	90	C6
Komodo	91	F7
Komoe	104	E4
Kom Ombo	103	F3
Komoran	91	K7
Komosomolets, Ostrov	81	L1
Komotini	75	H2
Komovi	74	E1
Kompong Cham	93	L6
Kompong Chhnang	93	K6
Kompong Som	93	K6
Kompong Speu	93	K6
Kompong Sralao	93	L6
Kompong Thom	93	K6
Komrat	79	D6
Komsomolets, Zaliv	79	J6
Komsomolsk	79	E6
Komsomolskiy	79	J6
Komsomolsk-na-Amure	85	P6
Konakovo	78	F4
Koncanica	72	D3
Konch	92	E3
Konda *Indonesia*	91	J6
Konda *Russia*	84	Ae4
Kondagaon	92	F5
Kondinin	112	D5
Kondinskoye	84	Ae5
Kondoa	107	G3
Kondon	85	P6
Kondoponga	78	E3
Konduz	92	C1
Kone	114	W16
Konevo	78	F3
Kong	104	E4
Kongan	89	J10
Kong Christian den X Land	120	W3
Kong Karls Land	80	D2
Kongolo	106	E4
Kongsberg	63	C7
Kongsvinger	63	E6
Kong Wilhelms Land	120	X2
Koniecpol	71	H3
Konigsberg	71	J4
Konigs Wusterhausen	70	E2
Konin	71	H2
Konitsa	75	F2
Koniya	89	B11
Konkamaalv	62	J2
Konkoure	104	C3
Konnern	70	D3
Konnevesi	62	M5
Konosha	78	G3
Konotop	79	E5
Konqi He	86	F3
Konskie	71	J3
Konstantinovsk	79	G6
Konstanz	68	B2
Konstyantynivka	79	F6
Kontagora	105	G3
Kontcha	105	H4
Kontiomaki	62	N4
Kontum	93	L6
Kontum, Plateau du	93	L6
Konya	76	E4
Konya Ovasi	76	E3
Konzhakovskiy Kamen , Gora	78	K4
Kootenai	122	G3
Kootenay	122	F3
Kootenay Lake	122	F3
Kopaonik	73	F4
Kopasker	62	W11
Kopavogur	62	U12
Koper	72	B3
Kopervik	63	A7
Kopet Dag, Khrebet	95	N2
Kopeysk	84	Ad5
Koping	63	F7
Kopka	124	F1
Kopmanholmen	62	H5
Koppang	63	D6
Kopparberg *Sweden*	63	F7
Kopparberg *Sweden*	63	F6
Koppi *Russia*	88	G1
Koppi *Russia*	88	H1
Kopru	76	D4
Koprubasi	76	C3
Koprulu	76	E4
Kopruoren	76	C3
Kopychintsy	73	H1
Kor	95	L6
Kora	77	K2
Korab	72	F5
Korahe	103	H6
Koraluk	121	P6
Korana	72	C3
Korba	69	C7
Korbach	70	C3
Korbu, Gunung	90	C5
Korce	75	F2
Korcula	72	D4
Korda	84	F4
Kord Kuv	95	M3
Korea Bay	87	N4
Korea, North	87	P4
Korea, South	87	P4
Korea Strait	89	B8
Korennoye	84	H2
Korenovsk	79	F6
Korf	85	V4
Korforskiy	88	E1
Korgan	77	G2
Korgen	62	E3
Korhogo	104	D4
Korido	91	K6
Korim	91	K6
Korinthiakos Kolpos	75	G3
Korinthos	75	G4
Koriyama	89	H7
Korkinitskiy Zaliv	79	E6
Korkodon	85	T4
Korkuteli	76	D4
Korla	86	F3
Kormakiti, Akra	76	E5
Kornat	72	C4
Koro	114	R8
Korocha	79	F5
Koroglu Daglari	76	E2
Koronia, Limni	75	G2
Koronowo	71	G2
Koros	72	F2
Korosten	79	D5
Korostyshev	79	D5
Korotaikha	78	L2
Korovin Volcano	118	Ad9
Korpilombolo	62	K3
Korsakov	88	J2
Korsnas	62	J5
Korsor	63	D9
Korti	103	F4
Kortrijk	64	E3
Korucu	76	B3
Koryakskaya Sopka	85	U6
Koryanskiy Khrebet	85	Z5
Koryazhma	78	H3
Korzybie	71	G1
Kos *Greece*	75	J4
Kos *Greece*	75	J4
Koschagyl	79	J6
Koscian	71	G2
Koscierzyna	71	G1
Kosciusco, Mount	113	K6
Kosciusko	128	H4
Kose	77	H2
Kos Golu	76	B2
Koshiki-retto	89	B10
Kosice	71	J4
Koski	63	K6
Koslan	78	H3
Koslin	71	G1
Kosma	78	H2
Kosong	88	B6
Kosong-ni	88	B5
Kossou, Lac de	104	D4
Kossovo	71	L2
Kostajnica	72	D3
Kosti	103	F5
Kostino	84	D3
Kostomuksha	62	P4
Kostopol	71	M3
Kostroma *Russia*	78	G4
Kostroma *Russia*	78	G4
Kostrzyn	70	F2
Kosu-dong	89	B8
Kosva	78	K4
Kosyu	78	K2
Kosyuvom	78	K2
Koszalin	71	G1
Kota	92	E3
Kotaagung	90	C7
Kota Baharu	90	C4
Kotabaru *Indonesia*	90	E6
Kotabaru *Indonesia*	90	F6
Kota Belud	90	F4
Kotabumi	90	C5

Name	Page	Grid
Kota Kinabalu	90	F4
Kotala	62	N3
Kotamubagu	91	G5
Kota Tinggi	90	C5
Kotel	73	J4
Kotelnich	78	H4
Kotelnikovo	79	G6
Kotelnyy, Ostrov	85	P1
Kotikovo	88	E2
Kotka	63	M6
Kot Kapura	92	D2
Kotlas	78	H3
Kotli	92	D2
Kotlik	118	C3
Koto	85	P7
Kotor	72	E4
Kotovo	79	G5
Kotovsk *Russia*	79	G5
Kotovsk *Ukraine*	79	D6
Kotri	92	C3
Kottagudem	92	F5
Kottayam	92	E7
Kotto	102	D6
Kotuy	84	G2
Kotyuzhany	73	K2
Kotzebue	118	C2
Kotzebue Sound	118	C2
Kouango	102	C6
Koudougou	104	E3
Koufonisi	75	J5
Koukajuak, Great Plain of the	120	M4
Kouki	102	C6
Koumac	114	W16
Koumenzi	86	F3
Koumra	102	C6
Koundara	104	C3
Koungou Mountains	106	B3
Kounradskiy	86	D2
Kourou	137	G2
Kouroussa	104	D3
Kousseri	105	J3
Koutiala	100	D6
Kouvola	63	M6
Kova	84	G5
Kovachevo	73	J4
Kovanlik	77	H2
Kovdor	62	P3
Kovdozero, Ozero	62	Q3
Kovel	71	L3
Kovernino	78	G4
Kovero	62	P5
Kovik Bay	121	L5
Kovno	71	K1
Kovrov	78	G4
Kovylkino	78	G5
Kowalewo	71	H2
Kowloon	87	L7
Koycegiz	76	C4
Koyda	78	G2
Koyuk	118	C3
Koyukuk	118	D3
Koyulhisar	77	G2
Koza	89	E9
Kozakli	76	F3
Kozan	77	F4
Kozani	75	F2
Kozekovo	71	M1
Kozelsk	78	F5
Kozhevnikovo	84	B5
Kozhikode	92	E6
Kozhim	78	K2
Kozhposelok	78	F3
Kozhva	78	K2
Kozlu	76	D2
Kozludere	77	G4
Kozluk	77	J3
Kozmodemyansk	78	H4
Kozu-shima	89	G8
Kpalime	104	F4
Krabi	93	J7
Kragero	63	C7
Kragujevac	73	F3
Krakow	71	H3
Krakowska, Jura	71	H3
Kral Chlmec	71	K4
Kralendijk	133	N8
Kraljevo	72	F4
Kralovvany	71	H4
Kralupy	70	F3
Kramatorsk	79	F6
Kramfors	62	G5
Krania	75	F3
Kranidhion	75	G4
Kranj	72	C2
Kranskop	108	F5
Krasavino	78	H3
Krasino	84	Ab2
Kraskino	88	C4
Krasneno	85	X4
Krasnoarmeyesk	84	Ae6
Krasnoarmeyskiy	85	W3
Krasnoborsk	78	H3
Krasnodar	79	F6
Krasnogorsk	88	J1
Krasnograd	79	F6
Krasnokamsk	78	K4
Krasnokutskoye	84	B6
Krasnolesnyy	79	F5
Krasnorechenskiy	88	E3
Krasnoselkup	84	C3
Krasnoslobodsk	78	G5
Krasnoturinsk	84	Ad5
Krasnoufimsk	78	K4
Krasnousolskiy	78	K5
Krasnovishersk	78	K3
Krasnovodsk	95	L2
Krasnovodskiy Poluostrov	79	J7
Krasnoyarsk	84	E5
Krasnoyarskiy Kray	84	E3
Krasnoye	78	G4
Krasnstaw	71	K3
Krasnyy Chikoy	84	H6
Krasnyye Okny	73	K2
Krasnyy Kholm	79	J5
Krasnyy Kut	79	H5
Krasnyy Luch	79	F6
Krasnyy Yar *Russia*	79	G5
Krasnyy Yar *Russia*	79	H6
Kratie	93	L6
Kraulshavn	120	Q3
Kravanh, Chuor Phnum	93	K6
Krefeld	70	B3
Kremenchugskoye Vodokhranilishche	79	E6
Kremenchuk	79	E6
Kremnets	79	D5
Krems	68	E1
Krenitzin Islands	118	Ae9
Kresevo	72	E4
Kresttsy	78	E4
Kresty	84	D2
Krestyakh	85	K4
Krestyanka	84	C2
Kretinga	63	J9
Kribi	105	G5
Krichev	79	E5
Krichim	73	H4
Krieza	75	H3
Krifovon	75	F3
Krilon, Mys	88	J3
Krios, Akra	75	G5
Krishna	92	E5
Krishnagiri	92	E6
Krishnanagar	93	G4
Kristdala	63	G8
Kristel	67	F5
Kristiansand	63	B7
Kristianstad *Sweden*	63	E8
Kristianstad *Sweden*	63	F8
Kristiansund	62	B5
Kristiinankaupunki	63	J5
Kristinestad	63	J5
Kristinovka	73	K1
Kriti	75	H5
Kritikon Pelagos	75	H5
Kriulyany	73	K2
Kriva Palanka	73	G4
Krivoye Ozero	73	L2
Krk	72	C3
Krnov	71	G3
Krokodil	108	E4
Krokom	62	F5
Krokong	90	E5
Krokowa	71	H1
Krolevets	79	E5
Kromy	79	F5
Kronach	70	D3
Krononberg	63	F8
Kronshtadt	63	N7
Kroonstad	108	E5
Kropotkin	79	G6
Krosno	71	J4
Krotoszyn	71	G3
Krsko	72	C3
Krugersdorp	108	E5
Krui	90	C7
Kruje	74	E2
Krumbach	70	D4
Krumovgrad	73	H5
Krung Thep	93	K6
Krusenstern, Cape	118	C2
Krusevac	73	F4
Krusevo	73	F5
Krustpils	63	M8
Kruzenshterna, Proliv	85	S7
Kruzof Island	118	H4
Krym	79	E6
Krymsk	79	F7
Krynki	71	K2
Kryry	70	E3
Kryvyy Rih	79	E6
Krzeszowice	71	H3
Ksabi	100	E3
Ksar El Boukhari	101	F1
Ksarel Kebir	100	D2
Ksar es Souk	100	E2
Ksenofontova	78	K3
Ksour Essaf	101	H1
Kstovo	78	G4
Kualakapuas	90	E6
Kuala Kerai	90	C4
Kuala Lipis	90	C5
Kuala Lumpur	90	C5
Kualapembuang	90	E6
Kuala Penyu	90	F4
Kuala Terengganu	90	C4
Kuandian	87	N3
Kuantan	90	C5
Kuba	89	D8
Kuban	79	G6
Kubenskoye Ozero	78	F4
Kubkain	114	C2
Kubokawa	89	D9
Kubonitu, Mount	114	J6
Kubor, Mount	114	C3
Kubrat	73	J4
Kubuang	90	F5
Kucevo	73	F3
Kuching	90	E5
Kuchinoerabu-jima	89	C10
Kuchinotsu	89	C9
Kuchurgan	73	K2
Kucuk	76	B3
Kucukcekmece	76	C2
Kucuk Kuyu	76	B3
Kudat	90	F4
Kudirkos-Naumiestis	71	K1
Kudus	90	E7
Kudymkar	78	J4
Kufi	76	C3
Kufstein	68	D2
Kugaly	86	D3
Kugi	84	Ad4
Kugmallit Bay	118	J2
Kuh-e Bul	95	L5
Kuh-e Garbosh	95	K5
Kuh Lab, Ra's	95	Q9
Kuhmo	62	N4
Kuhpayeh *Iran*	95	L5
Kuhpayeh *Iran*	95	N6
Kuhran, Kuh-e	95	P8
Kuh, Ra's-al-	95	N9
Kuito	106	C5
Kuji	88	H5
Kuju-san	89	C9
Kukalar, Kuh-e	95	K6
Kukes	75	F1
Kukhomskaya Volya	71	L3
Kukmor	78	J4
Kukpowruk	118	C2
Kukudu	114	H6
Kukup	90	C5
Kukushka	85	M6
Kula *Turkey*	76	C3
Kula *Yugoslavia*	72	E3
Kulagino	79	J6
Kulakshi	79	K6
Kulal, Mont	107	G2
Kulata	73	G5
Kuldiga	63	N8
Kule	108	D4
Kulebaki	78	G4
Kulgera	113	G4
Kulikov	71	L4
Kulinda *Russia*	84	G4
Kulinda *Russia*	84	H4
Kulmac Daglari	77	G3
Kulmbach	70	D3
Kuloy *Russia*	78	G3
Kuloy *Russia*	78	G2
Kulp	77	J3
Kulsary	79	J6
Kultay	79	J6
Kultuk	84	G6
Kulu	76	E3
Kulu Island	118	J4
Kulul	96	E9
Kulunda	84	B6
Kulundinskoye, Ozero	84	B6
Kulyab	86	B4
Kuma	79	H7
Kumagaya	89	G7
Kumakh-Surt	85	M2
Kumamoto	89	C9
Kumano	89	F9
Kumanovo	73	F4
Kumara	115	C5
Kumasi	104	E4
Kumba	105	G5
Kumbakonam	92	E6
Kum-Dag	95	M2
Kumertau	79	K5
Kuminki	62	L4
Kuminskiy	84	Ae5
Kumkuduk	86	F3
Kumluca	76	D4
Kummerower See	70	E2
Kumnyong	87	P5
Kumon Bum	93	J3
Kumru	77	G2
Kumsong	87	P4
Kumta	92	D6
Kumyr	86	C3
Kunas	86	E3
Kunas Chang	86	E3
Kunashir, Ostrov	88	L3
Kundelungu Mountains	107	E5
Kunduz	92	C1
Kungalv	63	H8
Kungar	78	K4
Kunghit Island	118	J5
Kungrad	51	U7
Kungsor	63	G7
Kungu	106	C2
Kunlun Shan	92	F1
Kunmadaras	72	F2
Kunming	93	K4
Kunsan	87	P4
Kununurra	112	F2
Kunu-ri	87	P4
Kuolayarvi	62	N3
Kuopio *Sweden*	62	M5
Kuopio *Sweden*	62	M5
Kupa	72	C3
Kupang	91	G7
Kuparuk	118	E2
Kupino	84	B6
Kupreanof Island	118	J4
Kupreanof Point	118	Ag8
Kupyansk	79	F6
Kuqa	86	E3
Kura	77	L2
Kurashasayskiy	79	K5
Kurashiki	89	D8
Kurayoshi	89	D8
Kurday	86	D3
Kurdzhali	73	H5
Kure	89	D8
Kure	76	E2
Kurecik	77	G3
Kure Daglari	76	F2
Kuresaare	63	M7
Kureyka	84	D3
Kurgan	84	Ae5
Kurganinsk	79	G7
Kurgan-Tyube	86	B4
Kurikka	62	N4
Kurilskiye Ostrova	85	S7
Kuril Trench	142	G3
Kurkcu	76	E4
Kurlek	84	C5
Kurmuk	103	F5
Kurnool	92	E5
Kuroi	89	E8
Kuroiso	89	G7
Kurow	71	K3
Kursk	79	F5
Kursumlija	73	F4
Kursunlu	76	E2
Kurtalan	77	J4
Kurtamysh	84	Ad6
Kurtun	77	H2
Kuru	63	K6
Kurucasile	76	E2
Kuruman *South Africa*	108	D5
Kuruman *South Africa*	108	D5
Kurume	89	C9
Kurunegala	92	F7
Kurzeme	63	K8
Kusadasi	76	B4
Kusadasi Korfezi	76	B4
Kusel	70	B4
Kusey Andolu Daglari	77	H2
Kushchevskaya	79	F6
Kushima	89	C10
Kushimoto	89	E9
Kushiro	88	K4
Kushka *Russia*	85	U4
Kushmurun	84	Ad6
Kushtia	93	G4
Kushva	78	K4
Kuskokwim	118	C3
Kuskokwim Bay	118	C4
Kuskokwim Mountains	118	D3
Kusma	92	F3
Kussharo-ko	88	K4
Kustanay	84	Ad6
Kustrin	70	F2
Kuta	105	G4
Kutahya	76	C3
Kutaisi	77	K1
Kutchan	88	H4
Kutima	84	H5
Kut, Ko	93	K6
Kutna Hora	70	F4
Kutno	71	H2
Kutu	106	C3
Kutubdia	93	H4
Kutum	102	D5
Kuujjuaq	121	N6
Kuujjuarapik	121	L6
Kuuli-Mayak	79	J7
Kuusamo	62	N4
Kuvango	106	C5
Kuvet	85	X3
Kuwait	94	H7
Kuwait	97	J2
Kuwana	89	F8
Kuya	78	G2
Kuybyshev *Russia*	84	B5
Kuybyshevskoye Vodokhranilishche	78	H4
Kuyeda	78	K4
Kuygan	86	C2
Kuytun	86	F3
Kuyucak	76	C4
Kuyumba	84	F4
Kuyus	84	D6
Kuzino	78	K4
Kuzitrin	118	C2
Kuzmovka	84	E4
Kuznetsk	79	H5
Kuznetsovo	88	G2
Kuzomen	78	F2
Kuzucubelen	76	F4
Kvaloy	62	H2
Kvaloya	62	K1
Kvalsund	62	L1
Kvarner	72	C3
Kvarneric	72	C3
Kvichak Bay	118	D4
Kvidinge	63	E8
Kvigtind	62	E4
Kvikkjokk	62	G3
Kvina	63	B7
Kvorning	63	C8
Kwa	106	C3
Kwale	105	G4
Kwamouth	106	C3
Kwangju	87	P4
Kwango	106	C3
Kwanso-ri	88	B5
Kwatisore	91	J6
Kwekwe	108	E3

Name	Page	Grid
Liddesdale	57	F5
Liden	62	G5
Lidingo	63	H7
Lidkoping	63	E7
Lidzbark Warminski	71	J1
Liebling	73	F3
Liechtenstein	70	C5
Liege	64	F3
Liegnitz	71	G3
Lielope	63	L8
Lienz	68	D2
Liepaja	63	L8
Lier	64	F3
Liestal	68	A2
Liezen	68	E2
Liffey	59	J6
Lifford	58	H3
Lifi Mahuida	139	C8
Lifou	114	X16
Ligger Bay	52	B4
Lighthouse Reef	132	D6
Ligonha	109	G3
Ligui	126	G8
Ligure, Appennino	68	B3
Ligurian Sea	68	B4
Lihir Group	114	E2
Lihou Reefs	113	L2
Lihue	126	R10
Lihula	63	K7
Lijiang	93	K3
Likasi	106	E5
Likhoslavl	78	F4
Liku	90	D5
Likupang	91	H5
L'Ile-Rousse	69	B4
Lille	64	E3
Lille Balt	63	C8
Lillebonne	64	D4
Lillehammer	63	D6
Lillesand	63	C7
Lillestrom	63	H7
Lillhamra	63	F6
Lillhardal	63	F6
Lillholmsjon	62	F5
Lillo	66	E3
Lillviken	62	G3
Lilongwe	107	F5
Liloy	91	G4
Lima Paraguay	138	E4
Lima Peru	136	B6
Lima Portugal	66	B2
Lima Montana	122	H5
Lima Ohio	124	H6
Limah	97	N4
Limankoy	76	C2
Limavady	58	J2
Limay	139	C7
Limbang	90	E5
Limbani	136	D6
Limbe Cameroon	105	G5
Limbe Malawi	107	G6
Limburg	70	C3
Limeira	138	G4
Limenaria	75	H2
Limen Vatheos	75	J4
Limerick Ireland	59	E8
Limerick Ireland	59	E7
Limfjorden	63	C8
Limin	75	H2
Limmen Bight	113	H1
Limni	75	G3
Limnos	75	H3
Limoeiro Ceara, Brazil	137	K5
Limoeiro Pernambuco, Brazil	137	K5
Limoges	65	D6
Limon	132	F9
Limon	123	N8
Limousin	65	D6
Limoux	65	E7
Limpopo	109	F4
Linaalv	62	J3
Linah	96	F2
Linapacan Strait	91	F3
Linares Chile	139	B7
Linares Mexico	128	C8
Linares Spain	66	E3
Lincang	93	K4
Lincoln New Zealand	115	D5
Lincoln U.K.	55	J3
Lincoln Illinois	124	F6
Lincoln Maine	125	R4
Lincoln Nebraska	123	R7
Lincoln City	122	B5
Lincoln Sea	140	R2
Lincolnshire	55	J3
Lincolnton	129	M3
Lindau	70	C5
Linde	85	L3
Linden Guyana	136	F2
Linden U.S.A.	129	J3
Linderodsasen	63	E9
Lindesberg	63	F7
Lindi	107	G4
Lindley	108	E5
Lindos	75	K4
Lindsay Canada	125	L4
Lindsay California	126	C2
Lindsay Montana	123	M4
Lindu Point	114	S8
Linfen	93	M1
Lingao	93	L5
Lingayen	91	G2
Lingen	70	B2
Lingfield	53	G3
Lingga	90	C6
Lingga, Kepulauan	90	C6
Lingle	123	M6
Lingling	93	M3
Lingshi	87	L4
Lingshui	93	M5
Lingsugur	92	E5
Linguere	104	B2
Ling Xian	93	M3
Lingyuan	87	M3
Lingyun	93	L4
Linhai	87	N6
Linhares	138	H3
Linhe	87	K3
Linh, Ngoc	93	L5
Linkoping	63	F7
Linkou	88	C3
Linlithgow	57	E5
Linnhe, Loch	57	C4
Linosa	74	B5
Linru	93	M2
Lins	138	G4
Linsell	63	E5
Linslade	53	G3
Lintao	93	K1
Linton U.K.	53	H2
Linton U.S.A.	123	P4
Linwu	93	M3
Linxi	87	M3
Linxia	93	K1
Linyi China	87	M4
Linyi China	87	M4
Linz Austria	68	E1
Linz Germany	70	B3
Linze	86	J4
Lion, Golfe du	65	F7
Liouesso	106	C2
Lipa Philippines	91	G3
Lipa Bos.	72	D3
Lipari, Isola	69	E6
Lipari, Isole	69	E6
Lipenska nadrz	70	F4
Lipetsk	79	F5
Lipiany	70	F2
Lipin Bor	78	F3
Liping	93	L3
Lipkany	79	D6
Lipljan	73	F4
Lipnishki	71	L2
Lipno	71	H2
Lippe	70	C3
Lipsoi	75	J4
Lipson	75	F3
Lipu	93	M4
Lipusz	71	G1
Lira	107	F2
Lircay	136	C6
Liri	69	D5
Lisabata	91	H6
Lisala	106	D2
Lisboa	66	B3
Lisbon Portugal	66	B3
Lisbon U.S.A.	123	R4
Lisburn	58	K3
Lisburne, Cape	118	B2
Liscannor Bay	59	D7
Lisdoonvarna	59	D6
Lishi	87	L4
Lishui	87	M6
Lisieux	64	D4
Liskeard	52	C4
Lismore Australia	113	L4
Lismore Ireland	59	G8
Lismore U.K.	57	C4
Liss	53	G3
Listowel	59	D8
Lit	62	F5
Litang	93	K3
Litani	137	G3
Litchfield	124	F7
Litherland	55	G3
Lithgow	113	L5
Lithinon, Akra	75	H5
Litos	66	C2
Lithuania	63	K9
Litovko	85	P7
Little	128	E4
Little Abaco	132	J1
Little Aden	96	G10
Little Andaman	93	H6
Little Bahama Bank	132	H1
Little Barrier Island	115	E2
Little Belt Mountains	122	J4
Littleborough	55	G3
Little Bow	122	H2
Little Cayman	132	G5
Little Colorado	126	G3
Little Falls Minnesota	124	C3
Little Falls New York	125	N5
Littlefield	127	L4
Littlehampton	53	G4
Little Inagua Island	133	L4
Little Karoo	108	D6
Little Minch, The	56	B3
Little Missouri	123	M5
Little Nicobar	93	H7
Little Ouse	53	H2
Little Pamir	92	D1
Littleport	53	H2
Little Red	128	G3
Little Rock	128	F3
Little Rocky Mountains	123	K3
Little Scarcies	104	C4
Little Sitkin Island	118	Ab9
Little Smoky	119	M5
Little Snake	123	K7
Little South-west Miramichi	125	S3
Little Strickland	55	G2
Littleton Colorado	123	M8
Littleton New Hampshire	125	Q4
Little Wabash	124	F7
Little Waltham	53	H3
Liulin	87	L4
Liupan Shan	93	L1
Liuyang	93	M3
Liuzhou	93	L4
Livani	63	M8
Live Oak	129	L5
Livermore	126	B2
Livermore, Mount	127	K5
Liverpool Australia	113	L5
Liverpool U.K.	55	G3
Liverpool Bay Canada	118	K1
Liverpool Bay U.K.	55	F3
Livingston Canada	121	N7
Livingston U.K.	57	E5
Livingston Montana	123	J5
Livingston Texas	128	E5
Livingstone	106	E6
Livingstone, Chutes de	106	B4
Livingstone Falls	106	B4
Livingstone Mountains	107	F4
Livingston Island	141	V6
Livingston, Lake	128	E5
Livno	72	D4
Livny	79	F5
Livojoki	62	M4
Livonia	124	J5
Livorno	68	C4
Liwiec	71	J2
Liwonde	107	G6
Li Xian	93	M3
Liyang	87	M5
Lizard	52	B4
Lizardo	137	H5
Lizard Point	52	B4
Ljosavatn	62	W12
Ljubinje	72	E4
Ljubisnja	72	E4
Ljubljana	72	C2
Ljungan	62	G5
Ljungby	63	E8
Ljusdal	63	G6
Ljusnan	63	F5
Llanarmon Dyffryn Ceiriog	52	D2
Llanbadarn Fynydd	52	D2
Llanbedr	52	C2
Llanberis	54	E3
Llanbrynmair	52	D2
Llandeilo	52	D3
Llandovery	52	D3
Llandrindod Wells	52	D2
Llandudno	54	F3
Llanelli	52	C3
Llanerchymedd	54	E3
Llanes	66	D1
Llanfaethlu	54	E3
Llanfair Caereinion	52	D2
Llanfairfechan	54	F3
Llanfair Talhaiarn	55	F3
Llanfyllin	52	D2
Llangefni	55	E3
Llanglydwen	52	C3
Llangollen	52	D2
Llangranog	52	C2
Llangurig	52	D2
Llanidloes	52	D2
Llanilar	52	C2
Llanos	136	D2
Llanquihue, Lago	139	B8
Llanrhystud	52	C2
Llanrwst	54	F3
Llantrisant	52	D3
Llanwenog	52	C2
Llanwrtyd Wells	52	D2
Llawhaden	52	C3
Llerena	66	C3
Lleyn Peninsula	52	C2
Lliria	67	F3
Llivia	67	G1
Llobregat	67	G2
Lloydminster	119	P5
Lluchmayor	67	H3
Llyswen	52	D2
Loa	138	C4
Loanhead	57	E5
Lobatse	108	E5
Lobau	70	F3
Loberia	139	E7
Lobez	70	F2
Lobito	106	B5
Lobos	139	E7
Lobos, Island	126	G7
Locarno	68	B2
Lochaber	57	D4
Lochailort	57	C4
Lochan Fada	56	C3
Loch Ard Forest	57	D4
Lochboisdale	57	A3
Lochearnhead	57	D4
Loches	65	D5
Lochgelly	57	E4
Lochgilphead	57	C4
Lochinver	56	C2
Lochmaben	57	E5
Lochmaddy	56	A3
Lochnagar	57	E4
Lochranza	57	C5
Loch Shin	56	D2
Lochy, Loch	57	D4
Lock	113	H5
Lockerbie	57	E5
Lockhart	128	D6
Lock Haven	125	M6
Lockport	125	L5
Locri	69	F6
Loddekopinge	63	E9
Loddon Australia	113	J6
Loddon U.K.	53	J2
Lodeve	65	E7
Lodeynoye Pole	78	E3
Lodge Grass	123	L5
Lodgepole	123	M7
Lodi Italy	68	B3
Lodi U.S.A.	126	B1
Lodingen	62	F2
Lodja	106	D3
Lodwar	107	G2
Lodz	71	H3
Loeriesfontein	108	C6
Lofoten	62	E2
Loftus	55	J2
Logan	122	J7
Logan, Mount	118	G3
Logansport Indiana	124	G6
Logansport Louisiana	128	F5
Loge	106	B4
Logishin	71	M2
Logone	102	C5
Logrono	66	E1
Logrosan	66	D3
Loh	114	T10
Lohardaga	92	F4
Loharu	92	E3
Lohit	93	J3
Lohja	63	L6
Lohtaja	62	K4
Loikaw	93	J5
Loimaa	63	K6
Loimijoki	63	K6
Loing	65	E5
Loi, Phu	93	K4
Loir	65	C5
Loire	65	B5
Loja Ecuador	136	B4
Loja Spain	66	D4
Lokantekojarvi	62	M3
Lokhpodgort	78	M2
Lokhvitsa	79	E5
Lokichokio	107	F2
Lokilalaki, Gunung	91	G6
Lokka	62	M3
Loknya	78	E4
Lokoja	105	G4
Lokshak	85	N6
Lokuru	114	H6
Lol	102	E6
Lola	104	D4
Lolland	63	D9
Lolo	122	G4
Loloda	91	H5
Lolo Pass	122	G4
Lolvavana, Passage	114	U11
Lom Bulgaria	73	G4
Lom Norway	63	C6
Lomami	106	D3
Lomas Coloradas	139	C8
Lomazy	71	K3
Lombarda, Serra	137	G3
Lombe	107	G4
Lombez	65	D7
Lomblen	91	G7
Lombok	90	F7
Lome	104	F4
Lomela	106	D3
Lomir	94	J2
Lomond Hills	57	E4
Lomond, Loch	57	D4
Lomonosov Ridge	140	A1
Lompobattang, Gunung	91	F7
Lompoc	126	B3
Lomza	71	K2
London Canada	125	K5
London U.K.	53	G3
Londonderry U.K.	58	H2
Londonderry U.K.	58	J3
Londonderry, Cape	112	F1
Londonderry, Isla	139	B11
Londoni	114	R8
Londrina	138	F4
Lone Pine	126	C2
Longa Angola	106	C5
Longa Angola	106	C6
Longa Island	56	C3
Long Akah	90	E5
Longa, Ostrova de	81	S2
Long Bay	129	N4
Long Beach California	126	C4
Long Beach New York	125	P6
Long Branch	125	P6
Longchang	93	L3
Longchuan	87	M7
Longde	93	L1
Long Eaton	53	F2
Longford Ireland	58	G5
Longford Ireland	58	G5
Longformacus	57	F5
Longframlington	57	G5
Longhoughton	55	H1
Longhua	87	M3

Name	Page	Ref
Longhui	93	M3
Long Island *Bahamas*	133	K3
Long Island *Canada*	121	L7
Long Island *New Zealand*	115	A7
Long Island *Papua New Guinea*	114	D3
Long Island *U.S.A.*	125	P6
Long Island Sound	125	P6
Longjiang	87	N2
Longjing	88	B4
Longlac	124	G2
Long Lake	124	G2
Longli	93	L3
Long, Loch	57	D4
Long Melford	53	H2
Longmen	87	L7
Long Mynd, The	52	E2
Longnan	87	L7
Longnawan	90	E5
Longney	52	E3
Long Point *Canada*	125	K5
Long Point *New Zealand*	115	B7
Long Preston	55	G2
Long Range	121	Q8
Long Range Mountains	121	Q7
Longreach	113	J3
Long Reef	114	E4
Longridge	55	G3
Longshan	93	L3
Longsheng	93	M3
Longs Peak	123	M7
Long Stratton	53	J2
Longton	55	G3
Longtown	57	F5
Longuyon	64	F4
Longview *Texas*	128	E4
Longview *Washington*	122	C4
Longwy	64	F4
Longxi	93	K2
Long Xuyen	93	L6
Longyan	87	M6
Longyao	87	L4
Lons-le-Saunier	65	F5
Looe	52	C4
Lookout, Cape	129	P3
Loongana	112	F5
Loop Head	59	C7
Lopatin	79	H7
Lopatino	79	H5
Lopatka	85	T6
Lopatka, Mys	85	T6
Lop Buri	93	K6
Lopevi	114	U12
Lopez, Cap	106	A3
Lop Nur	86	G3
Lopphavet	62	J1
Lopra	62	Z14
Lopydino	78	J3
Lora del Rio	66	D4
Lorain	124	J6
Loralai	92	C2
Lorca	67	F4
Lordegan	95	K6
Lord Howe Island	113	M5
Lordsburg	127	H4
Lore	91	H7
Lorengau	114	D2
Lorentz	91	K7
Lorenzo	136	B3
Loreto *Brazil*	137	H5
Loreto *Colombia*	136	C4
Loreto *Mexico*	126	G7
Lorica	133	K10
Lorient	65	B5
Lorillard	119	S3
Lorinci	72	E2
Lorn	57	C4
Lorne	113	J6
Lorn, Firth of	57	C4
Lorrach	70	B5
Lorraine	64	F4
Los	63	F6
Los Alamos	127	J3
Los Andes	139	B6
Los Angeles *Chile*	139	B7
Los Angeles *U.S.A.*	126	C4
Los Angeles Aqueduct	126	C3
Los Banos	126	B2
Los Blancos	138	D4
Los Filabres, Sierra de	66	E4
Losinj	72	C3
Los Mochis	127	H8
Los Pedraches	66	D3
Los Roques	136	D1
Lossie	56	E3
Lossiemouth	56	E3
Los Teques	136	D1
Los Testigos	133	R9
Lost Trail Pass	122	H5
Lostwithiel	52	C4
Lot	65	D6
Lota	139	B7
Lotfahad	95	P3
Lothian	57	E5
Lotta	62	N2
Lottorp	63	G8
Lo-tung	87	N7
Lotzen	71	J1
Loudeac	64	B4
Loudun	65	D5
Louga	104	B2
Loughborough	53	F2
Loughbrickland	58	K4
Lougheed Island	120	E2
Loughor	52	C3
Loughrea	59	E6
Loughsalt Mount	58	G2
Lough Swilly	58	G2
Louhans	65	F5
Louisa	124	J7
Louisiade Archipelago	114	T10
Louisiana	128	F5
Lou Island	114	D2
Louis Trichardt	108	E4
Louisville *Kentucky*	124	H7
Louisville *Mississippi*	128	H4
Loukhi	62	Q3
Loule	66	B4
Loup	123	Q7
Lourdes	65	C7
Louth *Ireland*	58	K5
Louth *U.K.*	55	K1
Louvain	64	F3
Louviers	64	D4
Lovanger	62	J4
Lovat	78	E4
Lovberga	62	F5
Lovech	73	H4
Loveland	123	M7
Lovell	123	K5
Lovere	68	C3
Loviisa	63	M6
Lovington	127	L4
Lovisa	63	M6
Lovnas	62	F4
Lovosice	70	F3
Lovua	106	D5
Low, Cape	120	J5
Lower Arrow Lake	122	E3
Lower Hut	115	E4
Lowestoft	53	J2
Lowicz	71	H2
Lowther Hills	57	E5
Lowther Island	120	G3
Loyal, Loch	56	D2
Loyaute, Iles	114	X16
Loyma	78	H3
Loyne, Loch	57	C3
Lozarevo	73	J4
Lozere, Mont	65	E6
Loznica	72	E3
Lozovaya	79	F6
Lualaba	106	E3
Luan	93	N2
Luanda	106	B4
Luang Prabang	93	K5
Luangwa	107	F5
Luan He	87	M4
Luanjing	87	K4
Luanping	87	M3
Luanshya	107	E5
Luapula	107	E5
Luarca	66	C1
Luashi	106	D5
Luau	106	D5
Lubalo	106	C4
Lubanas Ezers	62	M8
Lubang Islands	91	G3
Lubango	106	B5
Lubartow	71	K3
Lubawa	71	H2
Lubben	70	E3
Lubbock	127	M4
Lubeck	70	D2
Lubefu	106	D3
Lubenka	79	J5
Lubero	107	E3
Lubie, Jezioro	70	F2
Lubien	71	H2
Lublin	71	K3
Lubny	79	E5
Lubosalma	62	P5
Lubsko	70	F3
Lubtheen	70	D2
Lubudi	106	D4
Lubuklinggau	90	C6
Lubumbashi	107	E5
Lubutu	106	D3
Lucan	59	K6
Lucano, Appennino	69	E5
Lucaya	129	N7
Lucca	68	C4
Lucea	132	H5
Luce Bay	54	E2
Lucedale	128	H5
Lucena *Philippines*	91	G3
Lucena *Spain*	66	D4
Lucena del Cid	67	F2
Lucenec	71	H4
Lucera	69	E5
Lucerne	68	B2
Luchow	70	D2
Luckau	70	E3
Luckenwalde	70	E2
Lucknow	92	F3
Lucon	65	C5
Lucrecia, Cabo	133	K4
Luda	87	N4
Ludensheid	70	B3
Luderitz	108	C5
Ludford	55	J3
Ludgvan	52	B4
Ludhiana	92	E2
Ludington	124	G5
Ludlow *U.K.*	52	E2
Ludlow *U.S.A.*	126	D3
Ludogorie	73	J4
Ludus	73	H2
Ludvika	63	F6
Ludwigsburg	70	C4
Ludwigshafen	70	B4
Ludwigslust	70	D2
Ludza	63	M8
Luebo	106	D4
Luena	106	C5
Luepa	136	E2
Lufeng	93	L2
Lufeng	87	M7
Lufkin	128	E5
Luga	63	N7
Lugano	68	B2
Lugano, Lago di	68	B3
Luganville	114	T11
Lugela	109	G3
Lugenda	109	G2
Lugg	52	E2
Lugnaquilla	59	K7
Lugo *Italy*	68	C3
Lugo *Spain*	66	C1
Lugoj	73	F3
Lugovoy	86	C3
Lugton	57	D5
Luhansk	79	F6
Luiana	106	D6
Luichart, Loch	56	D3
Luik	64	F3
Luimneach	59	E7
Luing	57	C4
Luinne Bheinn	57	C3
Luiro	62	M3
Luiza	106	D4
Lujan	139	C6
Lujiang	87	M5
Lukashkin Yar	84	B4
Lukeville	126	F5
Lukovit	73	H4
Lukovo	72	F5
Lukow	71	K3
Lukoyanov	78	G4
Lukulu	106	D5
Lulea	62	K4
Lulealven	62	J3
Luleburgaz	76	B2
Lulo	106	C4
Lulong	87	M4
Lulonga	106	C2
Luluabourg	106	D4
Lulworth Cove	53	E4
Lumbala Nguimbo	106	D5
Lumberton	129	N3
Lumbovka	78	G2
Lumbrales	66	C2
Lumbreras	66	E1
Lumbres	64	E3
Lumijoki	62	L4
Lumphanan	57	F3
Lumsden	115	B6
Lumut, Tanjung	90	D6
Lunan	93	K4
Lunan Bay	57	F4
Lunayyir, Harrat	96	C4
Lunberger Heide	70	C2
Lund	63	E9
Lundar	123	Q2
Lundazi	107	F5
Lundy	52	C3
Lune	55	G2
Luneburg	70	D2
Lunel	65	F7
Luneville	64	G4
Lungga	114	K6
Lungwebungu	106	D5
Luni	92	D3
Luninets	71	M2
Lunsar	104	C4
Lunsemfwa	107	E5
Luntai	86	E3
Luobei	88	C2
Luobuzhuang	86	F4
Luocheng	93	L4
Luodian	93	L3
Luoding	93	M4
Luo He	93	L1
Luohe	93	M2
Luotian	93	N2
Luoyang	93	M2
Luqu	93	K2
Lure	65	G5
Lurgan	58	K4
Lurio *Mozambique*	109	G2
Lurio *Mozambique*	109	H2
Lusaka	107	E6
Lusambo	106	D3
Lusancay Islands	114	E3
Lushi	93	M2
Lush, Mountain	112	F2
Lushoto	107	G3
Lushui	93	J3
Lusignan	65	D5
Lusk	123	M6
Luspebryggan	62	H3
Lussac-les-Chateaux	65	D5
Lut, Bahrat	94	B6
Lut, Dasht-e	95	P6
Lut-e Zangi Ahmad	95	P7
Luthrie	57	E4
Luton	53	G3
Lutong	90	E5
Lutsk	79	D5
Lutterworth	53	F2
Luukkonen	63	N6
Luuq	107	H2
Luverne	124	B5
Luwingu	107	E5
Luwuk	91	G6
Luxembourg	64	F4
Luxembourg	64	G4
Luxeuil	65	G5
Luxi	93	J4
Luxor	103	F2
Luza *Russia*	78	H3
Luza *Russia*	78	H3
Luzern	68	B2
Luzhou	93	L3
Luziania	138	G3
Luzilandia	137	J4
Luzon	91	G2
Luzon Strait	91	G1
Lviv	71	L4
Lvovka	84	B5
Lwowek	71	G2
Lyadova	73	J1
Lyakhovskiye Ostrova	85	Q2
Lyall, Mount	122	G3
Lyallpur	92	D2
Lyapin	78	L3
Lybster	56	E2
Lyck	71	K2
Lycksele	62	H4
Lydd	53	H4
Lyddan Ice Rise	141	Y4
Lydenburg	108	F5
Lydford	52	C4
Lydney	52	E3
Lyell Range	115	D4
Lyman	123	J7
Lyme Bay	52	D4
Lyme Regis	52	E4
Lymington	53	F4
Lymm	55	G3
Lyna	71	J1
Lynchburg	125	L8
Lynd	113	J2
Lyndon	112	D3
Lyne	57	F5
Lyness	56	E2
Lyngdal	63	B7
Lyngseidet	62	J1
Lynher	52	C4
Lynn	125	Q5
Lynn Canal	118	H4
Lynn Lake	119	Q4
Lynton	52	D3
Lynx Lake	119	P3
Lyon *France*	65	F6
Lyon *U.K.*	57	D4
Lyon Inlet	120	K4
Lyon, Loch	57	D4
Lyonnais, Monts du	65	F6
Lyra Reef	114	E2
Lyskovo	78	H4
Lysva	78	K4
Lysychansk	79	F6
Lytham Saint Annes	55	F3
Lythe	55	J2
Lyttelton	115	D5
Lytton	122	D2
Lyubashevka	73	L2
Lyubcha	71	M2
Lyubertsy	78	F4
Lyubeshov	71	L3
Lyubimets	73	J5
Lyuboml	71	L3
Lyubotin	79	F6
Lyudinovo	79	E5
Lyushcha	71	M2

M

Name	Page	Ref
Maaia	109	H2
Maam Cross	59	C6
Maan	94	B6
Maanqiao	86	F3
Maanselka	62	N5
Maanshan	87	M5
Maarianhamina	63	G6
Maarrat an Numan	94	C4
Maas	64	F3
Maaseik	64	F3
Maasin	91	G3
Maastricht	64	F3
Maba	91	H5
Mabalane	109	F4
Mabar	96	G9
Mablethorpe	55	K3
Macachin	139	D7
McAdam	125	S4
Macedonia	73	F5
Macae	138	H4
McAlester	128	E3
McAllen	128	C7
McAllister, Mount	113	K5
MacAlpine Lake	119	Q2
Macapa	137	G3
Macara	136	B4
McArthur	113	H2
Macau	137	K5
Macaubas	138	J6
Macauley Islands	111	T8
McBeth Fjord	120	N4
McBride	119	L5
McCamey	127	L5
McCammon	122	H6
McCarthy	118	G3
Macclesfield	55	G3

Name	Page	Ref
Mashkid	95	R8
Masi	62	K2
Masilah, Wadi al	97	J9
Masi-Manimba	106	C3
Masindi	107	F2
Masirah	97	P6
Masirah, Khalij	97	N7
Masirah, Khawr al	97	P6
Masiri	95	K6
Masisi	107	E3
Masjed Soleyman	94	J6
Mask, Lough	58	D5
Maskutan	95	P8
Maslen Nos	73	J4
Masoala, Cap	109	K3
Mason Bay	115	A7
Mason City	124	D5
Ma, Song	93	K4
Masqat	97	P5
Massa	68	C3
Massachusetts	125	P5
Massachusetts Bay	125	Q5
Massakori	102	C5
Massa Marittima	68	C4
Massangena	109	F4
Massape	137	J4
Massava	84	Ad4
Massenya	102	C5
Massigui	100	D6
Massillon	124	K6
Massinga	109	G4
Massingir	109	F4
Masteksay	79	H6
Masterton	115	E4
Mastikho, Akra	75	J3
Mastuj	92	D1
Masturah	96	D5
Masuda	89	C8
Masulch	94	J3
Masurai, Bukit	90	C6
Masvingo	108	F4
Masyaf	94	C4
Mat	74	F2
Mataboor	91	K6
Mataca	109	G2
Matachel	66	C3
Matad	87	M2
Matadi	106	B4
Matafome	66	B3
Matagalpa	132	E8
Matagami *Ontario, Canada*	125	M2
Matagami *Quebec, Canada*	125	M2
Matagami, Lac	125	M1
Matagorda Bay	128	D6
Matagorda Island	128	D6
Matakana Island	115	F2
Matakaoa Point	115	G2
Matala	106	C5
Matale	92	F7
Matam	104	C2
Matamata	115	E2
Matamoros *Mexico*	128	D8
Matamoros *Mexico*	127	L8
Matane	125	S2
Mata Negra	136	E2
Matanzas	132	G3
Matapan, Cape	75	G4
Matapedia	125	S2
Matara	92	F7
Mataram	90	F7
Matarani	138	B3
Mataranka	112	G1
Mataro	67	H2
Matata	115	F2
Matatiele	108	E6
Mataura *New Zealand*	115	B6
Mataura *New Zealand*	115	B7
Matawai	115	F3
Matay	86	D2
Matcha	86	B4
Matehuala	131	J6
Matera	69	F5
Mateszalka	73	G2
Mateur	101	G1
Matfors	62	G5
Matheson	125	K2
Mathis	128	D6
Mathry	52	B3
Mathura	92	E3
Mati	91	H4
Matlock	55	H3
Mato, Cerro	133	Q11
Mato Grosso	136	F6
Mato Grosso do Sul	138	E3
Mato Grosso, Planalto do	138	E3
Matra	72	E2
Matrah	97	P5
Matrosovo	71	J1
Matruh	102	E1
Matsubara	89	J10
Matsue	89	D8
Ma-tsu Lieh-tao	87	M6
Matsumae	88	H5
Matsumoto	89	F7
Matsusaka	89	F8
Matsuyama	89	D9
Mattagami	121	K8
Mattancheri	92	E7
Mattawa	125	L3
Matterhorn *Switzerland*	68	A3
Matterhorn *U.S.A.*	122	G7
Matthews Peak	107	G2
Matthew Town	133	L4
Matti, Sabkhat	97	K10
Mattoon	124	F7
Matty Island	120	G3
Matua, Ostrov	85	S7
Matuku	114	R9
Maturin	136	E2
Matyushkinskaya	84	B5
Mau	92	F3
Maua	109	G2
Maubara	91	H7
Maubeuge	64	E3
Maubin	93	J5
Maubourguet	65	D7
Mauchline	57	D5
Maud	56	F3
Maues	136	F4
Mauganj	92	F4
Maui	126	S10
Maula	62	L4
Maule	139	B7
Mauleon-Licharre	65	C7
Maumere	91	G7
Maumtrasna	58	C5
Maumturk Mountains	59	C5
Maun	108	D4
Mauna Kea	126	T11
Mauna Loa	126	T11
Maungmagan Islands	93	J6
Maunoir, Lac	118	L2
Maures	65	G7
Mauriac	65	E6
Maurice, Lake	112	G4
Mauritania	100	C5
Mauritius	109	L7
Mauron	64	B4
Mauston	124	E5
Mautern	68	E2
Mavinga	106	D6
Mawbray	55	F2
Mawhai Point	115	G3
Mawlaik	93	H4
Mawson	141	E5
Maxaila	109	F4
Maxmo	62	K5
Maya	85	N5
Mayaguana Island	133	L3
Mayaguana Passage	133	L3
Mayaguez	133	P5
Mayak *China*	86	F2
Mayak *Russia*	71	H1
Mayak *Russia*	79	K5
Mayamey	95	M3
Mayas, Montanas	132	C6
Maybole	57	D5
May, Cape	125	N7
Maychew	96	D10
Maydh	103	J5
Mayenne *France*	64	C4
Mayenne *France*	65	C5
Mayero	84	G3
Mayfaah	97	H9
Mayfield *U.K.*	53	H3
Mayfield *U.S.A.*	124	F8
May, Isle of	57	F4
Maykop	79	G7
Maykor	78	K4
Maymakan *Russia*	85	N5
Maymakan *Russia*	85	P5
Maymyo	93	J4
Mayn	85	W4
Maynooth	59	J6
Mayo *Argentina*	139	B9
Mayo *Canada*	118	H3
Mayo *Ireland*	58	D5
Mayo *Mexico*	130	E4
Mayor Island	115	F2
Mayor, Pic	67	H3
Mayotte	109	J2
May Pen	132	J6
Mayraira Point	91	G2
Mayrata	75	F3
Maysville	124	J7
Mayumba	106	A3
Mayuram	92	E6
Mayville	123	R4
Mayyun Island	96	F10
Mazalat	73	H4
Mazamari	136	C6
Mazamet	65	E7
Mazar	92	E1
Mazar-e Sharif	92	C1
Mazarete	67	E2
Mazarredo	139	C9
Mazarron	67	F4
Mazarsu	86	C3
Mazaruni	136	F2
Mazatenango	132	B7
Mazatlan	130	F6
Mazdaj	95	K5
Mazeikiai	63	K8
Mazgirt	77	H3
Mazhur, Irq al	96	G3
Mazidagi	77	J4
Mazinan	95	N3
Mazirbe	63	K8
Mazury	71	J2
Mbabane	108	F5
Mbaiki	102	C7
Mbala	107	F4
Mbalavu	114	S8
Mbale	107	F2
Mbalmayo	105	H5
Mbalo	114	K6
Mbandaka	106	C2
MBanza Congo	106	B4
Mbanza-Ngungu	106	B4
Mbarara	107	F3
Mbengwi	105	G4
Mbeya	107	F4
Mbouda	105	H4
Mbour	104	B3
Mbout	100	C5
Mbuji-Mayi	106	D4
Mchinji	107	F5
MClintock	119	S4
Meade *Alaska*	118	D1
Meade *Kansas*	127	M2
Meadie, Loch	56	D2
Mead, Lake	126	E2
Meadow Lake	119	P5
Meadville	125	K6
Mealhada	66	B2
Meana	95	Q3
Meath	58	J5
Meaux	64	E4
Mebula	91	G7
Mecca	96	D6
Mechelen	64	F3
Mecheria	100	E2
Mechigmen	118	A2
Mechigmen Zaliv	118	A2
Mecidie	76	B2
Mecitozu	76	F2
Mecklenburger Bucht	70	D1
Mecsek	72	E2
Mecufi	109	H2
Mecula	109	G2
Medak	92	E5
Medan	90	B5
Medanos	139	D7
Medanosa, Punta	139	C9
Medea	101	F1
Medellin	136	B2
Medelpad	62	G5
Medenine	101	H2
Mederdra	100	B5
Medford	122	C6
Medgidia	73	K3
Medicine Bow Mountains	123	L7
Medicine Bow Peak	123	L7
Medicine Hat	123	J3
Medicine Lodge	127	N2
Medina *Saudi Arabia*	96	D4
Medina *N. Dakota*	123	Q4
Medina *New York*	125	L5
Medinaceli	66	E2
Medina del Campo	66	D2
Medina de Rioseco	66	D2
Medina Sidonia	66	D4
Medina Terminal Canal	125	L5
Medinipur	93	G4
Mediterranean Sea	98	D3
Medjerda, Monts de la	69	B7
Medkovets	73	G4
Mednyy, Ostrov	81	T4
Medoc	65	C6
Medole	68	C3
Medvezhl, Ostrova	85	U2
Medvezhyegorsk	78	E3
Medvyeditsa	78	F4
Medway	53	H3
Medyn	78	F5
Medynskiy Zavorot, Poluostrov	78	K2
Meeberrie	112	D4
Meechkyn, Kosa	85	Y3
Meekatharra	112	D4
Meeker	123	L7
Meerut	92	E3
Meeteetse	123	K5
Mega	91	J6
Megalo Khorio	75	J4
Megalopolis	75	G4
Megara	75	G3
Megeve	65	G6
Megget Reservoir	57	E5
Meghalaya	93	H3
Megion	84	B4
Megisti	76	C4
Megra *Russia*	78	F3
Megra *Russia*	78	G2
Mehamn	62	M1
Mehndawal	92	F3
Mehran	94	H5
Meig	56	D3
Meighen Island	120	G2
Meiktila	93	J4
Meiningen	70	D3
Meira	66	C1
Meissen	70	E3
Mei Xian	87	M7
Mejez El Bab	69	B7
Mejillones	138	B4
Mekambo	106	B2
Mekele	103	G5
Meknes	100	D2
Mekong	93	L6
Mekong, Mouths of the	93	L7
Mela	62	U12
Melaka	90	C5
Melambes	75	H5
Melanesia	142	F4
Melawi	90	E6
Melbourne *Australia*	113	J6
Melbourne *U.S.A.*	129	M6
Melbourne Island	119	Q2
Melbu	62	F2
Melchor Muzquiz	127	M7
Melenki	78	G4
Meleuz	78	K5
Melfi *Chad*	102	C5
Melfi *Italy*	69	E5
Melfort	119	Q5
Melgaco	137	G4
Melhus	62	D4
Melilla	100	E1
Melipilla	139	B6
Melita	123	P3
Melito di Porto Salvo	69	E7
Melitopol	79	F6
Melk	68	E1
Melksham	53	E3
Mellegue, Oued	101	G1
Mellerud	63	E7
Melle-sur-Bretonne	65	C5
Melling	55	G2
Mellish Reef	113	M2
Mellte	52	D3
Melnik	70	F3
Melo	138	F6
Melolo	91	G7
Melozitna	118	E2
Melrhir, Chott	101	G2
Melrose	124	C4
Melsungen	70	C3
Meltaus	62	L3
Melton Mowbray	53	G2
Melun	64	E4
Melut	103	F5
Melvern Lake	124	C7
Melville	123	N2
Melville Bugt	120	P2
Melville, Cape	113	J1
Melville Hills	118	L2
Melville Island *Australia*	112	G1
Melville Island *Canada*	120	D2
Melville, Kap	120	P2
Melville, Lake	121	Q7
Melville Peninsula	120	K4
Melvin, Lough	58	F4
Melykut	72	E2
Melyuveyem	85	W4
Memba	109	H2
Memberamo	91	K6
Memboro	91	F7
Memel	63	L9
Memmingen	70	D4
Mempawah	90	D5
Memphis *Tennessee*	128	H3
Memphis *Texas*	127	M3
Mena	128	E3
Menai Bridge	55	E3
Menaka	101	F5
Mendawai	90	E6
Mende	65	E6
Mendi	114	C3
Mendip Hills	52	E3
Mendocino, Cape	122	B7
Mendoza	138	C6
Menemen	76	B3
Menen	64	E3
Menfi	69	D7
Mengcheng	93	N2
Mengcun	87	M4
Mengen	76	E2
Mengene Dagi	77	L3
Menggala	90	D6
Menghai	93	K4
Mengjiagang	88	C2
Mengjiawan	87	K4
Mengla	93	K4
Mengshan	93	M4
Mengyin	87	M4
Meniet	101	F3
Menihek, Lac	121	N7
Meningie	113	H6
Menkya	78	L3
Menominee *U.S.A.*	124	G4
Menominee *U.S.A.*	124	G4
Menomonee Falls	124	F5
Menongue	106	C5
Menorca	67	J3
Mentawai, Kepulauan	90	B6
Mentawai, Selat	90	B6
Mentok	90	D6
Menton	68	A4
Mentor	125	K6
Menyamya	114	D3
Menzel Bourguiba	69	B7
Meon	53	F4
Meppel	64	G2
Meppen	70	B2
Mequinenza	67	G2
Merabellou, Kolpos	75	H5
Merak	90	D7
Merano	68	C2
Merauke	91	L7
Mercan Dagi	77	H3
Mercato Saraceno	68	D4
Merced	126	B2
Mercedario, Cerro	138	B6
Mercedes *Argentina*	139	C6
Mercedes *Argentina*	139	E6
Mercedes *Argentina*	138	E5
Mercedes *Uruguay*	138	E6
Mercimek	77	F4
Mercimekkale	77	J3
Mercurea	73	G3
Mercury Bay	115	E2
Mercy, Cape	120	P5
Mere	52	E3
Meredith, Cape	139	D10
Meredoua	100	F3

Name	Page	Grid
Mere Lava	114	U11
Mereworth	53	H3
Mergenovo	79	J6
Mergui	93	J6
Mergui Archipelago	93	J6
Meribah	113	J5
Meric	76	B2
Merida *Mexico*	131	Q7
Merida *Spain*	66	C3
Merida *Venezuela*	136	C2
Merida, Cordillera de	136	C2
Meriden	125	P6
Meridian	128	H4
Merig	114	T11
Merir	91	J5
Meriruma	137	G3
Merkys	63	L9
Mermaid Reef	112	D2
Merowe	103	F4
Merredin	112	D5
Merrick	57	D5
Merrill	124	F4
Merrillville	124	G6
Merrimack	125	Q5
Merritt	122	D2
Merritt Island	129	M6
Merriwa	113	L5
Mersa Fatma	96	E9
Mersea Island	53	H3
Merseburg	70	D3
Merse, The	57	F5
Mersey	55	G3
Merseyside	55	G3
Mersin	76	F4
Mersing	90	C5
Mersrags	63	K8
Merthyr Tydfil	52	D3
Mertola	66	C4
Mertvyy Kultuk, Sor	79	J6
Mertz Glacier	141	K5
Merzifon	76	F2
Merzig	70	B4
Mesa	126	G4
Mesaras, Kolpos	75	H5
Meschede	70	C3
Meselefors	62	G4
Meshik	118	D4
Meshraer Req	102	E6
Mesolongion	75	F3
Messina *Italy*	69	E6
Messina *South Africa*	108	F4
Messina, Stretto di	69	E6
Messingham	55	J3
Messini	75	F4
Messiniakos Kolpos	75	F4
Messo	84	B3
Messoyakha	84	B3
Mesta	75	H2
Mestiya	77	K1
Mestre	68	D3
Mesudiye	77	G2
Meta	136	D2
Metan	138	D5
Metapan	132	C7
Metaponto	69	F5
Metema	103	G5
Meteran	114	E2
Methven *New Zealand*	115	C5
Methven *U.K.*	57	E4
Methwin, Mount	112	E4
Metkovic	72	D4
Metlika	72	C3
Metropolis	124	F8
Metsovon	75	F3
Metu	103	G6
Metz	64	G4
Meulaboh	90	B5
Meureudu	90	B4
Meurthe	64	G4
Meuse	64	F3
Mexborough	55	H3
Mexia	128	D5
Mexicali	126	E4
Mexico	130	H6
Mexico *U.S.A.*	124	E7
Mexico City	131	K8
Mexico, Gulf of	117	K6
Meydancik	77	K2
Meydan e Gel	95	M7
Meydani, Ra's e	95	P9
Meymaneh	94	S4
Meymeh	95	K5
Meynypilgyno	85	X4
Meyrueis	65	E6
Mezdra	73	G4
Mezen *Russia*	78	G2
Mezen *Russia*	78	H2
Mezenc, Mont	65	F6
Mezenskaya Guba	78	G2
Mezenskiy	84	F2
Mezhdurechensk	84	D6
Mezhdusharskiy, Ostrov	80	G2
Mezhgorye	71	K4
Mezotur	72	F2
Mezquital	130	G6
Mezzana	68	C2
Mhangura	108	F3
Mhow	92	E4
Miahuatlan	131	L9
Miajadas	66	D3
Miami *Arizona*	126	G4
Miami *Florida*	129	M8
Miami *Ohio*	124	H7
Miami Beach	129	M8
Mianabad	95	N3
Miandowab	94	H3
Mianeh	94	H3
Miang, Pou	93	K5
Mianwali	92	D2
Mianyang	93	K2
Miarinarivo *Madagascar*	109	J3
Miarinarivo *Madagascar*	109	J3
Miass	84	Ad5
Miastko	71	G1
Micang Shan	93	L2
Michalovce	71	J4
Michelson, Mount	118	G2
Michigan	124	H5
Michigan City	124	G6
Michigan, Lake	124	G5
Michipicoten	124	H3
Michipicoten Island	124	H3
Michurinsk	79	G5
Mickle Fell	55	G2
Mickleton	53	F2
Micronesia	142	F4
Micurin	73	J4
Middelburg *Netherlands*	64	E3
Middelburg *South Africa*	108	E5
Middelburg *South Africa*	108	E6
Middle Andaman	93	H6
Middle Barton	53	F3
Middlebury	125	P4
Middlefart	63	C9
Middlemarch	115	C6
Middlesboro	124	J8
Middlesbrough	55	H2
Middleton *Greater Manchester, U.K.*	55	G3
Middleton *Strathclyde, U.K.*	57	B4
Middleton Cheney	53	F2
Middle Tongue	55	G2
Middleton-on-the-Wolds	55	J3
Middleton Reef	113	M4
Middletown *U.K.*	52	D2
Middletown *New York*	125	N6
Middletown *Ohio*	124	H7
Middlewich	55	G3
Mid Glamorgan	52	D3
Midhurst	53	G4
Midi	96	F8
Midland *Canada*	125	L4
Midland *Michigan*	124	H5
Midland *Texas*	127	M5
Midleton	59	F9
Midongy Atsimo	109	J4
Midsomer Norton	52	E3
Midwest	123	L6
Midwest City	128	D3
Midyan	96	B3
Midyat	77	J4
Mid Yell	56	A1
Midzor	73	G4
Miechow	71	J3
Miedwie, Jezioro	70	F2
Miedzyrzecz	70	F2
Mielec	71	J3
Miena	113	K7
Mieres	66	D1
Mieso	103	H6
Mieszkowice	70	F2
Miford Sound	115	A6
Mighan	95	P6
Miguel Aleman, Presa	131	L8
Miguel Alves	137	J4
Miguel Hidalgo, Presa	127	H7
Mihaliccik	76	D3
Mihara	89	D8
Miharu	89	H7
Mihrad, Al	97	L6
Miida	96	E9
Mijares	67	F2
Mikha Tskhakaya	77	J1
Mikhaylova	84	D1
Mikhaylovgrad	73	G4
Mikhaylov Island	141	F6
Mikhaylovka *Russia*	88	C4
Mikhaylovka *Russia*	79	G5
Mikindani	107	G5
Mikkeli *Finland*	63	M6
Mikkeli *Finland*	63	M6
Mikolajki	71	J2
Mikonos	75	H4
Mikri Prespa, Limni	75	F2
Mikulov	71	G4
Mikun	78	J3
Mikuni	89	F7
Mikuni-sammyaku	89	G7
Mikura-jima	89	G9
Milaca	124	D4
Milagro	136	B4
Milan *Italy*	68	B3
Milan *U.S.A.*	128	H3
Milano	68	B3
Milas	76	B4
Milazzo	69	E6
Milbank	123	R5
Mildenhall	53	H2
Mildurra	113	J5
Mile	93	K4
Mileh Tharthar	94	F5
Miles	113	L4
Miles City	123	M4
Milford *U.K.*	58	G2
Milford *U.S.A.*	125	N7
Milford Haven	52	B3
Milford Sound	115	A6
Milgun	112	D4
Milh, Bahr al	94	F5
Miliana	101	F1
Miliane, Oued	69	C7
Milk	123	L3
Millas	65	E7
Millau	65	E6
Milledgeville	129	L4
Mille Lacs, Lac des	124	E2
Mille Lacs Lake	124	D3
Miller	123	Q5
Millerovo	79	G6
Millers Flat	115	B6
Millford	58	J4
Millington	128	H3
Mill Island *Antarctic*	141	G5
Mill Island *Canada*	120	L5
Millisle	58	L3
Millnocket	125	R4
Millom	55	F2
Millport	57	D5
Mills Lake	119	M3
Milltown	58	K2
Milltown Malbay	59	D7
Millville	125	N7
Millwood Lake	128	F4
Milngavie	57	D5
Milogradovo	88	E4
Milolii	126	T11
Milos *Greece*	75	H4
Milos *Greece*	75	H4
Milowka	71	H4
Milparinka	113	J4
Milpillas	131	K9
Milton *New Zealand*	115	B7
Milton *Florida*	129	J5
Milton *Pennsylvania*	125	M6
Milton Abbot	52	C4
Milton Ernest	53	G2
Milton Keynes	53	G2
Miluo	93	M3
Milwaukee	124	G5
Mimizan	65	C6
Mimon	70	F3
Mina Abd Allah	97	J2
Minab	95	N8
Mina de San Domingos	66	C4
Minahassa Peninsula	91	G5
Minamata	89	C9
Minas *Indonesia*	90	C5
Minas *Uruguay*	139	E6
Mina Saud	97	J2
Minas Gerais	138	G3
Minas, Sierra de las	132	C7
Minatitlan	131	M8
Minbu	93	H4
Minch, The	56	C2
Mincio	68	C3
Mindanao	91	G4
Mindelo	104	L7
Minden *U.S.A.*	128	F4
Minden *Germany*	70	C2
Mindoro	91	G3
Mindoro Strait	91	G3
Mindra	73	G3
Minehead	52	D3
Mine Head	59	G9
Mineola	128	E4
Mineral Wells	128	C4
Minerva Reefs	111	T6
Minervino Murge	69	F5
Minfeng	92	F1
Mingechaur	79	H7
Mingela	113	K2
Minglanilla	67	F3
Mingshui *Gansu, China*	86	H3
Mingshui *Heilongjiang, China*	87	P2
Mingulay	57	A4
Minicoy	92	D7
Minigwal	112	E4
Min Jiang	93	K3
Minle	86	J4
Minna	105	G4
Minneapolis	124	D4
Minnedosa	123	Q2
Minnesota *U.S.A.*	124	C3
Minnesota *U.S.A.*	124	C4
Minnitaki Lake	124	E1
Mino	66	B1
Minorca	67	J3
Minot	123	P3
Minsk	78	D5
Minsk Mazowiecki	71	J2
Minsterley	52	E2
Mintlaw	56	F3
Minto	125	S3
Minto Inlet	119	M1
Minto, Lac	121	L6
Minturn	123	L8
Minusinsk	84	E6
Minwakh	97	J8
Min Xian	93	K2
Minyar	78	K4
Miquelon	125	M2
Mira *Italy*	68	D3
Mira *Portugal*	66	B4
Mirabad	95	Q6
Miracema do Norte	137	H5
Miraflores	136	C2
Miraj	92	D5
Miramichi Bay	121	N8
Miramont	65	D6
Miram Shah	92	D2
Miranda *Brazil*	138	E4
Miranda *Brazil*	138	E4
Miranda de Ebro	66	E1
Miranda do Douro	66	C2
Mirande	65	D7
Mirandela	66	C2
Mirandola	68	C3
Mirapinima	136	E4
Miravci	73	G5
Mirbat, Ra's	97	M8
Mirbut	97	M8
Mirear Island	96	B5
Mirebeau	65	D5
Mirgorod	79	E6
Miri	90	E5
Miri Hills	93	H3
Mirimire	136	D1
Mirim, Lagoa	138	F6
Mirjaveh	95	Q7
Mirnyy *Antarctic*	141	K5
Mirnyy *Russia*	85	J4
Mironovo	84	H5
Mirpur Khas	92	C3
Mirriam Vale	113	L3
Mirtoan Sea	75	G4
Mirtoon Pelagos	75	G4
Miryang	89	B8
Mirzapur	92	F3
Misgar	92	D1
Mishan	88	C3
Mi-shima	89	C8
Mishkino	78	K4
Misima Island	114	T10
Miskolc	73	F1
Misool	91	J6
Misratah	101	J2
Missinaibi	121	K7
Mission *Canada*	122	C3
Mission *U.S.A.*	123	P6
Mission Viejo	126	D4
Mississauga	125	L5
Mississippi *U.S.A.*	128	G4
Mississippi *U.S.A.*	128	G5
Mississippi Delta	128	H6
Missoula	122	G4
Missouri *U.S.A.*	124	D7
Missouri *U.S.A.*	124	E7
Missouri, Coteau de	123	P4
Mistassibi	121	M8
Mistassini *Canada*	125	P2
Mistassini *Canada*	125	P2
Mistassini, Lac	121	M7
Mistelbach	68	F1
Mistretta	69	E7
Mitatib	96	C9
Mitchell *Australia*	113	J2
Mitchell *Australia*	113	K4
Mitchell *U.S.A.*	123	Q6
Mitchell, Mount	129	L3
Mitchelstown	59	F8
Mithankot	92	D3
Mithimna	75	J3
Mitilini	75	J3
Mito	89	H7
Mitre	111	R4
Mitrofanovskaya	78	K3
Mitsio, Nosy	109	J2
Mitsiwa	103	G4
Mitsiwa Channel	96	D9
Mittelland Kanal	70	B2
Mittelmark	70	E2
Mitumba, Chaine des	107	E4
Mitwaba	107	E4
Mitzic	106	B2
Mixteco	131	K8
Miyah, Wadi al	77	H5
Miyake-jima	89	G8
Miyake-shoto	89	G11
Miyako	88	H6
Miyako-jima	89	G11
Miyakonojo	89	C10
Miyaly	79	J6
Miyazaki	89	C10
Miyazu	89	E8
Miyoshi	89	D8
Mizdah	101	H2
Mizen Head *Cork, Ireland*	59	C10
Mizen Head *Wicklow, Ireland*	59	K7
Mizhi	87	L4
Mizil	73	J3
Mizoram	93	H4
Mizpe Ramon	94	B6
Mjolby	63	F7
Mjosa	63	D6
Mlada Boleslav	70	F3
Mladenovac	72	F3
Mlawa	71	J2
Mljet	72	D4
Moa *Cuba*	133	K4
Moa *Indonesia*	91	H7
Moab	127	H1
Moa Island	114	C4
Moala	114	R9
Moate	59	F6
Moatize	109	F3
Moba	107	E4
Mobaye	102	D7
Mobayi-Mbongo	106	D2
Moberly	124	D7
Mobile	129	H5
Mobile Bay	129	H5
Mobridge	123	P5
Mobutu Sese Seko, Lake	107	F2
Moca	114	S9
Mocajuba	137	G4
Mocambique	109	H3

Name	Page	Grid	Name	Page	Grid	Name	Page	Grid	Name	Page	Grid
Mocamedes	106	B6	Monahans	127	L5	Monterey	126	B2	Mores Island	132	J1
Mocha, Isla	139	B7	Mona, Isla	133	P5	Monterey Bay	126	B2	Moreton Bay	113	L4
Mochudi	108	E4	Mona Passage	133	N5	Monteria	136	B2	Moreton-in-Marsh	53	F3
Mocimboa da Praia	109	H2	Monarch Mount	118	K5	Montero	138	D3	Moreton Island	113	L4
Moctexuma	127	H6	Monarch Pass	123	L8	Monterotondo	69	D4	Morez	65	G5
Moctezuma	131	K7	Monar, Loch	56	C3	Monterrey	128	B8	Morgan City	128	G6
Mocuba	109	G3	Monashe Mountains	122	E2	Monte Santu, Capo di	69	B5	Morganton	129	M3
Modder	108	E5	Monasterevin	59	H6	Montes Claros	138	E3	Morgantown	125	L7
Modena *Italy*	68	C3	Monastir *Albania*	73	F5	Montevideo *Uruguay*	139	E6	Morgongava	63	G7
Modena *U.S.A.*	126	F2	Monastir *Italy*	69	B6	Montevideo *U.S.A.*	124	C4	Mori *China*	86	F3
Modesto	126	B2	Monastir *Tunisia*	101	H1	Monte Vista	127	J2	Mori *Japan*	88	H4
Modica	69	E7	Monastyriska	73	H1	Montezuma Peak	127	J2	Moriarty	127	K3
Modigliana	68	C3	Monatele	105	H5	Montfort-sur-Meu	64	B4	Morioka	88	H6
Modling	68	F1	Moncalieri	68	A3	Montgomery *U.K.*	52	D2	Morlaix	64	B4
Modowi	91	J6	Moncao	66	B1	Montgomery *U.S.A.*	129	J4	Morley	55	H3
Moe	113	K6	Monchdorf	68	E1	Montguyon	65	C6	Morlunda	63	F8
Moelv	63	D6	Monchegorsk	62	Q3	Monti	69	B5	Mormanno	69	F6
Moengo	137	G2	Monchique	66	B4	Monticello *Arkansas*	128	G4	Mornington, Isla	139	A9
Moffat	57	E5	Monclova	127	M7	Monticello *Florida*	129	L5	Mornington Island	113	H2
Moffat Peak	115	B6	Moncontour	64	B4	Monticello *New York*	125	N6	Morobe	114	D3
Mogadishu	107	J2	Moncton	121	P8	Monticello *Utah*	127	H2	Morocco	100	D2
Mogadouro	66	C2	Mondego	66	C2	Montiel, Campo de	66	E3	Morogoro	107	G4
Mogdy	85	N6	Mondonedo	66	C1	Montignac	65	D6	Moro Gulf	91	G4
Mogilev-Podolskiy	79	D6	Mondovi	68	A3	Montilla	66	D4	Morokovo	85	W3
Mogi-Mirim	138	G4	Mondragone	69	D5	Mont-Joli	125	R2	Moroleon	131	J7
Mogincual	109	H3	Mondsee	68	D2	Mont Laurier	125	N3	Morombe	109	H4
Moglice	75	F2	Monemvasia	75	G4	Montlucon	65	E5	Moron	132	H3
Mogocha	85	L6	Moneron, Ostrov	88	H2	Montmagny	125	Q3	Moron *Mongolia*	86	J2
Mogoi	91	J6	Monesterio	66	C3	Montmedy	64	F4	Moron *Mongolia*	87	L2
Mogok	93	J4	Moneymore	58	J3	Montmirail	64	E4	Moronade, Cerro des	130	G7
Mogollon Plateau	126	G3	Monfalcone	68	D3	Montmorillon	65	D5	Morondava	109	H4
Mogotoyevo, Ozero	85	R2	Monforte	66	C3	Monto	113	L3	Moron de la Frontera	66	D4
Mogoyn	86	H2	Monforte de Lemos	66	C1	Montoro	66	D4	Moroni	109	H2
Mogoytuy	85	J6	Monga	106	D2	Montpelier	122	J6	Moron Us He	93	H2
Moguer	66	C4	Mongala	106	D2	Montpellier *France*	65	E7	Morotai	91	H5
Mohacs	72	E2	Mongalla	103	F6	Montpellier *U.S.A.*	125	P4	Moroto	107	F2
Mohaka	115	F3	Mong Cai	93	L4	Montraux	68	A2	Morozovsk	79	G6
Mohall	123	P3	Mongga	114	H5	Montreal	124	H3	Morpara	137	J6
Mohammadabad	95	Q6	Mongge	91	J6	Montreal	125	P4	Morpeth	55	H1
Mohammadia	100	F1	Mong Hang	93	J4	Montreal Lake	119	P5	Morrilton	128	F3
Mohawk	125	N5	Monghyr	92	G3	Montreal River Harbour	124	H3	Morrinhos	138	G3
Moheli	109	H2	Mong Lin	93	K4	Montrose *U.K.*	57	F4	Morrinsville	115	E2
Mohill	58	G5	Mongo	102	C5	Montrose *U.S.A.*	127	J1	Morris *Canada*	123	R3
Mohoro	107	G4	Mongolia	86	G2	Mont Saint-Michel	64	C4	Morris *U.S.A.*	124	C4
Moi	63	B7	Mongororo	102	D5	Montseny	67	H2	Morris Jesup, Kap	140	Q2
Moidart	57	C4	Mongu	106	D6	Montserrat	133	R6	Morris, Mount	112	G4
Moimenta da Beira	66	C2	Monhhaan	87	L2	Mont Wright	121	N7	Morristown	129	L2
Moindou	114	W16	Moniaive	57	E5	Monywa	93	J4	Morro Bay	126	B3
Mointy	86	C2	Monifieth	57	F4	Monza	68	B3	Morro do Chapeu	137	J6
Mo i Rana	62	F3	Moniquira	136	C2	Monzon	67	G2	Morro, Punta	139	B5
Moisie	121	N7	Monitor Range	122	F8	Moonie	113	K4	Morros, Punta	131	P8
Moissac	65	D6	Monkira	113	J3	Moopna	112	F5	Morrosquillo, Golfo de	133	K10
Moissala	102	C6	Monkland	52	E2	Moora	112	D5	Mors	63	C8
Mojave	126	C3	Monkoto	106	D3	Mooraberree	113	J4	Morshansk	79	G5
Mojave Desert	126	D3	Monmouth *U.K.*	52	E3	Moorcroft	123	M5	Mortagne	64	D4
Moji	89	C9	Monmouth *U.S.A.*	124	E6	Moore, Lake	112	D4	Mortain	64	C4
Mojones, Cerro	138	C5	Monnow	52	E3	Moorfoot Hills	57	E5	Mortara	68	B3
Moju	137	H4	Mono	105	F4	Moorhead	124	B3	Morteau	65	G5
Mokai	115	E3	Mono Lake	126	C2	Moorlands	113	H6	Morte Bay	52	C3
Mokelumne	122	D8	Monolithos	75	J4	Moorlinch	52	E3	Mortes	137	G6
Moknine	101	H1	Monopoli	69	F5	Moose	121	K7	Morton *U.K.*	53	G2
Mokohinau Island	115	E1	Monovar	67	F3	Moosehead Lake	125	R4	Morton *U.S.A.*	122	C4
Mokokchung	93	H3	Monreal del Campo	67	F2	Moose Jaw	123	M2	Morundah	113	K5
Mokolo	105	H3	Monreale	69	D6	Moose Lake *Canada*	119	Q5	Morven *Australia*	113	K4
Mokpo	87	P5	Monroe *Georgia*	129	L4	Moose Lake *U.S.A.*	124	D3	Morven *U.K.*	57	E3
Mokra Gora	72	F4	Monroe *Louisiana*	128	F4	Moose Mountain Creek	123	N2	Morvern	57	C4
Molaoi	75	G4	Monroe *Michigan*	124	J6	Moosonee	121	K7	Morwell	113	K6
Molat	72	C3	Monroe *N. Carolina*	129	M3	Mopeia Velha	109	G3	Mosakula	63	L7
Mold	55	F3	Monroe *Wisconsin*	124	F5	Mopti	100	E6	Mosby	63	B7
Moldavia	73	J2	Monrovia	104	C4	Moqor	92	C2	Moscow *U.S.A.*	122	F4
Molde	62	B5	Mons	64	E3	Moquequa	138	B3	Moscow *Russia*	78	F4
Moldova	73	J2	Monsaras, Ponta da	138	J3	Mora *Cameroon*	105	H3	Mosedale	55	F2
Moldova Noua	73	F3	Monselice	68	C3	Mora *Portugal*	66	B3	Mosel	70	B4
Moldoveanu	73	H3	Monserrat	67	F3	Mora *Sweden*	63	F6	Moselle	64	G4
Moldovita	73	H2	Montaigu	65	C5	Moradabad	92	E3	Moses Lake	122	E4
Mole *Devon, U.K.*	52	D4	Montalban	67	F2	Moradal, Sierra do	66	C3	Moseyevo	78	H2
Mole *Surrey, U.K.*	53	G3	Montalbo	66	E3	Mora de Rubielos	67	F2	Mosgiel	115	C6
Molepolole	108	E4	Montalcino	68	C4	Morafenobe	109	H3	Mosha	78	G3
Molfetta	69	F5	Montalto	69	E6	Morag	71	H2	Moshchnyy, Ostrov	63	M6
Molina de Aragon	67	F2	Montalvo	136	B4	Morales	132	C7	Moshi	107	G3
Molina de Segura	67	F3	Montamarta	66	D2	Moramanga	109	J3	Mosjoen	62	E4
Moline	124	E6	Montana	122	K4	Moran	123	J6	Moskenesoya	62	E3
Molkom	63	E7	Montanchez	66	C3	Morant Cays	132	K6	Moskosel	62	H4
Mollakendi	77	H3	Montanita	136	B3	Morant Point	132	J6	Moskva	78	F4
Mollaosman	77	K3	Montargis	65	E5	Moratuwa	92	E7	Mosonmagyarovar	72	D2
Mollendo	138	B3	Montauban	65	D6	Morava *Czech Rep.*	71	G4	Mosquera	136	B3
Molln	70	D2	Montauk Point	125	Q6	Morava	73	F3	Mosquitia	132	E7
Molnlycke	63	E8	Montbard	65	F5	Moraveh Tappeh	95	M3	Mosquito Lake	119	Q3
Molodechno	71	M1	Montbeliard	65	G5	Morawa	112	D4	Mosquitos, Costa de	132	F8
Molodezhnaya	141	D5	Montblanch	67	G2	Moray Firth	56	E3	Mosquitos, Golfo de los	132	G10
Molodo *Russia*	85	L3	Montbrison	65	F6	Morbi	92	D4	Moss	63	D7
Molodo *Russia*	85	L3	Montceau-les-Mines	65	F5	Mor Budejovice	70	F4	Mossaka	106	C3
Mologa	78	F4	Montcornet	64	F4	Morbylanga	63	G8	Mossburn	115	B6
Molokai	126	S10	Mont-de-Marsan	65	C7	Morden	123	Q3	Mosselbaai	108	D6
Moloma	78	H4	Montdidier	64	E4	Mordogan	76	B3	Mossley	58	L3
Molotov	78	K4	Monte Alegre	137	G4	Mordovo	79	G5	Mossman	113	K2
Moloundou	105	J5	Monte Azul	138	H3	Moreau	122	N5	Mossoro	137	K5
Molsheim	64	G4	Monte Bello	136	B5	Morebattle	57	F5	Most	70	E3
Molson Lake	119	R5	Montebello	125	N4	Morecambe	55	G2	Mosta	74	C5
Moluccas	91	H6	Monte Carlo	68	A4	Morecambe Bay	55	E2	Mostaganem	100	F1
Moma *Mozambique*	109	R3	Monte Caseros	139	E6	Moreda	66	E4	Mostar	72	D4
Moma *Russia*	85	Q3	Montecatini Terme	68	C4	Moree	113	K4	Mostiska	71	K4
Mombasa	107	R3	Monte Cristi	133	M5	Morehead *Papua New Guinea*	114	C3	Mosty	71	L2
Mombetsu	88	J3	Montecristo, Isola di	69	C4	Morehead *U.S.A.*	124	J7	Mostyn	55	F3
Momboyo	106	C3	Montego Bay	132	J5	Morehead City	129	P3	Mosul	77	K4
Momi, Ra's	97	P9	Montelimar	65	F6	Morelia	131	J8	Mosulpo	87	P5
Momol	71	L2	Montemaggiore Belsito	69	D7	Morella	67	F2	Mota	103	G5
Mompos	136	C2	Montemorelos	128	C8	More, Loch *U.K.*	56	D2	Mota	114	T10
Mon	63	E9	Montemor-o-Novo	66	B3	More, Loch *U.K.*	56	E2	Mota del Cuervo	66	E3
Monach Islands	56	A3	Montenegro	72	E4	Morena, Sierra	66	D3	Motala	63	F7
Monach, Sound of	56	A3	Montepuez	109	G2	Moreno	126	G6	Mota Lava	114	T10
Monaco	65	G7	Montepulciano	68	C4	Moreno, Bahia	138	B4	Motegi	89	H7
Monadhliath Mountains	57	D3	Monte Quemado	138	D5	More og Romsdal	62	C5	Motherwell	57	E5
Monaghan	58	J4	Montereau-faut-Yonne	64	E4	Moresby Island	118	J5	Motihari	92	F3

Name	Page	Grid
Motilla del Palancar	67	F3
Motovskiy Zaliv	62	G2
Motril	66	E4
Motueka *New Zealand*	115	D4
Motueka *New Zealand*	115	D4
Motupiko Blenheim	115	D4
Motykleyka	85	R5
Moudhros	75	H3
Moudjeria	100	C5
Mouka	102	D6
Mould Bay	120	C2
Moulins	65	E5
Moulmein	93	J5
Moulouya, Oued	100	E2
Moulton	55	H2
Moultrie	129	L5
Moultrie, Lake	129	M4
Mounda, Akra	75	F3
Mound City	124	C6
Moundou	102	C5
Moung	93	K6
Mountain	118	K2
Mountain Ash	52	D3
Mountain Home *Arkansas*	128	F2
Mountain Home *Idaho*	122	G6
Mountain Village	118	C3
Mount Airy	129	M2
Mount Ararat	77	L3
Mount Bellew	59	E6
Mount Desert Island	125	R4
Mount Doreen	112	G3
Mount Douglas	113	K3
Mount Elba	113	H5
Mount Gambier	113	J6
Mount Hagen	114	C3
Mount Isa	113	H3
Mount Magnet	112	D4
Mountmellick	59	H6
Mount Pleasant *Iowa*	124	E6
Mount Pleasant *Michigan*	124	H5
Mount Pleasant *Texas*	128	E4
Mount Pleasant *Utah*	126	G1
Mountrath	59	H6
Mount's Bay	52	B4
Mount Shasta	122	C7
Mount Thule	120	L3
Mount Vernon *Alabama*	129	H5
Mount Vernon *Illinois*	124	F7
Mount Vernon *Indiana*	124	G8
Mount Vernon *Ohio*	124	J6
Mount Vernon *Washington*	122	C3
Moura *Brazil*	136	E4
Moura *Portugal*	66	C3
Mourdi, Depression du	102	D4
Mourne Mountains	58	K4
Moussoro	102	C5
Moutong	91	G5
Movas	127	H6
Moville	58	H2
Moy	58	D4
Moyale	107	G2
Moyamba	104	C4
Moyen Atlas	100	E2
Moygashel	58	J4
Moyo *Indonesia*	91	F7
Moyo *Uganda*	106	F2
Moyobamba	136	B5
Moyu	92	E1
Mozambique	109	G3
Mozambique Channel	109	H3
Mozhaysk	78	F4
Mozhga	78	J4
Mozyr	79	D5
Mpanda	107	F4
Mpe	106	B3
Mpika	107	F5
Mporokoso	107	F4
Mpraeso	104	E4
Mrakovo	79	K5
M.R. Gomez, Presa	127	N7
Mrkonjic Grad	72	D3
Msaken	101	H1
MSila	67	J5
Msta	78	E4
Mstislav	78	E5
Mtsensk	79	F5
Mtwara	107	G5
Mualo	109	G2
Muang Chiang Rai	93	J5
Muang Khon Kaen	93	K5
Muang Lampang	93	J5
Muang Lamphun	93	J5
Muang Loei	93	K5
Muang Nan	93	K5
Muang Phayao	93	J5
Muang Phetchabun	93	K5
Muang Phichit	93	K5
Muang Phitsanulok	93	K5
Muang Phrae	93	K5
Muanza	109	F3
Muar	90	C5
Muara	90	E4
Muarabungo	90	D6
Muaraenim	90	D6
Muaralesan	91	F5
Muarasiberut	90	B6
Muarasigep	90	B6
Muarasipongi	90	B5
Muaratebo	90	D6
Muarateweh	90	E6
Mubende	107	F2
Mubi	105	H3
Mubrani	91	J6
Mucajai	136	E3
Muchinga Escarpment	107	F5
Much Wenlock	52	E2
Muck	57	B4
Muckanagh Lough	59	E7
Muckish Mount	58	G2
Muckle Roe	56	A1
Muckross Head	58	E3
Muconda	106	D5
Mucuim	136	E5
Mucur	76	F3
Mudanjiang	88	B3
Mudan Jiang	88	B3
Mudanya	76	C2
Mudayy	97	L8
Muddy Gap Pass	123	L6
Mudgee	113	K5
Mudurnu	76	D2
Mueda	109	G2
Muelas	66	D2
Mueo	114	W16
Mufulira	107	E5
Mufu Shan	93	M3
Muganskaya Step	94	J2
Mughar	95	L5
Mughshin	97	M7
Mugi	89	E9
Mugia	66	B1
Mugila, Monts	107	E4
Mugla	76	C4
Muhammad Qol	103	G3
Muhammad, Ras	103	F2
Muhaywir	77	J6
Muhldorf	70	E4
Muhlhausen	70	D3
Muhu	63	K7
Mui Bai Bung	93	K7
Muick	57	E3
Muirkirk	57	D5
Muite	109	G2
Mukachevo	79	C6
Mukah	90	E5
Mukawa	88	H4
Mukawwar	96	C6
Mukdahan	93	K5
Mukden	87	N3
Mukhen	88	F1
Mukhor-Konduy	85	J6
Mukomuko	90	D6
Mukur	79	J6
Mula	67	F3
Mulaly	86	D2
Mulan	88	B3
Mulanay	91	G3
Mulayit Taung	93	J5
Mulchatna	118	D3
Mulchen	139	B7
Mulde	70	E3
Muleshoe	127	L3
Mulga Downs	112	D3
Mulgrave	121	P8
Mulgrave Island	114	C4
Mulhacen	66	E4
Mulheim	70	B3
Mulhouse	65	G5
Muligort	84	Ad4
Muling *China*	88	C3
Muling *China*	88	C3
Muling He	88	D3
Mull	57	C4
Mullaghanattin	59	C9
Mullaghanish	59	D9
Mullaghareirk Mountains	59	D8
Mullaghcleevaun	59	K6
Mullaghmore	58	J3
Muller, Pegunungan	90	E5
Mullet, The	58	B4
Mullewa	112	D4
Mull Head *U.K.*	56	F2
Mull Head *U.K.*	56	F1
Mullinavat	59	H8
Mullingar	59	H5
Mullsjo	63	E8
Mull, Sound of	57	C4
Mulobezi	106	E6
Mulrany	58	C5
Multan	92	D2
Multanovy	84	A4
Multia	62	L5
Mulymya	84	Ad4
Mumbles, The	52	C3
Mumbwa	106	E6
Mumra	79	H6
Muna *Indonesia*	91	G7
Muna *Russia*	85	L3
Munayly	79	J6
Munchberg	70	D3
Munchen	70	D4
Munchengladbach	70	B3
Muncie	124	H6
Munda	114	H6
Mundesley	53	J2
Mundford	53	H2
Mundo	67	F3
Mundo Novo	138	J6
Mungbere	107	E2
Munich	70	D4
Muniesa	67	F2
Munkfors	63	E7
Mun, Mae Nam	93	K5
Munoz Gamero, Peninsula de	139	B10
Munster	70	B3
Munster	59	D8
Munsterland	70	B3
Muntenia	73	J3
Muntinlupa	91	G3
Munzur Daglari	77	H3
Muong Khoua	93	K4
Muong Ou Tay	93	K4
Muong Sing	93	K4
Muonio	62	K3
Muoniojoki	62	K3
Muqdisho	107	J2
Muqshin, Wadi	97	M7
Mur	68	E2
Mura	72	D2
Muradiye *Turkey*	76	B3
Muradiye *Turkey*	77	K3
Murallon, Cerro	139	B9
Muranga	107	G3
Murashi	78	H4
Murat *France*	65	E6
Murat *Turkey*	77	J3
Muratbasi	77	K3
Murat Dagi	76	C3
Muratli	76	B2
Muraysah, Ras al	101	K2
Murban	97	L5
Murcheh Khvort	95	K5
Murchison *Australia*	112	C4
Murchison *Canada*	120	H4
Murchison *New Zealand*	115	D4
Murchison Sund	120	M2
Murcia *Spain*	67	F4
Murcia *Spain*	67	F3
Murdo	123	P6
Murdochville	125	T2
Murefte	76	B2
Mures	73	F2
Muret	65	D7
Murfreesboro *N. Carolina*	129	P2
Murfreesboro *Tennessee,*	129	J3
Murgab *Tajikistan*	86	C4
Murgab *Turkmenistan*	95	R3
Muri	95	N3
Muriae	138	H4
Muriege	106	D4
Muritz See	70	E2
Murmansk	78	E2
Murmanskaya Oblast	62	P2
Murmansk Bereg	78	F2
Murmashi	62	Q2
Murnau	70	D5
Murom	78	G4
Muromtsevo	84	B5
Muroran	88	H4
Muros	66	B1
Muroto-zaki	89	E9
Murphy	129	L3
Murra Murra	113	K4
Murray *Australia*	113	H5
Murray *Kentucky*	124	F8
Murray *Utah*	122	J7
Murray Bridge	110	J9
Murray Harbour	121	P8
Murray, Lake *Papua New Guinea*	114	C3
Murray, Lake *U.S.A.*	129	M3
Murraysburg	108	D6
Murree	92	D2
Murrumbidgee	113	K5
Mursal	77	H3
Mursala	90	B5
Murud	90	F5
Murukta	84	G3
Murupara	115	F3
Murwara	92	F4
Murwillumbah	113	L4
Murz	68	E2
Murzuq	101	H3
Murzuq, Idhan	101	H4
Murzzuschlag	68	E2
Mus	77	J3
Musala	73	G4
Musan	88	B4
Musandam Peninsula	97	N3
Musayid	97	K4
Muscat	97	P5
Musgrave Ranges	112	G4
Mushash al Hadi	97	J3
Musheramore	59	D8
Mushie	106	C3
Musi	90	C6
Musian	94	H5
Muskegon *U.S.A.*	124	G5
Muskegon *U.S.A.*	124	H5
Muskingum	124	K7
Muskogee	128	E3
Musmar	103	G4
Musoma	107	F3
Mussau	114	D2
Musselburgh	57	E5
Musselshell	123	K4
Mussende	106	C5
Musserra	106	B4
Mussidan	65	D6
Mussuma	106	D5
Mussy	65	F5
Mustafakemalpasa	76	C2
Mustang	92	F3
Mustang Draw	127	L4
Musters, Lago	139	C9
Mustvee	63	M7
Musu-dan	88	B5
Muswellbrook	113	L5
Mut *Egypt*	102	E2
Mut *Turkey*	76	E4
Muta Ponta do	137	K6
Mutarara	109	G3
Mutare	109	F3
Mutki	77	J3
Mutnyy Materik	78	K2
Mutoko	109	F3
Mutoray	84	G4
Mutsu-wan	88	H5
Muurame	63	L5
Muurola	62	L3
Muwaffaq	97	M7
Muxima	106	B4
Muya	85	J5
Muyunkum, Peski	86	C3
Muzaffarabad	92	D2
Muzaffargarh	92	D2
Muzaffarnagar	92	E3
Muzaffarpur	92	G3
Muzon, Cape	118	J5
Muz Tagh Ata Range	92	E1
Mvuma	108	F3
Mwaniwowo	114	L7
Mwanza	107	F3
Mwaya	107	F4
Mweelrea	58	C5
Mwene Ditu	106	D4
Mwenezi *Zimbabwe*	108	F4
Mwenezi *Zimbabwe*	108	F4
Mwenga	107	E3
Mweru, Lake	107	E4
Mweru Wantipa, Lake	107	E4
Mwinilunga	106	D5
Myakit	85	S4
Myanaung	93	J5
Myanmar	93	J4
Myaundzha	85	R4
Myayangwa	93	H5
Myeik Kyunzu	93	J6
Myingyan	93	J4
Myinmu	93	J4
Myitkyina	93	J3
Myitnge	93	J4
Myittha	93	J4
Mykolayiv	79	E6
Myla	78	J2
Mymensingh	93	H4
Myre	62	F2
Myri	62	W12
Myrtle Beach	129	N4
Myrviken	62	F5
Mysen	63	H7
Mysliborz	70	F2
Mysore	92	E6
Mys Shmidta	85	Y3
My Tho	93	L6
Mytishchi	78	F4
Mzab	101	F2
Mze	70	E4
Mzuzu	107	F5

N

Name	Page	Grid
Naalehu	126	T11
Naantali	63	K6
Naas	59	J6
Nabao	66	B3
Nabavatu	114	R8
Naberezhnyye Chelny	78	J4
Nabeul	101	H1
Nabire	91	K6
Nablus	94	B5
Nabouwalu	114	R8
Naburn	55	H3
Nacala-a-Velha	109	H2
Nacaome	132	D8
Nachiki	85	T6
Nachvak Fjord	121	P6
Nacogdoches	128	E5
Nacozari de Garcia	127	H5
Nadachi	89	G7
Nadezhdinskoye	88	D1
Nadezhnyy, Mys	85	S2
Nadi	114	Q8
Nadiad	92	D4
Nadlac	72	F2
Nador	100	E1
Naduri	114	R8
Nadvornaya	71	L4
Nadym	84	A3
Naft-e Safid	94	J6
Nafud, An	96	E2
Nafy	96	F4
Naga	91	G3
Nagagami	124	H2
Nagahama	89	D9
Naga Hills	93	H3
Nagai	89	G6
Nagaland	93	H3
Nagano	89	G7
Nagaoka	89	G7
Nagappattinam	92	E6
Nagarjuna Sagar	92	E5
Nagasaki	89	B9
Nagashima	89	F8
Nagato	89	C8
Nagaur	92	D3
Nagercoil	92	E7
Nagishot	103	F7
Nagles Mountains	59	F8
Nagornyy	85	L5
Nagorsk	78	J4
Nagoya	89	F8
Nagpur	92	E4
Nagqu	93	H2

Name	Page	Grid
Nags Head	129	Q3
Nagykanizsa	72	D2
Nagykata	72	E2
Nagykoros	72	E2
Naha	89	H10
Nahariya	94	B5
Nahavand	94	J4
Nahe	70	B4
Nahoi, Cap	114	T11
Nahuel Huapi, Lago	139	B8
Naikliu	91	G7
Nailsea	52	E3
Nailsworth	52	E3
Naiman Qi	87	N3
Nain	95	L5
Nain	121	P6
Naini Tal	92	E3
Nairai	114	R8
Nairn	56	E3
Nairobi	107	G3
Najafabad	95	K5
Najd	96	E4
Najibabad	92	E3
Najin	88	C4
N Ajjer, Tassili	101	G3
Najran	96	G8
Najran, Wadi	96	G8
Nakadori-shima	89	B9
Nakajo	89	G6
Nakamura	89	D9
Nakano	89	G7
Nakano-shima	89	B11
Nakatay	84	Ad5
Nakatsu	89	C9
Nakatsugawa	89	F8
Nakfa	103	G4
Nakhichevan	77	L3
Nakhl *Eygpt*	96	A2
Nakhl *Oman*	97	N5
Nakhodka *Russia*	84	B3
Nakhodka *Russia*	88	D4
Nakhon Pathom	93	J6
Nakhon Phanom	93	K5
Nakhon Ratchasima	93	K6
Nakhon Sawan	93	K5
Nakhon Si Thammarat	93	J7
Nakina	121	J7
Nakiri	89	F8
Naknek Lake	118	D4
Nakskov	63	F9
Naktong	87	P4
Nakuru	107	G3
Nakusp	122	F2
Nalchik	79	G7
Nalgonda	92	E5
Nallamala Hills	92	E5
Nallihan	76	D2
Nalut	101	H2
Namaa, Tanjung	91	H6
Namacunde	106	C6
Namacurra	109	G3
Namak, Daryacheh-ye	95	K4
Namaki	95	M6
Namakzar	95	Q5
Namakzar, Daryacheh-ye	95	Q5
Namangan	86	C3
Namapa	109	G2
Namaponda	109	G3
Namarroi	109	G3
Namasagali	107	F2
Namatanai	114	E2
Nambour	113	L4
Nam Can	93	K7
Nam Co	93	H2
Nam Dinh	93	L4
Nametil	109	G3
Namib Desert	108	B4
Namibe	106	B6
Namibia	108	C4
Namlea	91	H6
Namoi	113	L5
Namosi Peak	114	R8
Nampa	122	F6
Nampula	109	G3
Namse La	92	F3
Namsen	62	E4
Namsos	62	D4
Namti	93	J3
Namtok	93	J5
Namuka-i-Lau	114	S9
Namuli	109	G3
Namur	64	F3
Namutoni	108	C3
Namwala	106	E6
Nana Barya	102	C6
Nanaimo	122	C3
Nanam	88	B5
Nanao	89	F7
Nancha	88	B2
Nanchang	87	M6
Nanchong	93	L2
Nancowry	93	H7
Nancy	64	G4
Nanda Devi	92	E2
Nandan	93	L3
Nanded	92	E5
Nandurbar	92	D4
Nandyal	92	E5
Nanfeng	87	M6
Nanga Eboko	105	H5
Nangahpinoh	90	E6
Nanga Parbat	92	D1
Nangatayap	90	E6
Nangong	87	M4
Nan Hai	83	K5
Nanjing	87	M5
Nanking	87	M5
Nan, Mae Nam	93	K5
Nanning	93	L4
Nanortalik	116	Q2
Nanpan Jiang	93	K4
Nanpara	92	F3
Nanpi	87	M4
Nanping	87	M6
Nansei-shoto	89	H10
Nansen Sound	120	H1
Nanshan Islands	90	E4
Nansha Qundao	90	E4
Nantais, Lac	121	M5
Nantes	65	C5
Nantong	87	N5
Nantua	65	F5
Nantucket Island	125	Q6
Nantucket Sound	125	Q6
Nantwich	55	G3
Nant-y-moch Reservoir	52	D2
Nanuku Passage	114	S8
Nanuku Reef	114	S8
Nanumanga	111	S3
Nanumea	111	S3
Nanusa, Kepulauan	91	H5
Nanyang	93	M2
Nanyuki	107	G2
Nao, Cabo de la	67	G3
Naococane, Lake	121	M7
Naousa	75	G2
Napa	126	A1
Napabalana	91	G6
Napalkovo	84	A2
Napas	84	C5
Nape	93	L5
Napier	115	F3
Naples *Italy*	69	E5
Naples *U.S.A.*	129	M7
Napo	136	C4
Napoleon	124	H6
Napoletano, Appennino	69	E5
Napoli	69	E5
Napoli, Golfo di	69	E5
Naqadeh	94	G3
Nar	53	H2
Nara *Japan*	89	E8
Nara *Mali*	100	D5
Nara *Pakistan*	92	C4
Naracoorte	113	J6
Naran	87	L2
Narasapur	92	F5
Narat	86	E3
Narathiwat	93	K7
Narayanganj	93	H4
Narberth	52	C3
Narbonne	65	E7
Narborough Island	136	A7
Narcea	66	C1
Nardin	95	M3
Narew *Poland*	71	J2
Narew *Poland*	71	K2
Narince	77	H4
Narken	62	K3
Narkher	92	E4
Narli	77	G4
Narmada	92	E4
Narman	77	J2
Narnaul	92	E3
Narodnaya, Gora	84	Ad3
Naro-Fominsk	78	F4
Narowal	92	D2
Narpes	62	J5
Narrabi	113	K5
Narrandera	113	K5
Narrogin	112	D5
Narromine	113	K5
Narsimhapur	92	E4
Narsinghgarh	92	E4
Nart	87	M3
Nartabu	91	J6
Naruko	88	H6
Narva	63	N7
Narvik	62	G2
Naryan Mar	78	J2
Narymskiy Khrebet	86	E2
Naryn *Russia*	84	F6
Naryn *Kyrgyzstan*	86	C3
Naryn *Kyrgyzstan*	86	D3
Nasarawa	105	G4
Naseby	115	C6
Nashua	125	Q5
Nashville	129	J2
Nasice	72	E3
Nasielsk	71	J2
Nasijarvi	63	K6
Nasik	92	D5
Nasir	103	F6
Nasir, Buhayrat	103	F3
Nasorolevu	114	R8
Nasrabad	95	K4
Nass	118	K3
Nassau	129	P8
Nasser, Lake	103	F3
Nassjo	63	F8
Nastapoka Islands	121	L6
Nastved	63	D9
Nata	108	E4
Natagaima	136	B3
Natal *Brazil*	137	K5
Natal *Indonesia*	90	B5
Natanz	95	K5
Natara	85	L3
Natashquan	121	P7
Natchez	128	G5
Natchitoches	128	F5
Natewa Bay	114	R8
National City	126	D4
Natitingou	105	F3
Natividade	137	H6
Natori	89	H6
Natron, Lake	107	G3
Nattavaara	62	J3
Natuna Besar	90	D5
Natuna, Kepulauan	90	D5
Naturaliste, Cape	112	D5
Naturaliste Channel	112	C4
Nauen	70	E2
Naueyi Akmyane	63	K8
Naujoji Vilnia	71	L1
Naul	58	K5
Naumburg	70	D3
Naungpale	93	J5
Nauru	111	Q2
Naurzum	84	Ad6
Nausori	114	R9
Nautanwa	92	F3
Nautla	131	L7
Nauzad	95	S5
Navadwip	93	G4
Navahermosa	66	D3
Naval	91	G3
Navalcarnero	66	D2
Navalmoral de la Mata	66	D3
Navalpino	66	D3
Navan	58	J5
Navarin, Mys	85	X4
Navarino, Isla	139	C11
Navarra	67	F1
Navars	67	G2
Navasota	128	D5
Navassa Island	133	K5
Navax Point	52	B4
Navenby	55	J3
Naver, Loch	56	D2
Navia *Spain*	66	C1
Navia *Spain*	66	C1
Naviti	114	Q8
Navlya	79	E5
Navojoa	127	H7
Navolato	130	F5
Navpaktos	75	F3
Navplion	75	G4
Navrongo	104	E3
Navsari	92	D4
Navua	114	R9
Nawabshah	92	C3
Nawada	92	G4
Nawah	92	C2
Nawasif, Harrat	96	F6
Naws, Ra's	97	M8
Nawton	55	J2
Naxos *Greece*	75	H4
Naxos *Greece*	75	H4
Nayagarh	92	G4
Nayau	114	S8
Nay Band	95	L8
Nay Band	95	N5
Nayoro	88	J3
Nazare	137	K6
Nazareth *Israel*	94	B5
Nazareth *Peru*	136	B5
Nazarovo	84	E5
Nazas	130	G5
Nazca	136	C6
Naze	89	B11
Nazerat	94	B5
Naze, The	53	J3
Nazik	94	G2
Nazik Golu	77	K3
Nazilli	76	C4
Nazmiye	77	H3
Nazwa	97	N5
Nazyvayevsk	84	A5
Ncheu	107	F5
Ndalatando	106	B4
Ndele	102	D6
Ndeni	114	N7
Ndjamena	102	C5
Ndjote	106	B3
Ndola	107	E5
Nea	62	D5
Nea Filippias	75	F3
Neagh, Lough	58	K3
Neah Bay	122	B3
Neale, Lake	112	G3
Nea Moudhania	75	G2
Neapolis *Greece*	75	F2
Neapolis *Greece*	75	H5
Nea Psara	75	G3
Near Islands	118	Aa9
Neath	52	D3
Nebine	113	K4
Nebit Dag	95	M2
Neblina, Pico da	136	D3
Nebraska	123	N7
Nebraska City	124	C6
Nebrodi, Monti	69	E7
Nechako	118	L5
Nechi	133	K11
Neckar	70	C4
Necochea	139	E7
Nedong	93	H3
Nedstrand	63	A7
Needles *Canada*	122	E3
Needles *U.S.A.*	126	E3
Needles Point	115	E2
Needles, The	53	F4
Neepawa	123	Q2
Neergaard Lake	120	L3
Nefedovo	84	A5
Nefta	101	G2
Neftechala	94	J2
Neftegorsk	79	J5
Neftekamsk	78	J4
Nefyn	52	C2
Nefza	69	B7
Negele	103	G6
Negev	94	B6
Negoiu	73	H3
Negombo	92	E7
Negotin	73	G3
Negrais, Cape	93	H5
Negra, Punta	136	A5
Negritos	136	A4
Negro *Argentina*	139	C7
Negro *Amazonas, Brazil*	136	E4
Negro *Santa Catarina, Brazil*	138	F5
Negro *Uruguay*	138	F6
Negros	91	G3
Negru Voda	73	K4
Nehavand	94	J4
Nehbandan	95	Q6
Nehe	87	N2
Nehoiasu	73	J3
Neijiang	93	K3
Nei Mongol Zizhiqu	87	L3
Neisse *Poland*	70	F3
Neisse *Poland*	71	G3
Neiteyugansk	84	A4
Neiva	136	B3
Neixiang	93	M2
Nekemte	103	G6
Neksikan	85	R4
Nekso	63	H9
Nelidovo	78	E4
Neligh	123	Q6
Nelkan	85	P5
Nellore	92	E6
Nelma	88	G2
Nelson *Canada*	122	F3
Nelson *New Zealand*	115	D4
Nelson *U.K.*	55	G3
Nelson, Cape *Australia*	113	J6
Nelson, Cape *Papua New Guinea*	114	D3
Nelson Lagoon	118	Af8
Nelspruit	108	F5
Nema	100	D5
Neman	78	C4
Neman	71	K1
Nemira	73	J2
Nemirov	73	K1
Nemiscau	121	L7
Nemours	64	E4
Nemun	63	J9
Nemuro	88	K4
Nemuro-kaikyo	88	K4
Nemuy	85	P5
Nenagh	59	F7
Nenana	118	F3
Nene	53	G2
Nen Jiang	87	P1
Nenjiang	87	P2
Nenthead	55	G2
Neokhorion	75	F3
Neon Karlovasi	75	J4
Neosho *Kansas*	124	C7
Neosho *Missouri*	124	C8
Nepa *Russia*	84	H5
Nepa *Russia*	84	H5
Nepal	92	F3
Nephi	126	G1
Nephin Beg Range	58	C4
Nera	69	D4
Nerac	65	D6
Nerchinsk	85	K6
Neretva	72	D4
Neriquinha	106	D6
Neris	63	L9
Nermete, Punta	136	A5
Neryuktey-l-y	85	K4
Neryuvom	84	Ad3
Nes	63	C6
Nesbyen	63	C6
Neskaupstadur	62	Y12
Nesna	62	E3
Nesscliffe	52	E2
Ness, Loch	56	D3
Nesterov *Russia*	71	K3
Nesterov *Ukraine*	71	K1
Nesterovo	84	H6
Neston	55	F3
Nestos	75	H2
Nesvizh	71	M2
Netanya	94	B5
Netherlands	64	F2
Neto	69	F6
Nettilling Lake	120	M4
Nettleham	55	J3
Netzahualcoyotl, Presa	131	N9
Neubrandenburg	70	E2
Neuchatel	68	A2
Neuchatel, Lac de	68	A2
Neufchateau *Belgium*	64	F4
Neufchateau *France*	64	F4
Neufchatel	64	D4
Neufelden	68	D1
Neumunster	70	C1
Neunkirchen *Austria*	68	F2
Neunkirchen *Germany*	70	B4

Neuquen *Argentina* **139** C7
Neuquen *Argentina* **139** C7
Neuruppin **70** E2
Neuse **129** P3
Neusiedler See **68** F2
Neuss **70** B3
Neustadt **70** C5
Neustettin **71** G2
Neustrelitz **70** E2
Neu-Ulm **70** D4
Nevada *Missouri* **124** C8
Nevada *U.S.A.* **122** F8
Nevada, Sierra *Argentina* **138** C5
Nevada, Sierra *Spain* **66** E4
Nevada, Sierra *U.S.A.* **126** C2
Nevado, Cerro **139** C7
Nevado, Sierra del **139** C7
Nevel **78** E4
Nevelsk **88** H2
Nevers **65** E5
Neve, Sierra da **106** B5
Nevesinje **72** E4
Nevezis **63** L9
Nevinnomyssk **79** G7
Nevis, Loch **57** C4
Nevsehir **76** F3
Nevyansk **84** Ad5
New **125** K8
New Abbey **55** F2
New Albany **124** H7
New Alresford **53** F3
Newark *New Jersey* **125** N6
Newark *Ohio* **124** J6
Newark-on-Trent **55** J3
New Bedford **125** Q6
New Bedford River **53** H2
New Bern **129** P3
Newberry **129** M3
Newbiggin **55** G2
Newbiggin-by-the-Sea **55** H1
Newbigging **57** E5
New Braunfels **128** C6
Newbridge **59** J6
New Britain **114** E3
New Brunswick *Canada* **121** N8
New Brunswick *U.S.A.* **125** N6
Newbuildings **58** H3
Newburgh *U.K.* **57** E4
Newburgh *U.S.A.* **125** N6
Newbury **53** F3
New Bussa **105** F4
Newby Bridge **55** G2
New Castle **125** K6
Newcastle *Australia* **113** L5
Newcastle *South Africa* **108** E5
Newcastle *U.K.* **58** L4
Newcastle *Indiana* **124** H7
Newcastle *Wyoming* **123** M6
Newcastle Emlyn **52** C2
Newcastleton **57** F5
Newcastle-under-Lyme **55** G3
Newcastle-upon-Tyne **55** H2
Newcastle Waters **113** G2
Newcastle West **59** D8
Newchurch **52** D2
New Cumnock **57** D5
Newdegate **112** D5
New Delhi **92** E3
Newell, Lake **122** J2
New England Range **113** L5
Newenham, Cape **118** C4
Newfoundland *Canada* **121** P6
Newfoundland *Canada* **121** Q8
New Galloway **57** D5
New Georgia **114** H6
New Georgia Island **114** H6
New Glasgow **121** P8
New Guinea **114** C2
New Halfa **96** B9
New Hampshire **125** Q5
New Hampton **124** D5
New Hanover **114** E2
Newhaven **53** H4
New Haven **125** P6
New Iberia **128** G5
Newick **53** H4
New Ireland **114** E2
New Jersey **125** N6
New Kandla **92** D4
New Liskeard **125** L3
New London **125** P6
Newman, Mount **112** D3
New Market **125** L7
Newmarket *Ireland* **59** D8
Newmarket *U.K.* **53** H2
Newmarket-on-Fergus **59** E7
New Martinsville **125** K7
New Meadows **122** F5
New Mexico **127** J3
Newmill **57** F5
Newmilns **57** D5
New Milton **53** F4
Newnan **129** K4
New Orleans **128** G5
New Philadelphia **125** K6
New Pitsligo **56** F3
New Plymouth **115** E3
Newport *Ireland* **58** C5
Newport *Dyfed, U.K.* **52** C2
Newport *Essex, U.K.* **53** H3
Newport *Gwent, U.K.* **52** E3
Newport *Isle of Wight, U.K.* **53** F4
Newport *Shropshire, U.K.* **52** E2
Newport *Arkansas* **128** G3
Newport *Kentucky* **124** H7
Newport *Rhode Island* **125** Q6
Newport *Tennessee* **129** L3
Newport *Vermont* **125** P4
Newport News **125** M8
Newport Pagnell **53** G2
New Providence **132** J2
Newquay **52** B4
New Quay **52** C2
New Richmond **125** T2
New Romney **53** H4
New Ross **59** J8
Newry **58** K4
Newry Canal **58** K4
New Smyrna Beach **129** M6
New South Wales **113** K5
Newton *Dumfries and Galloway, U.K.* **57** E5
Newton *Lancashire, U.K.* **55** G3
Newton *Iowa* **124** D6
Newton *Kansas* **128** D1
Newton *Mississippi* **128** H4
Newton Abbot **52** D4
Newton Aycliffe **55** H2
Newtonferry **56** A3
Newton Flotman **53** J2
Newtongrange **57** E5
Newtonmore **57** D3
Newton on Trent **55** J3
Newton Poppleford **52** D4
Newton Stewart **54** E2
Newtown **52** D2
New Town **123** N4
Newtownabbey **58** L3
Newtownards **58** L3
Newtownbreda **58** L3
Newtownbutler **58** H4
Newtown-Crommelin **58** K3
Newtowncunningham **58** G3
Newtownmountkennedy **59** K6
Newtownstewart **58** H3
New Ulm **124** C4
New York *U.S.A.* **125** M5
New York *U.S.A.* **125** P6
New York Erie Canal **125** M5
New Zealand **115** B3
Nexpa **130** H8
Neya **78** G4
Neybasteh **95** Q5
Neyland **52** C3
Neyriz **95** M7
Neyshabur **95** P3
Nezhin **79** E5
Ngabe **106** C3
Ngabordamlu, Tanjung **91** J7
Ngadda **105** H3
Ngangla Ringco **92** F2
Nganglong Kangri **92** F2
Ngangze Co **93** G2
Ngaoundere **105** H4
Ngaruawahia **115** E2
Ngaruroro **115** F3
Ngau **114** R9
Ngauruhoe **115** E3
Nggatokae **114** J6
Nggela Pile **114** K6
Nggela Sule **114** K6
Nggele Levu **114** S8
Ngoila **105** H5
Ngong **107** G3
Ngoring Hu **93** J2
Ngorongoro Crater **107** G3
NGouri **102** C5
Ngozi **107** E3
Nguigmi **101** H6
Ngulu Atoll **91** K4
Nguna **114** U12
Ngunju, Tanjung **91** G8
Nguru **105** H3
Nhamunda **136** F4
Nha Trang **93** L6
Nhill **113** J6
Niafounke **100** E5
Niagara **124** G4
Niagara Falls **125** L5
Niah **90** E5
Niamey **101** F6
Niangara **107** E2
Nias **90** B5
Nibe **63** C8
Nicaj Shale **74** E1
Nicaragua **132** D8
Nicaragua, Lago de **132** E9
Nicastro **69** F6
Nice **65** G7
Nichicun, Lake **121** M7
Nichinan **89** C10
Nicholas, Cape **120** G3
Nicholas Channel **132** G3
Nicholls Town **132** H2
Nicholl's Town **129** P8
Nicholson **113** H2
Nickol Bay **112** D3
Nicobar Islands **93** H7
Nicosia *Cyprus* **76** E5
Nicosia *Italy* **69** E7
Nicotera **69** E6
Nicoya, Golfo de **132** E10
Nicoya, Peninsula de **132** E10
Nida **71** J3
Nidd **55** H3
Nidzica **71** J2
Niebull **70** C1
Niederbronn **64** G4
Niedere Tauern **68** D2
Niefang **105** H5
Niemisel **62** J3
Nienburg **70** C2
Nieuw Amsterdam **137** F2
Nieuw Nickerie **137** F2
Nieuwpoort **64** E3
Nigde **76** F4
Niger **105** G4
Niger **101** G5
Nigeria **105** G4
Nigg **56** D3
Niigata **89** G7
Niihama **89** D9
Niihau **126** Q10
Nii-jima **89** G8
Niimi **89** D8
Nijar **66** E4
Nijmegan **64** F3
Nikaria **75** J4
Nikel **62** P2
Nikitas **75** G2
Nikki **105** F4
Nikolaev **71** K4
Nikolayevka **84** Ae6
Nikolayevsk-na-Amure **85** Q6
Nikolsk *Russia* **79** H5
Nikolsk *Russia* **78** H4
Nikolskiy **86** B2
Nikopol **79** E6
Niksar **77** G2
Nikshahr **95** Q8
Niksic **72** E4
Nikulino **84** D4
Nikumarora **111** U2
Nil **103** F2
Nila **91** H7
Nilgiri Hills **92** E6
Nil, Nahren **103** F2
Nilsia **62** N5
Nimach **92** D4
Nimba Mountains **104** D4
Nimes **65** F7
Nimmitabel **113** K6
Nimule **103** F6
Nina Bang Lake **120** L3
Nine Degree Channel **92** D7
Ninety Mile Beach **115** D1
Ninfas, Punta **139** D8
Ninfield **53** H4
Ningan **88** B3
Ningbo **87** N6
Ningde **87** M6
Ningdu **87** M6
Ningguo **87** M5
Ninghe **87** M4
Ninghua **87** M6
Ningjing Shan **93** J2
Ningqiang **93** L2
Ningshan **93** L2
Ningwu **87** L4
Ningxia **93** L1
Ningyang **87** M4
Ninh Hoa **93** L6
Ninigo Group **114** C2
Ninnis Glacier **141** K5
Ninyako Vogumma **84** B2
Nioaque **138** E4
Niobrara **123** P6
Niono **100** D6
Nioro du Sahel **100** D5
Niort **65** C5
Nios **75** H4
Nipigon **124** F2
Nipigon, Lake **124** F2
Nipisiguit **125** S3
Nipissing, Lac **125** L3
Niquelandia **137** H6
Nir **94** H2
Nirmal **92** E5
Nirmal Range **92** E5
Nis **73** F4
Nisa **66** C3
Nisab **96** H9
Nisava **73** G4
Nishinoyama **89** E8
Nishi-suido **89** B8
Nisiros **75** J4
Nisling **118** H3
Nisporeny **73** K2
Nissan **63** E8
Nisum Bredning **63** C8
Nitchequon **121** M7
Niteroi **138** H4
Nith **57** E5
Nithsdale **57** E5
Nitra **71** H4
Niuafoou **111** T5
Niuatoputapu **111** U5
Niue **111** V5
Niulakita **111** S4
Niulan Jiang **93** K3
Niutao **111** S3
Nivelles **64** F3
Nivernais **65** E5
Nivshera **78** J3
Niwbwrch **54** E3
Nizamabad **92** E5
Nizhneangarsk **84** H5
Nizhneimbatskoye **84** D4
Nizhnekamsk **78** J4
Nizhnekamsko Vodokhranilishche **78** J4
Nizhneudinsk **84** F6
Nizhnevartovsk **84** B4
Nizhneye Bugayevo **84** Ab3
Nizhniy Lomov **79** G5
Nizhniy Novgorod **78** G4
Nizhniy Yenangsk **78** H4
Nizhnyaya Bugayevo **78** J2
Nizhnyaya Chulym **84** B6
Nizhnyaya Omka **84** A5
Nizhnyaya Salda **84** Ad5
Nizhnyaya Shakhtama **85** K6
Nizhnyaya Tunguska **84** H5
Nizhnyaya Tura **78** K4
Nizhnyaya Voch **78** J3
Nizip **77** G4
Nizke Tatry **71** H4
Nizmennyy, Mys **88** E4
Njombe **107** F4
Njoroveto **114** H5
Njurundabommen **63** L5
Nkambe **105** H4
Nkayi **108** E3
Nkhotakota **107** F5
Nkongsamba **105** G5
Nmai Hka **93** J3
Noasca **68** A3
Noatak **118** C2
Nobeoka **89** C9
Nobres **137** F6
Nocera **69** E5
Nogales *Mexico* **126** G5
Nogales *U.S.A.* **126** G5
Nogata **89** C9
Nogent-le-Rotrou **64** D4
Nogent-sur-Seine **64** E4
Noginsk **78** F4
Noginskiy **84** E4
Nogoa **113** K3
Nogoya **138** E6
Noheji **88** H5
Noire **93** K4
Noire, Montagnes **64** B4
Noirmoutier **65** B5
Noirmoutier, Ile de **65** B5
Nok Kundi **92** B3
Nola *Central African Republic* **102** C7
Nola *Italy* **69** E5
Nolinsk **78** H4
Nomad **114** C3
Noma-misaki **89** C10
Nome **118** B3
Nomuka **111** U6
Nonburg **78** J2
Nonda **113** J3
Nondugl **114** C3
Nongan **87** P3
Nong Khai **93** K5
Nongoma **109** F5
Nonouti **111** R2
Nonthaburi **93** K6
Nontron **65** D6
Nookta Island **122** A3
Nootka Sound **122** A3
Nora **103** H4
Noranda **125** L2
Nordaustlandet **140** L2
Nordborg **63** E9
Nord Cap **62** T11
Norddepil **62** Z14
Norden **70** B2
Nordenham **70** C2
Nordenshelda, Arkhipelag **84** F1
Norderney **70** B2
Nordfjord **62** A6
Nordfjordeid **62** A6
Nordfold **62** F3
Nord-Friesische Inseln **63** C9
Nordhausen **70** D3
Nordhorn **70** B2
Nordkapp **62** L1
Nordkinn-halvoya **62** M1
Nord Kvaloy **62** H1
Nordland **63** E4
Nordmaling **62** H5
Nordostsee Kanal **70** C2
Nordoyar **62** Z14
Nordre Isortoq **120** R4
Nordre Strmfjord **120** R4
Nordstrand **70** C1
Nordurfjordur **62** U11
Nordvik **84** J2
Nordvik, Mys **84** J2
Nore **59** H8
Norfolk *U.K.* **53** H2
Norfolk *Nebraska* **123** R6
Norfolk *Virginia* **125** M8
Norfolk Island **111** Q7
Norfolk Lake **128** F2
Norheimsund **63** B6
Nori **84** A3
Norilsk **84** D3
Norlat **78** J5
Norman *Australia* **113** J2
Norman *U.S.A.* **128** D3
Normanby **113** J1
Normanby Island **114** E3
Normandes, Iles **64** B4
Normandie **64** D4
Normandie, Collines de **64** C4
Normanton *Australia* **113** J2
Normanton *U.K.* **55** H3
Norman Wells **118** K2
Nornalup **112** D5
Norra Storfjallet **62** F4
Norrbotten **62** M3

Norresundby 63 C8
Norrfjarden 62 J4
Norristown 125 N6
Norrkoping 63 L7
Norrland 62 F5
Norrtalje 63 H7
Norseman 112 E5
Norsjo 62 M4
Norsk 85 N6
Norsup 114 T12
Norte, Punta *Argentina* 139 D8
Norte, Punta *Argentina* 139 E7
Norte, Serra do 136 F6
Northallerton 55 H2
Northam 112 D5
Northampton *U.K.* 53 G2
Northampton *U.S.A.* 125 P5
Northamptonshire 53 G2
North Andaman 93 H6
North Arm 119 N3
North Astrolabe Reef 114 R9
North Battleford 119 P5
North Bay *Canada* 125 L3
North Bay *Ireland* 59 K8
North Bend 122 B6
North Berwick 57 F4
North Canadian 128 C3
North, Cape 121 P8
North Cape *New Zealand* 115 D1
North Cape *Norway* 62 L1
North Cape *U.S.A.* 118 A3
North Carolina 129 M3
North Cave 55 J3
North Channel *Canada* 124 J3
North Channel *U.K.* 58 L2
Northchapel 53 G3
North Charlton 55 H1
Northcliffe 112 D5
North Dakota 123 P4
North Dorset Downs 52 E4
North Downs 53 H3
Northeast Cape 118 B3
Northeast Providence Channel 132 J2
North Elmham 53 H2
Northern Ireland 58 H3
Northern Sporades 75 H3
Northern Territory 112 G3
North Esk 57 F4
Northfield 124 D4
North Flinders Range 113 H5
North Foreland 53 J3
North Geomagnetic Pole 140 S3
North Henik Lake 119 R3
North Korea 87 P4
North Kyme 55 J3
North Lakhimpur 93 H3
Northleach 53 F3
North Magnetic Pole 140 U3
North Miami Beach 129 M8
North Platte *U.S.A.* 123 N7
North Platte *U.S.A.* 123 P7
North Point *Canada* 121 P8
North Point *U.S.A.* 124 J4
North Pole 140 A1
North River 119 S4
North Roe 56 A1
North Ronaldsay 56 F1
North Ronaldsay Firth 56 F1
North Saskatchewan 119 P5
North Sea 50 H4
North Sentinel 93 H6
North Shields 55 H1
North Shoshone Peak 122 F8
North Sound 59 C6
North Sound, The 56 F1
North Stradbroke Island 113 L4
North Taranaki Bight 115 E3
North Tawton 52 D4
North Thoresby 55 J3
North Tolsta 56 B2
North Tonawanda 125 L5
North Twin Island 121 K7
North Tyne 57 F5
North Uist 56 A3
Northumberland 57 F5
Northumberland Islands 113 L3
Northumberland O 120 M2
Northumberland Strait 121 P8
Northwall 56 F1
North Walsham 53 J2
Northway Junction 118 G3
Northwest Cape 118 A3
North West Cape 112 C3
North West Highlands 56 C3
Northwest Providence Channel 132 H1
Northwest Territories 119 Q2
Northwich 55 G3
North York 125 L5
North Yorkshire 55 H2
Norton *U.K.* 55 J2
Norton *U.S.A.* 123 Q8
Norton Bay 118 C3
Norton Sound 118 C3
Norvegia, Cape 141 Z4
Norwalk 124 J6
Norway 63 C6
Norway House 119 R5
Norwegian Bay 120 H2
Norwegian Sea 62 A3
Norwich *U.K.* 53 J2
Norwich *U.S.A.* 125 Q6
Noshiro 88 G5
Noshul 78 H3
Nosok 84 C2
Nosop 108 D5
Nosovshchina 78 F3
Nosratabad 95 P7
Nossen 70 E3
Noss Head 56 E2
Noss, Island of 56 A2
Nosy-Varika 109 J4
Notec 71 G2
Noto 69 E7
Notodden 63 C7
Noto-hanto 89 F7
Notre Dame Bay 121 Q8
Notre Dame Mountains 121 N8
Nottingham 53 F2
Nottingham Island 120 L5
Nottinghamshire 55 H3
Notukeu Creek 123 L3
Nouadhibou 100 B4
Nouadhibou, Ras 100 B4
Nouakchott 100 B5
Noukloof Mountains 108 C4
Noumea 114 X17
Noup Head 56 E1
Noupoort 108 D6
Nouvelle-Caledonie 114 W16
Nouvelle Caledonie 114 W16
Nouvelle-France, Cap de 120 M5
Novabad 86 C4
Nova Bana 71 H4
Nova Cruz 137 K5
Nova Era 138 H3
Nova Friburgo 138 H4
Nova Iguacu 138 H4
Nova Lima 138 H4
Nova Mambone 109 G4
Novara 68 B3
Nova Remanso 137 J5
Nova Scotia 121 P8
Nova Sento Se 137 J5
Nova Sofala 109 F4
Nova Vanduzi 109 F3
Nova Varos 72 E4
Novaya Kakhovka 79 E6
Novaya Katysh 84 Ae5
Novaya Kazanka 79 H6
Novaya Novatka 84 G5
Novaya Odessa 79 E6
Novaya Sibir , Ostrov 85 R1
Novaya Tevriz 84 B5
Novaya Vodolaga 79 F6
Novaya Zemlya 84 Ab2
Novayo Ushitsa 73 J1
Nove Mesto 70 G4
Nove Zamky 71 H4
Novgorod 78 E4
Novgorod Serverskiy 79 E5
Novigrad 72 C3
Novikovo 88 J2
Novi Ligure 68 B3
Novi Pazar 72 F4
Novi Sad 72 E3
Novo Acre 137 J6
Novoaleksandrovsk 79 G6
Novoalekseyevka 79 K5
Novoanninskiy 79 G5
Novoarchangelsk 73 L1
Novo Aripuana 136 E5
Novobogatinskoye 79 J6
Novocheboksarsh 78 H4
Novocherkassk 79 G6
Novodolinka 84 A6
Novodvinsk 78 G3
Novograd-Volynskiy 79 D5
Novogrudok 71 L2
Novo Hamburgo 138 F5
Novoilinovka 85 P6
Novokazalinsk 86 A2
Novokhopersk 79 G5
Novokiyevskiy Uval 85 M6
Novokocherdyk 84 Ad6
Novokuybyshevsk 79 H5
Novokuznetsk 84 D6
Novolazareyskaya 141 A4
Novoletovye 84 G2
Novo Milosevo 72 F3
Novomitino 84 Ae5
Novomoskovsk *Russia* 78 F5
Novomoskovsk *Ukraine* 79 F6
Novopavlovka 84 H6
Novopokrovskaya 79 G6
Novopolotsk 63 N9
Novo Redondo 106 B5
Novo-Rokrovka 88 E3
Novoromanovo 84 C6
Novorossiysk 79 F7
Novorzhev 63 N8
Novo Sagres 91 H7
Novo Sergeyevka 79 J5
Novoshakhtinsk 79 F6
Novosibirsk 84 C4
Novosibirskiye Ostrova 85 Q1
Novospasskoye 79 H5
Novoukrainka 79 E6
Novo Uzensk 79 H5
Novo-Vyatsk 78 H4
Novoyeniseysk 84 E5
Novozhilovskaya 78 J3
Novozybkov 79 E5
Novska 72 D3
Novy Jicin 71 G4
Novyy 84 H2
Novyy Bor 78 J2
Novyy Bug 79 E6
Novyy Oskol 79 F5
Novyy Port 84 A3
Novyy Uzen 79 J7
Nowbaran 95 J4
Nowe 71 H2
Nowen Hill 59 D9
Nowgong 93 H3
Nowitna 118 E3
Nowograd 70 F2
Nowogrod 71 J2
Nowra 113 L5
Now Shahr 95 K3
Nowshera 92 D2
Nowy Sacz 71 J4
Nowy Targ 71 J4
Noyon *France* 64 E4
Noyon *Mongolia* 86 J3
Nozay 65 C5
Nsanje 107 G6
Nsukka 105 G4
Nsuta 104 E4
Ntem 105 H5
Ntwetwe Pan 108 E4
Nuba, Lake 102 F3
Nuba Mountains 102 F5
Nubian Desert 103 F3
Nubiya 102 E4
Nubiya, Es Sahra en 103 F3
Nudo Coropuna 136 C7
Nueces 128 C6
Nueltin Lake 119 R3
Nueva Florida 133 N10
Nueva Rosita 127 M7
Nueva San Salvador 132 C8
Nueve de Julio 139 D7
Nuevitas 132 J4
Nuevo, Bajo 132 H7
Nuevo Casas Grandes 127 J5
Nuevo Churumuco 130 J8
Nuevo Laredo 128 C7
Nugaruba Islands 114 E2
Nugget Point 115 B7
Nugrus, Gebel 96 B4
Nuhaka 115 F3
Nuh, Ra's 95 R9
Nui 111 S3
Nuits-Saint-Georges 65 F5
Nu Jiang 93 J3
Nukhayb 94 F5
Nukiki 114 H5
Nukualofa 111 T6
Nukufetau 111 S3
Nukuhu 114 D3
Nukulaelae 111 S3
Nukumanu Islands 111 N2
Nukunau 111 S2
Nukunono 111 U3
Nukus 51 U7
Nullarbor 112 G5
Nullarbor Plain 112 F5
Numan 105 H4
Numata 89 G7
Numazu 89 G8
Numedal 63 C6
Numfor 114 B2
Numto 84 A4
Nuneaton 53 F2
Nunivak Islands 116 C2
Nunligran 85 Y4
Nunney 52 E3
Nuomin He 87 N2
Nuoro 69 B5
Nupani 114 M7
Nuqdah, Ra's an 97 P6
Nuqrah 96 E4
Nur 95 K3
Nura 86 C2
Nurabad 95 K6
Nur Daglari 77 G4
Nure 68 B3
Nurek 86 B4
Nurhak 77 G4
Nurhak Dagi 77 G3
Nuristan 92 D1
Nurmes 62 N5
Nurnberg 70 D4
Nurri 69 B6
Nurzec 71 K2
Nusaybin 77 J4
Nusayriyah, Jebel al 77 G5
Nushagak Bay 118 D4
Nu Shan 93 J3
Nushki 92 C3
Nutak 121 P6
Nuugaatsiaq 120 R3
Nuuk 120 R5
Nuupas 62 M3
Nuwara 92 F7
Nuweveldreeks 108 D6
Nuyakuk, Lake 118 D4
Nuyts, Point 112 D6
Nuzayzah 77 H5
Nyahururu 107 G2
Nyainqentanglha Shan 92 G3
Nyaksimvol 84 Ad4
Nyala 102 D5
Nyamboyto 84 C3
Nyandoma 78 G3
Nyang 93 H3
Nyanza 107 E3
Nyasa, Lake 107 F5
Nyashabozh 78 J2
Nyaungu 93 H4
Nyayba 85 N2
Nyborg 63 D9
Nybster 56 E2
Nyeri 107 G3
Nyerol 103 F6
Nyima 93 G2
Nyirbator 73 G2
Nyiregyhaza 73 F2
Nyiru, Mont 107 G2
Nykarleby 62 N4
Nykobing *Denmark* 63 C8
Nykobing *Denmark* 63 D9
Nykoping 63 G7
Nylstroom 108 E4
Nymagee 113 K5
Nymburk 70 F3
Nynashamn 63 G7
Nyngan 113 K5
Nyong 105 H5
Nyons 65 F6
Nyrany 70 E4
Nyrud 62 N2
Nysa 71 G3
Nysh 85 Q6
Nyshott 63 N6
Nystad 63 J6
Nytva 78 K4
Nyuk, Ozero 62 P4
Nyuksenitsa 78 G3
Nyunzu 107 E4
Nyurba 85 K4
Nyurolskiy 84 B5
Nyuya 85 J4
Nyvrovo 85 Q6
Nzambi 106 B3
Nzega 107 F3
Nzerekore 104 D4
Nzeto 106 B4
Nzo 104 D4

O

Oadby 53 F2
Oahe Dam 123 P5
Oahe, Lake 123 P5
Oahu 126 S10
Oakdale 126 B2
Oakengates 52 E2
Oakes 123 Q4
Oakford 52 D4
Oakham 53 G2
Oak Hill 125 K8
Oakington 53 H2
Oakland *California* 126 A2
Oakland *Nebraska* 123 R7
Oak Lawn 124 G6
Oakley 123 P8
Oakover 112 E3
Oakridge 122 C6
Oak Ridge 129 K2
Oak Valley 125 N7
Oamaru 115 C6
Oa, Mull of 57 B5
Oates Land 141 L4
Oa, The 57 B5
Oatlands 113 K7
Oaxaca 131 L9
Ob 84 Ae3
Oban 57 D4
Oberammergau 70 D5
Oberhausen 70 B3
Oberlin 123 P8
Obidos *Brazil* 137 F4
Obidos *Portugal* 66 B3
Obihiro 88 J4
Obi, Kepulauan 91 H6
Obilnoye 79 G6
Obion 128 H2
Obninsk 78 F4
Obo 102 E6
Obock 103 H5
Obok-tong 88 B5
Oborniki 71 G2
Oboyan 79 F5
Obozerskiy 78 G3
Obregon, Presa 127 H6
Obruk 76 E3
Obryvistoye 85 Q7
Observatoire, Caye de l' 111 N6
Obskaya Guba 84 A3
Obuasi 104 E4
Ocala 129 L6
Ocana *Colombia* 136 C2
Ocana *Spain* 66 E3
Occidental, Cordillera *Colombia* 136 B3
Occidental, Cordillera *Peru* 136 B6
Occidental, Grand Erg 100 F2
Oceanside 126 D4
Ocejon, Pic 66 E2
Ochamchire 77 J1
Ochil Hills 57 E4
Ochiltree 57 D5
Ock 53 F3
Ockelbo 63 G6
Ocmulgee 129 L5
Ocna Mures 73 G2
Oconee 129 L4
Ocotlan 130 H7
Ocracoke Island 129 Q3
Ocreza 66 C3
Ocsa 72 E2
Oda 89 D8

Name	Page	Grid
Oda	104	E4
Odadhraun	62	W12
Odaejin	88	B5
Oda, Jebel	103	G3
Odate	88	H5
Odawara	89	G8
Odda	63	B6
Odemira	66	B4
Odemis	76	B3
Odendaalsrus	108	E5
Odense	63	D9
Oder	70	F2
Oderhaff	70	F2
Oderzo	68	D3
Odeshog	63	F7
Odessa *U.S.A.*	127	L5
Odessa *Ukraine*	79	E6
Odesskoye	84	A6
Odienne	104	D4
Odmarden	63	L6
Odorheiu Secuiesc	73	H2
Odra	70	F2
Odzaci	72	E3
Oeiras	137	J5
Oekussi	91	G7
Oelrichs	123	N6
Oena, Wadi	103	F2
Oenpelli Mission	113	G1
Of	77	J2
Ofanto	69	E5
Offaly	59	G6
Offenbach	70	C3
Offenburg	70	B4
Offord D'Arcy	53	G2
Ofidhousa	75	J4
Ofotfjord	62	G2
Ofunato	88	H6
Oga	88	G6
Ogaden	103	H6
Ogaki	89	F8
Ogasawara-shoto	83	N4
Ogbomosho	105	F4
Ogden	122	J7
Ogdensburg	125	N4
Ogea	114	S9
Ogeechee	129	M4
Ogho	114	H5
Ogi	89	G7
Ogilvie Mountains	118	H3
Oginskiy, Kanal	71	L2
Ogle Point	120	G4
Oglethorpe, Mount	129	K3
Oglio	68	C3
Ognon	65	F5
Ogoamas, Gunung	91	G5
Ogoja	105	G4
Ogoki	121	J7
Ogooue	106	B3
Ogoron	85	M6
Ogosta	73	G4
Ograzden	73	G5
Ogre	63	L8
Ogurchinskiy, Ostrov	79	J8
Oguz	77	H3
Oguzeli	77	G4
Ogwashi-Uku	105	G4
Ohai	115	A6
Ohakune	115	E3
Ohata	88	H5
O'hau, Lake	115	B6
O'Higgins, Lago	139	B9
Ohingaiti	115	E3
Ohio *Kentucky*	124	F8
Ohio *U.S.A.*	124	J6
Ohre	70	D2
Ohre	70	E3
Ohrid	73	F5
Ohridska Jezero	72	F5
Ohura	115	E3
Oiapoque *Brazil*	137	G3
Oiapoque *Brazil*	137	G3
Oikiqtaluk	120	L3
Oil City	125	L6
Oise	64	E4
Oita	89	C9
Oituz, Pasul	73	J2
Oiwake	88	H4
Ojinaga	127	K6
Ojo de Agua	138	D5
Ojos del Salado	138	C5
Oka *Russia*	78	G4
Oka *Russia*	84	G6
Okaba	114	B3
Okahandja	108	C4
Okahukura	115	E3
Okaihau	115	D1
Okanagan Lake	122	E3
Okanagan *U.S.A.*	122	E3
Okanogan *U.S.A.*	122	E3
Okara	92	D2
Okarem	95	M2
Okaukuejo	108	C3
Okavango	108	D3
Okavango Delta	108	D3
Okaya	89	G7
Okayama	89	D8
Okazaki	89	F8
Okeechobee, Lake	129	M7
Okehampton	52	C4
Okene	105	G4
Oketo	88	J4
Okha	85	Q6
Okhota	85	Q5
Okhotsk	85	Q5
Okhotskoye More	85	R5
Okhotsk, Sea of	85	R5
Okigwi	105	G4
Okinawa	89	H10
Okinawa-shoto	89	H10
Okinoerabu-shima	89	J10
Oki-shoto	89	D7
Okitipupa	105	F4
Oklahoma	127	N3
Oklahoma City	128	D3
Oklya	71	L3
Okmulgee	128	D3
Okondja	106	B3
Okoppe	88	J3
Oko, Wadi	103	G3
Oksfjord	62	K1
Oksino	78	J2
Okstindan	62	F3
Oktyabrskiy *Russia*	78	G3
Oktyabrskiy *Russia*	78	J5
Oktyabrskiy *Russia*	85	T6
Oktyabrskoye	79	K5
Oktyabrskoy Revolyutsii, Ostrov	81	L2
Oku	89	J10
Okulovka	78	E4
Okurchan	85	S5
Okushiri-to	88	G4
Okwa	108	D4
Olafsfjordur	62	V11
Olafsvik	62	T12
Oland	63	G8
Olanga	62	P3
Olathe	124	C7
Olavarria	139	D7
Olbia	69	B5
Old Bedford River	53	H2
Oldcastle	58	H5
Old Crow	118	H2
Old Deer	56	F3
Oldenburg *Germany*	70	C2
Oldenburg *Germany*	70	D1
Oldham	55	G3
Old Head of Kinsale	59	E9
Old Hickory Lake	129	J2
Oldman	122	H3
Old Man of Coniston	55	F2
Old Man of Hoy	56	E2
Oldmeldrum	56	F3
Old Nene	53	H2
Old Post Point	121	P8
Olds	122	G2
Old Tongy	113	K4
Old Town	125	R4
Old Wives Lake	123	L2
Olean	125	L5
Olekma	85	L5
Olekminsk	85	L4
Olekmo-charskoye Nagorye	85	L5
Olema	78	H3
Olen	63	A7
Olenegorsk	62	Q2
Olenek	85	L2
Olenekskiy Zaliv	85	N2
Oleniy, Ostrov	84	B2
Oleron, Ile d'	65	C6
Olesko	71	L4
Olesnica	71	G3
Olevsk	79	D5
Olevuga	114	K6
Olfjellet	62	F3
Olga	88	E4
Olgiy	86	G2
Olgopol	73	K1
Olhava	62	L4
Oliana	67	G1
Olib	72	C3
Olifants *Namibia*	108	C4
Olifants *South Africa*	108	C6
Olifants *South Africa*	108	F4
Olimbos *Greece*	75	G2
Olimbos *Greece*	75	J5
Olinda	137	L5
Olio	113	J3
Olite	67	F1
Oliva	138	D6
Olivares, Cerro del	138	C5
Olivia	124	C4
Olkhovka	79	G6
Ollague	138	C4
Ollague, Volcan	138	C4
Ollerton	55	H3
Ollila	62	M2
Olmedo	66	D2
Olmos	136	B5
Olney	124	F7
Olofstrom	63	F8
Olom	85	N3
Olomouc	71	G4
Olonets	78	E3
Olongapo	91	G3
Olot	67	H1
Olovo	72	E3
Olovyannaya	85	K6
Olpe	70	B3
Olsztyn	71	J2
Olsztynek	71	J2
Olt	73	H3
Olten	68	A2
Oltet	73	G3
Oltu *Turkey*	77	J2
Oltu *Turkey*	77	K2
Oltul	73	H3
Olu Deniz	76	C4
Olur	77	K2
Olvera	66	D4
Olympia	122	C4
Olympus *Cyprus*	76	E5
Olympus *Greece*	75	G2
Olympus, Mount	122	C4
Olyutorskiy, Mys	85	W5
Oma *Russia*	78	H2
Oma *Russia*	78	H2
Omachi	89	F7
Omae-zaki	89	G8
Omagari	88	H6
Omagh	58	H3
Omaha	124	C6
Omak	122	E3
Omakau	115	B6
Oman	97	M7
Oman, Gulf of	97	P4
Omarama	115	B6
Omaruru	108	C4
Oma-saki	88	H5
Ombrone	69	C4
Omchali	79	J7
Omdurman	103	F4
Omeath	58	K4
Omeleut	85	W4
Omeo	113	K6
Omerli	77	J4
Omerli Baraji	76	C2
Ometepe, Isla de	132	E9
Om Hajer	96	C9
Ominato	88	H5
Omineca Mountains	118	K4
Omis	72	D4
Omitlan	131	K9
Omiya	89	G8
Ommaney, Cape	118	J4
Ommanney Bay	120	F3
Omnogovi	86	G2
Omodeo, Lago	69	B5
Omolon	85	T3
Omoloy *Russia*	84	H5
Omoloy *Russia*	85	N2
Omono	88	H6
Omoto	88	H6
Omo Wenz	103	G6
Omsk	84	A6
Omsukchan	85	T4
Omu	88	J3
Omulevka	85	S4
Omulew	71	J2
Omura	89	B9
Omuramba Eiseb	108	C4
Omuramba Omatako	108	C4
Omurtag	73	J4
Omuta	89	C9
Omutinskiy	84	Ae5
Omutninsk	78	J4
Onalaska	124	E5
Onan	85	J6
Oncocua	106	B6
Ondaroa	66	E1
Ondava	71	J4
Ondjiva	106	C6
Ondo	105	F4
Ondorhaan	87	L2
Ondorkara	86	F2
Ondozero	78	E3
Ondverdarnes	62	S12
Oneata	114	S9
Onega *Russia*	78	F3
Onega *Russia*	78	F3
One Hundred Mile House	122	D2
Oneida Lake	125	N5
O'Neill	123	Q6
Onekotan, Ostrov	85	S7
Oneonta	125	N5
Onezhskaya Guba	78	F3
Onezhskiy Poluostrov	78	F3
Onezhskoye, Ozero	78	F3
Ongerup	112	D5
Ongole	92	F5
Ongon	87	L2
Ongt Gol	86	J3
Onguday	84	D6
Onich	57	C4
Oni-i-Lau	111	T6
Onilahy	109	H4
Onitsha	105	G4
Onjuul	87	K2
Onkivesi	62	M5
Ono	89	F8
Ono *Fiji*	114	R9
Ono *Japan*	89	H7
Onotoa	111	S2
Onslow	112	D3
Onslow Bay	129	P3
Onsong	88	B4
Ontario *Canada*	121	H7
Ontario *California*	126	D3
Ontario *Oregon*	122	F6
Ontario, Lake	125	M5
Onteniente	67	F3
Ontong Java Atoll	111	N3
Oodnadatta	113	H4
Oolagah Lake	128	E2
Ooldea	112	G5
Oostelijk-Flevoland	64	F2
Oostende	64	E3
Oosterschelde	64	E3
Oota Lake	118	K5
Opala	106	D3
Opanake	92	F7
Oparino	78	H4
Opatow	71	J3
Opava	71	G4
Opawica	125	N2
Opelika	129	K4
Opelousas	128	F5
Opheim	123	L3
Ophir, Gunung	90	B5
Opiscoteo, Lake	121	N7
Opobo	105	G5
Opochka	63	N8
Opole	71	G3
Opornyy	79	J6
Oporto	66	B2
Opotiki	115	F3
Opp	129	J5
Oppdal	62	C5
Oppeln	71	G3
Oppland	63	C6
Opua	115	E1
Opunake	115	D3
Oradea	73	F2
Orafajokull	62	W12
Orai	92	E3
Oran	138	D4
Oran	100	E1
Orange *Australia*	113	K5
Orange *France*	65	F6
Orange *Namibia*	108	C4
Orange *U.S.A*	128	F5
Orangeburg	129	M4
Orange, Cabo	137	G3
Orangeville	125	K4
Orange Walk	132	C5
Oranienburg	70	E2
Oranje	108	D5
Oranje Gebergte	137	F3
Oranjemund	108	C5
Oranjestad	136	C1
Oranmore	59	E6
Oras	91	H3
Oravita	73	F3
Oravska nadrz	71	H4
Orawia	115	A7
Orbec	64	D4
Orbetello	69	C4
Orbigo	66	D1
Orbost	113	K6
Orbyhus	63	G6
Orcadas	141	X6
Orcera	66	E3
Orchila, Isla	136	D1
Orchowo	71	G2
Orco	68	A3
Ord	112	F2
Orderville	126	F2
Ord, Mountain	112	F2
Ordu	77	G2
Orduna	66	E1
Ore	57	E4
Orealven	62	H4
Orebro *Sweden*	63	F7
Orebro *Sweden*	63	F7
Oregon	122	D6
Oregon City	122	C5
Orekhovo Zuyevo	78	F4
Orel	79	F5
Orem	122	J7
Oren	76	B4
Orenburg	79	K5
Orencik	76	C1
Orense	66	C1
Orestias	75	J2
Oreti	115	B6
Orford Ness	53	J2
Organ Peak	127	J4
Orgaz	66	E3
Orgeyev	79	D6
Orgiva	66	E4
Orgon Tal	87	L3
Orhaneli	76	C2
Orhangazi	76	C2
Orhon Gol	87	K2
Oriental, Cordillera *Colombia*	136	C2
Oriental, Cordillera *Peru*	136	B5
Oriental, Grand Erg	101	G2
Orihuela	67	F3
Orinoco	136	E2
Oriomo	114	C3
Oris	68	C2
Orissa	92	F4
Oristano	69	B6
Oristano, Golfo di	69	B6
Orivesi *Hame, Finland*	63	L6
Orivesi *Pohjois-karjala, Finland*	62	N5
Oriximina	137	F4
Orizaba	131	L8
Orizare	73	J4
Orje	63	D7
Orjen	72	E4
Orkanger	62	C5
Orkelljunga	63	E8
Orkla	62	C5
Orkney	56	E1
Orkney Islands	56	F1
Orla	71	G3
Orlando	129	M6
Orleanais	65	D5
Orleans	65	D5
Ormara	92	B3
Ormara, Ras	92	B3
Ormoc	91	G3
Ormond Island	120	K4

Name	Page	Grid
Ormos	75	H4
Ormskirk	55	G3
Ornain	64	F4
Orne	64	C4
Ornskoldsvik	62	H5
Oro	130	G4
Orobi, Alpi	68	B3
Orocue	136	C3
Orofino	122	F4
Oromocto	125	S4
Oron	85	K5
Orona	111	U2
Oronsay	57	B5
Oronsay, Passage of	57	B5
Orontes	77	G5
Oropesa	66	D3
Oroqen Zizhiqi	87	N1
Oroquieta	91	G4
Orosei, Golfo di	69	B5
Oroshaza	72	F2
Orotukan	85	S4
Oroville *California*	122	D8
Oroville *Washington*	122	E3
Oroville, Lake	122	D8
Orrin Reservoir	56	D3
Orsa	63	F6
Orsa Finnmark	63	F6
Orsaro, Monte	68	C3
Orsha	78	E5
Orsta	62	B5
Orta	76	E2
Ortabag	77	K4
Ortaca	76	C4
Ortakoy *Turkey*	76	F2
Ortakoy *Turkey*	76	F3
Ortatoroslar	76	F4
Ortega	136	B3
Ortegal, Cabo	66	C1
Ortelsburg	71	J2
Orthez	65	C7
Ortigueira	66	C1
Ortiz	133	P10
Ortles	68	C2
Ortona	69	E4
Orto-Tokoy	86	D3
Orumiyeh	77	L4
Orumiyeh, Daryacheh-ye	94	G3
Oruro	138	C3
Orvieto	69	D4
Orwell	53	J3
Oryakhovo	73	G4
Os	62	D5
Osa	78	K4
Osage	124	D7
Osaka *Japan*	89	E8
Osaka *Japan*	89	E8
Osaka-wan	89	E8
Osa, Peninsula de	132	F10
Osceola *Arkansas*	128	H3
Osceola *Iowa*	124	D6
Osh	86	B3
Oshamambe	88	H4
Oshawa	125	L5
O-shima	89	G8
Oshkosh	124	F4
Oshkurya	84	Ac3
Oshmarino	84	C2
Oshmyanskaya Vozvyshennost	71	M1
Oshmyany	71	L1
Oshnoviyeh	94	G3
Oshogbo	105	F4
Oshtoran Kuh	94	J5
Oshtorinan	94	J4
Oshwe	106	C3
Osijek	72	E3
Osimo	68	D4
Osinniki	84	D6
Osipovichi	79	D5
Oskaloosa	124	D6
Oskamull	57	B4
Oskara, Mys	84	F1
Oskarshamn	63	G8
Oskarstrom	63	E8
Oskoba	84	G4
Oskol	79	F5
Oslo *Norway*	63	D7
Oslo *Norway*	63	D7
Oslob	91	G4
Oslofjorden	63	H7
Osmanabad	92	E5
Osmancik	76	F2
Osmaneli	76	C2
Osmaniye	77	G4
Osmington	52	E4
Osmino	63	N7
Osmo	63	G7
Osnabruck	70	C2
Osogovska Planina	73	G4
Osorno *Chile*	139	B8
Osorno *Spain*	66	D1
Osoyro	63	A6
Osprey Reef	113	K1
Oss	64	F3
Ossa	75	G3
Ossa, Mount	110	L10
Ossett	55	H3
Ossian, Loch	57	D4
Ossokmanuan Lake	121	P7
Ostashkov	78	E4
Ostavall	62	F5
Ostby	63	E6
Oste	70	C2
Osterburken	70	C4
Osterdalalven	63	E6
Osterdalen	63	D5
Ostergotland	63	F7
Osterode	71	H2
Ostersund	62	F5
Ostfold	63	D7
Ost Friesische Inseln	70	B2
Ostfriesland	70	B2
Osthammar	63	H6
Ostiglia	68	C3
Ostra	68	D4
Ostrava	71	H4
Ostroda	71	H2
Ostrog	79	D5
Ostrogozhsk	79	F5
Ostroleka	71	J2
Ostrov	63	N8
Ostrovnoy, Mys	88	D4
Ostrow	71	G3
Ostrowiec	71	J3
Ostrow Mazowiecki	71	J2
Ostuni	69	F5
Osum	75	F2
Osum	73	H4
Osumi-kaikyo	89	C10
Osumi-shoto	89	C10
Osuna	66	D4
OsVan	78	K2
Oswaldtwistle	55	G3
Oswego	125	M5
Oswestry	52	D2
Otaki	115	E4
Otaru	88	H4
Otava	70	E4
Otavi	108	C3
Otawara	89	G7
Otchinjau	106	B6
Otelec	73	F3
Otelu Rosu	73	G3
Otematata	115	C6
Othe, Foret d'	65	E4
Othonoi	74	E3
Othris	75	G3
Oti	104	F4
Otira	115	C5
Otis	123	N7
Otish, Monts	121	M7
Otjiwarongo	108	C4
Otley	55	H3
Otlukbeli Daglari	77	J2
Otnes	63	D6
Otocac	72	C3
Otorohanga	115	E3
Otoskwin	121	H7
Otra	63	B7
Otranto	69	G5
Otranto, Capo d	69	G5
Otranto, Strait of	74	E2
Otsu	89	E8
Otsu	89	H7
Otta *Norway*	63	C6
Otta *Norway*	63	C6
Ottawa *Canada*	125	L3
Ottawa *Canada*	125	N4
Ottawa Islands	121	K6
Otter	52	D4
Otterburn	57	F5
Otter Rapids	125	K1
Otterup	63	D9
Ottery	52	C4
Ottery Saint Mary	52	D4
Ottumwa	124	D6
Oturkpo	105	G4
Otway, Bahia	139	B10
Otway, Cape	113	J6
Otway, Seno	139	B10
Otwock	71	J2
Otynya	71	L4
Otztaler Alpen	68	C2
Ouachita	128	F4
Ouachita, Lake	128	F3
Ouachita Mountains	128	E3
Ouadda	102	D6
Ouagadougou	104	E3
Ouahigouya	104	E3
Oualata	100	D5
Oua-n Ahagar, Tassili	101	G4
Ouanda Djaile	102	D6
Ouarane	100	D4
Ouargla	101	G2
Ouarra	102	E6
Ouarsenis, Massif de l'	67	G5
Ouarzazate	100	D2
Ouatoais	125	M4
Oubangui	106	C3
Oudenaarde	64	E3
Oude Rijn	64	F2
Oudtshoorn	108	D6
Oued Zem	100	D2
Oueme	105	F4
Ouen	114	X17
Ouessant, Ile d'	64	A4
Ouesso	106	C2
Ouezzane	100	D2
Oughterard	59	D6
Oughter, Lough	58	H4
Ouidah	105	F4
Oujda	100	E2
Oulainen	62	L4
Oulmes	100	D2
Oulu *Finland*	62	L4
Oulu *Finland*	62	M4
Oulujarvi	62	M4
Oulujoki	62	M4
Oulx	68	A3
Oum Chalouba	102	D4
Oum El Bouaghi	101	G1
Oum er Rbia, Oued	100	D2
Ou, Nam	93	K4
Ounasjoki	62	L3
Oundle	53	G2
Ounianga Kebir	102	D4
Oupu	87	P1
Ouricuri	137	J5
Ourinhos	138	G4
Ouro Preto	138	H4
Ourthe	64	F3
Ouse *Australia*	113	K7
Ouse *U.K.*	55	H3
Oust	65	B5
Outardes, Reservoir	121	N7
Outer Hebrides	56	A3
Outokumpu	62	N5
Out Skerries	56	B1
Outwell	53	H2
Ouvea	114	X16
Ouyen	113	J6
Ovacik *Turkey*	77	H4
Ovacik *Turkey*	77	J2
Ovada	68	B3
Ovalau Batiki	114	R8
Ovalle	138	B6
Ovau	114	H5
Ovejo	66	D3
Oven	115	X17
Overbister	56	F1
Overbygd	62	H2
Overkalix	62	K3
Overnas	62	G3
Overtornea	62	K3
Oviedo	66	D1
Ovinishche	78	F4
Ovre Ardal	63	B6
Ovruch	79	D5
Owahanga	115	F4
Owaka	115	B7
Owando	106	C3
Owase	89	F8
Owatonna	124	D4
Owbeh	95	R4
Owel, Lough	58	H5
Owenbeg	58	E4
Owenkillew	58	H3
Owenmore	58	C4
Owens	126	C2
Owensboro	124	G8
Owens Lake	126	D2
Owen Sound	125	K4
Owen Stanley Range	114	D3
Owerri	105	G4
Owo	105	G4
Owosso	124	H5
Owyhee *Nevada*	122	F7
Owyhee *Oregon*	122	F6
Oxbow	123	N3
Oxelosund	63	G7
Oxenholme	55	G2
Oxenhope	55	H3
Oxford *New Zealand*	115	D5
Oxford *U.K.*	53	F3
Oxford *U.S.A.*	128	H3
Oxfordshire	53	F3
Ox Mountains	58	E4
Oxnard	126	C3
Oxton	55	H3
Oyaca	76	E3
Oyali	77	J4
Oyapock	137	G3
Oyem	106	B2
Oykel	56	D3
Oykel Bridge	56	D3
Oymyakon	85	Q4
Oyo	105	F4
Ozalp	77	L3
Ozamiz	91	G4
Ozark Plateau	124	D8
Ozarks, Lake of the	124	D7
Ozd	72	F1
Ozernovskiy	85	T6
Ozernoye	84	A5
Ozersk	71	K1
Ozhogina	85	R3
Ozieri	69	B5
Ozinki	79	H5
Ozona	127	M5
Ozora	72	E2
Ozyurt	76	F3

P

Name	Page	Grid
Paama	114	U12
Paarl	108	C6
Pabbay *U.K.*	56	A3
Pabbay *U.K.*	57	A4
Pabellon de Arteaga	130	H6
Pabjanice	71	H3
Pabna	92	G4
Pabrade	63	L9
Pacaas Novos, Serra dos	136	E6
Pacaraima, Sierra	136	E3
Pacasmayo	136	B5
Pachino	69	E7
Pachora	92	E4
Pachuca	131	K7
Pacifica	126	A2
Pacific Ocean	87	P7
Pacific Ocean, North	143	H3
Pacific Ocean, South	143	J5
Pacitan	90	E7
Packwood	122	D4
Padang *Indonesia*	90	C6
Padang *Indonesia*	90	C5
Padangpanjang	90	D6
Padangsidimpuan	90	B5
Padasjoki	63	L6
Padauiri	136	E3
Paderborn	70	C3
Pades	73	G3
Padiham	55	G3
Padilla *Bolivia*	138	D3
Padilla *Mexico*	131	K5
Padina	73	J3
Padje-Ianta	62	G3
Padloping Island	120	P4
Padova	68	C3
Padrao, Pointa do	106	B4
Padron	66	B1
Padstow	52	C4
Padstow Bay	52	C4
Padua	68	C3
Paducah *Kentucky*	124	F8
Paducah *Texas*	127	M4
Padunskoye More	62	P2
Paekariki	115	E4
Paengnyong-do	87	N4
Paeroa	115	E2
Pag *Croatia*	72	C3
Pag *Croatia*	72	C3
Pagadian	91	G4
Pagasitikos Kolpos	75	G3
Pagatan	90	F6
Page	126	G2
Pagosa Springs	127	J2
Pagwa River	124	H2
Pagwi	114	C2
Pahala	126	T11
Pahang	90	C5
Pahia Point	115	A7
Pahiatua	115	E4
Pahlavi Dezh	95	M3
Pahoa	126	T11
Pahokee	129	M7
Pahra Kariz	95	Q4
Paia	126	S10
Paide	63	L7
Paignton	52	D4
Paijanne	63	L6
Pailolo Chan	126	S10
Paimpol	64	B4
Painswick	53	E3
Painted Desert	126	G2
Paisley	57	D5
Paita	136	A5
Paita	114	X17
Paittasjarvi	62	K2
Pajala	62	K3
Pakaraima Mountains	136	E2
Pakistan	92	C3
Pak Lay	93	K5
Pakokku	93	H4
Pakpattan	92	D2
Pakrac	72	D3
Paks	72	E2
Pakse	93	L5
Pala	102	B6
Palabuhanratu	90	D7
Palafrugell	67	H2
Palagruza	72	D4
Palaiokastron	75	J5
Palaiokhora	75	G5
Pala Laharha	92	G4
Palamos	67	H2
Palana	85	T5
Palanan Point	91	G2
Palanga	63	J9
Palangan, Kuh-e-	95	Q6
Palangkaraya	90	E6
Palanpur	92	D4
Palapye	108	E4
Palar	92	E6
Palata	69	E5
Palatka *U.S.A.*	129	M6
Palatka *Russia*	85	S4
Palau	69	B5
Palau Islands	91	J4
Palawan	91	F4
Palawan Passage	91	F4
Palayankottai	92	E7
Palazzola Acreide	69	E7
Paldiski	63	L7
Palembang	90	C6
Palena, Lago	139	B8
Palencia	66	D1
Palermo	69	D6
Palestine	128	E5
Paletwa	93	H4
Palghat	92	E6
Palgrave Point	108	B4
Palhoca	138	G5
Pali	92	D3
Palisade	127	H1
Palit, Kep i	74	E2
Palkane	63	L6
Palk Strait	92	E7
Pallaresa	67	G1
Pallas Grean	59	F7
Pallasovka	79	H5
Pallastunturi	62	K2
Palliser Bay	115	E4
Palliser, Cape	115	E4
Palma *Mozambique*	109	H2

Name	Page	Grid
Palma *Spain*	67	H3
Palma, Baia de	67	H3
Palma del Rio	66	D4
Pal Malmal	114	E3
Palmanova	68	D3
Palmares	137	K5
Palmar, Punta del	139	F6
Palmas	138	G5
Palmas, Cape	104	D5
Palmas, Golfo di	69	B6
Palma Soriano	132	J4
Palmatkina	85	V4
Palmeira	138	F5
Palmeiras	137	J6
Palmer *Antarctic*	141	V6
Palmer *U.S.A.*	118	F3
Palmer Land	141	V4
Palmerston	115	C6
Palmerston Island	111	W5
Palmerston North	115	E4
Palm Harbor	129	L6
Palmi	69	E6
Palmira	136	B3
Palm Springs	126	D4
Palmyra	94	D4
Palmyras Point	92	G4
Palo de las Letras	136	B2
Palomar, Mount	126	D4
Palopo	91	G6
Palos, Cabo de	67	F4
Palpetu, Tanjung	91	H6
Palu *Indonesia*	91	F6
Palu *Indonesia*	91	F6
Palu *Turkey*	77	H3
Palyavaam	85	W3
Pama	104	F3
Pamban	92	E7
Pamekasan	90	E7
Pameungpeuk	90	D7
Pamiers	65	D7
Pamisos	75	F4
Pamlico Sound	129	P3
Pampa	127	M3
Pampachiri	136	C6
Pampas *Argentina*	139	D7
Pampas *Peru*	136	C6
Pampilhosa da Serra	66	C2
Pamplona *Colombia*	136	C2
Pamplona *Spain*	67	F1
Pana	124	F7
Panaca	126	E2
Panagyurishte	73	H4
Panaji	92	D5
Panama	132	G10
Panama	132	H10
Panama, Bahia de	132	H10
Panama Canal	136	B2
Panama City	129	K5
Panama, Golfo de	136	B2
Panandak	95	K4
Panaro	68	C3
Panay	91	G3
Pancevo	72	F3
Panda	109	F4
Pandan *Philippines*	91	G3
Pandan *Philippines*	91	G3
Pandany	78	E3
Pandharpur	92	E5
Pando	139	E6
Pandunskoye More	78	E2
Panevezys	63	N9
Panfilov	86	E3
Pangalanes, Canal des	109	J4
Pangani	107	G4
Panggoe	114	H5
Pangi	106	E3
Pangkalanbuun	90	E6
Pangkalpinang	90	D6
Pangnirtung	120	N4
Pangong Tso	92	E2
Pangrango, Gunung	90	D7
Pangtara	93	J4
Pangururar	90	B5
Pangutaran Group	91	G4
Panhandle	127	M3
Paniai, Donau	114	B2
Panie, Mount	114	W16
Panipat	92	E3
Panjim	92	D5
Panna	92	F4
Panovo	84	G5
Pant *Essex, U.K.*	53	H3
Pant *Shropshire, U.K.*	52	D2
Pantar	91	G7
Pantelleria, Isola di	69	D7
Pantones	66	E3
Panuco *Mexico*	131	K6
Panuco *Mexico*	131	K6
Pan Xian	93	K3
Panyam	105	G4
Pao-de-Acucar	137	K5
Paola	69	F6
Paoua	102	C6
Papa	72	D2
Papakura	115	E2
Papantla	131	L7
Paparoa	115	E2
Paparoa Range	115	C5
Papa Stour	56	A1
Papatoetoe	115	E2
Papa Westray	56	F1
Papenburg	70	B2
Papigochic	127	J6
Papisoi, Tanjung	114	A2

Name	Page	Grid
Paps of Jura	57	B5
Paps, The	59	D8
Papua, Gulf of	114	C3
Papua New Guinea	114	C2
Papuk	72	D3
Papun	93	J5
Para	137	G4
Paracas, Peninsula	136	B6
Paracatu *Brazil*	138	G3
Paracatu *Brazil*	138	G3
Paracin	73	F4
Paradubice	70	F3
Paragould	128	G2
Paragua	136	E6
Paragua	136	E2
Paraguacu	137	J6
Paraguai	136	F7
Paraguana, Peninsula de	133	M8
Paraguari	138	E5
Paraguay	138	E4
Paraguay	138	E4
Paraiba	138	H4
Paraiba	137	K5
Parajuru	137	K4
Parakou	105	F4
Paralakhemundi	92	F5
Paralkot	92	F5
Paramaribo	137	F2
Paramillo	136	B2
Paramirim	137	J6
Paramonga	136	B6
Paramushir, Ostrov	85	T6
Parana	138	D6
Parana	138	H6
Paranagua	138	G5
Paranaiba *Maranhao, Brazil*	137	J4
Paranaiba *Mato Grosso do Sul, Brazil*	138	F3
Paranaiba *Minas Gerais, Brazil*	138	G3
Paranaidji	137	H5
Paranapanema	138	F4
Paranapiacaba, Serra	138	G4
Paranatinga	137	F6
Parangipettai	92	E6
Paraparaum	115	E4
Parapola	75	G4
Parauna	138	F3
Parbati	92	E4
Parbhani	92	E5
Parcel Islands	93	M5
Parchim	70	D2
Pardo	138	F4
Parecis, Serra dos	136	F6
Pareditas	139	C6
Pare Mountains	107	G3
Parengarenga Harbour	115	D1
Parepare	91	F6
Paria, Golfo de	133	R9
Pariaguan	136	E2
Paria, Peninsula de	133	R9
Paricutin, Volcan el	130	H8
Parigi	91	G6
Parikkala	63	N6
Parima, Serra	136	E3
Parintins	137	F4
Paris *France*	64	E4
Paris *Kentucky*	124	H7
Paris *Tennessee*	129	H2
Paris *Texas*	128	E4
Parkano	63	K5
Parker	126	E3
Parkersburg	125	K7
Parkes	113	K5
Parkgate	57	E5
Park Range	123	L7
Parksville	122	B3
Parma *Italy*	68	C3
Parma *U.S.A.*	125	K6
Parnaiba	137	J4
Parnamirim	137	K5
Parnassos	75	G3
Parnassus	115	D5
Parnis	75	G3
Parnon Oros	75	G4
Parnu	63	L7
Parnu	63	L7
Paro	93	G3
Paropamisus	95	R4
Paros *Greece*	75	H4
Paros *Greece*	75	H4
Parowan	126	F2
Parral	139	B7
Parras	127	L8
Parrett	52	E3
Parrsboro	121	P8
Parry Bay	120	K4
Parry Islands	120	C2
Parry, Kap	120	M2
Parry Peninsula	118	L2
Parry Sound	125	L4
Parseta	71	G2
Parshino	85	J5
Parsons	128	E2
Partabpur	92	F4
Parthenay	65	C5
Partizansk	88	D4
Parton	57	D5
Partry Mountains	58	C5
Paru	137	G4
Parys	108	E5
Pasa Barris	137	K6
Pasadena *California*	126	C3
Pasadena *Texas*	128	E6
Pasado, Cabo	136	A4

Name	Page	Grid
Pa Sak, Mae Nam	93	K5
Pasarwajo	91	G7
Pascagoula *U.S.A.*	128	H5
Pascagoula *U.S.A.*	128	H5
Pascani	73	J2
Pasco	122	E4
Pascua, Isla de	143	K5
Pasewalk	70	F2
Pashiya	78	K4
Pashkovo	88	C1
Pasig	91	G3
Pasinler	77	J3
Pasirpangarayan	90	C5
Paslek	71	H1
Pasley, Cape	112	E5
Pasmajarvi	62	L3
Pasman	72	C4
Pasni	92	B3
Paso de los Indios	139	C8
Paso de los Libres	138	E5
Paso de los Toros	138	E6
Paso Real	131	M9
Paso Rio Mayo	139	B9
Paso Robles	126	B3
Pasquia Hills	119	Q5
Passage East	59	J8
Passage West	59	F9
Passamaquoddy Bay	125	S4
Passau	70	E4
Passero, Capo	69	E7
Passo Fundo	138	F5
Passos	138	G4
Pastaza	136	B4
Pas, The	119	Q5
Pasto	136	B3
Pastol Bay	118	C3
Pastos Bons	137	J5
Pastrana	66	E2
Pasuruan	90	E7
Patache, Punta de	138	B4
Patagonia	139	C9
Patan *India*	92	D4
Patan *Nepal*	92	G3
Patani	91	H5
Patea	115	E3
Pateley Bridge	55	H2
Paternu	69	E7
Paterson	125	N6
Pathankot	92	E2
Pathfinder Reservoir	123	L6
Pathhead	57	F4
Patiala	92	E2
Patkai Bum	93	J3
Patman, Lake	128	E4
Patmos	75	J4
Patna	92	G3
Patnagarh	92	F4
Patnos	77	K3
Patomskoye Nagorye	85	J4
Patos	137	K5
Patos de Minas	138	G3
Patos, Lagoa dos	138	F6
Patquia	138	C6
Patrai	75	F3
Patras	75	F3
Patrasuy	78	L3
Patricio Lynch, Isla	139	A9
Patrington	55	J3
Patrocinio	138	G3
Pattani	93	K7
Patterdale	55	G2
Patti	69	E6
Patu	137	K5
Patuca	132	E7
Patuca, Punta	132	E7
Patzcuaro	130	J8
Patzcuaro, Laguna	130	J8
Pau	65	C7
Pau d'Arco	137	H5
Pau dos Ferros	137	K5
Pau, Gave de	65	C7
Pauini *Brazil*	136	D5
Pauini *Brazil*	136	D5
Paulilatino	69	B5
Paulista	137	K5
Paulistana	137	J5
Pauls Valley	128	D3
Paungde	93	J5
Pauni	92	E4
Pauri	92	E2
Pauto	136	C2
Pavarandocito	136	B2
Paveh	94	H4
Pavia	68	B3
Pavilosta	63	J8
Pavlikeni	73	H4
Pavlodar	84	B6
Pavlof Volcano	118	Af8
Pavlohrad	79	F6
Pavlovo	78	G4
Pavlovsk	79	G5
Pavlovskaya	79	F6
Pavullo nel Frigano	68	C3
Pavuvu	114	J6
Pawan	90	E6
Paxoi	75	F3
Paxton	57	F4
Payakumbuh	90	D6
Payette *U.S.A.*	122	F5
Payne, Lake	121	M6
Paynes Find	112	D4
Paysandu	138	E6
Payun, Volcan	139	C7
Pazanan	95	J6

Name	Page	Grid
Pazar	77	J2
Pazarbasi Burun	76	D2
Pazarcik	77	G4
Pazardzhik	73	H4
Pazaroren	77	G3
Pazaryeri	76	C2
Paz, Bahia de la	130	D5
Pazin	72	B3
Pcim	71	H4
Peabody Bugt	120	N2
Peace *Canada*	119	N4
Peace *U.S.A.*	129	M7
Peacehaven	53	M4
Peace River	119	M4
Peaima Falls	136	E2
Pea Island	129	Q3
Peak Hill	112	D4
Peale, Mount	123	K8
Pearl	128	H5
Pearl City	126	R10
Pearl Harbor	126	R10
Pearsall	128	C6
Peary Channel	120	F2
Pease	127	N3
Pebane	109	G3
Pec	72	F4
Pechenezhin	71	L4
Pechenga	62	P2
Pechora	78	J2
Pechorskaya Guba	78	J2
Pechorskoye More	78	J2
Pechory	63	M8
Pecos *U.S.A.*	127	L5
Pecos Plains	127	K4
Pecs	72	E2
Pedasi	132	G11
Pededze	63	M8
Pedernales	133	M5
Pedo La	92	F3
Pedorovka	79	J5
Pedra Azul	138	H3
Pedregal	132	F10
Pedreiras	137	J4
Pedro Afonso	137	H5
Pedro Cays	132	J6
Pedro Juan Caballero	138	E4
Pedro Luro	139	D7
Peebles	57	E5
Pee Dee	129	N3
Peel *Canada*	118	J2
Peel *U.K.*	54	E2
Peel Sound	120	G3
Peene	70	E2
Pegasus Bay	115	D5
Pegnitz *Germany*	70	D4
Pegnitz *Germany*	70	D4
Pegu	93	J5
Pegu Yoma	93	J5
Pegwell Bay	53	J3
Pegysh	78	J3
Pehlivankoy	76	B2
Pehuajo	139	D7
Peine	70	D2
Peipus, Lake	63	M7
Peixe	137	H6
Pei Xian	93	N2
Pekalongan	90	D7
Pekan	90	C5
Pekanbaru	90	C5
Pekin	124	F6
Peking	87	M4
Pekkala	62	M3
Pelabuanratu, Teluk	90	D7
Pelabuhan Kelang	90	C5
Pelagie, Isole	74	B5
Pelagos	75	H3
Pelat, Mont	65	G6
Peleaga	73	G3
Peleduy	85	J5
Pelee Island	124	J6
Peleng	91	G6
Peljesac	72	D4
Pelkosenniemi	62	M3
Pella	124	D6
Pellegrini	139	D7
Pello	62	L3
Pellworm	70	C1
Pelly	118	J3
Pelly Bay	120	J4
Pelly Mountains	118	J3
Peloponnisos	75	G4
Pelotas	138	F5
Pelplin	71	H2
Pelym	78	L3
Pemali, Tanjung	91	G6
Pematangsiantar	90	B5
Pemba	109	H2
Pemba Island	107	G4
Pemberton	122	C2
Pembina	119	M5
Pembroke *Canada*	125	M4
Pembroke *U.K.*	52	C3
Pembroke Dock	52	C3
Pena de Francia, Sierra da	66	C2
Penafiel	66	B2
Penafiel	66	D2
Penala	113	J6
Penalara, Pic de	66	E2
Penamacor	66	C2
Penapolis	138	F4
Penaranda de Bracamonte	66	D2
Penarroya	67	C2
Penarroya-Pueblonuevo	66	D3
Penarth	52	D3

Name	Page	Grid
Penas, Cabode	66	C1
Penasco, Puerto	126	F5
Pena, Sierra de la	67	F1
Pencader	52	C3
Pencaitland	57	F5
Pendalofon	75	F2
Pendembu	104	C4
Pendine	52	C3
Pendleton	122	E5
Pend Oreille Lake	122	F3
Pendra	92	F4
Penedo	138	K6
Penfro	52	C3
Penganga	92	E5
Pengkou	87	M6
Pengze	87	M5
Peniche	66	B3
Penicuik	57	E5
Peniscola	67	G2
Penistone	55	H3
Penitentes, Serra do	137	H5
Penmaenmawr	54	F3
Penmarch, Pointe de	65	A5
Penne	69	D4
Penner	92	E6
Penneshaw	113	H6
Pennine, Alpi	68	A2
Pennines	55	G2
Pennsylvania	125	L6
Penny Highlands	120	N4
Peno	78	E4
Penobscot	125	R4
Penobscot Bay	125	R4
Penonome	132	G10
Penrith	55	G2
Penryn	52	B4
Pensacola	129	J5
Pensamiento	136	E6
Pentecost Island	114	U11
Pentire Head	52	C4
Pentland Firth	56	E2
Pentland Hills	57	E5
Pen-y-ghent	55	G2
Penza	79	H5
Penzance	52	B4
Penzhina	85	V4
Penzhinskaya Guba	85	U4
Peoria	124	F6
Peqin	74	E2
Perak	90	C5
Perama	75	F3
Percival Lakes	112	E3
Perdido, Monte	67	G1
Peregrebnoye	84	Ae4
Pereira	136	B3
Perelazovskiy	79	G6
Perello	67	G2
Peremyshlyany	71	L4
Perenjori	112	D4
PereslavlZalesskiy	78	F4
Perevolotskiy	79	J5
Pereyaslavka	88	E2
Pergamino	139	D6
Pergamum	76	B3
Perhojoki	62	K5
Peri	77	J3
Peribonca	121	M8
Peribonca	125	Q2
Perigueux	65	D6
Perija, Sierra de	136	C2
Perim	96	F10
Peris	73	J3
Peristrema	76	F3
Perito Moreno	139	B9
Peritoro	137	J4
Perlas, Punta de	132	F8
Perlez	72	F3
Perm	78	K4
Pernambuca	137	K5
Pernik	73	G4
Peronne	64	E4
Perote	131	L8
Perote, Cofre de	131	L8
Perouse Strait, La	88	J3
Perpignan	65	E7
Perran Bay	52	B4
Perranporth	52	B4
Perros-Guirec	64	B4
Perry Canada	119	Q2
Perry Florida	129	L5
Perry Oklahoma	128	D2
Perryton	127	M2
Perryville Alaska	118	D4
Perryville Missouri	124	F8
Persembe	77	G2
Perseverancia	136	E6
Persian Gulf	97	K3
Pertek	77	H3
Perth Australia	112	D5
Perth Canada	125	M4
Perth U.K.	57	E4
Perth-Andover	125	S3
Pertominsk	78	F3
Pertugskiy	78	H4
Pertuis Breton	65	C5
Peru	136	B5
Peru Illinois	124	F6
Peru Indiana	124	G6
Peru-Chile Trench	143	L5
Perugia	68	D4
Perushtitsa	73	H4
Pervari	77	K4
Pervomaskiy	79	K5
Pervomaysk Russia	78	G5
Pervomaysk Ukraine	79	E6
Pervouralsk	84	Ac5
Pesaro	68	D4
Pescara	69	E4
Peschanyy, Mys	79	J7
Pesha	78	H2
Peshanjan	95	Q5
Peshawar	92	D2
Peshkopi	75	F2
Peski Belarus	71	L2
Peski Kazakhstan	84	Ae6
Pesqueira Brazil	137	K5
Pesqueria Mexico	127	N8
Pestovo	78	F4
Petah Tiqwa	94	B5
Petajavesi	62	L5
Petalcalco, Bahia	130	H9
Petalioi	75	H4
Petalion, Kolpos	75	H4
Petaluma	126	A1
Petatlan	131	J9
Petauke	107	F5
Peterborough Australia	113	H5
Peterborough Canada	125	L4
Peterborough U.K.	53	G2
Peterhead	56	G3
Peterlee	55	H2
Petermann Ranges	112	F3
Peter Pond Lake	119	P4
Petersburg Alaska	118	J4
Petersburg Virginia	125	M8
Petersfield	53	G3
Peterstow	52	E3
Petite Kabylie	67	J4
Petite Miquelon	121	Q8
Petit Mecatina, Riviere du	121	P7
Petitot	119	L4
Petkula	62	M3
Peto	131	Q7
Petoskey	124	H4
Petra Velikogo, Zaliv	88	C4
Petre Bay	115	F6
Petrila	73	G3
Petrodvorets	63	N7
Petrolandia	137	K5
Petrolina Amazonas, Brazil	136	D4
Petrolina Pernambuco, Brazil	137	J5
Petropavlovsk	84	Ae6
Petropavlovsk-Kamchatskiy	85	T6
Petropolis	138	H4
Petrovac	72	E4
Petrovsk	79	H5
Petrovskoye	78	K5
Petrovsk-Zabaykalskiy	84	H6
Petrozavodsk	78	E3
Petsamo	62	P2
Petteril	55	G2
Petukhovo	84	Ae5
Petworth	53	G4
Peureula	90	B5
Pevek	85	W3
Pewsey, Vale of	52	F3
Peza	78	H2
Pezenas	65	E7
Pezinok	71	G4
Pezmog	78	J3
Pfaffenhofen	70	D4
Pfarrkirchen	70	E4
Pforzheim	70	C4
Phalaborwa	108	F4
Phalodi	92	D3
Phaltan	92	D5
Phangan, Ko	93	K6
Phangnga	93	J7
Phan Rang	93	L6
Phan Thiet	93	L6
Phatthalung	93	K7
Phenix City	129	K4
Phet Buri	93	J6
Phetchabun, Thiu Khao	93	K5
Philadelphia Mississippi	128	H4
Philadelphia Pennsylvania	125	N6
Philip	123	P5
Philip Island	111	Q7
Philippeville	64	F3
Philippines	91	G2
Philippine Sea	91	G1
Philipstown	108	D6
Phillipsburg	123	Q8
Philpots Island	120	L2
Phnom Penh	93	K6
Phoenix	126	F4
Phoenix Islands	111	U2
Phong Saly	93	K4
Phong Tho	93	K4
Phu Cuong	93	L6
Phu Dien Chau	93	L5
Phuket	93	J7
Phuket, Ko	93	J7
Phulabani	92	F4
Phu Ly	93	L4
Phuoc Le	93	L6
Phu Tho	93	L4
Phyajoki	62	L4
Piacenza	68	B3
Piana	69	B4
Pianosa, Isola	69	C4
Piatra Neamt	73	J2
Piaui	137	J5
Piaui, Serra do	137	J5
Piave	68	D3
Piaya	90	F7
Piazza Armerina	69	E7
Pibor	103	F6
Pibor Post	103	F6
Pic	124	G2
Picardie	64	E4
Picayune	128	H5
Pichilemu	139	B6
Pickering	55	J2
Pickering, Vale of	55	J2
Pickle Lake	121	J7
Pico	69	D5
Picos	137	J5
Pico Truncado	139	C9
Picton	115	E4
Picun-Leufu	139	C7
Pidalion, Akra	76	F5
Pidurutalagala	92	F7
Piedecuesta	136	C2
Piedrabuena	66	D3
Piedrahita	66	D2
Piedralaves	66	D2
Piedras Negras	127	M6
Piedra Sola	138	E6
Pielavesi	62	M5
Pielinen	62	N5
Pierowall	56	F1
Pierre	123	P5
Pietarsaari	62	K5
Pietermaritzburg	108	F5
Pietersburg	108	E4
Pietrosu	73	H2
Pieve di Cadore	68	D2
Pigadhia	75	J5
Piggott	128	G2
Pihtipudas	62	L5
Pijijiapan	131	N10
Pikes Peak	123	M8
Pikeville	124	J8
Pikhtovka	84	C5
Pila	71	G2
Pilar	138	E5
Pilaya	138	D4
Pilcaniyeu	139	B8
Pilcomayo	138	D4
Pili	75	J4
Pilibhit	92	E3
Pilica	71	H3
Pilion	75	G3
Pilos	75	F4
Pilot Point	118	D4
Pilsen	70	E4
Pimenta Bueno	136	E6
Pimentel	137	G4
Pina	67	F2
Pinang Malaysia	90	C4
Pinang Malaysia	90	C4
Pinarbasi Turkey	76	E2
Pinarbasi Turkey	77	G3
Pinar del Rio	132	F3
Pinarhisar	76	B2
Pinawa	123	S2
Pincher Creek	122	H3
Pindare	137	H4
Pindhos Oros	75	F3
Pindi Gheb	92	D2
Pine Bluff	128	F3
Pine Bluffs	123	M7
Pine City	124	D4
Pine Creek	112	G1
Pine Creek Lake	128	E3
Pinedale	123	K6
Pine Falls	119	R5
Pinega Russia	78	G3
Pinega Russia	78	G3
Pine Island Bay	141	T4
Pine Pass	119	L5
Pine Point	119	N3
Pine Ridge	123	N6
Pinerolo	68	A3
Pines, Lake O' the	128	E4
Pinetop-Lakeside	127	H3
Pineville	124	J8
Pingban	93	K4
Pingdingshan	93	M2
Pingelly	112	D5
Pingeyri	62	T12
Pingguo	93	L4
Pingjiang	93	M3
Ping, Mae Nam	93	J5
Pingquan	93	L1
Pingtan Dao	87	M6
Ping-tung	87	N7
Pingwu	93	K2
Pingxiang Guangxi, China	93	L4
Pingxiang Jiangxi, China	93	M3
Pingyang	87	N6
Pingyao	87	L4
Pingyi	87	M4
Pingyin	87	M4
Pinhao	66	C2
Pinhel	66	C2
Pini	90	B5
Pinios Greece	75	F4
Pinios Greece	75	F3
Pinnes, Akra	75	H2
Pinos, Point	126	B2
Pinotepa Nacional	131	L9
Pinrang	91	F6
Pins, Ile des	114	X17
Pinsk	71	M2
Pintados	138	C4
Pinta, Isla	136	A7
Pinto	138	D5
Pinyug	78	H3
Pioche	126	E2
Piombino	69	C4
Pioner, Ostrov	81	L2
Pionerskiy Russia	84	Ad4
Pionerskiy Russia	71	J1
Piotrkow Trybunalski	71	H3
Piove di Sacco	68	D3
Piperi	75	H3
Pipestone	124	B5
Pipmudcan, Reservoir	125	Q2
Piracicaba	138	G4
Piracuruca	137	J4
Piraeus	75	G4
Pirahmet	77	H2
Piraievs	75	G4
Piranhas Amazonas, Brazil	136	E5
Piranhas Sergipe, Brazil	137	K5
Piranshahr	77	L4
Pirapora	138	H3
Pirara	136	F3
Pirgos Greece	75	F4
Pirgos Greece	75	H5
Pirimapun	114	B3
Pirineos	67	F1
Pirin Planina	73	G5
Piripiri	137	J4
Pirmasens	70	B4
Pirna	70	E3
Piro do Rio	138	G3
Pirot	73	G4
Pir Panjal Range	92	D2
Piru	91	H6
Piryatin	79	E5
Piryi	75	H3
Pisa	68	C4
Pisco	136	B6
Piscopi	75	J4
Pisek	70	F4
Pishan	92	E1
Pishin	95	Q8
Pishin-Lora	92	C3
Pistayarvi, Ozero	62	P4
Pisticci	69	F5
Pistilfjordur	62	X11
Pistoia	68	C4
Pisuerga	66	D1
Pit	122	D7
Pita	104	C3
Pitanga	138	E4
Pitcairn Island	143	J5
Pitea	62	J4
Pitealven	62	H4
Pitesti	73	H3
Pithiviers	64	E4
Pitkyaranta	78	E3
Pitlochry	57	E4
Pitlyar	84	Ae3
Pitt Island Canada	118	K5
Pitt Island New Zealand	115	F7
Pittsburg	124	C8
Pittsburgh	125	K6
Pittsfield	124	E7
Pitt Strait	115	F7
Piui	138	G4
Piura	136	A5
Pjorsa	62	N2
Pjorsa	62	V12
Placentia Bay	121	Q8
Placer	91	G3
Placerville	126	B1
Placido do Castro	136	D6
Plackoviea	73	G5
Plainview	127	M3
Plaka	75	H2
Plakenska Planina	73	F5
Plampang	91	F7
Plana	70	E4
Planeta Rica	133	K10
Plankinton	123	Q6
Plant City	129	L7
Plaquemine	128	G5
Plasencia	66	C2
Plastun	88	F3
Platani	69	D7
Plata, Rio de la	139	E6
Plati	75	G2
Plato	136	C2
Platte	123	R7
Platteville	124	E5
Plattling	70	E4
Plattsburgh	125	P4
Plattsmouth	124	C6
Plauen	70	E3
Plav	72	E4
Playa Azul	130	H8
Pleasanton	128	C6
Pleihari	90	E6
Pleiku	93	L6
Plenty, Bay of	115	F2
Plentywood	123	M3
Plesetsk	78	G3
Plessisville	125	Q3
Pleszew	71	G3
Pletipi Lake	121	M7
Pleven	73	H4
Plitra	75	G4
Pljevlja	72	E4
Plock	71	H2
Plockenstein	70	E4
Ploermel	65	B5
Ploiesti	73	J3
Plomb du Cantal	65	E6
Plombieres	65	G5
Ploner See	70	D1
Plonsk	71	J2
Ploty	70	F2

Plovdiv 73 H4
Plumpton 55 G2
Plym 52 C4
Plymouth *Devon, U.K.* 52 C4
Plymouth *Monserrat, U.K.* 133 R6
Plymouth *Indiana* 124 G6
Plymouth *New Hampshire* 125 Q5
Plymouth Sound 52 C4
Plynlimon 52 D2
Plyussa *Russia* 63 N7
Plyussa *Russia* 63 N7
Plzen 70 E4
Pniewy 71 G2
Po *Burkina Faso* 104 E3
Po *Italy* 68 C3
Pobeda, Gora 85 R3
Pobedy, Pik 86 D3
Pobiedziska 71 G2
Pobla de Segur 67 G1
Pocatello 122 H6
Pocatky 70 F4
Pochep 79 E5
Pochinok 78 E5
Pochutla 131 L10
Pocomoke City 125 N7
Pocone 138 E3
Pocos de Caldas 138 G4
Podcherye 78 K3
Po della Pila, Bocche del 68 D3
Podgorica 72 E4
Podgornoye 84 C5
Podkamennaya Tunguska 84 E4
Podlaska, Nizina 71 K2
Podolsk 78 F4
Podor 104 C2
Podporozhye 78 E3
Pofadder 108 C5
Poggibonsi 68 C4
Pohang 89 B7
Pohjois-Karjala 62 N5
Pohorela 71 J4
Pohorje 72 C2
Poiana Teiului 73 J2
Poinsett, Cape 141 H5
Pointe-a-Pitre 133 S6
Pointe-Noire 106 B3
Point Etienne 100 B4
Point Fortin 133 S9
Point Hope 118 B2
Point Lake 119 N2
Point Pleasant 124 J7
Poipet 93 K6
Poitiers 65 D5
Poitou 65 C5
Poix 64 D4
Pokataroo 113 K4
Pokhara 92 F3
Pokka 62 L2
Pokrovka *Kyrgyzstan* 86 D3
Pokrovka *Russia* 88 C4
Pokrovsk 85 M4
Pokrovskoye 84 Ae5
Polacca Wash 126 G3
Pola de Laviana 66 D1
Polan 95 Q9
Polana 71 H4
Poland 71 G2
Polar Plateau 141 A1
Polati 76 E3
Pole Khatun 95 Q3
Pol-e Safid 95 L3
Polesie Lubelskie 71 K3
Polessk 71 J1
Polesye 79 D5
Polgar 73 F2
Poliaigos 75 H4
Policastro, Golfo di 69 E6
Poligny 65 F5
Poligus 84 E4
Polikastron 75 G2
Polikhnitos 75 J3
Polillo Islands 91 G3
Polis 76 E5
Polisan, Tanjung 91 H5
Politovo 78 H3
Poliyiros 75 G2
Polkyko 84 F2
Pollachi 92 E6
Pollino, Monte 69 F6
Polmak 62 N2
Polmont 57 E5
Polna 63 N7
Polnovat 84 Ae4
Polonnoye 79 D5
Polotsk 63 N9
Polperro 52 C4
Polski Trumbesh 73 H4
Poltava 79 E6
Poltavka 84 A6
Poltsamaa 63 L7
Polunochnoye 84 Ad4
Poluostrov Shirokostan 85 P2
Poluy 84 Ae3
Polyanovo 84 Ae4
Polyarnik 85 Y3
Polyarnyy 62 Q2
Polynesia 143 H4
Polyuc 131 Q8
Pombal *Para, Brazil* 137 G4
Pombal *Paraiba, Brazil* 137 K5
Pombal *Portugal* 66 B3
Pomerania 70 E2
Pomona 126 D3
Pomorskie, Pojezierze 70 F2
Pomorskiy Proliv 78 H2
Pompano Beach 129 M7
Pompeyevka 88 C1
Pomyt 84 Ae4
Ponca City 128 D2
Ponce 133 P5
Ponce de Leon Bay 129 M8
Poncheville, Lac 125 M1
Pondicherry 92 E6
Pond Inlet 120 L3
Pondo 114 E2
Ponerihouen 114 W16
Ponferrada 66 C1
Pongoma 78 E2
Ponnaiyar 92 E6
Ponnani 92 E6
Pono 114 A3
Ponomarevka 78 J5
Ponoy *Russia* 78 F2
Ponoy *Russia* 78 G2
Pons 65 C6
Pont 57 G5
Ponta de Pedras 137 G4
Ponta Grossa 138 F5
Pont-a-Mousson 64 G4
Ponta Pora 138 E4
Pontardulais 52 C3
Pontarlier 65 G5
Pontchartrain, Lake 128 G5
Ponte de Barca 66 B2
Ponte de Pedra 137 F6
Pontedera 68 C4
Ponte de Sor 66 B3
Pontefract 55 H3
Ponteland 55 H1
Ponte Nova 138 H4
Ponterwyd 52 D2
Pontevedra 66 B1
Ponthierville 106 E3
Pontiac 124 J5
Pontianak 90 D6
Pontivy 64 B4
Pont-l'Abbe 65 A5
Pontoetoe 137 F3
Pontois 64 E4
Pontremoli 68 B3
Pontrilas 52 E3
Ponts 67 G2
Pontypool 52 D3
Pontypridd 52 D3
Ponziane, Isole 69 D5
Poole 53 F4
Poole Bay 53 F4
Poolewe 56 C3
Pooley Bridge 55 G2
Poona 92 D5
Poopo, Lago 138 C3
Poor Knights Islands 115 E1
Popayan 136 B3
Popigay *Russia* 84 H2
Popigay *Russia* 84 J2
Poplar Bluff 124 E8
Poplarville 128 H5
Popocatepetl, Volcan 131 K8
Popokabaka 106 C4
Popoli 69 D4
Popomanaseu, Mount 114 K6
Popondetta 114 D3
Porbandar 92 C4
Porcher Island 118 J5
Porcuna 66 D4
Porcupine 118 G2
Pordenone 68 D3
Pordim 73 H4
Pore 136 C2
Porec 72 B3
Pori 63 J6
Porirua 115 E4
Porjus 62 H3
Porkhov 63 N8
Porlakshofn 62 U13
Porlamar 136 E1
Porlock 52 D3
Porlock Bay 52 D3
Pornic 65 B5
Porog *Russia* 78 F3
Porog *Russia* 78 K3
Poronaysk 85 Q7
Poros *Greece* 75 G4
Poros *Greece* 75 G4
Porosozero 78 E3
Porozhsk 78 J3
Porozovo 71 L2
Porpoise Bay 141 J5
Porrentury 68 A2
Porsangen 62 L1
Porsanger-halvoya 62 L1
Porsgrunn 63 C7
porshofn 62 X11
Porsuk 76 D3
Porsuk Baraji 76 D3
Porsyakha 84 A3
Portachuelo 138 D3
Portadown 58 K4
Portaferry 58 L4
Portage 124 F5
Portage la Prairie 119 R5
Portal 123 N3
Port Alberni 122 B3
Port Albert 113 K6
Portalegre 66 C3
Portales 127 L3
Port Alfred 108 E6
Port Alice 122 A2
Port Angeles 122 C3
Port Antonio 132 J5
Portarlington 59 H6
Port Arthur *Australia* 113 K7
Port Arthur *U.S.A.* 128 F6
Port Askaig 57 B5
Port Augusta 113 H5
Port-au-Prince 133 L5
Port Austin 124 J4
Portavogie 58 M4
Port-Berge 109 J3
Port Blair 93 H6
Portboil 53 N7
Port Burwell 121 P5
Port Cartier 121 N7
Port Chalmers 115 C6
Port Charlotte 129 L7
Port Clarence 118 B2
Port Clinton 124 J6
Port Coquitlam 122 C3
Port Darwin 139 E10
Port-de-Paix 133 L5
Port Dickson 90 C5
Portel 66 C3
Port Elgin 125 K4
Port Elizabeth 108 E6
Port Ellen 57 C5
Port Erin 54 E2
Porterville 126 C2
Port-Eynon 52 C3
Port Francqui 106 D3
Port Gentil 106 A3
Port Glasgow 57 F4
Port Harcourt 105 G5
Port Hardy 118 K5
Porthcawl 52 D3
Port Heiden 118 D4
Port Herald 107 G6
Porthleven 52 B4
Porthmadog 52 C2
Porth Neigwl 52 C2
Port Huron 124 J5
Port Il'ich 94 J2
Portimao 66 B4
Port Isaac 52 C4
Port Isaac Bay 52 C4
Portishead 52 E3
Port Jackson 113 L5
Port Jervis 125 N6
Port Kaituma 136 F2
Port Kembla 113 L5
Port Kenney 113 G5
Portknockie 56 F3
Port Lairge 59 H8
Portland *Australia* 113 J6
Portland *New Zealand* 115 E1
Portland *Indiana* 124 H6
Portland *Maine* 125 Q5
Portland *Oregon* 122 C5
Portland Bay 113 J6
Portland, Bill of 52 E4
Portland, Cape 113 K7
Portland, Isle of 52 E4
Portland Point 132 J6
Portland Promontory 121 L6
Port Laoise 59 H6
Port Lavaca 128 D6
Port-Leucate 65 E7
Port Lincoln 113 H5
Portlock Reefs 114 C3
Port Loko 104 C4
Port Louis 109 L7
Port McArthur 113 H2
Port Macquarie 113 L5
Port Menier 121 P8
Port Moresby 114 D3
Portnacroish 57 C4
Portnahaven 57 B5
Port Nelson 119 S4
Port Nolloth 108 C5
Portnyagino, Ozero 84 H2
Porto 66 B2
Porto Alegre 138 F4
Porto Alexandre 106 B6
Porto Amboim 106 B5
Porto Camargo 138 F4
Porto d'Ascoli 69 D4
Porto dos Gauchos 137 F6
Porto Esperanca 138 E3
Porto Esperidiao 138 E3
Portoferraio 69 C4
Port-of-Spain 136 E1
Porto Grande 137 G3
Portogruaro 68 D3
Porto Lucena 138 F5
Portom 62 J5
Portomaggiore 68 C3
Porto Nacional 138 H6
Porto Novo *Benin* 105 F4
Porto Novo *Cape Verde* 104 L7
Port Orford 122 B6
Porto San Stefano 69 C4
Porto Sao Jose 138 F4
Porto Seguro 137 K7
Porto Socompa 138 C4
Porto Tolle 68 D3
Porto Torres 69 B5
Porto-Vecchio 69 B5
Porto Velho 136 E5
Portoviejo 136 A4
Portpatrick 54 D2
Port Pegasus 115 A7
Port Phillip Bay 113 J6
Port Pirie 113 H5
Portraine 59 K6
Portreath 52 B4
Portree 56 B3
Portrush 58 J2
Port Said 103 F1
Port Saint Joe 129 K6
Port Saint Johns 108 E6
Port-Saint-Louis 65 F7
Port Sandwich 114 T12
Port Saunders 121 Q7
Port Shepstone 108 F6
Portskerra 56 E2
Portsmouth *U.K.* 53 F4
Portsmouth *New Hampshire* 125 Q5
Portsmouth *Ohio* 124 J7
Portsmouth *Virginia* 125 M8
Portsoy 56 F3
Port Stephens 113 L5
Portstewart 58 J2
Port Sudan 103 G4
Port Talbot 52 D3
Porttipahdan tekojarvi 62 M2
Port Townsend 122 C3
Portugal 66 B3
Portuguesa 136 D2
Portumna 59 F6
Port Washington 124 G5
Port William 54 E2
Porvenir *Bolivia* 136 D6
Porvenir *Chile* 139 B10
Porvoo 63 L6
Posadas 138 E5
Posen 71 G2
Poshekhonye Volodarsk 78 F4
Posht-e Badam 95 M5
Poso 91 G6
Posof 77 K2
Post 127 M4
Postavy 63 M9
Poste Weygand 100 F4
Postmasburg 108 D5
Postojna 72 C3
Posusje 72 D4
Posyet 88 C4
Potamia 75 F4
Potamos 75 G4
Potapovo 84 D3
Potchefstroom 108 E5
Poteau 128 E3
Potenza 69 E5
Potes 66 D1
Potgietersrus 108 E4
Poti 77 J1
Potiskum 105 H3
Potlogi 73 H3
Potnarvin 114 U13
Potomac 125 M7
Potosi 138 C3
Potsdam *U.S.A.* 125 N4
Potsdam *Germany* 70 E2
Pott 114 V15
Potters Bar 53 G3
Pottstown 125 N6
Pottsville 125 M6
Pouebo 114 W16
Poughkeepsie 125 P6
Poulaphouca Reservoir 59 J6
Poulter 55 H3
Poulton-le-Fylde 55 G3
Poundstock 52 C4
Pouso Alegre 138 G4
Pouzauges 65 C5
Povenets 78 E3
Poverty Bay 115 G3
Povorino 79 G5
Povungnituk 121 L6
Povungnituk Bay 121 L6
Powder 123 M5
Powell 123 K5
Powell, Lake 126 F2
Powell River 122 B3
Power Head 59 F9
Powys 52 D2
Poya 114 W16
Poyang Hu 87 M6
Poyraz 77 H3
Poysdorf 68 F1
Poytya 63 K6
Pozanti 76 F4
Pozarevac 73 F3
Poza Rica 131 L7
Pozharskoye 88 E2
Poznan 71 G2
Pozoblanco 66 D3
Pozohondo 67 F3
Pozzuoli 69 E5
Prabumulih 90 D6
Prachin Buri 93 K6
Prachuap Khiri Khan 93 J6
Praded 71 G3
Pradelles 65 E6
Prades 65 E7
Prague 70 F3
Praha 70 F3
Prahova 73 H3
Praia 104 L7
Prainha *Amazonas, Brazil* 136 E5
Prainha *Para, Brazil* 137 G4
Prairie Dog Town Fork 127 L3
Prairie du Chien 124 E5
Prairies, Coteau des 124 C5
Prairie Village 124 C7
Prapat 90 B5
Prasonisi, Akra 75 J5

Prasto 63 E9
Prata 138 G3
Prato 68 C4
Pratt 127 N2
Pravets 73 G4
Pravia 66 C1
Predazzo 68 C2
Predcal 73 H3
Predeal, Pasul 73 H3
Predivinsk 84 E5
Predlitz 68 D2
Premer 113 K5
Premuda 72 C3
Prenai 71 K1
Prentice 124 E4
Prenzlau 70 E2
Preobrazhenka 84 H5
Preparis 93 H6
Preparis North Channel 93 H5
Preparis South Channel 93 H6
Prerov 71 G4
Prescot 55 G3
Prescott *Arizona* 126 F3
Prescott *Arkansas* 128 F4
Prescott Island 120 G3
Preseli, Mynydd 52 C3
Preservation Inlet 115 A7
Presevo 73 F4
Presho 123 Q6
Presidencia Roque Saenz Pena 138 D5
Presidente Dutra 137 J4
Presidente Epitacio 138 F4
Presidente Prudente 138 E4
Presidio 127 K6
Preslav 73 J4
Presnovka 84 Ae6
Presov 71 J4
Prespansko Jezero 75 F2
Presque Isle 125 S3
Pressburg 71 G4
Prestatyn 55 F3
Presteigne 52 D2
Preston *U.K.* 55 G3
Preston *Minnesota* 124 D5
Preston *Missouri* 124 D8
Prestonburg 124 J8
Prestonpans 57 F5
Prestwick 57 F4
Pretoria 108 E5
Preveza 75 F3
Prey Veng 93 L6
Pribilof Islands 118 Ad8
Pribinic 72 D3
Pribram 70 F4
Price 126 G1
Price, Cape 93 H6
Prichard 129 H5
Priego 66 E2
Priego de Cordoba 66 D4
Prieska 108 D5
Priest Lake 122 F3
Priest River 122 F3
Prievidza 71 H4
Prignitz 70 D2
Prijedor 72 D3
Prikaspiyskaya Nizmennost 79 J6
Prilep 73 F5
Priluki *Russia* 78 G3
Priluki *Ukraine* 79 E5
Primavera 141 V6
Primorsk *Azerbaijan* 79 H7
Primorsk *Ukraine* 79 F6
Primorsk *Russia* 79 H6
Primorsk *Russia* 63 N6
Primorskiy Kray 88 E3
Primorsko 73 J4
Primorsko-Akhtarsk 79 F6
Primrose Lake 119 P5
Prince Albert *Canada* 119 P5
Prince Albert *South Africa* 108 D6
Prince Albert Peninsula 119 N1
Prince Albert Road 108 D6
Prince Albert Sound 119 N1
Prince Alfred, Cape 120 B3
Prince Charles Island 120 L4
Prince Charles Mountains 141 E4
Prince Edward Island 121 P8
Prince Edward Islands 142 C6
Prince George 119 L5
Prince Gustav Adolph Sea 120 E2
Prince of Wales, Cape *Canada* 121 M5
Prince of Wales, Cape *U.S.A.* 118 B2
Prince of Wales Island *Australia* 114 C4
Prince of Wales Island *Canada* 120 G3
Prince of Wales Island *U.S.A.* 118 J4
Prince of Wales Strait 119 M1
Prince Patrick Island 120 B2
Prince Regent Inlet 120 H3
Prince Rupert 118 J5
Princes Risborough 53 G3
Princess Astrid Coast 141 A4
Princess Charlotte Bay 113 J1
Princess Elizabeth Land 141 F4
Princess Marie Bay 120 L2
Princethorpe 53 F2
Princeton *Canada* 122 D3
Princeton *Illinois* 124 F6
Princeton *Kentucky* 124 G8
Princeton *Missouri* 124 D6
Princeton *W. Virginia* 125 K8
Prince William Sound 118 F3
Principe 105 G5
Prineville 122 D5
Prins Karls Forland 80 C2
Prinzapolca 132 E8
Priozersk 63 P6
Pripet Marshes 79 D5
Pripyat 71 M2
Pristina 73 F4
Pritzwalk 70 E2
Privas 65 F6
Privolzhskaya Vozvyshennost 79 H5
Prizzi 69 D7
Prnjavor 72 D3
Probolinggo 90 E7
Proddatur 92 E6
Progreso 131 Q7
Prokhladnyy 79 G7
Prokletije 74 E1
Prokopyevsk 84 D6
Prokuplje 73 F4
Proletarsk 79 G6
Prome 93 J5
Proprad 71 J4
Propria 137 K6
Propriano 69 B5
Prorva 79 J6
Prosna 71 G3
Prospect 122 C6
Prosperous 59 J6
Prostejov 71 G4
Provence 65 G7
Providence *Seychelles* 82 D7
Providence *U.S.A.* 125 Q6
Providence, Cape *Canada* 120 D3
Providence, Cape *New Zealand* 115 A7
Providencia 136 B4
Providencia, Isla de 132 G8
Provideniya 81 V3
Provincetown 125 Q5
Provins 64 E4
Provo 122 J7
Prudhoe 55 H2
Prudhoe Bay 118 F1
Prum 70 B3
Pruszkow 71 J2
Prut 73 K2
Prutul 73 J2
Pruzhany 71 L2
Pryazha 78 E3
Prydz Bay 141 F5
Pryor 128 E2
Przechlewo 71 G2
Przemysl 71 K4
Przeworsk 71 K3
Przhevalsk 86 D3
Przysucha 71 J3
Psakhna 75 G3
Psara 75 H3
Pskov 63 Q8
Pskovskoye, Ozero 63 M7
Ptolemals 75 F2
Ptuj 72 C2
Puan 87 P4
Pucallpa 136 C5
Pucarani 138 C3
Pudai 95 R6
Pudasjarvi 62 M4
Puddletown 52 E4
Pudnya 63 N8
Pudozh 78 F3
Pudsey 55 H3
Puduchcheri 92 E6
Pudukkottai 92 E6
Puebla 131 K8
Puebla de Don Rodrigo 66 D3
Puebla de Sanabria 66 C1
Puebla de Trives 66 C1
Pueblo 127 K1
Pueblo Hundido 138 B5
Pueblo Nuevo 136 D1
Puelen 139 C7
Puente Alto 139 C6
Puerto Acosta 138 C3
Puerto Aisen 139 B9
Puerto Asis 136 B3
Puerto Ayacucho 136 D2
Puerto Ayora 136 A7
Puerto Barrios 132 C7
Puerto Cabello 136 D1
Puerto Cabezas 132 F7
Puerto Carreno 136 D2
Puerto Casado 138 E4
Puerto Coig 139 C10
Puerto Cortes *Costa Rica* 132 F10
Puerto Cortes *Honduras* 132 D7
Puerto Cumarebo 136 D1
Puerto del Rosario 100 C3
Puerto de Pollensa 67 H3
Puerto Deseado 139 C9
Puerto Escondido 131 L10
Puerto Estrella 136 C1
Puerto Eten 136 B5
Puerto Guarani 138 E4
Puerto Juarez 131 R7
Puerto La Cruz 136 E1
Puerto-Lapice 66 E3
Puerto Leguizamo 136 C4
Puerto Libertad 126 F6
Puertollano 66 D3
Puerto Lobos 139 C8
Puerto Madryn 139 C8
Puerto Maldonado 136 D6
Puerto Merazan 132 D8
Puerto Montt 139 B8
Puerto Natales 139 B10
Puerto Ordaz 133 R10
Puerto Paez 136 D2
Puerto Penasco 126 F5
Puerto Pico 138 E5
Puerto Plata 133 M5
Puerto Portillo 136 C5
Puerto Princesa 91 F4
Puerto Rey 132 J10
Puerto Rico *Bolivia* 136 D6
Puerto Rico *U.S.A.* 133 P5
Puerto Rico Trench 133 P5
Puerto San Antonio Oeste 139 C8
Puerto Santa Cruz 139 C10
Puerto Sastre 138 E4
Puerto Siles 136 D6
Puerto Suarez 138 E3
Puerto Tejado 136 B3
Puerto Vallarta 130 G7
Puerto Varas 139 B8
Puerto Villazon 136 E6
Puesto Arturo 136 C4
Pueyrredan, Lago 139 B9
Pugachev 79 H5
Pugachevo 88 J1
Pugal 92 D3
Puger 90 E7
Puget-Theniers 65 G7
Pui 73 G3
Puigcerda 67 G1
Pujehun 104 C4
Pukaki, Lake 115 C6
Pukchong 88 B5
Puke 74 E1
Pukekohe 115 E2
Pukeuri 115 C6
Puksa 78 F3
Pula 72 B3
Pular, Cerro 138 C4
Pulaski *New York* 125 M5
Pulaski *Tennessee* 129 J3
Pulaski *Virginia* 125 K8
Pulau Jos Sodarso 114 B3
Pulaupunjung 90 D6
Pulborough 53 G4
Pu-li 87 N7
Pulicat Lake 92 F6
Pulkkila 62 L4
Pullman 122 F4
Pulo Anna 91 J5
Pulog, Mount 91 G2
Pulonga 78 G2
Pulpito, Punta 126 G7
Pultusk 71 J2
Pulumur 77 H3
Pumasillo, Cerro 136 C6
Pumsaint 52 D2
Puna, Isla 136 A4
Punakha 93 G3
Pune 92 D5
Pungsan 88 B5
Punjab 92 E2
Puno 138 B3
Punta Alta 139 D7
Punta Arenas 139 B10
Punta, Cerro de 133 P5
Punta de Diaz 138 B5
Punta Delgada 139 D8
Punta Delgado 139 C10
Punta Gorda 132 C6
Punta Prieta 126 E6
Puntarenas 132 E9
Punta Saavedra 139 B7
Punto Fijo 136 C1
Puolanka 62 M4
Puquio 136 C6
Puquios 138 C5
Pur 84 B3
Pura 84 D2
Purari 114 D3
Purbeck, Isle of 53 E4
Purchena 66 E4
Purdy Islands 114 D2
Purepero 130 J8
Puri 92 G5
Purnia 93 G3
Pursat 93 K6
Purtuniq 120 M5
Puruliya 92 G4
Purus 136 E4
Puruvesi 63 N6
Purwakarta 90 D7
Purwokert 90 D7
Puryong 88 B4
Pusa 63 M8
Pusan 89 B8
Pushkino 94 J2
Pushlakhta 78 F3
Pusht-i-Rud 95 R6
Pustoshka 63 N8
Putao 93 J3
Putaruru 115 E3
Putian 87 M6
Putila 71 L5
Puting, Tanjung 90 E6
Putnok 72 F1
Putorana, Gory 84 F3
Putorino 115 F3
Puttalam 92 E7
Puttgarden 70 D1
Putumayo 136 C4
Putusibau 90 E5
Puulavesi 63 M6
Puuwai 126 Q10
Pu Xian 93 M1
Puyko 84 Ae3
Puyo 136 B4
Puzla 78 J3
Pweto 107 E4
Pwllheli 52 C2
Pyaozero, Ozero 62 P3
Pyapon 93 J5
Pyasina 84 D2
Pyasinado 84 B3
Pyasino, Ozero 84 D3
Pyatigorsk 79 G7
Pygmalion Point 93 H7
Pyhajarvi *Finland* 62 L5
Pyhajarvi *Finland* 62 L5
Pyhajarvi *Turku-Pori, Finland* 63 K6
Pyhajoki 62 L4
Pyhaselka 62 N5
Pyinmana 93 J5
Pylkaram 84 C4
Pyonggok-tong 89 B7
Pyonghae-ri 89 B7
Pyongyang 87 P4
Pyramid Lake 122 E7
Pyrenees 65 D7
Pyrzyce 70 F2
Pytalovo 63 M8

Q

Qaamiyat, Al 97 J7
Qabr Hud 97 J8
Qadimah 96 D5
Qadub 97 P10
Qaemshahr 95 L3
Qagan Tolgoi 87 K4
Qaidam Pendi 93 H1
Qaidam Shan 93 J1
Qaisar 94 S4
Qala Adras Kand 95 R5
Qalaen Nahl 96 B10
Qalamat ar Rakabah 97 L6
Qalamat Faris 97 K6
Qalansiyah 97 P10
Qalat 92 C2
Qalat Bishah 96 F6
Qalat Salih 94 H6
Qalat Sukkar 94 H6
Qala Vali 95 R4
Qaleh-ye Now 95 R4
Qamar, Ghubbat al 97 L8
Qamar, Jabal al 97 L8
Qaminis 101 K2
Qamsar 95 K5
Qandala 103 J5
Qapqal 86 E3
Qarabagh 95 Q4
Qara, Jabal al 97 M8
Qaratshuk 94 F3
Qardho 103 J6
Qareh Aqaj 94 H3
Qareh Su 94 H2
Qareh Su 94 H5
Qarqan He 86 F4
Qarqi 86 F3
Qaryat al Ulya 97 H3
Qasab 77 K4
Qasa Murg 95 S4
Qasr Amij 77 J6
Qasr-e-Qand 95 Q8
Qasr-e-Shirin 94 G4
Qatabah 96 G10
Qatah 77 J5
Qatana 94 C5
Qatar 97 K4
Qatrana 94 C6
Qattara Depression 102 E2
Qattara, Munkhafed el 102 E2
Qayen 95 P5
Qazvin 95 K3
Qeisum 96 A3
Qena 103 F2
Qeshm *Iran* 95 N8
Qeshm *Iran* 95 N8
Qeydar 94 J3
Qeys 95 L8
Qezel Owzan 94 J3
Qeziot 94 B6
Qianan 87 N2
Qianjiang 93 L3
Qianwei 87 N3
Qianxi 93 L3
Qianxinan 93 K3
Qiaowan 86 H3
Qidong *Hunan, China* 93 M3
Qidong *Jiangsu, China* 87 N5
Qiemo 92 G1
Qihe 87 M4
Qihreg 87 L3
Qijiaojing 86 F3
Qikou 87 M4
Qila Ladgasht 92 B3
Qila Saifullah 92 C2
Qilian Shan 86 H4
Qinab, Wadi 97 J8
Qingan 88 A2
Qingdao 87 N4
Qinggang 87 P2
Qinghai 93 J2
Qinghai Hu 93 K1
Qinghai Nanshan 93 J1
Qinghe 88 B2
Qing Xian 87 M4
Qingyang 93 L1
Qingyuan *Liaoning, China* 87 N3
Qingyuan *Zhejiang, China* 87 M6

Name	Page	Grid
Qinhuangdao	87	M4
Qin Ling	93	L2
Qinshui	93	M1
Qin Xian	87	L4
Qinyuan	87	L4
Qinzhou	93	L4
Qionglai	93	K2
Qionglai Shan	93	K2
Qiongzhong	93	L5
Qiongzhou Haixia	93	L4
Qiqihar	87	N2
Qir	95	L7
Qishn	97	K9
Qishran	96	E6
Qitai	86	F3
Qitaihe	87	Q2
Qitbit, Wadi	97	M7
Qixing He	88	D2
Qixingpao	88	C2
Qiyang	93	M3
Qizil Bulak	95	Q4
Qojur	94	H3
Qolleh-ye Damavand	95	L4
Qom	95	K4
Qomisheh	95	K5
Qomolangma Feng	92	G3
Qornetes Saouda	94	B4
Qorveh	94	H4
Qotbabad	95	N8
Qotur *Iran*	77	L3
Qotur *Iran*	77	L3
Quaidabad	92	D2
Quairading	112	D5
Quakenbruck	70	B2
Quanah	127	N3
Quang Ngai	93	L5
Quang Tri	93	L5
Quang Yen	93	L4
Quan Long	93	L7
Quannan	87	L7
Quan Phu Quoc	93	K6
Quantock Hills	52	D3
Quanzhou *Fujian, China*	87	M7
Quanzhou *Guangxi, China*	93	M3
Qu'Appelle	123	N2
Quaqtaq	121	N5
Quarai *Brazil*	138	E6
Quarai *Brazil*	138	E6
Quartu San Elena	69	B6
Quartzsite	126	E4
Quatsino Sound	122	A2
Quayti	97	J9
Quchan	95	P3
Qudaym	77	H5
Queanbeyan	113	K6
Quebec *Canada*	121	L7
Quebec *Canada*	125	Q3
Quedal, Cabo de	139	B8
Queen Bess, Mount	122	B2
Queen, Cape	120	L5
Queen Charlotte Islands	118	J5
Queen Charlotte Sound	118	K5
Queen Charlotte Strait	118	K5
Queen Elizabeth Islands	120	G2
Queen Mary Land	141	G4
Queen Maud Gulf	119	Q2
Queen Maud Land	141	A4
Queen Maud Mountains	141	N1
Queensbury	55	H3
Queens Channel	112	F1
Queensferry *Clwyd, U.K.*	55	F3
Queensferry *Lothian, U.K.*	57	E5
Queensland	113	J3
Queenstown *Australia*	113	K7
Queenstown *New Zealand*	115	B6
Queenstown *South Africa*	108	E6
Queija, Sierra de	66	C1
Queimadas	137	K6
Quela	106	C4
Quelimane	109	G3
Quelpart Island	87	P5
Quemado	127	H3
Quembo	106	C5
Quepos	132	E10
Que Que	108	E3
Queretaro	131	J7
Queshan	93	M2
Quesnel	119	L5
Quesnel Lake	119	L5
Quetena	138	C4
Quetta	92	C2
Quettehou	64	C4
Quevedo	136	B4
Quezaltenango	132	B7
Quezon City	91	G3
Quibala	106	B5
Quibaxi	106	B4
Quibdo	136	B2
Quiberon	65	B5
Quiberon, Baie de	65	B5
Quilengues	106	B5
Quillabamba	136	C6
Quillacollo	138	C3
Quillagua	138	C4
Quillan	65	E7
Quill Lakes	123	M2
Quillota	139	B6
Quilon	92	E7
Quilpie	113	J4
Quimbele	106	C4
Quimper	64	A4
Quimperle	65	B5
Quinag	56	C2
Quince Mil	136	C6
Quincy *California*	122	D8
Quincy *Illinois*	124	E7
Quincy *Massachusetts*	125	Q5
Quines	139	C6
Qui Nhon	93	L6
Quintanar de la Orden	66	E3
Quintero	139	B6
Quipungo	106	B5
Quiroga	66	C1
Quissanga	109	H2
Quita Sueno Bank	132	G7
Quito	136	B4
Quixada	137	K4
Qu Jiang	93	L2
Qujing	93	K3
Qulban Layyah	94	H7
Qumarleb	93	J2
Qumbu	108	E6
Qunayfidhah, Nafud	96	G4
Quoin Point	108	C6
Quorn	113	H5
Quorndon	53	F2
Quru Gol Pass	94	G2
Qus	103	F2
Quseir	103	F2
Qutiabad	94	J4
Qutu	96	E7
Quzhou	87	M6

R

Name	Page	Grid
Raab *Austria*	68	E2
Raab *Hungary*	72	D2
Raahe	62	L4
Raakkyla	62	N5
Raanes Peninsula	120	J2
Raanujarvi	62	L3
Raasay	56	B3
Raasay, Sound of	56	B3
Rab	72	C3
Raba	72	D2
Raba *Indonesia*	91	F7
Raba *Poland*	71	H4
Rabastens	65	D7
Rabat *Morocco*	100	D4
Rabat *Turkey*	77	J2
Rabaul	114	E2
Rabi	114	S8
Rabigh	96	D5
Rabor	95	N7
Rabyanah, Ramlat	101	K4
Race, Cape	121	R8
Rach Gia	93	L6
Raciborz	71	H3
Racine	124	G5
Rackwick	56	E2
Racoon	124	C5
Racoon Mountains	129	J3
Rada	96	G9
Radauti	73	H2
Radcliff	124	H8
Radde	88	C1
Radekhov	71	L3
Radford	125	K8
Radisson	121	L7
Radna	73	F2
Radnice	70	E4
Radnor Forest	52	D2
Radom	71	J3
Radomsko	71	H3
Radomyshl	79	D5
Radovis	73	G5
Radstadt	68	D2
Radstock	52	E3
Radstock, Cape	113	G5
Radzyn Podlaski	71	K3
Rae	119	M2
Rae Bareli	92	F3
Rae Isthmus	120	J4
Raetihi	115	E3
Rafaela	138	D6
Rafai	102	D6
Rafalovka	71	L3
Rafha	96	F2
Rafsanjan	95	M6
Raga	102	E6
Ragged Cays	133	K3
Raghtin More	58	H2
Raglan Harbour	115	E2
Ragusa *Croatia*	72	E4
Ragusa *Italy*	69	E7
Rahad	96	B10
Rahat, Harrat	96	E5
Rahimyar Khan	92	D3
Rahuri	92	D5
Raichur	92	E5
Raigarh *Madhya Pradesh, India*	92	F4
Raigarh *Orissa, India*	92	F5
Rainbow City	129	J4
Rainham	53	H3
Rainier, Mount	122	D4
Rainy	124	C2
Rainy Lake	124	D2
Raippaluoto	62	J5
Raipur	92	F4
Raisduoddarhaldde	62	J2
Raistakka	62	N3
Rajada	137	J5
Rajahmundry	92	F5
Rajanpur	92	D3
Rajapalaiyam	92	E7
Rajapur	92	D5
Rajasthan	92	D3
Rajasthan Canal	92	D3
Rajgarh	92	E4
Rajgrod	71	K2
Rajkot	92	D4
Rajmahal Hills	93	G4
Raj Nandgaon	92	F4
Rajpipla	92	D4
Rajshahi	92	G4
Rakaia	115	C5
Rakan, Ra's	97	K3
Rakbah, Sahl	96	E5
Raketskjutfalt	62	J2
Rakhes	75	G3
Rakhov	79	C6
Rakhovo	71	L4
Rakitnoye	88	E3
Rakkestad	63	D7
Rakops	108	D4
Rakov	71	M2
Rakusha	79	J6
Rakvere	63	M7
Raleigh	129	N3
Rama	132	E8
Ramallah	94	B6
Ramasaig	56	B3
Rambi	114	S8
Rambouillet	64	D4
Rambutyo Island	114	D2
Ramdurg	92	E5
Rameco	139	D7
Rame Head	52	C4
Rameswaram	92	E7
Ramgarh	92	F4
Ram, Jambal	96	B2
Ramor, Lough	58	H5
Ramos	130	G5
Ramos Island	114	K6
Rampart	118	E2
Rampur	92	E3
Ramree	93	H5
Ramsbottom	55	G3
Ramsele	62	G5
Ramsey *Cambridgeshire, U.K.*	53	G2
Ramsey *Essex, U.K.*	53	J3
Ramsey *Isle of Man, U.K.*	54	E2
Ramsey Bay	54	E2
Ramsey Island	52	B3
Ramsgate	53	J3
Ramsjo	63	F5
Ramtha	94	C5
Ramu	114	C3
Ramvik	62	G5
Ranau	90	F4
Rancagua	139	J6
Rance	64	B4
Rancha Cordova	126	B1
Ranchi	92	G4
Rancho California	126	D4
Randalstown	58	K3
Randazzo	69	E7
Randers	63	D8
Randolph	123	R6
Randsfjord	63	D6
Ranea	62	K4
Ranfurly	115	C6
Rangas, Tanjung	91	F6
Rangiora	115	D5
Rangitaiki	115	F3
Rangitata	115	C5
Rangkasbitung	90	D7
Rangkul	86	C4
Rangoon (Yangon)	93	J5
Rangpur	93	G3
Rangsang	90	C5
Ranibennur	92	E6
Raniganj	93	G4
Ranken	113	H3
Rankin Inlet *Canada*	119	S3
Rankin Inlet *Canada*	119	S3
Rankins Springs	113	K5
Rannoch Moor	57	D4
Rannoch, Loch	57	D4
Ranon	114	U12
Ranongga	114	H5
Ransiki	91	J6
Ranskill	55	H3
Rantau *Kalimantan, Indonesia*	90	F6
Rantau *Sumatera, Indonesia*	90	C5
Rantauprapat	90	B5
Rantoul	124	F6
Ranya	94	G3
Raohe	88	D2
Raon-l'Etape	64	G4
Raoul	111	T7
Rapallo	68	B3
Raper, Cape	120	N4
Rapid City	123	N5
Rapla	63	L7
Rapli	92	F3
Rapness	56	F1
Rappahannock	125	M7
Rapperswil	68	B2
Rapsani	75	G3
Rapulo	136	D6
Rapur	92	E6
Ras al Ayn	77	J4
Ras al Khafji	97	J2
Ra's al Khaymah	97	M4
Rasa, Punta	139	D8
Ras Dashen	96	D10
Raseiniai	63	K9
Ras el Ma	100	E5
Ras en Naqb	94	B6
Rashad	102	F5
Rasharkin	58	K3
Rashid	102	F1
Rasht	95	J3
Rask	95	Q8
Raska	72	F4
Raso, Cabo	139	C8
Rason, Lake	112	E4
Rasshua, Ostrov	85	S7
Rasskazovo	79	G5
Rassokha	84	H2
Rastenburg	71	J1
Rastigaissa	62	M1
Rasul	95	M8
Ratangarh	92	D3
Rat Buri	93	J6
Rathangan	59	J6
Rathcoole	59	K6
Rathdowney	59	G7
Rathdrum	59	K7
Rathen	56	F3
Rathenow	70	E2
Rathfriland	58	K4
Rathkeale	59	E7
Rathlin Island	58	K2
Rathlin Sound	58	K2
Rathluirc	59	E8
Rathmore	59	D8
Rathnew	59	K7
Rathoath	59	K5
Ratibor	71	H3
Ratisbon	70	E4
Rat Islands	118	Ab9
Ratlam	92	E4
Ratnagiri	92	D5
Ratnapura	92	F7
Ratno	79	C5
Raton	127	K2
Ratta	84	C4
Rattray	57	E4
Rattray Head	56	G3
Rattvik	63	F6
Ratzeburg	70	D2
Ratz, Mount	118	J4
Rauch	139	E7
Rauchua	85	V3
Raudales	131	N9
Raudhatain	97	H2
Raufarhofn	62	X11
Raufoss	63	D6
Raukumara Range	115	F3
Raul Leoni, Represa	133	R11
Rauma	63	J6
Raung, Gunung	90	F7
Raurkela	92	F4
Rausu	88	K3
Ravansar	94	H4
Ravar	95	N6
Rava Russkaya	79	C5
Ravenglass	55	F2
Ravenna	68	D3
Ravenscar	55	J2
Ravensthorpe	112	E5
Ravenstonedale	55	G2
Ravenswood	125	K7
Ravensworth	55	H2
Ravi	92	D2
Ravno	72	E3
Rawa	93	J3
Rawah	77	J5
Rawaki	111	U2
Rawalpindi	92	D2
Rawandiz	94	G3
Rawcliffe	55	J3
Rawdah	77	J5
Rawicz	71	G3
Rawlinna	112	F5
Rawlins	123	L7
Rawmarsh	55	H3
Rawson	139	C8
Rawtenstall	55	G3
Ray	53	F3
Rayachoti	92	E6
Rayadurg	92	E6
Rayagarha	92	F5
Rayakoski	62	N2
Ray, Cape	121	Q8
Raychikhinsk	85	M7
Rayen	95	N7
Rayeskiy	78	J5
Rayleigh	53	H3
Raymondville	128	D7
Ray Mountains	118	E2
Raysut	97	L8
Razan	94	J5
Razan	94	J4
Razdelnaya	79	E6
Razdolnoye	88	C4
Razgrad	73	J4
Razmak	92	C2
Raznas Ezers	63	M8
Raz, Pointe du	64	A4
Reading *U.K.*	53	G3
Reading *U.S.A.*	125	N6
Realico	139	D7
Rea, Lough	59	E6
Rearsby	53	F2
Reawick	56	A2
Rebecca, Lake	112	E5
Rebi	91	J7
Reboly	62	P5
Rebrikha	84	C6

Rebrovo 73 G4
Rebun-to 88 H3
Recanati 68 D4
Recea 73 G3
Recherche, Archipelago
of the 112 E5
Rechitsa 79 E5
Rechna Doab 92 D2
Recife 137 L5
Recklinghausen 70 B3
Recknitz 70 E2
Reconquista 138 E5
Recreio 136 F5
Red *Canada* 123 R2
Red *U.S.A.* 128 F5
Redalen 63 D6
Red Bay 121 Q7
Redbird 123 M6
Red Bluff 122 C7
Red Bluff Lake 127 L5
Redcar 55 H2
Redcliffe 113 L4
Red Cloud 123 Q7
Red Deer *Canada* 122 G2
Red Deer *Canada* 122 H1
Red Deer *Canada* 123 J2
Red Deer *Saskatchewan,*
Canada 119 Q5
Redding 122 C7
Redditch 53 F2
Redencao 137 J5
Redfield 123 Q5
Redhakhol 92 F4
Redhill 53 G3
Red Hills 127 N2
Red Lake *Canada* 123 S2
Red Lake *Canada* 123 T2
Red Lake *U.S.A.* 124 C3
Red Lake *U.S.A.* 123 R4
Red Lodge 123 K5
Redmond 122 D5
Redon 65 B5
Redondela 66 B1
Redondo 66 C3
Red Rock 124 F2
Redruth 52 B4
Red Sea 103 G3
Red Tank 113 K5
Red Wharf Bay 54 E3
Red Wing 124 D4
Redwood City 126 A2
Reed City 124 H5
Reedsport 122 B6
Ree, Lough 58 G5
Reetton 115 C5
Refahiye 77 H3
Refresco 138 C5
Rega 70 F2
Regen 70 E4
Regensburg 70 E4
Reggane 100 F3
Reggio di Calabria 69 E6
Reggio nell Amelia 68 C3
Regina *Brazil* 137 G3
Regina *Canada* 123 M2
Reguengos de Monsaraz 66 C3
Rehna 70 D2
Rehoboth 108 C4
Rehoboth Beach 125 N7
Rehovot 94 B6
Reidh, Rubha 56 C3
Reidsville 129 N2
Reiff 56 C2
Reigate 53 G3
Reighton 55 J2
Re, Île de 65 C5
Reims 64 F4
Reina Adelaida, Archipielago
de la 139 B10
Reindeer Lake 119 Q4
Reine 62 E3
Reinga, Cape 115 D1
Reinheimen 62 B5
Reinosa 66 D1
Reitz 108 E5
Relizane 100 F1
Remada 101 H2
Rembang 90 E7
Remeshk 95 P8
Remiremont 65 G4
Remontnoye 79 G6
Remoulins 65 F7
Remscheid 70 B3
Rena *Norway* 63 D6
Rena *Norway* 63 D6
Renaix 64 E3
Renard Islands 114 E4
Rendova Island 114 H6
Rendsburg 70 C1
Renfrew *Canada* 125 M4
Renfrew *U.K.* 57 D5
Rengat 90 D6
Rengo 139 B6
Renish Point 56 B3
Renk 103 F5
Renmark 113 J5
Renmin 87 P2
Rennell Island 114 K7
Rennes 64 C4
Reno *Italy* 68 C3
Reno *U.S.A.* 122 E8
Reo 91 G7
Repetek 95 R2
Repolovo 84 Ae4

Republican 123 R7
Repulse Bay *Australia* 113 K3
Repulse Bay *Canada* 120 J4
Requena *Peru* 136 C5
Requena *Spain* 67 F3
Rere 114 K6
Resadiye *Turkey* 76 B4
Resadiye *Turkey* 77 G2
Resen 73 F5
Resia, Passo de 68 C2
Resistencia 138 E5
Resita 73 F3
Resolution Island *Canada* 121 P5
Resolution Island *New*
Zealand 115 A6
Resolution Lake 121 P6
Restigouche 125 S3
Retalhuleu 132 B7
Rethel 64 F4
Rethimnon 75 H5
Retiche, Alpi 68 C2
Retsag 72 E2
Retuerta de Bullaque 66 D3
Reunion 109 L7
Reus 67 G2
Reuss 68 B2
Reut 73 J2
Reutlingen 70 C4
Revel 65 D7
Revelstoke 122 E2
Reventador, Volcan 136 B4
Revillagigedo Island 118 J5
Revillagigedo, Islas 130 D8
Rewa 92 F4
Rewari 92 E3
Rexburg 122 J6
Reyes, Point 122 C9
Reyhanli 77 G4
Rey, Isla del 132 H10
Reykjaheidi 62 W12
Reykjahhd 62 W12
Reykjanesta 62 T13
Reykjavik 62 U12
Reynivellir *Iceland* 62 U12
Reynivellir *Iceland* 62 W12
Reynosa 128 C7
Rezekne 63 M8
Rhatikon Pratigau 68 B2
Rhayader 52 D2
Rheda-Wiedenbruck 70 C3
Rhee 53 G2
Rhein 70 B3
Rheine 70 B2
Rhewl 55 F3
Rhiconich 56 D2
Rhine 64 G4
Rhinelander 124 F4
Rhino Camp 107 F2
Rhir, Cap 100 D2
Rho 68 B3
Rhode Island 125 Q6
Rhodes 75 J4
Rhodopi Planina 73 G4
Rhondda 52 D3
Rhone 65 F7
Rhoose 52 D3
Rhosneigr 55 E3
Rhuddlan 55 F3
Rhum 57 B3
Rhum, Sound of 57 B4
Rhydaman 52 C3
Rhyl 55 F3
Rhynie 56 F3
Riachao do Jacuipe 138 K6
Riacho de Santana 138 J6
Riano 66 D1
Riansares 66 E3
Riau, Kepulauan 90 C5
Riaza 66 E2
Ribadeo 66 C1
Ribadesella 66 D1
Ribas do Rio Pardo 138 F4
Ribat 95 R5
Ribatejo 66 B3
Ribble 55 G2
Ribe 63 C9
Ribeirao Preto 138 G4
Ribeiro do Pombal 137 K6
Riberac 65 D6
Riberalta 136 D6
Ribnica 72 C3
Ribnitz-Damgarten 70 E1
Riccall 55 H3
Rice Lake *Canada* 125 L4
Rice Lake *U.S.A.* 124 E4
Richard Collinson Inlet 119 N1
Richards Island 118 H2
Richardson 128 D4
Richardson Mountains 118 H2
Richelieu 125 P4
Richfield 126 F1
Richland 122 E4
Richlands 125 K8
Richmond *Australia* 113 J3
Richmond *New Zealand* 115 D4
Richmond *South Africa* 108 D6
Richmond *Greater London,*
U.K. 53 G3
Richmond *North Yorkshire,*
U.K. 55 H2
Richmond *Indiana* 124 H7
Richmond *Kentucky* 124 H8
Richmond *Virginia* 125 M8
Richmond Range 115 D4

Rickmansworth 53 G3
Ricla 67 F2
Ricobayo, Embalse de 66 D2
Ridgecrest 126 D3
Ridgeland 129 M4
Ridgway 125 L6
Riding Mountain 123 P2
Ridsdale 57 F5
Ried 68 D1
Rienza 68 C2
Riesa 70 E3
Riesco, Isla 139 B10
Rietfontein 108 D4
Rieti 69 D4
Rifle 123 L8
Rifstangi 62 W11
Riga 63 L8
Riga, Gulf of 63 K8
Rigan 95 P7
Rigistan 92 B2
Rigolet 121 Q7
Rihab, Ar 94 G6
Rihand 92 F4
Riiser-Larsen Sea 141 B5
Rijeka 72 C3
Rika 71 K4
Rika, Wadi al 96 G5
Rimah, Wadi al 96 E3
Rimal, Ar 97 L6
Rimavska Sobota 71 J4
Rimbo 63 H7
Rimini 68 D3
Rimna 73 J3
Rimnicu Sarat 73 J3
Rimnicu Vilcea 73 H3
Rimouski 125 R2
Rinca 91 F7
Rinchinlhumbe 86 H1
Ringe 63 D9
Ringebu 63 D6
Ringgold Isles 114 S8
Ringkobing 63 C8
Ringkobing Fjord 63 C9
Ringmer 53 H4
Ringselet 62 L3
Ringvassoy 62 H2
Ringwood 53 F4
Rinia 75 H4
Rinjani, Gunung 90 F7
Rinns Point 57 B5
Riobamba 136 B4
Rio Branco *Brazil* 136 D5
Rio Branco *Uruguay* 138 F6
Rio Bravo 128 D8
Rio Bueno 139 B8
Rio Caribe 136 E1
Rio Claro 136 E1
Rio Colorado 139 D7
Rio Cuarto 138 D6
Rio de Janeiro *Brazil* 138 H4
Rio de Janeiro *Brazil* 138 H4
Rio de Oro, Baie de 100 B4
Rio Gallegos 139 C10
Rio Grande *Argentina* 139 C10
Rio Grande *Brazil* 138 F6
Rio Grande *U.S.A.* 130 H6
Rio Grande City 128 C7
Rio Grande de Santiago 130 G7
Rio Grande do Norte 137 K5
Rio Grande do Sul 138 F5
Riohacha 136 C1
Rio Hato 132 G10
Rio Lagartos 131 Q7
Riom 65 E6
Riom-es-Montagnes 65 E6
Rio Mulatos 138 C3
Rionegro 136 C2
Rio Negro *Brazil* 138 G5
Rio Negro *Spain* 66 C1
Rio Negro, Embalse del 138 E6
Rio Negro, Pantanal do 138 E3
Rioni 77 J1
Rio Pardo de Minas 138 H3
Rio Primero 138 D6
Rio Sao Goncalo 138 H4
Riosucio *Colombia* 136 B2
Riosucio *Colombia* 136 B2
Rio Verde 138 F3
Ripley *Ohio* 124 J7
Ripley *Tennessee* 128 H3
Ripley *W. Virginia* 125 K7
Ripoll 67 H1
Ripon 55 H2
Ripponden 55 H3
Risca 52 D3
Rishiri-to 88 H3
Rishon le Zion 94 B6
Risle 64 D4
Risor 63 C7
Risoyhamn 62 F2
Ritchie's Archipelago 93 H6
Ritter, Mount 122 E9
Ritzville 122 E4
Riva 68 C3
Rivas 132 E9
Rivera 138 E6
River Falls 124 D4
Riverina 113 K5
Riversdale 108 D6
Riverside 126 D4
Riverton *Australia* 113 H5
Riverton *Canada* 123 R2
Riverton *New Zealand* 115 B7
Riverton *U.S.A.* 123 K6

Riviere-du-Loup 125 R3
Rivne 79 D5
Rivoli 68 A3
Riwaka 115 D4
Riwoqe 93 J2
Riyan 97 J9
Rize 77 J2
Rizhskiy Zaliv 63 K8
Rizokarpaso 76 F5
Rjukan 63 C7
Rjuven 63 B7
Roa 66 E2
Road Town 133 Q5
Roan Fell 57 F5
Roanne 65 F5
Roanoke *N. Carolina* 129 P2
Roanoke *Virginia* 125 L8
Roanoke Rapids 129 P2
Roan Plateau 123 K8
Robat 95 R6
Robat Karim 95 K4
Robat Thand 95 Q7
Robel 70 E2
Robert Brown, Cape 120 K4
Roberton 57 E5
Robertsbridge 53 H4
Robertsfors 62 J4
Robert S. Kerr Reservoir 128 E3
Robertson Range 112 E3
Robertsport 104 C4
Roberval 125 P2
Robinson 124 G7
Robinson Ranges 112 D4
Robledo 66 C2
Robledollano 66 D3
Robles La Paz 136 C1
Roblin 123 P2
Robore 138 E3
Rob Roy Island 114 H5
Robson, Mount 119 M5
Roca, Cabo da 66 B3
Roca Partida, Isla 130 C8
Roca Partida, Punta 131 M8
Roccella Ionica 69 F6
Rocha 139 F6
Rocha da Gale, Barragem 66 C4
Rochdale 55 G3
Rochechouart 65 D6
Rochefort 65 C6
Rochelle 124 F6
Rochester *Kent, U.K.* 53 H3
Rochester *Northumberland, U.K.* 57 F5
Rochester *New Hamshire* 125 Q5
Rochester *New York* 125 M5
Rochester *Winconsin* 124 D4
Rochford 53 H3
Rochfortbridge 59 H6
Rock 124 F5
Rockefeller Plateau 141 R3
Rock Falls 124 F6
Rockford 124 F5
Rockglen 123 L3
Rockhampton 113 L3
Rockingham *Australia* 112 D5
Rockingham *U.S.A.* 129 N3
Rockingham Bay 113 K2
Rock Island 124 E6
Rockland *Maine* 125 R4
Rockland *Michigan* 124 F3
Rock Springs *Montana* 123 L4
Rock Springs *Wyoming* 123 K7
Rockwood 125 R4
Rocky Ford 127 L1
Rocky Mount 129 P3
Rocky Mountain House 119 N5
Rocky Mountains 116 G3
Rocroi 64 F4
Rodberg 63 C6
Rodby 63 D9
Rodeby 63 F8
Rodel 56 B3
Roden 52 E2
Rodez 65 E6
Rodhos *Greece* 75 J4
Rodhos *Greece* 75 K4
Rodi Garganico 69 E5
Roding 53 H3
Rodinga 113 G3
Rodna 73 H2
Rodnei, Muntii 73 H2
Rodney, Cape *New Zealand* 115 E2
Rodney, Cape *U.S.A.* 118 B3
Rodonit, Kep i 74 E2
Rodosto 76 B2
Roebuck Bay 112 E2
Roermond 64 F3
Roeselare 64 E3
Roes Welcome Sound 120 J5
Rogachev 79 E5
Rogaland 63 B7
Rogatin 71 L4
Rogers 128 E2
Rogers, Mount 125 K8
Roggeveld Berge 108 D6
Rogliano 68 B4
Rognan 62 F3
Rogozno 71 G2
Rohri 92 C3
Rohtak 92 E3
Rois Bheinn 57 C3
Rojas 139 D6
Rojo, Cabo *Mexico* 131 L7
Rojo, Cabo *U.S.A.* 133 P6
Rokan 90 C5

Name	Page	Grid
Rokel	104	C4
Rokiskis	63	L9
Rolla	124	E8
Rolleston	113	K3
Roma *Australia*	113	K4
Roma *Italy*	69	D5
Roma *Sweden*	63	H8
Romain, Cape	129	N4
Romaine	121	P7
Romaldkirk	55	G2
Roman	73	J2
Romang	91	H7
Romania	73	G3
Romano, Cape	129	M8
Romanovka	85	J6
Romans-sur-Isere	65	F6
Romanzof, Cape	118	B3
Romao	136	E4
Romblon	91	G3
Rome *Italy*	69	D5
Rome *U.S.A.*	129	K3
Romerike	63	D6
Romilly	64	E4
Romney	125	L7
Romny	79	E5
Romo	63	C9
Romorantin	65	D5
Romsey	53	F4
Rona	56	C3
Ronay	56	A3
Roncador, Cayos	132	G8
Roncador, Serra do	137	G6
Ronco	68	D3
Ronda *India*	92	E1
Ronda *Spain*	66	D4
Ronda, Sierra de	66	D4
Ronde	63	D8
Rondeslottet	63	C6
Rondonia *Brazil*	136	E6
Rondonia *Brazil*	136	E6
Rondonopolis	138	F3
Ronge, Lac La	119	Q4
Rong Jiang	93	L4
Rong, Kas	93	K6
Rongshui	93	L3
Rong Xian	93	M4
Ronne	63	H9
Ronneby	63	F8
Ronne Entrance	141	U4
Ronne Ice Shelf	141	V3
Ronse	64	E3
Roodepoort	108	E5
Roof Butte	127	H2
Roosendaal	64	F3
Roosevelt	136	E5
Roosevelt Island	141	P3
Roosevelt, Mount	118	K4
Ropcha	78	J3
Roper	113	G1
Ropi	62	J2
Roquefort	65	C6
Rora Head	56	E2
Roraima	136	E3
Roraima, Mount	136	E2
Roros	62	D5
Rorvik	62	D4
Rosa, Cap	69	B7
Rosalia, Punta	126	E6
Rosa, Monte	68	A3
Rosario	137	J4
Rosario *Argentina*	138	D6
Rosario *Mexico*	130	G6
Rosario *Mexico*	127	H7
Rosario de la Frontera	138	D5
Rosarito	126	F6
Roscoe	127	M4
Roscommon *Ireland*	58	F5
Roscommon *Ireland*	58	F5
Roscrea	59	G7
Roseau	133	S7
Roseberth	113	H4
Rosebery	113	K7
Rosebud	122	H2
Roseburg	122	C6
Rosedale Abbey	55	J2
Rosehearty	56	F3
Rose Island	111	V4
Rosenburg	128	E6
Rosenheim	70	E5
Rose Point	118	J5
Roses	67	H1
Roses, Golfo de	67	H1
Roseto d'Abruzzi	69	D4
Rosetown	123	K2
Rosetta	102	F1
Roshkhvar	95	P4
Rosiori de Vede	73	H3
Rositsa	73	H4
Roskilde	63	E9
Roslavl	78	E5
Ross *New Zealand*	115	C5
Ross *U.K.*	57	G5
Rossall Point	55	F3
Rossano	69	F6
Rossan Point	58	E3
Rosscarbery Bay	59	D9
Ross Dependency	141	P7
Rossel Island	114	E4
Rosses Bay	58	F2
Rosses Point	58	E4
Rosses, The	58	F3
Ross Ice Shelf	141	N2
Rossington	55	H3
Ross Island	141	M3
Rosslare Harbour	59	K8
Ross-on-Wye	52	E3
Rossosh	79	F5
Ross River	118	J3
Ross Sea	141	N3
Rost	62	E3
Rostaq	95	L8
Rostock	70	E1
Rostonsolka	62	J2
Rostov	78	F4
Rostov-na-Donu	79	F6
Rostrevor	58	K4
Roswell *Georgia*	129	K3
Roswell *New Mexico*	127	K4
Rotemo	63	B7
Rotenburg	70	C3
Rothaargebirge	70	C3
Rothbury	57	G5
Rothbury Forest	57	G5
Rother *Kent, U.K.*	53	H3
Rother *W. Sussex, U.K.*	53	G4
Rothera	141	V5
Rotherham	55	H3
Rothesay	57	C5
Rothiesholm	56	F1
Rothwell *Northamptonshire, U.K.*	53	G2
Rothwell *W. Yorkshire, U.K.*	55	H3
Roti	91	G8
Rotja, Punta	67	G3
Roto	113	K5
Rotondella	69	F5
Rotorua	115	F3
Rottenberg	70	C3
Rottenburg *Germany*	70	C4
Rottenburg *Germany*	70	E4
Rotterdam	64	F3
Rottweil	70	C4
Rotuma	111	S4
Rotz	70	E4
Roubaix	64	E3
Rouen	64	D4
Rouge	93	K4
Rouillac	65	C6
Round Hill Head	113	L3
Roundup	123	K4
Roura	137	G3
Rousay	56	E1
Roussillon	65	E7
Rouxville	108	E6
Rouyn	125	L2
Rovaniemi	62	L3
Rovdino	78	G3
Rovereto	68	C3
Rovieng	93	L6
Rovigo	68	C3
Rovinj	72	B3
Rovnoye	79	H5
Rowan	94	J4
Rowlands Gill	55	H2
Rowley Island	120	L4
Rowley Shoals	112	D2
Roxas	91	G3
Roxboro	129	N2
Roxburgh	115	B6
Roxo, Cape	104	B3
Roxton	53	G2
Roy	123	K4
Royal Canal	59	J6
Royale, Isle	124	F3
Royal Geographical Society Islands	119	Q2
Royal Leamington Spa	53	F2
Royan	65	C6
Roy Hill	112	D3
Royston *Hertfordshire, U.K.*	53	G2
Royston *S. Yorkshire, U.K.*	55	H3
Royton	55	G3
Rozan	71	J2
Rozden	73	F5
Rozel Bay	53	M7
Rozewie	71	H1
Rozhishche	71	L3
Roznava	71	J4
Roztocze	71	K3
Rtishchevo	79	G5
Ruahine Range	115	F3
Ruapehu	115	E3
Ruapuke Island	115	B7
Ruawai	115	E2
Rubeho Mountains	107	G4
Rubio	133	L11
Rubtsovsk	84	C6
Ruby Dome	122	G7
Ruby Lake	122	G7
Ruby Mountains	122	G7
Rucheng	93	M3
Ruchi	78	G2
Rudan	95	N8
Ruda Slaska	71	H3
Rudbar	94	J3
Rudbar	95	R6
Rudkobing	63	D9
Rudnaya	88	K3
Rudnaya Pristan	88	E3
Rudnichnyy	78	J4
Rudnik	71	K3
Rudnitsa	73	K1
Rudnya	78	E5
Rudnyy *Kazakhstan*	84	Ad6
Rudnyy *Russia*	88	E3
Rudolfa, Ostrov	80	G1
Rudolf, Lake	107	G2
Rudolstadt	70	D3
Rudozem	73	H5
Rud Sar	95	K3
Rufaa	103	F5
Ruffec	65	D5
Rufiji	107	G4
Rufino	139	D6
Rugby *U.K.*	53	G2
Rugby *U.S.A.*	123	Q3
Rugen	70	E1
Rugozero	78	E3
Ruhengeri	107	E3
Ruhimaki	63	L6
Ruhnu	63	K8
Ruhr	70	B3
Ruijin	87	M6
Rujiena	63	L8
Rujmayn, Jbel Abu	77	H5
Rukumkot	92	F3
Rukwa, Lake	107	F4
Rul Dadnah	97	N4
Ruma	72	E3
Rumah	96	H4
Rumaylah, Uruq ar	96	H6
Rumbek	102	E6
Rum Cay	133	K3
Rumford	125	Q4
Rummelsburg	71	G1
Rumoi	88	H4
Runanga	115	C5
Runaway, Cape	115	F2
Runcorn	55	G3
Runde	108	F4
Rundu	108	C3
Running Water Creek	127	L3
Ruokolahti	63	N6
Ruoqiang	86	F4
Ruo Shui	86	J3
Rupat	90	C5
Rupea	73	H2
Rupert *Canada*	121	L7
Rupert *U.S.A.*	122	H6
Rupert Bay	121	L7
Rupununi	136	F3
Rurrenabaque	136	D6
Rusanovo	84	Ac2
Ruse	73	J4
Rush	59	K5
Rushden	53	G2
Rusk	128	E5
Ruskington	55	J3
Russas	137	K4
Russel, Cape	120	C2
Russell *Canada*	123	P2
Russell *New Zealand*	115	E1
Russell *U.S.A.*	123	Q8
Russell Island	120	G3
Russell Islands	114	J6
Russell Range	112	E5
Russell Springs	124	H8
Russellville *Alabama*	129	J3
Russellville *Kentucky*	124	G8
Russia	49	J3
Russian	122	C8
Russkaya	141	Q4
Russkaya Techa	84	Ad5
Russkiy-Kamlak	84	D6
Russkiy, Ostrov *Russia*	88	C4
Russkiy, Ostrov *Russia*	84	F1
Russkiy Zavorot, Poluostrov	78	J2
Rustavi	77	L2
Rustenburg	108	E5
Ruston	128	F4
Rutana	107	E3
Rute	66	D4
Ruteng	91	G7
Ruth	126	E1
Ruthin	55	F3
Rutigliano	69	F5
Rutland *India*	93	H6
Rutland *U.S.A.*	125	P5
Rutland Water	53	G2
Rutog	92	E2
Rutqa, Wadi	77	J6
Rutshuru	107	E3
Ruvuma	107	G5
Ruzayevka	84	Ae6
Ruzomberok	71	H4
Rwanda	107	E3
Ryan, Loch	54	D2
Ryazan	78	F5
Ryazhsk	79	G5
Rybachiy, Poluostrov	78	E2
Rybachye	86	F2
Rybinsk	78	F4
Rybinskoye Vodokhranilishche	78	F4
Rybnik	71	H3
Rybnitsa	73	K2
Rybnoye	84	E5
Ryd	63	F8
Rydaholm	63	F8
Ryde	53	F4
Rydet	63	E8
Rye *E. Sussex, U.K.*	53	H4
Rye *N. Yorkshire, U.K.*	55	H2
Rye Bay	53	H4
Rylsk	79	E5
Ryn Peski	79	H6
Ryotsu	89	G6
Rypin	71	H2
Ryukyu Islands	87	P6
Rzeszow	71	J3
Rzhev	78	E4

S

Name	Page	Grid
Saadatabad	95	L6
Saale	70	D3
Saalfeld	70	D3
Saar	70	B4
Saarbrucken	70	B4
Saarburg	70	B4
Saare	63	K8
Saaremaa	63	K7
Saarijarvi	62	L5
Saarikoski	62	J2
Saariselka	62	N2
Saarlouis	70	B4
Saatly	94	J2
Saba	133	R6
Sab Abar	94	C5
Sabac	72	E3
Sabadell	67	H2
Sabah	91	F4
Sabalana, Kepulauan	91	F7
Sabalan, Kuhhaye	94	H2
Sabana, Archipielago de	132	G3
Sabana de la Mar	133	N5
Sabanalarga	136	C1
Sabang *Sulawesi, Indonesia*	91	F5
Sabang *Sumatera, Indonesia*	90	B4
Sabanozu	76	E2
Sabarmati	92	D4
Sabatyn, Ramlat as	96	H9
Sabaya, Jabal	96	E7
Saberi, Hamun-e	95	Q6
Sabha	101	H3
Sabi	109	F4
Sabie	109	F5
Sabinal, Cayo	132	J4
Sabinas *Mexico*	127	M7
Sabinas *Mexico*	127	M7
Sabinas Hidalgo	128	B7
Sabine	128	F5
Sabine Peninsula	120	E2
Sabini, Monti	69	D4
Sabirabad	94	J1
Sabkhat al Jabbul	77	G5
Sable, Cape *Canada*	121	N9
Sable, Cape *U.S.A.*	129	M8
Sable Island	121	Q9
Sable Island Bank	121	P9
Sable-sur-Sarthe	65	C5
Saboia	66	B4
Sabon Birni	105	G3
Sabor	66	C2
Sabres	65	C6
Sabrina Coast	141	H5
Sabugal	66	C2
Sabulu	91	G6
Sæby	63	D8
Sabya	96	F8
Sabzevar	95	N3
Sabzvaran	95	N7
Sacaca	138	C3
Sacco	69	D5
Sacedon	66	E2
Sacel	73	H2
Sachigo	119	S5
Sachs Harbour	118	L1
Saco	123	L3
Sacramento *U.S.A.*	126	B1
Sacramento *U.S.A.*	122	D8
Sacramento Mountains	127	K4
Sacramento Valley	122	C8
Sadaba	67	F1
Sadabad	95	K7
Sadad	77	G5
Sadah	96	F8
Sada-misaki	89	D9
Sadani	107	G4
Sadarak	77	L3
Sadd al Aswan	103	F3
Sa Dec	93	L6
Sadgora	73	H1
Sadh	97	M8
Sadid	77	K5
Sadiya	93	J3
Sadiyah, Hawr as	94	H5
Sado	66	B3
Sado-shima	89	G6
Saeki	89	C9
Safa	94	C5
Safaga	96	B3
Safarabad	94	H2
Safarikovo	71	J4
Safed Khirs	92	D1
Saffaniyah, Ra's as	97	J3
Saffle	63	E7
Safford	127	H4
Saffron Walden	53	H2
Safi	100	D2
Safidabeh	95	Q6
Safid Kuh	95	R4
Safid Rud	95	J3
Safonovo	78	E4
Safranbolu	76	E2
Safwan	94	H6
Saga *China*	92	G3
Saga *Japan*	89	C9
Sagami-nada	89	G8
Sagamoso	133	L11
Saganthit Kyun	93	J6
Sagar *Karnataka, India*	92	D6
Sagar *Madhya Pradesh, India*	92	E4
Saggart	59	K6
Saginaw	124	J5

Name	Page	Ref
Shibotsu-jima	88	L4
Shibushi	89	C10
Shickshock Mountains	125	S2
Shiel Bridge	56	C3
Shieldaig	56	C3
Shiel, Loch	57	C4
Shihan, Wadi	97	L8
Shihezi	86	F3
Shiikh	103	J6
Shijiazhuang	87	L4
Shikarpur	92	C3
Shikoku	89	D9
Shikoku-sanchi	89	D9
Shikong	87	K4
Shikotan-to	88	L4
Shikotsu-ko	88	H4
Shildon	55	H2
Shilega	78	G3
Shiliguri	93	G3
Shilka *Russia*	85	K6
Shilka *Russia*	85	L6
Shillingstone	52	E4
Shillong	93	H3
Shilovo	78	G5
Shimabara	89	C9
Shimada	89	G8
Shimanovsk	85	M6
Shimian	93	K3
Shimizu	89	G8
Shimoda	89	G8
Shimoga	92	E6
Shimonoseki	89	C9
Shinano	89	G7
Shinas	97	N4
Shindand	95	R5
Shin Falls	56	D3
Shingu	89	E9
Shinjo	88	H6
Shinness	56	D2
Shinshar	77	G5
Shinyanga	107	F3
Shiogama	89	H6
Shiono-misaki	89	E9
Shiosawa	89	G7
Shiping	93	K4
Shipley	55	H3
Shippensburg	125	M6
Shippigan Island	121	P8
Shipston-on-Stour	53	F2
Shipton	55	H2
Shipton-under-Wychwood	53	F3
Shipunovo	84	C6
Shirakawa	89	H7
Shirane-san *Japan*	89	G8
Shirane-san *Japan*	89	G7
Shiraz	95	L7
Shire	107	F6
Shirebrook	55	H3
Shiretoko-misaki	88	K3
Shiriya-saki	88	H5
Shir Kuh	95	M6
Shirten Holoy Gobi	86	H3
Shirvan	95	N3
Shishaldin Volcano	118	Af9
Shivpuri	92	E3
Shivwits Plateau	126	F2
Shiwan Dashan	93	L4
Shiyan	93	M2
Shizhu	93	L3
Shizugawa	88	H6
Shizuishan	87	K4
Shizuoka	89	G8
Shkoder	74	E1
Shkumbin	74	E2
Shmidta, Ostrov	81	L1
Shobara	89	D8
Shokalskogo, Ostrov	84	A2
Shorapur	92	E5
Shorawak	95	S6
Shoreham-by-Sea	53	G4
Shorkot	92	D2
Shoshone	122	G6
Shoshone Mountains	122	F8
Shoshoni	123	K6
Shostka	79	E5
Shouguang	87	M4
Shouning	87	M6
Showa	141	C5
Showak	96	B9
Shozhma	78	G3
Shpikov	73	K1
Shpola	79	E6
Shrankogl	68	C2
Shreveport	128	F4
Shrewsbury	52	E2
Shrewton	53	F3
Shrigonda	92	D5
Shropshire	52	E2
Shrule	59	D5
Shuab, Ra's	97	P9
Shuanghezhen	87	P3
Shuangliao	87	N3
Shuangyashan	87	Q2
Shubar-Kuduk	79	K6
Shubra el-Khema	102	F1
Shucheng	87	M5
Shuga	84	B6
Shuicheng	93	K3
Shuikou	87	M6
Shujaabad	92	D3
Shulan	87	P3
Shumagin Islands	118	Af9
Shumen	73	J4
Shumerlya	78	H4
Shungnak	118	D2
Shuqrah	96	G10
Shura	77	K4
Shurab	95	K5
Shurab	95	N5
Shusf	95	Q6
Shush	94	J5
Shushenskoye	84	E6
Shushtar	94	J5
Shuswap Lake	122	E2
Shuya	78	G4
Shuya	89	G7
Shwebo	93	J4
Shwegyin	93	J5
Shweli	93	J4
Shyok	92	E2
Siahan Range	92	B3
Siah Koh	95	S5
Sialkot	92	D2
Siargao	91	H4
Siau	91	H5
Siauliai	63	K9
Sibenik	72	C4
Siberut	90	B6
Siberut, Selat	90	B6
Sibi	92	C3
Sibirskaya Nizmennost	84	G2
Sibirtsevo	88	D3
Sibiryakovo, Ostrov	84	B2
Sibiti	106	B3
Sibiu	73	H3
Sibolga	90	B5
Sibsagar	93	H3
Sibsey	55	K3
Sibu	90	E5
Sibut	102	C6
Sibutu	91	F5
Sibutu Passage	91	F5
Sibuyan	91	G3
Sibuyan Sea	91	G3
Sicasica	138	C3
Sichuan	93	K2
Sichuan Pendi	93	L3
Sicie, Cap	65	F7
Sicilia	69	D7
Sicilian Channel	69	C7
Sicily	69	D7
Sicuani	136	C6
Sidatun	88	E3
Sideby	63	J5
Sidheros, Akra	75	J5
Sidhirokastron	75	G2
Sidi Akacha	67	G4
Sidi Barram	102	E1
Sidi Bel Abbes	100	E1
Sidi Ifni	100	C3
Sidi Kacem	100	D2
Sidima	88	E1
Sidlaw Hills	57	E4
Sidmouth	52	D4
Sidmouth, Cape	113	J1
Sidney *Canada*	122	C3
Sidney *Montana*	123	M4
Sidney *Ohio*	124	H6
Sidon	94	B5
Sidorovsk	84	C3
Siedlce	71	K2
Siegen	70	C3
Siemiatycze	71	K2
Siem Reap	93	K6
Siena	68	C4
Sieniawa	71	K3
Sierpc	71	H2
Sierra Colorada	139	C8
Sierra Leone	104	C4
Sierra Vista	127	G5
Sierre	68	A2
Sifnos	75	H4
Sifton Pass	118	K4
Sigatoka *Fiji*	114	Q8
Sigatoka *Fiji*	114	Q9
Sigean	65	E7
Sighetu Marmatiei	73	G2
Sighisoara	73	H2
Sigli	90	B4
Siglufjordur	62	V11
Sigmaringen	70	C4
Signy	141	W6
Sigovo	84	D4
Sigtuna	63	G7
Siguenza	66	E2
Siguiri	104	D3
Sigulda	63	L8
Siikajoki	62	L4
Siikavuopio	62	J2
Siilinjarvi	62	M5
Siin	88	E2
Siipyy	63	J5
Siirt	77	J4
Sikar	92	E3
Sikasso	100	D6
Sikeston	124	F8
Sikhote Alin	88	E3
Sikinos	75	H4
Sikkim	93	G3
Sil	66	C1
Sila	97	K4
Silchar	93	H4
Sile	76	C2
Silesia	71	G3
Silgarhi	92	F3
Silifke	76	E4
Siligir	84	J3
Siling Co	93	G2
Silistra	73	J3
Silivri	76	C2
Siljan	63	F6
Silkeborg	63	C8
Sillajhuay	138	C3
Sillan, Lough	58	J4
Sillon de Talbert	64	B4
Siloam Springs	128	E2
Silom	114	E2
Silopi	77	K4
Silovayakha	78	L2
Silsbee	128	E5
Silute	63	J9
Silvan	77	J3
Silver Bay	124	E3
Silver City	127	H4
Silvermines Mountains	59	F7
Silver Spring	125	M7
Silverstone	53	F2
Silverton *U.K.*	52	D4
Silverton *U.S.A.*	127	J2
Simanggang	90	E5
Simard, Lac	125	L3
Simareh Karkheh	94	H5
Simav *Turkey*	76	C3
Simav *Turkey*	76	C2
Simayr	96	E8
Simcoe	125	K5
Simcoe, Lake	125	L4
Simeonovgrad	73	H4
Simeulue	90	B5
Simferopol	79	E7
Simi	75	J4
Simiti	136	C2
Simitli	73	G5
Simla	92	E2
Simleu Silvaniei	73	G2
Simmern	70	B3
Simojarvi	62	M3
Simojoki	62	L4
Simonka	71	J4
Simplicio Mendes	137	J5
Simplon Pass	68	B2
Simpson Bay	119	N2
Simpson Desert	113	H3
Simpson Peninsula	120	J4
Simrishamn	63	F9
Simsor	77	J3
Simushir, Ostrov	85	S7
Sinabang	90	B5
Sinabung	90	B5
Sinac	72	C3
Sinafir	96	B3
Sinaia	73	H3
Sinai Peninsula	103	F2
Sinaloa	130	F4
Sinanaj	74	E2
Sinaxtla	131	L9
Sincan *Turkey*	76	E3
Sincan *Turkey*	77	G3
Since	133	K10
Sincelejo	136	B2
Sinclair's Bay	56	E2
Sind	92	E3
Sinda	88	F1
Sindal	63	D8
Sindangbarang	90	D7
Sindel	73	J4
Sindhuli Garhi	92	G3
Sindirgi	76	C3
Sindominic	73	H2
Sindor	78	J3
Sind Sagar Doab	92	D2
Sinegorye	78	J4
Sinelnikovo	79	F6
Sines	66	B4
Sines, Cabo de	66	B4
Sinetta	62	L3
Sinfra	104	D4
Singa	103	F5
Singapore	90	C5
Singaraja	90	F7
Sing Buri	93	K6
Singida	107	F3
Singitikos, Kolpos	75	G2
Singkang	91	G6
Singkawang	90	D5
Singkep	90	C6
Singleton	53	G4
Singleton, Mount	112	G3
Singosan	87	P4
Siniatsikon	75	F2
Siniscola	69	B5
Sinj	72	D4
Sinjai	91	G7
Sinjajevina	72	E4
Sinjar	77	J4
Sinkat	103	G4
Sinnamary	137	G2
Sinnes	63	B7
Sinni	69	F5
Sinnicolau Mare	72	F2
Sinoe	104	D4
Sinoe, Lacul	73	K3
Sinop	76	F2
Sinpo	88	B5
Sinpung-dong	88	B5
Sintang	90	E5
Sint Maarten	133	R5
Sinton	128	D6
Sintra	66	B3
Sinu	136	B2
Sinuiju	87	N4
Sinyavka	71	M2
Sinyaya	63	N8
Siocon	91	G4
Siofok	72	E2
Sion	68	A2
Sionascaig, Loch	56	C2
Sion Mills	58	H3
Sioule	65	E5
Sioux City	124	B5
Sioux Falls	123	R6
Sioux Lookout	119	S5
Sipalay	91	G4
Siping	87	N3
Sip Song Chau Thai	93	K4
Sipul	114	D3
Sipura	90	B6
Siquia	132	E8
Siquijor	91	G4
Sira *India*	92	E6
Sira *Norway*	63	B7
Sir Abu Nuayr	97	M4
Siracusa	69	E7
Sirajganj	93	G4
Sir Alexander, Mount	119	M5
Siran	77	H2
Sir Bani Yas	97	L4
Sir Edward Pellew Group	113	H2
Siret *Romania*	73	J2
Siret *Romania*	73	J2
Sirhan, Wadi	94	D6
Siri Kit Dam	93	K5
Sirik, Tanjung	90	E5
Sir James McBrien, Mount	118	R3
Sirjan, Kavir-e	95	L6
Sirk	95	N8
Sirna	75	J4
Sirnal	77	K4
Sirohi	92	D4
Siros *Greece*	75	H4
Siros *Greece*	75	H4
Sirri	95	M9
Sirr, Nafud as	96	G4
Sirsa	92	D3
Sir Sanford, Mount	122	F2
Sirsi	92	D6
Sirte	101	J2
Sirte, Gulf of	101	J2
Sirvan	77	K3
Sisak	72	D3
Sisaket	93	K5
Sisophon	93	K6
Sisseton	123	R5
Sissonne	64	E4
Sistan	95	P8
Sistan, Daryacheh-ye-	95	Q6
Sisteron	65	F6
Sistig-Khem	84	F6
Sistranda	62	C5
Sitamau	92	E4
Sitapur	92	F3
Sitges	67	G2
Sithonia	75	G2
Sitia	75	J5
Sitian	86	F3
Sitidgi Lake	118	J2
Sitio da Abadia	138	H6
Sitka	118	H4
Sittang	93	J5
Sittingbourne	53	H3
Sittwe	93	H4
Situbondo	90	E7
Siuri	93	G4
Siuruanjoki	62	M4
Sivas	77	G3
Sivasli	76	C3
Siverek	77	H4
Siverskiy	63	P7
Sivrice	77	H3
Sivrihisar	76	D3
Sivrihisar Daglari	76	D3
Sivuk	85	Q6
Siwa	102	E2
Siwalik Range	92	F3
Siwan	92	F3
Si Xian	87	M5
Sixmilebridge	59	E7
Sixpenny Handley	53	E4
Siya	78	G3
Siyal Islands	96	C5
Sizin	84	F6
Sjælland	63	D9
Sjorup	63	C8
Skadarsko Jezero	74	E1
Skadovsk	79	E6
Skafta	62	V13
Skagafjordur	62	V12
Skagaflos	62	T12
Skagen	63	D8
Skagerrak	63	C8
Skagit	122	D3
Skagway	118	H4
Skaill	56	F2
Skala-Podolskaya	73	J1
Skanderborg	63	C8
Skanor	63	E9
Skansholm	62	G4
Skantzoura	75	H3
Skara	63	E7
Skaraborg	63	E7
Skarbak	63	C9
Skard	62	V12
Skardu	92	E1
Skarnes	63	D6
Skattkarr	63	E7
Skaudvile	63	K9

Stuart *Nebraska*	123 Q6	Sulu Archipelago	91 G4
Stuart Island	118 C3	Suluklu	76 E3
Stuart Lake	118 L5	Sulu Sea	91 F4
Stuart, Mount	122 D4	Suly	84 Ae6
Stung Treng	93 L6	Sulz	70 C4
Stura	68 A3	Sulzberger Bay	141 P3
Sturgeon	125 K3	Sumar	94 G5
Sturgeon Bay	124 G4	Sumarokovo	84 D4
Sturgeon Falls	125 L3	Sumatera	90 C6
Sturgeon Lake	124 E1	Sumba	91 F7
Sturgis	123 N5	Sumbar	95 H2
Sturovo	71 H5	Sumbawa	91 F7
Sturry	53 J3	Sumbawabesar	91 F7
Sturt Desert	113 J4	Sumbawanga	107 F4
Sturton by Stow	55 J3	Sumbe	106 B5
Stutterheim	108 E6	Sumburgh	56 A2
Stuttgart *U.S.A.*	128 G3	Sumburgh Head	56 A2
Stuttgart *Germany*	70 C4	Sumedang	90 D7
Stykkisholmur	62 T12	Sumenep	90 E7
Styr	71 L3	Sumgayyt	79 H7
Suakin	103 G4	Summan, As *Saudi Arabia*	96 H3
Suakin Archipelago	96 D7	Summan, As *Saudi Arabia*	97 J5
Suavanao	114 J5	Summer Isles	56 C2
Subashi	94 J4	Summer Lake	122 D6
Subay, Irq	96 F6	Summerside	121 P8
Subei	86 H4	Summit Lake	118 L4
Subi	90 D5	Sumner Lake	127 K3
Subiaco	69 D5	Sumperk	71 G4
Sublette	127 M2	Sumprabum	93 J3
Subotica	72 E2	Sumter	129 M4
Suceava	73 J2	Sumy	79 E5
Sucha	71 H4	Sunamganj	93 H3
Suchedniow	71 J3	Sunart, Loch	57 C4
Suck	59 F6	Sunaynah	97 M5
Sucre	138 C3	Sunaysilah	77 J5
Suda	78 F4	Sunbury	125 M6
Sudan	102 E5	Sunchon	87 P5
Sudbury *Canada*	125 K3	Sun City	126 F4
Sudbury *Derbyshire, U.K.*	53 F2	Sundance	123 M5
Sudbury *Suffolk, U.K.*	53 H2	Sundargarh	92 F4
Sudety	70 F3	Sunda, Selat	90 D7
Sudirman, Pegunungan	91 K6	Sunday Strait	112 E2
Sudr	96 A2	Sunde	63 D6
Sud, Recif du	114 X17	Sunderland	55 H2
Suduroy	62 Z14	Sundiken Daglari	76 D3
Sudzha	79 F5	Sundsvall	62 G5
Sue	102 E6	Sungaipenuh	90 D6
Suess Land	120 W3	Sungikai	102 E5
Suez	103 F2	Sungurlu	76 F2
Suez Canal	103 F1	Suning	87 M4
Suez, Gulf of	103 F2	Sunland Park	127 J5
Suffolk	53 H2	Sunlight Peak	127 J2
Sufian	94 G2	Sunndalsora	62 C5
Sugarloaf Mount	125 Q4	Sunne	63 E7
Sugla Golu	76 D4	Sunnyside	122 D4
Sugoy	85 T4	Sunnyvale	126 A2
Suhait	87 J4	Suntar	85 K4
Suhar	97 N4	Sun Valley	122 G6
Suhbaatar	87 K1	Sunwu	87 P2
Suhut	76 D3	Sunyani	104 E4
Suibin	88 C2	Suoirman, Pegunungan	114 B2
Suichuan	93 M3	Suomenlahti Finskij Zaliv	63 L7
Suide	87 L4	Suomussalmi	62 N4
Suidong	88 D2	Suo-nada	89 C9
Suifenhe	88 C3	Suonenjoki	62 M5
Suifen He	88 C4	Suoyarvi	78 E3
Suihua	88 A2	Supaul	92 G3
Suileng	88 A2	Superior *Arizona*	126 G4
Suining	93 L2	Superior *Nebraska*	123 Q7
Suiping	93 M2	Superior *Wisconsin*	124 D3
Suir	59 G8	Superior, Lake	124 G3
Suixi	93 M4	Suphan Dagi	77 K3
Sui Xian	93 M2	Supiori	91 K6
Suizhong	87 N3	Supsa	77 J1
Suj	87 K3	Suq ash Shuyukh	94 H6
Sukabumi	90 D7	Suqian	87 M5
Sukhinichi	78 F5	Suqutra	97 P10
Sukhona	78 G3	Sur	97 P5
Sukkertoppen	120 R5	Sura	78 H4
Sukkertoppen Iskappe	120 R4	Surab	92 C3
Sukkur	92 C3	Surabaya	90 E7
Sukma	92 F5	Surahammar	63 G7
Sukon	91 G6	Surak	95 P9
Sukpay	88 F2	Surakarta	90 E7
Sukpay Datani	88 F2	Suran	95 Q8
Suksun	78 K4	Surat *Australia*	113 K4
Sukumo	89 D9	Surat *India*	92 D4
Sulaiman Range	92 C3	Suratgarh	92 D3
Sula, Kepulauan	91 H6	Surat Thani	93 J7
Sulakyurt	76 E2	Surduc, Pasul	73 G3
Sulawesi	91 G6	Surendranagar	92 D4
Sulawesi, Laut	91 G5	Surgeres	65 C5
Sulaymaniyah	94 G4	Surgut	84 A4
Sulby	54 E2	Surigao	91 H4
Sulejow	71 H3	Surigao Strait	91 H3
Sulina	73 K3	Surin	93 K6
Sulina, Bratul	73 K3	Suriname	137 F3
Sulingen	70 C2	Surmene	77 J2
Sulitjelma	62 G3	Surnadalsora	62 C5
Sullana	136 A4	Surovikino	79 G6
Sullivan	124 E7	Surrah, Nafud as	96 G5
Sullivan Lake	122 J2	Surrey	53 G3
Sullom Voe	56 A1	Sur Sari	63 M6
Sullorsuaq	120 R3	Surt	101 J2
Sully	65 E5	Surt, Khalij	101 J2
Sulmona	69 D4	Surtsey	62 U13
Sulphur *Oklahoma*	128 D3	Suruc	77 H4
Sulphur *Texas*	128 E4	Suruga-wan	89 G8
Sulphur Springs	128 E4	Surulangun	90 D6
Sultandagi	76 D3	Susa *Italy*	68 A3
Sultanhani *Turkey*	76 E3	Susa *Japan*	89 C8
Sultanhani *Turkey*	77 F3	Susac	72 D4
Sultanhisar	76 C4	Susak	72 C3
Sultanpur	92 F3	Susaki	89 D9

Susami	89 E9	Swineshead	53 G2
Susangerd	94 J6	Swinoujscie	70 F2
Susanville	122 D7	Swinton *Borders, U.K.*	57 F5
Susehri	77 H2	Swinton *S. Yorkshire, U.K.*	55 H3
Susitna	118 E3	Switzerland	68 A2
Suso	93 J7	Swona	56 E2
Susquehanna	125 M6	Swords	59 K6
Susuka	114 H5	Syalakh	85 L3
Susurluk	76 C3	Syamzha	78 G3
Susuz	77 K2	Sybil Point	59 B8
Sutculer	76 D4	Sychevka	78 E4
Sutherland	108 D6	Sydney *Australia*	113 L5
Sutherlin	122 C6	Sydney *Canada*	121 P8
Sutlej	92 D2	Sydney Lake	123 S2
Sutterton	53 G2	Syeverodonetsk	79 F6
Sutton	53 G3	Sykehouse	55 H3
Sutton Bridge	53 H2	Syktyvkar	78 J3
Sutton Coldfield	53 F2	Sylacauga	129 J4
Sutton in Ashfield	55 H3	Sylene	63 E5
Sutton-on-the-Forest	55 H2	Sylhet	93 H4
Sutton Scotney	53 F3	Sylt	70 C1
Suttor	113 K3	Sylva	78 K4
Suttsu	88 H4	Sylvania	129 M4
Sutwik Island	118 D4	Sym	84 D4
Suva	114 R9	Synya	78 K2
Suvasvesi	62 N5	Synzhera	73 K2
Suverovo	88 E3	Syracuse *Italy*	69 E7
Suvorov Island	111 W4	Syracuse *Kansas*	127 M2
Suwalki	71 K1	Syracuse *New York*	125 M5
Suwannee	129 L6	Syr-Darya	86 C3
Suwanose-jima	89 B11	Syrdar-ya	80 H5
Suwar	77 J5	Syrdaryn	86 B3
Suwayqiyah, Hawr as	94 G5	Syria	94 C4
Suweis, Khalij-as-	103 F2	Syriam	93 J5
Suwon	87 P4	Sysola	78 J3
Suyevatpaul	78 L3	Syston	53 F2
Suyfun	88 C4	Sytomino	84 A4
Suzaka	89 G7	Syumsi	78 J4
Suzhou *Anhui, China*	93 N2	Syutkya	73 G5
Suzhou *Jiangsu, China*	87 N5	Syzran	79 H5
Suzu	89 F7	Szarvas	72 F2
Suzu-misaki	89 F7	Szczecin	70 F2
Suzun	84 C6	Szczecinek	71 G2
Svalbard	80 C2	Szczecinski, Zalew	70 F2
Svalyava	71 K4	Szczekociny	71 H3
Svappavaara	62 J3	Szczucin	71 J3
Svarta	63 F7	Szczuczyn	71 K2
Svartisen	62 E3	Szczytno	71 J2
Svartvik	63 G5	Szeged	72 F2
Svarvolthalvoya	62 M1	Szeghalom	73 F2
Svatovo	79 F6	Szekesfehervar	72 E2
Svatoy Nos, Mys	85 Q2	Szekszard	72 E2
Svay Rieng	93 L6	Szentes	72 F2
Sveg	63 F5	Szentgotthard	72 D2
Svelvik	63 D7	Szolnok	72 F2
Svencioneliai	63 M9	Szombathely	72 D2
Svendborg	63 D9	Szprotawa	70 F3
Svenstavik	62 F5		
Sventoji	63 N8	**T**	
Sverdrup Islands	120 G2		
Sverdrup, Ostrov	84 B2	Taal, Lake	91 G3
Svetlaya	88 G2	Tabaqah	94 D4
Svetlogorsk	79 D5	Tabar Islands	114 E2
Svetlograd	79 G6	Tabarka	69 B7
Svetlyy	85 K5	Tabas *Iran*	95 N5
Svetogorsk	63 N6	Tabas *Iran*	95 Q5
Svilajnac	73 F3	Tabasara, Serrania de	132 G10
Svilengrad	73 J5	Tabashimo	78 H4
Svir	63 M9	Tabatinga, Serra da	137 J6
Svirtsa	78 E3	Tabiteuea	111 R2
Svishtov	73 H4	Tablas	91 G3
Svisloc	71 L2	Tablas, Cabo	138 B6
Svitavy	71 G4	Table Cape	115 G3
Svobodnyy	85 M6	Taboleiro	137 K5
Svrljig	73 G4	Tabor	70 F4
Svyatoy Nos, Mys	78 H2	Tabora	107 F4
Swadlincote	53 F2	Tabou	104 D5
Swaffham	53 H2	Tabriz	94 H2
Swainby	55 H2	Tabuk	96 C2
Swain Reefs	113 L3	Tabuka	89 C9
Swainsboro	129 L4	Tabut	97 L9
Swains Island	111 U4	Tabwemasana	114 T11
Swakop	108 C4	Taby	63 H7
Swakopmund	108 B4	Tacheng	86 F2
Swale	55 H2	Tacloban	91 G3
Swaledale	55 H2	Tacna *Peru*	138 B3
Swale, The	53 H3	Tacna *U.S.A.*	126 F4
Swallow Falls	54 F3	Tacoma	122 C4
Swallow Island	114 N7	Tacora, Cerro de	138 C3
Swanage	53 F4	Tacuarembo	138 E6
Swan Hill	113 J6	Tadcaster	55 H3
Swan Islands	132 F6	Tademait, Plateau du	101 F3
Swankhalok	93 J5	Tadjoura	103 H5
Swanley	53 H3	Tadmur	77 H5
Swan Reach	113 H5	Tadoule Lake	119 R4
Swan River	119 Q5	Tadoussac	125 R2
Swansea	52 D3	Tadpatri	92 E6
Swansea Bay	52 D3	Tadworth	53 G3
Swanton	125 P4	Taegu	89 B8
Swatragh	58 J3	Taehuksan	87 P5
Swaziland	109 F5	Taejon	87 P4
Sweden	63 F8	Taf	52 C3
Sweet Home	122 C5	Tafahi	111 U5
Sweetwater *Texas*	127 M4	Tafalla	67 F1
Sweetwater *Wyoming*	123 K6	Tafassasset	101 G4
Swellendam	108 D6	Tafassasset, Tenere du	101 H4
Swidnica	71 G3	Taff	52 D3
Swiebodzin	70 F2	Taff, At	97 M4
Swietokrzyskie, Gory	71 J3	Tafila	94 B6
Swift Current	123 L2	Tafi Viejo	138 C5
Swinburne, Cape	120 G3	Tafresh	95 K4
Swindon	53 F3	Taft	95 M6
Swinemunde	70 F2	Taftan, Kuh-e-	95 Q7

Name	Page	Grid
Taganrog	79	F6
Taganrogskiy Zaliv	79	F6
Tagbilaran	91	G4
Taghmon	59	J8
Tagliamento	68	D3
Tagolo Point	91	G4
Tagounite	100	D3
Tagu	73	H2
Taguatinga	138	H6
Tagudin	91	G2
Tagula	114	E4
Tagula Island	114	E4
Tagum	91	H4
Tagus	66	C3
Tahan, Gunung	90	C5
Tahat, Mont	101	G4
Ta He	87	N1
Tahe	87	N1
Taheri	95	L8
Tahiryuak Lake	119	N1
Tahiti	143	J5
Tahlab, Dasht-i-	92	B3
Tahlequah	128	E3
Tahoe Lake *Canada*	119	P1
Tahoe, Lake *U.S.A.*	122	E8
Tahoka	127	M4
Tahoua	101	G6
Tahrud	95	N7
Tahta	102	F2
Tahtali Daglari	77	G3
Tahuamanu	136	D6
Tahulandang	91	H5
Taian	87	M4
Taibai Shan	93	L2
Taibus Qi	87	M3
Tai-chung	87	N7
Taier	115	C6
Taieri	115	C6
Taigu	87	L4
Taihape	115	E3
Taihe *Anhui, China*	93	N2
Taihe *Jiangxi, China*	93	M3
Tai Hu	87	N5
Taimba	84	F4
Tain	56	D3
Tai-nan	87	N7
Tainaron, Akra	75	G4
Taining	87	M6
Taipale	62	N5
Tai-pei	87	N6
Taiping	90	C5
Taipingbao	86	J4
Taipinggou	88	C1
Taira	89	H7
Taisei	88	G4
Taisha	89	D8
Taitao, Peninsula de	139	B9
Tai-tung	87	N7
Taivalkoski	62	N4
Taiwan	87	N7
Taiwan Haixia	87	M7
Taiyetos Oros	75	G4
Taiyuan	87	L4
Taiza	89	E8
Taizhou	87	M5
Taizz	96	G10
Tajabad	95	M6
Tajikistan	86	B4
Tajima	89	G7
Tajin-dong	88	B5
Tajito	126	F5
Tajo	66	D3
Tajrish	95	K4
Tajumuclo, Volcan de	132	B7
Tajuna	66	E2
Tak	93	J5
Takab	94	H3
Takada	89	G7
Takaka	115	D4
Takamatsu	89	E8
Takanabe	89	C9
Takaoka	89	F7
Takapuna	115	E2
Takasaki	89	G7
Takatshwane	108	D4
Takaungu	107	G3
Takayama	89	F7
Takefu	89	F8
Takengon	90	B5
Takeo	93	K6
Takestan	95	J3
Takhadid	94	G7
Takhi-i-Suleiman	95	K3
Takhta Bazar	95	R4
Takhtabrod	84	Ae6
Takikawa	88	H4
Takinoue	88	J3
Taklimakan Shamo	92	F1
Taku	118	J4
Takum	105	G4
Takwa	114	K6
Talagang	92	D2
Talamanca, Cordillera de	132	F10
Talangbetutu	90	C6
Talara	136	A4
Talar-i-Band	92	B3
Talas	86	C3
Talasea	114	E3
Talaton	52	D4
Talaud, Kepulauan	91	H5
Talavera de la Reina	66	D3
Talayuelas	67	F3
Talbot Inlet	120	L2
Talca	139	B7
Talcahuano	139	B7
Talcher	92	G4
Taldy-Kurgan	86	D2
Talgarth	52	D3
Taliabu	91	G6
Talihina	128	E3
Tali Post	102	F6
Talisay	91	G3
Talitsa	84	Ad5
Taliwang	91	F7
Talkeetna	118	E3
Talkeetna Mountains	118	F3
Talladega	129	J4
Tall Afar	77	K4
Tallahassee	129	K5
Tallinn	63	L7
Tall Kalakh	77	G5
Tall Kayf	77	K4
Tall Kujik	77	K4
Tallow	59	F8
Tall Tamir	77	J4
Talmenka	84	C6
Talnoye	79	E6
Taloda	92	D4
Talodi	102	F5
Talok	91	F5
Talovka	84	E5
Taloye	85	M4
Talsí	63	K8
Taltal	138	B5
Taltson	119	N3
Talu	114	F3
Taluma	85	L5
Talvik	62	K1
Tama	124	D6
Tamabo Range	90	F5
Tamale	104	E4
Tamames	66	C2
Tamana	111	S2
Tamano	89	D8
Tamanrasset *Algeria*	100	F4
Tamanrasset *Algeria*	101	G4
Tamar *Australia*	113	K7
Tamar *U.K.*	52	C4
Tamar, Alto de	133	K11
Tamarite de Litera	67	G2
Tamatave	109	J3
Tamaulipas, Llanos de	128	C8
Tamazunchale	131	K7
Tambacounda	104	C3
Tambangsawah	90	C6
Tambelan, Kepulauan	90	D5
Tambey	84	A2
Tambo	113	K3
Tambora, Gunung	91	F7
Tamboril	137	J4
Tambov	79	G5
Tambre	66	B1
Tambura	102	E6
Tamchaket	100	C5
Tame	136	C2
Tamega	66	C2
Tamiahua, Laguna de	131	L7
Tamil Nadu	92	E6
Tamis	72	F3
Tamit, Wadi	101	J2
Tammerfors	63	M6
Tammisaari	63	K6
Tampa	129	L7
Tampa Bay	129	L7
Tampere	63	M6
Tampico	131	L6
Tamsagbulag	87	M2
Tamuin	131	K7
Tamworth *Australia*	113	L5
Tamworth *U.K.*	53	F2
Tana *Chile*	138	C3
Tana *Kenya*	107	H3
Tana *Norway*	62	M1
Tanabe	89	E9
Tana bru	62	N2
Tanafjorden	62	N1
Tana Hayk	103	G5
Tanahbala	90	B6
Tanahgrogot	90	F6
Tanahjampea	91	G7
Tanahmasa	90	B6
Tanahmerah	114	C3
Tanah Merah	90	C4
Tanami	112	F3
Tanana	118	E2
Tananarive	109	J3
Tanchon	88	B5
Tandag	91	H4
Tandek	91	F4
Tandil	139	E7
Tando Adam	92	C3
Tandragee	58	K4
Taneatua	115	F3
Tanega-shima	89	C10
Tan Émellel	101	G3
Tanen Tong Dan	93	J5
Tanew	71	K3
Tanezrouft	100	E4
Tanf, Jbel al	77	H6
Tanga *Tanzania*	107	G4
Tanga *Russia*	85	J6
Tanga Islands	114	E2
Tanganyika, Lake	107	F4
Tangarare	114	J6
Tanger	100	D1
Tanggula Shan	93	G2
Tanggula Shankou	93	H2
Tangra Yumco	92	G2
Tangshan	87	M4
Tangwang He	88	B2
Tangwanghe	88	B1
Tangyuan	88	B2
Tan Hill	53	F3
Tanhua	62	M3
Taniantaweng Shan	93	J2
Tanimbar, Kepulauan	114	A3
Tanjung	90	F6
Tanjungbalai	90	B5
Tanjungkarang Telukbetung	90	D7
Tanjungpandan	90	D6
Tanjungpura	90	B5
Tanjungredeb	91	F5
Tanjungselor	91	F5
Tankapirtti	62	M2
Tankovo	84	D4
Tankse	92	E2
Tanlovo	84	A3
Tanna	114	U13
Tannu Ola	84	E6
Tannurah, Ra's	97	K3
Tanout	101	G6
Tan-shui	87	N6
Tanta	102	F1
Tan-Tan	100	C3
Tantoyuca	131	K7
Tanumshede	63	D7
Tanzania	107	G4
Taoan	87	N2
Tao He	93	K2
Tao, Ko	93	J6
Taolanaro	109	J5
Taormina	69	E7
Taos	127	K2
Taoudenni	100	E4
Taourirt	100	E2
Tapa	63	L7
Tapachula	131	N10
Tapah	90	C5
Tapajos	137	F4
Tapaktuan	90	B5
Tapan	90	D6
Tapanahoni	137	F3
Tapaua	136	D5
Taperoa	137	K6
Tappahannock	125	M8
Tappi-saki	88	H5
Tapsuy	78	L3
Tapti	92	D4
Tapuaenuku	115	D4
Tapul Group	91	G4
Taqah	97	M8
Taqtaq	94	G4
Taquari	138	E3
Taquari, Pantanal do	138	E3
Tara	84	A5
Tarabulus	101	H2
Taradale	115	F3
Tara, Hill of	58	J5
Tarakan	91	F5
Tarakli	76	D2
Tarakliya	73	K3
Taramana	91	G7
Taramo-jima	89	G11
Taran	84	A2
Tarancon	66	E2
Taransay	56	A3
Taransay, Sound of	56	A3
Taranto	69	F5
Taranto, Golfo di	69	F5
Tarapoto	136	B5
Tararua Range	115	E4
Tarascon	65	F7
Tarasovo	78	H2
Tarauaca *Brazil*	136	C5
Tarauaca *Brazil*	136	C5
Taravo	69	B5
Tarazona	67	F2
Tarazona de la Mancha	67	F3
Tarbagatay, Khrebet	86	E2
Tarbert *Ireland*	59	D7
Tarbert *Strathclyde, U.K.*	57	C5
Tarbert *Western Isles, U.K.*	56	B3
Tarbes	65	D7
Tarbet	57	D4
Tarbolton	57	D5
Tarboro	129	P3
Tarcaului, Muntii	73	J2
Tarcoola	113	G5
Tardienta	67	F2
Tardoki-yani, Gora	88	F1
Taree	113	L5
Tarendo	62	K3
Tareya	84	E2
Tarfa, Ra's at	96	F8
Tarfa, Wadi el	103	F2
Tarfaya	100	C3
Tarfside	57	F4
Targhee Pass	122	J5
Tarhunah	101	H2
Tarif	97	L4
Tarifa	66	D4
Tarija	138	D4
Tariku	114	B2
Tarim	97	J8
Tarim Basin	86	E3
Tarim He	86	E3
Tarim Pendi	86	E3
Taritatu	114	B2
Tarkasale	84	A3
Tarkastad	108	E6
Tarkhankut, Mys	79	E6
Tarkio	124	C6
Tarkwa	104	E4
Tarlac	91	G2
Tarlak	86	E3
Tarleton	55	G3
Tarma	136	B6
Tarn	65	D7
Tarna	72	F2
Tarnaby	62	F4
Tarnobrzeg	71	J3
Tarnow	71	J4
Tarnsjo	63	G6
Taro	68	B3
Taron	114	E2
Taroom	113	K4
Taroudannt	100	D2
Tarporley	55	G3
Tarragona	67	G2
Tarrasa	67	H2
Tarrega	67	G2
Tarsus	76	F4
Tartagal	138	D4
Tartas	65	C7
Tartu	63	P7
Tartung	90	B5
Tartus	94	B4
Tartus	77	F5
Tarutino	73	K2
Tarzout	67	G4
Tasci	77	F3
Tashakta	86	F2
Tashigang	93	H3
Tashk, Daryacheh-ye	95	L7
Tashkent	86	B3
Tashkepri	95	R3
Tashla	79	J5
Tashtagol	84	D6
Tasikmalaya	90	D7
Tasiujaq	121	N6
Taskesken	86	E2
Taskopru	76	F2
Tas-Kumsa	85	N3
Taslicay	77	K3
Tasman Bay	115	D4
Tasmania	113	K7
Tasman Mountains	115	D4
Tasnad	73	G2
Tasova	77	G2
Tas-Tumus	85	N2
Tasty	86	B3
Tasucu	76	E4
Tasuj	77	L3
Tataba	91	G6
Tatabanya	72	E2
Tatarbunary	73	K3
Tatarka	84	B6
Tatarsk	84	B5
Tataurovo	85	J6
Tateyama	89	G8
Tathlina Lake	119	M3
Tathlith	96	F7
Tathlith, Wadi	96	F6
Tatnam, Cape	119	S4
Tatry	71	H4
Tatsinskiy	79	G6
Tatsuno	89	E8
Tatta	92	C4
Tatum	127	L4
Tatvan	77	K3
Tau	111	V4
Tauari	137	F4
Taubate	138	G4
Tauchik	79	J7
Taumarunui	115	E3
Taung-gyi	93	J4
Taungnyo Range	93	J5
Taunton *U.K.*	52	D3
Taunton *U.S.A.*	125	Q6
Taunus	70	C3
Taupo	115	F3
Taupo, Lake	115	E3
Tauq	94	G4
Tauq	77	L5
Taurage	63	K9
Tauranga	115	F2
Tauroa Point	115	D1
Taurus	76	E4
Tauste	67	F2
Tauu Islands	114	F2
Tavalesh, Kuhha-ye	94	J3
Tavana-i-Tholo	111	T6
Tavas	76	C4
Tavda *Russia*	84	Ad5
Tavda *Russia*	84	Ae5
Taverner Bay	120	M4
Taveuni	114	S8
Tavira	66	C4
Tavistock	52	C4
Tavolara, Isola di	69	B5
Tavoy	93	J6
Tavrichanka	88	C4
Tavsanli	76	C3
Tavua	114	Q8
Tavuna-i-Ra	111	T6
Tavy	52	C4
Taw	52	D4
Tawakoni, Lake	128	E4
Tawau	91	F5
Tawe	52	D3
Taweisha	102	E5
Tawila	96	A3
Tawil, At	96	D2
Tawitawi Group	91	G4
Ta-wu	87	N7
Tawurgha, Sabkhat	101	J2

Name	Page	Grid
Taxco	131	K8
Taxkorgan	92	E1
Tay	57	E4
Tayandu, Kepulauan	91	J7
Tayastehus	63	L6
Tayeeglow	107	H2
Tay, Firth of	57	E4
Tayga	84	D5
Tayinloan	57	C5
Tay, Loch	57	D4
Taylor	123	Q7
Taylor Island	119	Q2
Taylor, Mount	127	J3
Taylorville	124	F7
Tayma	96	D3
Taymura	84	F4
Taymyr	84	E3
Taymyr, Ozero	84	G2
Taymyr, Poluostrov	84	F2
Tay Ninh	93	L6
Taynuilt	57	C4
Tayport	57	F4
Tayshet	84	F5
Tayshir	86	H2
Tayside	57	E4
Taysiyah, At	96	F2
Taytay	91	F3
Tayyebad	95	Q4
Taz *Russia*	84	B3
Taz *Russia*	84	C3
Taza	100	E2
Tazin Lake	119	P4
Tazirbu	101	K3
Tbilisi	77	L2
Tchad, Lac	102	B5
Tchibanga	106	B3
Tczew	71	H1
Teaca	73	H2
Te Anau	115	A6
Te Anau, Lake	115	A6
Te Anga	115	E3
Te Aroha	115	E2
Te Awamutu	115	E2
Tebesjuak Lake	119	R3
Tebessa	101	G1
Tebingtinggi *Indonesia*	90	B5
Tebingtinggi *Indonesia*	90	C6
Teboursouk	69	B7
Tecate	126	D4
Techirghiol	73	K3
Tecirli	77	G4
Tecoman	130	H8
Tecuci	73	J3
Tedelkynak	84	C4
Tedzhen	95	Q3
Teeapo, Lake	115	C5
Tees	55	H2
Tees Bay	55	H2
Teesdale	55	H2
Tefe *Brazil*	136	D4
Tefe *Brazil*	136	E4
Tefenni	76	C4
Tegal	90	D7
Tegid, Llyn	52	D2
Tegua	114	T10
Tegucigalpa	132	D7
Tehachapi Mountains	126	C3
Tehachapi Pass	126	C3
Te Haroto	115	F3
Tehek Lake	119	R2
Tehert	119	R2
Tehoru	91	H6
Tehran	95	K4
Tehuacan	131	L8
Tehuantepec *Mexico*	131	M9
Tehuantepec *Mexico*	131	M9
Tehuantepec, Golfo de	131	M10
Teign	52	D4
Teignmouth	52	D4
Tejo	66	C3
Te Karaka	115	F3
Tekes	86	E3
Tekeze	96	C9
Tekin	88	D1
Tekirdag	76	B2
Tekman	77	J3
Te Kopuru	115	D2
Te Kuiti	115	E3
Tela	132	D7
Tel Ali	77	K5
Telavi	77	L2
Tel Aviv-Yafo	94	B5
Telegraph Creek	118	J4
Telekhany	71	L2
Telemark	63	C7
Telemba	85	J6
Telen	139	C7
Telen	90	F5
Teleorman	73	H3
Telescope Peak	126	D2
Teles Pires	136	F5
Telford	52	E2
Teli	84	E6
Telimele	104	C3
Tell City	124	G8
Tellicherry	92	E6
Telposiz, Gora	78	K3
Telsen	139	C8
Telsiai	63	K9
Teluk Anson	90	C5
Telukbatang	90	D6
Telukdalam	90	B5
Tem	84	G5
Tema	104	E4
Temagami, Lake	125	K3
Temascaltepec	131	K8
Tembenchi	84	F4
Tembleque	66	E3
Tembo Aluma	106	C4
Teme	52	E2
Temerin	72	E3
Temerloh	90	C5
Temirtau	86	C2
Temiscamingve, Lac	125	L3
Temnikov	78	G5
Temnyy	85	K6
Tempe	126	G4
Tempio Pausania	69	B5
Temple	128	D5
Templemore	59	G7
Tempoal	131	K7
Tempue	106	C5
Temryuk	79	F6
Temuco	139	B7
Temuka	115	C6
Tena	136	B4
Tenali	92	F5
Tenasserim	93	J6
Tenbury Wells	52	E2
Tenby	52	C3
Tende	68	A3
Ten Degree Channel	93	H7
Tendelti	103	F5
Tendrovskaya Kosa	79	E6
Tenduruk Dagi	77	K3
Tenerife	100	B3
Tenes	100	F1
Tenevo	73	J4
Tengahdai	91	G7
Tengchong	93	J3
Tenggarong	90	F6
Tengiz, Ozero	84	Ae6
Teng, Nam	93	J4
Teng Xian	87	M4
Tenkasi	92	E7
Tenke	106	E5
Tenkodogo	104	E3
Tennant Creek	113	G2
Tennessee *U.S.A.*	129	H2
Tennessee *U.S.A.*	129	J2
Tennessee Pass	123	L8
Tenniojoki	62	N3
Tenosique	131	P9
Tenquehuen, Isla	139	B9
Tensift, Oued	100	D2
Tenterden	53	H3
Tenterfield	113	L4
Teofilo Otoni	138	E3
Teouta	114	X16
Tepasto	62	L2
Tepatitlan	130	H7
Tepebasi	76	E4
Tepecikoren	77	F4
Tepeji	131	K8
Tepelene	74	F2
Tepic	130	G7
Teplice	70	E3
Teplik	73	K1
Tepoca, Cabo	126	F5
Te Puke	115	F2
Ter	67	H2
Tera	66	C2
Teramo	69	D4
Terasa	93	H7
Tercan	77	J3
Teren-Uzyak	86	A2
Teresina	137	J5
Teresita	136	.D3
Teresopolis	138	H4
Teriberka	78	F2
Terme	77	G2
Termez	80	H6
Termini Imerese	69	D7
Terminillo	69	D4
Terminos, Laguna de	131	P8
Termoli	69	E4
Ternate	91	H5
Terneuzen	64	E3
Terney	88	F3
Terni	69	D4
Ternopil	79	D6
Terpeniya, Mys	85	Q7
Terpeniya, Zaliv	85	Q7
Terrace	118	K5
Terrace Bay	124	G2
Terracina	69	D5
Terrak	62	E4
Terralba	69	B6
Terre Adelie	141	K7
Terre Haute	124	G7
Terrell	128	D4
Terschelling	64	F2
Terskiy Bereg	78	F2
Teruel	67	F2
Terutao	93	J7
Tervel	73	J4
Tervo	62	M5
Teseney	103	G4
Teshekpuk Lake	118	E1
Teshio	88	H3
Teshio-sammyaku	88	H4
Tesica	73	F4
Tesiyn Gol	86	H2
Teslin *Canada*	118	J3
Teslin *Canada*	118	J3
Tesouro	138	F3
Tessalit	100	F4
Tessaoua	101	G6
Test	53	F3
Testa, Capo	69	B5
Testa del Gargano	69	F5
Tet	65	E7
Tetbury	53	E3
Tete	109	F3
Tetepare	114	H6
Tetere	84	G4
Teterow	70	E2
Tetouan	100	D1
Tetovo	73	F4
Te Tungano	114	K7
Teulada	69	B6
Teulada, Capo	69	B6
Teun	91	H7
Tevere	69	D4
Teverya	94	B5
Teviot	57	F5
Tevriz	84	A5
Te Waewae Bay	115	A7
Te Whanga Lagoon	115	H6
Tewkesbury	53	E3
Tewo	93	K2
Texada Islands	122	B3
Texarkana	128	E4
Texas	127	M5
Texas City	128	E6
Texcoco	131	K8
Texel	64	F2
Texoma, Lake	128	D4
Teykovo	78	G4
Teziutlan	131	L8
Tezpur	93	H3
Tha-anne	119	R3
Thabana Ntlenyana	108	E5
Thabazimbi	108	E4
Thadiq	96	G4
Thai Binh	93	L4
Thailand	93	K5
Thailand, Gulf of	93	K7
Thai Nguyen	93	L4
Thakhek	93	K5
Thal	92	D2
Thalab, Dasht-i	95	Q7
Thal Desert	92	D2
Thale Luang	93	K7
Thamarit	97	M8
Thame	53	G3
Thames *Canada*	124	J5
Thames *New Zealand*	115	E2
Thames *U.K.*	53	H3
Thamud	97	J8
Thane	92	D5
Thanet, Isle of	53	J3
Thanh Hoa	93	L5
Thanjavur	92	E6
Thankerton	57	E5
Thann	65	G5
Thano Bula Khan	92	C3
Tharabwin	93	J6
Tharad	92	D4
Thar Desert	92	D3
Thargomindah	113	J4
Tharrawaddy	93	J5
Tharthar	77	K5
Tharthar, Wadi ath	77	K5
Thasos *Greece*	75	H2
Thasos *Greece*	75	H2
Thatcham	53	F3
Thaton	93	J5
Thaungdut	93	H4
Thayetmyo	93	J5
Thazi	93	J4
Thebes	75	G3
Thedford	123	P7
Thelon	119	Q3
Thenia	67	H4
Theniet El Had	67	H5
Theodore Roosevelt Reservoir	126	G4
Thermaikos Kolpos	75	G2
Thermia	75	H4
Thermon	75	F3
Thermopolis	123	K6
Thessalon	124	J3
Thessaloniki	75	G2
Thetford	53	H2
Thetford Mines	125	Q3
Thiamis	75	F3
Thibodaux	128	G6
Thief River Falls	124	B2
Thiel Mountains	141	U1
Thierache	64	F4
Thiers	65	E6
Thies	104	B3
Thiladummathi Atoll	92	D7
Thimbu	93	G3
Thimphu	93	G3
Thio	114	X16
Thionville	64	G4
Thira *Greece*	75	H4
Thira *Greece*	75	H4
Thirasia	75	H4
Thirsk	55	H2
Thisted	63	C8
Thivai	75	G3
Thiviers	65	D6
Thlewiaza	119	R3
Thohoyandou	108	F4
Thomaston	129	K4
Thomastown	59	H7
Thomasville *Alabama*	129	J5
Thomasville *Georgia*	129	L5
Thompson *British Columbia, Canada*	119	L5
Thompson *Manitoba, Canada*	119	R4
Thompson *U.S.A.*	124	C6
Thompson Sound	115	A6
Thomson *Australia*	113	J3
Thomson *U.S.A.*	129	L4
Thonon-les-Bains	65	G5
Thornaby	55	H2
Thornbury	52	E3
Thornby	53	F2
Thorndon	53	J2
Thorne	55	J3
Thorney	53	G2
Thornhill	57	E5
Thornley	55	H2
Thornton	55	F3
Thouars	65	C5
Thouet	65	C5
Thrakikon Pelagos	75	H2
Thrapston	53	G2
Three Forks	122	J5
Three Kings Islands	111	R8
Three Points, Cape	104	E5
Three Rivers *Michigan*	124	H6
Three Rivers *Texas*	128	C6
Three Sisters Islands	114	K7
Threshfield	55	G2
Throsell Range	112	E3
Thueyts	65	F6
Thuin	64	F3
Thule	120	N2
Thun	68	A2
Thunder Bay	124	F2
Thunder Mount	118	C2
Thung Song	93	J7
Thuringer Wald	70	D3
Thurles	59	G7
Thurloo Downs	113	J4
Thurnscoe	55	H3
Thursby	55	F2
Thurso *U.K.*	56	E2
Thurso *U.K.*	56	E2
Thurston Island	141	T4
Thusis	68	B2
Thwaites Glacier	141	S3
Tiancang	86	H3
Tianchang	87	M5
Tiandong	93	L4
Tiane	93	L3
Tiangua	137	J4
Tianjin	87	M4
Tianjun	93	J1
Tianqiaoling	88	B4
Tianshui	93	L2
Tianyang	93	L4
Tianzhen	87	L3
Tianzhu	93	K1
Tiaret	100	F1
Tibati	105	H4
Tiber	69	D4
Tiberias	94	B5
Tibesti	102	C3
Tibet	92	F2
Tibet, Plateau of	92	F2
Tiboku Falls	136	F2
Tiburon, Isla	126	F6
Tichitt	100	D5
Ticino	68	B3
Ticul	131	Q7
Tidaholm	63	E7
Tidjikdja	100	C5
Tieli	88	B2
Tieling	87	N3
Tien Shan	86	D3
Tien Yen	93	L4
Tierp	63	G6
Tierra Amarilla	127	J2
Tierra Blanca	131	L8
Tierra del Fuego, Isla Grande de	139	C10
Tietar	66	D2
Tiete	138	F4
Tifton	129	L5
Tifu	91	H6
Tiger	122	F3
Tigharry	56	A3
Tighina	79	D6
Tigil *Russia*	85	T5
Tigil *Russia*	85	T5
Tignish	121	P8
Tigre *Peru*	136	B4
Tigre *Venezuela*	136	E2
Tigres, Baia dos	106	B6
Tigris	94	H6
Tigzerte, Oued	100	D3
Tigzirt	67	J4
Tihamat ash Sham	96	E7
Tihamat Asir	96	F8
Tihsimir	77	J3
Tijoca	137	H4
Tijuana	126	D4
Tikal	132	C6
Tikamgarh	92	E4
Tikanlik	86	F3
Tikhoretsk	79	G6
Tikhvin	78	E4
Tikitiki	115	G2
Tikopica	111	Q4
Tikrit	77	K5
Tiksi	85	M2
Tilburg	64	F3
Tilbury	53	H3
Tilemsi, Vallee du	100	F5

Name	Page	Ref
Till	57	F5
Tillaberi	100	F6
Tillanchang	93	H7
Tillicoultry	57	E4
Tilomar	91	H7
Tilos	75	J4
Tilsit	71	J1
Tilt	57	E4
Timanskiy Kryazh	78	H3
Timar	77	K3
Timaru	115	C6
Timashevsk	79	F6
Timbakion	75	H5
Timbedra	100	D5
Timbo *Guinea*	104	C3
Timbo *Liberia*	104	D4
Timbuktu	100	E5
Timfristos	75	F3
Timimoun	100	F3
Timiris, Cap	100	B5
Timis	73	G3
Timisoara	73	F3
Timkapaul	84	Ad4
Timmernabben	63	G8
Timmins	125	K2
Timok	73	G3
Timolin	59	J7
Timor	91	H7
Timor, Laut	91	H7
Timoshino	78	F3
Timsher	78	J3
Tinaca Point	91	H4
Tinaco	133	N10
Tinahely	59	K7
Tinakula	114	M7
Tindivanam	92	E6
Tindouf	100	D3
Tineo	66	C1
Tinglev	63	C9
Tingo Maria	136	B5
Tingsryd	63	F8
Tingvoll	62	C5
Tinhare, Ilha de	137	K6
Tinogasta	138	C5
Tinompo	91	G5
Tinos *Greece*	75	H4
Tinos *Greece*	75	H4
Tintinara	113	J6
Tinto *Spain*	66	C4
Tinto *U.K.*	57	E5
Tinto Hills	57	E5
Tinwald	115	C5
Tiomilaskogen	63	E6
Tipaza	67	H4
Tipitapa	132	D8
Tippecanoe	124	G6
Tipperary *Ireland*	59	F8
Tipperary *Ireland*	59	G7
Tipton	124	H6
Tiptree	53	H3
Tiquicheo	131	J8
Tiracambu, Serra do	137	H4
Tiran	96	B3
Tirana	74	E2
Tirane	74	E2
Tirano	68	C2
Tiraspol	79	D6
Tire	76	B3
Tirebolu	77	H2
Tiree	57	C4
Tirga Mor	56	B3
Tirgoviste	73	H3
Tirgu Bujor	73	J3
Tirgu Carbunesti	73	G3
Tirgu Frumos	73	J2
Tirgu Jiu	73	G3
Tirgu Mures	73	H2
Tirgu Neamt	73	J2
Tirgu Ocna	73	J2
Tirich Mir	92	D1
Tirnava Mare	73	H2
Tirnava Mica	73	H2
Tirnavos	75	G3
Tirol	68	C2
Tirpul	95	Q4
Tirso	69	B6
Tirua Point	115	E3
Tiruchchirappalli	92	E6
Tirumangalam	92	E7
Tirunelveli	92	E7
Tirupati	92	E6
Tiruppur	92	E6
Tiruvannamalai	92	E6
Tisa	72	F3
Tisisat Falls	103	G5
Tissa	71	K4
Tissington	55	H3
Tista	93	G3
Tisza	72	F2
Tit-Ary	85	M2
Titchfield	53	F4
Titicaca, Lago	138	C3
Titograd	72	E4
Titova Mitrovica	73	F4
Titovo Uzice	72	E4
Titovo Velenje	72	C2
Titov Veles	73	F5
Titran	62	C5
Tittmoning	70	E4
Titu	73	H3
Titusville	129	M6
Tiumpan Head	56	B2
Tivaouane	104	B2
Tiveden	63	F7
Tiverton	52	D4
Tivoli	69	D5
Tiwi	97	P5
Tiyas	77	G5
Tizimin	131	Q7
Tizi Ouzou	101	F1
Tiznit	100	D3
Tjamotis	62	H3
Tjornuvik	62	Z14
Tjotta	62	E4
Tlaltenango	130	H7
Tlapa	131	K9
Tlapehuala	131	J8
Tlaxiaco	131	L9
Tlemcen	100	E2
Toad River	118	K4
Toamasina	109	J3
Tobago	133	S9
Toba Kakar Ranges	92	C2
Tobercurry	58	E4
Tobermory *Canada*	125	K4
Tobermory *U.K.*	57	B4
Toberonochy	57	C4
Tobi	91	J5
Tobin Lake	112	F3
Tobi-shima	88	G6
Toboali	90	D6
Tobol	84	Ae5
Tobolsk	84	Ae5
Tobseda	78	J2
Tobysh	78	J3
Tocache Nuevo	136	B5
Tocantins	137	H4
Toccoa	129	L3
Toco	133	S9
Toconao	138	C4
Tocopilla	138	B4
Tocuyo	133	N9
Todeli	91	G6
Todi	68	B2
Todi	69	D4
Todmorden	55	G3
Todog	86	E3
Todos os Santos, Baia de	137	K6
Todos Santos *Bolivia*	138	C3
Todos Santos *Mexico*	130	D6
Todos Santos, Bahia de	126	D5
Toe Head *Ireland*	59	D10
Toe Head *U.K.*	56	A3
Toetoes Bay	115	B7
Tofino	122	B3
Toft	56	A1
Tofte	63	D7
Tofua	111	T5
Toga	114	T10
Togi	89	F7
Togiak	118	C4
Togian, Kepulauan	91	G6
Togni	96	B7
Togo	104	F4
Togtoh	87	L3
Toguchi	89	H10
Togur	84	C5
Tohamiyam	103	G4
Tohatchi	127	H3
Tohma	77	G3
Toi-misaki	89	C10
Tojo	89	D8
Tok	118	G3
Tokachi	88	J4
Tokachi-Dake	88	J4
Tokaj	73	F1
Tokanui	115	B7
Tokar	103	G4
Tokara-kaikyo	89	C10
Tokara-retto	89	B11
Tokat	77	G2
Tokelau	111	U3
Tokiwa	88	J3
Tokke	63	C7
Toklar	77	G3
Tokmak	86	D3
Tokolon	84	H5
Tokoro	88	K3
Tokoroa	115	E3
Toksun	86	F3
Tok-to	89	C7
Toktogul	86	C3
Tokuno-shima	89	J10
Tokushima	89	E8
Tokuyama	89	C8
Tokyo	89	G8
Tolar, Cerro	138	C5
Tolbonuur	86	G2
Tolbukhin	73	J4
Toledo *Spain*	66	D3
Toledo *U.S.A.*	124	J6
Toledo Bend Reservoir	128	F5
Toledo, Montes de	66	D3
Tolentino	68	D4
Toliara	109	H4
Tolitoli	91	G5
Tolka	84	C4
Tolmezzo	68	D2
Tolmin	72	B2
Tolochin	78	D5
Tolosa	67	E1
Tolo, Teluk	91	G6
Tolsta Head	56	B2
Tolstoye	73	H1
Tolstoy, Mys	85	T5
Toluca	131	K8
Toluca, Nevado de	131	K8
Tolyatti	79	H5
Tomah	124	E4
Tomahawk	124	F4
Tomakomai	88	H4
Tomani	90	F5
Tomaniivi	114	R8
Tomar *Portugal*	66	B3
Tomar *Kazakhstan*	86	D2
Tomari	88	J2
Tomarza	77	F3
Tomasevo	72	E4
Tomashevka	71	K3
Tomaszow Lubelski	71	K3
Tomaszow Mazowiecka	71	J3
Tombador, Serra do	136	F6
Tombe	103	F6
Tombigbee	129	H5
Tomboco	106	B4
Tombouctou	100	E5
Tombua	106	B6
Tomelilla	63	E9
Tomelloso	66	E3
Tomini, Teluk	91	G6
Tomioka	89	H7
Tomkinson Ranges	112	F4
Tomma	62	E3
Tommot	85	M5
Tomo	136	D2
Tomochic	127	J6
Tompa	84	H5
Tompo	85	P4
Tomsk	84	D5
Tonbridge	53	H3
Tondano	91	G5
Tonder	70	C1
Tone	52	E3
Tonelagee	59	K6
Tonga	111	U6
Tonga *Sudan*	102	F6
Tongariro	115	E3
Tongatapu	111	U6
Tongatapu Group	111	T6
Tonga Trench	143	H5
Tongcheng	93	M3
Tongchuan	93	L1
Tongdao	93	L3
Tonggu	93	M3
Tongguan	93	M2
Tonghai	93	K4
Tonghe	88	B2
Tonghua	87	P3
Tongjiang	88	D2
Tongking, Gulf of	93	L5
Tongliao	87	N3
Tongling	87	M5
Tonglu	87	M6
Tongnae	89	B8
Tongoa	114	U12
Tongren	93	L3
Tongtianheyan	93	H2
Tongue *U.K.*	56	D2
Tongue *U.S.A.*	123	L5
Tongue, Kyle of	56	D2
Tongue of the Ocean	132	J2
Tong Xian	87	M4
Tongxin	93	L1
Tongyu	87	N3
Tongzi	93	L3
Tonichi	127	H6
Tonk	92	E3
Tonkabon	95	K3
Tonle Sap	93	K6
Tonneins	65	D6
Tonnerre	65	E5
Tono	88	H6
Tonopah	126	D2
Tonosi	132	G11
Tonsberg	63	D7
Tonstad	63	B7
Tonya	77	H2
Tooele	122	H7
Toowoomba	113	L4
Topeka	124	C7
Toplane	74	E1
Toplica	73	F4
Toplita	73	H2
Topocalma, Punta	138	B6
Topola	72	F3
Topolcani	73	F5
Topoli	79	J6
Topolkki	63	N6
Topolovgrad	73	J4
Topozero, Ozero	62	P4
Toppenish	122	D4
Toprakli	76	F3
Toraka Vestale	109	H3
Tora-Khem	84	F6
Torbali	76	B3
Torbat-e-Heydariyeh	95	P4
Torbat-e Jam	95	Q4
Tor Bay *Australia*	112	D5
Tor Bay *U.K.*	52	D4
Tordesillas	66	D2
Tore	56	D3
Tore	62	K4
Torfastadir	62	U12
Torgau	70	E3
Torgo	85	K5
Torhout	64	E3
Torino	68	A3
Torkaman	94	H3
Tormes	66	D2
Tornealven	62	K3
Tor Ness	56	E2
Torne-trask	62	H2
Torngat Mountains	121	P6
Tornio	62	L4
Toro, Cerro de	138	C5
Toroiaga	73	H2
Torokina	114	F3
Torokszentmiklos	72	F2
Toronaios, Kolpos	75	G2
Toronto	125	L5
Toropets	78	E4
Tororo	107	F2
Toros Dagi	76	F4
Toros Daglari	76	E4
Torpoint	52	C4
Torquay	52	D4
Torrance	126	C4
Torrao	66	B3
Torre Annunziata	69	E5
Torre Baja	67	F2
Torreblanca	67	G2
Torrecilla en Cameros	66	E1
Torre del Greco	69	E5
Torrelaguna	66	E2
Torrelavega	66	D1
Torremolinos	66	D4
Torrens Creek	113	K3
Torrens, Lake	113	H5
Torrente	67	F3
Torreon	127	L8
Torres Island	114	T10
Torres Novas	66	B3
Torres Strait	114	C4
Torres Vedras	66	B3
Torrevieja	67	F4
Torr Head	58	K2
Torridge	52	C4
Torridon, Loch	56	C3
Torrijos	66	D3
Torrington *Connecticut*	125	P6
Torrington *Wyoming*	123	M6
Torrox	66	E4
Torsas	63	F8
Torsby	63	E6
Torshavn	62	Z14
Torsken	62	L2
Tortkuduk	84	A6
Tortola	133	Q5
Tortona	68	B3
Tortosa	67	G2
Tortosa, Cabo de	67	G2
Tortue, Ile de la	133	L4
Tortuga, Isla	126	G7
Tortuga, Isla la	136	D1
Tortum	77	J2
Torul	77	H2
Torun	71	H2
Tory Island	58	F2
Torysa	71	J4
Tory Sound	58	F2
Torzhok	78	F4
Torzym	70	F2
Tosa-shimizu	89	D9
Tosa-wan	89	D9
Toscaig	56	C3
Tosco-Emiliano, Appennino	68	C3
Tostado	138	D5
Tosya	76	F2
Totana	67	F4
Totes	64	D4
Totma	78	G4
Totnes	52	D4
Totness	137	F2
Totora	138	C3
Totota	104	C4
Totoya	114	S9
Totton	53	F4
Tottori	89	E8
Touba	104	D4
Toubkal, Jebel	100	D2
Tougan	104	E3
Touggourt	101	G2
Touho Ouegoa	114	W16
Toul	64	F4
Toulon	65	F7
Toulouse	65	D7
Toummo	101	H4
Toumodi	104	D4
Toungoo	93	J5
Touraine	65	D5
Tourcoing	64	E3
Tournai	64	E3
Tournon *France*	65	D5
Tournon *France*	65	F6
Tournus	65	F5
Touros	137	K5
Tours	65	D5
Tousside, Pic	102	C3
Touws River	108	D6
Tovarkovskiy	79	F5
Towada	88	H5
Towanda	125	M6
Towcester	53	G2
Tower Island	136	B7
Towie	56	F3
Townsend	122	J4
Townshend Island	113	L3
Townsville	113	K2
Towson	125	M7
Toxkan He	86	D3
Toya-ko	88	H4
Toyama	89	F7
Toyama-wan	89	F7
Toyohashi	89	F8
Toyonaka	89	E8
Toyooka	89	E8

Name	Page	Grid
Tyanya	85	K5
Tychany	84	F4
Tychy	71	H3
Tygda	85	M6
Tyler	128	E4
Tyloskog	63	F7
Tym	84	C5
Tymovskoye	85	Q6
Tynda	85	L5
Tyndall, Mount	115	C5
Tyndrum	57	D4
Tyne	55	H2
Tyne and Wear	55	H2
Tynemouth	55	H1
Tynset	62	D5
Tyr	85	P6
Tyre	94	B5
Tyret	84	G6
Tyrma	85	N6
Tyrone *U.K.*	58	H3
Tyrone *U.S.A.*	125	L6
Tyrrhenian Sea	69	D5
Tysnesoy	63	A7
Tyukalinsk	84	A5
Tyulgan	79	K5
Tyuli	84	Ae4
Tyung	85	L4
Tywi	52	C3
Tywyn	52	C2
Tzaneen	108	F4
Tzoumerka	75	F3

U

Name	Page	Grid
Uainambi	136	C3
Uapao, Cape	114	X16
Uapes	136	D4
Uatuma	136	F4
Uaupes	136	D3
Uava	137	K5
Uba	138	H4
Ubaitaba	137	K6
Ube	89	C9
Ubeda	66	E3
Ubekendt O	120	R3
Uberaba	138	J3
Uberaba, Laguna	138	E3
Uberlandia	138	G3
Ubinskoye	84	B5
Ubolratna Reservoir	93	K5
Ubombo	109	F5
Ubon Ratchathani	93	K5
Ubundu	106	E3
Ucayali	136	C4
Ucdam	77	J3
Uch Adzhi	95	R2
Uchami	84	F4
Ucharal	86	F2
Uchiura-wan	88	H4
Uchte	70	C2
Uchur	85	N5
Uckermark	70	E2
Uckfield	53	H4
Ucluelet	122	B3
Uda	85	N6
Udachnyy	84	J3
Udaipur	92	D4
Udayd, Ra's al	97	K4
Udbina	72	C3
Uddevalla	63	D7
Uddjaur	62	G4
Udine	68	D2
Udon Thani	93	K5
Udskoye	85	N6
Udupi	92	D6
Ueckermunde	70	F2
Ueda	89	G7
Uele *Russia*	84	J2
Uele *Zaire*	106	D2
Uelen	81	V3
Uelkal	85	Y3
Uelzen	70	D2
Ufa *Russia*	78	K4
Ufa *Russia*	78	K5
Ugab	108	B4
Uganda	107	F2
Ugashik Bay	118	D4
Ugashik Lakes	118	D4
Ughelli	105	G4
Ugijar	66	E4
Uglich	78	F4
Ugljane	72	D4
Ugra	78	E5
Ugun	85	M5
Ugurlu	77	J2
Ugurludag	76	F2
Ugut	84	A4
Uherske Hradiste	71	G4
Uhlava	70	E4
Uhrusk	71	K3
Uig	56	B3
Uige	106	C4
Uil *Kazakhstan*	79	J6
Uil *Kazakhstan*	79	J6
Uinskoye	78	K4
Uinta Mountains	122	J7
Uisong	89	B7
Uitenhage	108	E6
Ujiji	107	E3
Uji-shoto	89	B10
Ujjain	92	E4
Ujpest	72	E2
Ujscie	71	G2
Ujung Pandang	91	F7
Uka	85	U5
Ukholovo	79	G5
Ukhta	78	J3
Ukhunku	85	L3
Uki	114	K7
Ukiah	122	C8
Ukmerge	63	L9
Ukraine	79	D6
Ukta	71	J2
Uku	106	B5
Uku-jima	89	B9
Ukuma	106	C5
Ula	76	C4
Ulaangom	86	G2
Ulan Bator	87	K2
Ulan-Erge	79	G6
Ulanhad	87	M3
Ulan-Khol	79	H6
Ulan Tohoi	86	J3
Ulan-Ude	84	H6
Ulan Ula	93	H2
Ulas	77	G3
Ulawa	114	K6
Ulchin	89	B7
Ulcinj	74	E2
Uled Saidan	101	J3
Ulfborg	63	C8
Ulgumdzha	85	K4
Ulhasnagar	92	D5
Uliastay	86	H2
Ulithi Atoll	91	K4
Uljan	72	C3
Uljma	73	F3
Ulla	66	B1
Ullaanbaatar	87	K2
Ullanger	62	H5
Ullapool	56	C3
Ullock	55	F2
Ullswater	55	G2
Ullung-do	89	C7
Ulm	70	C4
Ulog	72	E4
Ulongue	109	F2
Ulricehamn	63	E8
Ulsan	89	B8
Ulsta	56	A1
Ulsteinvik	62	A5
Ulster	58	H3
Ulster Canal	58	H4
Ulubat Golu	76	C2
Ulubey *Turkey*	76	C3
Ulubey *Turkey*	77	G2
Uluborlu	76	D3
Ulucinar	77	F4
Uludag	76	C2
Ulu Dagi	76	C2
Uludere	77	K4
Uluguru Mountains	107	G4
Ulukisla	76	F4
Ulunkhan	85	J6
Ulus	76	E2
Ulva	57	B4
Ulverston	55	F2
Ulyanovsk	78	H5
Ulysses	127	M2
Ulzburg	70	C2
Umala	138	C3
Uman	79	E6
Uman	131	Q7
Umanak Fjord	120	R3
Umari	114	B2
Umarkot	92	C3
Umba	78	E2
Umbertide	68	D4
Umboi Island	114	D3
Umbro-Marchigiano, Appennino	68	D4
Umea	62	J5
Umealven	62	H4
Umm al Qaywayn	97	M4
Umm as Samim	97	M6
Umm Bel	102	E5
Umm Keddada	102	E5
Umm Lajj	96	C4
Umm Ruwaba	102	F5
Umm Said	97	K4
Umm Urumah	96	C4
Umnak Island	118	Ae9
Umred	92	E4
Umtali	109	F3
Umtata	108	E6
Umzingwani	108	E4
Una *Brazil*	137	K7
Una *Bosnia-Herzegovina*	72	C3
Unalaska Island	118	Ae9
Unare	133	Q10
Unayzah	96	F3
Uncia	138	C3
Uncompahgre Peak	123	L8
Uncompahgre Plateau	122	K8
Underwood	123	P4
Unecha	79	E5
Uneiuxi	136	D4
Ungava Bay	121	N6
Ungave, Péninsule d'	121	L5
Unggi	88	C4
Uniao dos Palmares	137	K5
Uniao do Vitoria	138	E5
Unije	72	C3
Unimak Island	118	Af9
Unimak Pass	118	Ae9
Unini	136	E4
Union	129	M3
Union City	128	H2
Uniondale	108	D6
Union Springs	129	K4
Uniontown	125	L7
United Arab Emirates	97	L5
United States of America	116	H4
Unity	122	E5
Universales, Montes	67	F2
University Park	127	J4
Unnao	92	F3
Unst	56	B1
Untaek	88	A5
Unye	77	G2
Unzha	78	G4
Uodgan	96	D8
Uoyan	85	J5
Upata	133	R10
Upavon	53	F3
Upemba, Lake	106	E4
Upernavik	120	Q3
Upernavik Isfjord	120	R3
Upington	108	D5
Upolu	111	U4
Upolu Point	126	T10
Upper Arrow Lake	122	F2
Upper Broughton	53	G2
Upper Hutt	115	E4
Upper Klamath Lake	122	D6
Upper Seal Lake	121	M6
Uppingham	53	G2
Uppsala *Sweden*	63	G6
Uppsala *Sweden*	63	L7
Upsala	124	E2
Upstart Bay	113	K2
Uqla Sawab	77	J6
Urad Qianqi	87	K3
Urad Zhongqi	87	K3
Urak	85	Q5
Urakan	84	H5
Urakawa	88	J4
Ural	79	J6
Ural Mountains	78	K3
Uralsk	79	J5
Uralskiy Khrebet	78	K3
Urandangi	113	H3
Urandi	137	J6
Uranium City	119	P4
Uraricoera	136	E3
Urawa	89	G8
Urayirah	97	J4
Urayq, Al	96	D2
Urayq, Nafud al	96	F4
Urbana	124	J6
Urbino	68	D4
Urda	79	H6
Urdzhar	86	E2
Uren	78	H4
Urengoy	84	B3
Ureparapara	114	T10
Ures	126	G6
Urfa	77	H4
Urgal	85	N6
Urgel, Llanos de	67	G2
Urgench	80	G5
Urgup	76	F3
Urho	86	F2
Uritskiy	84	Ae6
Urkan	85	M6
Urla	76	B3
Urlingford	59	G7
Urmi	88	D1
Urosevac	73	F4
Urr Water	57	E5
Ursatyevskaya	86	B3
Uruacu	137	H6
Uruapan	130	H8
Urubamba	136	C6
Urubu	136	F4
Urucui	137	J5
Urucuia	138	G3
Urucui, Serra do	137	J5
Uruguaiana	138	E5
Uruguay	138	E6
Urumchi	86	F3
Urumqi	86	F3
Urupadi	137	F4
Urup, Ostrov	85	S7
Uruti Point	115	F4
Urville, Tanjung d'	114	B2
Uryupinsk	79	G5
Urzhum	78	H4
Urziceni	73	J3
Usa	78	K2
Usak	76	C3
Usambara Mountains	107	G3
Usedom	70	F1
Ushant	64	A4
Ushitsa	73	J1
Ushtobe	86	D2
Ushuaia	139	C10
Usk *Gwent, U.K.*	52	E3
Usk *Powys, U.K.*	52	D3
Usk Reservoir	52	D3
Uskudar	76	C2
Uslar	70	C3
Usman	79	F5
Usolye	78	K4
Usolye-Sibirskoye	84	G6
Uspenka	84	B6
Ussel	65	E6
Ussuri	88	E2
Ussuriysk	88	C4
Ust-Barguzin	84	H6
Ust-Belaya	85	W3
Ust-Chara	85	L4
UstChizhapka	84	B5
Ustica, Isola di	69	D6
UstIlimsk	84	G5
Ust-Ilimskiy Vodokhranilishche	84	J4
Ust-Ilych	84	Ac4
Usti nad Lebem	70	F3
Ustka	71	G1
UstKamchatsk	85	U5
Ust-Kamenogorsk	86	E2
Ust-Kamo	84	F4
Ust-Kan	84	E5
Ust-Kara	84	Ad3
Ust-Karenga	85	K6
UstKatav	78	K5
Ust-Kulom	78	J3
Ust-Kut	84	H5
Ust-Kuyga	85	P3
Ust-Labinsk	79	F6
UstLuga	63	N7
UstMaya	85	N4
Ust-Mayn	85	W3
Ust-Mil	85	N5
Ust-Muya	85	K5
UstNem	78	J3
Ust-Nera	85	Q4
UstNiman	85	N6
UstOmchug	85	R4
Ust-Ordynskiy	84	G6
Ustovo	73	H5
Ust-Ozernoye	84	D5
UstPenzhino	85	V4
Ust-Pit	84	E5
Ust-Port	84	C3
UstReka	78	H3
UstSara	78	E3
UstTapsuy	78	L3
Ust-Tatta	85	N4
Ust-Tsilma	78	J2
Ust-Tym	84	C5
UstTyrma	85	N6
UstUra	78	G3
UstUsa	78	K2
UstVaga	78	G3
UstVyyskaya	78	H3
UstYuribey	84	Ae3
Ustyurt, Plato	51	T7
Usuki	89	C9
Usulatan	132	C3
Usumacinta	131	P9
Utah	122	H8
Utah Lake	122	J7
Utajarvi	62	M4
Utara	90	C6
Ute Creek	127	L2
Utena	63	N9
Uthal	92	C3
Utiariti	136	F6
Utica	125	N5
Utiel	67	F3
Utikuma Lake	119	M4
Utkholok	85	T5
Utrecht	64	F2
Utrera	66	D4
Utsera	77	K1
Utsjoki	62	M2
Utsonomiya	89	G7
Utta	79	H6
Uttaradit	93	K5
Uttar Pradesh	92	F3
Uttoxeter	53	F2
Uttyakh	85	N3
Utubulak	86	F2
Utukok	118	C2
Utupua	114	N7
Uuldza	87	L2
Uummannaq	120	R3
Uusikaarlepyy	62	K5
Uusikaupunki	63	J6
Uusimaa	63	L6
Uvac	72	E4
Uvalde	127	N6
Uvarovo	79	G5
Uvea	111	T4
Uvinza	107	F4
Uvira	107	E3
Uvol	114	E3
Uvs Nuur	86	G1
Uwajima	89	D9
Uwayrid, Harrat al	96	C3
Uy	84	Ad6
Uyak	118	E4
Uyandina	85	Q3
Uyeg	78	J2
Uyuni	138	C4
Uyuni, Salar de	138	C4
Uz	71	K4
Uzaym, Nahr al	94	G4
Uzbekistan	86	B3
Uzda	71	M2
Uzen	79	J7
Uzerche	65	D6
Uzes	65	F6
Uzhgorod	79	C6
Uzhok	71	K4
Uzlovaya	78	F5
Uzumlu	76	D4
Uzun	84	D6
Uzundere	77	J2
Uzungol	77	J2
Uzunisa	77	G2
Uzunkopru	76	B2
Uzunkuyu	76	B3

V

Name	Page	Ref.
Vaajakoski	62	L5
Vaal	108	E5
Vaala	62	M4
Vaal Dam	108	E5
Vaasa *Finland*	62	J5
Vaasa *Finland*	62	K5
Vacaria	138	F5
Vacha	70	D3
Vache, Ile-a-	133	L5
Vadodara	92	D4
Vadso	62	N1
Vadu	73	K3
Vaduz	68	B2
Vaga	78	G3
Vagar	62	Z14
Vagay *Russia*	84	Ae5
Vagay *Russia*	84	Ae5
Vage	63	A6
Vaghena	114	H5
Vagnharad	63	G7
Vah	71	G5
Vaich, Loch	56	D3
Vainikkala	63	N6
Vaitupu	111	S3
Vakarel	73	G4
Vakfikebir	77	H2
Valaam, Ostrov	63	P6
Valandovo	73	G5
Valcheta	139	C8
Valday *Russia*	78	E4
Valday *Russia*	78	F3
Valdayskaya Vozvyshennost	78	E4
Valdemarsvik	63	G7
Valdepenas	66	E3
Valderaduey	66	D2
Valderrobres	67	G2
Valdes, Peninsula	139	D8
Valdez	118	F3
Valdivia	139	B7
Val-d'Or	125	M2
Valdosta	129	L5
Valdres	63	C6
Valea Lui Mihai	73	G2
Valenca	66	B2
Valenca	138	K6
Valenca do Piaui	137	J5
Valencay	65	D5
Valence	65	F6
Valencia *Spain*	67	F3
Valencia *Venezuela*	136	D1
Valencia de Alcantara	66	C3
Valencia de Don Juan	66	D1
Valencia, Golfo de	67	G3
Valencia Island	59	B9
Valencia, Lago de	133	P9
Valenciennes	64	E3
Valentim, Serra do	137	J5
Valentin	88	E4
Valentine	123	P6
Valenzuela	91	G3
Valera	136	C2
Valga	63	M8
Valiente, Peninsula	132	G10
Valjevo	72	E3
Valkininkay	71	L1
Valladolid *Mexico*	131	Q7
Valladolid *Spain*	66	D2
Vallasana de Mena	66	E1
Vallay	56	A3
Valle de la Pascua	136	D2
Valle de Santiago	131	J7
Valledupar	136	C1
Valle Grande	138	D3
Valle Hermosa	128	D8
Vallejo	126	A1
Vallenar	138	B5
Valletta	74	C5
Valley Falls	122	D6
Valleyview	119	M4
Vallgrund	62	J5
Vallimanca	139	D7
Vallo di Lucania	69	E5
Valls	67	G2
Valmiera	63	L8
Valognes	64	C4
Val-Paradis	125	L2
Valparaiso	129	J5
Valparaiso *Chile*	139	B6
Valparaiso *Mexico*	130	H6
Valpovo	72	E3
Valsjobyn	62	F4
Vals, Tanjung	114	B3
Valtos	56	B2
Valurfossen	63	B6
Valuyki	79	F5
Valverde	100	B3
Valverde de Jucar	66	E3
Valverde del Camino	66	C4
Van	77	K3
Vanadzor	77	L2
Vanajanselka	63	L6
Vanavona	114	H6
Van Buren *Arkansas*	128	E3
Van Buren *Maine*	125	S3
Van Canh	93	L6
Vancouver *Canada*	122	C3
Vancouver *U.S.A.*	122	C5
Vancouver Island	122	A2
Vanda	63	N6
Vandalia	124	F7
Vanderhoof	118	L5
Van Diemen, Cape	112	G1
Van Diemen Gulf	112	G1
Vanern	63	E7
Vanersborg	63	E7
Vanga	107	G3
Vangaindrano	109	J4
Van Golu	77	K3
Vangou	88	D4
Vangunu	114	J6
Van Horn	127	K5
Vanikoro Islands	114	N7
Vanimo	114	C2
Vanna	62	H1
Vannas	62	H5
Vannes	65	B5
Van Rees, Pegunungan	114	B2
Vanrhynsdorp	108	C6
Vanrock	113	J2
Vansbro	63	F6
Vanset	77	K4
Vansittart Island	120	K4
Vantaa	63	N6
Vanua Balavu	114	S8
Vanua Lava	114	T10
Vanua Levu	114	R8
Vanua Levu Barrier Reef	114	R8
Vanuatu	114	T12
Vanwyksvlei	108	D6
Vanzevat	84	Ae4
Vapnyarka	73	K1
Varallo	68	B3
Varamin	95	K4
Varanasi	92	F3
Varandey	78	K2
Varangerfjorden	62	P1
Varangerhalvoya	62	N1
Varazdin	72	D2
Varazze	68	B3
Varberg	63	E8
Vardar	73	F5
Varde	63	C9
Vardo	62	P1
Varena	71	L1
Varennes	65	E5
Varese	68	B3
Varfolomeyevka	88	D3
Vargarda	63	E7
Vargas Guerra	136	B4
Varginha	138	G4
Varilla	138	B4
Varkaus	63	L5
Varmland	63	E7
Varmlands-nas	63	E7
Varna	73	J4
Varnamo	63	F8
Varnek	84	Ad3
Varnya	84	A3
Varoy	62	E3
Varto	77	J3
Vartry Reservoir	59	K6
Varzea Grande	137	J5
Varzino	78	F2
Varzuga	78	F2
Varzy	65	E5
Vasa	62	J5
Vascao	66	C4
Vascongadas	66	E1
Vashkovtsy	73	H1
Vasilishki	71	L2
Vasilkov	79	E5
Vasilyevka	79	F6
Vaskha	78	H3
Vaslui	73	J2
Vassdalsegga	63	B7
Vasteras	63	G7
Vasterbotten	62	G4
Vasterdalalven	63	E6
Vastergotland	63	E7
Vasterhaninge	63	H7
Vasternorrland	62	G5
Vastervik	63	G8
Vastmanland	63	G7
Vasto	69	E4
Vasyugan	84	B5
Vatersay	57	A4
Vathi *Greece*	75	F3
Vathi *Greece*	75	J4
Vaticano, Capo	69	E6
Vatilau	114	J6
Vatnajokull	62	W12
Vatneyri	62	A2
Vatoa	111	T5
Vatomandry	109	J3
Vatra Dornei	73	H2
Vattern	63	F7
Vatu-i-Ra Channel	114	R8
Vatulele	114	Q9
Vaughn	127	K3
Vaupes	136	C3
Vavatenina	109	J3
Vavau Group	111	U5
Vavuniya	92	F7
Vaxholm	63	H7
Vaxjo	63	F8
Vayalpad	92	E6
Vaygach	84	Ac2
Vaygach, Ostrov	84	Ac2
Veberod	63	E9
Vebomark	62	J4
Vecht	64	G2
Vechta	70	C2
Vechte	70	B2
Veddige	63	E8
Vega *Norway*	62	D4
Vega *U.S.A.*	127	L3
Vegorritis, Limni	75	F2
Vegreville	119	N5
Veidholmen	62	B5
Veinge	63	E8
Vejen	63	C9
Vejer de la Frontera	66	D4
Vejle	63	C9
Velanidhia	75	G4
Velas, Cabo	132	E9
Velasco, Sierra de	138	C5
Velay, Monts du	65	E6
Velebit Planina	72	C3
Velestinon	75	G3
Velez Malaga	66	D4
Velez Rubio	67	E4
Velhas	138	H3
Velichayevskoye	79	H7
Velika Gorica	72	D3
Velika Kapela	72	C3
Velikaya *Russia*	78	H2
Velikaya *Russia*	85	W4
Velikaya Kema	88	F3
Veliki Kanal	72	E3
Velikiy Bereznyy	71	K4
Velikiye Luki	78	E4
Velikonda Range	92	E6
Veliko Turnovo	73	H4
Veliky Ustyug	78	H3
Velingara	104	C3
Velingrad	73	H4
Velizh	78	E4
Vella Gulf	114	H5
Vella Lavella	114	H5
Velletri	69	D5
Vellore	92	E6
Velsk	78	G3
Velt	78	J2
Velvestad	62	E4
Venado Tuerto	139	D6
Venafro	69	E5
Venaria	68	A3
Venda Nova	66	C2
Vendas Novas	66	B3
Vendome	65	D5
Vendsyssel	63	D8
Venecia	136	D6
Venezia	68	D3
Venezia, Golfo di	68	D3
Venezuela	136	D2
Venezuela Basin	134	C1
Venezuela, Golfo de	136	C1
Vengurla	92	D5
Veniaminof Volcano	118	Ag8
Venice *Italy*	68	D3
Venice *U.S.A.*	128	H6
Venkatapuram	92	F5
Venlo	64	G3
Vennesla	63	C7
Venta	63	J8
Ventimiglia	68	A4
Ventnor	53	F4
Ventry	59	B8
Ventspils	63	N8
Ventuari	136	D3
Ventura	126	C3
Venus Bay	113	K6
Venustiano Carranza *Mexico*	130	G5
Venustiano Carranza *Mexico*	131	N9
Vera *Argentina*	138	D5
Vera *Spain*	67	F4
Veracruz	131	L8
Veranopolis	138	F5
Veraval	92	D4
Verbania	68	B3
Vercelli	68	B3
Verdalsora	62	D5
Verde *Mexico*	131	L9
Verde *U.S.A.*	126	G3
Verden	70	C2
Verdigris	124	C8
Verdinho, Serra do	138	F3
Verdon	65	G7
Verdun	64	F4
Vereeniging	108	E5
Vereshchagino	78	J4
Verga, Cap	104	C3
Verin	66	C2
Verin Talin	77	K2
Verkhne-Avzyar	78	K5
Verkhnedvinsk	63	M9
Verkhne-Imanskiy	88	E3
Verkhneimbatskoye	84	D4
Verkhne Matur	84	D6
Verkhne Nildino	84	Ad4
Verkhne Skoblino	84	D5
Verkhnetulomskiy	62	P2
Verkhne Tura	78	K4
Verkhnevilyuysk	85	L4
Verkhniy Baskunchak	79	H6
Verkhniy Shar	78	J2
Verkhnyaya Amga	85	M5
Verkhnyaya Inta	78	L2
Verkhnyaya Toyma	78	H3
Verkhoturye	84	Ad5
Verkhovye	79	F5
Verkhoyansk	85	N3
Verkhoyanskiy Khrebet	85	M3
Verkhyaya Nildino	78	L3
Vermilion	119	N5
Vermilion Bay	128	G6
Vermilion Lake	124	D3
Vermillion	123	R6
Vermillion Bay	124	D2
Vermont	125	P5
Vernal	123	K7
Verneuil	64	D4
Vernon *Canada*	122	E2
Vernon *France*	64	D4
Vernon *U.S.A.*	127	N3
Veroia	75	G2
Verona	68	C3
Versailles	64	E4
Vert, Cape	104	B3
Verviers	64	F3
Vervins	64	E4
Veryan Bay	52	C4
Veryuvom	78	L2
Veshenskaya	79	G6
Veslos	63	C8
Veslyana	78	J3
Vesoul	65	G5
Vest-Agder	63	B7
Vesteralen	62	F2
Vestfjorden	62	F2
Vest-Fold	63	D7
Vestre Jakobselv	62	N1
Vestvagoy	62	E2
Vesuvio	69	E5
Vesyegonsk	78	F4
Veszprem	72	D2
Vetekhtina	85	K5
Vetlanda	63	F8
Vetluga *Russia*	78	H4
Vetluga *Russia*	78	H4
Vetluzskiy	78	H4
Vettore, Monte	69	D4
Veun Kham	93	L6
Veurne	64	E3
Vevey	68	A2
Veyatie, Loch	56	C2
Vezelay	65	E5
Vezere	65	D6
Vezirkopru	76	F2
Viacha	138	C3
Viamao	138	F6
Viana	137	J4
Viana do Castelo	66	B2
Viangchan	93	K5
Viareggio	68	C4
Viaur	65	E6
Viborg	63	C8
Vibo Valentia	69	F6
Vicecomodoro Marambio	141	W6
Vicente Guerrero	130	H6
Vicenza	68	C3
Vich	67	H2
Vichada	136	D3
Vichuga	78	G4
Vichy	65	E5
Vicksburg	128	G4
Vico	69	B4
Vicosa	137	K5
Victor Emanuel Range	114	C3
Victor Harbor	113	H6
Victoria *Argentina*	138	D6
Victoria *Northern Territory, Australia*	112	G2
Victoria *Victoria, Australia*	113	J6
Victoria *Cameroon*	105	G5
Victoria *Canada*	122	C3
Victoria *Chile*	139	B7
Victoria *Hong Kong*	90	E1
Victoria *Malaysia*	90	F4
Victoria *Seychelles*	82	D7
Victoria *U.S.A.*	128	D6
Victoria de las Tunas	132	J4
Victoria Falls	108	E3
Victoria Island	119	P1
Victoria, Lake	107	F3
Victoria Land	141	L4
Victoria, Mount *Myanmar*	93	H4
Victoria, Mount *Papua New Guinea*	114	D3
Victoria Nile	107	F2
Victoria Peak	118	K5
Victoria Strait	119	Q2
Victoriaville	125	Q3
Victoria West	108	D6
Victorica	139	C7
Victorville	126	D3
Vicuna	138	B6
Vidago	66	C2
Vidalia	129	L4
Vidareidi	62	Z14
Vididalur	62	X12
Vidim	84	G5
Vidimyri	62	V12
Vidin	73	G4
Vidisha	92	E4
Vidivellir	62	X12
Vidomlya	71	K2
Vidsel	62	J4
Viedma	139	D8
Viedma, Lago	139	B9
Viella	67	G1
Vienna *Austria*	68	F1
Vienna *Illinois*	124	F8
Vienna *Ohio*	125	K7
Vienne *France*	65	D5
Vienne *France*	65	F6
Vientiane	93	K5
Vieques	133	Q5
Vierwaldstatter See	68	B2
Vierzon	65	E5
Vieste	69	F5
Vietnam	93	L5
Vif	65	F6

Name	Page	Grid
Vigan	91	G2
Vigevano	68	B3
Viggiano	69	E5
Vigia	137	G4
Viglio, Monte	69	D5
Vigo	66	B1
Vigrestad	63	A7
Viiala	63	K6
Vijayawada	92	F5
Vijose	74	E2
Vik	62	E4
Vik	62	V13
Vikajarvi	62	M3
Vikersund	63	D7
Vikhorevka	84	G5
Vikna	62	D4
Viksoyri	63	B6
Vila	114	U12
Viladikars	77	K2
Vila Franca	66	B3
Vilaine	65	C5
Vilaller	67	G1
Vilanculos	109	G4
Vila Nova	137	F4
Vila Nova de Famalicao	66	B2
Vila Pouca de Aguiar	66	C2
Vila Real	66	C2
Vila Real de Santo Antonio	66	C4
Vila Velha	138	H4
Vila Velha de Rodao	66	C3
Vila Vicosa	66	C3
Vilcheka, Zemlya	80	H1
Viled	78	H3
Vileyka	71	M1
Vilhelmina	62	G4
Vilhena	136	E6
Viliga-Kushka	85	T4
Viljandi	63	L7
Vilkitskogo, Proliv	81	M2
Vilkovo	73	K3
Villa Abecia	138	C4
Villa Angela	138	D5
Villa Aroma	138	C3
Villa Bella	136	D6
Villa Bens	100	C3
Villablino	66	C1
Villacarrillo	66	E3
Villacastin	66	D2
Villach	68	D2
Villa Cisneros	100	B4
Villa Constitucion	138	D6
Villa de Cura	136	D2
Villadiego	66	D1
Villa Dolores	139	C6
Villafranca del Bierzo	66	C1
Villafranca de los Barros	66	C3
Villafranca del Penedes	67	G2
Villafranca di Verona	68	C3
Villaguay	138	E6
Villa Hayes	138	E5
Villahermosa	131	N9
Villa Huidobro	139	D6
Villa Iris	139	D7
Villajoyosa	67	F3
Villalba	66	C1
Villalon de Campos	66	D1
Villalpando	66	D2
Villa Maria	138	D6
Villamayor de Santiago	66	E3
Villa Montes	138	D4
Villanueva	130	H6
Villanueva de Cordoba	66	D3
Villanueva del Fresno	66	C3
Villanueva de los Castillejos	66	C4
Villanueva de los Infantes	66	E3
Villanueva y Geltru	67	G2
Villaputzu	69	B6
Villarcayo	66	E1
Villarejo	66	E2
Villarrica	138	E5
Villarrobledo	66	E3
Villasandino	66	D1
Villa Union Argentina	138	C5
Villa Union Mexico	127	M6
Villavicencio	136	C3
Villaviciosa	66	D1
Villazon	138	C4
Villedieu	64	C4
Villefort	65	E6
Villefranche-de-Rouergue	65	E6
Villefranche-sur-Saone	65	F6
Villena	67	F3
Villeneuve-sur-Lot	65	D6
Villeneuve-sur-Yonne	65	E4
Ville Platte	128	F5
Villers-Bocage	64	C4
Villers-Cotterets	64	E4
Villeurbanne	65	F6
Villodrigo	66	D1
Vilna	71	L1
Vilnius	71	L1
Vilnya	71	L1
Vilshofen	70	E4
Vilyuy	85	M4
Vilyuysk	85	L4
Vilyuyskoye Plato	84	H3
Vimmerby	63	F8
Vimperk	70	E4
Vina del Mar	139	B6
Vinaroz	67	G2
Vinas	63	F6
Vincennes	124	G7
Vincennes Bay	141	H5
Vinchina	138	C5
Vindelalven	62	J4
Vindeln	62	H4
Vindhya Range	92	E4
Vineland	125	N7
Vinga	73	F3
Vinh	93	L5
Vinh Loi	93	L7
Vinh Long	93	L6
Vinh Yen	93	L4
Vinica	73	G5
Vinkovci	72	E3
Vinnytsya	79	D6
Vinogradov	71	K4
Vipiteno	68	C2
Vir	72	C3
Virac	91	G3
Viramgam	92	D4
Virandozero	78	F3
Viransehir	77	H4
Virarajendrapet	92	E6
Virden	123	P3
Vire France	64	C4
Vire France	64	C4
Virfurile	73	G2
Virgenes, Cabo	139	C10
Virgin	126	E2
Virgin Gorda	133	Q5
Virginia Ireland	58	H5
Virginia Minnesota	124	D3
Virginia U.S.A.	125	L8
Virginia Beach	125	N8
Virginia Falls	118	L3
Virgin Islands	133	Q5
Virmasvesi	62	M5
Virovitica	72	D3
Virrat	63	K5
Virudunagar	92	E7
Vis	72	D4
Visalia	126	C2
Visayan Sea	91	G3
Visby	63	H8
Viscount Melville Sound	120	E3
Visegrad	72	E4
Viseu Brazil	137	H4
Viseu Portugal	66	C2
Vishakhapatnam	92	F5
Vishera	78	K3
Vishnevets	71	L4
Vislanda	63	F8
Visoko	72	E4
Viso, Monte	68	A3
Vista	126	D4
Vistonis, Limni	75	H4
Vit	73	H4
Vitava	70	F4
Viterbo	69	D4
Viterog Planina	72	D3
Vitiaz Strait	114	C3
Vitichi	138	C4
Vitigudino	66	C2
Viti Levu	114	Q9
Vitim Russia	85	J5
Vitim Russia	85	J5
Vitina	75	G4
Vitoria	66	E1
Vitoria	138	H4
Vitoria da Conquista	137	J6
Vitoria de Santa Antao	137	K5
Vitre	64	C4
Vitry-le-Francois	64	F4
Vitsyebsk	78	E4
Vittangi	62	J3
Vittel	64	F4
Vittoria	69	E7
Vittorio Veneto	68	D3
Vivarais, Monts du	65	F6
Viver	67	F3
Vivero	66	C1
Vivi Russia	84	F4
Vivi Russia	84	F4
Vizcaino, Desierto de	126	E7
Vizcaino, Sierra	126	E7
Vize	76	B2
Vizhas	78	H2
Vizianagaram	92	F5
Vizinga	78	J3
Vizzavona	69	B4
Vladicin Han	73	G4
Vladikavkaz	77	L1
Vladimir	78	G4
Vladimirets	71	M3
Vladimirovka	79	J5
Vladimir Volynskiy	71	L3
Vladivostok	88	C4
Vlakherna	75	G4
Vlasenica	72	E3
Vlieland	64	F2
Vlissingen	64	E3
Vlore	74	E2
Vodice	72	C4
Vodlozero, Ozero	78	F3
Vogan	105	F4
Voghera	68	B3
Voh	114	W16
Vohemar	109	J2
Vohilava	109	J4
Vohimarina	109	J2
Vohipeno	109	J4
Voi	107	G3
Voiron	65	F6
Vojens	63	C9
Vojmsjon	62	G4
Vojnic	72	C3
Volary	70	E4
Volborg	123	M5
Volchansk	79	F5
Volda	62	B5
Volga	79	H6
Volgodonsk	79	G6
Volgograd	79	G6
Volgogradskoye Vodokhranilishche	79	H6
Volgsele	62	G4
Volissos	75	H3
Volkhov Russia	78	E4
Volkhov Russia	78	E4
Volklingen	70	B4
Volkovysk	71	L2
Volksrust	108	E5
Volnovakha	79	F6
Volochankao	84	E2
Volochayevka	88	E1
Volochisk	71	M4
Volodskaya	78	G3
Vologda	78	F4
Volokon	84	H5
Volonga	78	H2
Volos	75	G3
Voloshka	78	F3
Volovets	71	K4
Volozhin	71	M1
Volpa	71	L2
Volsk	79	H5
Volta	104	F4
Volta, Lake	104	E4
Volta Redonda	138	H4
Volterra	68	C4
Volteva	78	G3
Volturno	69	E5
Volvi, Limni	75	G2
Volynskaya Vozvyshennost	71	L3
Volynskoje Polesje	71	L3
Volzhskiy	79	G6
Von Martius, Cachoeira	137	G6
Vopnafjordur	62	X12
Voras, Oros	75	F2
Vordingborg	63	D9
Voriai Sporadhes	75	H3
Vorkuta	78	L2
Vormsi	62	K7
Voronezh	79	F5
Voronovo	71	L1
Vorontsovo	63	N8
Voronya	78	F2
Voroshno	78	H4
Vortsjarv	63	M7
Voru	63	M8
Vosges	64	G4
Voskresensk	78	F4
Voss Norway	63	B6
Voss Norway	63	B6
Vostochno-Sibirskoye More	85	T2
Vostochnyy Russia	88	D4
Vostochnyy Russia	88	J1
Vostock	141	H3
Vostretsovo	88	E3
Votice	70	F4
Votkinsk	78	J4
Votkinskoye Vodokhranilishche	78	K4
Vot Tande	114	T10
Vouga	66	C2
Vouziers	64	F4
Vowchurch	52	E2
Voxnan Sweden	63	F6
Voxnan Sweden	63	F6
Voynitsa	62	P4
Voy Vozh	78	J3
Voyvozh	78	K3
Voza	114	H5
Vozhayel	78	H3
Vozhega	78	G3
Vozhe, Ozero	78	F3
Voznesensk	79	E6
Voznesenye	78	F3
Vozvyshennost Karabil	95	R3
Vrancei, Muntii	73	J3
Vrangelya, Mys	85	P6
Vrangelya, Ostrov	81	U2
Vranje	73	F4
Vranov	71	J4
Vratsa	73	G4
Vrbas	72	D3
Vrbovsko	72	C3
Vrede	108	E5
Vrhnika	72	C3
Vrindavan	92	E3
Vrlika	72	D4
Vrondadhes	75	J3
Vrsac	73	F3
Vrsacki Kanal	73	F3
Vryburg	108	D5
Vryheid	108	F5
Vucitrn	73	F4
Vukovar	72	E3
Vulavu	114	J6
Vulcan	73	G3
Vulcano, Isola	69	E6
Vung Tau	93	L6
Vunisea	114	R9
Vuokatti	62	N4
Vuollerim	62	J3
Vyartsilya	62	P5
Vyatka	78	J4
Vyatskiye Polyany	78	J4
Vyazemskiy	88	E2
Vyazma	78	E4
Vyazniki	78	G4
Vyborg	63	N6
Vychegda	78	H3
Vydrino	84	F5
Vygoda	73	L2
Vygozero, Ozero	78	F3
Vyhorlat	71	K4
Vyksa	78	G4
Vym	78	J3
Vyrnwy	52	D2
Vyshniy-Volochek	78	E4
Vysokoye	71	K2
Vytegra	78	F3
Vyzhva	71	L3

W

Name	Page	Grid
Wa	104	E3
Waal	64	F3
Waat	103	F6
Wabana	121	R8
Wabasca	119	N4
Wabash	124	G7
Wabe Gestro Wenz	103	H6
Wabe Shabele Wenz	103	H6
Wabigoon Lake	124	D2
Wabowden	119	R4
Wabush	121	N7
Waccasassa Bay	129	L6
Waco	128	D5
Wad Banda	102	E5
Waddan	101	J3
Waddeneilanden	64	F2
Waddenzee	64	F2
Waddesdon	53	G3
Waddington, Mount	118	K5
Wadebridge	52	C4
Wadena	124	C3
Wadi Gimal	96	B3
Wadi Halfa	102	F3
Wad Medani	103	F5
Wadomari	89	J10
Wad Rawa	103	F4
Wafra	97	H2
Wager Bay	120	J4
Wagga Wagga	113	K6
Wagin	112	D5
Wahai	91	H6
Waharoa	115	E2
Wahiawa	126	R10
Wahibah, Ramlat ahl	97	P6
Wahidi	96	H9
Wahoo	123	R7
Wahpeton	123	R4
Waialua	126	R10
Waianae	126	R10
Waiau New Zealand	115	A6
Waiau New zealand	115	D5
Waiau New Zealand	115	D5
Waibeem	91	J6
Waidhofen Austria	68	E2
Waidhofen Austria	68	E1
Waigeo	91	J6
Waiheke Island	115	E2
Waihi	115	E2
Waikabubak	91	F7
Waikato	115	E3
Waikerie	113	H5
Waikouaiti	115	C6
Wailuku	126	S10
Waimakariri	115	D5
Waimamaku	115	D1
Waimate	115	C6
Wainganga	92	E4
Waingapu	91	G7
Waini Point	136	F2
Wainwright	118	D1
Waiotapu	115	F3
Waiouru	115	E3
Waipa	115	E2
Waipahi	115	B7
Waipara	115	D5
Waipawa	115	F3
Waipiro	115	G3
Waipu	115	E1
Waipukurau	115	F3
Wairau	115	D4
Wairau Valley	115	D4
Wairio	115	B7
Wairoa	115	F3
Waitaki	115	C6
Waitangi	115	F6
Waitara	115	E3
Waitoa	115	E2
Waiuku	115	E2
Wajima	89	F7
Wajir	107	H2
Wakasa-wan	89	E8
Waka, Tanjung	91	H6
Wakatipu, Lake	115	B6
Wakaya	114	R8
Wakayama	89	E8
Wake	89	E8
Wakeeny	123	Q8
Wakefield	55	H3
Wakkanai	88	H3
Wakool Australia	113	J6
Wakool Australia	113	J6
Waku Kungo	106	C5
Walachia	73	H3
Walade	114	K6
Walagan	87	N1
Walbrzych	71	G4
Walcha	113	L5

Walcheren 64 E3
Walcz 71 G2
Waldenburg 71 G3
Waldon 52 C4
Waldron 128 E3
Waldshut 70 C5
Wales 118 A2
Wales Island 120 J4
Walgett 113 K4
Walikale 107 E3
Walinga 114 D3
Walker 122 E8
Walkeringham 55 J3
Walker Lake 122 E8
Wallace 129 P3
Wallaceburg 124 J5
Wallal Downs 112 E2
Wallasey 55 F3
Walla Walla 122 E4
Walldurn 70 C4
Wallhallow 113 H2
Wallingford 53 F3
Wallis, Iles 111 T4
Wallowa 122 F5
Walls 56 A1
Wallsend 55 H2
Walney, Island of 55 F2
Walpole 114 Y17
Walsall 53 F2
Walsenburg 127 K2
Walsingham, Cape 120 P4
Walsrode 70 C2
Walterboro 129 M4
Walter F. George Reservoir 129 K5
Waltham Abbey 53 H3
Walton 53 G3
Walvis Bay 108 B4
Wama 106 C5
Wamba *Nigeria* 105 G4
Wamba *Zaire* 106 C4
Wami 114 A2
Wana 92 C2
Wanaaring 113 J4
Wanaka 115 B6
Wanaka, Lake 115 B6
Wanapiri 91 K6
Wanapitei 124 K3
Wanda Shan 88 C3
Wandel Sea 140 P2
Wandingzhen 93 J4
Wanganui *New Zealand* 115 E3
Wanganui *New Zealand* 115 E3
Wangaratta 113 K6
Wangary 113 H5
Wangerooge 70 B2
Wangiwangi 91 G7
Wangjiadian 88 C2
Wangkui 87 P2
Wang, Mae Nam 93 J5
Wangqing 88 B4
Wanie-Rukula 106 E2
Wankaner 92 D4
Wankie 108 E3
Wanlaweyn 107 H2
Wanquan 87 L3
Wantage 53 F3
Wanxian 93 L2
Wanyuan 93 L2
Wanzai 93 M3
Wapenamanda 114 C3
Wapsipinicon 124 E5
Warangal 92 E5
Waratah Bay 113 K6
Warboys 53 G2
Warbreccan 113 J3
Warburg 70 C3
Warburton 113 H4
Ward 115 E4
Wardha 92 E4
Ward Hunt, Cape 114 D3
Ward Hunt Strait 114 E3
Ware *Canada* 118 K4
Ware *U.K.* 53 G3
Ware *U.S.A.* 125 P5
Wareham 53 E4
Waren *Germany* 70 E2
Waren *Indonesia* 91 K6
Warka 71 J3
Wark Forest 57 F5
Warkworth 115 E2
Warlingham 53 G3
Warmbad 108 C5
Warminster 53 E3
Warm Springs 126 D1
Warner Robins 129 L4
Warnow 70 D2
Warora 92 E4
Warracknabeal 113 J6
Warrego 113 K5
Warren *Minnesota* 124 B2
Warren *Ohio* 125 K6
Warren *Pennsylvania* 125 L6
Warrenpoint 58 K4
Warrenton *South Africa* 108 D5
Warrenton *U.S.A.* 125 M7
Warri 105 G4
Warrina 113 H4
Warrington *U.K.* 55 G3
Warrington *U.S.A.* 129 J5
Warrior Reefs 114 C3
Warrnambool 113 J6
Warroad 124 C2
Warsaw 71 J2
Warshiikh 107 J2
Warsop 55 H3
Warszawa 71 J2
Warta 71 G2
Waru 91 J6
Warwick *Australia* 113 L4
Warwick *U.K.* 53 F2
Warwick *U.S.A.* 125 Q6
Warwick Channel 113 H1
Warwickshire 53 F2
Wasbister 56 E1
Wasco 126 C3
Wasdale Head 55 F2
Washburn Lake 119 P1
Washim 92 E4
Washington *U.K.* 55 H2
Washington *District of Columbia* 125 M7
Washington *Georgia* 129 L4
Washington *Indiana* 124 G7
Washington *Missouri* 124 E7
Washington *N. Carolina* 129 P3
Washington *Pennsylvania* 125 K6
Washington *U.S.A.* 122 D4
Washington Cape 141 M4
Washington Land 120 N1
Washington, Mount 125 Q4
Wash, The 53 H2
Wasian 91 J6
Wasior 91 J6
Wasisi 91 H6
Waskaganish 121 L7
Waspan 132 E7
Wast Water 55 F2
Watam 114 C2
Watampone 91 G6
Watansoppeng 91 F6
Watchet 52 D3
Waterbeach 53 H2
Waterbury 125 P6
Wateree 129 M3
Waterford *Ireland* 59 G8
Waterford *Ireland* 59 H8
Watergrasshill 59 F8
Waterloo *Belgium* 64 F3
Waterloo *U.S.A.* 124 D5
Waterlooville 53 F4
Waternish 56 B3
Waternish Point 56 B3
Waterside 57 D5
Watertown *New York* 125 N4
Watertown *S. Dakota* 123 R5
Watertown *Wisconsin* 124 F5
Waterville *Ireland* 59 B9
Waterville *U.S.A.* 125 R4
Watford 53 G3
Watford City 123 N4
Watheroo 112 D5
Watkaremoana, Lake 115 F3
Watling Island 133 K2
Watlington 53 F3
Watroa 115 F3
Watsa 107 E2
Watseka 124 G6
Watson 123 M1
Watson Lake 118 K3
Watsonville 126 B2
Watten 56 E2
Watten, Loch 56 E2
Watton 53 H2
Watubela, Kepulauan 91 J6
Wau *Papua New Guinea* 114 D3
Wau *Sudan* 102 E6
Wauchope 113 G3
Waukarlycarly, Lake 112 E3
Waukegan 124 G5
Waurika 128 D3
Wausau 124 F4
Wave Hill 112 G2
Waveney 53 J2
Waverly 125 M5
Wavre 64 F3
Wawa 124 H3
Waxahachie 128 D4
Waya 114 Q8
Wayabula 91 H5
Waycross 129 L5
Way, Lake 112 E4
Waynesboro *Georgia* 129 L4
Waynesboro *Mississippi* 128 H5
Waynesboro *Pennsylvania* 125 M7
Waynesburg 125 K7
Waynesville *Missouri* 124 D8
Waynesville *Tennessee* 129 L3
Waynoka 128 C2
Wda 71 H2
We 90 B4
Wé 114 X16
Weald, The 53 H3
Wear 55 H2
Weardale 55 H2
Weasenham 53 H2
Weatherall Bay 120 E2
Weatherford 128 C3
Weaver 55 G3
Webi Shabeelle 103 J7
Webster 123 R5
Webster City 124 D5
Weda 91 H5
Weddell Sea 141 W4
Wedel 70 C2
Weduar, Tanjung 91 J7
Weeley 53 J3
Weemelah 113 K4
Wegorzewo 71 J1
Wegorzyno 70 F2
Weichang 87 M3
Weiden 70 E4
Weifang 87 M4
Weihai 87 N4
Weihe 88 B3
Wei He 93 L2
Weilu 87 L3
Weimar 70 D3
Weinan 93 L2
Weingarten 70 C5
Weiser 122 F5
Weissenburg 70 D4
Weissenfels 70 D3
Weiss Lake 129 K3
Weitra 68 E1
Weixin 93 K3
Wejherowo 71 H1
Welch 125 K8
Welcome Kop 108 C6
Welda 70 E3
Weldiya 103 G5
Welkom 108 E5
Welland 53 G2
Wellesley Islands 113 H2
Wellingborough 53 G2
Wellington *New Zealand* 115 E4
Wellington *South Africa* 108 C6
Wellington *Shropshire, U.K.* 52 E2
Wellington *Somerset, U.K.* 52 D4
Wellington *Kansas* 128 D2
Wellington *Texas* 127 M3
Wellington Channel 120 H2
Wellington, Isla 139 B9
Wells *U.K.* 52 E3
Wells *U.S.A.* 122 G7
Wellsford 115 E2
Wells-next-the-Sea 53 H2
Welney 53 H2
Wels 68 D1
Welshpool 52 D2
Welwyn Garden City 53 G3
Wemindji 121 L7
Wenasaga 123 T2
Wenatchee 122 D4
Wenchang 93 M5
Wenchuan 93 K2
Wendover 122 G7
Wengen 68 A2
Wenling 87 N6
Wenlock Edge 52 E2
Wenshan 93 K4
Wensleydale 55 H2
Wensu 86 E3
Wen Xian 93 K2
Wenzhou 87 N6
Wepener 108 E5
Weri 91 J6
Wernigerode 70 D3
Werra 70 D3
Werris Creek 113 L5
Wertach 70 D4
Weser 70 C2
Weslaco 128 D7
Wessel Islands 113 H1
West Auckland 55 H2
West Bay 128 H6
West Bengal 93 G4
West Branch Susquehanna 125 M6
West Bromwich 53 E2
Westbrook 125 Q5
West Burra 56 A2
Westbury 53 E3
Westbury-sub-Mendip 52 E3
Westby 124 E5
West Calder 57 E5
West End 129 N7
Westerdale 55 J2
Westerham 53 H3
Westerland 70 C1
Western Australia 112 E3
Western Desert 103 E2
Western Ghats 92 D5
Western Isles 56 A3
Westernport 125 L7
Western Ross 56 C3
Western Sahara 100 C4
Western Samoa 111 U4
Westerschelde 64 E3
Westerstede 70 B2
Westerwald 70 B3
West Falkland 139 E10
Westfield *U.K.* 56 E2
Westfield *Massachusetts* 125 P5
Westfield *New York* 125 L5
West Frankfort 124 F8
Westgate 55 G2
West Gerinish 56 A3
West Glamorgan 52 D3
West Glen 53 G2
West Harptree 52 E3
West Heslerton 55 J2
West Hoathly 53 G3
West Indies 48 D4
West Kilbride 57 D5
West Kirby 55 F3
West Linton 57 E5
Westlock 119 N5
Westmeath 59 G6
West Memphis 128 G3
West Meon 53 F3
West Mersea 53 H3
West Midlands 53 F2
West Moors 53 F4
Westmoreland 113 H2
Weston 125 K7
Weston-Super-Mare 52 E3
West Palm Beach 129 M7
West Plains 124 E8
West Point *Mississippi* 128 H4
West Point *Nebraska* 123 R7
Westport *Ireland* 58 C5
Westport *New Zealand* 115 C4
Westport Quay 58 C5
Westray 56 F1
Westray Firth 56 E1
West Road 118 L5
West Sussex 53 G4
West Tavaputs Plateau 122 J8
West Virginia 125 K7
West Wellow 53 F4
West Wyalong 113 K5
West Yellowstone 122 J5
West Yorkshire 55 H3
Wetar 91 H7
Wetar, Selat 91 H7
Wetaskiwin 119 N5
Wetherby 55 H3
Wewahitchka 129 K5
Wewak 114 C2
Wexford *Ireland* 59 J8
Wexford *Ireland* 59 K8
Wexford Bay 59 K8
Wey 53 G3
Weybridge 53 G3
Weyburn 123 N3
Weyhill 53 F3
Weymouth 52 E4
Weymouth Bay *Australia* 113 J1
Weymouth Bay *U.K.* 52 E4
Whakataki 115 F4
Whakatane 115 F2
Whalsay 56 A1
Whanganui Inlet 115 D4
Whangaparaoa 115 G2
Whangarei 115 E1
Whangaruru Harbour 115 D1
Whaplode 53 G2
Wharanui 115 E4
Wharfe 55 H2
Wharfedale 55 H3
Wharton 128 D6
Whataroa 115 C5
Wheatland 123 M6
Wheatley *Nottinghamshire, U.K.* 55 J3
Wheatley *Oxfordshire, U.K.* 53 F3
Wheeler Peak 122 G8
Wheeling 125 K6
Whernside 55 G2
Whidbey, Point 113 H5
Whitburn *Lothian, U.K.* 57 E5
Whitburn *Tyne and Wear, U.K.* 55 H2
Whitby 55 J2
Whitchurch *Avon, U.K.* 52 E3
Whitchurch *Hampshire, U.K.* 53 F3
Whitchurch *Shropshire, U.K.* 52 E2
White *Canada* 118 G3
White *Arkansas* 128 G3
White *Indiana* 124 G7
White *Missouri* 124 D8
White *S. Dakota* 123 P6
White *Texas* 127 M4
Whiteadder Reservoir 57 F5
White Bay 121 Q7
Whitecourt 119 M5
Whitefish 122 G3
Whitefish Lake 119 P3
Whitefish Point 124 H3
White Gull Lake 121 P6
Whitehall 125 P5
White Handkerchief, Cape 121 P6
Whitehaven 55 F2
Whitehead 58 L3
Whitehorse 118 H3
Whitehorse Hill 53 F3
White Island 115 F2
White, Lake 112 F3
White Lake 128 F6
Whiteman Range 114 E3
White Mountains 118 F2
White Mount Peak 122 E9
Whitemouth 124 B2
Whiten Head 56 D2
Whiteparish 53 F3
White Pass 118 H4
White River 124 H2
White River Plateau 123 L8
White Salmon 122 D5
White Sea 78 F2
White Sulphur Springs 122 J4
White Volta 104 E4
Whitewater 124 F5
Whitewood 123 N2
Whitfield Moor 55 G2
Whithorn 54 E2
Whiting Bay 57 C5
Whitley Bay 55 H1
Whitmore 52 E2
Whitney, Mount 126 C2
Whitney-on-Wye 52 D2
Whitsand Bay 52 C4
Whitstable 53 J3
Whittlesey 53 G2
Whitton 55 J3
Whittonstall 55 H2
Whitworth 55 G3

Name	Page	Grid
Wholdaia Lake	119	Q3
Whyalla	113	H5
Wiarton	125	K4
Wiay	56	A3
Wichita	128	D2
Wichita Falls	127	N4
Wichita Mountains	128	C3
Wickenburg	126	F4
Wickford	53	H3
Wickham	55	H2
Wickhambrook	53	H2
Wickham, Cape	113	J6
Wicklow *Ireland*	59	K7
Wicklow *Ireland*	59	K7
Wicklow Head	59	L7
Wicklow Mountains	59	K6
Widawka	71	H3
Wide Firth	56	E1
Widnes	55	G3
Widyan, Al	94	E6
Wielen	70	G2
Wielun	71	H3
Wien	68	F1
Wiener Neustadt	68	F2
Wieprz	71	K3
Wieren	70	D2
Wiesbaden	70	C3
Wigan	55	G3
Wiggins	128	H5
Wighill	55	H3
Wigmore	52	E2
Wight, Isle of	53	F4
Wigston	53	F2
Wigton	55	F2
Wigtown	54	E2
Wigtown Bay	54	E2
Wil	68	B2
Wilbur	122	E4
Wilcannia	113	J5
Wild Spitze	68	C2
Wilhelm II Land	141	F4
Wilhelm, Mount	114	D3
Wilhelm-Pieck-Stadt	70	F3
Wilhelmshaven	70	C2
Wilkes-Barre	125	N6
Wilkes Land	141	J4
Wilkhaven	56	E3
Wilkins Sound	120	D2
Willamette	122	B5
Willard	126	G6
Willaumez Peninsula	114	D2
Willemstad	136	D1
Willeroo	112	G2
William, Mount	113	J6
Williams *Australia*	112	D5
Williams *U.S.A.*	122	C8
Williamsburg	125	M8
Williams Lake	119	L5
Williamson	124	J8
Williamsport	125	M6
Williamston	129	P3
Willingboro	125	N6
Willington *Derbyshire, U.K.*	53	F2
Willington *Durham, U.K.*	55	H2
Willipa Bay	122	B4
Willis Group	110	M5
Williston *South Africa*	108	D6
Williston *Florida*	129	L6
Williston *N.Dakota*	123	N3
Williston Lake	118	L4
Williton	52	D3
Willmar	124	C4
Willoughby-on-the-Wolds	53	F2
Willow Bunch	123	M3
Willowmore	108	D6
Willow Springs	124	E8
Wills, Lake	112	F3
Wilmington *Australia*	113	H5
Wilmington *Delaware*	125	N7
Wilmington *N. Carolina*	129	P3
Wilmot Passage	115	A6
Wilmslow	55	G3
Wilson	129	P3
Wilson's Promontory	113	K6
Wilstedt	70	C2
Wilton	53	F3
Wiltshire	53	F3
Wiluna	112	E4
Wimbleball Lake	52	D3
Wimborne Minster	53	F4
Wincanton	52	E3
Winchcombe	53	F3
Winchelsea	53	H4
Winchester *U.K.*	53	F3
Winchester *Kentucky*	124	H8
Winchester *Tennessee*	129	J3
Winchester *Virginia*	125	L7
Wind	118	H2
Winder	129	L4
Windermere *Canada*	122	G2
Windermere *U.K.*	55	G2
Windermere, Lake	55	G2
Windhoek	108	C4
Windischgarsten	68	E2
Windom	124	C5
Windorah	113	J4
Wind River Range	123	K6
Windrush	53	F3
Windsor *Australia*	113	L5
Windsor *Newfoundland, Canada*	121	Q8
Windsor *Ontario, Canada*	124	J5
Windsor *Quebec, Canada*	125	Q4
Windsor *U.K.*	53	G3
Windsor *U.S.A.*	129	P3
Windsor, Lake	133	L4
Windward Islands	133	S7
Windward Passage	133	K5
Winfield *Alabama*	129	J4
Winfield *Kansas*	128	D2
Winisk *Canada*	121	J7
Winisk *Canada*	121	J6
Winkler	123	R3
Winneba	104	E4
Winnemucca	122	F7
Winnenvicca, Lake	122	E7
Winner	123	Q6
Winnfield	128	F5
Winnibigoshish Lake	124	C3
Winning Pool	112	C3
Winnipeg *Canada*	123	R3
Winnipeg *Canada*	123	S2
Winnipeg, Lake	123	R2
Winnipegosis, Lake	119	Q5
Winnipesaukee, Lake	125	Q5
Winnsboro	128	G4
Winona *Minnesota*	124	E4
Winona *Mississippi*	128	H4
Winschoten	64	G2
Winsford	55	G3
Winslow *U.K.*	53	G3
Winslow *U.S.A.*	126	G3
Winslow Reef	111	U2
Winston-Salem	129	M2
Winterbourne Abbas	52	E4
Winter Garden	129	M6
Winterthur	68	B2
Wintinna	113	G4
Winton *Australia*	113	J3
Winton *New Zealand*	115	B7
Wiqia	86	C4
Wirksworth	55	H3
Wirraminna	113	H5
Wisbech	53	H2
Wisconsin *U.S.A.*	124	E5
Wisconsin *U.S.A.*	124	E4
Wisconsin *U.S.A.*	124	F4
Wisconsin Rapids	124	F4
Wishaw	57	E5
Wislany, Zalew	71	H1
Wislok	71	K3
Wisla	70	D2
Wismar	70	D2
Wissembourg	64	G4
Wistanstow	52	E2
Witbank	108	E5
Witham *Essex, U.K.*	53	H3
Witham *Lincolnshire, U.K.*	55	J3
Witheridge	52	D4
Withernsea	55	J3
Withington *Gloucestershire, U.K.*	53	F3
Withington *Hereford and Worcester, U.K.*	52	E2
Witney	53	F3
Witten	70	B3
Wittenberg	70	E3
Wittenberge	70	D2
Wittingen	70	D2
Witti Range	90	F5
Wittstock	70	E2
Witu	107	H3
Witu Islands	114	D2
Wkra	71	J2
Wladyslawowo	71	H1
Wloclawek	71	H2
Wlodawa	71	K3
Wloszczowa	71	H3
Wodzislaw	71	J3
Wodzislaw Slaski	71	H3
Woitape	114	D3
Wokam	91	J7
Woken	88	C2
Woking	53	G3
Wokingham	53	G3
Wolds, The	55	J3
Wolf	124	F4
Wolf Point	123	M3
Wolfsberg	68	E2
Wolfsburg	70	D2
Wolf, Volcan	136	A7
Wolin	70	F2
Wollaston, Cape	119	M1
Wollaston, Islas	139	C11
Wollaston Lake	119	Q4
Wollaston Peninsula	119	M2
Wollongong	113	L5
Wologisi Mountains	104	C4
Wolomin	71	J2
Wolstenholme, Cape	120	L5
Wolsztyn	70	G2
Wolverhampton	53	E2
Wolverton	53	G2
Wolviston	55	H2
Wombourne	53	E2
Wombwell	55	H3
Wondoola	113	J2
Wonju	87	P4
Wonosobo	90	D7
Wonsan	87	P4
Wonthagg	110	L9
Wood	123	L3
Woodbourne	115	D4
Woodbridge	53	J2
Woodburn	113	L4
Woodhall Spa	55	J3
Woodland	126	B1
Woodlark Island	114	E3
Woodlark Islands	114	E3
Woodroffe, Mount	112	G4
Woodside	113	K6
Woods, Lake	113	G2
Woods, Lake of the	124	C2
Woods Point	113	K6
Woodstock *Australia*	113	J3
Woodstock *New Brunswick, Canada*	125	S3
Woodstock *Ontario, Canada*	125	K5
Woodstock *U.K.*	53	F3
Woodville *New Zealand*	115	E4
Woodville *U.S.A.*	128	E5
Woodward	128	C2
Woody Head	115	E2
Wooler	57	F5
Woonsocket	125	Q6
Wooramel	112	C4
Woore	52	E2
Wooton Wawen	53	F2
Wootton Bassett	53	F3
Worcester *South Africa*	108	C6
Worcester *U.K.*	52	E2
Worcester *U.S.A.*	125	Q5
Worgl	68	D2
Workington	55	F2
Worksop	55	H3
Worland	123	L5
Worms	70	C4
Worms Head	52	C3
Worth	70	C4
Worthing	53	G4
Wotu	91	G6
Wowoni	91	G6
Wragby	55	J3
Wrangel Island	116	B1
Wrangell	118	J4
Wrangle	55	K3
Wrath, Cape	56	C2
Wray	123	N7
Wreake	53	G2
Wreck Reef	113	M3
Wrecsam	55	G3
Wrexham	55	G3
Wrington	52	E3
Wroclaw	71	G3
Wronki	71	G2
Wrottesley, Cape	120	B3
Wroxham	53	J2
Wrzesnia	71	G2
Wubin	112	D5
Wubu	87	L4
Wuchang	87	P3
Wuchuan	87	L3
Wudayah	96	H8
Wudinna	113	H5
Wudu	93	K2
Wufeng	93	M2
Wugang	93	M3
Wuhai	87	K4
Wuhan	93	M2
Wuhu	87	M5
Wu Jiang	93	L3
Wukari	105	G4
Wuliang Shan	93	K4
Wuliaru	91	J7
Wulin	88	B3
Wumeng Shan	93	K3
Wundsiedel	70	E3
Wuning	93	M3
Wunstorf	70	C2
Wuntho	93	J4
Wuping	87	M6
Wuppertal	70	B3
Wurarga	112	D4
Wurmsee	70	D5
Wurno	105	G3
Wurzburg	70	C4
Wurzen	70	E3
Wushi	86	D3
Wutonggou	86	H3
Wuvulu Island	114	C2
Wuxi *Jiangsu, China*	87	N5
Wuxi *Sichuan, China*	93	L2
Wuxing	87	N5
Wuxuan	93	L4
Wuyiling	88	B1
Wuying	88	B1
Wuyuan	87	K3
Wuzhi Shan	93	M5
Wuzhou	93	M4
Wye *Derbyshire, U.K.*	55	H3
Wye *Gwent, U.K.*	52	E3
Wylye	53	E3
Wymondham	53	J2
Wynard	123	M2
Wynbring	113	G5
Wyndham *Australia*	112	F2
Wyndham *New Zealand*	115	B7
Wynne	128	G3
Wyoming	123	K6
Wyoming Peak	122	J6
Wyre	55	G3
Wyre Forest	52	E2
Wyrzysk	71	G2
Wysokie	71	K3
Wyszogrod	71	J2
Wytheville	125	K8

X

Name	Page	Grid
Xaafuun	103	K5
Xaafuun, Raas	103	K5
Xai-Xai	109	F5
Xambioa	137	H5
Xangongo	106	C6
Xanten	70	B3
Xanthi	75	H2
Xapuri	136	D6
Xarardheere	103	J7
Xavantes, Serra dos	137	H6
Xegil	86	D3
Xenia	124	J7
Xiachengzi	88	C3
Xiaguan	93	K3
Xiahe	93	K1
Xiamen	87	M7
Xian	87	L4
Xian	93	L2
Xianfeng	93	L3
Xiangfang	93	M2
Xiang Jiang	93	M3
Xiangquan He	92	F2
Xiangtan	93	M3
Xiangyang	88	A3
Xianning	93	M3
Xian Xian	87	M4
Xianyang	93	L2
Xiaobai	88	B2
Xiao Hinggan Ling	87	P1
Xiaojiahe	88	D2
Xiao Shui	93	M3
Xicotepec	131	L7
Xieng Khouang	93	K5
Xifeng	93	L3
Xigaze	93	G3
Xiji	88	A2
Xi Jiang	93	M4
Xilin *Guangxi, China*	93	L4
Xilin *Heilongjiang, China*	88	B2
Xilin Hot	87	M3
Xilokastron	75	G3
Ximiao	86	H3
Xin Barag Youqi	87	M2
Xin Barag Zuoqi	87	M2
Xinchang	87	N6
Xinfeng *Guangdong, China*	87	L6
Xinfeng *Jiangxi, China*	87	L7
Xingan	93	M3
Xingcheng	87	N3
Xinglong *Hebei, China*	87	M3
Xinglong *Heilongjiang, China*	87	P1
Xinglongzhen	88	A2
Xingtai	87	L4
Xingtang	87	L4
Xingu	137	G4
Xingwen	93	K3
Xingxingxia	86	H3
Xinhua	93	M3
Xining	93	K1
Xinjiang	93	M1
Xinjiang Uygur Zizhiqu	92	F1
Xinjin	87	N4
Xinlin	87	M3
Xinmin	87	P2
Xinpu	87	M5
Xintai	87	M4
Xinwen	87	M4
Xinxiang	93	M1
Xinyang	93	M2
Xinyi *Guangdong, China*	93	M4
Xinyi *Jiangsu, China*	87	M5
Xinyl He	87	M5
Xinyuan	86	E3
Xinzhou	87	L4
Xiqing Shan	93	K2
Xique-Xique	137	J6
Xisha Qundao	93	M5
Xi Ujimqin Qi	87	M3
Xiushan	93	L3
Xixia	93	M2
Xixiang	93	L2
Xizang Gaoyuan	92	F2
Xizang Zizhiqu	92	F2
Xochimilco	131	K8
Xpujil	131	Q8
Xuanwei	93	K3
Xuchang	93	M2
Xuddur	107	H2
Xuefeng Shan	93	M3
Xunke	87	P2
Xuru Co	92	G2
Xushui	87	M4
Xuwen	93	M4
Xuyong	93	L3
Xuzhou	93	N2

Y

Name	Page	Grid
Yaan	93	K2
Yabassi	105	G5
Yablanitsa	73	H4
Yablis	132	F7
Yablonitse, Pereval	71	L4
Yablonov	71	L4
Yablonovyy Khrebet	85	J6
Yabrai Yanchang	86	J4
Yabrud	77	G6
Yabuyanos	136	C4
Yada	84	A3
Yadgir	92	E5
Yadkin	129	M2
Yadua	114	R8
Yaeyama-shoto	89	F11
Yafran	101	H2

Name	Page	Ref
Yu Xian	87	L4
Yuzha	78	G4
Yuzhno Kamyshovyy Khrebet	88	J2
Yuzhno-Sakhalinsk	88	J2
Yuzhnoye	88	J2
Yuzhnyy Bug	79	E6
Yverdon	68	A2
Yvetot	64	D4

Z

Name	Page	Ref
Zaandam	64	F2
Zabal Saghir, Nahr al	77	K5
Zabaykalsk	85	K7
Zab-e Kuchek	94	G3
Zabid	96	F9
Zabok	72	C2
Zabol	95	Q6
Zaboli	95	Q8
Zabren	71	G4
Zabrze	71	H3
Zaburunye	79	J6
Zacapa	132	C7
Zacapu	130	J8
Zacatecas	130	H6
Zacatecoluca	132	C8
Zacoalco	130	H7
Zadar	72	C3
Zadetkyi Kyun	93	J7
Zafora	75	J4
Zafra	66	C3
Zagan	70	F3
Zagazig	102	F1
Zagreb	72	C3
Zagros, Kuhha-ye	95	K6
Zagubica	73	F3
Zagyva	72	F2
Zahedan	95	Q7
Zahle	77	F6
Zahran	96	F8
Zahrat al Batin	94	F6
Zaindeh	95	L5
Zaire	106	C3
Zaire	106	D3
Zajecar	73	G4
Zakamensk	84	G6
Zakatly	79	H7
Zakharovka	86	C2
Zakhmet	95	R3
Zakho	94	F3
Zakho	77	K4
Zakinthos *Greece*	75	F4
Zakinthos *Greece*	75	F4
Zakros	75	J5
Zala	72	D2
Zalaegerszeg	72	D2
Zalalovo	72	D2
Zalau	73	G2
Zaleshchiki	73	H1
Zalim	96	F5
Zalingei	102	D5
Zamakh	97	H8
Zambales Mountains	91	G2
Zambeze	109	F3
Zambezi	106	D5
Zambia	107	E5
Zamboanga	91	G4
Zambrow	71	K2
Zamora *Ecuador*	136	B4
Zamora *Spain*	66	D2
Zamora de Hidalgo	130	H7
Zamosc	71	K3
Zancara	66	E3
Zanesville	124	K8
Zangezurskiy Khrebet	94	G2
Zanjan	94	J3
Zanjon	138	C6
Zante	75	F4
Zanthus	112	E5
Zanule	78	H3
Zanzibar	107	G4
Zanzibar Island	107	G4
Zaoyang	93	M2
Zaozernyy	84	E5
Zaozhuang	87	M5
Zapadna Morava	72	F3
Zapadnaya Dvina	78	E4
Zapadno Sibirskaya Ravnina	84	Ae4
Zapadnyy Chink Ustyurta	79	J7
Zapadnyy Sayan	84	E6
Zapata	128	C7
Zapata, Peninsula de	132	G3
Zapatosa	136	C2
Zapatoza, Cienaga de	133	L10
Zapiga	138	C3
Zapolyarnyy	62	P2
Zaporizhzhya	79	F6
Zapotlanejo	130	H7
Zap Suyu	77	K4
Zara *Turkey*	77	G3
Zara *Croatia*	72	C3
Zaragoza *Colombia*	136	C2
Zaragoza *Spain*	67	F2
Zarand *Iran*	95	K4
Zarand *Iran*	95	N6
Zarandului, Muntii	73	G2
Zaranj	95	Q6
Zarasai	63	M9
Zarate	139	E6
Zaraysk	78	F5
Zaraza	136	D2
Zardak	95	P4
Zard Kuh	95	K5
Zaria	105	G3
Zarnesti	73	H3
Zarqa	94	C5
Zarqan	95	L7
Zary	70	F3
Zarzaitine	101	G3
Zarzis	101	H2
Zashchita	84	C6
Zaskar Mountains	92	E2
Zaslavl	71	M1
Zastron	108	E6
Zatec	70	E3
Zatishye	73	K2
Zator	71	H4
Zavitinsk	85	M6
Zavodskoy	84	C6
Zawiercie	71	H3
Zawr, Ra's az	97	J3
Zaysan	86	E2
Zaysan, Ozero	86	E2
Zbarazh	71	L4
Zbaszyn	70	F2
Zborov	71	L4
Zbruch	71	M4
Zdolbunov	71	M3
Zdunska Wola	71	H3
Zebak	92	D1
Zebirget	96	C5
Zeebrugge	64	E3
Zeerust	108	E5
Zefat	94	B5
Zehdernick	70	E2
Zei Badinan	94	F3
Zei Koya	94	F4
Zeitz	70	E3
Zelenoborskiy	62	Q3
Zelenodolsk	78	H4
Zelenogorsk	63	N6
Zelenogradsk	71	J1
Zelenokumsk	79	G7
Zelina	72	D3
Zella Mehlis	70	D3
Zell am See	68	D2
Zelva	71	L2
Zemaitija	63	K9
Zemetchino	79	G5
Zemgale	63	L8
Zemio	102	E6
Zemlya Bunge	85	Q1
Zemmora	67	G5
Zempoala	131	K8
Zempoaltepec	131	M9
Zemun	72	F3
Zenica	72	D3
Zepce	72	E3
Zerbst	70	E3
Zerkow	71	G2
Zermatt	68	A2
Zernograd	79	G6
Zerqan	75	F2
Zestafoni	77	K1
Zetouji	87	N4
Zeya *Russia*	85	M6
Zeya *Russia*	85	M6
Zeysk	85	M6
Zeytinbagi	76	C2
Zeytinlik	77	J2
Zezere	66	C2
Zgierz	71	H3
Zgorzelec	70	F3
Zhabe	71	L4
Zhalanash	84	Ae6
Zhamansor	79	J6
Zhamshi	86	C2
Zhanabas	86	B2
Zhanatas	86	B3
Zhangbei	87	L3
Zhangdian	87	M4
Zhangguangcai Ling	88	B3
Zhangiz-Tobe	86	E2
Zhangjiakou	87	L3
Zhangping	87	M6
Zhangpu	87	M7
Zhangzhou	87	M7
Zhanjiang	93	M4
Zhaoan	87	M7
Zhaoguang	88	A1
Zhaoqing	93	M4
Zhaotong	93	K3
Zhaoxing	88	C2
Zhaoyuan	87	P2
Zharbulak	86	F2
Zharma	86	E2
Zharyk	86	C2
Zhashkov	79	E6
Zhatay	85	M4
Zhaxigang	92	E2
Zhejiang	87	M6
Zhelaniya, Mys	80	H2
Zheldyadyr	84	Ae7
Zheleznodorozhnyy *Russia*	84	G5
Zheleznodorozhnyy *Russia*	71	J1
Zheleznodorozhnyy *Russia*	78	J3
Zheleznogorsk	79	F5
Zhenan	93	L2
Zhengan	93	L3
Zhenglan Qi	87	M3
Zhengzhou	93	M2
Zhenjiang	87	M5
Zhenyuan	93	L3
Zherdevka	79	G5
Zhigalovo	84	H6
Zhigansk	85	L3
Zhijiang	93	L3
Zhilaya Kosa	79	J6
Zhiloy, Ostrov	79	J7
Zhitkovichi	79	D5
Zhlobin	79	E5
Zhmerinka	79	D6
Zhob *Pakistan*	92	C2
Zhob *Pakistan*	92	C2
Zhodino	78	D5
Zhokhova, Ostrov	85	S1
Zholymbet	84	A6
Zhongba	92	F3
Zhongdian	93	J3
Zhongwei	93	L1
Zhong Xian	93	L2
Zhongyaozhan	87	P1
Zhoushan Dao	87	M6
Zhovten	73	L2
Zhucheng	87	M4
Zhukovka	79	E5
Zhulong	87	M4
Zhuozi	87	L3
Zhuxi	93	L2
Zhuzhou	93	M3
Zhytomyr	79	D5
Ziama-Mansouria	67	J4
Zibo	87	M4
Zicavo	69	B5
Zidani Most	72	C2
Zidarovo	73	J4
Ziel, Mount	112	G3
Zielona Gora	70	F3
Ziesar	70	E2
Zigazinskiy	78	K5
Zigong	93	K3
Ziguinchor	104	B3
Zihuatanejo	131	J9
Zilair	79	K5
Zile	77	F2
Zilina	71	H4
Zima	84	G6
Zimapan	131	K7
Zimbabwe	108	E3
Zimkan	94	H4
Zimnicea	73	H4
Zimniy Bereg	78	G2
Zimovniki	79	G6
Zinapecuaro	131	J8
Zindajan	95	Q4
Zinder	101	G6
Zinjibar	96	G10
Zipaquira	136	C2
Zirje	72	C4
Zi Shui	93	M3
Zitacuaro	131	J8
Ziyun	93	L3
Zizhong	93	K3
Zlatibor	72	E4
Zlitan	101	H2
Zloczew	71	H3
Zlutice	70	E3
Zmigrod	71	G3
Zmiyevka	79	F5
Znamenka *Russia*	84	B6
Znamenka *Ukraine*	79	E6
Znamenskoye	84	A5
Znin	71	G2
Znojmo	70	G4
Zohreh	95	K6
Zoige	93	K2
Zolochev *Ukraine*	79	F5
Zolochev *Ukraine*	71	L4
Zolotinka	85	L5
Zolotonosha	79	E6
Zolotoy, Mys	88	G2
Zomba	107	G6
Zongo	106	C2
Zonguldak	76	D2
Zongyang	87	M5
Zonza	69	B5
Zorleni	73	J2
Zouar	102	C3
Zouerate	100	C4
Zrenjanin	72	F3
Zubayr, Jazair az	96	F9
Zuenoula	104	D4
Zufaf	96	E8
Zufar	97	M8
Zug	68	B2
Zugdidi	77	J1
Zugspitze	70	D5
Zujar	66	D3
Zula	96	D9
Zulia	133	L10
Zumbo	108	F3
Zumpango	131	K8
Zungeru	105	G4
Zuni	127	H3
Zuni Mountains	127	H3
Zunyi	93	L3
Zuo Jiang	93	L4
Zupanja	72	E3
Zuqaq	96	E7
Zurich	68	B2
Zurichsee	68	B2
Zuru	105	G3
Zut	72	C4
Zutphen	64	G2
Zuwarah	101	H2
Zuyevka	78	J4
Zvishavane	108	F4
Zvornik	72	E3
Zwedru	104	D4
Zweibrucken	70	B4
Zwettl	68	E1
Zwickau	70	E3
Zwiesel	70	E4
Zwolen	71	J3
Zwolle	64	G2
Zyrardow	71	J2
Zyryanka *Russia*	84	C2
Zyryanka *Russia*	85	S3
Zyryanovsk	86	E2